I0814357

NUREMBERG'S CITIZEN PROSECUTOR

Democratic Ideals in Global Perspective

Jacqueline Arthur-Montagne and
Emily S. Burrill, Editors

NUREMBERG'S CITIZEN PROSECUTOR

Benjamin Ferencz and the Birth of International Justice

Gregory S. Gordon

University of Virginia Press • *Charlottesville and London*

Published in association with the University of Virginia's Karsh Institute of Democracy

The University of Virginia Press is situated on the traditional lands of the Monacan Nation, and the Commonwealth of Virginia was and is home to many other Indigenous people. We pay our respect to all of them, past and present. We also honor the enslaved African and African American people who built the University of Virginia, and we recognize their descendants. We commit to fostering voices from these communities through our publications and to deepening our collective understanding of their histories and contributions.

University of Virginia Press

Printed in the United States of America on acid-free paper

First published 2025

9 8 7 6 5 4 3 2 1

Library of Congress Cataloging-in-Publication Data

Names: Gordon, Gregory S., author.

Title: Nuremberg's citizen prosecutor : Benjamin Ferencz and the birth of international justice / Gregory S. Gordon.

Description: Charlottesville : University of Virginia Press, 2025. | Series: Democratic ideals in global perspective | Includes bibliographical references and index.

Identifiers: LCCN 2024060656 (print) | LCCN 2024060657 (ebook) | ISBN 9780813953090 (hardback) | ISBN 9780813953106 (ebook)

Subjects: LCSH: Ferencz, Benjamin B., 1920–2023. | Public prosecutors—United States—Biography. | Lawyers—United States—Biography. | Jewish lawyers—United States—Biography. | Einsatzgruppen Trial, Nuremberg, Germany, 1947–1948. | War crime trials—Germany—Nuremberg—History. | International Military Tribunal. | International Criminal Court.

Classification: LCC KF373.F395 G67 2025 (print) | LCC KF373.F395 (ebook) | DDC 340.092 [B]—dc23/eng/20250110

LC record available at https://lccn.loc.gov/2024060656

LC ebook record available at https://lccn.loc.gov/2024060657

Cover photo: Benjamin Ferencz at the *Einsatzgruppen* trial, 1947. (United States Holocaust Memorial Museum Photo Archives)
Cover design: Cecilia Sorochin

CONTENTS

Part V. Providing

Part VI. Preventing

FOREWORD

Professor Gregory Gordon's biography *Nuremberg's Citizen Prosecutor: Benjamin Ferencz and the Birth of International Justice* makes an important contribution to the literature on the history of international criminal law and constitutes a fresh and serious examination of my life's work. While people may be aware of my work as a prosecutor at Nuremberg, Professor Gordon shows the full range of my lifelong efforts to end the scourge of war and protect and provide for the victims of atrocity. Although others have written about my life's work, I know of no other author whose research and writing style combined have borne such satisfying results. His recounting of my life is still a work in progress, but he has shared with me substantial extracts from the first few parts of the book. Based on this, I have formed quite a favorable impression.

What really stands out is the quality of the research. Professor Gordon has made every effort to unearth all available archival records to tell my story. I have been telling that story myself for one hundred years now. But naturally, over time, certain details can become a bit fuzzy. If I might be hazy on some of the finer points, Professor Gordon has made sure to chronicle them with crystal-clear precision based on extensive digging. My online Benny Stories are intended to provide anecdotes about some of the key events in my life. They are a helpful starting point, but Professor Gordon has filled in some of the gaps in these stories, giving important information about my school days, my US Army experience, my time in Nuremberg, the period devoted to Holocaust reparations issues in Germany, my years in private practice, and my efforts as an author and advocate working for the criminalization of aggression and the establishment of an International Criminal Court.

One of the book's key achievements is how it fleshes out my non-Nuremberg experience, especially as regards my work on behalf of atrocity victims, and puts it into better context vis-à-vis my entire career. That said, the research regarding my Nuremberg experience is impressive. In addition to my personal correspondence and diaries, Professor Gordon has scoured, among other sources, the available materials at the National Archives and Records Administration, the Telford Taylor Papers at the Columbia Rare Book & Manuscript Library, the Sheldon Glueck Papers at the Harvard Law School Library, the Paul H. Gantt Nuremberg Trial Papers at the Towson University Special Collections and University Archives, and, of course, the Benjamin B. Ferencz Collection at the United States Memorial Museum Archives. Thanks to this research, we now have a much better sense of my Nuremberg timeline and specific activities. A good example of this is the material on the Berlin Branch—Professor Gordon has laid out all the important details and identified the full cast of characters in reference to my activities in Berlin, making it very clear that I was wearing several hats and, through memoranda and correspondence, showing exactly what I did, and with whom, when I was wearing those various hats.

Another aspect of the biography that stands out is the context it gives. If he is describing my time during the 1930s, Professor Gordon gives the reader a sense of how that fits into the timeline and important facts concerning the Great Depression. If he is writing about my time in the US Army, he provides the surrounding key events of World War II that frame and contextualize my military service. Nuremberg and my work on Holocaust reparations issues are recounted through the lens of the Cold War events and tensions affecting what I was doing and coloring how I was perceiving it at the time. Equally important, in terms of contextualization, is the emphasis placed in the book on the role of my wife, Gertrude, as a partner in my life and work. The Berlin Branch is another good example of this. Gertrude had joined me in Germany by that time and was an extremely important part of our team in Berlin. Chronicling the important contributions she made there and going forward, as our work in international criminal justice progressed, also gives the book great historical authenticity and a sense of being complete.

But I would be remiss here if I failed to comment on the stellar writing through which Professor Gordon presents his research. I know of no other author who has chronicled my life whose style and technique are as compelling and as moving as Professor Gordon's. By way of example, he has shared with me passages regarding my experience investigating crimes at Nazi concentration camps. I can say unequivocally that his writing style is exceptionally poignant, informative, and powerful. I am extremely impressed by the high-caliber writing, which is the fruit of Professor Gordon's research efforts on the project thus far.

As I have understood it from Professor Gordon, among other things, the book is meant to show how persons of humble origins, such as myself, can work hard, dedicate themselves to higher causes, and make an important difference. I believe one can encapsulate my philosophy into a simple slogan: "Law Not War." And my advice to younger people is "Never Give Up." I believe Professor Gordon's account of my life will inspire readers to apply this philosophy and advice to their own lives. In that sense, during this period when the rule of law around the world is being eroded and dictators are rising again, I believe Professor Gordon's biography can make a vital contribution toward helping humanity pull back from the brink and work toward a global system of true peace and security.

Benjamin B. Ferencz

PREFACE

This project was born seven years ago in The Hague, the Netherlands, fittingly the global seat of international law. I was at a luncheon after an event there honoring the last living Nuremberg prosecutor, Benjamin Ferencz, a legend in my field whom I had had the privilege of meeting years previously. He had recently written the foreword to my book *Atrocity Speech Law: Foundation, Fragmentation, Fruition* (2017), and I was having a nice chat with his son, Donald, who had invited me to the event. We were speaking about his dad's historic accomplishments and how terrific it would be if someone were to publish a well-researched, comprehensive account of his life. I remarked that this would be a dream assignment. The following month, I received a note from Don asking me to call him. Apparently there had been some post-Hague discussion about the idea of a Ben Ferencz biography, and Don was now encouraging me to take on the project, promising unfettered access. I was incredibly honored, but I was in the middle of a new scholarly project (a monograph on the philosophy of Michel Foucault and its relation to international criminal law), and it would be difficult for me to switch gears. I asked Don to let me reflect on it.

It occurred to me that Ben, though still spry and energetic, was then ninety-eight years old and might not have much longer to live. So it would be best if someone could begin work on such a book right away. Perhaps, I wondered, it was worth putting aside my existing project even if it meant losing crucial momentum. The idea of working on a Ben Ferencz biography was beginning to grow on me. Still, I decided to do a little research to see what existing life accounts might be out there. I soon discovered that, ostensibly, a biography of Ben had already been published—Tom Hoffman's *Benjamin Ferencz, Nuremberg Prosecutor and Peace Advocate* (2014). I asked Don about this, and he told me that Hoffman had a family connection (he was married to one of Ben's cousins) and was not a professional writer (he was a retired US defense industry consultant). Besides, Ben was not enthusiastic about the end product. So I read the book and thought I might have an inkling why—it seemed largely a rendering in the third person of Ben's online memoirs (the "Benny Stories," now titled simply "Stories"). Don also revealed that a Swiss journalist, Philipp Gut, was working on a Ferencz biography in German (published in 2020 as *Jahrhundertzeuge Ben Ferencz*).

So I had a lot to ponder. Would it be worthwhile for me to take on this project given what I had discovered? After much soul searching, I decided to do it. Gut's biography would be in a different language. And I could provide the larger historical context missing from Hoffman's book, I thought, as well as emphasize a key aspect of Ben's career: his work on behalf of victims. Apart from all that, I could do this from a lawyer's perspective. (I was wondering, for instance, why there was so little out there on Ben's specific contributions to the *Einsatzgruppen* trial, beyond his oft-quoted opening statement—certainly he would have done more, such as conduct cross-examinations.) I told Don that I was on board and would apply for sabbatical leave so I could really plunge into the project.

To help, Don provided me with a letter expressing his and Ben's support for the project, and The Chinese University of Hong Kong, my home institution at the time, granted me sabbatical leave. I would like to thank Dean Christopher Gane for his encouragement and guidance. Don then arranged for me to visit his father in Delray Beach, Florida, and take a tour of the Benjamin B. Ferencz Collection (that is, Ben's personal papers) at the United States Holocaust Memorial Museum (USHMM) in Washington, DC. Thus, huge thanks to Don Ferencz, who, in the years to follow, continued to supply me with documents, photographs, and contacts—without him, this project would never have seen the light of day. Sandra Schulberg, Ben's media consultant when I started the project, was also very helpful during that initial phase in getting me acquainted with the important resources and persons of interest—I have not forgotten her generosity and am pleased to thank her here. I am also very grateful to the USHMM, especially its incredible Senior Advisor on Archives, Henry Mayer; its Photo Archivist, Caroline Waddell Koehler; and Anna Cave, then Director of the USHMM's Ferencz International Justice Initiative (part of the Simon-Skjodt Center), as well as Elizabeth Little of the Initiative.

I took my 2019–20 sabbatical leave in Florence, Italy, as a Visiting Fellow with the European University Institute (EUI), which had acquired a complete microfiche set of the USHMM's Ferencz Collection and had excellent resources for researching atrocity victim issues. (I would tell people that this was my year of doing "Ferencz in Firenze"!) I would like to thank my EUI "Sherpa," Professor Martin Scheinin, as well as the EUI's amazing Library Director, Pep Torn Poch. Professor Marina Aksenova was my initial EUI liaison and remained an invaluable sounding board throughout the project—thanks to her and Professor Neha Jain of the EUI, who helped in many of the same ways. Part of the year was also spent as a Research Fellow at Georgetown University Law Center—I am grateful to Professor David Luban for making this possible. Thanks as well to Morten Bergsmo, Director of the Center for International Law Research and Policy (where I am also a Research Fellow), who linked me up with Georgetown (as well as other important research sources) and helped me appreciate the importance of victim justice issues in Ferencz's career.

Along the way; I got fantastic research assistance from students and young lawyers who asked to volunteer, including Lukas Buchholz, Ann HY Lee, Roshan Melwani, Daisy Chu, Armani Cheng, Alpha Ngai, and Francisco Quintana. I am truly in their debt. Professor John Barrett, Robert Jackson's biographer, was also unfailingly generous with his time and ideas (as well as his couch on visits to New York City!). And I was very lucky to consult with certain illustrious Nuremberg/international criminal law experts—Professors Kevin Jon Heller, Diane Marie Amann, Kim Priemel, Mark Drumbl, Stan Goldman, Roger Clark, Michael Bazyler, Jonathan Bush, and Hilary Earl. I am so appreciative for what they have contributed. I feel the same way about the crucial assistance of Professor Geoffrey Corn, George R. Killam Jr. Chair of Criminal Law and Director of the Center for Military Law and Policy at Texas Tech University School of Law, who previously served as the US Army's senior law of war expert advisor and provided outstanding quality control for the book's military-related passages.

Many thanks as well to Ben's daughters, Keri Ferencz, Robin Ferencz Kotfica, and Nina Dale. They were all generous with their time, but I am particularly grateful to Keri for giving me access to documents and recordings that really helped illuminate the past.

I would also like to thank those involved in the publishing process. My dear old friend Marc Ashley got me back in touch with his older brother Bennett, someone I looked up to so much in my childhood, and who is now General Counsel and Managing Director of Janklow & Nesbit Associates, one of the nation's premier literary agencies. Bennett was such an amazing and generous guide as I started the publishing process. And without him I would have never met my agent extraordinaire, Paul Lucas, who helped guide me to the University of Virginia Press and negotiate our contract. When it was time to choose a publisher, Paul wisely arranged a phone call with UVA Press's ubertalented history and politics editor (and now editor in chief), Nadine Zimmerli. Within a few minutes of our chat, I was sold. Nadine was German/English bilingual, had an impressive education/work pedigree, and her passion was acquiring books about Americans who have gone overseas and made history. We clicked instantly, and I could not wait to start working with her. In the seven years since, the relationship has actually managed to exceed my expectations. Enormous and heartfelt thanks to you, Nadine, and your other colleagues at UVA Press, including Ellen Satrom, Jason Coleman, Clayton Butler, Susan Murray, and Fernando Campos, who have helped bring this biography to life. Special thanks as well to the University of Virginia's Karsh Institute of

Democracy for partnering with UVA Press to make this the inaugural book in their new partnership series Democratic Ideals in Global Perspective.

I would also like to express my appreciation to a long list of others (and apologies to anyone overlooked), including Professors Claus Kress, Noah Weisbord, Toby Golick, Jocelyn Getgen Kestenbaum, Michael Scharf, Ryan Mitchell, and Daley Birkett; lawyers Philipp Ambach, Kathy Roberts, Gilbert Bitti, Stefan Barriga, Joanna Frivet, Dolph Hellman, Dion Cominos, Kip Hale, and Antonio Angotti; as well as Liechtenstein Ambassador to the United Nations Christian Wenaweser, former Ambassador-at-Large for War Crimes Issues David Scheffer, former International Criminal Court Judge Marc Perrin de Brichambaut, former ICC Chief Prosecutor Luis Moreno Ocampo, International Nuremberg Principles Academy Deputy Director Viviane Dittrich, and Columbia University Library Archivist Christopher Laico.

I also received invaluable editorial assistance from my lifelong friend Marc Ballon, a superb journalist, teacher, and professional writer who understood the book's nuances and really helped me find my voice when it mattered most. But no one was more valuable throughout this project, and on so many levels, than the incomparable law librarian and lawyer Jan Stone. I cannot begin to express my appreciation for what she has done and helped make possible throughout this project. Stellar research, great writing insights, resourceful logistical assistance, warm encouragement during various dark moments (and even light ones), and clear-eyed perspective—she gave me all of that and much, much more. She has truly been a partner in this project, and words alone cannot express my appreciation to her.

And I am certainly at a loss for words when it comes to thanking my two favorite people in the world, my wife and indispensable life partner, Annie, as well as our daughter, Genevieve, an amazing young lady and my greatest pride. Not only did they let me go on that sabbatical year, but they gave me the kind of support that kept me going. And they inspired me, through seven years of ups and downs, including COVID-19 and all its attendant problems and delays. It has been a long haul, but we have done it together. My deep love and gratitude to both of you.

NUREMBERG'S CITIZEN PROSECUTOR

PROLOGUE

A PLEA OF HUMANITY TO LAW

SEPTEMBER 29, 1947. Nuremberg, Germany. Six years previously, to the day, the Jewish children of Kiev had been rounded up by German invaders and forced to march two miles north of the city to a ragged ravine called Babi Yar. There, trembling with terror, they were stripped of their clothes and forced on top of other naked bodies already lying lifeless in the gully. Those who resisted were beaten until they lay prostrate on the mound of corpses, their ears filled with the surrounding screams of abject fear; their noses with the ubiquitous stench of unnatural death. And then they were shot at close range on the nape of the neck or the back of the head, only to serve as the gruesome final resting place for the next layer of humanity to be piled upon them. They, along with the mostly Jewish women and the elderly who accompanied them on the death march, were among the 34,000 murdered during that interminable day and the next, victims of the largest single massacre of Jews in the Holocaust.

Now, in the Palace of Justice, Courtroom 600, before the Nuremberg Military Tribunal, those who had supervised that ghastly operation, and many others like it during the initial German invasion of the Soviet Union, were seated in the dock. They were the chieftains of specially organized Nazi mobile killing units attached to Adolf Hitler's invading armies and tasked with liquidating the Third Reich's "enemies," primarily Jews. The Schutzstaffel, or SS, had dubbed those detachments "Einsatzgruppen," and by the time they were done with their grisly work, they had murdered approximately 1.5 million innocent civilians.

It was 9:30 a.m. on that late September morning in 1947. The court clerk called the case, and Nuremberg Military Tribunal II-A asked the prosecution to begin. A well-groomed young man with wavy, light-brown hair in a crisp white shirt, a conservative tie, and a dark civilian pinstripe suit approached the lectern, his penetrating blue eyes fixed on the men in robes before him. His name was Benjamin Berell Ferencz. He was just under five foot two, barely clearing the podium.[1] And he was only twenty-seven years old. Later that day the Associated Press would refer to this proceeding as "the biggest murder trial in history."[2] It was that young man's first trial, and he was about to deliver the opening statement.

The previous day, a Sunday, aware of his imminent rendezvous with history, he had sat in this same august space, reflected on what was at stake, and begun drafting his opening. "I was sitting in the courtroom [that] Sunday," he would later recall. "I was alone in the courtroom. And I wrote it out by hand."[3] Less than a year before, in that same chamber, the International Military Tribunal had convicted of war crimes the top surviving Nazi leaders, including Hermann Göring, Rudolf Hess, Joachim von Ribbentrop, and Ernst Kaltenbrunner. That proceeding began with Chief US Prosecutor Robert Jackson voicing words that were now seared into the young man's psyche: "That four great nations, flushed with victory and stung with injury stay the hand of vengeance and voluntarily submit their captive enemies to the judgment of the law is one of the most significant tributes that Power ever has paid to Reason."[4]

In complete solitude that Sunday afternoon, with autumnal sunlight filtering in like mote-speckled movie projections through the vast mullioned casement windows and the faint echo of Jackson's rhetoric filling the empty expanse, he thought about the million-plus innocent victims slaughtered by the men he would face in that courtroom the next day. And words started to flow onto the blank pad: "It is with sorrow and with hope that we here disclose the deliberate slaughter of more than a million innocent and defenseless men, women, and children. This was the tragic fulfillment of a program of intolerance and arrogance. Vengeance is not our goal, nor do we seek merely a just retribution. We ask this Court to affirm by international penal action man's right to live in peace and dignity regardless of his race or creed. The case we present is a plea of humanity to law."[5]

Now it was Monday morning, and he was back in Courtroom 600, standing before those Nazi butchers—surrounded by a bevy of fellow jurists, interpreters, stenographers, and members of the public and press—plaintively vocalizing the words he had penned in the same space, entirely empty, less than twenty-four hours before. But his statement to the Tribunal revealed not merely the substance of his case against the Nazi killing squad leaders; in ways that were likely not even apparent to him in that watershed moment, as whirring movie cameras captured his eloquence for posterity, the opening lines of his peroration revealed so much about where this young man had come from and where he would be going.

Significantly, and powerfully, his very first sentence was about victims. That he had been, up to that day, and would continue to be, well beyond that moment, a tireless champion for the victims of persecution, one might have divined from the details of his own life story. He was born to a Jewish family in a little peasant cottage in Transylvania, which had had a long history of persecution and pogroms against Jews. At the time of his birth in March 1920,

Transylvania was part of Romania (but had been part of Hungary as recently as 1918). He would later observe, "My family had been subjected to persecution. Romania was . . . noted for its persecution of the Jews. [It] was a good idea for Jews and Gypsies to leave."[6] And that is what his family did. So, his flight to the United States with his parents and sister, when he was a newborn baby, was an exodus of victims seeking, as he now articulated in court, "to live in peace and dignity regardless of . . . race or creed."[7]

But his common cause with victims of violence had much deeper roots than simply having sought safe haven from pogroms in the Old Country. For after streaming through the processing portals of Ellis Island, his landing spot in America was not much more tranquil than the antisemitic villages of Transylvania; with limited means and connections, the Ferencz family had to settle in Hell's Kitchen, New York City. At that time, as its name perfectly suggested, it was one of the nation's worst crime-infested slums. And young Benny, as his family called him, lived in the dank cellar of a tenement house, growing up in an atmosphere of pervasive violence. The shakedowns, muggings, beatings, and murders on the streets of his childhood also went a long way toward shaping the young man who spoke on behalf of the "innocent and defenseless men, women, and children" in that Nuremberg courtroom in 1947.

In fact, his compassion for the victims of Nazi depravity was at the root of more than just his eloquent opening statement before the Nuremberg Military Tribunal. It was also responsible for the trial even taking place at all. In late 1946, in an abandoned Nazi ministry building in Berlin, it was Ferencz and his team who had discovered the only remaining complete set of Einsatzgruppen daily field reports laying out, with grim statistical precision, all the activities of these murder squads. At the time, following the trial of the highest-level Nazi leaders, the United States had been planning to conduct eleven "subsequent trials" in Nuremberg, which would prosecute remaining leaders across various subdivisions of the Third Reich, such as its medical, judicial, industrial, police, and military sectors. On discovering the Einsatzgruppen field reports, Ferencz pored over them and started doing the math. They indicated that more than one million innocent civilians had been cold-bloodedly executed by the special units. Something had to be done.

He hopped on the next plane to Nuremberg and implored Brigadier General Telford Taylor, head of the US Office, Chief of Counsel for War Crimes (OCCWC), that there needed to be a twelfth trial of the Einsatzgruppen leaders. Taylor balked, saying that already stretched resources had been allocated for only eleven trials—there could be no additional proceeding. But Ferencz was thinking of the victims and would not back down. "Look," he later recalled shouting, "I've got this evidence here. . . . A million murders! You can't let these guys go. This is mass murder on a scale never before seen in human history."[8] The heated exchange finally moved Taylor to reconsider. He asked Ferencz if he could take charge of the trial while continuing to lead the investigative unit in Berlin. Having to work around the clock would not deter Ben Ferencz from seeking justice for more than a million lost souls—he was on board. With that, after some persuasion of his superiors in the Pentagon, General Taylor authorized the Nuremberg proceeding against the Einsatzgruppen leaders—what ended up being the ninth of the twelve so-called Subsequent Nuremberg Trials.

And now the young lawyer's powerful opening statement was setting the stage for an epic trial that would conclude several months later, with guilty verdicts against all of the twenty-two who sat in the dock that late September day. This would include several well-educated SS generals, such as the infamous lead defendant, SS-Brigadeführer (Brigadier General) Otto Ohlendorf, an economist with a PhD who also happened to be the commander of Einzatzgruppe D, which murdered nearly 100,000 innocent civilians through the killing fields of Bessarabia, southern Ukraine, and the Caucasus during those dark days of 1941–42. Another top-ranked SS commander was Paul Blobel, a former architect, who planned and directed the Babi Yar massacre.

For any attorney, let alone a newly minted one still in his twenties, the work on *Einsatzgruppen* would likely be a career pinnacle. Indeed, for his work on that case, Ferencz became a figure of history. His role as chief prosecutor in the adjudication of Nuremberg's bloodiest crimes made headlines around the world. His exploits in court were captured on film, and his words were recorded for posterity. Eleanor Roosevelt sent him a note of congratulation after the trial's conclusion. He was, after all, a principal player in one of legal history's most epochal and impactful chapters—the Nuremberg Trials. By the time those proceedings had concluded in the spring of 1949, by which point he had been promoted to executive counsel of the OCCWC and had recently transitioned into Holocaust restitution work, he was twenty-nine years old. Most of his career still lay ahead of him.

AND IT was quite a career. In fact, when asked what he considered the proudest accomplishment of his professional life, Ferencz would not point to his Nuremberg work (or his work in the US Army as an innovative war crimes investigator before Nuremberg); rather, he identified his important role in obtaining compensation for victims of crimes against humanity as his "crowning achievement" and the "proudest period" of his life.[9] As one expert has noted: "Ferencz's idea of the centrality of victims and the need for their redress, protection and empowerment has been a staple of his vision for justice and accountability. Disturbed by the horrors seen while liberating Nazi concentration camps, [he] could not stop at bringing a handful of war criminals to trial."[10]

For what followed Nuremberg was the construction of an entire reparations program for victims of the Holocaust. In 1948, while still working out of his OCCWC office, Ferencz took leadership of the Jewish Restitution Successor Organization (JRSO), whose mission was to locate, and return to the rightful owners, Jewish property that had been confiscated or sold under duress by the Nazis during the war. His innovative strategy would later take root in human rights law and can be seen in the judgments of modern tribunals.

After years of tracking down individual items of Nazi plunder, he helped devise a more global approach to reparations for the crimes of the Hitler regime. Ferencz took a leading role in negotiating the Reparations Agreement between Israel and the Federal Republic of Germany, which was signed in Luxembourg City Hall on September 10, 1952. Then he headed up the organization that assisted survivors in securing their shares of the indemnity settlement, the United Restitution Organization (URO). And on his return to the United States several years later, he eventually formed a law partnership with his old Nuremberg boss, Telford Taylor, and continued to represent Holocaust victims seeking reparations for Nazi crimes in courts around the world.

While he may have considered this work the pinnacle of his professional life, by the time he started winding down his law practice in the 1970s, he still had much left to accomplish. His career had already consisted of *probing* Nazi atrocities, *prosecuting* them, and *providing* for their victims. He was now prepared to embark on the fourth major phase of his life's work—*preventing* future such atrocities. This period is marked by a supernova of activity and campaigning to define the crime of aggression and establish a permanent international criminal court with jurisdiction over that crime. In the 1970s, Ferencz played a key role in the United Nations formulating a definition of aggression. And by 1998, his dream of prosecuting that offense suddenly seemed within reach when diplomats from across the globe gathered in Rome to determine whether they should sign a treaty to create the kind of court Ben had been advocating for. They invited him to address the assembly, and his words, as well as his subsequent contributions to the negotiations, helped inspire adoption of the treaty.

BUT THERE is even more to Ben Ferencz than this string of additional non-Nuremberg achievements. For if, toward the end of his long life, seeing him myopically as merely the "last living Nuremberg prosecutor" would have reduced his career to a caricature; so too would lionizing him as a perfect saint of international justice miss the true essence of his character. He was a man of incredible depth, complexity, and sometimes, contradiction.

Paradoxically, for instance, this tireless crusader for the rule of law spent many of the most important years of his life flouting the law. The product of a broken home, he was often lonely and depressed. As a child left to his own devices on the streets of Hell's Kitchen, he participated in crime before realizing he was ultimately more interested in preventing it. In high school, he was nearly expelled for running a gambling scheme and, in the end, never earned his high school diploma. But he managed to finagle his way into the City College of New York without it. And despite his short stature and fine intellect, with his pugnacious nature and street savvy, for a time he was a boxer during his university days.

As a soldier in the US Army, he routinely violated rules and regulations and committed prosecutable offenses. Commandeering materials to make fabricated leave passes, which he distributed as he saw fit; conspiring with other soldiers to steal shipments of food; routinely disobeying orders from his superiors—such conduct was an integral part of the Ferencz military experience. On more than one occasion, he was threatened with an actual court-martial, and, on various others, he was punished with demeaning labor, such as digging latrines. When Telford Taylor interviewed him for the job at Nuremberg, as Ferencz later recounted, Taylor had "uncovered some of my military records that, understandably, caused him some concern. He noted that my army file indicated that I was occasionally insubordinate. 'That is not correct, Sir,' I replied. 'I am not occasionally insubordinate. I am usually insubordinate.'"[11]

And Ben Ferencz, the indefatigable campaigner for human rights, due process, and fairness was often guilty of shunting aside those values. In conducting his war crimes investigations, he has acknowledged, he was "mad. . . . There was some sense of outrage."[12] While probing at Ebensee concentration camp, for example, he came upon a group of inmates chasing down an SS guard, whom they caught and then roasted alive in an oven. Ferencz watched and did nothing. He later wrote that, even had he been able to stop this torture, "frankly, I was not inclined to try."[13]

He paid little heed to human rights or due process in other instances too. When investigating war crimes committed against downed American pilots in Germany, Ferencz would coerce statements and confessions by brandishing a .45 pistol before those he interrogated and threatening to shoot them if they were not forthcoming.[14]

But rule-upholder versus rule-violator has not been the only contradiction at the heart of his character. In fact, there have been many. He had what seemed like a fairy-tale romance with his childhood sweetheart, Gertrude. They were together for nearly eighty-five years and married for almost seventy-five before Gertrude passed away in 2019. In many ways, it was a model relationship, each of them truly in love with the other. And Ben would often brag how they never even had a fight. And yet, as revealed publicly for the first time in these pages, Ferencz was not monogamous. Tortured by his wartime experiences and lonesome for long stretches on the road, he found solace in the arms of others, Gertrude found out, and the couple nearly divorced.

Similarly, he has had a topsy-turvy relationship with his children. His early years of fatherhood could almost be described as idyllic—with the paterfamilias lovingly wrestling with the kids, teaching them about the arts, taking them on excursions, and even cooking for them at times. But as the youngsters—Keri, Robin, Don, and Nina—began reaching adolescence and developing distinct personalities, tensions surfaced. This was especially true with the eldest daughters, Keri and Robin, who were sent away to boarding school at one point and, at another, ran away from home. And as Ferencz's reparations work ramped up and he was increasingly immersed in the dark details of Hitler's genocide against the Jews, he began exposing his younger children, Don and Nina, via graphic photos and anecdotes, to gruesome details about the Holocaust that traumatized them. And Don, as the only son of a man with traditional patriarchal views, particularly felt the pressure and bore the burden of living up to his father's high standards, rigorous expectations, and legacy. Ben Ferencz has admitted that, in certain respects, his role as a parent has brought him "grief."[15]

Over the years, he managed to thrive financially, making millions of dollars successfully playing the stock market. But he lived as modestly as he did before he achieved such affluence, residing most of his adult life in the humble abode in New Rochelle, New York, that he purchased on his return to the United States in the 1950s. Toward the end, his dwelling was an unadorned bungalow-style home in Delray Beach, Florida, that he bought for a modest sum. Despite striving for great wealth through investments, he completely eschewed a life of luxury and gave away most of his fortune to charity.

And perhaps even more perplexing has been the role played by his Jewish identity. From his immigrant roots, his strong family ties, and his success in overcoming antisemitism at various junctures in his career, Ben Ferencz's Jewish heritage was clearly a great source of self-identity and pride. Indeed, he championed the cause of literally hundreds of thousands, if not millions, of Jews around the world with his innovations in Holocaust reparations. And yet, he felt a certain ambivalence about his religion. Despite the seemingly central role of Judaism in his biography, it did not figure prominently in his writings, speeches, or even his daily life. He did not belong to a synagogue. He did not observe the Jewish holidays. If pressed about this, he would show clear discomfort and try to change the subject. The phantasmagoric suffering he witnessed in the concentration camps always haunted him. It shook his faith in God, in reference to whom, he would observe wryly, "We are not on speaking terms."[16] He was, more than anything else, a humanist who happened to be Jewish.

But arguably the man's complexity is no better demonstrated than in the way he controlled his personal narrative. He is best known for his exploits at Nuremberg; however, he gave a rather circumscribed account of it. He always emphasized that, on arriving in Nuremberg in 1946, Telford Taylor sent him straightaway to Berlin to take over the OCCWC's most important investigative office. Then, according to his standard telling of the story, the Einsatzgruppen reports were eventually discovered, and he transferred back to Berlin to become chief prosecutor in the case against the mobile killing squad defendants. From there, he would routinely explain, he became Taylor's executive counsel and then left the office to do reparations work.

Amazingly, though, he would always leave out an important, even essential, aspect of his OCCWC contributions in Nuremberg. In fact, as my research revealed, Taylor first assigned him to be an investigator on the Nazi industrialist cases—that is, those against, inter alia, Alfried Krupp (a key arms manufacturer for Hitler, plunderer, and exploiter of Jewish slave labor) and the executives of IG Farben (slavers and plunderers too, but also directors of the conglomerate that developed Zyklon B, the lethal chemical used in Nazi gas chambers). It was after proving himself for months as a star investigator on these cases that Taylor elevated him to Berlin Branch chief. And this omission is not just an historical oddity, curiously left out of his life story. In fact, it is a key missing part of the puzzle, which helps explain the great results he achieved in Berlin, where the industrialist investigations assumed great importance. Indeed, it is an essential Nuremberg backstory as it foreshadows Ferencz's service post-*Einsatzgruppen* as a trial attorney for the *Krupp* prosecution. In other words, his in-court trial experience at Nuremberg was not limited to *Einsatzgruppen;* it also included *Krupp.*[17] And this work on the industrialist cases is essential for contextualizing his later civil litigation campaign against Nazi industrialists for their exploitation of Jewish slave labor. Even more importantly, it may be the key to fully understanding his later crusade to criminalize the aggression offense.

And there are other curious omissions in Ferencz's standard narrative, including important details regarding his Nazi art-plundering investigations, which filtered into Hermann Göring's prosecution at Nuremberg, his dealings with Hannah Arendt on the Holocaust restitution cases, his communications with Israeli prosecutors during the Adolf Eichmann trial preparations, the true extent of his brilliant defense of Vietnam War protesters against serious criminal charges in Hawaii, and his éminence grise role in crafting victims provisions in the International Criminal Court treaty.

And yet, at times, he would exaggerate or embellish elsewhere—giving the impression, for example, that he was among those who stormed the beaches at Normandy on D-Day. Rather, he tranquilly disembarked at Omaha Beach the following month, well after active fighting there had ceased.[18] Similarly, he has related that, based on high-level, back-channel communications from his former Harvard Law professor, for whom he had conducted war crimes research in school, he was plucked out of obscurity from his combat unit and transferred to Patton's Judge Advocate (JA) Section to head up a new war crimes investigation unit.[19] Instead, as I found in my research, he applied for a position with the JA Section as a paralegal specialist, got the job, and then merit and circumstances on the ground conspired to eventually convert him into a pioneer war crimes investigator.

So THERE is a complexity and depth of character to Ben Ferencz that has escaped public appreciation and helps properly humanize him. *Einsatzgruppen* trial expert Hilary Earl has described him as a "fantastically complicated personality";[20] indeed, he was so much more than the "Nuremberg prosecutor." Perhaps it is fair to ask, then, why that moniker features so prominently in the title of this story of his life. It is a perfectly good question, and a word of explanation is in order.

Put simply, while Nuremberg was not *all* that the man was about, it was *central* to all he accomplished. For when he stood in the courtroom making his opening argument on that early autumn day in 1947, everything about that moment summed up the life he had led as he laid out his case to the Tribunal. That he had been an underdog could be seen symbolically in the way he scarcely cleared the lectern. That he had been a war crimes investigator who personally witnessed the types of cruelty, inhumanity, and suffering that he was describing for the court could be gleaned from his eloquence and passionate pleas for justice. That he was a voice for the victims who had a disdain for military rigidity and hierarchy could be seen in his civilian attire and his earnest, youthful face and could be heard in his thick Hell's Kitchen accent.

At the same time, this moment of perfect equipoise in his life—not chronologically but experientially, thematically—would telegraph everything that was to come, in terms of both victim advocacy and atrocity prevention. As observed by Canadian Supreme Court Justice Rosalie Abella: "[If] all he had done was argue at the age of twenty-seven in front of the Nuremberg Tribunal, I would've said, 'That's a remarkable person.' To go on and use that as the fire that ignites his soul and his brain on behalf of humanity is what makes him an iconic figure."[21]

So there are good reasons for the emphasis on Nuremberg. But why refer to Ben Ferencz as Nuremberg's "citizen prosecutor"? In the main, the American "chief prosecutors" of the Nuremberg Trials—those who were there in prominent positions at the birth of international criminal law—arrived at this watershed moment of history as the product of privileged circumstances or exalted positions in society. Robert Jackson himself, although born on a farm and never having formally earned a law degree, came to Nuremberg having already served, successively, as US solicitor general, attorney general, and associate justice of the US Supreme Court.

Even those American chief prosecutors lower in the hierarchy than Jackson had come to Nuremberg from relatively advantaged backgrounds or high stations in life. This is easy to see from a quick sampling of the various personal histories of some of them. Telford Taylor himself, a descendant of the seventeenth-century settlers of Massachusetts, was born to a physicist and had been a prominent New Deal lawyer before the war began.[22] James McHaney, lead prosecutor in the so-called *Medical* case, was the son of an Arkansas Supreme Court justice and had worked at a white-shoe New York City law firm.[23] Charles M. La Follette, who ran the *Justice* case, had previously been a US congressman and was the cousin of the great Progressive icon Senator Robert M. La Follette.[24] Before Nuremberg, *Ministries* chief prosecutor Robert M. Kempner, the son of two prominent German scientists, had served as the senior legal advisor to the Prussian police and was fired by Hermann Göring himself.[25]

Certainly, Taylor's staff was generally quite young, and not all came from society's upper strata.[26] But even among the rank and file, Ben Ferencz's humble origins stood out. He had been a dirt-poor immigrant child, the diminutive son of a one-eyed janitor, initially raised in poverty on the mean streets of Hell's Kitchen; a man whose education and command of the English language was late in coming. Despite later being a scholarship student at Harvard Law School (where he barely had enough money to feed himself), he had been initially rejected from the armed forces and, even once inducted, relegated to the rank of buck private, serving as a lowly supply clerk in an artillery unit.

He eventually became an army investigator but hated military pomp and the mistreatment of ordinary soldiers and was constantly on the outs with his superiors, nearly court-martialed on several occasions. When Telford Taylor hired him, he was unemployed.

In one sense, "citizen" is defined as "an ordinary person."[27] Former president Barack Obama has referred to "citizens" as "ordinary men and women" who can rise up to do "extraordinary things" and help pull the "arc of the moral universe in the direction of justice."[28] He might have been speaking of Benjamin Ferencz in the wake of World War II—an ordinary man trying his first case under extraordinary circumstances, who rose to the occasion in Courtroom 600 and helped bend the trajectory of human history in the direction of justice. It is in this sense that we can think of him as Nuremberg's "citizen" prosecutor. And having assumed that role, he worked tirelessly for the rest of his life, continuing to help steer the world in the direction of justice.

But while he may have represented the everyman, his long journey was filled with an incredible cast of larger-than-life figures. In addition to the great philosopher Hannah Arendt, former First Lady Eleanor Roosevelt, General George Patton, Justice Robert Jackson, German chancellor Konrad Adenauer, and legal pioneer Raphael Lemkin, this includes movie star Marlene Dietrich, presidential advisor John J. McCloy, Senator Edward Kennedy, Harvard Law School legend Roscoe Pound, Nobel laureate and author Elie Wiesel, and actress Angelina Jolie, among others. But through it all, Benjamin Ferencz never lost touch with his poor immigrant roots, his humble origins—even when moving in the most privileged corridors of power and having accumulated great wealth, to his core, he was still that impoverished kid trying to survive on the streets of Hell's Kitchen, that cherubic, earnest-faced young lawyer, remaining among the ranks of the common folk and fighting for justice on their behalf.

And this is a particularly poignant time to tell his story. When, all around the world, the shrill voices of intolerance now seek to conjure up the ghosts of old hatreds and the pall of new persecutions, laying out the full panorama of Ben Ferencz's life journey is quite timely. Those who might be tempted to listen to the rants of today's demagogues, who tell us that the norms and the customs, even the architecture, of the international rule of law are the product of the privileged, the province of the powerful, and the pox of the people, should examine the life of Ben Ferencz. The remarkable story of this everyman who rose to such great heights as an icon of international justice, but who never forgot where he came from, may remind us that the core values and aspirations of the international rule of law, as well as the democratic ideals underlying it, are shared by all strata of society. But his story may also serve to warn us of the dangers we face in returning to the ugly climate of the 1930s and the first half of the 1940s. Thus, the life of Benjamin B. Ferencz should be an inspiration for the masses, and a beacon of hope for the oppressed, especially as the specter of a new era of global aggression looms on the horizon. Let us now consider how that life unfolded.

PART I
PRELUDE

1

FROM DRACULA'S CASTLE TO HELL'S KITCHEN

> The happy and powerful do not go into exile, and there are no surer guarantees of equality among men than poverty and misfortune.
>
> —Alexis de Tocqueville, *Democracy in America*

To modern ears, the name Transylvania conjures up an almost mystical land of medieval hamlets, mountainous borders, gothic fortresses, dark churches, howling wolves, and bloodthirsty vampires, including Count Dracula, the most legendary of those fanged creatures. Many think Transylvania is only a figment of the imagination of horror-fiction writers. But it is a real place. Situated in eastern Europe, in the modern-day nation of Romania, it is nestled in the Carpathian Mountains region, not far from the Hungarian and Ukrainian frontiers.

After the Ottomans subjugated Hungary in 1541, Transylvania became a vassal of its empire, maintaining a degree of Romanian autonomy by paying tribute to the sultan in Constantinople. In 1683, an Ottoman invasion of the Holy Roman Empire was halted at the gates of Vienna, and, ultimately, rule over Transylvania transferred to the Habsburgs in 1687. In practice, this meant that Transylvania fell within the dominion of the Hungarians (or Magyars, in the local tongue), who "offered a higher guarantee of security to Jews than [the governments of] other countries" in the region.[1] Thus, "Transylvanian Jews enjoyed the same rights as the empire's other citizens, suffering neither discrimination nor marginalization."[2]

As a result, the region became a magnet for Jews fleeing persecution, and the northern Transylvanian town of Şomcuta Mare was one of the focal points of that migration. The Jewish community there began developing at the beginning of the nineteenth century, many of the settlers arriving from Galicia (a region that now consists of parts of contemporary Poland and Ukraine). Şomcuta Mare's first synagogue was built in 1862. By the time of World War I, the Jewish community in the town had grown to nearly 1,000 persons, or roughly 30 percent of the population. By then, they played a diverse role in the regional economy, owning flour mills, exporting grains and fruit, and working in the local trades.[3]

In 1920, one of those tradesmen was Josef Ferencz, a cobbler. He was born in the region in 1894, during the reign of Habsburg monarch Franz Joseph. Perhaps reflecting the gratitude of Transylvania's Jewish people for the tolerance and rights they enjoyed in the realm, the shoemaker went by a Magyar inversion of the Austro-Hungarian emperor's name. Unfortunately, by the time of Josef Ferencz's twenty-fourth birthday, the situation for Jews in Transylvania had changed for the worse. Austria-Hungary, one of the Central powers during World War I, had suffered defeat at the hands of the Entente powers, which precipitated the empire's collapse.

Among the raft of passionate irredentist claims made in the wake of Austria-Hungary's demise was that of Romania for Transylvania. And the claim was honored. Via the 1920 Treaty of Trianon, Josef Ferencz's birth region was officially ceded to the Land of Count Dracula. Of course, Bram Stoker's infamous vampire was inspired by a real-life historical figure from the region, Vlad Dracula, a fifteenth-century nobleman whose gory sobriquet was "Vlad the Impaler," as he would run pikes through his enemies' innards and then vertically hoist them on the sharpened poles so they would die in slow agony. For the Jews of Transylvania, the return of the region to Romanian rule might have evoked comparisons to Vlad. The new overlords were reluctant to even grant citizenship to their Hebraic neighbors, who were once again subject to physical and economic persecution.

The year 1920 was significant for Josef Ferencz in other ways too. Most importantly, his first and only son was born. In Ciolt (a small village on the outskirts of Şomcuta Mare), on March 11 of that year, "Berrel" Ferencz, who would later be known as Benjamin Berell Ferencz,[4] entered the world in his parents' small cottage, a simple structure with a clay floor.[5] Eighteen months earlier, in the same peasant dwelling, his twenty-two-year-old mother, Shari (née Legman and known as "Sara"), had given birth to Ben's sister, Perril (who would later be called "Pepi" and then "Pearl"). The young couple, who were second cousins in an arranged marriage, saw which way the wind was blowing for Şomcuta Mare's vulnerable Jewish community and decided that staying would put Perril and Berrel in too much peril; so they decided to leave.

Their instincts were good. Just up the road, in the small Transylvanian town of Sighetu Marmației, during the same decade, a Jewish boy named Elie Wiesel would be born to Sarah Feig and Shlomo Wiese. A little over two decades later, Sarah, Shlomo, and Elie would find themselves in the death camp the Nazis called Auschwitz; only Elie would survive, barely. If Josef, Sara, Pearl, and Benjamin Ferencz had remained in Transylvania, the same fate would have likely befallen them (in fact, Ben's grandmother and various aunts, uncles, and cousins were murdered at Auschwitz). Still, amazingly, Ben Ferencz and Elie Wiesel would both end up together at Buchenwald concentration camp, Ben as an American liberator, and Elie as an Auschwitz death march survivor. One would become a famous Holocaust prosecutor and the other, a famous Holocaust author. And, as we shall see, their lives would intersect again and again, well into the twenty-first century.

Unfortunately, the historical record does not disclose the exact nature of the first leg of the Ferencz family's exodus from Transylvania. But one thing is certain—they began the journey on land sometime at the beginning of 1921. And the little family might have gone in two different directions. They may have headed southeast, toward the Black Sea, where they would have secured passage on a vessel navigating through the Bosphorus and the Dardanelles to the Sea of Marmara, then the Aegean, the Mediterranean, the Tyrrhenian, through the Strait of Gibraltar, and on to England. Ironically, this is the route Count Dracula took to the British Isles in Bram Stoker's fictionalized account.

More likely, however, the Ferencz family headed due west by train and eventually found themselves at one of the French ports on the English Channel. They would have embarked from places such as Calais, Cherbourg, Dunkirk, or Le Havre and ended up at Dover or Portsmouth or one of the other English endpoints. Another train journey would have taken them north, to their final destination—Liverpool—before finally leaving Europe.

A ship manifest shows they paid for passage on a boat belonging to the White Star Line, the same company whose RMS *Titanic,* the largest sea vessel in the world, had tragically sunk off the coast of Newfoundland a bit over eight years previously. The Ferenczes' Atlantic passage on the White Star Line ship RMS *Cedric* would not end so tragically, but it was not smooth sailing all the same. The Ferencz family were placed in the *Cedric*'s lowest bowels. As Ben himself wryly noted later, "The only reason we traveled in third-class steerage across the cold Atlantic in January was that there was no fourth-class."[6]

The ship manifest lists the date of departure from Liverpool as "19th January 1921" and indicates its final destination as "New York." Below that, a section titled "Names and Descriptions of ALIEN Passengers Embarked at the Port of Liverpool" lists, among the "aliens" on board "Ferencz, Josef." And then, under his name, those of his spouse and two children appear—"Sara," "Pepi," and "Bela." Ben later noted humorously that "the records of the immigration authorities on Ellis Island showed that I came into the country from the town of Ciolt, in Romania, on January 29, 1921 as a 4-month-old single female by the name of Bela."[7] He went on, evidently quite amused: "The truth is that I am, and always have been, a male. I was at least two-and-a-half-times older than the record stated, and no one has ever called me Bela, although my Jewish name was Berrel. The indication that I was unmarried at that time is probably accurate. I doubt whether even the Immigration and Naturalization Service would treat the errors on the ship's manifest as valid cause for deportation. I shall always be grateful for the generous immigration policies of the United States at that time."[8]

In fact, all humor aside (as well as name inaccuracy), in Romania/Hungary, "Bela" designates a male, and, to add another Count Dracula reference, it was used by the most famous actor to play the Transylvanian vampire, Bela Lugosi. But the ties to Transylvania were about to end there. For Ben's voyage on the RMS *Cedric* was a miserable infantile rite of passage to the New World. And he survived it thanks to his Uncle Leppold. Per Ben: "The oldest of my mother's five brothers came with us. His name was Leppold, but Americans called him Leopold. He often reminded me in later years that he had saved my life when he stopped my father, who became enraged by my incessant crying, from throwing me overboard. Frankly, I did not recall the event, but I was always grateful nevertheless to my Uncle Leppold."[9]

Things would not get much better on arrival in New York. On passing through Ellis Island, they were met by Sara's older sister Fani, who escorted them to temporary shelter provided by the Hebrew Immigrant Aid Society. But soon the family was sharing crowded spaces on the Lower East Side of Manhattan with indigent relatives while Josef went job hunting. And the search for employment was not going well. In later years, Ben would aptly analyze his father's job prospects: "He was only a one-eyed Jewish shoemaker who couldn't possibly find a job in America in the vocation to which he was apprenticed. Despite having lost an eye as a youth, and very limited schooling, he boasted that he could make a pair of boots from a single piece of cowhide. No one had told him that there weren't many cows in New York City, and even fewer customers for boots hand-made by a Transylvanian cobbler."[10]

Desperate, Josef jumped at the chance to work as a janitor tending three apartment houses on the West Side of Midtown Manhattan. If his English had been better, perhaps the name of his new workplace's neighborhood would have convinced him to hold out for better prospects. He would be toiling in a slum known as "Hell's Kitchen." From the mid-1800s into the 1980s, this bleak quarter of the city was, as described by the *New York Times* (which coined the area's satanic moniker in its pages), "one tough neighborhood" with a history "that's rich with gangsters and ghosts, streetwalkers and speakeasies, mysterious disappearances and gruesome murders."[11] The *Times* article describes what the neighborhood would have been like when the Ferencz family moved there in 1921:

> Tenements to house the workers and their families were hastily thrown up from the 1850s on, and out of them roamed gangs of youths who ruled the streets after the Civil War. The Hell's Kitchen Gang, whom Herbert Asbury called "a collection of the most desperate ruffians in the city" in his 1927 book "The Gangs of New York" (inspiration for the Martin Scorsese film), fought constantly with the police and with rivals like the Gorillas, the Parlor Mob, and the Gophers. . . . The block of West 39th Street between 10th and 11th Avenues saw so much fighting it was nicknamed Battle Row.[12]

Ben's later research determined that it was "the highest density crime area in the nation at the time."[13] And this bleak quarter is where Ben Ferencz would experience his initial awakenings as a sentient being and form his first impressions of humanity and the world around him. It was not an auspicious beginning. As he has noted about his first American residence, "It was there that I learned to muse about life and death, the spirit of free enterprise, business ethics, the perils of gambling and alcoholism, the advantages of law over crime, and similar subjects taught primarily in the school of hard knocks."[14]

Living quarters for the Ferencz family consisted of a small portion of the subterranean cellar of one of Josef's three janitorial sites, at 346 West Fifty-Sixth Street. Tiny, dank, and dark (with only two small windows taking in limited light from the base of the building's rickety stoop in an alley), Sara did her best to make it habitable. The cavernous digs could at least be faintly illuminated via match-lit gas lamps. Other than those, the main amenities were a wood-burning stove that had both culinary and thermal utility as well as a nearby sink that served as a washing basin and makeshift bathtub for the children (weekly ablutions for the adults were performed in a portable metal tub filled with pails of hot water).

The only privacy afforded the occupants was via dug-out portions of the cold stone wall, referred to by the family as "niches" (which would have been spoken in Yiddish, the Ferencz lingua franca). These narrow nooks served as "bedrooms"—one for the parents and one for the children—and, as there were more than two such cubbyholes, the Ferenczes supplemented their meager income by letting boarders sleep in the other ones. Sara also padded the tight weekly budget by cooking homestyle meals for Hungarian immigrants.

Perhaps Ben's first lessons in public service came via his parents' charitable practice of letting vagrants come in from the cold to sleep on beds of newspapers taken from a stack piled against the stone wall. But Sara would still exercise caution and warn the children to stay away from the "bums."

One way for Sara to keep them away from the "bums" on their floor was to take Benny and Pearl outside "for an airing at the head of the dozen iron steps that led up from [their] basement apartment."[15] Pearl was the classic older child—incredibly responsible, conservative, obedient, a stickler for the rules. Benny viewed her as "an orderly child who would stay put."[16] Her younger sibling was the opposite. Ignoring his sister's stern threats to "tell on him," he would sally forth into the neighborhood and soak up all its sordid sights and sounds.

During these excursions into Hell's Kitchen, the little immigrant boy gradually began developing a deviant streak that would stay with him throughout his life. His walk on the wild side began innocently enough—he spied a gaggle of boys on Eighth Avenue with stacks of papers under their arms shouting "Extra, Extra! Get your papers!" Pedestrian commuters hurrying home from work were being handed copies of these dailies and robotically giving the vendors coins in exchange. Benny soon realized that his could be a pretty lucrative venture. And he wanted in on the action.

He flashed in his mind to the supply of old newspapers stacked against the stone wall in their cellar. They normally served as mattresses for the tramps who slept on their floor, but the enterprising child concluded that they could be put to better use. So he removed the top part of the stack, placed the pile under his arm, and hightailed it to Eighth Avenue. Once there, he began parading up and down the thoroughfare with the other boys shouting, in his thick Hungarian/Yiddish accent, "Getcher papers!" And the scheme was working, as the rushed passersby never stopped to notice that they were buying last week's news. Unfortunately, a one-eyed janitor returning home to 346 West Fifty-Sixth Street ended up being one of his customers. Joe Ferencz quickly put the kibosh on his son's new "business."

But other opportunities beckoned. At one point, Benny auditioned to be the paid subject of a portrait of a girl to be painted by a young artist. Previewing the movie *Tootsie* by decades, Benny thought he could get the part. His blonde hair was on the long side at that point, and he wore one of his sister's blouses for the audition. And he won the gig! He later walked to the studio and posed in his feminine garb while holding a large peppermint candy cane. His reward was $2.50 in nickels and dimes. He was beginning to conclude that perhaps crime paid.

That was reinforced somewhat by his father's own example. Because, as it turned out, Joe Ferencz had also been soaking up the neighborhood ethos and decided to become a bootlegger. In 1919, not long before the arrival of the Ferencz family in New York, the Eighteenth Amendment to the United States Constitution had been ratified. That modification of the nation's charter criminalized the production, transport, and sale of intoxicating liquors and was made federally enforceable via Congress's passage of the 1920 Volstead Act. In spite of this, Janitor Joe sought to supplement his income by converting a mash of boiling potatoes into a "fiery liquid" that dripped from a copper distillery hidden in the cellar. Although Ben would later joke that there was no risk that his old man "was going into competition with Al Capone,"[17] the homemade booze was still turning a pretty profit, being sold to many of the neighborhood's increasingly "thirsty" Irish residents, including certain of those in the police force. Little Benny was in on the conspiracy and swore to keep the bootlegging operation a secret.

And so the stage was set for deeper exploration of the dark side. Eventually, Benny's excursions into the neighborhood brought him into contact with older kids, juvenile delinquents who befriended him and wanted him to share in their life of crime on the streets. Whether it was through theft or gambling, the young Ben Ferencz began regularly breaking the law as a "mascot" member of various Hell's Kitchen gangs.

One of their favorite tactics was to send their little charge into a small grocery store as an advance party. He was instructed to make enough noise while purloining food that the proprietor would notice him. Then, he would swiftly scurry out of the establishment with the store owner in hot pursuit. But, with his tiny stature and agile gait, he could move like a jackrabbit and always managed to evade capture. In the meantime, the other boys in the gang would enter the store and calmly help themselves to whichever merchandise they liked.

Otherwise, the conspiracy to steal was quite straightforward—in passing, gang members would simply swipe potatoes roasting on sidewalk braziers—a delicacy they called "Mickeys"—and make a run for it while the enraged spud-seller screamed and chased them in vain. Benny was enjoying the camaraderie and the material benefits of this life of thievery: "I was priding myself on . . . stealing things, you know, and getting away with it."[18]

But at some point, Benny started to sour on the idea of a life of crime, realizing he "would rather be on the side of the law, than on the side of the criminals."[19] Part of his sense of disillusionment with the criminals stemmed from all the brutality he was seeing on the streets: the muggings, beatings, stabbings, and often-fatal bloody gang brawls. Even as a child, in time, he realized that the criminal life would swallow him up in its dark, ugly maw; it was surely a path to oblivion. And that life-altering epiphany began with an incident outside a movie theater.

THE FERENCZ family could not afford babysitters, and, while both parents were working (Sara doing odd jobs, sewing, and cleaning houses to help make ends meet), the ideal solution was to drop both kids off at the neighborhood movie theater, the Chalona, on Ninth Avenue. Benny and Pearl could be accompanied in by an adult, and for the ten-cent cost of admission, they could remain there for as long as was needed. In fact, Benny recalls one occasion where his father deposited him at the theater early in the day and, when retrieving him at midnight, found his son asleep under a seat in one of the front rows. But mostly the cinema thrilled him, and sleep was rarely on the agenda. These were the days of silent films, and the children were treated to features with stars such as Charlie Chaplin, Buster Keaton, and Mary Pickford.

One rainy day, when both parents were otherwise occupied, the children had to walk to the movie theater themselves and then ask any adult in the vicinity (that is, a stranger) to accompany them in (perhaps not the best idea in Hell's Kitchen). Soon a young man passed by and offered to buy the children tickets and walk them into the cinema. But once Pearl gave the man the quarter she had been clutching, he walked toward the box office, and then pivoted in the other direction, laughing and running away with the movie money. The two children were devastated. And they started bawling at the top of their lungs as an increasingly intense rain fell on them. It was a pitiful scene, but their luck was about to change.

An elderly gentleman soon passed by and asked them what was wrong. When they explained what had happened, the kind senior motioned them toward the theater marquis to get them out of the rain. Even better, he offered to purchase their movie tickets and accompany them into the cinema. A few minutes later, the man returned with ice cream cones for both Benny and Pearl. The children were deeply moved, with the younger sibling later reporting, "Neither my sister nor I ever forgot that kindness. Not everyone is mean and rotten. The world is not such a bad place after all."[20]

In fact, the incident had a profound effect on the young Ben Ferencz. In the first place, he felt the sting of being a crime victim, and that left a profoundly bad taste in his mouth. More importantly, though, he gained an appreciation for the value of helping other people in need. And he dedicated himself to doing that for others.

Almost instinctively, he began gravitating toward the underdogs in his neighborhood. One of them was "Tony the Shoeshine Man" on Fifty-Sixth Street. Tony was an immigrant from Italy who missed his family terribly. The other kids in the neighborhood, perhaps sensing this and being cruel as kids can be, would pass by and shout insults at him. But Benny took on the role of protector—he would defend Tony. "He was a nice man," he recounted later. "And I resented the fact that the other kids would come make fun of him."[21]

So Benny would lurk around the neighborhood, keeping a protective eye on Tony and monitoring whether his two customer high chairs were empty. If they were, he would stop by and keep Tony company. And the shoeshine man would always reciprocate with a Tootsie Roll or two. They were an odd couple, Tony and Benny—the old man, who mainly spoke Italian, and the young kid, who conversed primarily in Yiddish. But they developed a strong bond as fish-out-of-water immigrants looking for kinship in a hostile environment.

In that same spirit, another outcast to whom Benny was drawn was a retired medical doctor who had gone blind and was now living in their tenement house. Feeling depressed over his sightlessness and abandoned because of his age, he would spend most of his time moping alone on the stoop above the Ferencz basement. So the little boy would join him there and help raise his spirits. On other occasions, he would serve as the poor soul's eyes, taking him for a walk around the block while the man rested his hand on Benny's shoulder. Just as with Tony the Shoeshine Man, despite the vast age difference, a bond developed between Benny and the sightless physician. Ferencz learned years later that this octogenarian had bequeathed him his entire book collection, including his old medical texts. They held no real value for the young man, but Ben was touched by the gesture—after all, his would-be benefactor had nothing else to give. The relationship further reinforced his belief in devoting himself to doing good deeds for others.

As this new ethic was being reinforced in his mind, he was becoming more and more disenchanted with the criminal element in his neighborhood. One of the inextricable associations with crime in Hell's Kitchen was the abuse of alcohol. And, as his character was evolving, Benny was also developing a strong distaste for spirits, what he called "the evils of drink." That aversion began in earnest when his father was attacked in their neighborhood by someone severely under the influence.

The man was throwing bricks from the roof of one of Janitor Joe's tenement houses, and, with Benny in tow, the protective father ordered the man to desist. But the response was violent. The inebriated brick-heaver came toe to toe with Joe and threw a roundhouse punch. Joe then pulled the hefty cover off a nearby garbage can "and held it up like the shield of a Roman gladiator." But the man rushed at Joe again with another punch, and the janitor "smashed his opponent squarely in the face."[22] There could not have been a more powerful reminder of the evils of the drink.

But Benny really began to channel his inner Carrie Nation after a religious holiday dinner that followed this incident. As he described it in his later written recollections:

> It was Passover [and the] prayer ritual requires repeated sips of wine. The kosher purple grape juice was sufficiently fermented and sweet to make it very palatable and I did my religious duty with gusto and glee. I was soon feeling quite happy and even more talkative than usual—much to the amusement of all present. They kept pouring more wine and I kept drinking it. Soon, I was what experts call "drunk as a skunk." I recall vividly how the room kept spinning round and round while I got sicker and sicker. That was the first time in my life that I ever became inebriated. It was also the last.

With his newfound animosity toward alcohol and crime, his father's copper still in the basement was soon within Benny's crosshairs. Now channeling his inner Eliot Ness, he started telling everyone in the neighborhood about the "fiery liquid" his father was secretly brewing in the cellar. When that did not have the desired effect, he took it one step further: "I told [my father] I was going to turn him in."[23] And that did the trick—in short order, the distillery disappeared from the cellar, and the moonshine operation was effectively dismantled. Benny's initial encounter with law enforcement was exhilarating, and he would describe it as his "first victory over organized crime."[24]

He was now resolved to earn a clean living himself. His main vocation, in this regard, was serving as Joe's "Assistant Janitor." In effect, his main task, none too glamorous, was helping with garbage collection. This was accomplished with a dumbwaiter and rope. Each kitchen in the tenement houses had a small closet-like door that opened onto a shaft, which contained the small garbage-receptacle-lift. The tenants would deposit trash on the dumbwaiter shelf, which was hoisted up to them—and then brought down—by the janitor using a rope pulley in the basement. Once collected, the garbage would be placed in a large metal can and then hauled up the cellar steps to the sidewalk for collection. It is safe to say that, in his long and varied career, this was not among his favorite jobs.

Far more gratifying than garbage collection was bottle recycling. Benny eventually realized that he could return the empty milk receptacles to the grocer for two or three cents a pop. As an adult, he recorded this as one of the great triumphs of his early life: "Eureka! That is how I started to make my fortune. I became an independent entrepreneur in the environmental conservation business!"[25]

But as poor as the Ferenczes were, life in Hell's Kitchen did not revolve solely around earning an extra buck. On certain weekends, Joe and Sara would bring the kids to Central Park to hear the famous Goldman Band (primarily a wind/brass ensemble) playing free concerts on the mall. Another family favorite was taking in plays and musicals at theaters on the Lower East Side's "Jewish Rialto" (also called the "Jewish Broadway").[26]

In fact, the family was able to scrape together enough money to buy a cheap gramophone, and they would play records of their favorite Yiddish theater singers on it. Ben recalls that, when "the singer's voice began to slow to a southern drawl," it was his duty "to start winding up the machine furiously to accelerate him back to a peppy Yiddish ending."[27]

But mostly the kids preferred diversions that took place outside of the dank tenement cellar they called home. And they were able to find them. One of the boarders was a kind Hungarian immigrant by the name of Dave Schwartz. He would often take Pearl and Benny for Sunday rides on a Fifth Avenue bus with an open upper deck from which they "could look down on the fancy shops and people."[28] The kids loved exploring Manhattan this way and were thrilled to know they could stay on the bus as long as they liked, without having to pay any extra fare. And the excursions were even better when Mr. Schwartz would buy them ice-cream cones, which he typically did.

For Benny and Pearl, escaping from 346 West Fifty-Sixth Street was not just about avoiding the ugly physical surroundings. The personal dynamics in the cellar were equally bleak. While arranged consanguineous marriages in the Jewish community were not uncommon in the Old Country, the one between Joe and Sara did not seem to be working out in the New World. As their son cleverly quipped, "Hell's Kitchen would never qualify as a setting for marriages made in heaven."[29] The young couple was apparently mismatched from the start, and their problems were only aggravated by their poverty, hard work, and slum surroundings on the West Side of Midtown Manhattan. According to their son, "My father and mother would spend much time just shouting at each other; which rather disturbed my tranquility."[30]

Adding to the tension was the announcement that Sara was pregnant again. It was a difficult pregnancy, and it resulted in the birth of a quite tiny and frail girl. Things grew direr still when, soon after her birth, she fell seriously ill. In some ways, the fate of Benny's new little sister would be the determining factor in whether Joe and Sara could save their marriage. The concerned parents wanted to devote all their time and resources to aid in the recovery of the new family addition. To do that, they sent Pearl and Benny to spend some time with their Uncle Leppold in upstate New York.

By then, Leppold was living on a small farm well outside of the city—in Port Jervis, approximately three hours northwest by train. Sara's eldest brother was married and had his own kids. It was a nice respite from Hell's Kitchen, and the Ferencz children benefited from wide-open spaces, fresh air, and the company of well-behaved young ones who posed no risk of beating them up or taking their valuables. Unfortunately, this idyllic interlude was cut short by some very bad news—Joe and Sara's newborn did not make it. Both Benny and Pearl were devastated; so were their parents. And that proved to be the undoing of the marriage.

The first phase of Ben Ferencz's life in America was now coming to an end. The family would move out of the clammy confines of 346 West Fifty-Sixth Street, and his parents would go their separate ways. Until that time, little Benny's education had been exclusively on the streets. In moving out of Hell's Kitchen, he would graduate from the School of Hard Knocks and eventually make it all the way to Harvard Law School. As he said goodbye to gangs, gamblers, and grifters, he was getting ready to say hello to girls, grades, and gravitas. A new world was about to open up for him, and he was quite eager to enter. But hard times still lay ahead.

2

DIVORCE, DEPRESSION, AND DELIVERANCE

It's not the size of the dog in the fight, it's the size of the fight in the dog.

—Arthur G. Lewis, popularly attributed to Mark Twain

The split between Joe and Sara brought an escape from the tenement cellar but also a new life of rootlessness. Ben referred to these as his "lost years" when he and Pearl were "shuttling between [our] father and [our] mother, and from apartment to apartment."[1] At first, Benny and Pearl were shipped off to the residence of Sara's older sister, Fani, who was married to a tailor named Sam. Tante (Aunt) Fani and Uncle Sam lived in their own house in Brooklyn and had two older children.

Ben would later describe the period with Tante Fani as a "tough time."[2] She was gruff and too quick to resort to corporal punishment (Ben recounted her slapping him in the face upon her finding him after he lost her in a crowd at Coney Island). "I didn't like her," he confided as an adult.[3] But he "never forgot that she took us in when we didn't have a roof over our heads."[4]

And he found ways to make the yearlong stay in Brooklyn tolerable, such as developing a bond with Tante Fani's son, Sidney, who would give his younger cousin rides around Brooklyn on his bike handlebars. Sometimes this would include trips to Sam's tailor shop, where the kindly uncle would allow his nephew the "great fun" of jumping up and down on the pressing machine and watching the steam pour out.[5] Benny really loved Uncle Sam, and, in many ways, he could sympathize with him in terms of having a strained relationship with Tante Fani. Like Joe and Sara, Sam and Fani were in an arranged marriage, and the chilled relations between them could be felt in the Brooklyn abode. Also living there as a lodger was a nice Greek man named Albert, who cleaned felt hats. Fani and Albert were having an affair, and Benny was wise to it. So was the lonely Uncle Sam, who "found his happiness in a bottle."[6]

During this difficult period in his life, Benny had trouble finding happiness anywhere. And, as is often the case for lost souls seeking solace, he might have turned to religion. In fact, the young Ben Ferencz did seriously explore his Jewish roots. That had begun in the family's Hell's Kitchen cellar. At first, Judaism provoked a kind of juvenile spiritual awakening. And it started with the Jewish tradition of Yahrzeit, a yearly commemoration of the anniversary of a loved one's death. Propped on a shelf at the foot of Benny's bed in the cellar were "Yahrzeit glasses" filled with paraffin and containing a candle that would burn for many hours. The boy was fascinated by the flickering lights in the glasses and asked his mother why they were there. She told him that each one "reflected the soul of a dear departed, and it was a way of remembering and communicating with that loved one."[7]

But he was skeptical. He studied the flames very carefully but "never detected any souls or spirits."[8] And even if he could, he wondered, "How could [they] get through the ceiling?!?"[9] Nevertheless, watching the flames stirred something deep within his own soul (and this stayed with him since, as he would later recount, he went on to study "all religions" and was "taken by Buddhism").[10] As he described this moment in his memoirs:

> What was particularly striking was the fact that very often, when it seemed that the fire was about to go out, it would ignite again with a bright flare and continue burning. That might happen several times before the flame finally disappeared in swirling black smoke and then was gone forever. I concluded that the flickering candle was a true reflection of real life. When it looks like there is no hope and the end is near, there may still be life left and it can keep on burning for a while longer. I learned never to blow out the candle of life before its time has come.[11]

This was arguably the origin of his lifelong "never say die" attitude, which would inspire him to persevere through so many professional and personal obstacles in the coming decades. But he experienced no *Jewish* spiritual epiphany regarding the flickering candles. Still, he kept his mind open to his family's faith. Thus, he would accompany his father to a local synagogue on the sabbath, a time of rest when Jews are supposed to refrain from engaging in work and related physical tasks (including the kindling of fire). Once at the synagogue, so as to comply with this injunction, his father would have him go outside and "hire" a "goy" (non-Jewish) boy to put a match to the gas flames found under grates that would illuminate the chapel's interior.[12] Benny felt that it was "a waste of five cents" since he "could handle the job for less."[13] On another occasion, the temple cantor asked the young boy to buy him a corned beef sandwich at the neighborhood deli. But the eatery was closed, and all Benny could rustle up was a very unkosher ham sandwich from another shop. When he brought it back, the kashrut-devoted cantor stated he could eat it nonetheless since no one else in the congregation could see him do it. The adult Ferencz later noted that he "had great fun thinking about [the] kosher [cantor] eating a ham sandwich."

His skepticism regarding Judaism was somewhat reinforced by Dave Schwartz, the Ferenczes' Hungarian lodger in the Hell's Kitchen cellar, who would take the children on weekend excursions. Benny and Dave had developed a close relationship. That Dave "came from Budapest, which was considered an 'enlightened' city, and did not share the orthodoxy of Jews from the East" made a significant impression on the little boy. When it was time for his bar mitzvah (a Jewish coming-of-age ritual held when a boy turns thirteen), Benny went through the motions to please his family. And by the end of the experience, he had become disenchanted. As he later described it:

> We couldn't afford to send me to Hebrew school except for a few weeks to learn to read, but not understand, the prayers needed for my Bar Mitzvah. . . . I dutifully composed a customary Bar Mitzvah speech in praise of my parents and teachers. My Hebrew instructor, understandably, was not satisfied with the paucity of the gift he received for his efforts. He made his dissatisfaction plain in the presence of my classmates. Of course, I was very embarrassed. If that was what being a religious Jew meant, I wanted no part of it.[14]

WITHOUT BEING able to draw on his Jewish faith for succor, the small child was nevertheless able to find large reserves of inner strength to deal with the tribulations of the broken home that awaited him after the year interlude at Tante Fani's. By this time, both his parents had already remarried. Not long after the split with Sara, Janitor Joe met and married a fellow Transylvanian Jew named Rose Fried. Ben later described Rose as a "quiet and kind lady."[15] In quick succession, she would soon bear Joe two sons, Benny and Pearl's half brothers, David and Eddie. And Dave Schwartz turned out to be more than a lodger—a few weeks after Joe's nuptials, Sara wed Dave.

Although his parents, and their respective new spouses, remained cordial toward one another, there was lingering discord.[16] To make matters worse, both households were still struggling economically, never able to stay in one apartment because "our inability to pay the rent inspired us to move."[17]

But the economic problems were about to get much worse. On October 24, 1929, now known as "Black Thursday," the US stock market crashed. Its value had been artificially inflated via a frenzy of unregulated, speculative buying on margin in the previous months. On that dark day, panicked investors, suspecting the bubble was about to burst, began trading millions of shares at precipitously falling prices. The market completely cratered four days later, on "Black Tuesday," when investors traded a record 16.4 million shares and lost $14 billion on the New York Stock Exchange. Between Black Thursday and Black Tuesday, the Dow Jones Industrial Average dropped 25 percent, and investors lost $30 billion, ten times more than the 1929 federal budget and the total of US spending for World War I. This economic meltdown is paired in the collective consciousness with images of ruined financiers pitching themselves from window ledges into the canyons of Wall Street below. By mid-November, more than $100 billion had disappeared from the American economy.

The stock market crash precipitated a downward economic spiral that ushered in the Great Depression. By 1933, the unemployment rate reached a catastrophic 25 percent, with nearly thirteen million Americans out of work. Few cities were hit harder than the Big Apple, where it all began.[18] In the New York City of 1932, 50 percent of manufacturing plants were shuttered, one in three city residents was out of work, and roughly 1.6 million were receiving some type of relief. Ben remembered "people in crowds around the banks, saying, 'I need money for my children.' And the bank presidents didn't have the money." And he saw lawyers on the streets of Manhattan "selling apples."[19]

The now-divided Ferencz family, which had already been on shaky financial grounds, was hit particularly hard. They were among the millions of New Yorkers surviving on the largesse of public assistance programs. Ben remembered the "bread lines, soup kitchens. It was a hard time. Well, we didn't have any money to begin with. We were always poor."[20] And it was a humiliating experience. Ben recalled, "It was a time of deep depression in more ways than one. I hated to go to the US Government 'home relief' station where surplus food was given away in the form of two-pound loaves of bread and blocks of frozen butter or American cheese. Once they gave away surplus green woolen sweaters. I was too embarrassed to wear one because all the other kids had the same garment and could recognize the source."[21]

And this spurred persistent efforts to find a steady job and ease the family's financial burdens. He applied for a stock boy position at the neighborhood grocery store and, as part of the job interview, was asked how many eggs were in a crate. He had absolutely no idea, so he guessed. "And they said, 'No—wrong number. There are twenty dozen.' I haven't forgotten the number."[22] Not giving up, he would rise early in the morning and make his way to the local golf course to volunteer as a caddie. But he was continually rebuffed, with the course manager reminding him that "the bag is as big as you."[23]

What proved to be his best employment prospect entailed a return to bonding with a fellow immigrant underdog trying to eke out a living on the mean streets of New York City. If that underdog in Hell's Kitchen had been Tony the Shoeshine Man, in the Bronx it was Mr. Lee the Laundry Man. Like Tony, Mr. Lee spoke no English, but he taught Benny how to use an abacus and cuss in Chinese. The latter would inform customers when the laundry would be finished, how much it would cost, and that if they failed to return on the appointed day without their receipts, they would lose their laundry. In cases when customers requested the cleaned clothes be taken to them, Benny would oblige (and earn tips).

He might have sought out more lucrative jobs, but his loyalty to Mr. Lee prevented him from doing so. He later explained:

> To be perfectly frank, I stayed with Mr. Lee because I was sorry for him. He worked very hard for long hours and slept on a small cot in the back room that contained only a deep tub for washing clothes by hand. Several large sacks of rice seemed to be his only source of nourishment. Each Sunday, he would put on his black suit and take the elevated train to Chinatown to exchange news with friends from home. Japan invaded Manchuria in 1931 and China was at war. My friend was worried about the safety of his family and decided to go home. He asked me to accompany him to Woolworth's "five-and-ten-cents store" to help him buy some gifts for his family in China. He could not resist the call of family and country. I never saw him again. I often thought of how unfortunate it was that such a hard-working man could not live in peace and dignity because of conflicts in another part of the world.[24]

This initial Japanese invasion of China could be considered the opening act of World War II, the conflict that became so central in the life of Benjamin Ferencz. And, in essence, Mr. Lee was the first victim of the war personally known to him. So one could say that his lifelong crusade to help the oppressed "live in peace and dignity" after conflicts in other parts of the world began with his Chinese friend and benefactor.

While the Great Depression may not have been an ideal environment to start one's working life, it proved not too much of a hindrance for getting an education. Surprisingly, in terms of learning the ABCs, the period before the economic collapse had been more trying. When they still lived in Hell's Kitchen, Janitor Joe had tried to enroll his six-year-old son in the local public school, but the principal refused him admission owing to his preternaturally tiny size and his broken English (at that point, his only proficient language was Yiddish). When he moved in with Tante Fani, she was able to enroll him in her local Brooklyn public school. But he still struggled with English and did not know how to read.

There were promising signs of his potential, however. If he heard a story once, he could repeat it verbatim. In fact, on one occasion, he got into trouble when a teacher caught him "reading" correctly from the wrong page! But he started realizing that he loved to read and worked very hard at it—spending many hours at various neighborhood libraries in the Bronx, wherever they happened to be living at the time (due to economic hardship, they moved around a lot). He also started to gain a greater deontological perspective of the world: "I also remember going to the New York Society for Ethical Culture on Sundays to hear sermons that stressed the brotherhood of all people. Even at an early age, I felt a deep yearning for universal friendship and world peace."[25]

Once his reading improved and outlook expanded, he started to excel at school and was allowed to skip a couple of grades and be placed with students his own age. Eventually, the family became rooted enough in one Bronx location, on Bainbridge Avenue, in the Norwood neighborhood, that Benny was able to settle into Public School (P.S.) 80 (on Mosholu Parkway), which would also educate such future luminaries as fashion designers Calvin Klein and Ralph Lauren, actress Penny Marshall, and pianist Joshua Rifkin.

The neighborhood around P.S. 80 at that time has been described as "rough New York streets surrounded by rustic parks" and populated by hardworking "sons and daughters of the old Lower East Side" benefiting from "street-smarts, resilience, ambition, and humor."[26] Ben would later describe P.S. 80 as merely a "cement campus."[27] In the very warm months, the spartan asphalt grounds would be doused with showers to give students relief from the heat, and in the colder months they would sled down a small hill next to the campus.[28]

Ben seemed to adjust to this neighborhood much more effectively than he had to Hell's Kitchen. And, as his grades improved, he was able to branch out into other extracurricular activities. But that did not include athletics—his pint-sized stature prevented his participation in popular sports such as baseball, football, or basketball. Even had it not, his mother felt that such "violent" games were not meant for a "nice Jewish boy." For similar reasons, Sara objected to his joining the Boy Scouts, which she thought was a "military organization."[29]

He tried his hand at muckraking, though (or a crude, sidewalk version of it). Aware of Tammany Hall corruption in the early 1930s, he turned a milk crate into his "soap box" and set it up on Fremont Avenue in the Bronx. There he stood on the makeshift podium bellowing that then New York City mayor Jimmy Walker, as well as his police commissioner, were breaking the law. "They're all a bunch of crooks," Ben declaimed.[30] A large crowd gathered and egged him on, and, in the end, Walker was forced to resign due to a corruption scandal. While the young Ben Ferencz might have wanted to take credit for Mayor Walker's downfall, he seems to have abandoned his muckraking career (although one might see this as the encore to his Eliot Ness turn in Hell's Kitchen and another augur of his future career in law enforcement).

In the end, his niche seemed to be as an entertainer. This began at the local movie house, where the enterprising owner established a "Mickey Mouse Club," which predated the popular television version by a couple of decades. The idea was to show Disney animated shorts before the regular feature film. In advance of the cartoons, the kids would sing a medley of Disney-related songs. Probably because of his small stature, he speculated, Benny was chosen as the "Chief Mickey," and was given a membership pin evidencing his elevated status within the club. He got free admissions to the movies and VIP treatment from fellow classmates at school and was even voted "secretary" of the graduating class. But, alas, these perks were not long-lived—the management of the theater was caught in the middle of a battle between two rival unions, both run by gangsters, and had to close.

Still, he was able to parlay his fleeting fame into another choice role. His eighth-grade drama teacher invited him to join the cast of the graduation play, which was a variation of the Italian folktale *The Happy Man's Shirt.* The theatrical production revolved around a king who was so horribly melancholy that his health was failing, and his life was in danger. His advisors told him that, to lift his spirits and save his life, he needed to wear the shirt of a "happy man." His courtiers eventually found a shepherd in the fields (played by Ben) who seemed incredibly content. He was wearing a sheepskin coat, and, when asked for his shirt, he opened the coat to reveal a bare chest and legs, sporting only a pair of small black bathing trunks under his "wool" coat. When he lifted it, the audience howled in laughter and clapped vociferously at the spectacle of the nearly nude Ferencz. So did the monarch in the drama when he found out that the happiest man in the kingdom owned no shirt. As the play ended, his laughter cured him of his melancholy, and, from that point forward, Ben Ferencz, the bathing beauty, acquired the P.S. 80 nickname "The Happy Man."

But the sobriquet somewhat belied his true emotional state during that period. Perhaps because of his family's peripatetic existence post–Hell's Kitchen, Benny had trouble making friends and, to the end of his life, described himself "by inclination, as well as necessity, very much a loner." He added, in reference to his teenage years, "I don't recall ever having been a normal adolescent."[31] Still, he was not a complete misanthrope. He did have one "buddy"—his stepmother's nephew, Lou Perlman, who went by "Mutchy." During the summers, the two families spent time together in the Catskill Mountains, where the two boys would entertain themselves tossing horseshoes and "killing hordes of mosquitoes."[32]

By LATE 1932, Americans had suffered through three years of the Great Depression and voted out of office the president who had been presiding over the economic catastrophe, Republican standard-bearer Herbert Hoover. He was replaced by a progressive New Yorker promising them a "New Deal"—Democratic nominee Franklin Delano Roosevelt. At the end of January 1933, not long after FDR's election as president, the German people also found a new leader in their midst—a former army corporal from Austria and head of a party called the National Socialist German Workers' Party (NSDAP, or "Nazi" Party, for short). His name was Adolf Hitler, and he immediately set out persecuting the object of his deep, irrational hatred—the Jews. In May, after a Nazi boycott of Jewish businesses and book burnings of the works of Jewish and other "subversive" authors, upward of 100,000 Americans attended an anti-Nazi rally in New York City. It was the largest political demonstration in the city's history, and Ben's parents were there.

Around the same time, Josef and Sara's only son was nearing the end of middle school at P.S. 80 and remained mired in a funk of loneliness and depression. He still felt like the "misfit" little scamp from Hell's Kitchen whose family was torn apart, and he perceived the world as a hostile and threatening place. So when his teacher, Mrs. Connelly, told him he needed to bring in his parents for a meeting with her and the principal, Mr. Stantial, Ben feared the worst. Only his mother was available to accompany him for what he perceived would be a kind of academic firing squad. The two school representatives began, "slowly and carefully," by telling Sara that they wanted to talk to her "about the future of her only son." According to Ben: "They explained that I was an unusual child . . . [and we] expected a lesson on how to discipline unruly children. It sounded ominous."[33] And their worst fears came to pass when the principal and teacher informed them that Ben ought to be sent to a "special school"—with mother and son both gleaning that this was an institution for problem children.

And then, just when all seemed dark and lost, Sara and her son received the most wonderful surprise. The school being described was not for "juvenile delinquents," as they feared, but rather for "gifted boys." It was called Townsend Harris High School, a "preparatory" school, designated as such because a student completing studies there was automatically entitled to admission into the City College of New York. And tuition for City College was waived—this meant Ben would be the recipient of a free college education!

This was a life-altering encounter. Ben later described his emotions: "No one in my parents' family had ever gone to college. Everyone we knew went to work as soon as they could find a job. To finish high school was regarded as the highest possible academic achievement for immigrants like us. Now my mother was being told that her little boy might go to college and it would cost nothing, which was about all we could afford. Only in America! I have been a grateful patriot ever since."[34]

Now his moniker "The Happy Man" began matching his actual emotions. As he prepared to embark on this new life adventure, the former "Chief Mickey" got some memorable parting words from his classmates, as reflected in his P.S. 80 "Autograph Book" from June 1933. The little keepsake begins with Ben's poetic introduction: "Go little Album, far and near, To all my friends I love so dear, Tell them all to write a page, That I may remember them, in my old age."[35] The messages left by his classmates ran the gamut. There were words of wisdom, like this note from Arthur Blechman: "May you learn every day of your life. Take heed or gain in wisdom from this: 'It is the knowing man who knows enough to know he doesn't know it all.'" Some of his classmates gave him mere doggerel, such as this offering from Harold Sachs: "To Little Benny/as round as a penny/and small as a mouse/If you ever grow big/as big as a pig/You'll be doing good for your age/and all ready to start on the stage." Henry Friedman contributed the following: "Coffee in the coffee pot/Pancakes on the griddle/How you got out of 80/Sure is a riddle." But many left sweet and heartfelt parting sentiments, such as Arthur Goldman: "May your success be as bright as Edison's light."[36]

Ben Ferencz graduated from Public School 80 on June 27, 1933. And the move to Townsend Harris meant a change in residence. As much as the family appreciated being in the Norwood neighborhood of the Bronx, it would have greatly burdened Benny to commute to Townsend Harris, located on Twenty-Third Street and Lexington in Manhattan. (He would have had to travel alone on the Third Avenue El train for almost an hour a day.) Such an onerous trajectory would have made the accelerated program at Townsend (graduating in three years, instead of four, with rigorous college-level classes) undoable.

So Benny, Sara, Pearl, and Dave picked up and moved to 129 East Sixty-Fourth Street in Manhattan—"a good address in a good neighborhood."[37] They could afford the higher rent only because Ben's mother took an entrepreneurial approach—she leased the entire brownstone townhouse and then rented the ten furnished rooms within as sublets. As Ben described it: "We lived on the ground floor, in what had been a kitchen, rented out the other rooms, kept the house clean, and in essence carried on the noble traditions of janitoring we had learned in Hell's Kitchen. Uncle Dave tended the furnace and did repairs when he came home from his job as an ironworker. I was experienced as an Assistant Janitor and was now on my way to becoming something more."[38]

That "something more" would entail graduating from high school and college and, eventually, a ticket to Harvard Law School. He had survived Hell's Kitchen, a broken home, broken English, a rootless, isolated existence, and the darkest days of the Great Depression. Townsend Harris High School would be his deliverance, and he was ready to make his mark there.

3

OF RESILIENCE, ROMANCE, AND REVOLUTIONARIES

> The experiment is to be tried, whether the children of the people, the children of the whole people, can be educated; and whether an institution of the highest grade, can be successfully controlled by the popular will, not by the privileged few.
>
> —Dr. Horace Webster, on the opening of the Free Academy, 1849

The final phase of Ben Ferencz's education in the Bronx coincided with Franklin Roosevelt's first one hundred days in office. In fact, the one-hundredth day of the New Deal was marked in June 1933, the same month that Ben graduated from P.S. 80. In that breathtaking period from March through midyear, FDR pushed through fifteen pieces of major legislation, including, among others, the National Recovery Administration (NRA), the Federal Emergency Relief Administration (FERA), the National Industry Recovery Act (NIRA), the Agricultural Adjustment Administration (AAA), and the Civilian Conservation Corps (CCC). He implemented a bank holiday and sponsored the Emergency Banking Act to provide federal deposit insurance when the banks reopened. He then used a series of radio addresses called "Fireside Chats" to explain the "New Deal" measures he was taking and to calm a still anxious American public. And it worked.[1]

By September, when classes were under way for the new academic year at Townsend Harris High School, American optimism was still on the upswing. That month, there was a parade down Manhattan's Fifth Avenue, with more than a quarter million marchers showing support for the NRA, which, among other things, set fair wage and labor standards. New Yorkers were eager to go back to work, and Ben Ferencz was equally eager to start his prep school studies.

They would take place not far from the NRA parade route as Townsend Harris was located a couple of avenues over, on Lexington. Its small physical plant consisted of three floors of what is now Baruch College. And, within these tight confines, the recent Bronx transplant discovered that the study habits that led to success at P.S. 80 would not yield similar results at this elite academy. His rude awakening was in the form of F grades in algebra, history, and French.

But Ben's problems were not only academic. Since his family was still struggling economically, he could not afford to buy lunch at the school cafeteria. This sting of financial hardship somehow fused with a streak of the old Hell's Kitchen deviance. And he devised a scheme to get rich quick—a game called "penny-a-punch," wherein students would fork over one cent in exchange for a "punch hole" in a card. Each hole contained a little paper with a prediction of good fortune or a prize ranging from one to ten cents. By way of scissors, Benny would remove enough of the cash prizes embedded in the top portion of the card (and then repaste it) that he would be assured of making a profit from one-cent purchases. This would leave a "fifteen cent surplus that would buy a hamburger and some mashed potatoes for lunch" and "would have made [his] Hell's Kitchen gang proud."[2]

Unfortunately, he got caught. The building custodian noticed all the paper slips scattered on the ground and reported it to the dean, Dr. Robert H. Chastney, a humorless martinet whose investigation identified the young Ferencz as the culprit. He called Ben into his office and immediately went on the attack with a demand: "Don't say a word! I want your father here tomorrow morning! One more word out of you and you're expelled!"[3] The chastened student later recollected that he was "quivering" and quite concerned because he had not seen his father for at least a year.

But Ben managed to reach him on the telephone, explained that he was on the verge of being expelled, and "begged him to come to the rescue." Joe wanted to know, as expressed in his unadulterated Old Country accent, "What means expelled?" It was "the academic equivalent of being shot," came the reply. When Joe asked him for what, Ben responded that he was only "trying to earn [his] lunch money." Joe's rejoinder: "For this they want to shoot you?!?"[4] The father's response gave the son some hope. And the former's cool demeanor proved to be critical at the appointed hour. As described by the younger Ferencz: "Dr. Chastney began to work him over in an uninterrupted tirade: he was not running a school for gamblers and crooks! Gambling was illegal! Fathers should train their children to obey the law! He would give me one last chance! God bless America! My bewildered Dad, on my advice, listened quietly and simply nodded. He wondered what the burly man was raving about. We were dismissed by the Dean with the repeated sharp warning that this was my last chance!"[5]

The confrontation with Dean Chastney seemed to scare him straight. He buckled down in his studies, retook algebra and French, and passed them with flying colors. He also did well in English, history, and hygiene. And, although math was not his favorite subject, he also earned relatively decent grades in geometry, calculus, and advanced trigonometry. Whereas studying for math was more of a chore, he realized he had a knack for languages. And he began to excel in French.

But this was not strictly rooted in a love of learning; rather, it was for love of a certain sultry French actress, Danielle Darrieux. He was able to find a nearby "arts theater" where he could see the features of this "Ingrid-Bergman-type movie star." Having kept "one eye glued on her and one on the large English subtitles," he would exit the theater looking "a bit cockeyed." But it was better than hearing his French professor's "incomprehensible explanation of how he had fought the battle of the Marne."[6] And it was quite effective, bringing him to the point of speaking "almost as a Parisian."[7] He would take advantage of this skill throughout his career, culminating in his service as a translator for René Cassin, the Nobel Prize–winning author of the Universal Declaration of Human Rights, when the Frenchman visited the United States.

Physical education was also an area of achievement for the young Ferencz. In particular, he did quite well in the swimming pool (where, at the all-boys school, for some inexplicable reason, it was mandatory to swim naked!). But there was one required aquatic skill he could never master—floating motionless in the water for one minute. When instructed to roll over, knees clasped to the chest, face down in the water and "float like a cork," he would sink to the pool floor "as though I had rocks in my head," amazing his instructors.[8]

Ben also displayed unusual talents in the gymnasium. He was quite the tumbler and "could shinny up a rope faster than a monkey."[9] For his stunts on the rings, he was known as "The man on the flying trapeze." Barely over 100 pounds in weight, he was also "much sought after to be top man on the human pyramid."[10] Ironically, though, it was gym class that brought him back into conflict with Dean Chastney (whose name Ben soon began to associate with the similar-sounding word "chastise").

The taskmaster called Ben into his office during his senior year, informing him that he was in trouble again for failure to attend gym class. Ben explained that his scheduled gym session conflicted with the only time he had available for lunch. He had been making up for his absences by going to the gym at other times and the teachers could all confirm his regular attendance. The dour dean gave him an ultimatum: attend the scheduled classes, or there would be no graduation or admission to City College. Ben did not take kindly to this, later noting that he "didn't like ultimatums," and thus, as uttered later in Ben's inimitable gruff voice, "The wrath of Ferencz was upon him!"[11]

He was soon meeting with the City College dean of admissions, a "jolly

Irishman" who referred to the Townsend Harris senior as "Terrence" upon learning that his name was "Ferencz" (putting the stress on the first syllable, instead of the customary second-syllable stress). "Well, Terrence m'boy," he said, putting his arm around Ben's shoulder, "what can I do for you?" The indignant teenager asked whether he could be admitted to CCNY from the prep school without having passed gym class. "Why, of course, we would admit you Terrence m'boy. We'd be glad to have you," the administrator replied. Ben recalled that he "thanked him profusely and scooted away before he could discover that my name was Benny and I wasn't Irish." He then headed back downtown and marched into Dr. Chastney's office. "Sir," he told the dean, "I have just come from City College and they will admit me without having passed gym. You lied to me!" Chastney "turned red, gripped his teeth and snapped, 'You'll get no diploma from this school!'"[12]

And so, in the official records, Benjamin B. Ferencz never formally graduated from Townsend Harris High School (although, quite belatedly, Townsend Harris sent him a diploma in October 2019). Thus, in transitioning to City College, he learned a valuable lesson. As he put it himself when reflecting on his career after earning the Harvard Law School Medal of Freedom: "If the courthouse door is locked, I'm going to go through the window. And if the window is locked, I'm going to go through the roof. And if the roof is blocked, I'm going to take another route."[13]

ALTHOUGH NOT an Ivy League institution, the City College of New York (CCNY) has an illustrious academic history. Founded as the Free Academy in 1847, it is the City University of New York's oldest institution as well as its flagship. Its iconic Gothic Revival spires loom over the Manhattan neighborhood of Hamilton Heights and span Convent Avenue from 130th to 141st Streets. Among other notable achievements, its hallowed halls have graduated ten Nobel Prize winners and served as Albert Einstein's preferred venue to present his theory of general relativity for the first time outside of Europe. In an era when the finest private schools were the exclusive province of the wealthy Protestant establishment, multitudes of gifted students (especially Jewish ones) attended City College because they had no other option. CCNY's superior scholastic reputation and renown as a working-class institution brought it comparisons with a certain famous Cambridge, Massachusetts, Ivy League school and associated monikers such as the "Harvard of the Proletariat" and "Harvard-on-the-Hudson."

Being enrolled there was a great source of pride for Ben Ferencz. But as his college studies got under way in 1937, it was becoming increasingly difficult to appreciate one's individual life and accomplishments at the local level. For all around, the signs were clear that the world was sliding inexorably toward war. Italy had recently invaded Abyssinia (1935), and Germany, in direct and provocative violation of the Treaty of Versailles, had remilitarized the Rhineland (1936). The Second Sino-Japanese War, essentially the opening phase of World War II's Pacific Theater, began in earnest that year. And the Spanish Civil War—pitting Nationalists against Republicans—was raging. Having started in 1936, it was perceived as a twilight struggle between the global forces of dictatorship versus democracy, or fascism against communism.

The CCNY student body of 1937 was somewhat like the Republican side in the Spanish Civil War—it was solidly on the left and distinctly animated by antifascist fervor.[14] And while these left-leaning students, with their frequent on-campus protests, clashed with the administration, they often received encouragement from more junior faculty members, many of whom were themselves CCNY graduates and had the same poor Jewish immigrant roots as their students. That said, radical political leanings within the teaching ranks were frowned on by the administration even more than those of the students. The New York State Rapp-Coudert Committee, which convened in 1940 to weed out Communists from institutions of higher education, precipitated the firing of more than fifty CCNY faculty and staff. Dozens more testified in private and public hearings in what was "a state-sanctioned anti-communist witch hunt that foreshadowed the larger federal efforts of the 1950s."[15]

Remarkably, given how widespread it was, Ben Ferencz seemed, at first, to exist in an academic and social bubble, hermetically sealed off from the revolutionary ferment on campus. As he later remarked: "Many considered CCNY to be a hotbed of radicalism. One of the courses offered was 'Dialectical Materialism.' Since I had not the slightest idea what that meant, and it did not interfere with my lunch schedule, I enrolled. The assigned readings dealt with debates between Bolsheviks and Mensheviks, and correspondence between Bukharin, Zinoviev, and other revolutionaries whose names also meant nothing to me. I dropped the course. Revolutions and revolutionaries was not my thing."[16]

Instead, as he began his college career, he appeared to be more concerned about logistics. The family digs on the eastern side of Midtown Manhattan that had accommodated a short commute to Townsend Harris did not work as well for a college located on the west side of the borough's upper reaches. So the family moved back to the Bronx, "where there were fewer pretentious people" and where he could board a streetcar from the new apartment that would take him close to City College.

But living arrangements were not quite as settled as that. In particular, Ben had become increasingly frustrated with his overbearing sister. Per his mother's commands, he had to do chores under Pearl's "glaring eye." On one occasion, she ordered him to do something he felt was unreasonable, and, when he refused, instead of using her usual tactic of "venting her ire by slapping or scratching" him, she reported him to Sara, who was working as a seamstress nearby. His mother got on the phone and told him that he needed to obey his sister, since she was older. If he refused, his mother added, he "had to leave the house." Sara probably never anticipated that her son would actually take her up on it. Within a couple of hours, though, after packing his bags, he was at his father's doorstep and announced that he was moving in.

In some ways, this was the "Benny Declaration of Independence"—it was summer, he had finished an academic year at CCNY, and he was feeling a greater sense of autonomy. But his sudden departure left his mother utterly dumbfounded—again, she never really thought her threat would be taken seriously. She was soon at Janitor Joe's doorstep, explaining that, on returning from work, she and "Uncle Dave" had been "shocked" to discover that Ben had turned in his key and departed, and she demanded an explanation. "I always treated my mother with respect and we discussed the situation in quiet detail," he recalled. But he refused to apologize to his sister "for not obeying her unreasonable demands. We were at an impasse. I said I would have to think about it."[17]

Perhaps more important than that conversation's impact on Ben's living arrangements was the effect it had on a certain eavesdropper. As it happened, listening furtively to the dialogue out of the side of her ear was one Gertrude Fried. Like Ben, she had been born into Transylvania's Jewish community (on November 5, 1919, about six months before her future husband) but left for the United States much later in life, in 1936, at the age of sixteen.

As a result, she was subjected to the kind of antisemitic persecution that Ben and his nuclear family escaped thanks to their earlier migration. She grew up being called a "stinky Jew." She later remembered that "the churches were speaking out against the Jews . . . they were really beating up the Jews." And she and her family "lived behind locked doors."[18] Sometime in the 1920s, Gertrude's father, Shulem (later changed to Sam), went to the United States to seek a better life; he would get settled and send for his family later. But her mother refused to go as she was "very, very religious . . . neurotically religious" and could not bring herself to leave the Old Country.[19] Gertrude's two siblings also refused to be uprooted.

But Gertrude's sentiments were different from those of her mother and siblings. Over the years, her father would return to visit the family, and Gertrude became "obsessed" with the idea of relocating to America. By 1936 she was ready to leave. When her father returned for a visit, she decided that she would be going back with him to the United States. So she joined Shulem for the steerage-class passage to New York on the old Polish liner, the *Batory*. On arrival, she moved in with her father's sister, who had also emigrated earlier. Of course, that sister, Eva Perlman (also known as Chava), was the mother of Ben's best buddy, Lou "Mutchy" Perlman. Chava was, in turn, the sister of Ben's stepmother Rose Ferencz (née Fried). Rose and Chava were best friends, lived in close proximity to one another, and spent much time together. For their daily coffee klatches, Chava was occasionally accompanied by her niece, Gertrude.

Ben and Gertrude had first met when the young man was still a student at Townsend Harris. The initial encounter was not auspicious. As Ben later described it: "A new Hungarian in town moved in with Lou's family. 'Gizi' [short for Gizella], whose name was Americanized as Gertrude, and pronounced Goity, did not impress me. 'She sure looks like a greenhorn!' [he told Lou]. Her reaction to me was, 'A silly kid!' Hardly enough to distract me from my studies."[20]

But roughly two years later, initial impressions had changed. Listening to Ben speak to his mother about why he had moved out, the girl previously referred to as "the Greena Cousina" was "touched" by his "gentle and persuasive reasoning." As a result, according to the young Ferencz:

> I may thereby have won my most important case. It was not too long thereafter that I was impressed by her language skills and knowledge and her determination to go to night school to complete her education. The "Green" began to take on a rosy glow. In fact, I began to notice that she was very pretty. I was in no rush to return to my sister's domination. I stayed with Pop until school started. Meanwhile Gertie and I began to take long walks, hand in hand. We became close friends. Being a proper Jewish girl, she saw to it that it was not too close.[21]

Apart from the apparent chemistry between the two, their attraction to one another made sense on many levels. They were both from the Transylvanian immigrant Jewish community and could bond over having left Romania to escape persecution (even though Ben could not remember it firsthand). Each was strong with languages and put a premium on education. And they shared an interest in social justice—Gertie would go on to become a social worker and Ben, a pioneer in seeking justice for victims of crimes against humanity.

The relationship began turning serious. And despite the fact that they both lived in a near impoverished state (the pall of the Great Depression still hung over them), they found ways to have fun. Ben would later wax nostalgic about this period: "[Our] favorite recreation was to go to Cooper Union to listen to lectures that were very enlightening—and free. We could afford the subway fare which was only five cents, and we might even 'go Dutch' and share the costs. Sometimes I could be a sport and invite her to a hot chocolate at Stubies Ice Cream Parlor on Tremont Avenue.... We found we had much in common and saw each other whenever we could."[22]

As HIS LOVE life began to take form, so too did his career aspirations. And, once again, his Hell's Kitchen roots played a part. "Being distressed" by what he saw in his old neighborhood, he wanted a career that would enable him "to prevent juvenile delinquency."[23] That he could do so as a lawyer was first suggested to him when he was living in Brooklyn with Tante Fani. Her husband, the beloved Uncle Sam, noticed how good Benny was at arguing with everyone, and thus he "was the guy who said I would be a good lawyer. And I thought, well I want to be a lawyer; I don't want to be a crook."[24]

This had a bearing on his undergraduate studies, as he decided to major in sociology to prepare himself for law school. But his interest in the major was not strictly an interest in the law per se, for he was also deeply concerned with issues such as race relations, poverty, and other forms of social injustice. Not surprisingly, one of his favorite courses at CCNY was the major's flagship class, sociology itself. His love for the course, though, was not rooted merely in its intellectual content.

What also fascinated him was the opportunity afforded to engage in hands-on fieldwork. In particular, students enrolled in the class worked on finding solutions to the problem of juvenile truancy. Ben took a leadership role in the project and devised "a program of evening activities" to attract young truants. Those with a record of absences were invited to come voluntarily to participate in "popular games and workshop activities." Ben later explained that they "provided lots of building materials [and the] idea was to teach the little dears the joys of peaceful cooperation." He added: "Occasionally, one kid would try to hit another in the head with a hammer, but that was unusual."[25]

Further real-world opportunities presented themselves. He was recommended for an unpaid summer job, as a counselor at a reform school, "The Children's Village," in Dobbs Ferry, New York. The seemingly innocuous name of the institution belied the nature of the people it was serving—the eponymous "children" were persistent truants, runaways, thieves, or even murderers. The "Village" consisted of small homes with "cottage parents," who were meant to give guidance to the delinquents. Ben served as such a "cottage parent."

On weekends, he would hitchhike home to the Bronx and return with candy for his wards. After his gifts were stolen on a couple of occasions, before they could even be distributed, he set a trap, lacing the bag of treats with "pungent peppermints." He soon lined up his charges and had them exhale—the olfactory senses of Ben, and the boys themselves, alerted them to the offender. The cottage parent then "left it to [the thief's] bunk buddies to decide on the appropriate response." A half hour later, the crook "had been tried by a jury of his peers and justice had obviously been done. He might have had trouble sitting, or even standing, for a while, but the crime was never repeated." From this, Ben concluded that "experience is often the best teacher" and "peace and justice go hand in hand."[26]

He learned other important lessons as part of an internship in the New York City criminal court system. His assignment was to arrange the court records of interviews by psychologists, psychiatrists, or social workers who gave written opinions about felons being processed through the system. It was a sobering experience, as he later recounted:

> I was surprised, and even shocked, to discover that some citizens who appeared quite respectable were capable of the most atrocious crimes. It became clear that some sex offenders were habitual criminals where imprisonment seemed to have no deterrent effect. [The] professional habitual criminals were well known to the police and were frequently subjected to coercive techniques. . . . It seldom worked, but sometimes it did. It was clear to me that progress toward a more humane and peaceful world would be a slow and difficult process. For many intransigent problems, there are no easy answers.[27]

As with many of his previous jobs, though, these unpaid gigs failed to defray his meal, transportation, or dating expenses, so he needed to find remunerated employment as well. Once again, drawing on his Hell's Kitchen instincts, he decided to skirt the rules and academic integrity to earn his keep. This came in the form of "ghostwriting" papers for students at CCNY and other campuses around New York City. He was paid by an enterprising (and not too morally scrupulous) CCNY senior who served as the middleman—the senior would field requests from students in need and farm out assignments to his stable of surrogate writers. Ben later described how the process worked and how much he learned from it:

> I would accept an assignment in any of the social sciences. . . . By collecting a pile of relevant books from the library . . . I could type out a requested paper for an unknown recipient on any acceptable subject for the sum of one hun-

> dred dollars—no questions asked. Not only did it provide me with a means of sustenance, I developed a skill at speed reading and writing, and learned more than I ever absorbed in school. It is not necessary to sit in a classroom to become a learned person, just as not all of those who flaunt academic degrees are well educated.[28]

Despite his busy schedule with studies, internships, work, and a budding romance, he still found time to enjoy leisure/self-improvement activities for himself. As he did at Townsend Harris (even if not then at the hours preferred by Dean Chastney), he continued to be a frequent visitor to the gym. And eventually he took up boxing. Fighting at 115 pounds, as a light-side bantamweight, he learned technique and developed punching power but could never overcome the reach advantage of most of his opponents. He was advised to slim down to qualify for the flyweight class, but his mother got wind of his pugilistic pursuits and badgered him into quitting. Still, the sport helped develop Ben's Hell's Kitchen toughness, and it came in handy when he had to deal with those unruly juvenile delinquents as an intern at "The Children's Village."

In the end, however, his studies took priority over everything else. This was especially true since, just as at Townsend Harris, he struggled in the early years and needed to work hard to pull up his grades. His CCNY transcript reflects this. In his first semester, for example, with the exception of an A in English and a B in French, he earned C grades in courses such as economics, history, and science. He even earned a D in mathematics. But there was steady improvement from that point forward—never receiving a grade as low as a D again. A smattering of C marks remained, in courses such as biology, hygiene, and botany. (He hated botany as a discipline, later grousing that its expensive textbook was written primarily in Latin.)[29]

By his third semester, he was earning more As and Bs than Cs. He described earning an A in Professor Bonaro Overstreet's class since the only course requirement was reading Aldous Huxley's *Ends and Means,* which allowed for "endless philosophical discussions" in which he "excelled." Perhaps his favorite course at CCNY was philosophy with Professor Morris Rafael Cohen, who was also a great mathematician. "He taught ethics," Ben later explained, "except what impressed me was that he was rather cynical in his outlook."[30]

And, in his last two semesters, when he was mostly taking courses directly in his major, he earned nearly straight As (with only a couple of Bs and no Cs). He wrote a senior honors thesis titled "The Theory of Responsibility in Criminal Law," and his thesis advisor was the great criminologist Harry Shulman, director of the Community Service Division of CCNY and well known for conducting field studies in gang treatment. Ferencz thrived under his tutelage. Over the course of his three years at CCNY, he had grown quite a bit as a student.[31]

AND BEN's emerging penchant for "excelling in philosophical discussions," especially those related to the subject of war versus peace, eventually brought him back to the world of radical leftist politics at the CCNY campus. "All social problems," he recalled, "were being solved, or at least debated, in one of the City College alcoves known as 'The Kremlin.'"[32] From his perspective, it was all about "Young Communists" duking it out with "Young Socialists" over the best way to maintain peace. He would chime in and try to convince both sides that "the primary goal of the communists was to kill the socialists and vice versa." Somehow, this only earned him the reputation of being a Trotskyite, much to his amusement as he "didn't know that Leon Trotsky was a leading counterrevolutionary whose career ended abruptly when he was murdered with an ice pick by one of Stalin's agents."[33]

Despite his relative ignorance and misfit status among the group, he stuck with them. "Undaunted," he reported, he marched "with a mob of City College activists who paraded about two miles to Columbia University holding high our banners calling for world peace."[34] When they arrived at the "high-brow" college, hoping to be joined by hundreds of other intellectuals, they were "assaulted with a barrage of chalk and blackboard erasers tossed from windows" by Columbia students who "declared war" on them. From this, he learned that "there are differing views about how to run the world, and that trying to maintain peace can be a thankless, and even hazardous, endeavor."[35]

In fact, toward the end of his time at CCNY, it started becoming clear that maintaining peace would not be possible at all. Ben later noted that "the world seemed to be in constant turmoil and on the brink of war. . . . Japan had recently invaded China; the Russian revolution after World War I had provoked there civil strife as Red Russians were killing White Russians, and the Marxists fighting with the Leninists. Germany was preparing for aggression."[36]

In particular, after remilitarizing the Rhineland in 1936, Hitler annexed Austria in 1938 and swallowed up Czechoslovakia by the beginning of the next year. In fact, the Nazi threat was especially clear in Ben's world as he and other New Yorkers were subjected to the spectacle of twenty thousand American Nazis on February 20, 1939, grouped under the name of the "German American Bund," holding a rally in Madison Square Garden. But the streets surrounding the arena were equally packed with anti-Nazi demonstrators, reported to have included "everyone from veterans to housewives to members of the Socialist Workers Party."[37]

By the start of his senior year, Germany moved to acquire its next territorial prize—Poland. In defiance of Great Britain and France, which had guaranteed Polish sovereignty after Hitler mocked Neville Chamberlain's "peace in our time" pledge, Hiter's forces breached Poland's frontiers on the morning of September 1, 1939. Soon the Poles were engulfed in the destruction inflicted by Nazi blitzkrieg tactics. Two days later, on September 3, the British and French made good on their promises and declared war on Hitler's state. By the time Ben graduated from CCNY with a bachelor of science degree in social sciences in June 1940, the Germans had successfully invaded and were occupying Denmark, Norway, Holland, Belgium, and France. Humanity was, by then, engulfed in World War II. Thus, as Ben Ferencz entered Harvard Law School in the fall of 1940, his legal education would be in the context of, and undeniably impacted by, the bloodiest conflict in human history.

PART II

PREPARING

4

THE WORLD WAR II WAITING GAME AT HARVARD

Life is what happens to you while you're busy making other plans.

—JOHN LENNON, "Beautiful Boy (Darling Boy)"

BEN HAD known for quite some time that he wanted to be a lawyer, but as the end of his studies at City College of New York approached, he had done very little to prepare himself for the next phase of his education. The stakes were high, but the calculus was simple. "I didn't know any lawyers," he explained later. "And I wanted to go to the best school. . . . Somebody told me it was Harvard Law School."[1] So with that bit of crack research, he applied to that school, and that school only—there were no "insurance school" applications. Miraculously, despite an overall GPA that was not stellar, he was admitted to the Harvard Law School Class of 1943. He always marveled at his good fortune, confessing, "I still don't know why I was admitted."[2]

Given its considerable reputation, Ben's astonishment was understandable. Harvard Law alumni include nineteen Supreme Court justices, ten US attorneys general, former president Barack Obama, and countless professors and partners in top law firms.[3]

So how was Ben Ferencz's 1940 admission into this Valhalla of legal education possible? The answer is as simple as it is surprising—the Harvard Law School (HLS) classes admitted in those days were enormous. Due to "tuition dependence," even a prestigious school such as Harvard had to "live from hand to mouth" with no support from endowment income or philanthropy.[4] In addition to constraining finances, HLS's tuition-dependence syndrome fostered a combative and competitive culture, as depicted in John Osborn's 1971 novel *The Paper Chase* (and the famous 1973 movie that followed). Faculty deliberately tried to flunk students out of the law school, treating the attrition rate as an index of its academic quality.[5]

Ben experienced this firsthand in the fall of 1940. "When I arrived at Harvard," he recollected, "[Dean James Landis] made a speech, and he said 'look to the right and look to the left of you, a year from now, one of you three won't be here.' And we were all . . . petrified and very intimidated."[6]

The import of the dean's message was clear: the bottom third of the class was going to flunk out by the summer of 1941. But avoiding that fate was not necessarily a recipe for happiness either. Those who managed to survive would continue to be terrorized by an aggressive "inquisition" style of classroom instruction known as the Socratic method. The "method" bearing the great philosopher's name consists of an open-ended string of questions, which, step by step, seeks to expose tensions and contradictions in the students' responses. Eventually, in theory, it leads them to formulate sound, defensible conclusions. At its best, it represents a cooperative dialogue that encourages student engagement, spurs critical thinking, and fleshes out cogent ideas. At its worst, it resembles intellectual boot camp more than legal education, a tool used to intimidate and demoralize students in front of their peers as seen in the fictional classroom of Harvard Law contracts professor Charles Kingsfield in *The Paper Chase*.

During Ben's time at HLS, this second "dark" version of the Socratic method was prevalent. And perhaps its most sadistic exponent was property professor Edward H. "Bull" Warren (the inspiration for the filmic Kingsfield character), who codified his system of terror in a 1942 treatise titled *Spartan Education*. Beyond the garden-variety Socratic torture, Bull Warren, later described by the *Harvard Crimson* as the school's "intellectual drillmaster,"[7] would "shout out a grade for every answer received in class from a trembling student." Ben painted a fairly grim picture of the classroom experience: "His greatest joy seemed to be to heap scorn and humiliation on his helpless victims. I witnessed when he called one poor classmate forward, handed him a dime, and directed him to phone home and advise his parents that they were wasting their money since he would never become a lawyer. I was never one to revel in the misery of others [and] was saddened to see the pain he inflicted when he responded to some hapless student by moaning, 'Am I to breathe the breath of life into this lump of clay?'"[8]

Sadness turned to personal outrage when the Bull directed his sadism toward Ben himself. One early morning, running into property class just as the bell was sounding, the empty lecture hall soon revealed, to his horror, that the session had been moved to another building. He hightailed it to the new location, opened the door cautiously, and walked gingerly into an ongoing lecture. But the Bull, looking every bit like the scariest version of his nickname, halted his discourse midsentence and glared at the tardy 1L as if he were a Spanish matador dangling a red cape. Then he verbally gored him: "You! Get Out! Get

Out! Get Out!" Ben complied and ran out of the door "as though being chased by the Devil."[9]

And from that day forward, whenever Ben would provide an answer in class, the Bull shouted out "D"! From this, young Ferencz learned an invaluable lesson for that course: "Better never than late."[10] Still, when he buttonholed the Bull in the hallowed halls just after the course ended and inquired about his grade, the sadistic educator told him he narrowly missed earning an A in property. His downfall was a failure to demonstrate an understanding of the difference between "personalty" and "realty." "He was absolutely right," Ben later noted. "Since I had never owned any property and had never heard the term 'personalty.'"[11]

Other professors made a much more positive impression. Ben's favorite was Harvard legend Lon Fuller, who joined the faculty the very year Ben started there. Fuller taught Ben contracts in his first year, but he was famous for his theories on jurisprudence. Along with Oliver Wendell Holmes, Roscoe Pound, and Karl Llewellyn, "Fuller was one of the four most important American legal theorists" of the last century—a secular natural law adherent who was critical of legal positivism.[12]

Interestingly, in light of Ben Ferencz's later career, part of Fuller's fame stemmed from his 1958 debate with the preeminent British legal philosopher H. L. A. Hart, the so-called "Hart-Fuller Debate" involving the Nazi-tinged "Grudge Informer Case." The hypothetical "case" involved a woman during the time of the Third Reich who, unhappy in her marriage, having had an affair and wanting to get rid of her husband, told authorities that her spouse had criticized Adolf Hitler. Under a Nazi law criminalizing statements "inimical to the welfare of the Third Reich," the husband was prosecuted, found guilty, and sentenced to death. The positivist Hart advocated recognizing the statute as valid law and punishing the wife under a later-adopted stricture, retroactively making criminal what before had been legal. Fuller, taking the naturalist position, argued that consideration of the "inner morality of law" would be sufficient to declare the Nazi statute invalid: "To me there is nothing shocking in saying that a dictatorship which clothes itself with a tinsel of legal form can so far depart from the morality of order, from the inner morality of law itself, that it ceases to be a legal system."[13]

Through osmosis, this contempt of Nazi-style "law" was passed by Professor Fuller to Ben Ferencz in contracts class. Former HLS dean Albert Sacks has noted that the natural law thinker "transformed the first-year course in contracts so that it successfully combined the virtues of first-year Socratic and developmental teaching with preliminary exposure to some of the profound philosophic dilemmas and insights that interested him."[14] Indeed, Ben later recollected that the contracts professor "was a real philosopher. . . . I learned from him . . . which way [a case should] tilt in terms of justice and right."[15]

Ben also very much appreciated another of the four twentieth-century American legal philosophy giants at HLS: Roscoe Pound. Founder of the school of "sociological jurisprudence" and one of the most cited legal scholars of all time, Pound was originally a professor of botany from the University of Nebraska (ironic, considering Ben Ferencz's well-earned disdain for that topic during his college days!). His sociological approach stressed the actual effects of the law within society and, from the other side of the telescope, the influence of social phenomena on law's substantive and procedural facets.

For example, Pound undertook a famous study of crime in Cleveland with fellow HLS professor (and later Supreme Court justice) Felix Frankfurter in which they proved that, during 1922, increased coverage of crime in Cleveland newspapers, despite no increase in reported crime, led to disproportionate sentencing outcomes. By exposing this, they managed to spark positive change in the local criminal justice system. Pound thus conceptualized law as a kind of social engineering tool used to manufacture positive communal change. And this resonated with Ben since his undergraduate studies in sociology focused on such phenomena and suggested reforms.

Sadly, by the 1940s, according to Ben, Pound was a poorly aged septuagenarian, and close to blind. "Reading his old notes, he was a bore." Still, he was the most "learned scholar" of all Ben's teachers, and his ability "to categorize all knowledge into legal systems" as well as his "prodigious memory" were "truly phenomenal."[16]

Yet another inspiration was Pound mentee Zechariah Chafee, Ben's ethics professor. Chafee was considered a pioneering civil rights scholar, especially regarding freedom of speech. A man of conscience whom Harvard nearly fired for critiquing *Abrams v. United States* (which upheld the 1918 Sedition Act criminalizing the printing of advocacy materials meant to hinder US prosecution of World War I),[17] Professor Chafee eloquently defended himself before a special committee and managed to save his job. In fact, his work on free speech heavily influenced Oliver Wendell Holmes and Louis Brandeis in their shaping of post-1918 First Amendment doctrine. And his ethics course "espoused human rights long before Human Rights was taught." From him, Ben learned concepts crucial to his later war crimes and reparations work—in particular, principles "about tolerance and the need to treat all human beings justly."[18]

All of this inspired in the young man a much deeper love of intellectual pursuits, a greater appreciation of law and justice, and an unquenchable thirst for understanding how the world worked. As he recounted later:

> My dream of paradise was to find myself lost in the stacks of the Harvard law library. I found such wonderful books to study and so much wisdom in the decisions of towering Judges like Benjamin Nathan Cardozo, Learned Hand, and Oliver Wendell Holmes. . . . [In] my first law office, I hung portraits of those three inspiring legal giants on the wall above my desk. When a visiting judge remarked that the legal greats looked down on me, I replied, "No, I look up to them." The rough edges of my earlier education began to wear off as I found inspiration in some of the great jurists I most admired.[19]

UNFORTUNATELY, AS before, an integral part of the Ben Ferencz educational experience also included financial hardship. Although he earned a scholarship for his outstanding first-year performance in criminal law (among the top three in the class), putting a roof over his head and rustling up meals remained an onerous burden. As for the former, he lived in an attic on Mellen Street, for which rent was eight dollars per week, and he shared it "with another poor boy from the Bronx," Austin Graham.[20] From his attic window, he could see certain classmates driving "fancy red convertibles."

> [They had names that] began with an initial and ended with a Roman numeral. They wore argyle socks and brown loafers and belonged to fraternities where they drank cocktails. On Sundays they could be seen punting their little boats on the Charles River. [Joseph P. Kennedy Jr., son of the millionaire Ambassador to the Court of St. James and brother of the future US president, was at Harvard Law at the same time as Ben and had been on the crew]. Many of those who came from military or private schools could be identified by the fact that they always said "Sir" to begin and end every sentence.[21]

Like the "other Jewish boys from City College,"[22] Ben felt somewhat like a fish out of the Charles River in this world of privilege. Apart from his studies, his main concern was nutritional sustenance. And, in this regard, he was quite resourceful. For instance, the Commander Hotel, opposite the Law School, featured a special Sunday buffet brunch—all one could eat for fifty cents. Ben would gorge on that, permitting survival for another couple of days. But how to fatten himself for the rest of the week? Once again, his entrepreneurial instincts and budding negotiation skills saved him. He worked out a deal with the Harvard Divinity School whereby he would operate as a kind of busboy, clearing tables after meals. In return, he could eat his choice of leftovers.

But he still had to hustle for the other sundry expenses not covered by the scholarship. This, along with the intense studies, made life a real "grind," as he described it; yet he managed to eke out an existence. His successful campaign for election to the Board of Student Advisers, for example, brought a stipend for coaching students in brief writing. Even better, after doggedly pursuing leads, he discovered a federal program offering small grants to needy students for employment as professorial research assistants. Ben applied, was accepted, and did not hesitate in choosing his preferred scholar. He made a beeline to the library, where he found Roscoe Pound "wearing his green visor while peering closely into some ancient text."[23] Pound's refusal was delivered "kindly," explaining to Ben that "knowledge cannot be transmitted second hand through someone else's head."[24]

His second choice was Professor Sheldon Glueck. That Glueck became the consolation prize is somewhat surprising given the many life parallels between professor and student. Glueck was twenty-four years older than Ferencz but was Jewish and had also emigrated to the United States from eastern Europe (Warsaw, Poland) as a child. Like Ferencz, he grew up on rough streets (in Milwaukee, in the same neighborhood and time as Golda Meir) and soon became fascinated with the subject of juvenile delinquency. Glueck was naturalized as a US citizen in 1920, the year Ferencz was born.

Like Ferencz, Glueck was a gifted student rising from humble roots to earn an undergraduate degree at Georgetown University, a law degree from National University (since merged into George Washington University Law School), and a master's and PhD from Harvard University in criminology. Glueck served in the US Army in World War I, and Ferencz did the same in World War II. And, as World War II neared its apex, both men turned away from studying juvenile delinquency toward studying war crimes.

In fact, by then, Glueck was probably America's leading expert on youth criminality, so studying Nazi atrocities represented quite the detour. But with World War II raging and reports of such horrific offenses circulating, the London International Assembly of the League of Nations Union had formed the Commission on Trial and Punishment of War Criminals. Eventually, the Commission's agenda included inviting to join its ranks one of America's most prominent criminal law experts at arguably its top university. Glueck apparently concluded that this would not be a bad career move and accepted. As he became more involved in the Commission's work, he resolved to write a book on the investigation and prosecution of war crimes.

Enter Benjamin Berell Ferencz. Having been rebuffed by Pound (who, ironically, was later suspected of being a Nazi sympathizer),[25] Ben arrived at Glueck's office doorstep just as the juvenile criminologist was about to embark on the research for his planned book on Nazi war crimes. It was a propitious moment for both men that resulted in an offer to conduct the research, which Ben gladly accepted. That meeting, along with the decision to accept the research assistant offer, turned out to be a life-altering event for the young Harvard Law student.

Professor Glueck gave Ben the Commission reports he had been receiving detailing Nazi atrocities and would funnel him new ones as they came in. "I was very much aware that Jews [in Poland] were [being] exterminated," he later recollected.[26] Thus, quite conscious of what was at stake, Ben set about piecing together for Glueck the fragments of the pre-1940 law related to international crimes.

Relative to the modern legal landscape, there was very little, and most centered on violations of the law of war. Highlights included Peter von Hagenbach's trial in 1474 for offenses committed while governing territory in the Upper Alsace region on behalf of the Duke of Burgundy. Considered history's first international war crimes trial (and later cited at the Nuremberg Trials), its ad hoc panel of twenty-eight judges representing different regional polities is noted for rejecting the defense of superior orders and considering an embryonic version of crimes against humanity.[27]

After a considerable caesura, and an awakening regarding the horrors of modern armed conflict via the US Civil War, the international community began a serious effort to formulate a systematic law of war. The 1863 Lieber Code, drafted by the Prussian-born jurist Francis Lieber and promulgated by President Abraham Lincoln, represented the first written codification of the laws and customs of war, stipulating specific rules for protecting civilians and their property, treating prisoners and enemy wounded humanely, and limiting military targets to those deemed essential.

This laid the groundwork for perhaps the most significant legal instrument that Ben would examine during his research—the Geneva Convention of 1864. Its origin was a book about the gruesome 1859 Battle of Solferino in Italy, written by the Swiss eyewitness Henri Dunant (*A Memory of Solferino*), which led to the 1863 creation of the International Committee of the Red Cross. In turn, the Committee convened a sixteen-nation conference that adopted the 1864 Convention for the Amelioration of the Condition of the Wounded in Armies in the Field. Among other things, the Convention provided for: (1) relief to the wounded regardless of nationality; (2) neutrality/inviolability of medical personnel; and (3) the distinctive sign of the red cross on a white ground. The subsequent Geneva Conventions of 1906 (extending protections for the wounded and those caring for them) and 1929 (extending protections to prisoners of war) built on this platform. The Hague Conventions of 1899 and 1907 complemented this burgeoning body of law by imposing limits on the means and methods of warfare (such as prohibiting certain weapons and tactics).

Additionally, the relevant universe would have included a series of war crimes-related instruments arising from World War I, including the 1915 Allied Joint Declaration, which concerned the systematic mass slaughter of Armenians (later to be properly designated as the Armenian Genocide). In it, France, Great Britain, and Russia asserted that "in the presence of these new crimes of Turkey against humanity and civilization, the allied Governments publicly inform the [Ottoman Government] that they will [be held] personally responsible for the said crimes."[28] Within an international law context, this is likely the first use of the term "crimes against humanity."

In its Article 227, the 1919 Treaty of Versailles provided for creation of an ad hoc international criminal tribunal to prosecute Germany's Kaiser Wilhelm II for initiating the war; and its Article 228 called for prosecuting German military personnel for atrocities. Yet the Kaiser tribunal was never established, and merely twelve low-level German war criminals were tried before the Leipzig Supreme Court (the Reichsgericht) by Allied prosecutors, and only lightly punished. Known as the Leipzig War Crimes Trials, these proceedings did help clarify certain laws and customs of war but were roundly condemned as a failed justice enterprise.

Similarly, the 1920 Treaty of Sèvres provided for the trial by the Allies of Turkish war criminals in connection with the Armenian Genocide, but it was superseded by the 1923 Treaty of Lausanne, which reversed Sèvres and provided for amnesty. Instead, an interim Turkish government conducted a limited number of domestic courts-martial, punishing a small number of low-level Ottoman offenders, while high-level genocide organizers escaped justice. A culture of impunity was established that would ultimately lead to the horrors of World War II and the Holocaust.

Nevertheless, the post–World War I legal regime did lay down strictures regarding the launching of war. Article 10 of the 1919 League of Nations Covenant, the predecessor to the United Nations Charter, declared that member states would "respect and preserve as against external aggression the territorial integrity and existing political independence" of the other member states. The 1928 Kellogg-Briand Pact went further—renouncing war as a solution for international controversies and dictating that all disputes be settled by pacific means.[29]

Finally, apart from the tribunals contemplated by the Treaties of Versailles and Sèvres, the state of the relevant law at the beginning of the century's fifth decade also included the template for creating another international criminal court. On November 16, 1937, in response to King Alexander of Yugoslavia's assassination, a Convention for the Creation of an International Criminal Court was opened for signature in Geneva under the auspices of the League of Nations. But this Convention, along with its companion Convention for the Prevention and Punishment of Terrorism, did not secure the minimum number of ratifications necessary to enter into force.

On first getting his brief to summarize the germane law circa 1940, Ben Ferencz knew nothing of these precedents. So he took a very thorough and systematic approach, summarizing every war crimes–related book in the Harvard Law Library. This was a Herculean task, even requiring him to stay in Cambridge an additional month after classes ended to conduct research. In the end, he put his results on cards that synopsized every tome he had read and presented the resulting thick stack to Glueck.

Glueck then combined this with the atrocity reports he had received from the Commission and wrote a book titled *War Criminals: Their Prosecution and Punishment,* published by Alfred A. Knopf. All these years later, the book, which focuses more on the European Theater than the Pacific, makes for a fascinating read. It is incredible to realize that, at the time of its release in the fall of 1944, Hitler was still alive and directing the Nazi military effort. One can only imagine, as the book does, what it would have been like to apprehend and prosecute the Führer himself, as well as some of his top henchmen who also ultimately cheated the hangman's noose, such as Joseph Goebbels and Heinrich Himmler. In the fall of 1944, well before the Nuremberg International Military Tribunal Charter had been drafted, it would have been fair to pose the question, as the book did, "Can Heads of State (e.g., Hitler) legitimately be subjected to trial and punishment by the United Nations [referring to the UN before it was officially created by treaty]; or are such high-placed malefactors exempt from legal liability and trial by a foreign jurisdiction?"[30] Glueck, with the benefit of Ferencz's research, answered the former cutting-edge question in the affirmative—heads of state could be subject to trial and punishment by the international community.

In fact, *War Criminals: Their Prosecution and Punishment,* which is largely forgotten today, should be considered a pioneering work. At a time when it was not entirely clear what kind of justice would await Axis mass murderers, with Churchill favoring summary execution for top leaders and Stalin, kangaroo-court show trials, Glueck's analysis was prophetic and likely had an impact on eventual Allied justice efforts at Nuremberg.

For instance, prophesying some of the bedrock principles of the Nuremberg Trials, the book did a solid job of laying out the elements of the key war crimes. It explained why "acts of state" should not shield individuals from criminal liability, favored subjecting heads of state to liability and punishment, rejected the defense of superior orders, and advocated in favor of prosecuting the "big fish" before an international tribunal. In particular, Glueck recommended "prosecution of ordinary offenders in the victim's domestic tribunals (military or civil, as locally provided) and leading culprits (Heads of State, members of general staffs and certain other high-placed classes . . .) in an International Criminal Court to be established by the United Nations and such neutral states as wish to participate."[31]

Glueck's work was well reviewed. The *Virginia Law Review* praised the book's "earnest and timely plea that the most precious thing to be salvaged from the ruins of war is man's hard-won heritage of justice through law" so that "the protean forces of evil, which have almost succeeded in turning the world into a slave-pen and charnel-house, meet their just fate in a manner that will demand the decent respect of mankind and that will stand well in the judgment of history."[32]

Given Ben's enormous contribution to the monograph, it is rather astonishing that Glueck failed to even acknowledge him in its preface—although he did thank "his students . . . for the opportunity of discussing with them some views and doubts regarding the problems involved."[33] Still, making matters worse, Glueck sent Ferencz a copy of the book with an invoice asking to be reimbursed for its cost! Fortunately, Ben was in the army by then and could afford to remit the three-dollar price. Regardless, Glueck's former research assistant had the satisfaction of knowing that he had contributed to something that could significantly impact the postwar justice trajectory. And, once he became a key figure in the Nuremberg Trials, he could see with his own eyes how his work with Glueck was bearing fruit (including via Ben's own well-informed efforts). At the same time, despite his former professor's selfishness, Ferencz was always a good sport in terms of dealing with Glueck from that point forward. And his magnanimity would ultimately pay dividends as Glueck's whispering in the ears of Pentagon players likely played a role in Ben's becoming a prosecutor at Nuremberg.

BEN FERENCZ's work with Sheldon Glueck was certainly a significant thread in his Harvard Law School experience. But another one, even more significant, was playing out parallel to this—the United States' entry into World War II and Ben's efforts to enlist. Those who were alive on December 7, 1941, and old enough to understand what was going on around them, remember well what they were doing that day. It was a Sunday. At 7:48 a.m. local time on the Hawaiian island of Oahu, at the American naval base at Pearl Harbor, Japanese naval and air forces launched a preemptive military strike. Having completely surprised the Americans, 353 Imperial Japanese aircraft, including fighters, level and dive bombers, as well as torpedo bombers, unleashed an attack in two waves from six aircraft carriers.

In addition to killing 2,403 Americans and injuring another 1,178, the Japanese managed to sink or seriously damage eight battleships, three cruisers, three destroyers, an anti-aircraft training ship, and one minelayer. Within hours, there were also coordinated Japanese attacks on the US-held Philippines, Guam, and Wake Island and on the British Empire in Malaya, Singapore, and Hong Kong. Before the end of the week, Japan, Germany, and Italy had exchanged declarations of war against the United States, with Franklin Delano Roosevelt famously describing the "day that will live in infamy" before a joint session of Congress on December 8. The United States was at war in the Pacific and in Europe.

When the first wave of Japanese airplanes began raining down destruction on the US naval base at Pearl Harbor, it was 12:48 p.m. in Cambridge, Massachusetts. Ben Ferencz was sitting at his desk in his small attic room, studying. The radio was on, and he and his roommate Austin Graham were stunned to hear reports flooding in about a Japanese attack. Like the rest of their classmates, as well as persons from across all corners of the campus, they followed a converging mass of students streaming into Harvard Yard, where an impromptu assembly joined in a spontaneous "rally and support for our government." According to Ben, "Everyone I met was ready to enlist in defense of our country."[34]

And Ben wanted nothing more than to join them. But destiny would not bend to his will. In fact, in retrospect, his efforts to enlist may be seen as a kind of comical movie montage, with each segment representing another failed attempt to join the war effort.

The montage began with somewhat of a prelude. During law school, even before Pearl Harbor, Ben "had been trying to sabotage Germany." He would write to the German consulate requesting material to distribute that would explain Germany's side in the war. And they would send him hundreds of copies of pamphlets, which Ben immediately burned in the garbage.

Post–Pearl Harbor, his efforts were more explicitly geared toward returning to the continent of his birth and participating in the fight. And this is where the actual first scene of the comic montage unfolds. He sent a letter to the War Department volunteering for the intelligence services. With his fluent French, he suggested, he could be dropped behind enemy lines in France. In addition, he informed them, "I could probably get by on my skills in Hungarian, Yiddish, and possibly German."[35] But his précis of prodigious language skills did not do the trick. Washington informed him that no one could serve in the intelligence services who had not been a US citizen for at least fifteen years. His citizenship was derived from his father's papers, which had been issued in 1933. It had been fewer than ten years.

Cue up the montage's next scene: Ben sending an inquiry to the US Army paratroopers, which was also rejected forthwith given the inquirer's pint size, which meant that he was "more likely [to] go up than down."[36]

The montage is interspersed with metaphorical images of Ben throwing up his hands in exasperation. The first of these is a snapshot from his first year of law school. On returning home for winter break between the first and second semesters, he carried a letter from Dean Landis to US military officials noting that he was a "student of promise" and should be allowed to finish his first year (the document was needed as a peacetime draft had been in place since October pursuant to the Selective Training and Service Act of 1940). Ben presented this epistle to the clerk of the draft board in the Bronx, where he had been registered. The latter queried him briefly and assured young Ferencz that there would be no problem in deferring his induction.

At the end of the second term, he packed up his books and went home, expecting to be called up for military service before the end of the summer. But by the time September rolled around, no induction notice had arrived. In the meantime, Sara prevailed upon her son to return to Cambridge and carry on his legal studies.

Back at Harvard, Ben endured the next segment of the failed-enlistment montage. This time it centered on the US Navy, into which service his roommate, Austin Graham, had been inducted as an ensign. But that ended abortively too: "Although I had qualified as a Red Cross lifeguard, despite my inability to float, the idea of drowning at sea did not particularly appeal to me."[37] And he was convinced that the navy's sister service, the US Marines, would not take him either because he was too small. The army was unappealing as well because he had just "considered the war wounds" described in Eric Remarque's great book *All Quiet on the Western Front,* which had made "quite a profound impression" on him.[38]

The final shots of the montage relate to his efforts vis-à-vis the US Army Air Corps, which for him "had great appeal" with its "attractive" slogan "Your first mistake will be your last" (per Ben, "a nice, quick, clean way to go").[39] This part of the montage is the most comical, with the quickest shots of failure in rapid succession as his "love affair with the Air Corps was not mutual." As he phrased it later, "no matter how hard I tried, they would not have me." First, he went the conventional route of requesting to be a pilot. Rejection—he was so short, his feet would never reach the airplane pedals![40]

Next shot in the montage: the air corps lowered the height requirement, he reapplied, but he still failed to qualify—an eye missed one of the letters on the 20/20 chart. His own description of what followed perfectly captures the absurdity of the situation: "An optometrist suggested that I try eye exercises such as following the point of a moving pencil for hours. When my classmates observed my peculiar gyrations in class, some wondered whether I had been studying too hard and had gone out of my mind. The exercises didn't help; on my next physical exam for an assignment for pilot training, my left eye missed two letters rather than one."[41]

The closing montage scene unfolds at the Boston airfield, where Ben arrived at the invitation of an examiner, who felt sorry for him after his second failed eye test. The examiner told him an army representative there could do what was needed to help the Harvard Law student become a pilot. The officer at the airfield told him to sign a sheaf of papers on various dotted lines and he would be on his way to fighting for the United States in the skies above Europe. But Ben hesitated: "Now, if there is one thing you learn at Harvard, it is not to sign anything without reading it first. The paper would sign me up for training as a Glider Pilot. I didn't know what a Glider Pilot was. When he explained, I respectfully declined his kind offer. I consider myself a patriot, but if I am going to fly, I want a machine that can go up and not merely down."[42]

And that represented his last try. So he resigned himself to the idea that perhaps he would not be taking up arms against Axis forces before graduating from Harvard Law School. But he was never quite certain. That potential induction notice still hung over his legal studies like a sword of Damocles. Unfortunately, being in this state of limbo did him no favors in terms of his grade point average. His law school effort for the last two years "suffered from the anticipation" that he would have to leave at any moment. He "sent all his books home" after the first year and would not even "buy the expensive law books" that exceeded his budget.[43] "My primary focus was on trying to get into military service where I could do the most good," he recounted later. "The thought that others might risk their lives for me, while I remained at home, was not something I could live with. I was waiting for the draft call that never came."[44]

Still, he was able to leave Harvard with his head held high, earning excellent grades in subjects such as torts, contracts, jurisprudence, and, most importantly, criminal law. In certain courses, like evidence, for which his marks were impressive, even if not at the very acme of the roster, he learned invaluable lessons that would serve him well throughout his career (especially for his work in the *Einsatzgruppen* trial, where the expertise gained would help him determine that he could submit the entire prosecution case in just two court days). In that regard, one course in particular stands out—Professor

Glueck's "special seminar" on war crimes, held during Ben's last semester of law school.[45]

In the end, although he may have benefited from a relaxation of Harvard Law attrition quotas with the start of World War II, when retaining students going off to war proved a challenge, Ben never fell victim to the Day 1 "look to your right, look to your left, one-third-will-flunk-out" threat. To the contrary, in June 1942, HLS instituted a special wartime policy to expedite the degree process for students who completed their second year in June 1942. They were permitted to do fifteen hours of classroom work per week during the summer of 1942 and fourteen hours during the fall term (as well as complete the written work requirement), qualifying them for the degree by January 1943 rather than the following June. These students then officially graduated on the next university commencement date, March 1943. And that is what Ben did. His transcript declares that, on March 1, 1943, Benjamin Berell Ferencz graduated from Harvard Law School with an LLB (or bachelor of laws—in those days, the standard American law school degree, as opposed to the modern JD, or juris doctor).

Immediately upon graduation, Ben proceeded with haste to his draft board back in the Bronx. He reminded the clerk that he had been given a brief deferment to complete the second semester of his first year of law school and had heard nothing since. Interestingly, it was the same clerk who had initially taken his letter from Dean Landis and asked him some questions back in 1941. The clerk said he would send Ben his induction notice soon. Ben thanked him and left the room.

Quite oddly, however, the clerk began following him out the door. When they reached the elevator, he started speaking to Ben, who had noticed him on his heels and was feeling quite apprehensive. "Ferencz," he said, "how did you do in law school?" Ben replied that he had "done all right." The clerk then asked, "Do you want some more time to take your bar exam?" Now Ben was feeling really uncomfortable. He told the clerk he could take the exam while he was serving in the military.

Then, as the two of them stood awkwardly in the hallway, the clerk unburdened himself to the younger man. He explained that he had been enrolled at Yale Law School when the United States entered World War I. He had enlisted in the air corps and "had been a bit of a hero" but had lost a leg in combat. He lamented that he had never been able to return to his legal studies and had regretted it ever since. He confessed that when Ben tendered him the letter from Dean Landis, he resolved to spare the Harvard Law student the same fate that had befallen him. So he had held the Ferencz file in his desk drawer until that day. Ben was bowled over by the confession, at a loss for words. But soon it struck him how much impact this man had likely had upon his life—he probably owed him his legal education and law degree. Perhaps, it dawned on him in a flash, if he had been inducted to serve in World War II after his first year at Harvard, as had this man had during World War I while at Yale, he would have never earned his LLB. As this occurred to him, words of appreciation started coming out, haltingly, but powerfully, with genuine emotion.

Ben called for the elevator again, it came, he got in, and that was the last time he ever saw his hitherto unknown guardian angel. "The stranger who had quietly taken me under his wing certainly changed the course of my life," he later penned. And then he concluded with a rhetorical question: "Was Fate saving me for something else?"[46] As he was about to embark on a course that would see him become a pioneer in war crimes investigation and a figure of history at Nuremberg, the answer was most assuredly yes.

5

PRIVATE BENJAMIN

> The soldier's heart, the soldier's spirit, the soldier's soul, are everything.
>
> —George C. Marshall

After visiting his "guardian angel" at the local draft board, Ben Ferencz was offered a position as crime investigator for the New York Legal Aid Society, the oldest and largest provider of legal services to the indigent in the United States. He explained in a letter to Sheldon Glueck that he found "covering the slums and the Harlem hideouts a very interesting experience."[1] He added that the work opened "doors that would normally be closed" and allowed him to speak with "the most disreputable characters." As well, it helped him refine his understanding of the criminal justice system's machinery as he "got a glimpse of the operation of the courts, the D.A.'s office, and the work of the defense attorney."[2]

Later in the spring of 1943, though, Ben finally received his draft notice, quit his job with the Legal Aid Society, and reported for duty. In his dotage, he would delight in telling people, just a bit facetiously, that, "During the course of World War II, the Army recognized my talent as a Harvard Law graduate [with expertise in the law of war]" and in "its infinite wisdom made me a buck private in the artillery!"[3]

Comically, if not sadly, after nearly three years of efforts to join the military, foiled, as it turned out, so he could earn his LLB, the newly minted Harvard Law graduate was assigned to be a *typist* in the US Army's 115th AAA Gun Battalion (an anti-aircraft artillery unit). His law degree mattered not a whit in the assignment. And, as he wryly noted in his memoirs, "I never did learn how to type or how to fire a cannon."[4]

But he was schooled in the essential functions of soldiering as part of a time-honored American tradition—boot camp. After an introduction to the army and a brief stay at Fort Dix, New Jersey, basic training began in earnest in North Carolina, at an anti-aircraft artillery training facility called Camp Davis, which he described as "a miserable swamp and completely out of contact with civilization."[5] He hated his life not only because of the location but also because what they were doing there was "a dehumanizing process . . . where, as part of the training, the first thing you do is take human beings and make robots out of them. And I refused to become a robot and that caused me endless grief in the Army."[6]

The key player in the dehumanization process was the master sergeant, "a massive brute from Texas who boasted of beating his wife."[7] Upon their arrival, this sadist warned the new inductees that they could "go nowhere, see no one, get no transfers, and no, no, no everything." Ben later noted in his diary that the experience felt like "a sentence to life imprisonment."[8] But he began to adjust. His work in college as an intern helping juvenile delinquents at the Children's Village came "in most handy in adjusting to army life."[9]

And, after a while, he came to believe that his peers were giving highly exaggerated accounts about the rigors of basic training. Weapons instruction, obstacle courses, infiltration courses, twenty-five-mile hikes "have been temporary inconveniences," he said with some bravado in his diary. "Nothing more."[10] In fact, the army was cultivating in him an appreciation for the smaller pleasures of life that he had always taken for granted: "Who would have thought a year ago, that I would find pleasure in putting my hand in *warm* water, or having a bed sheet, or a bed, or a coat hanger, or a million other things?"[11]

After all the initial drilling, he even grew to make peace with his later transition into his supply clerk post: "There is very little work attached to the job (typing and filing) [and there] is plenty of food . . . and plenty of time to write letters, read, and loaf."[12] And although many of the men in his battalion had a "loud façade," were "immature" (focused primarily on beer and women), and "afraid to think," the people he worked with in the supply clerk's office were downright "pleasant."[13] So, in large part, his new life was starting to agree with him.

However, there was one aspect of boot camp to which he could never reconcile himself: marching. And that turned out to be his downfall. The new recruits were obliged to spend "hour after hour marching around in the hot sun" with the Texas mauler shouting, "Turn right, turn left, column right, column left . . ." Ben noted sarcastically that the invaluable "basic lesson" in all this was "to teach adults how to distinguish the right foot from the left foot."[14] At some point, Private Benjamin Ferencz decided he had had enough. With his Harvard-honed sense of justice most grievously offended, he resolved to give the Lone Star lout a lecture on the history and purpose of marching. "Close order drill," he informed him, "was invented by the Romans for a reason that was valid in [ancient] times." He continued:

> Those on the right of a marching unit carried their shields on their right arm, those on the left carried shields on their left and those in the middle held their shields overhead. Thus, like a modern tank, they were protected on all sides against the spears that might be thrown from an enemy on a hill. I pointed out that we were not likely to encounter spears thrown from a hill. A solid block of American foot soldiers approaching the machine guns of an entrenched enemy position would be mowed down if we did what he was training us to do. The "Sarge" listened with obvious contempt and retaliated by declaring war on me![15]

The first salvo in the Sarge's "war" against Private Ferencz was directed at the latter's scalp. "Your fucking hair is too fucking long," he barked in his Texas drawl. "No higher than one inch, soldier!" Ben dutifully went to the barber, where, with thoughts of sabotage permeating the organ under the area to be shaved, he requested that all his hair be removed. No sooner was he bald than he visited the medics and complained that, as a teenager, he had once been camping in the hot sun with a shaved head "and the result was that his cranium swelled up like a pudgy balloon." He asked whether marching in the hot North Carolina sun might have the same effect on his then-exposed pate. The doctor put it in medical terms: fatal sunstroke was a real risk. So, at Ben's request, he wrote out an order that Private Ferencz was not to march outdoors until his hirsute protection against the solar orb resprouted. And then, as only the private's own arch voice could properly express it, he "thanked [the doctor] profusely for his great medical acumen and marched out singing in loud military cadence, 'Left right, left, right . . . left, right . . .'"[16]

The next morning, not surprisingly, the drill master was none too amused. And more swearing, followed by the ordering of punitive measures, ensued: "OK you fucking wise guy. I'll fix your fucking wagon!" The idyllic days of basic training were about to end. The "wagon fixing" consisted of "a special assortment of tortures," including scouring the wooden barrack floor with a toothbrush, wiping out the toilets, and scrubbing the "stinking grease pits" of the officers' mess. For the latter, when he was through, he later chuckled, "it really earned the name 'mess.'" The utensils were "even more grimy and greasy" than when he started. He told his superiors that his subpar work was excused because his "hands were not used to near-boiling water," and his "tender skin could only tolerate lukewarm immersion." He was fired "as an incompetent dishwasher" and given even more demeaning assignments, including chopping down trees and planting them around the sandy barracks only to deracinate them again immediately after the commanding officer's inspection. This is when he reached the unalterable conclusion that the military experience was dehumanizing. And engaging in such exercises was the type of "revolting stupidity," he later wrote indignantly, "that encouraged me to revolt."[17]

The "revolt" was carried out via his "non-drilling" regular duties as supply clerk. And his version of a Spartacus-style uprising modestly centered on "the official rubber stamps needed to authenticate every military action." He had been directed to request one of each of these for the battalion commander and the company commander, respectively. And so, he realized, with a bit of the old Hell's Kitchen creative juices flowing, that if it were "such a vital instrument," it might be "prudent to request an extra one as a reserve." But he would keep it in his own pocket "for safekeeping" and would be willing to "sooner part with [his] rifle" than this illicit seal. It, along with an extra book of blank passes, ordered as well for good measure, "became [instruments] of justice."[18] Ben elaborated: "When all the officers and the Sergeant had left the camp for the weekend, a line formed around my bunk. My buddies knew that a pass from Benny, validated with the official seal, would get them past all of the MPs. I was simply demonstrating the equality of all men as guaranteed by our noble constitution. There was no limit to my patriotism."[19]

Months elapsed between the procurement of the bogus stamp and the unit's dispatch overseas. For Private Ferencz, always more of a loner, an observer, than a socialite or joiner, this afforded ample time to study his surroundings. It was his first visit to the "South," and from it he learned to "love New York."[20] Rather than spend his weekends at the camp or in nearby Wilmington, North Carolina, as most of his battalion peers did, he took a more anthropological approach, exploiting "every opportunity to hitch-hike around the countryside and get acquainted with the people and customs."[21] At times this could be a cheerful experience as he was occasionally the recipient of "Southern hospitality" that was much appreciated.[22]

There was a dark side, though. Writing in his diary, he observed that many of the locals felt superior to the "Yankees"—those who were white, that is. For those of color, and for residents of color as well, the "church-going, peace-loving Southerners" were "determined 'to keep the nigga in his place' and it is a violent determination." He added, with disgust, that "Anyone championing the cause of freedom for the Negro is bitterly hated." And he concluded this section of his diary ominously, if not prophetically (in light of the widespread race riots that took the United States to the brink of civil war in the 1960s), by noting "Perhaps this will be the spark in the powder keg to set off the Spanish Civil war in America."[23]

By mid-September 1943, the new recruits of the 115th AAA Gun Battalion had finished their time at "Swamp" Davis (Ben's derisive name for the facility). The next phase of their training would take place at a base called Camp Pickett, located outside of Blackstone, Virginia (per Ben, "a pretty typical small town—one main street and little else").[24] Although named after the martyred Confederate general of failed "Charge" fame, Private Ferencz and his fellow Yankees much preferred Pickett to Davis. The Ferencz Diary notes somewhat humorously: "I don't know what's happened to our cooks, but the food suddenly tastes good." In addition, the kitchen was "nice," the barracks were "large," and "this looks like a good deal." He predicted that "morale will undoubtedly be higher here."[25]

It did not hurt morale either that Ben and many of his brothers in arms were given leave the following weekend. Eighteen hours of Gertie and his nuclear family was blissful, even if it was "pretty disappointing" to find no one waiting for him when he arrived, and his return to camp was forty minutes after the leave deadline because the train was late.[26]

Not wanting to take his chances with another leave request on the heels of this infraction, for his next foray off base, he decided to use his "extra" approval stamp and supplemental supply of passbooks to self-authorize the egress/ingress. His destination was not very far—the Camp Pickett Rehabilitation Center. The enterprising Roscoe Pound acolyte wanted to study a new criminological phenomenon in the military context. Certain army personnel were committing offenses (e.g., absence without leave or disrespect toward a superior officer) that violated the army's Articles of War but would not amount to crimes in civilian life. Traditionally, though, if found guilty, they would carry a criminal record with them into civilian life, post–dishonorable discharge. This could doom them long-term to lives on the margins and deprive the military of potentially still valuable soldiers who merely needed cost-effective reform. To avoid such outcomes, the army had recently established a series of Rehabilitation Centers, to which offenders could be sentenced and given training and a chance to be restored to their army units.

At the Camp Pickett Center, Ferencz inspected the premises, examined the facility's relevant policies, interviewed the executive officer, Lieutenant Colonel A. E. Hesler, and spoke with certain offenders. He then used the "really swell"[27] Camp Pickett library to conduct related research and took advantage of any additional spare time he had to draft an article titled "Rehabilitation of Army Offenders." He managed promptly, and impressively, to place it in one of America's oldest and best-regarded legal publications, the *Journal of Criminal Law & Criminology*.

It is a short piece, but well researched and written, with the author concluding that the collected data on the Rehabilitation Centers to that point "already indicate that the results have more than justified the efforts exerted. These men, who would have been lost to the service in the last war, are now returning as members of fighting units, many have been given positions of trust and leadership, and all are being given the opportunity to wear with pride the uniform of the United States Army."[28]

Unfortunately, the Camp Pickett idyll could not last forever. Soon, the unit was packing up and heading to Camp Bradford, still in Virginia, but outside Norfolk, on the commonwealth's southeastern shore. In contrast to Camp Pickett, the new base was a "strictly-business place"—no "brass and polish," limited entertainment, and a "long beer line which keeps moving till they stop serving."[29] The coastal location was not selected haphazardly—the battalion was there to train for amphibious landings.

Private Ferencz practiced jumping from invasion boats into small landing craft or directly into the surf and then racing to the shore. He learned how to scale cargo nets and demonstrated his technique for digging foxholes on the beach (even during a ferocious rainstorm, no less).[30]

Ben pointed out in his diary that training for the amphibious landings "may be very important to me someday in the near future."[31] Yet, for reasons inexplicable to him, his first sergeant did not allow him to participate in the full range of training. During portions of the exercises, the self-described wife beater randomly ordered Private Ferencz to rake leaves or take up KP duty.[32] When he tried to explain to the Sarge why it was vital for him to participate in all the amphibious training, he was brusquely rebuffed. "The First Sgt. has a nasty disposition," he explained in his diary, "particularly toward someone he can't completely dominate—and I can't get a civil answer out of him." He added that his superior kept "trying to belittle my Harvard education—guess it gives him an inferiority complex."[33]

Mercifully, the stay at Camp Bradford was short, and the unit returned to the beloved Camp Pickett. It was now mid-October 1943, and there was a sense in the air that they would soon be shipping out to start fighting in the war. Axis forces in Europe were up against it by then. The Germans had finally lost the epic Battle of Stalingrad earlier in the year, and now the Soviets were gradually driving west, retaking lost territory (winning significant engagements, such as Kursk in July-August, the biggest tank battle in history) and slowly pushing through western Russia and then eastern Europe to eventually reach the German frontier.

British and American forces had prevailed in North Africa (with the late-1942 decisive Battle of El Alamein), had conquered Sicily and landed in Italy, where they pushed north and were driving back Axis forces. Mussolini had been deposed and arrested in July, and, by September, the new government had sued for peace, even declaring war on Germany (something Ben noted in his diary). Winston Churchill had gotten what he wanted in terms of persuading Franklin Roosevelt to attack the "soft underbelly of the Axis" before making any landings in France.[34] But now Normandy was beckoning, and the soldiers of the 115th AAA, done with their amphibious training, were bracing themselves for a final exodus to liberate "Fortress Europe."

Ben seemed instinctually to seize these valedictory moments of his stateside training interval. He was granted leave for another weekend in the Bronx. And he voted in a local election (presumably for offices in his home borough—it was the first time he had ever voted in his life—and he was one of the few soldiers at Camp Pickett to exercise his franchise right). As he noted in his diary: "Much debate and bloodshed for the principle of free elections. Wonderful theory, but when it comes to casting the ballot not many people are interested."[35]

And, during a late-October "field trip" to New Point Comfort, Virginia, where the unit went for five days of weapons training (not one of the core functions of a supply clerk), Ben was again able to take advantage of some downtime. He scouted out a "cozy refuge behind a hidden sand bar" that "provided many hours of just loafing and reading in the sunshine" (he was, at the time, working his way through the autobiography of the New Deal secretary of the interior Harold Ickes).[36]

Even better was an impromptu trip to the adjacent town of Mathews, Virginia. He took an unauthorized morning ride on a rations truck headed to a distant camp to collect needed victuals. The driver deposited Ben in the tiny town's center and promised to retrieve him on the way back. The only activity Private Ferencz could detect in this little enclave was groups of children walking to school. So he decided to join them. It turned out to be a good move. The teachers, all seven of them, "seemed delighted to have a visitor." And the kids were "practically in ecstasy to have a real honest-to-goodness soldier in their classroom."[37] Ben then recorded the lovely vignettes of the day:

> After shaking hands with every youngster in the first grade, listening to the school sing songs and reciting poems, I had to sit in on every class. I was grinning from ear to ear all morning. The Principal insisted that I have lunch with them and the school cook prepared a special plate for me. It was swell. The kids were pushing and pulling me everywhere. They got an obvious kick out of it when I let them all autograph my helmet liner. . . . I don't think I've enjoyed myself so much since I've been in the army.[38]

One of the teachers stood out—Johanna Crittenden, who was "particularly pleasant." "The kids adored her and I've always felt that children's sentiments are an infallible test of a person's character," he observed in his diary. He felt something very strong for her. And on his return to the barracks, he wrote her a letter baring a vulnerable part of his soul. Shedding the "brave soldier" persona of the previous day, he confessed that the army was not treating soldiers as "humans," and the end result was often "a very callous soul." He went on to explain: "We forget that there are places where people are busy learning other things than 'How to Kill.' We forget the sound of pleasant voices, polite requests, and the sound of children laughing. I explained that her classroom brought all these back to me and gave a new fire to the old ideals. I thought of similar happy schoolrooms sprinkled everywhere over this great country and the spark of hope started jumping."[39] Johanna promptly responded, and soldier and teacher stayed in touch for a time, but the correspondence eventually petered out. One wonders what might have developed between her and Ben Ferencz if a certain Gertrude Fried had not already come into his life.

His magical moment with Johanna came at a good time. He would soon need it to brace himself for the imminent bad news regarding his efforts to transfer out of the 115th and into Officer Candidate School (OCS). He had applied for OCS admission on arrival at Fort Dix. He was soon summoned to appear before the OCS Board and pleasantly surprised to see that its presiding officer was an old Harvard Law School friend, George Hickman. One of the rare West Point graduates at HLS, Hickman had never made Ben feel out of place in those Waspish environs. Having embarked on a great career that would eventually see him become the army judge advocate general, he was still then just "Major Hickman," and he and Private Ferencz expressed mutual joy at finding one another again. He assured Ben immediately that his application would be approved. But Ben heard nothing further until the 115th was ready to sail off to war.

By then it was December, and the unit was at Camp Shanks, its final bivouac point before boarding a large troop-transport ship heading to Europe. Immediately before their arrival there, the 115th had returned to Fort Dix, where the men, in groups of five, lived in "tents with wooden floors."[40] If Ben had had downtime during the amphibious landing and shooting range exercises, when most of the other soldiers in the unit were fully engaged, the opposite was true at Camp Dix. He and the other supply clerks were "preparing a Battalion for overseas shipment" and thus working "day and night."[41] Fortunately, he managed to squeeze in one last visit home to say "goodbye" to the folks and Gertie. That helped restore him physically and emotionally just as they were about to depart for Camp Shanks.

That sense of having recharged his battery, along with the lingering good feeling from his interaction with Johanna and her students, did not last long, though; he was about to get blindsided regarding his OCS application. The

Sarge, referred to in Ben's diary at that time as the "drunken whoremonger," called him into his office "with a happy sneer." "Well," he said, "we've finally received orders to ship overseas. I've been holding some papers here that may interest you," he said sarcastically. "I see you want to be an officer. I also see that a request has been made to transfer you to another outfit [by the officers Ben had impressed at the Camp Pickett Rehabilitation Center]." The Sarge paused and then concluded, in a tone of mock sympathy, stressing each word, "All transfers are now prohibited." He ripped up both documents before Ben's eyes and "tossed them into the trashcan with a flourish." His last words were, "The only way you'll get out of this outfit is in a box!"[42]

Ben was crushed but bereft of options. So he decided to find a more uplifting message before sailing across the Atlantic, taking in the *Why We Fight* movie series, then being shown on base. These were seven films, commissioned by the US War Department and made by director Frank Capra (of *It's a Wonderful Life* fame), meant to put the war into context, explain American aims, and inspire the troops to fight. They had the desired effect on Ben. What he saw on-screen reminded him that this twilight struggle was about whether humanity would live in "a free world vs. a slave world."[43] Many of the scenes of "sorrow and destruction" brought "tears to his eyes." But he could not help wondering what the many Black soldiers in the auditorium were thinking and whether "they will continue to fight for freedom after the war is over."[44] Again, he was presciently anticipating the postwar civil rights movement.

And he had been having other, similar, thoughts about life after the war for America's fallen enemies. These reflections, recorded in his diary, would foreshadow his eventual work at Nuremberg and, more generally, in the field of transitional justice. Pondering Italian and possible German surrenders, Ben offered that he did not believe "a Fascist nation can become a Democracy by a simple declaration." The key to "establishing a decent system" "is to replace the psychology of greed and hate with simple Christian ethics. It's a problem in 'How to Think' but no one seems concerned with psychological reconstruction." But who should take charge of such a project? "The formal church has been handing out too much bugaboo," he noted. And "the politicians don't understand. The businessmen are not interested in world improvement, and the philosophers are locked in their ivory towers."[45] But perhaps those in his chosen profession, the lawyers, could contribute toward bringing about the needed change? The accumulated musings in the diary indicate he had an inkling of that as he prepared to embark at long last for the battlefields of Europe.

THE ACTUAL date of departure was December 5, 1943, in the early-morning hours (they left Camp Shanks at 3:00 a.m., took a train to the port, and then a ferry to Pier 90, where the ship was waiting). As they prepared to board, they were greeted by a band playing martial tunes, and women from the Red Cross were handing out chocolate bars, doughnuts, and coffee. It seemed like the wrong ambience for 4:00 a.m., but they took what was offered, climbed a "short" gangplank ("so fast I didn't have time for an emotion," Ben later recalled),[46] and found their places on the ship.

Benjamin Ferencz originally came to the United States from England in the lower bowels of an enormous seafaring vessel, and he returned to England the same way, nearly twenty-three years later. The 1940s version of the vessel was called the RMS *Strathnaver.* Prior to being dragooned for the war, the British liner had been used for civilian ocean travel (it was huge, 23,000 tons, and not very old, with a 1931 maiden voyage to Australia). Now the ship was being commanded by British naval officers who, along with the commanders of the American troops onboard, "were living like kings" in the "neat cabins and staterooms" above deck.[47] Otherwise, the *Strathnaver* was staffed by an Indian crew. And, as Ben later explained, the rest of the ship was "jammed with Yanks being transported to an unnamed secret destination."[48] Overall, there were four thousand souls packed into the *Strathnaver.*

Of them, the 115th AAA Gun Battalion was consigned to almost the ship's lowest reaches—the "G" Deck—only "H" was lower, and that was the other side of the ship's hull bottom. In fact, Ben had the impression of being in a "tub" down there. Despite close quarters, Battalion personnel were allowed topside for air only one hour per day. Apart from "tedious boat drills," the balance of ship life for the 115th was spent crouched on the floor of the galley (playing cards, shooting craps, or reading), or perched on hammocks that were unfurled at night to serve as sleeping quarters. Via hook supports, the mesh-net hammocks were stacked in groups of five or six from floor to ceiling, with one man per hammock. "If the soldier in the net above was heavy," Ben later wrote, "some part of his anatomy was bound to rest on the man below. I scurried for the hammock on top."[49]

Below the hammocks, a row of long tables served as eating spaces during meals. The tables were not the problem; the meals were. The typical repast consisted of British-supplied "olive green color" frankfurters washed down with "gasoline-like water." So, inevitably, a black market developed where "an apple pie cost as much as five dollars." In the meantime, the British naval officers, as well as the US commanders of the American units on board, were dining on fresh fruit, salmon, and steaks. "This crass discrimination," Ben noted, "soon gave rise to rumbling in the ranks." Ben colorfully described what happened next as "Mutiny on the Strathnaver":

> We had on board members of the 101st Airborne Division, known as some of the toughest men in the army. . . . One late afternoon, the 101st took flight and landed in the galley. As one of the ship's half-naked Indian crew members was carrying a crate of oranges on his shoulder up the ladder, a paratrooper was waiting at the top. "I'll take that," said the husky soldier, pushing the Indian down the steps with his paratrooper boot. That was the signal. Paratroopers swooped down like the screaming eagles on their insignia. The doors to the storerooms were broken open. Crates of oranges and apples were lifted wholesale and hauled away. Within minutes, everything edible had disappeared. The mutiny on the Strathnaver was over without firing a shot.[50]

There were personal scores settled on the ship's passage too. The Sarge, as it happened, was not cut out for life at sea. During a particularly tempestuous stretch of weather, he turned "a sickly green to match the frankfurters." He was groaning on the floor, prostate, and leaning his head into a bucket with every heave of the ship. With just a touch of sarcasm, Ben later recorded: "So, out of my spirit of loving kindness, I offered to get him some more frankfurters, or maybe even a plate of nice greasy pork chops. Each time I mentioned food he seemed to retch some more. So I kept mentioning different delicacies, like baked reptiles or Chinese fried dog, to see if I could find one that might tempt him. No luck."[51]

While the voyage may have been miserable for the Sarge, it could have been fatal for all of them. Mere days after the 115th AAA Gun Battalion and its comrades in arms set sail, Nazi submarines attacked convoys in the North Atlantic. In fact, the captain of the *Strathnaver* later told certain men onboard that the convoy ahead of them and the one behind them had both been attacked. Wisely, the *Strathnaver* took a southern route and reached England via undisturbed passage up the Iberian Peninsula (still, Ben, who had been promoted to the rank of corporal by then, was obligated to take guard duty on the ship's deck at night—at least he could marvel at the thousands of twinkling stars in the clear skies overhead). On December 16, 1943, the great vessel dropped her anchor into the Bay of Liverpool, remarkably completing the reverse symmetry of Ben's personal voyage: this was the place from which he had originally set sail for the States as a baby. On disembarking the next evening, a "strange train" whisked the soldiers through the night to Manchester, which they would call home for the next several weeks.

"HOME" WAS the grounds of a large menagerie cum amusement park called Belle Vue Zoological Gardens, which was located to the east of the city center in what struck Ben as a pretty seedy area of town. If the surroundings were not particularly agreeable, the sleeping quarters were even worse. The men in Ben's group were assigned to makeshift beds in what had been the park's elephant house (with certain desiccated droppings left on the straw floor unpleasantly reminding them of the structure's previous inhabitants).

For the 115th AAA, Manchester was merely a transit point. Thus, the soldiers had much time on their hands, and local women were not in short supply either. En route to their landings on the beaches of Normandy, despite being in the land of Churchill, this would not be their finest hour. Most of their lives revolved around preparing for and recovering from each night's boozy, carnal hoopla.

Even Ben got in on the act, albeit in a much more wholesome way, having met a young lady at "one of the better dance halls."[52] She worked at a telegraph office and "seemed very nice."[53] Going out and fraternizing like this was better than being lonely, especially since "mail from that certain female at home" seemed to be "very slow" in arriving.[54] He concluded that "some pleasant female" would "do wonders for [his] morale."[55] So he started dating the "telegraph girl,"[56] seeing her in the evenings and taking her on at least one Sunday excursion to Wythenshawe Park on the outskirts of town. When he dropped the young lady off at home, her mother invited him in, and they all chatted over hot cocoa and cake. He noted in his diary that he would never have the opportunity to know if things might have worked out with Telegraph Girl—the 115th was about to pull up stakes.

The next day, February 19, the 115th AAA said goodbye to Manchester and hello to Freckleton, where, only six months later, the infamous Freckleton Air Disaster would occur (a military plane, attempting to land in stormy weather at a nearby airbase, crashed into a schoolhouse, killing sixty-one people, including many children and teachers). Their new location was near that soon to be benighted airbase. And, immediately upon arrival, they were put "in action," with their gun batteries placed in static defense positions so as to guard airfields near the western coast of England. In addition to his normal supply clerk duties, as well as serving as "fireman" in the boiler room, Corporal Ferencz was assigned to stand guard at the driveway into their position. He bemoaned the "senselessness" of this job, given that if "the enemy should penetrate this far," he could "easily slip in" and the "sentry [curiously not given ammunition] would be helpless and useless." And yet, he fumed in conclusion, "1/3 of my time is spent on guard."[57]

He was none too thrilled with the living accommodations either. They were put into small Quonset huts; with sixteen soldiers crammed into one, "it's pretty hard to keep the place clean—or quiet," and "there's not a very homelike atmosphere."[58] Far from the urban decay of Manchester, the area around them now was all muddy farmland, and they had to trudge through the muck in galoshes just to reach their mess hall about three blocks away.

Fortunately, those pastoral environs were home for just under three weeks. Their next destination was Camp Blandford, in the south-central part of England. On the way, Corporal Ferencz and his comrades had occasion to visit a prisoner of war (POW) camp filled with Italian POWs. And it inspired Ben to record his impressions regarding the fleeting fortunes of war and the long-term effects of propaganda, ideology, as well as the power of ethnic solidarity: "Our boys crowded around the barbed wire fence and spoke to the prisoners in Italian. From what I could hear they seemed a group of typical young fascists, who, like everyone else, were fed up with war but whose political opinions remained unchanged. Our Italian boys were very friendly and gave the prisoners cigarettes and bought brass rings from them at fancy prices. Not long ago these prisoners were killing Americans and Englishmen, but the naive Americans didn't seem to realize or care."[59]

By March 17, they had reached southern England, in the area of Salisbury, and decamped at Blandford, where the order of the day was "mobile training." As Ben explained, "90 mm. [anti-aircraft artillery] outfits must learn to move quickly or be destroyed and we sure can use the instruction."[60] After a month of preparing for it, the mobile training began in earnest by the middle of April. The plains around Salisbury were flat and ideal for the assembly of the countless tanks and vehicles that would be needed to teach the soldiers how to synchronize all the different moving parts. Much of the time was spent in the field, away from the camp, where the men pitched tents in the freezing-cold wind on the impenetrable chalk plain. There was no plumbing or electricity, and it was nearly impossible to get warm or, given the diamond-hard earth, even dig a latrine. In an almost surreal contrast to the GIs' personal misery, they could see the magnificent Salisbury Cathedral off in the distance (at various points during their perambulations on the plain, Ben had an opportunity to visit the Gothic edifice and "study its beautiful architecture").[61]

At one overnight stop on this inhospitable heath, Ben's tent was literally pitched against one of the famous prehistoric rocks at Stonehenge, one of southern England's great tourist sites. He later described a comic scene that ensued: "[At] daybreak, I was awakened to find my tent surrounded by a circle of people chanting in white robes. It looked more like the Ku Klux Klan than the German army, but I grabbed my rifle anyway. It turned out that they were harmless pilgrims come to celebrate at what they believed was an ancient religious shrine."[62]

In the waning days of the spring of 1944, on the Salisbury Plain, Ben's unit seemed to be in perpetual motion. The 115th was not fixed to any one hierarchical unit higher on the food chain (for example, brigade, division, corps, or army). It eventually reached France under the aegis of the First Army and later was moved to the Third. Such units were utilized to reinforce the capabilities of subordinate commands when and where needed. Accordingly, it was designated a "mobile" battalion, the artillery equivalent of a hired gun for actual combat situations where enemy aircraft were spotted and needed to be shot out of the sky, or where vital friendly assets needed enhanced air defense protection. Thus, for the purposes of these exercises, on as little as fifteen minutes' notice, the men, their guns, and their equipment would all have to pick up and relocate rapidly, moving herky-jerky from one staging area to the next. But there was method to this seeming madness—Allied commanders were preparing for a campaign of rapid maneuver following the invasion. Moreover, their zigging and zagging did seem to have one directional commonality—they were generally moving toward their final point of embarkation on the English coast.

Before they got there, Ben would continue to take advantage of leave passes. There was a dreary trip to London that included a visit to the famed Brighton Beach, which was unfortunately covered with barbed wire and steel barricades designed to thwart any possible German invasion.[63] He took refuge from the inclement weather by visiting the Old Bailey, where he watched criminal proceedings but could not always understand the "whispers" in a strange accent (contrasted with the bellowing heard in courts back home).

Giving up on the English legal system, he made his way to the Churchill Club, to which he had previously applied and been admitted. But he was snubbed on arrival at this snobbish "officers association" because he was the only enlisted man present. It was another reminder of how much he hated elitism.

Meanwhile, after what seemed an interminable wait, despite the constant frenetic movement, the 115th finally gathered on the Salisbury Plain and learned about what it was they had been so intensely preparing for. An army general addressed the assembly and explained that, at the start of the invasion on "D-Day" (formally Operation Overlord), they would cross the channel and hit the beach in France once engineers had cleared the mines and barriers under the water. Troops would go ashore with barrage balloons that would be released with hanging cables to intercept low-flying enemy aircraft. The 115th would take positions on the sand and set up its guns to shoot down high-flying German airplanes attacking any US personnel or equipment located on the beach.

So now they knew their roles in the imminent invasion of "Fortress Europe." But there was yet another delay—the weather was not cooperating. While they waited for the skies to clear, they began to run out of supplies, as everything had been put in waterproof containers and placed in the seafaring vessels that would be transporting them. It soon became apparent that the most pressing shortage was toilet paper. So the ever-enterprising Ferencz snapped into action. He took an enormous supply of soft onion-skin carbon copy paper and had a nearby butcher take a meat cleaver to it, chopping it into sections. "With a truckload of improvised toilet tissue," he mused later, he returned to the base "in triumph," joking that he "was responsible for 'wiping out' a whole battalion."[64]

Little by little, the men were positioning themselves closer to the English Channel. Finally, "at the very tip of England," at a place called Land's End, the 115th was standing by for the initiation of D-Day. Ben later recorded his powerful recollection of that epochal moment: "I recall the early morning hours of June 6, 1944. . . . I was on guard duty, as usual. I watched the sky turn black with planes. Many of them dragged one or two gliders behind them. I knew that the ships that I had seen clogging the harbors all along the British coast had set sail for the beaches of France. The tension of the waiting, the excitement of what was happening, and the knowledge that we were finally engaging a hated enemy caused a surprising sensation to rise in my breast. I let out a loud cheer. I wanted to be with the invading force."[65]

His turn would come soon. He was about to experience war firsthand and become a legal chronicler of its horrors. In a little over a year, an awkward, gangly Private Benjamin Ferencz had transformed into the more seasoned, savvy Corporal Benjamin Ferencz, who was about to join one of the greatest invading armadas in human annals. And in the year to come, after a kinetic and bloody race across France, he would find himself within Germany's frontiers, a newly minted war crimes investigator about to embark on a personal rendezvous with history.

6

PATTON'S SOLDIER

> Wars may be fought with weapons, but they are won by men. It is the spirit of men who follow and of the man who leads that gains the victory.
>
> —General George S. Patton, *Cavalry Journal*

By the time Benjamin Ferencz crossed the English Channel, whose surface on that summer day was as calm as a "Bronx Park lake," and reached the beaches of Normandy, it was D+28 from the initiation of Operation Overlord.[1] If further removed, and certainly less heroic, than D-Day itself, the date was at least auspicious from a different American history perspective—it was Independence Day, July 4, 1944. The 115th AAA Gun Battalion ought to have been there on June 6 with the rest of the initial landing craft and partaken of the glory, if not also the gore, of facing the first salvos of Nazi ordnance. But for reasons never explained to Corporal Ferencz, at the last minute, the 115th AAA was replaced for the June 6 operation by the 116th AAA.

This artillery unit numbers switch had a significant impact on Corporal Ferencz's Normandy Beach landing experience. As his portion of the 115th disembarked from the SS *James B. Weaver* into LCIs (landing craft infantry—smaller amphibious assault craft), traces of the tragic human sacrifice and ghostly detritus of the previous month's battle (including hundreds of wrecked ships and smaller landing craft) were scattered all around Omaha Beach, Ben's landing spot. On D-Day itself, apart from Omaha, a sector whose taking was the responsibility of the Americans, the targeted fifty-mile stretch of Normandy's coast had been divided by the Allies into four other "Beach" divisions: Utah (an American sector as well), Gold (a British sector), Sword (British too), and Juno (a Canadian sector).

Strong winds had blown the landing craft east of their intended positions, particularly at Utah and Omaha (the two sectors with the most carnage). The troops had approached the beaches under hails of German bullets from gun emplacements perched on the bluffs above the shore. And the sea front was densely populated with mines and other obstacles, such as wooden stakes, metal tripods, and barbed wire, which impeded forward progress from the landing crafts and saddled beach-clearing teams with a Herculean, as well as hazardous task. In all, casualties from that hellish day have been estimated at 10,000, including 2,500 dead. The Americans bore the brunt, with approximately 6,603 dead or wounded (the British counted 2,700, and the Canadians, 946 casualties).

Corporal Ferencz could sense the presence of all those lost souls as his LCI approached the shore and docked in the surf (at the same spot, a portion of the 115th—its "Light Scale"—had landed at D+6).[2] The ramp was lowered, and through about two feet of water, the unit's jeeps raced to dry land. Ben stepped out into the sea and waded ashore with the rest, somewhat more submerged owing to his diminutive frame (waist high, as opposed to knee high). Before them, about one hundred yards inland, rose a large hill, into whose sides the German defenders had burrowed to fend off the Allied onslaught. Now the enormous hummock was a "shell-scarred mess."[3] Its expertly concealed positions had been blown to smithereens. But one enormous concrete pillbox stood out—its camouflage had been blasted away, and its steel reinforcement protruded "like a shattered skeleton."[4] Just then, a summer thunderstorm "tore the heavens open" while the men of the 115th marched single file up the hill. "It was as though the heavens were weeping," Ferencz later wrote.

Shambling up that mucky footpath, he and his brothers in arms passed the crushed remains of German 88 positions (that is, those using 88 mm guns). At the ascent's summit, the freshly painted crosses of a large, makeshift American cemetery "gave mute testimony to the fact that getting to that grave had not been easy."[5] While catching his breath atop the peak, Ben could hear the truck engines churn on their slip-sliding climb up the river-of-mud road. And, looking down, he could see the other soldiers plodding along on either side of the vehicles, absorbing the wet, brown earth splattering from the tires while, all at once, getting washed under the heavy sheets of rain. Looking farther down onto the busy beachhead and beyond, he beheld the spectacle of the barrage balloon flotilla, each nondirigible blimp tethered to a ship and floating steadily in the rain-soaked skies, seemingly in defiance of the downpour. Looking behind, farther along the top of the massive muddy knoll, a landing strip had been constructed, and he could see a steady stream of ascending and descending P-47 Thunderbolt fighter-bomber planes leaving on patrol and coming back.

Soon, the trucks of the battery's Light Scale arrived and took them through the rain farther inland. Along the way, through the wet, pastoral fields, Ben noticed that only a single farmhouse still stood intact. In its yard, a middle-aged French woman, seemingly oblivious to the destroyed Norman infrastructure all around her, smiled at the passersby. Twenty minutes after leaving the Omaha Beach escarpment, and having navigated a series of windy roads after seeing the farmhouse woman, Ben and the other soldiers who had so recently alighted from the LCIs in the surf rejoined the rest of their battery mates. They had been engaged at the Battle of Cherbourg, where the town and port had been liberated after fierce fighting. The reunited battery's new position was now near Saint-Laurent-sur-Mer, between Bayeux and Isigny.

But within days, Ben and his unit were involved in one of the most significant engagements after the Allied breakout from the Normandy beaches—the Battle of Saint-Lô. The town where the battle was fought, and from which it derives its name, was about twenty miles inland from the coast and served as a strategic transportation hub and German defensive stronghold. After initial success in establishing a foothold on the coast, Allied progress toward the French interior had ground to a virtual halt, with hundreds of thousands of soldiers boxed in along the narrow Normandy beachhead and its vicinity. American forces under General Omar Bradley found themselves in a grueling war of attrition "among the dreaded hedgerows."[6]

These were massive bands of shrubbery, lined by mud walls and creating sunken lanes, which were prominent features on the Norman bocage landscape that enclosed fields but also stymied effective fighting. Every bocage represented a kind of vegetal hindrance that had to be cleared lest the Germans exploit it to halt Allied forward progress, even with no air cover. These leafy nuisances were negating significant advantages in tanks, planes, and motorized maneuver, which Supreme Allied Commander Dwight D. Eisenhower was counting on for a rapid breakout from the Normandy region. Even worse, the unusual landscape was enabling German guerrilla raids against American forces, after which the enemy would slip away undetected. One could say that this terrain made for a new kind of botanical trench warfare. Thus, Bradley's First Army, to which the 115th AAA Gun Battalion was then attached, needed to take Saint-Lô not only to deprive the German Seventh Army of this strategic crossroads but also to overcome the hedgerows and then drive into the French heartland.

The beginning of the American assault was set for July 11, about one week after Corporal Ferencz's Normandy arrival. To overcome the bocage barriers, Ben later noted, American ingenuity was responsible for creating the "Sherman Hedgerow Cutter." Made by welding segments of steel railroad tracks along the sides and front of a tank, it was "a big pitchfork on wheels" that could "cut through the massive mounds as easily as picking up a pork chop."[7] This conferred on US forces an important new advantage. Still, additional help was needed. As the battle progressed, to further soften enemy resistance, eight battalions of artillery were to pound the city, supplemented by air strikes from nearly two hundred P-47 Thunderbolt fighter-bombers. The 115th was ordered to move to the city's outskirts "and be ready to roll."[8] "Soon," Ben reported, "the sky was darkened by long waves" of bombers "as far as the eye could see." He described what happened next:

> The massive bombs fell like heavy hail soaking the city below. Although I must have been several kilometers away, the ground shook so fiercely that I could not stand. We all lay flat and watched as St. Lo was pummeled into ruin. When the order came to "Start rolling!" our trucks and guns could find no road; and no house or building was left standing. The French city of St. Lo was reduced to a pile of rubble. I still wonder how many innocent human beings lay buried beneath those smoldering ruins.[9]

Ben was right—the air and ground attacks razed up to 95 percent of Saint-Lô, according to most estimates. The Irish playwright Samuel Beckett dubbed the city the "Capital of the Ruins." But its capture was critical to the success of what was called Operation Cobra and to the subsequent closing of the so-called Falaise Gap, another key victory, where scores of demoralized German units were encircled and captured. These operations ultimately permitted Allied forces to expel the Nazis from northern France and complete their march across the Gallic countryside toward the German border.

After Operation Cobra, the 115th was transferred from the First to the Third Army, under the command of General George S. Patton. Even before taking over the Third, Patton was already one of the most colorful figures in US military history. Urges for both political and military glory were in his DNA. Born in San Gabriel, California, in 1885, his grandfather on his mother's side had been the mayor of Los Angeles. And coming from a long line of prominent Virginia military men on his father's side, including forebears who had fought for the Confederacy during the Civil War, Patton graduated forty-sixth in his US Military Academy class at West Point in 1909. Three years later, he represented the United States at the Stockholm Olympic Games, where he finished fifth in the modern pentathlon (swimming, pistol shooting, running, riding, and fencing). He was a superb fencer and swordsman, eventually becoming an instructor of swordsmanship and designing the US Model 1913 Enlisted Cavalry Saber, known as the Patton Sword.

In 1916, Patton joined the staff of Brigadier General John J. Pershing and accompanied him on a punitive expedition into Mexico to capture the notorious outlaw Pancho Villa, after he launched one of the last attacks on US soil, in Colombus, New Mexico. Patton personally shot and killed a couple of Villa's lieutenants and tied them to the hoods of his detachment's cars when driving back to Pershing's headquarters. This brought him his first taste of fame, and he found it intoxicating. He then joined Allied Expeditionary Forces Commander Pershing's staff in France when the United States entered World War I, and ultimately became the first officer to be appointed to the US Army Tank Corps, personally leading US tank units into battle. In the process, he earned the Distinguished Service Cross for bravery under fire after being gravely wounded by machine gun bullets but refusing evacuation until his unit prevailed in the battle.

By the time the United States entered World War II, Patton was known for his expertise in rapid mobile tank warfare, his brash personality (including a foul mouth, polished helmet, riding crop, and pistols with his initials carved into the ivory handles), and his belief that he had been reincarnated as a soldier in many previous lives, including as a Roman legionnaire and as part of the fourteenth-century army of John the Blind of Bohemia. Before the Allied invasion of Sicily, British General Harold Alexander said to Patton, "You know, George, you would have made a great marshal for Napoleon if you had lived in the 19th century." Patton replied, "But I did."[10] After the Allies landed in Sicily in early July 1943, he employed his armor in a lightning-quick drive that resulted in the US Seventh Army's capture of Palermo on July 22 and Messina on August 17. After his military brilliance on the Mediterranean's largest island, he gained more notoriety for having slapped two shell-shocked soldiers in field hospitals for not participating in combat. In the resulting uproar, General Eisenhower temporarily removed him from battlefield command.

But, with his nickname of "Old Blood and Guts" (from telling his troops before battle that they would be "up to their necks" in the enemy's blood and guts), he had gained the respect of the Germans, and Eisenhower used him as a decoy in the lead-up to D-Day (running a phantom army, complete with plywood aircraft and inflatable rubber tanks, in southeast England, and successfully deceiving the Germans into thinking he would strike at the channel's narrowest point—the Pas de Calais). When it was time to drive deep into France after Operation Cobra, Eisenhower turned to a rehabilitated Patton and gave him control of the Third Army. And it is from the campaign that followed, all the way through France, Belgium, and Germany, that Patton became a legend in military annals.

That was at the beginning of August 1944. And Corporal Benjamin Ferencz's diary intimates that Patton's troops were about to make history. "The Americans have launched a vast offensive," he wrote.[11] According to Stanford historian Victor Davis Hanson, "The Third Army took off in a type of American blitzkrieg not seen since Union General William Tecumseh Sherman's rapid marches through Georgia and the Carolinas during the Civil War."[12]

When Patton's new unit had finally become operational seven weeks after D-Day, it was supposed to play only a subsidiary role—guarding the southern flank of the armies of General Bradley and British Field Marshall Bernard Montgomery, while securing the Atlantic ports. But "Old Blood and Guts" had other ideas, and he convinced his superiors to give him free rein. His troops began in Lower Normandy, with a slight detour south for certain detachments to capture the province of Brittany. But the bulk of his forces, including Ben Ferencz's unit, sped in an easterly direction through France. And Ben's diary reflects this amazing race across the Gallic countryside.

At the very beginning of the odyssey, he wrote: "At 2 p.m. out of a clear blue sky, we received our march order [and we were] to take up positions at the front. We loaded our vehicles quickly [and] moved toward the front with much eagerness and anticipation."[13] Not long thereafter, they reached the city of Avranches but did not linger, pulling "into an area past Avranches. The tanks had gone through two days before, but from the many truckloads of prisoners passing, it was apparent that there were still plenty of Germans in the area."[14]

Indeed, Nazi forces were still making their presence felt. The following evening, as the 115th AAA continued its pursuit of the Third Army's forward-moving tanks, a full moon came out, and the Luftwaffe brought the pall of death to the lunar-lit skies. As Ben described it: "In the distance we could hear a machine gun firing. Then we saw the planes. Perhaps a dozen planes—German planes—were dropping flares over the front. We could hear the bombs and Jerry [that is, the Germans] seemed to have complete mastery of the air. We understood then why we were sent for so hurriedly. The road was jammed with a steady stream of vehicles going forward. It was a perfect target for strafing, and Jerry didn't miss the opportunity."[15]

Heading southeasterly, toward the town of Saint-Hilaire-du-Harcouët, they faced further German resistance. Their new position had them guarding the flank of advancing tank columns: "German planes came over regularly. They bombed Allied roads, bridges and concentrations."[16] The 115th tried to shoot them out of the sky, but they kept coming in waves. Eventually, the unit made its way to a farm, where it would spend the night, and Ben had to "chase the goats away" before he could dig his foxhole. Later on, well after the sun had set, the Luftwaffe came again. And when the battery's .90-millimeter cannons opened fire, the sky was lit with "an enormous display of fireworks." But the ground attack gave them no immunity from "being strafed, or hit by flak or bombs." Still, the guns were having their effect, and many German planes were "hurtling down in flames."[17]

Unfortunately, German planes were not the only ones being shot out of the sky. Many US fliers also lost their lives to Allied "friendly fire." The Americans and Brits tried to avoid this as best they could by using radar to distinguish their airplanes from the enemy's. But the Germans devised a kind of cloaking mechanism by dropping strips of aluminum into the sky so as to scramble the radar readings. Thus, in the confusion, as Ben later painfully recounted:

> Allied aircraft, often returning still carrying bombs or ammunition, were blown to smithereens. Our tracer bullets reaching for the planes, and the ensuing "fireworks" that exploded into the sky left a painful image in my mind. Those of us who were not manning the guns fanned out over the terrain desperately and hopelessly searching for survivors. I carried a cardboard carton into which I sadly placed pieces of a finger or a clump of hair that might help to identify a human body so we could notify the next of kin. I don't want to be considered unpatriotic and I hope I will be forgiven, but "the rockets' red glare, the bombs bursting in air" evoke memories I would rather forget. Like many veterans of war, I never go to any celebrations where fireworks are featured.[18]

Unfortunately, the Americans were still taking heavy casualties. But, as August's calendar days were being x-ed out, the tide began to turn. German resistance was gradually crumbling. Tracking that time period, Ben's diary gives various accounts of Wehrmacht soldiers surrendering. For example, at one point, five were taken prisoner on the roads near their encampment and were brought into the battalion office. Two of them, looking haggard and frightened, seemed to be about sixteen years old.[19]

By mid-August, the Germans were "retreating faster" than the Third Army "could keep up with them."[20] It got to the point where they had encircled "about 20 German divisions," and it was "often difficult to discover just where the American or enemy lines" were located. The German dead were also beginning to pile up along the roads. Ben recalled, "Their bodies were black and bloated, and I could smell them as I approached. There had been no time to bury them, and dozens lay strewn along the road to glory. Before I saw one, I thought I'd spit on him, but after one look I changed my mind. The truck slowed down and I got a good look. A million maggots were crawling at his face, forming blacker splotches on the black background. It all seemed unhuman, unreal, and nauseating."[21]

DESPITE THESE grotesque scenes, there was a sense that the retaking of France was a fait accompli, and the tension started to ease among Ben and his battery mates. In fact, Corporal Ferencz started to appreciate that he found himself in the country whose language and culture he had studied so intensely back in New York. During this sweep across France, Patton's men were wont to bivouac on farms. Ben would enjoy speaking with the Norman cultivators, and they would shower him with the best gifts they could find, such as boxes of fresh eggs and bottles of their best cognac. And, when the soldiers were on the move, French civilians would stand along the sides of the roads and wave at the advancing liberators. If the unit stopped for maintenance or supplies, Ben would regale passersby in their native tongue with stories of Patton's advance south and east from Avranches.

But his language skills really came in handy once they passed Alençon (on the edge of Normandy) and were heading into the Loire Valley chateau region. One day, while tracking a German sniper, an officer in Ben's battery "spotted two pretty girls" near a chateau. The officer immediately shouted out to Ben, and they walked onto the chateau grounds. "It did not take long," Ben later wrote, "to get acquainted and to discover that the girls, aged 16 and 23, were daughters of the estate owner."[22]

The property was perched atop a hill affording a view for "hundreds of miles around." There were beautiful lawns and a small lake nearby. Ben, who had spent the first part of his childhood in a New York City slum, thought it was all quite breathtaking. But his breath was taken away even more by the beauty of the lord of the manor's twenty-three-year-old daughter, whose name was equally beautiful—Geneviève. She invited him to go swimming in the lake and they really hit it off. She was a college graduate who was "intelligent, attractive, and just [his] size." Besides all that, he found her to be "an excellent swimming companion."[23] As they were bivouacking in that area for a comparatively long time, he returned on several occasions to see the alluring Geneviève. Although she was a "devout Catholic" and "very restrained in her conduct" at first, over time she found herself quite enamored of the American corporal and started to ease up. On Ben's final night in the area, romance blossomed. As the American swain described it: "Geneviève led me to what was obviously a lover's lane around the lake's edge. There we managed to slip away from the others by swimming through the woods to a secluded spot. No sooner had we stopped to catch our breath than the lovely miss, whom I had never ever touched before, threw her arms around me and started kissing me passionately. . . . One thing led to the other, and it must be admitted that this surprise affair was very pleasant."[24]

His dalliances since becoming a soldier had gotten progressively more serious. In the United States there had been a spark with Johanna; in England, there were dates with "Telegraph Girl"; and, finally, in France, there was an actual "affair" with Geneviève. It was romance with someone other than Gertrude, and it would not be the last time he would experience that during the war. But there was hardly any time to ponder all that as Ben's battery was again on the move. And now he could feel a growing sense of confidence, and joy, among the French citizenry that they were finally being freed from their Nazi oppressors. He waxed nostalgic about this in his diary: "Travelling along the roads to our new position was an unforgettable thrill. French men, women, and children, all dressed in their Sunday finery lined the roads to cheer us on. Flowers, apples, pears, cucumbers, squash, and cider were only some of the things they threw at us. Jubilation oozed from every pore as the population was being liberated."[25]

As German resistance was breaking down, the Third Army's pace quickened in entering the Loire Valley. The men of the 115th AAA Gun Battalion soon found themselves in Le Mans, home of what is now the world's oldest active endurance car race, the "24 Hours in Le Mans," which had started in 1923. Ferencz and his battery mates were there for less time than the race.

But that did not mean that the Nazi menace had disappeared entirely. In Blois, while on the grounds of another chateau, Ben heard shots being fired in the courtyard. He peered around a wall cautiously and saw what appeared to be German soldiers firing rifles toward a field. A closer look revealed that beneath those German helmets were civilian Frenchmen, wearing brassards of the FFI (Forces Françaises de l'Intérieur), identifying themselves as members of the French resistance military wing. They were donning helmets taken from captured Wehrmacht soldiers and were firing at a distant German artillery encampment. It was clear that the enemy was outside the range of the old rifles.[26] Meanwhile German mortar shells kept exploding in the courtyard where they were hiding. Ben feared for their lives. Fortunately, some American jeeps were patrolling the area, and Corporal Ferencz alerted them to the situation. They signaled the air corps, which sent in planes that took out the German unit and their mortars.

Soon thereafter, Ben's battalion was speeding off to chase Nazis at the place of Joan of Arc's greatest military triumph, Orléans. There, along with other Third Army units, they helped protect General Bradley's southern flank and dashed German hopes for a defense of the Paris-Orléans gap (Paris was liberated on August 25, with help from the Fourth US Infantry Division of the First Army).

By then, the Nazis were either being captured en masse or clearing out of France in rearguard action to mount an eventual defense of the "Fatherland." Thus, in quick succession, the 115th AAA passed rapidly through Sens (where Ferencz had enough time for another fling with a "buxom little blonde"),[27] Châteaudun, Vitry-le-François, and St. Dizier. Ben described this as Patton's "lightning advance" and noted that, in terms of combat, France had become a "hollow shell."[28] He went on: "The Germans left hurriedly for Germany—where we expect to meet again." And then, in words evoking animal imagery that would have made Patton proud, he concluded, "The scent of blood is in our nostrils and we are all panting for the kill."[29]

Unfortunately, as it entered France's far eastern province of Lorraine, close to the German frontier, the Third Army's progress slowed considerably. It was the middle part of September, and Patton was running out of fuel while fleeing German forces were regrouping and stiffening their resistance.[30]

This was felt most keenly during the September-December Lorraine Campaign, in which Patton's troops prevailed only after nearly four months of protracted fighting. While the Third Army's capture of Metz and Nancy during these pitched battles has garnered more publicity, for Ben Ferencz, the liberation of the smaller Lunéville earlier on was personally much more meaningful. In October, while guarding a recently captured bridge, the diminutive corporal rushed to the rescue of a young lady, about twenty years old, who attempted a crossing on her bicycle. The powerful guns of the German Panzer tanks, which were on the outskirts of town in a nearby forest, were leaving shrapnel all around the bridge. Ben urged this mademoiselle to turn around, but she insisted that she had to rush home and bolted across the bullet-pocked span.

The next day, by chance, they ran into each other at the gate of the 115th's quarters, where Ferencz had been standing guard. He scolded her for ignoring his warnings at the bridge. And she apologized by inviting him to her house for dinner. He gladly accepted. Once there, her little family told Ben that they were celebrating "Lunéville Liberation Day." It was just the young lady, a kindergarten teacher; her father, a professor at the University of Nancy; and her mother. "Papa" had caught a rabbit, cooked it in wine, and even managed to rustle up two eggs. Added to that were flowers, wine, fruits, and Ben's US Army rations. "They had been saving the ingredients of that meal for 4 years," Ben noted in his diary.[31] They sang French songs and offered toasts for the Allied armies. At the end, "Papa" went down to the cellar, brought up a bottle of champagne, and said it was his last. But it would be opened if, and only if, "Le Petit Benjamin" would return. "Of course, I returned," Ferencz later wrote. "And we all shared the last bottle of champagne together. It touched my heart."[32] And he continued to spend evenings with the family (having only a platonic relationship with the daughter—something he noted explicitly in his diary) until the Third Army pulled out of Lunéville.

By then, Patton's forces were at a standstill close to the German frontier. And, with a lot of time on his hands, Ferencz reverted to his penchant for bucking army authority and getting into trouble. Not all of it was his fault. At one point, as he was standing guard in front of his unit's camp and reading a book in the rain, a general's staff car approached. He saluted and waved the car through. But the next day he was summoned to appear and answer the charge that he had been sitting while on guard duty, in violation of army regulations. He was told he could be court-martialed for this offense. But calling upon his "legal acumen," he noted later, he successfully argued "beyond reasonable doubt" that while he was wearing his army raincoat "it was utterly impossible for anyone in a passing vehicle to detect whether [he] was sitting or standing. Case dismissed!"[33]

The raincoat saved him again when he had actually violated the rules. While standing guard duty on the German border in the freezing cold, he did not wish to be "immobile for four hours in the snow on a dark and stormy night peering into the darkness for any sign of enemy movement or to see if I could spot someone trying to kill me."[34] So he used his capacious mackintosh as a kind of tent. Under it, he started a fire in an old ration can containing gasoline. On that, he placed his canteen cup, half filled with water. From his cartridge belt, he withdrew a bouillon cube borrowed from the kitchen. He dropped it into the water and made hot chicken soup. The enormous slicker concealed all of this and allowed him to illegally light a fire to stay warm.

On another occasion, when enlisted men, but not officers, were denied some Scotch that had been gifted to the unit, Ferencz's "sense of justice" compelled him to "correct the imbalance."[35] So he stole ingredients from the unit's supply room and gave them to a local ice cream parlor, which then used them to make vanilla ice cream—enough to feed all four companies of the 115th.

Similarly, he was found to have disobeyed an order issued to the unit of "no individual cooking in the area." He flouted the injunction by purchasing a chicken from a local farmer and then cooking it in his tent for some of his comrades. Once again, he was called before the colonel and threatened with a court-martial. But Ferencz had the perfect defense—it was not "individual" cooking because he had guests; thus, it was "group" cooking. "He seemed to be thinking over what I said," Ben later wrote. "It finally sank in. He turned red, then white, then blue. A real patriot. Then he screamed at the top of his voice, 'Get out of here! Get out! Get out! I ran." Owing to this incident, when everyone else in his unit earned a Good Conduct medal to boost their morale, Ferencz was denied the distinction.

While being the only person in the battery not to earn the medal might have stung, it was nothing compared to the treatment he received at the hands of a new warrant officer, who was temporarily assigned to the 115th headquarters. The unit's roster listed him as Harvey Bligh. Without knowing anything more about him, his surname alone should have raised an eyebrow. William

Bligh, of course, was the tyrannical captain of *Mutiny on the Bounty* fame. Harvey did justice to his apparent forebear's infamous reputation. He began by asking Ferencz to perform unreasonable tasks, such as cleaning Bligh's trousers, digging Bligh's foxhole, removing Bligh's bedroll from a truck, and assembling his tent. For the penultimate task, Ben said he would comply but, in disgust, "dropped" the bedroll in the mud while unloading it, dragged it through the mud to the foxhole, dumped it in the foxhole and then covered that with mud. When Bligh saw this, he exploded, cursing at the corporal and, it would seem, silently vowing revenge.

He got it soon enough. One night, Bligh was on duty in the headquarters barracks and Ferencz was the orderly. He commanded the former to sweep the floor. Ben did. "Do it again!" Bligh then shouted. And Ben did. Then he screamed, "You're a Harvard man! You can do better than that!" Ben did it again. But Bligh was still not satisfied, and the attack became antisemitic. "OK, Jew Boy," he bellowed, "do it again!" Ben did as he was told but something deep inside of him snapped. He wanted out of the unit.

His desire to transfer out was helped considerably by the fact that he had very little to do now that the Third Army was stalled at the German border. Moreover, he was in an air-defense unit, and the Allies had gained complete control of the skies. Through the many lulls, he was able to research and draft an article titled "Hostile French Civilians," dealing with the legal treatment of civilian-dressed spies left behind by the retreating Germans and French citizens who had been collaborating (with descriptions of rough local justice meted out by the French Resistance, such as shaving the hair of women with German lovers and parading them in public). As with his previous article, this one was also published by the prestigious *Journal of Criminal Law & Criminology.*[36]

Still, by the middle of November, "there wasn't enough work around to keep me busy," he wrote in his diary, "and time hung heavy on my hands. . . . I put in a request for transfer."[37] A certain Captain Klatte, the new battery commander, accompanied him to Third Army headquarters, where he was interviewed by the staff judge advocate and the deputy staff judge advocate, who were running Patton's Judge Advocate (JA) Section.

The staff judge advocate served as Patton's principal military legal advisor, akin to a general counsel. The section he supervised was manned by a good number of military lawyers, or judge advocate officers, supported by enlisted personnel serving as "paralegal specialists." The office handled all legal issues related to the command, ranging from military discipline (including prosecuting and reviewing courts-martial), to claims, legal aid, all the way to international law.

Ferencz interviewed for a paralegal specialist position. His interviewers were "very friendly" but explained that, unfortunately, there were no openings available. All the same, they asked that Ben send them a formal written request for the position, with a letter of recommendation and a copy of his *Journal of Criminal Law & Criminology* article ("Rehabilitation of Army Offenders"). He did so (with a letter of recommendation from Professor Sheldon Glueck), and, less than two weeks later, as the 115th, along with the rest of Patton's troops in the field, were planning to breach the border and head into Germany, an order came through from higher headquarters to transfer Corporal Benjamin B. Ferencz to the Third Army's JA Section.[38]

PART III

PROBING

7

WAR CRIMES INVESTIGATOR

In improvisation, there are no mistakes.

—Miles Davis

The order transferring Corporal Benjamin Ferencz from the 115th AAA Gun Battalion to the Judge Advocate Section of the Third Army was received on Friday, December 1, 1944. As he had been told there were no openings, the object of the order was quite astonished to learn of the transfer.[1] According to his diary, he bid everyone a "hasty farewell" and with "beating heart" left for Patton's headquarters in Nancy.[2] Arriving the same day, he was put to work at once, and, by the end of the weekend, he concluded that everything there was "wonderful."[3] The officers and enlisted men were very friendly, and the ambience was "more like that of a regular law office than an army position."[4] He added, "Almost everyone around is a lawyer, or a court reporter, and the level of intelligence is immeasurably higher than in the 115th."[5]

And the work was "very interesting and pleasant." Along with two other lawyers, he noted in his diary, he was tasked with writing reviews of "General Court-Martial cases." This entailed "a criticism of the procedure, laws and sentence applied, and is similar to the opinion of an appellate judge."[6] Typical cases centered on charges of desertion, absence without leave (AWOL), attempted rape, robbery, insubordination, and similar offenses. Officers could also be charged with "conduct unbecoming an officer" (an ill-defined charge rarely yielding convictions). The workload was large, and, he noted, although there would be "little free time," he knew that he was going to enjoy it. "At long last," he rejoiced, "I am working with the law again."[7] During his first weeks there, in addition to "writing a few reviews and memoranda on legal problems," he conducted research on "international law and the problem of war criminals."[8]

But this period of relative tranquility was not to last. In Berlin, Adolf Hitler had been preparing for a great offensive on the Western Front meant to turn the tide against the Allies. He sought a return to the glories of 1940 by dispatching troops to the Ardennes Forest and smashing through the weakest point on the Allied line, which was quite thin in that area. Hitler meant to exploit this, hoping his forces would have any easy path all the way to the Belgian port of Antwerp, where he could cut off the Allies' key supply harbor. At the same time, in breaking through this weak link, Hitler ultimately aimed to encircle the US and British armies and, by isolating them from one another, destroy them. Then, he reckoned, he could direct his remaining forces to the east and turn back the advancing Soviets.

In preparation for launching the offensive, the Germans dressed fluent English speakers in American uniforms and dropped them behind the lines to sow confusion. They hoped, too, that the terrible winter weather would work to their advantage by negating Allied air dominance. On December 16, 1944, at 5:30 a.m., Hitler's forces launched the assault with a massive artillery barrage and then a ground thrust spearheaded by two key tank units—Wehrmacht General Hasso von Manteuffel's Fifth Panzer Army and SS General (Oberst-Gruppenführer) Sepp Dietrich's Sixth Panzer Army.

At the outset of this Battle of the Bulge (named for the massive protrusion it created in the Allied line), the Germans reaped the benefits of their planning. Because the nearly impenetrable woods made for difficult fighting terrain, the Americans and British were not expecting a German offensive there. At the same time, the thick woods offered cover for the massing of troops, whereas the high ground provided a drier surface for tank maneuvers. And inclement weather brought in layers of thick, misty precipitation, which provided a natural cloak, checking Allied airpower.

On the ground, the Germans managed to wreak havoc among the American and British ranks through the disguised soldiers, who cut communications lines, manipulated road signage, and engaged in other acts of sabotage. Powerful German Panzer IV and Tiger tanks, accompanied by spirited infantry who knew this could be their last chance to reverse the fortunes of war, crashed through the thin Allied phalanxes.

Approximately one week after the start of the German push, Manteuffel and his Fifth Panzer Army reached the strategic crossroads of Bastogne, a transportation hub sometimes referred to as the Paris of the Ardennes. Along with the badly depleted Tenth Armored Division and Twenty-Eighth Infantry Division, tenaciously spearheading the defense of the city was the US 101st Airborne Division under the cool leadership of General Anthony McAuliffe. Despite being heavily outnumbered, the Americans responded to the siege "with cheery defiance. 'They've got us surrounded—the poor bastards!' became a common refrain among the town's GI defenders."[9] On December 22, the Germans presented McAuliffe with a surrender demand, and his simple, but audacious and now famous, reply was "NUTS." The 101st, a paratrooper unit with only light arms and no tanks or armored vehicles, now faced the full force of battle-hardened German armored and mechanized units, the type of force ratio no commander ever hopes to encounter.

By then, most of Patton's staff, including his Judge Advocate Section, had relocated to his forward headquarters in Luxembourg. And that is where Ben Ferencz spent Christmas 1944. Given the disaster that was unfolding in the Ardennes Forest, the men chowed down an appropriately no-frills holiday repast—"slabs of cold turkey" buried under "a pile of cool mashed potatoes."[10]

Christmas may have been dour, but there was little time to enjoy it anyway. Behind the scenes the Allies had been planning and initiating their counterattack to the surprise German offensive. And those plans largely revolved around the tactical and operational prowess of Old Blood and Guts. If Patton's historical 1944 achievements auspiciously began in the warm French countryside, they were gloriously crowned in the freezing Belgian forest. In fact, Patton was about to realize the greatest triumph of his storied career. He had been positioned on the German border tilting eastward, preparing to cut a bloody swath across the Third Reich which, he hoped, would eventually take him to Berlin. Instead, on a moment's notice, he directed his massive Third Army forces to execute a 90-degree pivot and race north toward Bastogne to relieve its beleaguered American defenders and deprive the Germans of control of the region's vital transportation hub.

To accomplish this remarkable feat, when a portion of Patton's troops were still guarding positions in France on the German frontier, and during one of the coldest winters in European history, with roads frozen over with ice and snow, required an "all-hands-on-deck" effort from Third Army personnel. As the Germans reached the crescendo of their offensive and the 101st was at the end of its rope in Bastogne, Ben Ferencz reported that "Patton gave the order, 'Every man who can carry a gun, get going to Bastogne! Now!!' That included me."[11] Ferencz was "jammed into an open truck" crowded with other shivering soldiers. As they raced north to the front, he later described the drama (and comedy) that ensued: "Bits of paper were stuffed into the barrels of our M1 rifles to keep out the snow and pouring rain. We were warned not to leave the vehicles since all roads and adjacent areas had been thoroughly mined by the meticulous Krauts. I learned an important lesson: never piss against the wind or you may get it in the face."[12]

Before they could reach Bastogne, the weather had cleared, and the US Army Air Corps had gone to work. By the time Ben's truck arrived, the Paris of the Ardennes had been leveled. Ben described the macabre scene:

> The Belgian inhabitants who survived were dazed and desolate. Their homes were in ruins. German prisoners of war were being transported to the rear.

> There was total chaos in the battered city. In a bombed-out basement, some of the guys from Patton's HQ found what they thought were cases of wine. To me it tasted like vinegar. Victory had to be celebrated. A few hungry young Belgian ladies eagerly accepted the invitation to join in the festivities. A party was arranged in the pitch-black cellar that was gaily decorated with an American flag on the wall and U.S. army blankets on the floor. The weary soldiers drank the vinegar to lift their spirits, and they did whatever they could to console the ladies in their hour of need.[13]

Patton's forces, aided by massive Allied air attacks, had indeed liberated Bastogne by December 26. But the history books clarify that the Battle of the Bulge dragged on through the last part of January. In fact, the Fifth Panzer Army had advanced to within four miles of the Meuse River. And the Americans had to spend the better part of a month executing their counteroffensive and removing the "bulge" from the Allied line.

But it came at a great cost. In the miserably arctic conditions, where GIs initially suffered from exposure and lack of supplies and then bore the brunt of savage German fighting in the dense woods, the Battle of the Bulge was one of the most brutal skirmishes in US history. It was one of the bloodiest too. Nineteen thousand US soldiers lost their lives during the engagement, and more than seventy thousand were wounded or went missing. Even Corporal Benjamin Ferencz of the Judge Advocate Section experienced some of the battle's misery and witnessed some of its horrors. But by the time it was over, and the Germans had mounted their last true offensive of the war, Corporal Ferencz had long since returned to the JA Office and prepared for a new phase of operations.

In the wake of his savior heroics during the Battle of the Bulge, General Patton made his way back to base headquarters and resumed planning for the march across Germany. But he was starting all over again, and he still had a long way to go before penetrating the Third Reich's frontier. For although the Germans' Ardennes gambit had failed, they were still full of fight. And as American forces returned to their pre-Bulge positions in France, it remained for them to breach the redoubtable Siegfried Line, a long string of pillboxes, antitank dragon teeth, and other strongpoints built along the German border opposite the French Maginot Line. After a couple months of vicious fighting, on March 22, 1945, Patton finally pierced the Nazi "Western Wall" (as Hitler called the Siegfried Line) and crossed the Rhine River, over the Ludendorff Bridge at Remagen, into the "Fatherland."

Judge Advocate Section attorney Benjamin Ferencz moved along with him, as Third Army headquarters relocated to Germany. And it was there, not very long after Patton's breach of the Nazi fortifications, that the diminutive corporal had his first brush with the rich and famous. The encounter was with the German cinema icon Marlene Dietrich. The great movie star had first gained notoriety as the vamp Lola-Lola in director Joseph von Sternberg's 1930 film *The Blue Angel.* Dietrich went on to star in a string of motion pictures playing glamorous and mysterious femmes fatales. She was known for haunting Berlin's demimonde establishments, sometimes dressing as a man, and for her risqué sexual practices (in the 1930 film *Morocco,* a tuxedo-clad Dietrich gave the silver screen one of its first lesbian kisses). A staunch antifascist, "when approached by the Nazi Party to perform in propaganda films, she turned them down with a ferocious 'NEIN.'"[14]

In fact, during Hitler's dictatorship, she traded in her German passport for an American one and moved to Hollywood. There, she created a fund with Jewish American director Billy Wilder to assist Jews and dissidents seeking haven on US shores. She sold war bonds and had become so patriotic that she entertained American GIs via extensive USO tours. One of those tours brought her to General Patton's headquarters, within spitting distance of the German front lines when her native country had placed a seven-figure bounty on her head and capture meant probable execution. When asked why she would put herself so close to harm's way, she replied, "Aus Anstand."[15] Out of decency. And it was in this time of potential peril that Ben Ferencz briefly entered her life.

Corporal Ferencz, as the odd enlisted man in a JA Section populated primarily by officers, drew the glamorous assignment of cleaning the unit's toilets. One morning, he learned that Marlene Dietrich would be staying at Third Army headquarters. When she appeared on the floor where Ben was doing "valued latrine duty," she was shown to a room which, along with a toilet, had a real bathtub.[16] Notwithstanding his mandate to clean the toilet in that room, Ferencz was instructed to ensure that the movie star's ablutions not be disturbed. So, with these conflicting directives in mind, he waited what he thought was a reasonable amount of time before entering to clean the commode.

Evidently, however, he had not waited long enough. The great Marlene Dietrich still sat in the tub, "calmly immersed only in her splendor."[17] "Oh, pardon me Sir!" he gasped, with much humiliation, turning on a dime to vacate the premises (the gender faux pas only heightening the comedy, especially given Dietrich's famous androgynous persona).[18]

He stood guard at the door until she had finished with her bath and came out. He apologized for the intrusion. But she was extremely gracious, smiling mischievously and letting him know how much she enjoyed his calling her "Sir." They both laughed, and, in her inimitable Bavarian nonrhotic accent, she asked where he was from and how it was that he got stuck cleaning toilets. When he explained that he was a Harvard-trained lawyer, she was incredulous. How had he been assigned as an orderly?!? She heartily laughed again. And, by then charmed by the spunky New Yorker, she kindly invited him to join her at the Third Army's upcoming luncheon, which had been planned by the officers.

But as fraternization between officers and enlisted personnel was prohibited, he suggested that she "describe him as an old friend from her hometown" and insist that he accompany her. Amazingly, she obliged (and even more incredibly, the officers accepted Dietrich's claim that the young New Yorker was an old friend from her hometown). And so Ben Ferencz had the distinct honor of being Marlene Dietrich's lunch date that afternoon.

He sat opposite her during the meal, and she gave him her "calling card," which also included, toward the bottom, the title of her 1939 film *Destry Rides Again*. He wondered, for a moment, what it would be like, in real life, for him to be the movie's eponymous Jimmy Stewart character to her German showgirl, Frenchy. This little idyll was made more magical when she intimated that she would much prefer chatting with him than with the dozen or so officers invited to the repast. But as the dessert plates were being cleared, she dutifully maneuvered to the other end of the table to thank General Patton, who then escorted her away, and out of Ben Ferencz's Third Army life. As he could never muster the courage to use her calling card, his short but titillating relationship with Marlene Dietrich reached its abrupt end. Fittingly, he would go on to become a chief prosecutor for one of the famous Nuremberg Trials (*Einsatzgruppen*), and she would go on to star in a famous movie about one of those proceedings, *Judgment at Nuremberg* (depicting the *Justice* trial).

It was just as well that Marlene Dietrich did not continue to be a distraction. The Judge Advocate Section's work was about to become much more labor-intensive and substantially grimmer. As early as September 25, 1944, in a letter whose upper portion read, "Subject: 'Punishment of War Criminals,'" Secretary of War Henry L. Stimson had directed Judge Advocate General Myron C. Cramer to establish an agency under his direction, which would at once (1) collect all evidence of atrocities or other grave crimes committed against members of the US Armed Forces and/or other Americans; (2) examine and sift through such evidence; (3) arrange for the apprehension and prompt trial of persons against whom a prima facie case was made out; and (4) provide for the execution of sentences that might be imposed.[19]

On the same day, the judge advocate general established an office in his War Plans Division implementing this policy. By the end of the following week, the War Crimes Division had been created. And on March 22, 1945, the date Patton's troops crossed the Rhine, the agency was designated the War Crimes Office.

In the Twelfth Army Group, under which Patton's Third Army was placed in the command structure, Colonel Claude B. Mickelwaite served as judge advocate and thus had operational responsibility for the Third Army's implementation of the new war crimes investigation mandate from higher headquarters. This was carried out through a War Crimes Branch that was subdivided into an Evidence Branch, Prosecution Branch, Post-Trial Branch, and Administrative Branch. The Evidence Branch, which encompassed investigations, was run by Colonel Burton F. Ellis (who would later supervise the Dachau Trials). And under him in the hierarchy was Colonel Charles E. Cheever of the Third Army JA Section and then Lieutenant Colonel Robert E. Joseph, who would be Ben Ferencz's direct superior with respect to war crimes investigations.

The timing of this launch of the American war crimes program was propitious. As US forces finally set foot on German soil, a multiplicity of serious crime scenes became available to them. That said, they had been aware of Nazi atrocities even before their arrival in Germany. As early as January, as Ferencz and his fellow JA soldiers were making their post-Bastogne return to headquarters, they were hearing about a massacre that had occurred near a town called Malmédy.

At a crossroads only a bit south of the town, on December 17, 1944, just as the Battle of the Bulge was getting under way, the First SS Panzer Division captured an unprepared American artillery unit whose 113 soldiers had offered no resistance, immediately surrendering to the Germans. Nevertheless, the Americans were assembled in a field, and then German machine-gunners opened fire on them. In the following moments, SS men walked among the bleeding Americans, shooting at the heads of those who were writhing. Eighty-four GIs were murdered, but some escaped by feigning death.

The perpetrators of this "Malmédy Massacre" were later apprehended, tried, and convicted at the Dachau Trials (see chapter 9). They had violated Part I, Article 2, of the 1929 Geneva Convention, to which both Germany and the United States were then parties. Pursuant to that provision, "Prisoners of war are in the power of the hostile Government, but not of the individuals or formation which captured them. They shall at all times be humanely treated and protected, particularly against acts of violence, from insults and from public curiosity. Measures of reprisal against them are forbidden."[20]

As Ben Ferencz and his fellow JA lawyers were hearing about the Malmédy Massacre, unbeknownst to them, scores of other American POWs, fliers who had been shot down over German territory and compelled to surrender, had also been unlawfully denied quarter and summarily executed. This was pursuant to directives collectively known as the Nazi "Lynch Law," which were promulgated over time via various upper-echelon Hitlerite decrees and communications.

As early as 1940, the Führer's deputy, Rudolf Hess, had demanded that enemy parachutists be "arrested or rendered harmless." This was interpreted to mean "arrested or liquidated."[21] Hitler himself issued the "Commando Order" on October 18, 1942, giving authority to German troops to execute any captured enemy soldiers who were "acting like bandits."[22] The Nazi dictator believed that this would deter future commando raids. The following year, Reichsführer-SS Heinrich Himmler sent out a circular to all higher SS and police leaders (who informed subordinates only verbally, because it was known to be criminal) that read: "It is not the task of the police to meddle with skirmishes between German nationals and parachuted English or American *terror* fliers."[23]

The following year, in June 1944, Nazi propaganda minister Joseph Goebbels said in a nationally broadcast speech: "It so happened that in a few villages or towns the population took the law into their own hands against the *terrorist* fighter pilots. They battered them to death [cheering, applause] or cut their throats, or similar. We're not shedding crocodile tears over that, and those who did this will not be led to the scaffold for it; we're not as stupid as that."[24] This was "a blatant instigation to kill."[25] Finally, in July 1944, what had been indirectly communicated was made direct: "[Police] received secret orders which amounted practically to the order to kill all Allied airmen, without regard for the circumstances of the case."[26]

As Nazi communications crystalized into an overall normative injunction for the liquidation of grounded POWs, the number of these victims was steadily rising. By the end of the war, hundreds had lost their lives to angry lynch mobs. At the Dachau Trials alone, the United States tried approximately two hundred of these cases, many of them multidefendant, of which eighty-two ended in execution by hanging.[27] At no small number of those trials, the evidence used to prosecute the defendants had been collected by Corporal Benjamin B. Ferencz.

THAT THE Third Army JA Section was gearing up for war crimes investigations was apparent from the moment Ben Ferencz joined the unit. Indeed, reference at the December job interview to his Sheldon Glueck–derived war crimes expertise likely went a long way toward assuring his transfer into the unit. And, as noted, immediately upon his arrival he was tasked with conducting war crimes legal research in apparent anticipation. Now that Patton and his troops were marching east through the crumbling Third Reich, it was time to put his know-how to the test. He would do so through HQ stops in Trier, Frankfurt, Erlangen, and Munich, with the JA Section following the moving front.

As the war crimes probes began, it soon became clear that nearly all of the unit's on-the-ground investigatory duties would be assumed by Corporal Ferencz—exclusively. Ben reckoned this was due to the small size of the JA Section at the Third Army headquarters. According to his memoirs, this skeletal crew "consisted of about five Lt. Colonels led by Colonel Cheever" (and Ferencz's direct superior, Lieutenant Colonel Joseph).[28] His memoirs also indicate that, of these officers, only Cheever had legal training and that Ben informed his superiors that the unit needed "men who had more familiarity with the law."[29]

Still, Ferencz's contemporaneous diary paints a different picture. It plainly records that there were enlisted men in the unit as well.[30] And, as mentioned at the outset of this chapter, Ben noted too that "almost everyone around is a lawyer" and "the atmosphere is more like that of a regular law office."[31]

Be that as it may, regardless of the unit's specific roster composition, Ben Ferencz was likely one of the few who had specialist knowledge regarding grave violations of international humanitarian law, that is, war crimes. And his diary reflects the leadership position he was assuming. In a March 26, 1945, entry, he reported, "For the past several weeks I have been in charge of war crimes prosecutions. It has meant directing investigations of reported atrocities, questioning witnesses and 'grilling' the accused."[32] In other words, he was conducting these investigations himself.

But given the volume of reports flooding into the Third Army JA Section by then, the burden of doing this solo began to overwhelm him. So he asked for help. And soon he got it—in the form of a fellow Ivy League product, Private Jack Nowitz. Ben described their initial encounter:

> I was in my office when a soldier appeared and saluted. He was completely covered with mud and had a rifle slung over his back. "Private Jack Nowitz, reporting Sir," he said. "Sit down, soldier," I said, "I'm only a Corporal, and you don't have to salute me. Who are you?" It turned out that he was a Yale law graduate, had practiced law in Connecticut, and spoke several languages. He

was told to be under my direct command, and I was the only one who had any idea about what he was supposed to do. His past military service had focused on digging ditches for the Corps of Engineers.[33]

With Nowitz in tow, the investigations began in earnest. At first, Ferencz and Nowitz worked together. This was no easy feat as they were literally blazing new trails in terms of war crimes investigation practice. As Ferencz later lamented, "I had no one to tell me what to do."[34] However, he and Nowitz gradually gained proficiency and developed investigative procedures and protocols. Soon, they were ready to split up so as to cover more ground.

And the cases began to take on a similar pattern. A file would be opened after receipt of an intelligence report that US fliers had been captured on the ground and then beaten to death by local mobs. Ferencz would take a jeep to the crime scene, summon the town's *Bürgermeister* (mayor) or police chief, and order whomever was in charge to convene a gathering of all civilians living within a hundred yards of the beating. "[I would tell the mayor or police chief that] I was here on orders from General Patton, carrying out orders of the President of the United States."[35]

Ferencz would then find the person in town with the best English and dragoon him as an interpreter (or, if none were available, Nowitz would do the honors). Next: "I'd line them up, maybe 20–30 people. I'd tell them to sit down and write out exactly what happened: what they heard, what they saw. 'Anyone who lies will be shot.' As I talked to them, [Nowitz or the interpreter] would say, 'You can't say that.' I said, 'I have a .45 caliber gun. What am I going to tell them? "Please be nice. Tell me the truth? Are you happy?" What the hell are you expecting me to do?'"[36]

The forms in question, which had been prepared prior to his arrival at the crime scene, began with a German declaration that the witness swore to tell the whole truth under penalty of death (he later wryly dubbed this the "Ferencz Miranda Rule").[37] After taking in the English translation of a dozen or so such affidavits, he could glean with fairly decent precision the who, the how, the why, and the where of the case, including the location of the corpses.

Dealing with those cadavers was often the most challenging part of the experience. As Ben later recounted: "Then we would have to find the bodies. The body was very seldom there. They'd throw them into the river, and they moved downstream. I think that was the toughest job I ever did. I had to really go into a trance to locate the body in those conditions because you had to—you'd come to a hole, a mound of dirt. The ground was hard; it was [still] wintertime."[38]

The dead soldiers would have to be photographed and positively identified. The problem was that diamond-hard earth. How could the bodies be brought to the surface? The tiny New Yorker was not very good at traditional shovel digging, and he dared not use a pickax lest he mar the cadavers in ways that would obscure the fatal wounds or other salient crime data. So he came up with two possible alternative solutions. The first was fairly simple—brandish the .45 again and shanghai the locals to dig with their shovels. In Ben's words: "The Germans were very intimidated. They would say 'Jawohl!' when I would give them the clear order. They would move, you know. And they weren't dealing with an officer. I had no insignia on. I pretended. I'd give that impression. First thing, I'd say, 'I'm delivering orders from General Patton and you'd better obey.'"[39]

If the locals, or their shovels, were not available, then he devised his own self-help technique. He would locate the deceased by putting his hands in the soil. From there, he would "dig in the dirt and see if [he] could locate a portion of the body . . . an elbow or something else . . . [or he tried] to locate the ankle and get two feet together."[40] Next, a rope would be tied around the limb or bony protrusion and attached on the other end to the jeep. Finally, the vehicle would be put in motion and the body slowly extracted, with fingerprints intact, for positive identification by the Quartermaster corps. This was followed by splashing pails of water on the bodies to remove the grime and facilitate an identification. "Sometimes they were naked. If they had pants on, I could look for the serial number on the inside of their pants."[41]

Ben later explained that, "Under these very difficult circumstances," he tried to treat the deceased "with every possible respect. This somber duty has always laid heavy on my mind."[42] On another occasion he noted that, in treating the deceased this way, he was being "very mindful" of the feelings of the victims' family members, adding "that's why I was so apprehensive."[43]

Once the victims were located and dealt with, he would return to headquarters and draft a full report. It would provide a thorough factual account of the offense, specify the law of war violations, the names and addresses of important witnesses, and the identity of the offenders, who were placed on a list of persons wanted for immediate apprehension and trial.

ALTHOUGH so many cases with such similar fact patterns began to blur, certain ones stood out. At first blush, one of the incidents, where three fliers had been shot down and killed on the ground by a mob, looked like all the rest. The suspects cited the Nazi Lynch Law and begged for forgiveness as they were only "acting under orders from Berlin to treat all bombardiers as war criminals."[44] Ferencz was able to solve much of the case via meticulous records of the local Gestapo (Geheime Staatspolizei, or Secret State Police, Hitler's ruthless political enforcers), which helped him determine that the murdered airmen had been dumped in a hole at the edge of the local cemetery.

He had to threaten the graveyard's sexton with orders to dig up the entire plot before the latter would disclose the specific burial site. After the three bodies were disinterred, Ferencz washed them down with buckets of water and found the ID numbers of two of them on the inside of their fatigues. The third one was completely naked. He had a crew cut and "looked like a typical American boy."[45] Ferencz reported to the adjutant general that he could notify the next of kin that the three men had been murdered and their bodies found. But there was a surprise twist ending to the story, as Ben explained: "Several months later, when the perpetrators of those crimes were on trial before a Third U.S. Army Military Commission, I learned by chance that the dead flier who was naked with no ID, was in fact alive and well in the United States. I suggested that he be interrogated to see if he had some clue regarding the misidentified third man. I never found out the answer. It taught me to never again rely on circumstantial evidence—and I never did."

On another occasion, a message came into headquarters from the Counter-Intelligence Corps about an American crewman whose plane had been shot down in Gross-Gerau (near Frankfurt) two days after an Allied bombing raid. The airman had bailed out of his airplane and parachuted to the ground, only to be bludgeoned to death by an enraged mob. Ferencz was assigned to the case. While investigating, he was surprised to find a woman who admitted that her own daughter had repeatedly beaten the victim on the head with a shoe. She confessed that she had unsuccessfully tried to persuade her daughter to back off, "since that was no way for a German girl to behave."[46]

Ferencz located the daughter, "an attractive young woman," who explained "through her tears" that, during the bombing raid two days previously, her two children had been killed. In her grief and rage, she admitted, she had joined the mob. But the fatal blow, she revealed, had been struck by a local fireman using a crowbar. Since the woman appeared repentant, Ferencz merely placed her under house arrest. "The truth is," he later confided, "I felt sorry for her."[47]

His next task was to track down the fireman who had boasted to the crowd that "he loved being covered with American blood."[48] Through his sleuthing, Ferencz pinpointed the location of his house and discovered that he had fled. Under questioning, his wife pled ignorance as to his whereabouts, and a search of the premises yielded nothing. But Ferencz figured out a way to crack the case, nonetheless. "Do you do his laundry?" he asked the unsuspecting wife. "Of course," she retorted with great pride. Ferencz was then able to wring a confession out of her to the effect that she had washed the shirt worn on the night in question and that it was soaked with blood. He got her to swear this out in an affidavit, and he took the shirt as evidence. Case closed, he thought, as he left the residence. And the fireman was eventually apprehended.

As a postscript, several months later, he attended a session of the Gross-Gerau war crimes trial before a Third Army Military Commission. Among the group of defendants, he recognized both the fireman and the young mother whose children had been killed in the raid. The former was sentenced to death. When the young woman's punishment of two years imprisonment was announced, she fainted in the prisoner's dock. Afterward, Ferencz inquired about her health, and the medic who had treated her indicated she would be fine. But, he added, she was pregnant. And the father was one of the US soldiers assigned to guard her. "Strange things happen in times of war," Ferencz concluded.

Still, the pregnant woman reminded him of the basic humanity of many individual Germans, despite their country's collective criminality. As he recorded in his diary: "I am personally convinced . . . that there are millions of Germans who are good people. They went along with the Nazi party line and slogans the same as millions of people do back home. Thoughtless yes, but people are that way. They may have inwardly deplored the plight of the Jews, but they took no more action than the average Northerner who deplores the treatment of the Negro in America."[49]

Back at headquarters, the JA brass started taking to heart the long-standing complaints of Ferencz and Nowitz that the serious uptick in war crimes probes exceeded their collective capacity to conduct proper investigations—they had reached their breaking point. Fortunately, relief was soon at hand. Three qualified enlisted men joined the unit. One of them, a certain Morris Wright, had been "a good lawyer in Atlanta before he entered the army as a Private," and he made the biggest difference in lightening their load. Two Dutchmen, Jan Fenijn and Jan Black, serving as interpreters, also helped immeasurably as it was becoming increasingly difficult to deputize local interpreters.

The other additions were not as useful. They were former tank commanders now suffering from what appeared to be alcoholism or what they then called shell shock—post-traumatic stress disorder. Ferencz felt certain that these officers had been sent to a nonfighting JA unit as a substitute for standard R&R (Recreation and Rehabilitation). And he facetiously observed that "Some of them were usually sober enough to sign the reports prepared by the enlisted men."[50]

These officers may have been damaged by their service and limited to clerical tasks, but even they would be desperately needed as the calendar pages turned to the later part of spring. The "flier murder" cases would soon recede into the background as Patton's forces continued their sweep eastward. They were about to reach the entrance gates to hell on earth—the bloody, barb-wired archipelago of the Nazi concentration camp network. And the Third Army war crimes investigation unit would need every bit of manpower it could muster.

8

LIBERATING THE CONCENTRATION CAMPS

A dark flame had entered into my soul and devoured it.

—Elie Wiesel, *Night*

Well before the end phases of the war, the Allies already had an inkling of the almost phantasmagorical nature and scale of Nazi atrocities. By late 1942, the Polish government-in-exile informed the world of the Holocaust by publishing a brochure titled *The Mass Extermination of Jews in German Occupied Poland.* That document was based in part on intelligence collected by the courageous Polish resistance fighter Jan Karski, who had infiltrated and escaped both the Warsaw Ghetto and the Nazi concentration camp network.[1] The next year, in Moscow, Franklin Roosevelt, Winston Churchill, and Joseph Stalin issued the Declaration on German Atrocities in Occupied Europe (or the Moscow Declaration), which put the Nazis on notice that, at war's end, they would be facing justice for their depredations.

But it was not until July 1944, as Soviet armies swept west, that the Allies witnessed firsthand the evidence of Nazi gulag mass murder. At that time, the Russians discovered the abandoned Majdanek concentration camp, whose prisoners had already been herded off on a death march with the retreating Germans. The emptied charnel house had been set aflame to eliminate evidence, but the remains of gas chambers confirmed Allied reports of industrial-scale extermination. In the weeks that followed, Soviet troops encountered the genocidal killing centers of Belzec, Sobibor, and Treblinka, before reaching the biggest one of all, Auschwitz, in January 1945. Its prisoners had begun their death march several days previously, but the Russians were nevertheless presented with residual inventories of horror, including 348,820 men's suits and 836,515 women's dresses neatly folded, pyramids of dentures and eyeglasses, and seven tons of women's hair.[2]

Comparable grim discoveries on the Western Front did not occur until April of that year, after Allied forces had crossed over the Rhine. The concentration camp in Ohrdruf was the first to be liberated by US forces. So gruesome was the evidence the Nazis left behind that General Dwight D. Eisenhower himself was called to the scene to bear witness. He would later write: "The things I saw beggar description. . . . The visual evidence and the verbal testimony of starvation, cruelty and bestiality were so overpowering. . . . I made the visit deliberately, in order to be in a position to give first hand evidence of these things if ever, in the future, there develops a tendency to charge these allegations to 'propaganda.'"[3]

Ohrdruf had been discovered and liberated by Patton's Third Army. And its most experienced war crimes investigator, Corporal Benjamin B. Ferencz, had been an integral part of the operation. In a way, he had been preparing for that hellish encounter for quite some time. As Patton's tanks rolled farther east into Germany during the nightmarish thaw of those first days of spring, intelligence reports started streaming into headquarters regarding masses of dead and decomposing bodies, badly emaciated prisoners, and ovens burning the corpses. These ghoulish scenes were presided over by SS men, the reports relayed. And they particularly caught the attention of investigator Ferencz. He was already contemplating how he would take a lead role in collecting evidence of these atrocities.

Toward that end, he approached his commanding officer, newly promoted Colonel Robert E. Joseph. The latter had been riding high on the string of successes by his unit in investigating war crimes committed against downed Allied airmen. Much of that success was due to the knowledge and hard work of Ben Ferencz, which Joseph readily acknowledged.

"Corporal," he said to Ferencz soon after attaining his new rank, "I know that my promotion is due largely to your work. In appreciation, I am promoting you to Sergeant!" In his extended hand was a three-stripe sergeant emblem meant to adorn Ferencz's epaulets. But the corporal flatly refused the new adornment; his by now deep-seated disdain for the military extended to all its pomp and circumstance, including promotions and insignia. And so he contemptuously dropped the stripes into a nearby trashcan. Colonel Joseph looked on in slack-jawed amazement. (Ferencz later admitted that he had gone too far and owed his benefactor an apology—and, in fact, he could not reject the promotion itself, only its sartorial symbols.)

But the rejection of the new stripes was not all for show—Ferencz had a very practical reason for refusing them. As he later recounted telling the colonel: "Sir, I'm sorry, but as you know, I have been trying to do my job without wearing any insignia or reference to rank. If it be known that I am only a sergeant, I will be unable to do the things that must be done. My only wish now is to get into the concentration camps that our army is liberating. Major war crimes are occurring, and I know how to prove it. These stripes would only be a handicap."[4]

Still flabbergasted, Colonel Joseph ultimately assented to his subordinate's plan—giving him a "free hand" to pursue investigations—and Ferencz sprang into action. Comparing notes with Nowitz, Wright, and the other active investigators, he set up a large war map in headquarters with US Army troop movements and reported locations of Nazi concentration camps. The key logistical question for him was how to gain access to the camps and be given sufficient leeway to carry out the necessary probes. Complete cooperation from the advancing combat forces entering these newly liberated slaughterhouses would be essential, he concluded.

So he resorted to one of his favorite, and most effective, military practices: forgery. He fabricated an "official authorization" document giving him permission "to interrogate any suspects, enter any premises, and do all things necessary to carry out a war crimes assignment."[5] Pursuant to this passe-partout, onto which, without authorization, Ben affixed General Patton's seal, all units and commanders were ordered to assist investigator Ferencz in whatever way he asked. And, to make it look even more official, he stamped "Secret" on the top and bottom. He then found an officer to sign it, suggesting later, wryly, that the signer may not have even been inebriated.[6]

This investigative operation was marked by another classic Ferencz feature—he would be operating on his own. Taking even more liberties with army bureaucracy, he had himself classified as a "Jeep driver" and took sole possession of one of the iconic military vehicles. He had it adorned with the large, white, German words (all in capital letters) "IMMER ALLEIN" (always alone), so that there would be no doubt about who was running the show (although he was often accompanied by an interpreter, driver, or officer). Even if joined by fellow lawyers-in-arms, he perceived himself as in charge and working as a "Lone Ranger" Nazi war crimes investigator. Armed with his "orders" from Patton and his custom-painted jeep, he studied his wall map carefully and prepared to embark on the darkest journey of his life.

His macabre odyssey began with the aforementioned Ohrdruf, a satellite camp of the bigger and more infamous Buchenwald concentration camp. Located in the Reich's Weimar region, near the towns of Gotha and the eponymous Ohrdruf itself, it was a later addition to the Nazi camp network, constructed only in November 1944. Still, in fewer than six months of operation, it facilitated the imprisonment, enslavement, torture, and extermination of countless innocent souls (nearly 12,000 had been confined there by March 1945).

That was not apparent as the first US soldiers stumbled on its threshold. They were members of the Third Army's Fourth Armored Division and had been surveying the surrounding environs of nearby captured towns. On April 4, 1945, they came upon the inconspicuous gate of the camp after descending a small hillock. One of the soldiers described the scene: "From the outside, the camp was unremarkable. It was surrounded by a high barbed wire fence and had a wooden sign which read, 'Arbeit Macht Frei' [Work leads to freedom—a cruelly ironic sign affixed to the gates of most Nazi concentration camps]. The swinging gate was open, and a young soldier, probably an SS guard, lay dead diagonally across the entrance."[7] Once past the threshold, however, a hellish landscape presented itself to the unsuspecting GIs. The stunned troops beheld "a pile of dead prisoners, all in striped uniforms. The corpses were fleshless, and at the back of each skull a bullet hole. . . . [N]ext to the parade ground, was a shed with corpses stacked like lumber. On the edge of the camp was a large pit where bodies were burned."[8] The sickened soldiers called in what they had seen to Third Army headquarters.

Sargeant Ferencz was soon aware of the report. He consulted his map, plotted his course, took the necessary papers and equipment, and hopped into his jeep (likely joined by an interpreter and/or another investigator from the unit). As he drove through the war-ravaged Thuringian countryside to Ohrdruf, the deep and permanent psychic scarring of Benjamin Ferencz was about to begin.

He would later describe a "scene of horror." There were "hundreds of dead bodies, naked or clad only in tattered rags that looked like pajamas. . . . [M]any others seemed to be on the verge of starvation and death."[9] A medical unit administered first aid while Ferencz took notes and collected evidence. Members of the Signal Corps, who were also present and using their cameras to document the hitherto inconceivable images, provided Ferencz with photographic evidence. He tried to speak with survivors, but they were too delirious with disease and hunger to give coherent testimony.

In fact, those who remained were there only because the SS did not have enough time to dispatch them with bullets. Ohrdruf's overlords had been ordered to evacuate immediately as American troops were about to arrive, and they hastily forced those who could move on a death march to the satellite's main camp, Buchenwald. Ben Ferencz wanted to retrace their steps. So he and his crew got back into the IMMER ALLEIN and followed the jagged line of corpses that had fallen during the death march, like an infernal trail of crumbs, to the gates of Buchenwald.

BUCHENWALD WAS the nerve center of a vast 139-subcamp network. The Weimar region, where it was located, had been associated with Germany's most progressive tendencies—it was the adopted home of Johann Wolfgang von Goethe, one of the nation's Enlightenment icons, as well as the source of the name Weimar Republic, the liberal-democratic manifestation of everything the Nazis hated about the pre-1933 German interwar period. The region's traditional image of tolerance would be effectively eradicated by placing a concentration camp in its midst. "Buchenwald"—the camp's name chosen by Heinrich Himmler himself—means "beech tree forest" in German, and, quite symbolically, the Nazis chopped down a beautiful woodland of such timbers, located on the northern slopes of the Ettersberg forest, to build their ugly persecution complex.

With a peak of 112,000 prisoners in February 1945, Buchenwald was the largest Nazi concentration camp erected within the pre-Anschluss German borders of 1937. In effect, it was Ohrdruf writ large—more infrastructure, more prisoners, more guards, and more atrocities. The latter included forced medical experimentation on prisoners. An untold number of them were slain to test vaccines and treatments against contagious diseases, such as typhus, cholera, and diphtheria. Between its opening and liberation, the Third Reich imprisoned in Buchenwald approximately 250,000 persons from all countries of Europe, of whom SS administrators murdered at least 56,000 prisoners, approximately 11,000 of them Jews.

Ohrdruf had not anesthetized Ferencz to the nightmare that was Buchenwald. He later described it as "a charnel house of indescribable horrors" and an "incredible scene of death and inhumanity deliberately imposed by the Nazis on helpless civilians." He also noted that it powerfully reinforced General Eisenhower's comment, on seeing Ohrdruf, that "American soldiers could now see why they had to leave home to fight in Germany."[10]

Elie Wiesel was there, having barely survived Auschwitz and then a death march. He is captured in a now famous photograph lying on a multitiered wooden structure suitable for warehousing farm animals, surrounded by other skin-and-bones survivors, his hollowed-out face spectrally staring into the camera. Whether consciously or not, Ferencz likely crossed paths with him there, the Transylvanian Jewish boy who left and became an iconic Holocaust liberator happening upon the one who stayed and became an iconic Holocaust survivor.[11]

The sights and sounds and smells of this new and terrible phase of his war experience had already been chipping away at Ben Ferencz's mental well-being. "There was no time for emotion. No time for being shocked, for tears—for anything like that," Ferencz later recounted.[12] To come out in one piece, he knew he had to compartmentalize and focus on the task at hand—collecting evidence to enable prosecution of the perpetrators. And evidence abounded. Most infamously, Ferencz found lampshades that had been made of tattooed human skin, to please SS Commandant Karl-Otto Koch's wife, Ilse (later tried and convicted as the notorious "Bitch of Buchenwald").[13] And he discovered two shrunken skulls of prisoners, entirely black and with full manes of hair, which were kept by SS officers as ornaments (photos of these were later widely distributed to the press).

But the most valuable evidence by far was discovered in the *Schreibstube,* the camp office, where Ferencz found Buchenwald's "Totenbücher," the death registries recording the names of inmates who had perished on the premises. He also found there a brave and invaluable witness. This Frenchman had fought for the Republicans in the Spanish Civil War, had worked in the *Schreibstube,* and approached Ferencz when the latter was poring over the Totenbücher. "I've been waiting for you," he said, and then escorted Ferencz to an area near the facility's electrified fence.

Once there, he surveyed the ground, littered with bone fragments and other atrocity detritus, and homed in on a particular spot. He then started digging. Eventually, he disinterred a small wooden box, which he handed to Ferencz. The camp's SS men had formed a kind of social club, the prisoner explained, where they could imbibe spirits and swap tales of barbarity. Each SS man in the "club" had a "membership folder" showing his photo, date of birth, home address, and similar personal particulars. Each time a member attended one of the club get-togethers, his folder was marked with a stamp on the back page. When the folder was filled, a replacement had to be issued. It was the Frenchman's job to prepare the new folder.

However, rather than destroy the old ones, as directed, he covertly placed them underground in that spot by the electrified fence, risking almost certain torture and murder had he been discovered. Fortunately, he never was, and his plan paid off—Ferencz now had a veritable "who's who" ledger of Buchenwald SS guards. The grateful war crimes investigator later wrote that the Frenchman's "outstanding courage marked the faith, shared by many other suffering victims, that there would one day be a day of reckoning when justice would be done."[14]

A LONG STRING of concentration camps followed Buchenwald, as the Third Army swept through the Third Reich. And Ferencz began to form a composite of what he experienced as liberator cum investigator at each one of them:

> [There were] dead bodies strewn across the camp grounds, piles of skin-and-bones cadavers piled up like cordwood before the burning crematoria, helpless skeletons with diarrhea, dysentery, typhus, TB, pneumonia, and other ailments, retching in their louse ridden bunks or on the ground with only their pathetic eyes pleading for help. Few had enough strength to muster a smile of gratitude. My mind would not accept what my eyes saw. It built a protective barrier to enable me to go on with my work in what seemed an incredible nightmare. I had peered into Hell.[15]

The work, which kept him focused and essentially sane, also took on a kind of settled investigative routine. After Buchenwald, he realized that his first stop at every camp had to be the *Schreibstube,* where he could secure camp records. The key documents to be retrieved there were the Totenbücher, the aforementioned death registries identifying deceased inmates and their dates of demise. A cause of death, most likely fictitious, would always be listed. Typical pretexts included disease, such as typhus, or the extremely popular "auf der Flucht erschosssen"—shot while trying to escape. Nazi bureaucratic order required that each part of the form be filled out, regardless of the apparent falsity and repetitious absurdity.

Despite the repetitive tasks and the investigative fruits they yielded, however, Ferencz found the work hellacious and morbidly depressing. "There is no doubt that I was indelibly traumatized by my experiences as a war crimes investigator of Nazi extermination centers," he acknowledged years later. "I still try not to talk or think about the details."[16]

Fortunately, there were distractions along the way. After Buchenwald, Ferencz and his small team encountered some advance units of the Red Army that had occupied a German house. As the Americans had been moving on Weimar from the west, Soviet troops had been approaching it from the east. They were finally linking up.

Ferencz entered the house and was immediately shaken from his dark Buchenwald stupor. The Russians swarmed him, grabbing him by the lapels and pushing him into a celebration already in progress. He was still trying to process the extreme contrast between the concentration camp inferno he had just walked away from and the raucous revelry that now enveloped him. The revelers meant to speed the transition by plying him with vodka. Ben quickly washed down a shot of what, to him, tasted like gasoline. And then the party was on.

Joyful stomping and dancing were punctuated by the sudden movement of a burly Soviet soldier, with pants stuffed into big black boots. He grabbed Ferencz, lifted him off his feet, and started swinging him around the room like a rag doll. But only once his barely-over-five-feet frame was again earthbound did he realize that his husky dancing partner was a woman! Unlike the US Army, the USSR's included both genders within its fighting units.

Having escaped the clutches of this formidable female, Ferencz was soon confronted by another Soviet soldier—and this one shared his gender, if not his views on justice. After being asked what he did in the US Army, Ferencz explained that he was a war crimes investigator seeking evidence of SS crimes. The Russian soldier was incredulous. "Don't you know what they did?" he asked. Ferencz shot back, "Of course, I do." "So why are you asking them?" the Russian soldier demanded in further disbelief. "Just shoot them!" The American had been struggling with a lot of overpowering emotions after already having visited Ohrdruf and Buchenwald. He was categorically opposed to what the man was proposing ("Being a lawman, I couldn't accept it"), but, on a strictly emotional level, he found it intriguing ("but I often wondered if he was right").[17]

Another important, and healthy, distraction along the way was his continued correspondence with Gertrude, whom he often sweetly addressed as "Trudy" in the letters. On April 16, 1945, after his initial forays into the concentration camps, he sent her a letter in which he referenced "mass murders" and "gruesome and horrible exterminations," which he could not describe. Without specifically referencing the concentration camps, he let her know about the emotional impact these new investigations were having on him. "It is all part of the crazy fantastic thing that is happening over here. I shut my eyes and think that it is unreal, dear. That it is all a mad dream that will disappear when I open my eyes. Then I open my eyes and there it is. The temptation to be blind is great, but the pathos is so deep that I cannot tear myself away."[18]

Four days later, he let her know how much her missives were helping him survive these travails. "There have been loads of wonderful letters from you in the past few days, dear, to keep my morale from sagging." By then censorship restrictions seemed to have eased somewhat, because he began to specifically identify to Trudy the horrible Nazi detention centers: "Things around the office have really been popping lately. We have been uncovering dozens of Nazi murder camps. By the time you receive this, you will have probably read all about them in the newspapers, and they may strike you as being incredible.

It is really horrible and fantastic. Millions of people starved to death, beaten, tortured and burned." He then gave more details of his investigation:

> We are now working on a case—and this is the absolute truth—in which hundreds of men with tattooed skin were slaughtered and skinned so that the wife of the death camp could have lampshades made of the colored human tissues. A story? No. We have the proof. We have the skins, the lampshades, the dead bodies of the unfortunate victims,—and also the names of the perpetrators. We just apprehended a Dr. whose specialty was injecting typhus germs into hundreds of people (death absolutely certain) just to see the results.[19]

In between messages about the horrors of the concentration camps, there were expressions of a wide range of emotions that the homesick war crimes sleuth wanted to share with his beloved. Soon after US forces began liberating these Nazi slaughterhouses, the central figure of American leadership through the dark days of the Great Depression to the attack on Pearl Harbor and then the most trying of the war years, President Franklin Delano Roosevelt, finally succumbed to the rigors of the office and died on Thursday, April 12, 1945. At 7:00 p.m. that night, Vice President Harry S. Truman took his place. Although there was goodwill toward, and justifiable confidence in, the new commander in chief, the nation was stung with a profound sense of loss and anguish.

And Ben and Trudy shared in that grief through their letters. Soon after helping liberate Buchenwald, he let Trudy know that her "letters following the death of the president have served to impress me more than anything else around here of the great loss we have suffered. When the news was first received, I was in the midst of a war-criminal hunt and had no time to measure its significance. . . . I have been too dazed with work and wranglings . . . to let the actuality sink in. No need now to prolong your sadness, dear. Things will work out, and there is nothing we can do about it, so there is certainly no sense in letting it get us down."[20]

And he shared with her his distress over the antisemitism he perceived in the Third Army's war crimes investigation unit. One way this manifested itself was in personnel policies. There was by then, for instance, a shortage of commissioned officers in the unit. Ferencz was aware of this and felt he could help by assuming such a role. But when he applied for a commission, it was refused.[21] Given the excellent work he had been doing, he could not understand why. Not long after this, a fellow soldier he knew who had been offered a commission in another unit was told that if he withdrew from consideration in the other unit and applied for a commission in the war crimes investigation unit, it would be granted. But the commission was denied. Ferencz learned from the applicant that this happened because, after withdrawing from consideration in the other unit, the war crimes investigation unit learned that the man was Jewish. "Will you ask me," he wrote to Trudy, "why I [don't] like the army?"

Antisemitism manifested itself in other ways, too. For example, the unit learned through an informant that the chief surgeon in a hospital they were investigating had been an "arch Nazi" who had "brutally castrated at least dozens of Jews." But the case was not pursued. Ben wrote to Trudy, in a fit of pique, that they would have to tell "our well-meaning informant that castrating thousands of Jews is none of our business and no use getting excited about it because we're not interested. I wonder what these people will think of Allied justice after the war."[22] But communicating with Trudy helped him keep his perspective: "[But] for so many millions it is far more tragic and we can't complain. When I compare you, or myself, with some poor miserable bewildered who roams the roads of the world seeking something to which to attach the remnants of his beaten soul, I cannot find it in me to moan my own misfortunes."[23]

Despite a heavy dose of such work-diary-flavored passages, often laced with gallows humor, the letters always ended tenderly, sweetly (sometimes even in French): "Bonne nuit ma chérie. Je vous aime. Always, Ben" (April 16);[24] "With all my heart, Ben" (May 15); and "Here's a kiss goodbye. Love, Ben" (June 14).

Sergeant Ferencz needed to tap into the deep emotional reserves born of his love for Trudy as he descended further into the Hades of the Nazi concentration camp system. After he helped liberate and investigate numerous camps and subcamps after Ohrdruf and Buchenwald, three additional ones stood out for the unique horrors he witnessed while investigating them, as well as his own conduct while bearing witness: Flossenbürg, Mauthausen, and Ebensee.

Post Buchenwald, the general movement of the Third Army was in a southeasterly direction. As Patton's forces were approaching the Czech border in the northeastern Bavaria region, they came upon another large Nazi detention center. This one was located in the remote Upper Palatinate Forest area, in the neighborhood of the Fichtel Mountains, adjacent to the eponymous small town of Flossenbürg. Somewhat incongruously, the town was overlooked by the ruins of a picturesque medieval castle.

Flossenbürg was chosen for its location near a granite quarry, whose minerals the prisoners could extract for Nazi building projects. Constructed in May 1938 on orders from Reichsführer-SS Heinrich Himmler himself, it was unique within the concentration camp system because its inmate population did not consist exclusively of political prisoners or persecuted group members; it also included a large number of street criminals, many of whom had been convicted of sexual offenses. The SS put those deviants in charge of camp administration, as "kapos" (trustees), and they would sexually prey on young male prisoners, who were raped in droves.

By the time of its liberation by the Third Army in late April 1945, nearly 97,000 prisoners had passed through the Flossenbürg camp system, of whom an estimated 30,000 prisoners perished, including 3,515 Jews. So many died in Flossenbürg, at such a high rate, that a crematorium had been added in 1940. In addition to the harsh forced labor conditions in the granite quarries, causes of death included exposure to the elements, disease, beatings, and executions. There were only just over 1,500 prisoners left alive in the camp; as many as 200 of them expired soon after the arrival of US soldiers.

One of those soldiers was Sergeant Benjamin Ferencz. But his route to this Nazi prison facility was rather circuitous. It began with a call into Third Army headquarters on April 27, 1945—a concentration camp had been discovered next to a town called Flossenbürg, about four miles from the Czech border. A small team of Ferencz, a lieutenant, and a driver hopped into the IMMER ALLEIN and took off in the direction of the provided coordinates. At this late stage of the war, travel from headquarters to campsites was beginning to reflect the near total collapse of the Nazi armed forces. As Ferencz and his small team proceeded toward Flossenbürg, they passed thousands upon thousands of dispirited German POWs, jammed into trucks and escorted by only handfuls of their American captors tagging behind them in jeeps.

What followed this spectacle was less heartening. As the war crimes investigative team approached the *Konzentrationslager* (concentration camp), the convoys of German prisoners were soon replaced by the Nazis' own erstwhile prisoners. These were mere shadows of men—so emaciated and exhausted that they could barely stand up, let alone move forward. They shambled zombie-like along the road, clad in the telltale blue-and-white striped "pajamas" with numbers stenciled on the jacket pocket. These wraiths had managed to peel off from the SS-directed death procession out of Flossenbürg. That they had survived at all to this point was something of a miracle given the brutality of the Nazi evacuation. In a letter to Trudy, Ben described their ordeal:

> There were about 20,000 [evacuated prisoners]. In groups of between 3 and 5 thousand men the Nazis herded the victims to their doom. The stated destination was Dachau, another concentration lager about 200 miles to the south. About 100 SS men accompanied each group of prisoners, as they marched toward their new home. There was no food. Most of the prisoners were already

> suffering from malnutrition and many were on the verge of starvation. Thousands were ill from a multiplicity of diseases. Typhus and the deadly lice accompanied the pilgrimage. The SS men surrounded the herd of victims, and a special group followed behind to take care of those who faltered.[25]

As the war crimes investigators passed these death march survivors, the latter could not even muster the energy required to wave or smile.[26] But Ferencz's attention was soon diverted elsewhere when a French soldier jumped onto the road and pleadingly gestured for the jeep to stop. The man breathlessly recounted that he had been a prisoner in the village for two years, along with fifteen other French soldiers under his command. They had noticed the Flossenbürg evacuees making their macabre pilgrimage toward Dachau. The next thing they knew, the SS rushed at them and ordered them to dig a trench deep in the nearby forest. They did as they were told, hightailed it back to the village (because they knew what was about to happen), and then saw the Nazis frog-march a group of about forty to fifty weary skeletal figures in blue-and-white-striped tatters toward the direction of their freshly dug grave. They could then hear gunfire emanating from the wooded area.

Ferencz told the French officer to hop into the jeep to show them where the makeshift mass tomb had been ploughed. Only a thin layer of dirt covered the cadavers, and, on its removal, Ferencz could see the head of one of them. "The glaring dead eye was all I had to see," he later recounted. He told the Frenchman to replace the covering soil because "these dead had suffered enough."[27] He then went to a nearby farmhouse to collect witness statements. The farmer's wife confirmed what the French officer had reported and added that her husband and son were the ones who threw dirt over the corpses to prevent the spread of disease.

After taking each family member's sworn statement, Ferencz was appalled to hear the father, mother, and son complain about certain Russian Flossenbürg survivors who had been to their farm and taken some of their food and clothing. As she lodged her grievance, the farmer's wife started crying. Ferencz was incredulous. "I was in no mood for tears," he related to Trudy in a letter. "I told her, in my best broken German, that she could only thank Hitler for anything that happened to her, and that she should be thankful that she wasn't in the place of those poor political prisoners."[28]

After this "side investigation," Ferencz and his colleagues resumed their onward push toward what was still the main objective, the Flossenbürg concentration camp. Much of the same scenery repeated itself—German POWs crammed into passing trucks as well as death march survivors and displaced persons wearily plodding down the roads. But some of the human, and barely human, forms were not moving at all. For the thoroughfares, byways, and paths the Americans traversed were littered with corpses, those who could simply bear no more. Ben would tell Trudy that "the emaciated sprawling blue bodies had me crying from my heart."[29]

The Ferencz party would sometimes slow down and interview weary passersby—some of them had valuable information regarding the various camps in which they had been imprisoned and from which they had been herded on death marches. Other survivors were to be found in the many abandoned houses along the way. Most Germans had fled by then, and the camp refugees were squatting in their empty domiciles. Those Germans who stayed were being raped and plundered, mostly by vengeful Russians. These targets of pent-up Russian fury complained of Russian criminality to Ferencz and his associates. For example, an elderly woman approached Ferencz and asked him if he could retrieve her cow, which had been stolen by the Russians. And, she had the temerity to ask whether he could punish them while he was at it. Ferencz's belligerent retort: "The Russians lost much more than a cow. If you want your cow back, you can go ask Hitler for it!"[30]

On tips they had received, they stopped at certain houses hoping to find witnesses. In those dwellings taken over by Russians, most of the liberated prisoners were willing to answer questions but too weak to do anything but lie limply on the floor and wait for either medical attention or expiration. Ferencz noted that, despite the wretched condition of the men, "each nationality [Poles, Czechs, Hungarians, Romanians, Russians, Dutchmen, Frenchmen, Luxembourgers, Belgians, and Norwegians] had some sort of organization. An elected leader was in charge of each group, and he made the distribution of food and clothing as it was brought in."[31] Many of the squatters had been taken on death marches from Buchenwald to Flossenbürg and had only recently escaped from the latter. They told the Americans that the camp they were about to enter was much worse than the one they had investigated near Weimar. Although filled with dread, Ferencz and his team were now extremely eager to reach Flossenbürg.

And they finally did. By the time Ben Ferencz started his Flossenbürg investigation, only 1,400 prisoners clung to life in the camp. Throughout the premises, small fires were burning piles of lice-infested clothing—and those little infernos, interspersed among the dead bodies lying crumpled across the camp's grounds, made for a rather apocalyptic scene. Bucking his standard protocol, Sargeant Ferencz's first visit was not to the *Schreibstube* but to the crematorium. The latter was located at the foot of a long hill behind the camp. Something akin to a railroad track had been constructed on the incline (through a long, low tunnel) and a trolley car cum coffin, moving on small gauge railroad wheels, would transport cadavers down the slope. Approximately thirty prisoners a day were still dying at that time, and so, to avoid the spread of disease, the crematorium was still in active use. Ferencz and his crew walked down the low tunnel, stooping, and keeping astride the rail tracks, with Ben wondering "how many hundreds of thousands had come down the easier way—in the wagon."[32]

The crematorium was a small "horror building," as Ben described it, which consisted of four rooms. As he set the scene in his letter to Trudy:

> In one room was a large oven. No fire was going, and the ashes and bones were plainly visible. The adjoining room had about 60 dead bodies piled up like cordwood. Those emaciated corpses had ceased to breathe within the past few days, and the absence of fuel had prevented their cremation. They were nothing but skin and bones, and yet their taut skin showed the welts and scars of their beatings. The buttocks were black and blue, where the rubber hose of the SS had left its mark, even unto death. The stench was revolting, but the sight of these beaten and starved bodies, and the realization of the manner in which they met their death was even more sickening.[33]

After inspecting the crematorium, team Ferencz moved on to the barracks, which were only slightly less horrific. The "beds," a series of dank, wooden warrens, more fitting for a chicken coop or rabbit hutch, filled the room. They were touching each other and aligned in tiers of three. The "mattress" for each "bed" was a louse-infested straw sack. From floor to ceiling, between twelve to fifteen persons were stacked like cartons on this putrid shelving after back-breaking labor in the elements. Worse, they were only allowed inside the barracks for the purpose of "sleeping." At all other times, regardless of weather, the inmates had to wait outside in the open court.[34]

After a cursory tour of the rest of the camp, it was time to collect evidence. Toward that end, the officer accompanying Ferencz took the IMMER ALLEIN and went in search of a telephone to request additional help, including stenographers, photographers, and movie camera operators. In the meantime, Ferencz remained on-site and got to work doing what he could on his own. The Flossenbürg camp commander, a Soviet captain who had been imprisoned there for several years and took charge of the camp as the SS abandoned it, was cooperating fully. He gave Ferencz the use of two large offices and, as an assistant, a twenty-two-year-old Yugoslav medical student who was fluent in seven languages.

Ferencz then deputized a number of other detainees to help him with the work: some tabulated data from the books that had been secreted away in nooks and crannies by prisoners that contained inmate statistics and names; two longtime French detainees as well as a Polish journalist were tasked with writing a complete history of the camp; another volunteer compiled the names of all the camp's known SS men; and a doctor was gathering statements from persons in the hospital. Ferencz himself went to work furiously taking statements of a representative cross-section of detainees. He had previously deputized a group of prisoners, fluent in either French or English, to serve as interpreters for the many languages spoken by the witnesses.

Even if extremely productive, it had been a long and trying day for Sergeant Ferencz. Little did he know that, at some point during the afternoon of his second day at Flossenbürg, Adolf Hitler had shot himself in the head in his Berlin bunker. The criminal at the apex of the malevolent hierarchy he was investigating had managed to evade justice, and the Third Reich was now under new, provisional leadership.

The next day at the camp, May 1, 1945, was devoted to more of the same investigative business, with Ferencz sorting out logistics, gathering physical evidence, and taking witness statements. But what stood out in his memory about that day had nothing to do with atrocities or collecting evidence of them. The key image seared into his memory was a huge platform built in the center of the prison yard to celebrate May Day. Standards of the United States, Great Britain, and the Soviet Union festooned the front, and before them were painted portraits of Stalin, Churchill, and the recently departed FDR. To that backdrop, the inmates paraded around the square, with each nationality forming a separate group and carrying its own state flag. But Ferencz noticed "one particularly emaciated group assembling without any flag."[35] He asked one of the inmates who they were. "Oh," he said, "those are the Jews." And, in response, he reflected ruefully that the "Jewish inmates, who had no national flag, were segregated out—even in liberated concentration camps."[36]

THE NEXT major concentration camp that Ben Ferencz would investigate was not in Germany. The Third Army continued along its southeasterly trajectory and crossed the border into Austria. And on the banks of the Danube River, near the Wiener Graben stone quarry, on May 5, 1945, they came upon a Nazi incarceration site known as Mauthausen. It was located on a hill above the market town bearing the same name, twelve miles east of Linz, Upper Austria. Once this alpine country was incorporated into Nazi Germany via the March 1938 Anschluss, it apparently wished to ape all the worst tendencies of the "Fatherland." Thus, for purposes of locking up "traitors to the people," Austrian

Gauleiter August Eigruber[37] would soon boast of the Führer's homeland having one of the great badges of distinction in the perverted world of National Socialism—a concentration camp.

Like Flossenbürg, the site for Mauthausen was scouted out by Himmler (with the help of subordinates) and was also selected for purposes of quarry exploitation (in fact, the SS founded a company, German Earth and Stone Works Inc., to exploit the granite they intended to extract with Mauthausen slave labor). Similar to Flossenbürg as well, Himmler and his lieutenants decided to let street criminals serve as the kapos of the Austrian camp. Also following the template of the other camp, Mauthausen became the epicenter of an explosion of subcamps as the SS demand for wartime production via brutal bondage rapidly accelerated. By war's end, nearly one hundred Mauthausen satellite camps had been set up. Approximately 197,464 victims were imprisoned in the Mauthausen camp system during its existence. At least 95,000 perished there; more than 14,000 of them were Jewish.

As with the other concentration camps, Ferencz had learned of Mauthausen when Third Army troops, this time from the Eleventh Armored Division, reported happening upon yet another massive Nazi detention complex. What ensued was yet another long jeep expedition, with another translator (this one Czech), on roads once again choked with refugees and corpses. Now it seemed as if all the continent's survivors were trudging along those forlorn, dusty byways, seeking to reclaim old lives or establish new beginnings. Ferencz observed that "Every nation in Europe was represented, and every conveyance imaginable was being used. Old women pulled loaded carts, Hungarian soldiers rode slowly in stolen horse drawn wagons, Spanish loyalists pushed their dilapidated auto up a hill and Austrian mothers and children just plodded along with a load on their backs."[38]

At last, they arrived at Mauthausen. And it struck Ferencz as different from the other camps he had investigated:

> I had never . . . seen one so imposing. The little Jeep churned up the narrow and steep road. Again, hundreds of people lined the way. But many of these were not walking. They were lying in the dust, their hollow eyes staring out of their bony faces. At the top of the long ascent was a massive wall of huge stone blocks. Turrets interrupted the wall at regular intervals, and behind this monumental stone fortress were 25,000 dying and dead souls. The other camps I had seen seemed to be built just for a short while. They had been made of wood with wire fencing. But this one was built to last forever. A permanent place for the destruction of "enemies of the Reich."[39]

As before, he then toured the premises. And this time, if it could even be imagined, the parade of horribles was worse. The stone wall he had seen entering the camp had a necklace made of iron chains affixed to it on the interior. Inmates had been collared to the wall, drawn up to their tip toes, and then bludgeoned across the head and face with the other end of the heavy chain. Many of these wretches, along with most sectors of the camp's population, were then dispatched in one of the camp's four crematoria. Promised a shower, about 200 men, women, and children would be led into what seemed like a place for washing. But the heavy, airtight doors would then be bolted shut, and lethal gas would be introduced into the chamber. Within six minutes—360 seconds of agony and screaming—those crammed into the cell would give up the ghost. Victims with gold teeth had been previously marked with an iodine "X" across the chest on the way in. And before joining the other victims in the ovens, the precious metal in their mouths would be extracted.

Others perished in frightful numbers in the stone quarry. Several prisoners pointed to the imposing Mauthausen walls, which were made from the rocks quarried there, and told Ferencz that "Each stone has cost a life." For sport, the Nazis would order their prisoners to jump off the high cliff into the granite pit. Those who refused were pushed over the precipice. Inspecting the scene, Ferencz could see that smashed bones were still mingled with the smashed rock. "The stockholders in the quarry were the SS and the leaders of the Nazi party," he wrote to Trudy. "The blood of the slaves were their dividends, and the fat grew rich on human misery."[40]

The barracks were more appalling here, too, because there were children in them. "I saw little infants, only two and three weeks old, who were wrapped in rags; living in dirt, without food, and with nothing but their wails." One girl made a particularly strong impression on him. She had been "torn away from her parents a few years ago and had finally ended on the death block, where the arrival of the Americans saved her. Her only crime, as well as that of the dozens and dozens of other children, was that she was Jewish."[41]

The adults were not in much better shape. "Everyone was starved," Ferencz explained in his letter to Trudy. "The food was scarce and what there was abominable. Filthy hovels—as many as fifty persons were jammed in a room. Here they lay sharing their diseases until they were removed to the hospital. In the hospital 'trained' doctors decided on the most practical cure. Benzene was injected into the veins as a cure and death was almost instantaneous."[42] With his tour of the hideous facility over, Ben noted in his diary that, "of the Nazi murder camps, Mauthausen was the worst and my mind still refuses to believe the things I've seen."[43]

Disease was too rampant to stay in close proximity to the camp's grounds so Ben found an apartment in nearby Linz that belonged to a family of Nazi adherents. He ordered them to leave, then removed the National Socialist flags and song books that he found in the dresser drawers, as well as the portrait of Adolf Hitler that adorned one of the walls. He also "emptied all of the clothing in the closets . . . and put [it] in my jeep to deliver [it] to the near-naked Mauthausen inmates."[44]

With the donation of the clothes, his instincts regarding attention to victim welfare during the investigation phase were developing further. He had already been providing them food, including soup and sardines. But, through experience, he realized he had to start out with only the very simplest nutrition: "You had to begin by feeding them soup for a week, begin with a very light soup until their stomachs and systems were built up."[45]

Meanwhile, efforts to collect evidence at Mauthausen were ongoing. For this investigation, there was a larger Third Army logistical presence, with a dedicated team on-site conducting witness interviews and securing physical evidence. In addition, "An international committee had been organized with representatives of each nation," Ben explained in correspondence to Trudy, "and they were all busy writing sworn testimonials of the things that happened to them and their countrymen."[46] Ferencz was one of those who worked on collecting those statements.

Remarkably, one of the declarations he took at Mauthausen survives. It is from Lucien Vanherle, a Belgian political prisoner who worked as an accountant in the "political bureau" at Mauthausen's subcamp Gusen, which gave him access to adminstrative statistics. As with the other concentration camp survivor affidavits taken by Ferencz, this one was "sworn" to a commissioned officer—Major Eugene S. Cohen of the Third Army JA Section—but Ferencz took the statement in French (and then translated it into English). The statement began dramatically: "The veil is lifted. [Here is] the truth about the concentration camp at Mauthausen, a modern Dante's Inferno."[47]

Vanherle then broke down the number of prisoners and fatalities. Many of the internees, he explained, died from the hard labor, disease, or hunger. Of the latter, Vanherle reported the Nazis would point to the "sight of the piles and piles of cadavers and say, '*Zu faul zum essen*' (Too lazy to eat)."[48] The others were victims of the ordinary criminals working as kapos for the SS. They were put in charge of lower-tier prison administration and, under the watchful and approving eye of the SS, terrorized their fellow inmates. Of their excesses of bestiality and sadism, he testified:

> There was death by whipping, forced exercises, by injections of poison, by gas, by driving them to suicide, by shooting, by hanging. Other processes consisted of bathing the unfortunates until they died under the showers which alternated from ice cold to boiling hot. . . . . A particularly effective method used by some sadists was drowning (the victim) in a tub of water or of human excrement, as well as the remains of the victims. [Many of them] carried the name "N!N!" on their dossiers. That means "Nacht und Nebel" "Night and Fog." In other words [they were disappeared].[49]

Vanherle then concluded with a plea for justice: "In the name of all the political prisoners who died for their country in these baths of Satan, we demand justice for them, for their heirs, and their families. We demand just treatment with extreme severity for those who bear responsibility for this frightful carnage."[50] That plea resonated with Ben Ferencz as he prepared to leave Mauthausen and investigate one of its key subcamps—Ebensee.

EBENSEE WAS "considered to be one of the most diabolic concentration camps ever built."[51] Established in November 1943, at the southern tip of a lake named Traunsee (about fifty miles southwest of Linz in the Upper Austrian Salzkammergut region), Ebensee's chief purpose was to furnish slave labor for the construction of enormous underground tunnels in which armament works were to be housed. After rising at 4:30 a.m., the prisoners would dig away at the tunnels until late at night. Their striped pajama uniforms gave them no protection against the elements during the harsh Austrian winters. And, as at Mauthausen, they were put through the unimaginable ordeals of overcrowding (barracks designed to house 100, crammed in 750), hunger, disease, and torture. The latter included the usual whippings and beatings. But the violence at Ebensee was even more deranged and sadistic than at the mother camp.

One of the preferred methods of torture for the camp's first commandant, SS-Hauptsturmführer Georg Bachmayer, was to tie a prisoner's arms behind him, with the hands side by side and thumb to thumb and then suspend him from a tree about eighteen inches off the ground. Bachmayer would then release his favorite dog, a German shepherd called "Lord," to maul the prisoner, who would be left to die a slow and agonizing death. Bachmayer was succeeded by SS-Obersturmführer Otto Riemer, who, unimaginably, was even more sadistic. He "personally beat, shot, and tortured prisoners daily. He openly offered extra cigarettes and leave to those sentries who could account for the largest number of deaths. If a sentry at the end of a day did not have a sufficient number to his credit, he would knock off the cap of a prisoner and throw it into a forbidden area. When the prisoner went to retrieve it, he would be shot dead."[52]

Ebensee's death toll was staggering. Corpses were tossed into piles, and every three to four days they were taken to the Mauthausen crematoria to be incinerated. If the mother camp's ovens could not accommodate the additional bodies, the cadavers would simply remain in ever-growing piles. "The smell of the dead, combined with sickness, phlegmon, urine, and feces, was unbearable."[53] By mid-1944, Ebensee had installed its own crematorium, but the death rate was increasing exponentially (350 per day in the spring of 1945), and the crematorium could not keep pace. Once again, the mountains of cadavers were growing. In the end, nearly 28,000 prisoners endured the Ebensee experience.

When the Eightieth Infantry Division of the Third Army liberated the camp on May 6, 1945, it held about 18,500 prisoners. Roughly one-third of them were Jewish, but there were also Russians, Poles, Czechs, and Roma and Sinti. Approximately 11,000 of them perished by the time Ebensee was liberated.

Ben Ferencz chronicled much of this in his investigation of the camp. But what stood out to him was the brutal extent of starvation there, and its attendant suffering. In his diary, he was in despair as he described the complex's "emaciated skeletons" and resolved that the "thousands upon thousands" who were "systematically starved to death, can never be forgotten."[54] Writing to Trudy in powerfully evocative prose, he provided a glimpse of the inhuman state and extreme suffering of these skeletal survivors:

> In front of one of the barracks was a big pail of water and in it some of the prisoners were bathing some of the patients. It was a fantastic sight. The patients, nothing but skin and bones, were carried out to the tub. They were carried like babies, and none of them could have weighed more than 80 lbs. They were placed standing in the tub and water run over their bodies. Like lifeless marionettes these former humans fell over the arms of their bather. Their heads flapped loosely, and their arms hung limp. Yet these skeletons being held up in a tub were live human beings—men who may have been prominent and influential at one time. Now they were but helpless animal-like puppets who might not die. No one who has not seen it can visualize the scene. It is all a wild nightmare.[55]

After weeks of being on this incredibly dark path, a fierce rage had welled up inside of Ben. While conducting his investigation at Ebensee, an infuriated Ferencz ordered a group of passing Germans to halt and forced them to bury the bodies of inmates strewn along the camp's grounds. And, toward the end of his time there, he apparently reconnected with those nascent vigilante-justice feelings he first experienced when, after Buchenwald, the Russian soldier asked him why he refrained from simply shooting SS men instead of investigating them and giving them a trial. While at Ebensee, he saw a group of prisoners savagely attack and brutally torture an SS officer. And he stood by and did nothing. As Ferencz later described the scene: "First, he was beaten mercilessly. Then the mob tied him to one of the metal trays used to slide bodies into the crematorium. There he was slowly roasted alive, taking him in and out of the oven several times. I watched it happen and did nothing. It was not my duty to stop it, even if I could have, and frankly, I was not inclined to try. There seemed to be no limit to human brutality in wartime."[56]

By the time Ben Ferencz's jeep rolled out of the perimeter of Ebensee, the war in Europe had come to an end. On May 8, 1945, led by Hitler's handpicked successor, Reichspräsident (formerly Grand Admiral) Karl Dönitz, Nazi Germany unconditionally surrendered to the Allies. The continent lay in ruins, submerged under tidal wave upon tidal wave of displaced and miserable humanity. Approximately seven to eleven million refugees had been deracinated, finding themselves in wastelands such as Germany, Italy, Austria, and Poland, and they had nowhere to go. Tens of millions in Europe had died during the war, including six million Jews targeted for genocide by the Third Reich.

By then, all the Nazi concentration camps had been overrun and their victims ministered to by the Allies. In addition to those already mentioned, the Soviets liberated Ravensbrück, Sachsenhausen, and Theresienstadt. The British liberated concentration camps in northern Germany, including Neuengamme and Bergen-Belsen. And the Americans also liberated Dachau (which Ben Ferencz passed through and inspected on his way to Flossenbürg/Mauthausen) and Dora-Mittlebau, as well as a multitude of other subcamps. In all, Allied forces discovered roughly 1,500 concentration and labor camps throughout Nazi-occupied territory.

What was needed to clean up, repair, and heal this fractured continent was beyond the capacity of any one individual, organization, or nation. It would take years, billions of dollars, and a massive collective effort to restore some kind of normalcy and vitality to Europe. But among the wreckage and carnage that lay before those who survived the bloodletting and could take stock of all the devastation, individual resolve was being mustered and plans were being made. Sergeant Benjamin Ferencz was one of those survivors. And he was already dedicating himself to seek justice for the inhuman, and indescribable, deeds he had been chronicling during that horrible spring of 1945. As Ebensee receded further into his jeep's rearview mirror, he recorded later, all he could think of was heading "back to Munich to write my reports. They would serve as the basis for later war crimes prosecutions."[57] And all he had experienced in those months would set him on a permanent course of seeking to vindicate the rights of the victims of crimes against humanity from that day forward.

At the same time, though, he had been badly scarred by what he had just lived through. As he explained in one of his final letters to Trudy from this extended, ugly road trip: "There were a million other things I saw and did, but I can't describe them now, dear. It's horrible and pathetic. I don't even want to think of what the sight of all these things is doing to me." He would be traumatized by those sights for the rest of his days.

9

MONUMENTS MAN AT THE EAGLE'S NEST AND THE DACHAU TRIALS

Mountaintops inspire leaders but valleys mature them.

—Winston Churchill

After the nightmarish spring of 1945, Ben Ferencz was exhausted—physically, psychologically, emotionally, spiritually. He confided in his diary that he was a victim of "war fatigue."[1] In work terms, he needed something akin to a break. And he got one. Actually, he got two. The first was to investigate the top Axis war criminal of them all—Adolf Hitler. The second was to investigate the art that the Führer and his henchmen had looted from collections across Europe. Both investigations took him to the bucolic mountainous regions of Bavaria and Austria with gorgeous alpine scenery and no concentration camps. That was exactly what he needed.

Toward the end of the war, before learning that the founder of National Socialism had committed suicide in his Berlin bunker, General Eisenhower was convinced the Nazi plan for the end game was to withdraw the cream of the SS and Gestapo into the mountains of southern Bavaria. There, the Allied supreme commander expected that Hitler would block the tortuous mountain passes and hold out indefinitely against their enemies. (It was for this reason that Ike had ordered Patton's Third Army to march toward the southeast of Germany when Patton would have preferred fighting his way into Berlin.)

Eisenhower referred to this area of southwest Germany as the Nazi "National Redoubt," and "Hitler's Eagle's Nest was the presumed HQ for this combination last stand and beginning of guerrilla war against the occupiers."[2] There, the Allies feared, the dictator "would be well protected and have radio facilities he could use."[3] The 101st Airborne, now assigned to the Seventh Army, had secured the Nazi fortress (fittingly, given the unit's logo and "Screaming Eagles" nickname) just before Ferencz and his team of investigators arrived to "find documents and other evidence of crime."[4]

What the Screaming Eagles had seized was a stylish fortress erected atop the summit of the Kehlstein, a rocky outcrop at the apex of the mountainous Obersalzberg region above Berchtesgaden. It was commissioned in 1937 by Martin Bormann, Deputy Führer Rudolf Hess's personal secretary at the time (who would go on to become Hitler's personal secretary and head of the Party Chancellery, replacing Hess after the latter's May 1941 solo flight across the English Channel to seek peace negotiations with the British government). Bormann's aerie for Hitler was visually stunning—with a main reception room lined with enormous triple-paned mountain-view picture windows and dominated by a fireplace of Mussolini-supplied oxblood-red Italian marble laced with alabaster. And, unusually for the late 1930s, its state-of-the-art kitchen was equipped entirely with electrical appliances.

Paid for by the Nazi Party at a cost of 30 million Reichsmarks (approximately US$200 million today), the great expense was due not only to the opulent design touches but also the challenging construction logistics. The structure was perched atop a 6,108-foot peak (well over one mile high). The precipitous path leading up to the summit included various tunnels and hairpin turns so difficult to navigate that twelve workers died during construction. The complex also featured a brass-plated elevator, built into the mountain (thus allowing visitors to avoid the dangerous mountain), and was adorned with circular Venetian mirrors and green-leather benches. Hitler inaugurated this Kehlsteinhaus, as it was typically called in German, on his fiftieth birthday, April 20, 1939.

Ben Ferencz would be approaching this supposed last stronghold of National Socialism from the movement's birthplace, Munich. He expected to collect no small quantity of evidence so, in addition to his jeep, he commandeered a two-wheeled trailer from the army chaplain. A private from the war crimes investigation unit accompanied him. En route, they met up with another team of investigators who had been collecting evidence at concentration camps in the region. That team would join Ferencz and the private for the Eagle's Nest probe. Ferencz's trailer-hitched jeep had left Munich in the morning, and, by the afternoon, the two teams of investigators found themselves at the base of the Kehlstein.[5]

Ferencz's vehicle then started the ascent, trailer in tow, following the other team's vehicle. And it was rough going. Unfortunately, the diminutive New Yorker had had no previous experience driving a car with a two-wheeled carriage bringing up the rear (let alone on such a steep incline). When he wanted the trailer to go to the left, he had to turn his steering wheel to the right, and vice versa. Not only did this seem extremely dangerous on a ridiculously steep ascent like the Kehlstein road, but it was slowing him and the other team down considerably. Moreover, the road was coarse and bumpy, pocked with bomb divots and craters and covered in debris.

The jeep was being severely tested, and its engine started to strain and sputter—finally, it gave out. And since the men could not bring it back to life, they decided to scrap the trailer. The private accompanying Ferencz unhooked it and pushed it into the woods adjoining the road. Then the investigators instructed the closest group of American sentries in the vicinity "to keep an eye on it."[6] Eventually, they were able to restart Ferencz's auto, resume their little caravan, and snake their way up to the summit.

What they found there was quite disappointing. The gnarled state of the mountain road, which was evidence of a serious preassault bombing campaign, foretold of further damage to the Eagle's Nest itself. Through a combination of Nazi attempts at evidence destruction, the air strikes, as well as looting and vandalism, the place had been trashed. File cabinets, which might have contained valuable evidence, had been raided and their documents removed or rendered illegible. In Ferencz's own words, "the creative GIs of the 101st had been using the second drawer up from the bottom of the cabinets as very convenient toilet seats."[7] The SS guardhouses in the vicinity had also been thoroughly vandalized. In short, Hitler's mountaintop hideaway yielded no valuable evidence. The investigative teams started their descent down the mountain feeling rather dejected.

That sense of gloom was amplified considerably when they discovered that the chaplain's trailer was no longer in the spot where they had left it. In fact, it was nowhere to be found at all. Thus, on returning to headquarters, the complete absence of useful evidence from the Eagle's Nest was not the only concern of Ferencz's superior officers. The real problem was the missing trailer. And, once again, Ben faced the prospect of a court-martial.

Alternative charges were prepared accusing Sargeant Ferencz of either losing or stealing government property. As usual, though, he succeeded in getting them dismissed, cleverly arguing that the property was neither lost nor stolen because it was necessarily taken by other US troops (as the American military had exclusive control of the mountain road). And the Harvard Law grad was on to his next investigation.

THAT SECOND probe concerned Nazi-looted art. Historical overviews of Germany's World War II transgressions tend to focus on the tremendous loss of innocent human life and attendant suffering. But National Socialist criminality went well beyond offenses against people. Among the Third Reich's untold property crimes, the theft, plundering, and destruction of art and related cultural relics and treasures loomed large, to the tune of billions of dollars in damage. Artwork looted by the Nazis "exceeded the collections amassed by the Metropolitan Museum in New York, the Louvre in Paris, and the Treitiaskov Gallery in Moscow."[8]

And in reference to the Holocaust in particular, it should not be forgotten that the Nazis stole some 600,000 paintings from Jews, at least 100,000 of which are still missing. In France alone, almost 70,000 homes of Jews and French war resisters were emptied during World War II.

The Allies became quite interested in this aspect of Nazi wrongdoing as they began taking back German-conquered territory in 1943. That year, at the instigation of Franklin D. Roosevelt, the Allied armies created the Monuments, Fine Arts, and Archives (MFAA) program to help protect and preserve war-affected cultural property. The members of this unit were informally known as "Monuments Men" (the subject of the 2014 George Clooney/Matt Damon film), and they worked with military forces to safeguard art and other cultural objects from war damage. And, as the conflict was winding down, they concentrated on locating Nazi-plundered art so it could be returned to its rightful owners.

But the Monuments Men were not alone in tracing stolen art after the war. The Third Army war crimes investigation unit was asked to help, too, and it assigned Sergeant Benjamin Ferencz to certain of those investigations. The main target of Ferencz's efforts, Karl Haberstock, had been Hitler's personal art dealer. To understand exactly how Haberstock fit into the vast Nazi art-looting conspiracy, Ferencz first studied the origins of the plundering campaign.

It could be traced back to 1933, during the very earliest days of National Socialist Germany. From the start, Hitler sought to purge so-called "degenerate art," such as cubism, expressionism, and impressionism, from German public institutions. These pieces were seized without compensation and sold overseas to generate revenue for the party, which preferred works from the old masters. Soon, art looting, which had originally been a manifestation of short-term ideological urges, became a systematic, organized government program. For ambitious Hitler acolytes, acquiring admired works of art, by whatever means, and especially if taken from Jews, confirmed a dedication to promoting long-term Nazi racial ideologies in the Reich.

Apart from Hilter himself, the failed Austrian painter who directed seizure of numerous masterpieces for his planned revenge-fantasy Führermuseum in his hometown of Linz, the Third Reich's art-plunderer-in-chief was the dictator's second in command, Reichsmarschall Hermann Göring. The corpulent Luftwaffe chief had a hand in the regime's first extraterritorial looting that occurred in 1938, with the Nazi Anschluss of Austria. Two years later, Göring helped establish the Einsatzstab Reichsleiter Rosenberg (ERR), directed by party ideologist Alfred Rosenberg, which was housed in Paris's Jeu de Paume Museum.

The ERR, which operated from 1940 to 1944, was the official Nazi office tasked with confiscating prominent, mainly Jewish, art collections in Nazi-occupied territories. All treasures seized were designated as either going to Hitler's planned museum in Linz or to Göring's personal collection at his country estate Carinhall. Ideologically acceptable works not selected for Linz or Carinhall were set aside for German museums. And pieces deemed "decadent" (that is, too modern or licentious) were auctioned off outside of Nazi territory.

FROM THE outset, Karl Haberstock was an important figure in this Nazi spoliation program. Born in 1878 into a large, middle-class Augsburg Catholic family, he began his career as a bookkeeper and then a banker before he opened a porcelain store in Würzburg in 1903. From porcelain, he branched out into art dealing and moved to Berlin. There he found great success and, as of the 1920s, was selling high-priced paintings to an international clientele. By the time Hitler became German chancellor in 1933, Haberstock had made a name for himself in the art world; seeing which way the wind was blowing, he joined the Nazi Party that same year and ingratiated himself with its power brokers, including the NSDAP leader himself. In 1936, he sold his first picture to the Führer (Paris Bordone's *Venus and Amor*), and Hitler became his most important client, buying more than one hundred works from Haberstock between 1936 and 1938. At the same time, the former banker served as art dealer to other top-tier Nazi leaders, including Göring, Joseph Goebbels, Albert Speer, and Wilhelm Frick.

One of Haberstock's key allies in the Nazi network was art historian and curator Hans Posse, whom he had recommended to Hitler as the first director of his Linz Führermuseum. Haberstock, in turn, was appointed by Hitler as Posse's chief advisor. In addition to this role, and along with his associate Baron Gerhard von Pöllnitz, Haberstock participated in confiscating Jewish-owned art so that it could be "Aryanized." And he played a key role in selling off the "degenerate" art that had been confiscated from German state museums (including conceiving of the infamous 1939 auction of such art in Lucerne, Switzerland, which was organized by the auctioneer and Nazi accomplice Theodor Fischer, and included works by Vincent Van Gogh, Pablo Picasso, Paul Matisse, Georges Braque, Marc Chagall, Wassily Kandinsky, Emil Nolde, and Paul Klee).

That said, Haberstock's pull within the Nazi hierarchy weakened considerably after Posse unexpectedly succumbed to cancer in December 1942. The ERR, into whose inner circles Haberstock had failed to insinuate himself, served as advisor to Hitler in the selection of Posse's replacement, Hermann Voss, who disliked Haberstock and marginalized him. Thus, from then until the end of the war, cut off from access to Hitler and the Linz museum project, Haberstock became a bit player, selling some Nazi-looted art but none directly connected to the Reich's major power brokers. Haberstock's prospects dimmed even further when, in January 1944, his Berlin gallery, which also served as his home, was bombed to smithereens in an Allied air raid. He and his wife, Magdalene, were taken in by Baron Gerhard von Pöllnitz, a committed National Socialist who dabbled in looted art. And the accommodations were quite grand, a castle in Aschbach, located between Würzburg and Bamberg in Upper Franconia.

Still, despite his diminished stature, in an American report prepared to assist investigators capture war criminals, Haberstock was assigned great culpability. Per the report, his entire career was based on two principles: antisemitism and Germanic chauvinism. His "position in the Nazi Party and his leadership role in the purchase and distribution of stolen art led [the Americans to conclude] that he should be tried at the same level of severity as the leading Linz officials."[9]

As a result, Haberstock was included in the Allied Central Registry of War Crimes and Security Suspects (CROCAS). And this is when Ben Ferencz entered the picture. Haberstock, along with the other Nazi art-dealer residents of Baron von Pöllnitz's castle, had already been interviewed concerning the whereabouts of various priceless artworks by Monuments Man Captain Robert K. Posey. Another Monuments Man, Captain Thomas Giuli, then visited the castle and put certain residents under house arrest, while taking Haberstock to nearby Würzburg for questioning. Giuli then reported the investigation to the Third Army Judge Advocate Section so that war crimes investigators could be brought in to assist. The JA Section, in turn, assigned the case to First Lieutenant Dwight McKay and Sergeant Benjamin Ferencz. On arrival in Würzburg, McKay and Ferencz were given a debriefing by Giuli, who then gave them custody of Haberstock.

McKay and Ferencz found Haberstock in the local Würzburg jail, which had been badly damaged, along with the rest of the city's structures, in a March 1945 British firebombing.[10] They needed a suitable place to question their war crimes suspect. So they commandeered a villa on the outskirts of town, formerly owned by a high-ranking Nazi official, and took Haberstock there. In a June 6 letter to Trudy, Ben described his initial impression of the

Nazi art dealer: "White haired and with a curling mustache the aged Haberstock immediately looked very harmless. The portly gentleman bowed and looked at us rather wistfully."[11]

At first, the old man was frightened and not very forthcoming. And so Ferencz and McKay transitioned into the role of "good cop, bad cop" to help elicit answers. Ferencz's description of his partner to Trudy in the June 6 letter goes a long way toward explaining why McKay was cast in the "bad cop" role:

> At this point let me introduce Lt. Dwight McKay a G.F.U. [General Fuck Up] from way back. (That's army lingo for a bad boy.) He has only been in the section for about a month. The first day he was assigned he was arrested for being drunk and disorderly and waving a gun at a nurse in her quarters at 1 A.M. . . .
>
> Every once in a while, during the questioning, the crazy McKay would jump out of his seat and shout at the old man, in unintelligible English, "Don't lie to me, you son-of-bitch, or I'll kill you!". . . Then McKay would explain in fumbling French that he was trying to decide whether the old man would be hung this week or the next. The old boy never knew [if McKay was] seriously threatening his life.[12]

In his "good cop" role, though, Ferencz plied the aging art looter with fine Franconian wine (Buxbeidl) previously procured from the town's mayor, and Haberstock began to loosen up. For three days, the war crimes investigators recorded the story of Hitler's former art dealer. Haberstock explained that the Nazis had four methods of acquiring valuable art. First, they would simply seize the treasures and send their owners to concentration camps. Ultimately, however, this method fell into disfavor, as wealthy art owners tended to be persons of influence in the community, and their shabby treatment created bad optics for the regime.

The second method was to "purchase" the masterpieces. The payment would be by check drawn on the German ministry and payable to the Bank of France. Then, through a simple process of diplomatic financial negotiation, the price of the painting was subtracted from the war debt the Germans imposed on the French, and, as Ferencz put it in the letter to his girlfriend: "The Germans had 'bought' a painting, and France had lost one and was not a cent richer."[13] The third method was that the Germans would offer ridiculously low prices for paintings under an implied threat of imprisonment or death. The fourth method was almost as simple and brutally efficient—the Gestapo would approach owners and ask if they had any charitable "contributions" to make. The feared Nazi secret police operatives, cynically asking for benevolence, would never be rebuffed. In short, as Ferencz summed it up in his letter:

"Never in history were there more successful collectors. The wealthy Jews who had art treasures had to flee for their lives. They tried to sell whatever they could and get out of the country. So the fortune of the Rothschilds, and dozens of prominent citizens fell to the hands of the Third Reich. By 1943 France was completely plundered, and every land in which the Nazis had set foot had made its contribution to the New Order."[14]

The next stage in the Haberstock investigation was to examine the records related to the confiscated art, as well as any of the remaining art pieces themselves. Those were located at Haberstock's temporary residence—Baron von Pöllnitz's castle. So, after filling out the necessary paperwork, that is where Ferencz and McKay took their prisoner. The castle, overlooking the quaint farming village of Aschbach, was like something out of a fairy tale. Its estate included a lake and several hundred hectares of forest; its facade was covered in sepia-toned plaster and surrounded by wild grape vines.

Inside the chateau itself was a motley assortment of displaced Nazi culture vultures—it was something like a sea-level art-theft version of Thomas Mann's *Magic Mountain*. There was the French double agent Roger Dequoy, who represented Paris Jewish collector Georges Wildenstein in buying and selling Nazi-looted art in France during the war (while Wildenstein was seeking refuge in the United States). At the same time, Duquoy worked on behalf of the Germans (including Haberstock) and often served as the middleman in dealings implicating the interests of both Wildenstein and the Nazis.

There was also Bruno Lohse, an SS-Hauptsturmführer who, at 6 foot four and more than 350 pounds, cut quite an imposing figure. He had served as Hermann Göring's chief art looter in Paris during World War II, aiding and abetting the Reichsmarschall in some of his most egregious plundering. Among other cultural crimes, Lohse raided the works of Jewish collector Alphonse Schloss, which included numerous seventeenth-century Dutch chefs d'oeuvre.

Not to be outdone, Hildebrand Gurlitt was also calling the castle home. Perhaps the most notorious, and devious, Nazi art grifter of them all, he somehow managed to thrive despite being of Jewish heritage. Classified as "one-quarter" (or "Mischling Second Degree") under the Nuremberg Laws because of his Jewish grandmother, he had originally dealt in "degenerate art" as curator of the König Albert Museum in Zwickau, where his exhibitions of Die Brücke artists such as Erich Heckel, Karl Schmidt-Rottluff, and Emil Nolde fell afoul of the Militant League for German Culture. He was once again accused of promoting "degenerate art" as curator of the Kunstverein in Hamburg, where he also had to resign.

In spite of this inauspicious National Socialist debut, he somehow managed to reinvent himself as an antisemitic art dealer who learned to curry favor with the Nazis by exploiting Jewish collectors, who were coerced into selling at bargain-basement prices. Having built a sterling reputation as a Jew-hating art profiteer among Hitler's paladins, he became one of Göring's chief World War II art agents. In Nazi-occupied territories, he bought masterpieces for the Reichsmarschall from Jews under duress, while picking up other treasures via implicit threat, also for peanuts, for the planned Führermuseum in Linz.

Gurlitt, along with the other art peddlers on-site, were good friends with the lord of the manor, who was not present—Baron von Pöllnitz had been arrested the previous week given his high-level status within the Nazi Party and the SS. Despite his absence, Ferencz and McKay had plenty to work with. In addition to questioning the Aschbach castle's "who's who" of Nazi art dealers, their spouses, and other assorted high-society relatives and friends sheltering in the enormous manor, the Third Army war crimes investigators brought in other witnesses, including Göring's private secretary, Gisela Limberger. During her time working for the Luftwaffe commander in chief, she was often occupied with matters related to his art collection. In a letter to Trudy, Ben provided insights into how the interrogation proceeded:

> I spent today conversing with Goering's private secretary, and she had many amazing things to tell me. Our talks were on a very friendly plane, for the lady was simply an efficient secretary and personally honest. She admired her former boss considerably, and by the time we were through, she had written down and sworn to such remarks as he travelled in all the occupied countries where he took all objects, and when we parted, she hadn't even realized she had made many damaging remarks against him, and I was smiling like a fox.[15]

Apart from meeting with persons of interest, Ferencz and McKay were also able to take an inventory of the art stored inside the castle and in various locations on its spacious grounds. They found an impressive hoard. The German magazine *Der Spiegel* described the complex as "an immense art warehouse" consisting of "suspicious private property," including some thirteen crates of artwork and suitcases and bags full of art.[16] Apart from magnum opus works from the usual "degenerate" artists, this "warehouse" included more obscure but valuable paintings, such as *The Studio of the Painter Grossmann* by the Bulgarian expressionist Jules Pascin.[17] In his memoirs, Ferencz described their daily life conducting this investigation of the castle and its inhabitants:

> Mornings were spent questioning those who had been in the art "business." Afternoons were spent searching places where they might have hidden stolen

> paintings. At teatime, we assembled in the dining room where we sat around a large table while old "Tanta Thea," who had been a Baroness, poured tea from a samovar. Since food was rather scarce, I managed to scrounge a big box of U.S. army hot dogs that was very well received in the land that gave us the frankfurter. Much to my chagrin, I was referred to as "Our dear American God." My mother would have been proud; providing I didn't tell her that my fans were all German.[18]

SINCE THEY had done such a thorough job in Bavaria, the Third Army asked Ferencz and McKay to represent its war crimes investigation unit for more art-looting probes in the Tyrol region of Austria. In particular, they wanted Patton's gumshoes to work in Altaussee, where the Nazis had warehoused a vast portion of their plundered treasures in a capacious salt mine complex. The investigation would be jointly conducted with the Monuments Men as well as agents of the Art Looting Investigation Unit (or ALIU, under the aegis of the Office of Strategic Services, the CIA's precursor). On arriving, Ferencz was eager to inspect the subterranean grottoes sheltering the Nazi spoils and provided an evocative account of them in a letter to Trudy:

> I trudged along the dark trails, the moist and cold salt covered stone on all sides, until I reached a large cavern. Here several rooms had been constructed of huge cross beams, and the rooms had been sealed by a series of doors. A guard stood outside each door. Within were parts of the hidden loot. . . . From top to bottom this vast room was loaded with paintings, neatly arranged side by side. In one corner stood a dozen Rembrandts, in another a large number of paintings by Van Gogh. Neatly stacked they looked like another bunch of frames; taking the "frames" apart revealed a fabulous fortune.[19]

The Allies had gathered in Altaussee the cream of the Nazi art-pillaging suspects picked up in various locations around Europe so they could question them about the salt mine hoard in a systematic way. Along with Third Reich art pooh-bahs like Hermann Voss, this included persons initially debriefed by Ferencz and McKay, such as Haberstock and Lohse, who remained under house arrest, as well as Göring's personal secretary, Gisela Limberger.[20] Although the investigations were being spearheaded by the ALIU, the Monuments Men and army war crimes investigators, including the Third Army's representatives, Ferencz and McKay, played a vital supporting role in the interrogations and inspections. The probes were roughly divided into three: (1) the

Linz Führermuseum Investigation; (2) the ERR Investigation; and (3) the Hermann Göring Collection Investigation, to which Ferencz and McKay were assigned.

And there was much to do. In collaboration with the ALIU and the Monuments Men, there were witness interrogations, art inspections, and document sorting. On the weekends, though, there was also time to enjoy the rustic environs. As Ben noted in his diary:

> The best part of the job down here, however, has been the place and the people around it. It is the most beautiful country I have ever been in. Here in the Tyrol and the Salzkammergut the towering snow-capped Alps drop sharply into serene blue lakes, and the countryside is bathed in the greenness of trees and plants. The wooden, balconied homes, with their gaily painted fronts, and the colorful clothing of the population, the short leather pants, green jackets and feathered felt caps of the men, and the colorful skirts of the women make the place exceedingly picturesque.[21]

It would seem that he much preferred admiring the skirts. He stressed in his diary that there was "a critical shortage of males" in the area and that he had never seen "such a land of lonely women."[22] As a result, the "non-fraternization policy completely collapsed." And Ben Ferencz contributed thereto. He was living "regally" in this "quiet paradise," and after each day of interviewing witnesses, examining art, or dealing with paperwork, he would take a jeep, and with one or two other soldiers, tour the countryside and "make friends."[23] His American cigarettes, chocolate, and food were very helpful in this regard. And he found it "ironic to be romancing with the still-Nazi wife of some ardent Nazi."[24]

While it may seem shocking to contemplate Ben Ferencz romancing certain Nazi women, he was also helping compile strong dossiers against certain Nazi men. Thanks, in part, to his work at Würzburg, Aschbach, and Altaussee, a compelling case of crimes against humanity for art looting and spoliation of cultural property was made against Hermann Göring before the International Military Tribunal at Nuremberg, where Karl Haberstock's testimony was incorporated into the prosecution case (along with an ALIU report prepared by Theodore Rousseau to which Ferencz and McKay had contributed).[25] Of the report, which benefits throughout from the Ferencz/McKay baseline investigations, the Monuments Men Foundation has said: "the wealth of intelligence data . . . greatly expedited the restitution process for millions of looted works of art and cultural objects."[26] Thus, the artwork investigations of Ben

Ferencz, the Third Army's unofficial "Monuments Man" during the summer of 1945, can ultimately be seen as his earliest contribution to the prosecutions at Nuremberg as well as to Holocaust reparations.

NOTWITHSTANDING HIS excellent "summer vacation" in the Alps, Sergeant Ferencz was eager to get out of the army. So he applied for a job with a new organization, the United Nations Relief and Rehabilitation Administration (UNRRA), which had recently been established to help war victims by providing food, clothing, shelter, and other basic necessities. While UNRAA only lasted for four years, in that short time, it received funding of nearly $4 billion, and many of its functions were transferred to various United Nations agencies, including the International Refugee Organization and the World Health Organization.

Ben interviewed for the UNRRA position toward the end of the summer and was successful—he was offered a contract as social welfare director. But his ability to accept the offer hinged on his being discharged from the army, which required at least 85 "points" (or credits for time in, overseas stationing, battle stars, etc.)—Ben had only 68. So, in the end, the offer was torment, not opportunity. "My recent failure in regard to that UNRRA matter sorta [*sic*] dimmed my spirits awhile," he wrote to Trudy.[27] He realized that he would have to gut it out until at least the end of the war.

But the end was near. On August 6, 1945, an American B-29 bomber dropped the world's first deployed atomic bomb (nicknamed "Little Boy") on the Japanese city of Hiroshima, annihilating approximately 90 percent of the city and instantly killing about 80,000 of its residents. Three days later, a second B-29 dropped another A-bomb (called "Fat Man") on Nagasaki, wiping out roughly 40 percent of the city and killing an estimated 40,000. The Japanese were ready to sue for peace. Cessation of hostilities was announced on August 15, 1945 (Victory over Japan Day, or V-J Day), and on September 2, a formal surrender ceremony was performed aboard the battleship USS *Missouri,* in Tokyo Bay.

By then, Ferencz had returned to Third Army headquarters from Altaussee and found he had a new superior. Colonel Joseph had been shipped home, and the new boss, a younger lieutenatnt colonel, had bad news for the returning art-looting investigator. He was going to be subject to court-martial yet again—this time for being AWOL (absent without leave) based on an unauthorized extension of stay in Altaussee. And there was more—his rank was going to be reduced to private. Ferencz was livid—he felt he was being picked on again. As before, he was going to fight it—with gusto. He submitted a detailed response explaining the nature of his assignment at Altaussee and how authorization had been implied. Once again, after weeks of procedural skirmishes, he was cleared, and his rank preserved.

In the meantime, in the background, ongoing efforts were being made to bring Nazi war criminals to justice. On May 2, 1945, President Harry S. Truman had appointed Associate Supreme Court Justice Robert H. Jackson as chief prosecutor for the United States in the proposed trials of the major Nazi war criminals. Truman gave Jackson discretion to choose his own staff and to establish and initiate the trials program. Jackson arrived in London in late June 1945 to negotiate an agreement for the trials with the British, the Soviets, and the French.

Less than two months later, on August 8, the United States, the Union of Soviet Socialist Republics, Great Britain, and France signed what has become known as the London Agreement, providing for prosecution of the major German war criminals by the International Military Tribunal (IMT) in Nuremberg. The constitution, jurisdiction, and functions of the IMT were set forth in an attached Charter, which provided that each signatory would exercise a prosecutorial and judicial role in the proceedings, and that the defendants would have certain basic rights. The offenses to be prosecuted were defined as Crimes against Peace, War Crimes, Crimes against Humanity, and Conspiracy to Commit each of those underlying crimes. The Charter provided that Nazi organizations could be indicted along with individual Nazi leaders.

On October 18, 1945, in Berlin (officially the IMT's headquarters), the four chief prosecutors for the Allies—Jackson (United States), Francois de Menthon (France), Roman A. Rudenko (Soviet Union), and Sir Hartley Shawcross (Great Britain)—handed down indictments against twenty-four Nazi officials, including top politicians such as Göring and Hess; highest-ranking military men, such as Wilhelm Keitel and Alfred Jodl; governors of conquered territory, such as Arthur Seyss-Inquart and Hans Frank; as well as bankers (Walther Funk); police (Ernst Kaltenbrunner); and propagandists (Julius Streicher). And the indictment named six organizations or groups as criminal: the Reich Cabinet, Leadership Corps of the Nazi Party; the SS (Schutzstaffel); the SD (Sicherheitsdienst, the SS intelligence service); the Gestapo; the SA (Sturmabteilungen); and the General Staff and High Command of the German Armed Forces.

When the trial began on November 20, 1945, only twenty-one defendants appeared in court. The elderly German industrialist Gustav Krupp was excluded based on failing health, and Nazi Party secretary Martin Bormann was tried and convicted in absentia. German Labor Front head Robert Ley committed suicide on the eve of the trial. The proceeding was presided over by Sir Geoffrey Lawrence (UK, IMT president), Francis Biddle (US), Henri Donnedieu de Vabres (France), and Iona T. Nikitschenko (USSR). The verdicts would be issued on October 1, 1946.

From the time it was established, the IMT at Nuremberg garnered much publicity around the world and dominated discussions about justice for Nazi war criminals. But, from an American perspective, it was not the only jurisdiction for the prosecution of such offenders. In fact, in Europe, the United States conducted such prosecutions under three separate jurisdictions: (1) the IMT pursuant to its Charter; (2) the US Military Tribunals at Nuremberg pursuant to Allied Control Council Law No. 10 (the so-called Subsequent Nuremberg Proceedings—covered in the chapters to come); and (3) military commissions and provost courts established by US military commands to try captured enemy personnel for precapture war crimes.[28]

Although listed last, the third jurisdiction brought perpetrators to justice first and was the one most commonly exercised by victorious Allied military commanders throughout Europe. There were on-the-fly military trials of Germans who murdered downed US pilots as early as the late spring of 1945.[29] Then, in October 1945, the *Hadamar* case was tried before a US military commission at the War Crimes Branch's headquarters in Wiesbaden, Germany.[30] Hadamar was the site of a Nazi euthanasia center not far from Frankfurt where thousands of mentally and physically disabled persons were gassed between 1941 and 1945.

The Americans first came upon the Hadamar facility in late March, not long after breaching the Siegfried Line. They wanted to try the chief administrators and medical staff of the facility for crimes against German citizens, but "war crimes" charges would not permit it—at that time, instances of persons of one nationality mass-murdering persons of the same nationality were not recognized as war crimes or offenses subject to military commission jurisdiction (this problem would be fixed with the adoption of "crimes against humanity" in the IMT Charter and Control Council Law No. 10, later in 1945). Thus, on October 8, 1945, Chief US Prosecutor Leon Jaworski, who would go on to great fame as the Watergate special prosecutor, opened the trial with charges of war crimes committed against tubercular Soviet and Polish forced laborers, who had been euthanized at the facility in the last months of the war. On October 15, 1945, the six-man US military tribunal issued guilty verdicts against all seven defendants, sentencing three of them to death by hanging.

A little less than one month later, on November 13, 1945, the Dachau Trials began (also exactly one week before the IMT proceeding started at Nuremberg, which was only about sixty-five miles up the road). This represented the first large-scale American trials program devoted to prosecuting Nazi atrocity crimes. All 489 of the inquests, charging 1,672 war crimes suspects, were held through December 1947 on the grounds of the infamous concentration camp. These were the proceedings at which the lion's share of Ben Ferencz's Third Army war crimes investigations bore fruit.

The US Army had two reasons for choosing Dachau, the Nazis' oldest concentration camp, as the site for its first large-scale war crimes trials. Most importantly, as a matter of principle, the 1943 Moscow Declaration, signed by FDR, Churchill, and Stalin, had pledged that Germans would be sent back to the countries where they had committed their crimes and "judged on the spot by the peoples whom they have outraged."[31] In other words, trials would take place at the scenes of the crimes, and Dachau was a major crime scene.[32] Second, for more practical reasons, the Dachau physical plant, with its spacious buildings and operable plumbing and heating, made for a good court facility.[33]

The concentration camp infrastructure equipment, such as machinery and workbenches, were removed, and three courtrooms—A, B, and C—were carved out of the resulting space. In turn, those courtrooms would be used for four separate categories of proceedings: (1) "parent" concentration camp trials (that is, Dachau, Mauthausen, Flossenbürg, and Buchenwald) were for the large Courtroom A; (2) subcamp trials (for example, Nordhausen, Mühldorf, and Kaufering) would be heard in the smaller Courtrooms B or C; (3) downed airmen or "flier murder" cases were also meant for the two smaller courtrooms; and (4) catch-all cases, such as the Malmédy Massacre matter, would also be tried in Courtrooms B or C.

Ben Ferencz's investigative results supported charges in case categories one through three and he was ordered to Dachau to help the prosecution team, led by Lieutenant Colonel William D. Denson, prepare. In fact, Ferencz was the staff member who hammered the sign "United States Army, War Crimes Division" over the Dachau courtroom door. He assisted however he could with trial preparations and attended some of the proceedings, including the very first one, concerning crimes committed in the Dachau concentration camp itself. This was perhaps the most seminal inquest of the program and set the stage, both in terms of substance and procedure, for the trials that followed.

All the cases were heard by a military commission—seven commissioned US Army officers appointed by the commander as well as a "law member," normally a JAG officer who advised the commission members on questions of law and procedure. In essence, the commission was a jury convened by the commander. This arrangement mirrored the structure of a general court-martial (that is, felony level court) used to try US service members at that time.

For the *Dachau* trial itself, prosecutors charged forty defendants, including camp administrators, guards, and medical personnel, with violations of the

Laws and Usages of War (such as killings, beatings, torture, starvation, abuse, and other mistreatment and indignities). There were two separate counts—one for violations committed against civilians and the other for violations committed against prisoners of war.

Lieutenant Colonel Denson, who worked tirelessly for two years in prosecuting the major concentration camp cases at Dachau, deserves great credit for how the mode of liability was charged. Instead of trying to pin specific murders, beatings, or other mistreatment on each of the forty defendants, he innovatively accused them of general perpetration of such acts as part of a "common design" when the defendants were aware of that common design. In particular, he sought to prove that, in various ways, each defendant actively participated in the enforcement of a system of repression, combined with knowledge of the system's existence and an intent to further its common design of ill-treating inmates. The strategy worked, and, after a one-month trial, all forty defendants, including camp commandant and lead defendant Martin Gottfried Weiss, as well as kapo Emil Erwin Mahl and camp doctor Claus Schilling (who infamously performed malaria experiments on prisoners) were found guilty. Thirty-six were sentenced to death by hanging.

The other major concentration camp trials—*Mauthausen, Flossenbürg,* and *Buchenwald*—were conducted pursuant to a like template and yielded similar results, with Denson, the chief prosecutor in each, racking up a 100 percent conviction rate (there were excellent outcomes for the two hundred or so "flier murder" inquests too). As the three camp trials just mentioned involved evidence collected by Ben Ferencz (as did many of the downed airmen cases), one might have anticipated his approval of the proceedings. Surprisingly, he took a dim view of them. As he later told an interviewer:

> I thought [those trials] were terrible. . . . They bore very little resemblance to a normal due process of law. . . . [T]he judges were officers with no legal training, usually, who had no better assignment. The procedures were very informal. I'm not suggesting that we tried and punished innocent people: on the contrary, they were all guilty as hell, otherwise you wouldn't have tried them in the first place. You had too many guilty ones let loose, but . . . I was not very impressed with the quality of the law work being done at Dachau.[34]

But some might view Ferencz's assessment as too harsh given what certain Holocaust justice experts have described as a "commitment to fair procedure." In particular, defendants benefited from high-quality legal representation (paid for by the Americans, when necessary), cross-examination of prosecution witnesses that was "extensive, never curtailed, . . . an opportunity to testify [or refuse to] and present defense witnesses," and rules of evidence that often tracked what "would be followed in a [US domestic] courtroom."[35] Although Ben Ferencz criticized the trials for being too summary in nature,[36] some stretched into weeks or even months.

The *Flossenbürg* trial, for example, which had fifty-two defendants, lasted from June 1946 through January 1947. Ironically, Ben Ferencz himself spent two days on the stand in that case (in July 1946) and reported a positive impression of the proceedings in a letter to his wife.[37] This favorable perception was due, in no small part, to the efforts of Lieutenant Colonel Denson, who pushed for greater due process at a time when the Pentagon was demanding swift justice. (Still there were legitimate complaints about certain trials being too summary in nature as well as lawyers representing multiple clients resulting in lack of individualized attention and potential conflicts of interest.)[38]

Regardless, the Dachau Trials marked an important step in the development of international criminal law. Apart from setting influential precedents, such as contributing toward what would become the "Joint Criminal Enterprise" doctrine via Lieutenant Colonel Denson's brilliant "common design" charging strategy, the proceedings at the site of Nazi Germany's first concentration camp meted out punishment to some of the Third Reich's most vile criminals, including Gauleiter August Eigruber (also an SS-Obergruppenführer and Landeshauptmann of Upper Austria) described in chapter 8 (found guilty at the *Mauthausen* trial) and SS-Standartenführer Joachim Peiper (found guilty in the *Malmédy Massacre* trial).

By December 1945, Ben Ferencz had earned enough points to be discharged. But the army wanted to keep him. Brigadier General Edward C. Betts, the theater judge advocate himself, wrote to him personally, praising his excellent work and promising to transfer him to higher HQ as a commissioned officer, if he wished. But the homesick sergeant refused (Jack Nowitz accepted a similar offer and returned home two years later, as a captain). Instead, Sergeant Ferencz used his remaining leave time for a ten-day Swiss vacation that featured hitchhiking, sleeping in train overhead luggage racks, palling around with a gang of smugglers, and gazing at gorgeous mountain scenery.

On his return to France, having missed his unit's scheduled homebound departure on the RMS *Queen Mary* from the port of Cherbourg, Ferencz improvised and hitchhiked to Antwerp, where he talked his way onto a battered Liberty Ship called the *Fitzhugh Lee*. Once on board, he found an unused bunk near a stairwell and settled in. During the voyage, he earned money teaching fellow soldiers how to do magic tricks (one of the cash-generating skills he had taught himself during the Great Depression to help scrape by). He also managed to send a cable to his mother, Uncle Dave, and Trudy notifying them of his expected arrival date in New York harbor. Unfortunately, the cable did not arrive before the *Queen Mary.* Sara, Dave, and Trudy were devastated to learn that Ben was not on the boat with the rest of his unit. They feared the worst. Trudy, thinking she had lost the only man she had ever loved, was inconsolable, barricading herself in her room and crying into her pillow until the arrival of Ben's telegram.

The same welcoming party as the previous day was there to greet him ecstatically at the appointed hour. He was promptly whisked away to the Bronx, where the whole clan was gathered to receive him at his mother's home. Over the next few days, he basked in the glow of familial adoration, then presented himself at Fort Dix in New Jersey on December 26, 1945. His long odyssey had begun there nearly three years before, and now it was finally coming to an end. On being discharged, he was awarded five battle stars and handed a letter with President Truman's facsimile signature expressing a grateful nation's appreciation for his service.

He could not reciprocate the sentiment. "I was glad that I had been able to do my share," he later reflected. But he looked back on all the battlefield carnage and the concentration camp horrors, mingled with the daily ordeal of unreasonable orders and demands for blind obedience, and concluded that his three years in the U.S. Army were easily the most miserable of his life. Never again, he resolved on Boxing Day 1945, did he want to witness such horrors or endure such a dehumanizing experience. He yearned for the life of a civilian in the United States. And he would soon have it—but not for long.

PART IV

PROSECUTING

10

FROM THE PENTAGON TO THE PALACE OF JUSTICE

> I seldom end up where I wanted to go, but almost always end up where I need to be.
>
> —Douglas Adams

The war was over. And Ben Ferencz was among the droves of soldiers living through the demobilization process at the end of 1945. Those being ferried back stateside were part of Operation Magic Carpet, the War Shipping Administration's effort to repatriate more than eight million American servicemen via an armada of Liberty ships, Victory ships, and troop transports. Once on American shores, these discharged GIs needed to reintegrate into the domestic economy and social fabric of a changed nation. Despite the positive economic changes brought on by the war years, memories still lingered of the trying reintegration of the Dough Boys in 1918 (amid the Spanish flu pandemic) as well as the struggles of the Great Depression in the 1930s.

Anticipating the likely challenges, the government took a proactive stance and enacted the Servicemen's Readjustment Act of 1944, commonly known as the GI Bill. To ease veterans back into the labor market as smoothly as possible, the legislation offered an unprecedented range of assistance, including unemployment compensation and help in finding jobs; funded tuition for college and vocational training; loans for homes, businesses and farms; and treatment at specialist hospitals.

On his arrival in New York at the end of 1945, Ben Ferencz sought to take full advantage of these benefits. He wanted to build a new life with Gertrude and devised a rough plan—he would begin by enrolling in school and then look for law firm jobs while earning an advanced degree—eventually, the supplemental education credential would improve prospects for subsequent employment. Within practically no time, he applied for and gained admission to Columbia Law School, where he started in the master's program (and received tuition and unemployment compensation from the GI Bill). He decided to take business law–related courses in Morningside Heights to enhance his credentials for white-shoe firms on Wall Street. Then he started putting out feelers for employment opportunities in downtown New York City.

And that's when something unexpected happened. On the stairs leading to the magnificent Beaux-Arts facade of the New York Public Library, somewhere near one of the pedestaled marble lions, as Ben was taking a break from pounding the pavement in the financial district, he ran into one of his old Harvard Law School classmates, Murray Gartner. They caught up, and Ben explained that he was back from the war and looking for a job. Murray mentioned he was clerking for US Supreme Court Justice Robert Jackson, who was then on leave in Nuremberg serving as chief US prosecutor. Ben mentioned that he had been investigating Nazi war criminals as part of his work with the Third Army Judge Advocate Section. Gartner seemed impressed, and the two exchanged contact information.

Within the week, Ben received a telegram from the Pentagon, inviting him there to discuss job prospects—at the government's expense.[1] It is possible that Murray Gartner had sent word to Jackson's office in the Pentagon that his old Harvard classmate would be an ideal person to help out in Germany. But, if so, Gartner was not the only reason for the Pentagon's interest in Ferencz. At the same time, working behind the scenes, Ben's old law school professor, Sheldon Glueck, had been pulling strings there on Ben's behalf too.[2]

The behind-the-scenes efforts yielded two interviews. The first was with the US Army, represented by Colonel David "Mickey" Marcus. His goal was to convince Ferencz that he would slot back perfectly into a prosecutor's role for the Dachau Trials. This was a tall order given Ferencz's contempt for the army and those particular proceedings, but Marcus was the ideal person to make the pitch. He was older than Ferencz, but, like Ben, he was the son of Jewish Romanian immigrants who had fled to America to escape persecution. Marcus also grew up on the mean streets of New York City, developed an interest in law enforcement, earned degrees via full-ride scholarships at West Point and Brooklyn Law School (different schools, but both he and Ben became lawyers), and, of course, he had seen combat during World War II.

But Marcus was also a larger-than-life character with an incredible range of experiences that must have impressed the younger man. Before the war, he rose to prominence as a gang-busting federal prosecutor who secured convictions against the ruthless mobster Lucky Luciano. In gratitude, Mayor Fiorella LaGuardia appointed him commissioner of corrections for New York City. In 1940, he returned to the army and, post–Pearl Harbor, served as the governor of Hawaii's executive officer, where he developed innovative jungle-fighting tactics for Pacific Theater troops. He was then sent to Europe and, on D-Day, parachuted into Normandy with the 101st Airborne Division. Later assigned to the JAG Corps, he accompanied the FDR/Truman delegations to the conferences at Yalta and Potsdam, took the lead in drafting the surrender terms for Italy and Germany, played a pivotal role in establishing the Nuremberg and Dachau Trials programs, and worked closely with General Lucius Clay in governing Berlin. Then, at the invitation of President David Ben-Gurion in 1948, he became the new state of Israel's first general and would be tragically killed by friendly fire after leading a successful defense against the fledgling nation's attackers. By the end of his life, Marcus had become a legend, and Kirk Douglas portrayed him in the 1966 Hollywood film *Cast a Giant Shadow.*

Ferencz's Pentagon encounter with him was after his work helping establish the Dachau/Nuremberg Trials programs and before he left for Israel. Then chief of the army's War Crimes Division and wholly invested in the success of the Dachau Trials, Marcus began the meeting in a very friendly manner. "Call me Mickey," he said in a warm, baritone voice. The two men shook hands, and Marcus started his pitch. There was a critical shortage of attorneys with the expertise needed to conduct war crimes trials. "Benny," he said earnestly, "we want you to go back to Germany. We'll make you a Colonel."[3] The younger man was nonplussed. "I thought he was kidding," Ferencz later wrote. With only partial sarcasm, he replied that he would only rejoin the army if there were a renewed armed conflict with Germany, and the United States was losing.

But Marcus was "a good salesman," Ferencz later recollected.[4] "Benny," he said with even more conviction, "you've been there, you've seen it—you've got to go back." So he presented a compelling counteroffer: a "simulated rank" equivalent to a full colonel, with all of its privileges, yet Ferencz could remain a civilian employee who could quit at any time. The former Third Army war crimes investigator was impressed—not only was Marcus an effective advocate, but he struck the cynical Ferencz as "a shrewd and tough cookie—my kind of guy."[5] The offer was intriguing and helped shift his frame of mind toward a possible return to Germany.

Still, there was that other appointment at the Pentagon. Mickey Marcus was representing the army. But Ben's second interview that day would be with the office that had been prosecuting the major war criminals before the International Military Tribunal (IMT) in Nuremberg, an at-large federal government initiative under the leadership of Chief US Prosecutor Robert Jackson. Ben was scheduled to speak with one of Jackson's deputies, Colonel Telford Taylor, who had been appointed to succeed Jackson in a series of "subsequent trials" that would bring to justice additional Nazi leaders in "themed" proceedings divided according to the different sectors of the Third Reich—for example, jurists, doctors, industrialists, security personnel, ministers, military commanders.

Taylor was quite a different character from Marcus. The son of an upstate New York physicist, he was descended from Elder Estabrook of the Plymouth Colony and from Edward Bellamy, the nineteenth-century author who penned the utopian romance *Looking Backward.* He had earned degrees from preppy Williams College and then Harvard Law School, where he was elected to the *Law Review* and received his LLB in 1932. Having clerked for Second Circuit Court of Appeals Judge Augustus Hand (cousin of the legendary Judge Learned Hand), he went into government service as a New Deal lawyer, working from 1933 to the early 1940s in a succession of federal offices, including the Department of the Interior, the Agricultural Adjustment Administration, the Senate Interstate Commerce Committee, the Department of Justice (where he got to know Robert Jackson), and the Federal Communications Commission.

In 1942, he received a major's commission and went into Army Intelligence, where he helped decipher secret German codes at Bletchley Park. A year later, he was promoted to lieutenant colonel and became a military attaché in the US embassy in wartime London. He was made a full colonel in 1944 and joined Jackson's staff the following year, where he distinguished himself through excellent work on one of the Nazi "criminal organization" charges—the General Staff and High Command of the German Armed Forces. With his star rising, he was ultimately tapped to succeed Jackson as chief prosecutor for the Subsequent Proceedings. And his Pentagon meeting with Ben Ferencz was part of a brief Washington, DC, trip to recruit lawyers to work on those cases.

Surprisingly, the short, feisty, Jewish Ferencz established immediate chemistry with the tall, cold, Waspish Taylor. Having checked on the latter's background, with his Harvard Law degree and distinguished career in public service, Ben was already inclined to be impressed. Of course, Taylor had also scrutinized the dossier of his fellow Harvard Law grad and even referred to the letter of recommendation from Glueck. Then he caught Ferencz off guard, breaking into the language of Molière to test his résumé claim of fluency in the Gallic tongue. "In French, he asked me to say something in French. I did, and it seemed to make a favorable impression."[6]

Then their dialogue revealed a shared sense of humor. "Your Army file indicates that you are occasionally insubordinate," Taylor said, reverting back to English. "That is not correct, Sir," Ferencz retorted. "I am not occasionally insubordinate. I am usually insubordinate." Ferencz then paused before adding, "When asked to obey orders that I know are manifestly stupid or illegal." There was another brief pause. "But I've been checking up on you too and I don't anticipate that you would give such orders."[7] Taylor could barely conceal a chuckle. The palpable, visceral connection between these two men, which would survive a baptism by fire at Nuremberg, deepen with a law partnership, and be tested again and again through McCarthyism, the civil rights movement, Vietnam, marital problems, and old age, was forged at that moment. "You come with me," Taylor said, unwittingly inviting the younger man on a life's journey rather than mere passage to Germany.

Ben could feel in his bones that this is where he was meant to go. He all but agreed, only needing to confirm it with Gertrude, he told Taylor. So he placed a call to the Bronx forthwith and got straight to the point, asking his beloved whether she would like to go to Europe for a "brief" honeymoon. "Oh," she exclaimed, "this is so sudden. I'd love it!" He took the job.

But behind the scenes, not everything was as straightforward for Gertie.[8] In interviews and in his memoirs, Ben always portrayed the relationship as a fairy-tale romance—but their liaison was far more complicated. At various junctures over the years, they had broken up and gotten back together again.[9] Ben had a strong personality, and Gertrude found herself needing to accommodate it, often at the expense of her own needs and desires. (She later told her daughter Keri that, in the relationship, it was best "to be like Jell-O—there could be no fighting with Jell-O.")[10] But she was fiercely intelligent and had serious career ambitions for herself (being an excellent student, strong with languages, and wanting to seek social justice in her own right). How much autonomy was she willing to give up on a permanent basis? Was she ready to make a lifelong commitment to putting her mate's needs and plans over her own?

Another complicating factor was the attitude of Gertie's family, especially her father. The Fried clan liked Ben but did not entirely trust him. They feared that he appreciated the opposite sex a bit too much and worried he would be, in their words, a "wolf."[11] And their suspicions were not entirely unfounded. Ben had strayed in Europe during the war. Could he be trusted to honor the lifelong commitment of marriage? Gertie confronted him about his previous dalliances, and he assured her that, once they were married, he would remain monogamous.[12]

Ultimately, it was her decision to make. And her instincts told her she could live happily ever after with this man. So, like Ben's decision to join Taylor, his invitation to Gertie for the "brief honeymoon" was about a lot more than just a trip to Germany. She would accept Ben's proposal, and, although the pledge of marital fidelity was not ultimately kept, and there would be painful moments in the relationship, she would not regret her decision. After an unanticipated delay of ten years in Germany and the birth of four children whom she adored, the Ferencz family would return to the United States, where Gertie would realize her educational dreams, ultimately qualifying as a social worker. She would also become an indispensable partner in, and steadfast supporter of, the important life work of the only man she ever loved.

So a wedding was planned in great haste. On March 31, 1946, Ben and Gertie exchanged their vows in the living room of the dwelling she had called home since she moved to the United States—the house of Eva Perlman (that is, Tante Chava). Only a few family members were present, including the steadfast Lou Perlman, who was best man. After Ben and Gertie experienced a blissful month of matrimony, the groom sailed for Germany on the fittingly named USS *General Taylor* (so dubbed in tribute to the World War I general Harry Taylor, not Ben's soon-to-be boss).

So WHY WAS Gertrude not on the boat with Ben? The relevant military regulations at that time forbade spouses from accompanying their husbands to overseas duty stations for this kind of work—she would try to find a job of her own in Germany and join him as soon as possible. In the meantime, the new bride, wearing a red coat on that cold spring morning, saw her husband off to the harbor. He sadly climbed on board the "black bucket" and then watched his beloved's crimson garment slowly fade away as the USS *General Taylor* headed out to sea. About one week later, the ship reached the continent of Ben's birth.

It had briefly dropped anchor in England before docking in Bremerhaven very late on the night of May 9. After lodging in the German port city, Ferencz left for Nuremberg and arrived on the evening of May 11. He had a quick meal at the restaurant of the assigned digs, the city's tired and fading high-end hospitality venue, the Grand Hotel (located in the town center, near the railway station), and then he enjoyed the sound sleep of an exhausted wayfarer.

The following morning, he awoke to the terrible sights that the daylight revealed—a city in utter ruins. Nuremberg had been a favorite target of Allied bombing raids not only because of its symbolic importance as the city of the annual Nazi Party rally but also because it was an important southern German transportation and infrastructure hub. The deadliest paroxysm of explosives and incendiaries had been unleashed on January 2 of the previous year, when 521 British planes released 6,000 high-payload bombs and one million fire-igniting devices on the city. In the resulting inferno, approximately 1,800 Germans lost their lives and another 100,000 their homes.

Located about one hundred miles north of Munich and serving as the capital of the north Bavarian Franconia region, Nuremberg was Bavaria's second-largest city. Long before the Nazis designated it as the preferred site for their annual party gathering, it was a town of great historical importance. Considered the "unofficial capital" of the Holy Roman Empire as early as the fourteenth century, the Imperial Diet and courts met at Nuremberg Castle, an imposing fortress on a hill overlooking the old city center. As a key crossroads for the empire, the area at the foot of the hill developed into one of Europe's most enchanting medieval enclaves, something resembling a gingerbread village, with half-timber *Fachwerk* dwellings whose lovely, framed windows sported flower boxes, gold-plated fountains, fairy-tale church spires and stone towers with arches, a maze of narrow cobblestone lanes leading to open-air markets, and single-arch masonry footbridges spanning the town's Pegnitz River. Cradle of the Northern Renaissance, this is where Albrecht Dürer painted his greatest masterpieces and Johann Pachelbel composed his Canon in D and Chaconne in F minor. It was home to some of the most prestigious guilds, including Hans Sachs's fourtheenth- to sixteenth-century league of balladeers, who were the inspiration for Richard Wagner's opera *Die Meistersinger von Nürnberg.*

Unfortunately, given its reputation as a postcard-perfect physical representation of the German First Reich (that is, the Holy Roman Empire), and as the site of the Kaiser's official castle (giving him the title of "Burgrave of Nuremberg") during the Second Reich (that is, the German Empire), the Third Reich was naturally drawn to the quaint "Volk" setting of Wagner's Renaissance-era (and antisemitic) opera. At the beginning of Hitler's rule, the Franconian capital was officially selected for the annual Nazi Party convention. But even before the Führer took power in Germany, there had been National Socialist rallies there in 1923, 1927, and 1929.

The gatherings became a fixed event every September, themed so as to trumpet some supposed Nazi "achievement" each year: "Rally of Victory" (1933, for the seizure of power); "Rally of Unity and Strength" (1934, for the consolidation of power—this one was featured in Leni Riefenstahl's documentary *Triumph of the Will*); "Rally of Freedom" (1935, compulsory military service introduced—thus, freedom from the Versailles Treaty); "Rally of Honor" (1936, for restoring "honor" via remilitarization of the Rhineland); "Rally of Labor" (1937, for the reduction in unemployment); and "Rally of Greater Germany" (1938, for the Austrian Anschluss). Ironically, the 1939 Party Congress was to be titled "Rally for Peace," but the invasion of Poland one day before its scheduled start meant it had to be scuppered.

This annual spectacle was held at the Nazi Party Rally Grounds, located in the Langwasser District, southeast of the city center and covering about eleven square kilometers, which were specially constructed to host the event. The grounds included a stadium, the Zeppelin Field tribune and grandstand, and Congress Hall. They were primarily designed by Hitler's personal architect, Albert Speer. And on them, assemblies of up to a half million fanatics would gather for multiday spectacles featuring a long stream of Nazi propaganda speeches interspersed with earsplitting Wagner overtures, rousing martial songs, banner displays, goose-step marches, human swastika formations, torchlight processions, bonfires, stunning pyrotechnic displays, and "cathedrals of light" (that is, more than one hundred anti-aircraft searchlights, at intervals of several meters, pointed skyward to form a series of vertical bars encircling the spectators).

As part of their international propaganda campaign, the Nazis generously shared these disturbing images of fascist pageantry with the world, and this, along with the Franconian capital's reputation as the place where the infamous 1935 antisemitic racial strictures (the so-called Nuremberg Laws) were promulgated, inspired the Allies to go over the top in targeting the city, carpet-bombing it and blasting it to smithereens. This cradle of National Socialism became its grave.

The ancient city's medieval walls had been almost entirely razed. The few gingerbread structures left standing inside of them now looked like they had been left in the oven for far too long. The once mighty castle became a charred, smoldering mess; the Hauptmarkt at its base, site of the city's renowned Christmas Market, annually festooned with lights, garlands, and ornaments, was now just a pile of rubble; the Rathaus (town hall) was gutted; the majestic fourteenth-century Frauenkirche was nothing more than a singed facade with a rickety skeleton behind it. Against this backdrop, forlorn women in rags navigated the debris trying to carry on some semblance of normal life. Barely clad children scurried around the ruins looking for scraps of food. Able-bodied men scooped up horse droppings for heating and fuel.

These were among the sights that would have greeted Ben Ferencz as he walked out of the Grand Hotel and emerged into the sunlight on the morning of May 11, 1946. As he soon learned, a few structures had survived the area bombing attacks, including the Grand Hotel itself (one wing of which was damaged and undergoing repairs) and the Schöner Brunnen (or Beautiful Fountain). The latter, an ornamental structure as old as the Frauenkirche, still stood in an octagonal water basin and rose proudly among the surrounding wreckage as a sixty-five-foot gilded gothic spire adorned with forty Holy Roman sculpted figures and fenced by a wrought-iron grill fastened with golden locks. One of the most beautiful of Nuremberg's prewar structures, it was now a symbol of the possible reclamation of the city's glorious past.

But there was another edifice left standing, damaged but capable of being restored, which also represented a chance to redeem Nuremberg's uncertain near future—the Palace of Justice. Constructed between 1909 and 1916 and situated in the Weststadt District, about three kilometers northwest of the old town on the other side of the Pegnitz River, it was a "large and heavily constructed complex" located on the Fürtherstrasse, the main thoroughfare running northwest of the closely adjacent city of Fürth-im-Bayern.[13] The hulking structure had been erected during the Second Reich to house the regional court of appeals, and among the rubble of the Third Reich, during the first week of July 1945, General Clay had recommended it to Robert Jackson as the site for the trial of the major Nazi war criminals. It was perfect, Clay told the chief US prosecutor, given its location in the American Zone (that is, the southern portion of Germany), in a city rife with symbolic importance for National Socialism, and it could be modified to suit their logistical needs for the trial.[14]

The Americans were able to convince the other Allied representatives, as part of the ongoing negotiations in London that summer, that the IMT trial should take place in the Franconian capital. This was over the objection of the Soviets, who wanted the proceeding in Berlin, within their own zone of occupation. Jackson cleverly negotiated around this by agreeing to designate Berlin as the Tribunal's "headquarters" (almost strictly of symbolic value), with Nuremberg as its first trial venue (other trials before a quadripartite bench were being contemplated at that time but ultimately never took place).

Otherwise, as we have seen, the June-August 1945 negotiations between the Americans, British, French, and Soviets yielded the London Agreement, attached to which was the Charter establishing the International Military Tribunal's essential features, jurisdiction, crimes, and procedures. Importantly, Articles 6, 7, and 8 of the Charter laid out the main substantive provisions, arguably representing the doctrinal birth of international criminal law.

Nearly all of the familiar concepts regarding the trial of war criminals, to which the modern world is now so well inured, are found in these three provisions: (1) per Article 6, *individual* criminal responsibility for offenses committed on behalf of the state (in the IMT's later pithy words in its Judgment, "Crimes . . . are committed by men, not by abstract entities");[15] (2) also per Article 6, the expansion of delicts beyond war crimes (broadly, mistreatment of civilians, wounded combatants, and prisoners of war) to include crimes against peace (waging of aggressive war) and, more importantly, crimes against humanity (focusing on atrocities and persecutions against a "civilian population," permitting prosecution of mass crimes committed by a government against its own people); (3) per Article 7, official position does not shield an individual from liability; and (4) per Article 8, following orders is not a defense.

Pursuant to these principles, and on charges arising from them, the four Allied prosecutors began the trial of the major Nazi war criminals on November 20, 1945. Sitting in the dock that morning, and listening to the reading of the indictment, were Hermann Göring (Reichsmarschall and Hitler's second in command), Rudolf Hess (Nazi Party deputy leader), Joachim von Ribbentrop (foreign minister), Wilhelm Keitel (chief of the Armed Forces High Command), Wilhelm Frick (minister of the interior), Ernst Kaltenbrunner (chief of the Reich Main Security Office), Hans Frank (governor-general of occupied Poland), Konstantin von Neurath (governor of Bohemia and Moravia and prewar minister of foreign affairs), Franz von Papen (prewar vice chancellor and wartime ambassador); Walther Funk (minister of economics); Hjalmar Schacht (prewar Reichsbank president and minister of economics); Erich Raeder (navy grand admiral), Karl Dönitz (Raeder's successor), Alfred Jodl (chief of the operations staff of the Armed Forces High Command), Alfred Rosenberg (head of the Reich Ministry for the Occupied Eastern Territories), Baldur von Schirach (Gauleiter and Reichsstatthalter of Vienna and head of the Hitler Youth), Hans Fritzsche (head of the Propaganda Ministry's Radio Division); Julius Streicher (editor in chief of the radical Nazi antisemitic newspaper *Der Stürmer*), Fritz Sauckel (general plenipotentiary for labor deployment), Albert Speer (minister of armaments and war production), and Arthur Seyss-Inquart (Reichskommissar of the Occupied Netherlands).

The next day, after the defendants entered pleas of "not guilty" (*nicht schuldig*), Robert Jackson approached the lectern to make the trial's initial opening statement and delivered one of the great orations in world history. He began by clarifying that the focus of the justice enterprise was prosecuting aggressive war: "The privilege of opening the first trial in history for crimes against the peace of the world imposes a grave responsibility." Then he put the stakes of that enterprise into perspective: "The wrongs which we seek to condemn and punish have been so calculated, so malignant, and so devastating that civilization cannot tolerate their being ignored because it cannot survive their being repeated." However, he reminded his audience, the fact that the defendants were being granted a trial was a significant watershed in global affairs: "That four great nations, flushed with victory and stung with injury, stay the hand of vengeance and voluntarily submit their captive enemies to the judgment of the law is one of the most significant tributes that Power has ever paid to Reason."[16]

After acknowledging that the Tribunal was "novel" but geared toward the practical end of seeking justice via international law, he shone the spotlight on the defendants themselves. "The common sense of mankind demands that law shall not stop with the punishment of petty crimes by little people," he noted. "It must also reach men who possess themselves of great power and make deliberate and concerted use of it to set in motion evils which leave no home in the world untouched." Then he concerned himself with these specific defendants:

> Merely as individuals their fate is of little consequence to the world. What makes this inquest significant is that these prisoners represent sinister influences that will lurk in the world long after their bodies have returned to dust. We will show them to be living symbols of racial hatreds, of terrorism and violence, and of the arrogance and cruelty of power. . . . Civilization can afford no compromise with the social forces which would gain renewed strength if we deal ambiguously or indecisively with the men in whom those forces now precariously survive.[17]

Jackson later confronted the critique of "victor's justice" and implored the Tribunal to be "fair and temperate" even in minor matters because the "worldwide scope of the aggressions carried out by these men has left but few real neutrals."[18]

The balance of the opening statement is full of other soaring rhetoric, but, in the main, it laid out the substance of the Americans' case, which would focus on Count 1 of the Indictment, that is, the Common Plan or Conspiracy to commit the substantive crimes (the British would handle Count 2, Crimes against Peace; the French and Soviets, Count 3, War Crimes, and Count 4, Crimes against Humanity). Interestingly, in alluding to "undeniable proofs of incredible events" and a "catalog of crimes [that] will omit nothing that could be conceived by a pathological pride, cruelty, and lust for power," he cited to evidence of mass slaughter committed by special Nazi paramilitary murder squads known as Einsatzgruppen. These units followed the Wehrmacht into conquered Soviet territory and murdered perceived enemies of the Third Reich, primarily Jews, Roma and Sinti, and Communist functionaries.

Jackson specified that in "Vitebsk, 3,000 Jews were liquidated because of the danger of epidemics. In Kiev 33,771 Jews were executed on September 29 and 30 [this was the massacre at Babi Yar] in retaliation for some fires which were set off there. In Zhitomir 3,145 Jews had to be shot because, judging from experience, they had to be considered as the carriers of Bolshevik propaganda."[19] Indeed, as part of the prosecution's case-in-chief, Otto Ohlendorf would later testify before the Tribunal that his unit, Einsatzgruppe D, murdered 90,000 innocent men, women, and children, primarily Jews, in southern Ukraine between June 1941 and June 1942.[20]

The Allied prosecution teams presented evidence such as this, as well as compelling proof of aggression and war crimes, for several months, through the first week of March 1946. On March 8, the defense cases began, and through the end of the first part of May the Tribunal heard testimony from Göring, Ribbentrop, Kaltenbrunner, Frank, Streicher, Schacht, Funk, and Dönitz. It was after Dönitz testified that Ben Ferencz arrived in Nuremberg. And after surveying the rubble that Sunday upon his arrival, he made his way to the Palace of Justice on Monday, May 13, where he met the American prosecution staff and received a letter from Justice Jackson, stating that he was a member of his team and should be accorded all the privileges enjoyed by other American prosecution lawyers (an International Military Tribunal, OCC [Office, Chief of Counsel] identification card—Pass No. 4564—was issued to him a couple days later, on May 15, 1946).

Ben took a tour of the premises and was given an overview of the progress of the IMT proceeding to that point. In a letter to Gertrude, he marveled at "Justice Jackson's tremendous organization," which he described as being "about 25 times the size of the Third Army group." He added that "they have really done an amazing job of assorting and organizing documentary material."[21] As part of his orientation over the next couple of months, he attended several trial sessions during the period when the Tribunal was hearing the defense cases of Raeder, von Schirach, Sauckel, Jodl, Seyss-Inquart, von Papen, and Speer. The place was a hive of activity and energy. "The enormity of it all," he wrote to Gertrude, "stems from its international aspects." The four major powers "have complete staffs here, including counsel, research and document men, interpreters, investigators, etc. Then I guess a thousand other nations have representatives and the press of the world is also present. So it makes a very interesting multitude, not to mention the hundreds of guards."[22]

Apart from orientation and watching portions of the IMT trial, Ben Ferencz's initial few weeks in Nuremberg were devoted to adjusting to life in the bombed-out city. Unfortunately, he and the other new Subsequent Proceedings Division (SPD) recruits were not long for the Grand Hotel, which was being requisitioned as billets exclusively for transiting high-rank officers. When he first learned about his imminent eviction, Ferencz was depressed about leaving the Grand, which had offered "excellent meals, floor show and all the modern improvements of a large New York hotel."[23]

As luck would have it, though, he was soon offered excellent alternative lodgings—four other SPD lawyers, including Drexel Sprecher and Alexander Hardy, had found a place on the other side of the Pegnitz, in Fürth, and invited him to become the fifth occupant. The proposed lodgings, essentially a "villa" located on the Lindenstrasse, about ten miles from the Palace of Justice, made for "an excellent home with several baths, dining rooms, large living room and all the comforts of a cozy mansion."[24] In a letter to Gertrude, he humorously described his "married man" interaction with his unattached new housemates:

> The four gentlemen . . . desire to have as a housemate one who would not be shocked at their carryings on or one who would not be surprised to see a strange face around the house at strange hours. . . . I explained that, though I was of liberal mind, I was most desirous of leading a chaste and simple existence, that my only purpose in living anywhere was to be with you. Undaunted, they insisted and I, weak creature, accepted. [So I will] move from my secluded hotel room to a den of quiet iniquity. Ye who have prayers to say, prepare to say them now![25]

Apart from his bridegroom "fish out of water" presence in this large "bachelor pad," his biggest concern was food supply. Ferencz's new house was not designated as a "mess" so, according to army regulations, no army-supplied victuals could be obtained. Sustenance could be had from the Grand Hotel, but Ben and his housemates did not have a vehicle to pick it up.

So the wily former supply clerk from Hell's Kitchen came to the rescue. The first order of business was securing transportation. He made his way to the nearest army motor pool and explained his situation to the sergeant on duty. The latter told him that he could not help as the "table of organization" contained no vehicles for civilians employed by the SPD. But Ferencz would not be so easily deterred. At the back of the motor pool, he spotted a German command car that looked like an oversized jeep with a nine-passenger capacity. When he inquired as to whom the strange looking megajeep had been assigned, the sergeant explained it was captured booty and could not be allocated to any US soldier. Ferencz countered that he was a civilian and would be willing to take "the heap" off his hands. With some relief, the duty sergeant agreed. Ferencz thanked him for his "ingenuity" and drove off in his new Nazi command car.

Step two was about getting his new dwelling designated as a mess. This proved to be somewhat messy. At first, he only wanted enough food to feed five, and this is what he forthrightly admitted to the friendly sergeant at his next stop—the Quartermaster Depot. But the man informed him that "There has to be a minimum of twenty-five. I can't help you."[26] Some awkward small talk ensued, through which Ben discovered that the sergeant would be going off duty in about a half hour and would be replaced by a corporal. Ben thanked the sergeant for his trouble, wished him well, and then left. After driving around for thirty minutes, he returned and reinitiated his mess application with the corporal.

This time, the persona of Private Benny Ferencz, 115 AAA supply clerk formerly of 346 West Fifty-Sixth Street, Manhattan, submitted the request. When it came to the question about how many men were to be fed, he was ready with a Machiavellian reply in his thick New York accent: "Well it's a new mess and the number varies. Let's take the minimum of twenty-five and if I need more, I'll come back." It worked. And now his Hell's Kitchen brain kicked into overdrive. He would have sufficient surpluses, he reckoned, to manage trades with nearby farmers, offering genuine American canned goods in exchange for fresh fruits, vegetables, and eggs, a real luxury in spring 1946 Germany.

But it got better—mess privileges also came with a beer ration, which would have to be picked up directly from the local brewery. Ben's new household only needed beer for four men (as the former supply clerk himself did not partake)—a quantity meant for twenty-five far exceeded their demand. But the crafty Ferencz was already scheming about how to deal with the excess. He located the *Bierstube* closest to their Lindenstrasse quarters and struck a bargain with the proprietor. Ferencz asked the brewery to deposit his kegs at this neighborhood beer garden, which could keep half of it for its own use. The proprietor, in return, would bottle the beer and put it on ice pending pickup and transportation of the other half by the newly procured Nazi command car.

Hard liquor could be purchased by Americans for fifty cents a bottle at the PX, but, Ferencz noticed, they could never find enough beer, the locally preferred alcohol. So having spotted a great business opportunity, he devised something he called the "Benny Beer Distribution System." Per his later account: "If any of my friends . . . urgently needed a few cases of beer, all they had to do was phone me. . . . I [then] phoned my partner at the local bistro and authorized him to hand over a set number of cases. . . . Soon I had a great reputation. My initial fame came not for my skill as a lawyer but for my mysterious ability to provide unlimited quantities of free beer."[27]

And the "Benny" beer flowed freely at parties in and around Ferencz's new villa lodgings. As it happened, Justice Jackson and most of his top staff working on the IMT trial, including Press Officer Gordon Dean, Executive Officer Robert Gill, Executive Trial Counsel Robert Storey and Thomas Dodd, as well as Associate Counsel John Harlan Amen (Ohlendorf's examiner during the trial), and Assistant Trial Counsel Whitney Harris lived as well in villas on the Lindenstrasse, not far from Ferencz. Also in the vicinity were prominent IMT lawyers such as Associate Counsel Telford Taylor himself and Sidney Alderman, who lived a few blocks away on the Schwedenstrasse. Jackson and his team, as well as Taylor and his, including certain lawyers who worked on both the IMT and Subsequent Trials, like Drexel Sprecher and Robert Kempner, would attend these shindigs. It was at such mixers that Ben Ferencz had the chance to speak with Robert Jackson at greater length and gain a greater appreciation for his dedication to the work in which they were all engaged.

But as spring transitioned to summer, Telford Taylor had less and less time for parties. He was still fulfilling his duties as a member of Jackson's IMT staff while ramping up the activities of his own team to prepare for the prosecution of additional Nazi war criminals. On May 17, 1946, about a week after Ben Ferencz's arrival in Nuremberg, Taylor issued "Subsequent Proceedings Division Organizational Memo No. 1." The Subsequent Proceedings Division, the name of Taylor's operation under Jackson's aegis, would become the Office, Chief of Counsel for War Crimes (OCCWC, under the jurisdiction of the Office of the Military Government of the United States, or OMGUS) in October of 1946, once Jackson resigned and Taylor took over as chief counsel.

In the memo, Taylor informed his legal staff that they would be divided into six teams: (1) the "Registry Group" (tasked with compiling a "register" of "leading German personalities," that is, those most responsible in each Reich enterprise or government activity);[28] (2) the "Military Group"; (3) the "SS/Doctors Group"; (4) the "German Foreign Office Group"; (5) "Industrialists Group No. 1," covering the general structure of German industry and finance; and (6) "Industrialists Group No. 2," which would handle the investigations of the Krupp AG Armaments Firm and the chemical concern IG Farben, the manufacturers of Zyklon B, the toxic substance used to murder millions of Jews in the gas chambers. This team, under the direction of James Heath, included Benjamin Ferencz.[29]

Pursuant to Organizational Memo No. 2, of June 25, 1946, a Legal and Research Staff was set up, which, among other tasks, would prepare the necessary orders for establishment of Zonal Courts and their procedures—this was eventually codified in Military Government Ordinance No. 7. Additionally, an "Interrogation Section" was formed.[30] Taylor would also later create an "Evidence Division" into which the Interrogation Section would be folded and to which to new units would be added—an "Apprehension and Locator Section" and a "Document Control Section." The office would also form a "Service Segment" with the Administrative, Reproduction, Signal (communications equipment) and Language Divisions. There was also a "Public Information Office" and a "Special Projects Division"—the latter being the idea of Ben Ferencz (see chapter 14). (A Publications Division would later be added.)

Apart from assigning Ferencz to "Industrialists Group No. 2," the May 17 memo was noteworthy for concluding that "The organization of the Subsequent Proceedings Division will be kept flexible and will from time to time be adapted to changing circumstances and the arrival of new personnel."[31] Indeed, Ben's role would change several times over the next two years. For someone who had cut his teeth on flier-murder and concentration camp cases, his first assignment meant gaining expertise in a hitherto unknown area—the criminality of Nazi industrial titans. In fact, although Ferencz was wont to tell audiences that his Nuremberg career had three main parts—heading the Berlin Branch, prosecuting the *Einsatzgruppen* case, and serving as Taylor's executive counsel—there were in fact two other important stages of his 1946–48 Nuremberg experience that both relate to this work on the industrialist cases: investigating Krupp and IG Farben upon his arrival and serving as a courtroom attorney when the *Krupp* defendants were being prosecuted.

Significantly, in a May 24, 1946, letter to Gertie, he explained how vital he sensed his work was on the Nazi industrialist investigations:

> You know we are now busy trying to prove that IG Farben and Krupp and their officials should be hung as war mongers and murderers. It is very interesting going into the details of the organization and finding out how efficiently these sinister forces operated. I'm sure we'll be able to prove that they desired and planned for war and that they headed the looting of foreign industries as well as used concentration camp inmates for their experiments on poison gases, etc. And these are the distinguished white-collar gentlemen of finance. . . . I feel a certain satisfaction in the work as though we are groping for the roots of war causes. And perhaps we may move a little closer thereby toward permanent peace.[32]

His lines of inquiry led him to various parts of the German-speaking world, including Vienna, Linz, and Frankfurt. In a June 15, 1946, memorandum addressed in humorous Teutonic fashion to the respective Industrialists Group leaders ("Lieber Jim [Heath] und/oder [Drexel] Sprecher"), Ferencz summarized the results of his Frankfurt investigation (conducted with Esther Glassman, who had transferred to Industrialist Group No. 2 in June). It is quite revealing of his ingenuity, guile, hard work, and humor:

> Lest it be thought that I have expired in the gutters of Frankfurt, I am making . . . a report of activities since we parted company. For a few days, Miss Glassman and I waded and wobbled through the personal files of the now notorious [Hermann] Schmitz [IG Farben CEO and an eventual convicted defendant in the *IG Farben* trial]. This revealed many delightful photographs of his childhood and family life . . . dentist bills, insurance receipts and sundry similar disillusions.

> "This," I thought, "will never do." Yet the 5 buildings of Farben files did not invite my probing. It behooved me thereupon to call a meeting of the I.G. Farben Board and discuss my problems with them. Inasmuch as most of these gentlemen are now unavailable, for obvious reasons, I had to be content with the presence of a Dr. Kugler, Director of Chemicals and Dyes, a Dr. Struss, head of the Tea-Bureau (Technical) and [the] head of the financial and statistics department.
>
> I carefully explained to these gentlemen that I was from Nooorember'g, letting it roll significantly off my tongue. . . . Somehow the idea became prevalent that if they played ball in the right way, they might possibly be the new top men in their beloved industrie [*sic*]. (So help me I made no promises!) The effect was most amazing.
>
> Before I could say "Heil Hitler" these 3 characters start bringing me the most amazing reports. Complete lists of the contributions of Farben to the Nazi organizations . . . statistics on the use of slave labor, lists of companies financed jointly by Farben and the Wehrmacht, the periodic rise in Farbens [*sic*] assets lists, [and a] complete report on [Farben] acquisitions . . . in German occupied territory. . . . While perusing Schmitz's 100 folders of little notes I also found a chart showing the rise of his personal and family wealth, and congratulations from Goring [*sic*], Goebbels, Ribbentrop, Keitel, etc. etc. (Hitler sent an autographed photo) on his 60th birthday.[33]

Results like this were earning Ben Ferencz a sterling reputation in Nuremberg, even more so than his beer distribution scam. But the latter was an important part of his social life, which he valued greatly during those early days, while separated from Gertrude. Of great satisfaction was the quality time he was spending with his immediate supervisor, Jim Heath, as well as one of the other team leaders, Werner Peiser (Registry Group), and his wife. These three were becoming fast friends, and Ben described a memorable outing they had in his Nazi command car to the nearby countryside, where they visited the picturesque town of Rothenberg: "As we crossed the heavy cobblestones approaching the city, we passed beneath the massive arches of the outer wall. . . . The old moat was now dry and so we rolled on to the inner wall with its winding stairway to the top where, once, metal-laden warriors waited for the spears of the enemy. It was as something from a 16th century novel to find this little city so well preserved with its ancient and quaint structures."[34]

Apart from work and socializing, he was distracting himself through two different side projects. One was to help his cousin Tibor "Tibby" Legman, who had been a US serviceman in Europe during the war but had run afoul of the law and was now being detained in Giessen, Germany (near Frankfurt), awaiting court-martial. In a letter to Gertie, he described Tibby's dire circumstances: "This morning I traveled out to Giessen. . . . He was in a little pen and the conditions were terrible, . . . the seriousness of this situation cannot be overestimated. I have been running around wildly to every colonel or general in the JA section who could possibly help. It looks pretty bad. And the only recourse now is Washington. It means that I will have to write all kinds of briefs and appeals. And even then I don't know how much good I can do."[35]

But his interventions did help, and Tibby was eventually spared a court-martial—dishonorably discharged and allowed to return to the United States. At the same time, Ben was also trying to help extended members of his wife's family. Her cousins Erna and Julie were in Displaced Persons camps, dreading the prospect of being sent back to Romania. In a June 3, 1946, letter to his spouse, he explained that he had "received assurances that no one will be sent back to their origin unless they want to go. . . . I'll try to do something more concrete as soon as I can."[36] Her relatives eventually made it into the American Zone and later found passage to the United States.

He also returned to Dachau in July to testify in the *Flossenbürg* case. In another letter to Gertie, he described his positive impressions of the experience: "I was on the stand for two days, gave them hell, had a lot of fun and met many old friends. There was much excitement over my testimony, as I described the scenes of death in my disinterring dozens of murdered souls. The accused, all 52, howled. But it won't help them. The trial should be over in a few weeks. And I will see if I have contributed to the cause."[37]

Of greater concern to Ben, though, was the question of how to arrange for his wife to join him in Germany. In his many missives to her during this period, he poured out his heart, letting her know how dearly he missed her. His chief priority in life, he emphasized again and again, was arranging for them to be reunited. Toward that end, he wrote many letters of introduction on her behalf, to be used for securing interviews in the nation's capital.

And Gertie had legitimate prospects, having taken night courses at Hunter College, studied German, and become a proficient stenographer and typist. She and Nancy Fenstermacher, the wife of one of Ben's fellow SPD colleagues, Ted, went on a job-hunting trip to Washington, DC. Nancy, a Vassar College graduate and, like Gertie, proficient in German, steno, and typing, was the source of invaluable moral support (and would later make a significant contribution to Ben's team when he prosecuted the *Einsatzgruppen* case).

Gertie and Nancy presented a united job-seeking front at the Pentagon and other government agencies in Washington, DC. Unfortunately, neither was able to land a gig in Germany—both becoming finalists for secretarial jobs but never passing the rigorous typing tests. In the end, they had to wait until regulations changed and made it possible for dependents to join their husbands in duty stations overseas. That change took place later in the summer. And by then, Ben Ferencz's job description was about to undergo a fundamental change as well.

11

THE BERLIN BRANCH

Our honeymoon will shine our life long: its beams will only fade over your grave or mine.

—Charlotte Brontë, *Jane Eyre*

As it happened, while Gertrude Ferencz was preparing to embark on a ship to cross the Atlantic and join her husband at long last, the latter was being considered for promotion. His outstanding work on the Nazi industrialist cases was paying off. Ben told her via letter dated August 14, 1946, that the Subsequent Proceedings Division (SPD) was setting up a "Berlin Branch" to scour bombed-out Nazi government buildings for evidence, and "none other than Mrs. Ferencz's husband has been appointed as chief of the branch."[1] There would be from twenty to forty persons working for him, he explained, "and I have no doubt that my troubles will be multiplied from 20 to 40 times. It is a big responsibility, though a very flattering one."[2] SPD branch offices would also operate in Frankfurt, Paris, and Washington, DC.

Of these off-site branches, the one in Berlin would be the "primary satellite," given its location as the former Nazi capital and thus its breadth and variety of captured document collections.[3] The office would also serve as OCCWC's OMGUS liaison. In assigning young Ferencz to run this pivotal unit, the prosecutors in Nuremberg were giving him a great vote of confidence. As he explained it to Gertie in an August 15 letter: "I have discovered the tricks they're playing with me now. I am chief troubleshooter. And when they have a particularly tough nut, I am sent to crack it. I wouldn't be a bit surprised to find out that once the Berlin branch is organized and running smoothly, they will find another major problem for my so-called talents."[4]

The problem was that he was not sure his wife would be receiving these letters before shoving off. And, in fact, she did not. He knew the important details regarding her passage, however. She would be sailing on the US Army Transport Ship *Willard A. Holbrook* and arriving in Bremerhaven during the first week of September. On board with her would be Nancy Fenstermacher and Betty King, the wife of fellow OCCWC prosecutor Henry King. (Gertrude had written to Ben that she did not care for Mrs. King, and he reassured her that she should feel no guilt over it: "The opinion you expressed about her is the same one I feel for her husband. There's little love here, so don't go out of your way on the boat to be her bosom buddy.")[5]

Ben officially transferred to Berlin, on Saturday, August 17, 1946, hopping on a plane only hours after writing his last letter to Gertrude addressed to her Bronx residence. He was dubious that she would receive it before her departure so Ben had been tracking the Holbrook's progress and resolved to be at the Bremerhaven port when it docked. But there was a serious obstacle—infernal army regulations (his hated enemy for nearly four years) forbade husbands from being at the Hanseatic seaport when the vessel arrived. Still, Ben Ferencz had spent nearly four years honing the high art of flouting army regulations—he would put his refined skills to the test once again.

His feint on this occasion was to notify the Berlin Military Command of probable cause as to the presence of wanted Nazi malefactors in Bremerhaven and thereby induce issuance of orders to proceed to the German port city "to arrest any war crimes suspects."[6] Once he arrived at water's edge, orders in hand, he was stopped at a Military Police checkpoint. The fraudulently obtained orders were produced, and Ben requested the MP on duty issue him a special security pass so he could board the ship. Toward that end, Gertrude's husband was asked for his name, office, purpose, and the name of the person to be removed from the ship. When the MP realized that the surnames of the identified war crimes suspect and war crimes investigator matched, a chary eyebrow was raised. But Ben assured the man that "it was a secret operation and it was OK."[7] The pass was issued, and Ben drove onto the dock. The *Holbrook* was tied to the pier as he sauntered toward the gangplank. Then a cry went out from a gaggle of excited wives leaning over the rail, "It's Benny! It's Benny!" they shouted. The cunning saboteur of army regulations smiled and waved. The ladies cheered even more ecstatically.

Mr. Ferencz later discovered that Mrs. Ferencz, who had been regaled for years with countless anecdotes about her husband's deviance vis-à-vis the army, had assured the other wives, who were well aware of the regulations and had no hopes of seeing their own husbands at the dock, that her man would be there waiting for her. Many of them had placed bets on show versus no-show and had been waiting anxiously to see if the diminutive Nuremberg lawyer would appear. The no-show wagers were being paid as Gertie's spouse "galloped up the gangplank amid hurrahs and slaps and hugs from all the ladies."[8] Mrs. Ferencz rushed toward him and fell into his arms "amid laughter, tears, and kisses—until spotted in amorous embrace by the Captain of the ship."[9]

"Who let that man on board?" the skipper thundered. Ben produced his Berlin orders and the MP pass. "That's not worth the paper it's written on," he hollered. That was followed by, "Get that man off my ship!" With two "glowering MP giants" hovering over him, Ben was frog-marched back down the gangplank. Before slinking off, however, he was able to warn Gertie not to go to Nuremberg and said that he would meet her at the Berlin Bahnhof (train station).[10]

Then it was Round 2 of Ferencz vs. Army. Given his eleventh-hour transfer to Berlin as Gertrude was first boarding the *Holbrook*, he was told that it had been too late to change her transport destination from Nuremberg to Berlin. She would first have to be taken by train to the Franconian capital, processed there, and then given rail passage to the former Nazi capital. But Ben was willing to bet against army inefficiency in favor of army incompetence. He had been informed that Gertrude and her luggage were on a train en route to Nuremberg. But that report itself may have been the product of bungled tracking. He reckoned it was worth a trip to the Bahnhof to see if incompetence trumped inefficiency.

He imagined the odds were slightly in favor of inefficiency, so he rather glumly took in the sights and sounds of the special celebration that the Berlin Command had prepared for this first arrival of wives. The station was festooned with American flags, and every soldier awaiting his loved one was assigned a car and driver to take them home. A military band was in place and ready to break into festive marches upon the train's arrival. Ben stood dejectedly on the platform as the train chugged into the station and the band broke into its tunes. Still, his head "kept turning like a spectator at a tennis match as the windows of each car came and drifted by."[11] Suddenly, to his "surprise and delight," there was Gertrude "standing in the train's doorway, shouting, and waving furiously." Incompetence had indeed triumphed over inefficiency. He and his Berlin Branch chief-chauffeur brought the recent bride home to the new "little villa" her husband had recently scouted out in the Dahlem neighborhood, in the southeastern portion of the bombed-out city. Gertrude's luggage was delivered the next day. "Finally," he wrote, "our honeymoon began."[12]

But its start was none too idyllic. On the train from the port town to her new city of residence, Gertrude was first introduced to the desolate, postapocalyptic landscape of war-ravaged 1946 Germany. She had never witnessed anything like the cratered and scarred topography, the blasted edifices, or the despondent, hollowed-out faces moving zombie-like across these scenes of devastation. What she saw on entering Berlin was even worse. The city's people had been "slowly starving to death in horrific conditions that included a relentless bombing campaign by the Allied air forces."[13] A once proud metropolis, Berlin had been "reduced to smoking rubble." Its residents struggled "merely to survive another day" and had been subjected to the "collective wrath of the Russians," which amounted to an "entirely uncharted sphere of a mass psychosis of horrific savagery." German women, all civilians ranging from very young to old, had been "gang raped, mutilated, humiliated and then frequently murdered by Red Army soldiers."[14] Apart from the visual evidence of destruction, the stench of these evil deeds still hung over the city and rudely greeted Gertrude Ferencz upon her arrival. From Bremerhaven to Berlin, she did not stop crying.

Unfortunately, she would need to remain in this desolate place indefinitely—the "honeymoon" could involve no travel at first as her husband was working overtime to get the new Berlin Branch up and running. Its location was not ideal—a shabby floor in the Harnack House in the US occupation sector of southwest Berlin (in the Dahlem district—not far from where he lived). Ferencz later recollected that "the Harnack House had been bombed, had been destroyed. And there were broken chairs."[15] So soon after arriving, he telephoned the responsible US military officer, a general, and said, "I want you to come over here right away. I'm here on orders of the President of the United States [his usual ruse]." And the man said, "Yes, sir."[16]

In the interim, Ferencz found a photograph of President Harry S. Truman lying on the floor, in a broken frame. He removed the photo and wrote on it, "From your friend, Harry."[17] He then patched up the frame as best he could, placed it on the wall behind his desk, and, when the officer in charge arrived, invited him to rest his rump on a chair with no legs or back—the general could thus only tilt back while seated. The photo was strategically placed in a spot where the man would have no choice but to peer at it, and its new inscription. Ben recalled what happened next: "I said, 'Look at this place!' I said, 'I'm here on orders of the President and we've got a big problem. We can't work in a place like this. Chairs are broken . . . everything else.' And I put him in a chair and he's looking right up at Truman. . . . So, he got us a whole building next to General [Lucius] Clay! [then the US deputy military governor]."[18]

Ferencz had outfoxed the US Army again, and it earned his new branch an office in prime Berlin real estate—the Armed Forces Building. General Clay's headquarters were located on Kronprinzenallee in Berlin-Zehlendorf—part of an 85,000-square-meter multibuilding complex erected between 1935 and 1937.[19] It was from here that General Clay directed the rebuilding of the city and played a central role during the Soviet blockade of Berlin and the 1948–49 Berlin Airlift, which alleviated its consequences. It had been one of the few capital city structures damaged only slightly during World War II and offered

Ferencz's team a set of clean suites with intact furniture. In no time, the former artillery battalion clerk had requisitioned office supplies, filing cabinets and typewriters.

His next order of business was finding the proper personnel to fill the new space. This proved to be more of a challenge. Some, such as Ferencz himself, had transferred from Nuremberg. Others had to be recruited locally based on familiarity with the German language as well as German history and bureaucracy. An organizational chart from the early days of the Berlin Branch (approximately September 1946) shows a total of twenty-nine staff, including Ferencz himself.[20] By the end of the year, an updated chart reveals a significant personnel increase—twenty-eight additional staff added for a total of fifty-seven.

The December organizational chart is also revealing in terms of the scope of the branch's functions. It roughly divides into three sections: (1) Office of the Chief; (2) Thematic Investigations; and (3) Clerical. The Office of the Chief consisted of Ferencz, a secretary, and a "Liaison Officer"—Lieutenant Colonel William Wuest (the point person for US military interactions). The Clerical section, divided into three subsections—Documents Processing, Legal Clerical, and Administrative and Personnel—provided administrative and research assistant support and was not insubstantial, at twenty-one employees. The "research assistant" function resided in the "Documents Processing" subsection, which had a "Research Analyst" sub-subsubsection and included Gertrude Ferencz (who seemed to focus on industrialist cases and eventually became a dedicated analyst for the *IG Farben* case).

But the bulk of the Berlin Branch personnel consisted of investigators (thirty-four), each of whom was placed in one of the "thematic" subsections: (1) SS Division; (2) Economics Division; and (3) Ministries Division. Many of the investigators in these units were native German speakers who were also proficient in English. As Telford Taylor himself explained, "Most of the documentary evidence was German, so that [many of the American] attorneys . . . were helpless unless assisted by analysts and research workers who were qualified, both linguistically and by general education and intelligence, to screen extensive files and other large collections of documents and select such as were or might be relevant evidence."[21] Therefore, most of these investigators "were highly qualified; the Ministries Division, for example, required not only fluency in German and knowledge of French but also knowledge of Nazi history, legal experience plus a knowledge of 'international law,' and 'acquaintance with criminal investigation techniques.'"[22]

Exemplary of this was the Berlin Branch's Ministries Division chief, Ossip

Flechtheim, the eventual founder of the influential school of "Futurology." In 1909, Flechtheim had been born into a Jewish family near Odessa, in what is now Ukraine. His mother was Russian, but the family soon moved to his father's birth country, Germany, and the multilingual Flechtheim studied law and political science at universities in Freiburg, Heidelberg, Paris, and Berlin, under eminent professors such as Edmund Husserl. He passed the state law examination in Düsseldorf in 1931 and was employed by the German civil service. Three years later, he obtained a doctorate in Cologne for a thesis on Hegel's criminal theory (after Nazi legal theorist Carl Schmitt refused to supervise him on antisemitic grounds). Having been dismissed from the civil service on the NSDAP's ascension to power, he was arrested in 1935 and fled to Switzerland before emigrating to the United States in 1939. Postwar, he returned to Germany and joined the Berlin Branch, where, among other accomplishments, he took the lead in investigating Carl Schmitt and having him arrested.[23]

The work performed by investigators such as Flechtheim was efficient because the investigative divisions in the branch offices mirrored the SPD trial divisions that were forming in Nuremberg while the IMT trial was wrapping up. That proceeding closed on August 31, 1946, as Ben Ferencz was settling into his new role in Berlin. During the month of September, the judges retired to chambers to discuss the evidence, and they announced their verdict on October 1. Eleven of the twenty-one defendants were sentenced to death. Three defendants received terms of life in prison—Rudolf Hess, Erich Raeder, and Walther Funk. Karl Dönitz (ten years), Konstantin von Neurath (fifteen years), Baldur von Schirach (twenty years), and Albert Speer (twenty years) each received prison sentences of less than life. The Tribunal acquitted the remaining three defendants—Hans Fritzsche, Franz von Papen, and Hjalmar Schacht. The IMT also declared that four of the charged groups—the Nazi Leadership Corps, the Gestapo, the SD, and the SS—were criminal while not reaching that conclusion with regard to the others: the Reich Cabinet, the German General Staff and High Command, and the SA (Sturmabteilung—Storm Division).

The death sentences were largely viewed as condign retribution for the most culpable defendants, such as Göring and Kaltenbrunner, while the prison sentences and acquittals of the other defendants created an impression within the international community of individualized and well-considered justice. At the same time, the IMT's judgment upheld the principles elucidated in its Charter. Aspersions of "victors' justice" were still being cast on the proceeding but, in general, it ended on a high note.

On October 11, the sentences were confirmed by the Allied Control Council, and, five days later, those defendants sentenced to death were hanged in the prison's gymnasium (Hermann Göring evaded the headman's rope by committing suicide via a smuggled cyanide pill only hours before his scheduled execution). The following day, October 17, Robert Jackson resigned as chief of counsel, and exactly one week later, Telford Taylor was appointed to replace him by General Joseph McNarney, the US military governor.

By this point, Taylor had the newly renamed Office, Chief of Counsel for War Crimes (OCCWC) running on all cylinders. Again, vis-à-vis the Berlin Branch's investigative organizational chart, the trial teams in Nuremberg, which were a "divisions" mirror, had come into focus. The SS Division—both in Nuremberg (where it was headed by James McHaney) and the branch offices—had responsibility for preparing and presenting *Medical, Pohl,* and *RuSHA* (Cases Nos. 1, 4, and 8 respectively). Under the aegis of the Economics Division, teams prepared the trials against *Flick* (Case No. 5), *IG Farben* (Case No. 6), and *Krupp* (Case No. 10).[24] The Ministries Division (later bifurcating into a Political Ministries Division and Economic Ministries Division) handled *Justice* (Case No. 3) and *Ministries* (Case No. 11). Finally, the brief of the Military Division included *Milch* (Case No. 2), *Hostage* (Case No. 7), and *High Command* (Case No. 12) (the Berlin Branch did not have a Military Division because the evidence for those cases would be coming from Paris and Washington, DC). Case No. 9, *Einsatzgruppen,* will be discussed in much greater detail in the next two chapters.

The trial dates, general description of the defendants, and key prosecutors for each of these cases are broken down below (Telford Taylor and division chiefs will not be mentioned unless taking a lead role throughout the trial—Taylor gave the opening and closing statements in many of them).[25] Each case involved charges of war crimes and crimes against humanity—in certain cases defendants were also charged with membership in criminal organizations (such as the Gestapo, the SS, and its Intelligence Service, the SD). In a small number of cases, defendants were charged with crimes against peace/ conspiracy related thereto (as indicated below):

NO. 1, THE *MEDICAL* CASE: *US vs. Karl Brandt, et al.* (Trial Dates: December 9, 1946, to August 20, 1947)
DEFENDANTS: Nazi physicians accused of carrying out Hitler's euthanasia program and conducting inhumane experiments on POWs and civilians. PROSECUTORS: James McHaney (chief prosecutor), Alexander Hardy, Arnost Horlik-Hochwald, Glen Brown, Esther Johnson, Jack Robbins, and Daniel Shiller.

NO. 2, THE *MILCH* CASE: *US vs. Erhard Milch* (Trial Dates: January 2 to April 17, 1947)
DEFENDANT: Luftwaffe Field Marshall Erhard Milch, whose alleged crimes centered on use of slave labor, mistreatment/murder of POWs, and medical experimentation on civilians and POWs. PROSECUTORS: Clark Denny (chief), Henry King, James Conway, Dorothy Hunt, Raymond McMahon, and Maurice Myers.

NO. 3, THE *JUSTICE* CASE: *US vs. Joseph Alstötter, et al.* (Trial Dates: March 5 to December 4, 1947)
DEFENDANTS: Members of the Reich Ministry of Justice or the People's and Special Courts—accused of using their positions to perpetrate Nazi crimes. PROSECUTORS: Charles La Follette (chief), Robert King, Alfred Wooleyhan, and Sadie Arbuthnot (the 1961 Academy Award–winning movie *Judgment at Nuremberg* was based on this trial).

NO. 4, THE *POHL* CASE: *US vs. Oswald Pohl, et al.* (Trial Dates: April 8 to November 3, 1947)
DEFENDANTS: Administrators (with Oswald Pohl in charge) of the SS-Wirtschafts-und Verwaltungshauptamt (SS Main Economic and Administrative Office), the unit that operated the concentration camps. PROSECUTORS: Jack Robbins (chief), George Baucum Fulkerson, Peter Walton, Hans Froelich, William Hart, James Higgins, and Julius Rudolph.

NO. 5, THE *FLICK* CASE: *US vs. Friedrich Flick, et al.* (Trial Dates: April 19 to December 22, 1947)
DEFENDANTS: Executives of the Flick Concern, a group of industrial enterprises (including coal mines and steel plants), accused, inter alia, of using slave labor, plundering private property, and participating in the "Aryanization" of Jewish properties. PROSECUTORS: Charles Lyon (chief), Thomas Ervin (deputy chief counsel), Rawlings Ragland (deputy chief counsel), Norbert Barr, Paul Gantt, Ralph Goodman, Richard Lansdale, Edwin Sears, Joseph Stone, and Blake Woodson.

NO. 6, THE *IG FARBEN* CASE: *US vs. Carl Krauch, et al.* (Trial Dates: August 27, 1947, to July 30, 1948)
DEFENDANTS: Directors of a large chemical firm conglomerate accused of, inter alia, plundering/spoliating private property, committing medical experiments on concentration camp prisoners, and assisting Hitler in preparing

for aggression (for which they were charged with crimes against peace/conspiracy). PROSECUTORS: Drexel Sprecher (chief), Josiah DuBois (deputy chief counsel), Morris Amchan, Jan Charmatz, Mary Kaufman, Albert Levy, Belle Mayer, Emanuel Minskoff, Randolf Newman, and Virgil Van Street.

NO. 7, THE *HOSTAGE* CASE: *US vs. Wilhelm List, et al.* (Trial Dates: July 15, 1947, to February 19, 1948)
DEFENDANTS: German Armed Forces officers whose troops committed war crimes (e.g., murdering civilians, especially via reprisal killings, and POWs, in denying them quarter, as well as engaging in wanton destruction of civilian property not justified by military necessity) during the German occupation of Greece, Yugoslavia, Albania, and Norway, in addition to murdering protected persons on the Russian front. PROSECUTORS: Clark Denny (chief, initially), Theodore Fenstermacher (chief—took charge when Denny became ill), George Baucum Fulkerson, and Walter Rapp.

NO. 8, THE *RuSHA* CASE: *US vs. Ulrich Greifelt et al.* (Trial Dates: October 20, 1947, to March 10, 1948)
DEFENDANTS: Officials of various SS organizations accused of, inter alia, implementing the Nazi "pure race" programs via racial cleansing and resettlement schemes. PROSECUTORS: James McHaney (chief), Daniel Shiller, Edmund Schwenk, Knox Lamb, Hans Froehlich, Esther Johnson, and Harold Neely.

NO. 9, THE *EINSATZGRUPPEN* CASE: *US vs. Otto Ohlendorf, et al.* (Trial Dates: September 29, 1947, to April 10, 1948)
This case, for which Ben Ferencz served as chief prosecutor, will be dealt with extensively in chapters 12 and 13.

NO. 10, THE *KRUPP* CASE: *US vs. Alfried Krupp, et al.* (Trial Dates: December 8, 1947, to July 31, 1948)
DEFENDANTS: Executives of a weapons manufacturer accused of, inter alia, aiding the Nazis in preparing for aggressive war (supporting crimes against peace charges), using captured civilians as slave laborers and plundering/spoliating property. PROSECUTORS: H. Russell Thayer (chief, through April 1948) Joseph Kaufman (deputy chief counsel through December 1947), Rawlings Ragland (deputy chief counsel from December 1947 and chief from April 1948), Cecilia Goetz, Max Mandellaub, John Bowler, Irving Brilliant, Herbert Goldenberg, Maurice Huebsch, Maximilian Koessler, Maurice Myers, and Benjamin Ferencz (see chapter 14).

NO. 11, THE *MINISTRIES* CASE: *US vs. Ernst von Weizsäcker, et al.* (Trial Dates: January 6 to April 13, 1949)
DEFENDANTS: The group included Reich ministers as well as state secretaries and members of the Nazi Party hierarchy, who were accused of, inter alia, participation in acts of aggression (for which crimes against peace charges were brought) and/or responsibility for numerous atrocities committed both in Germany and in occupied countries during the war. PROSECUTORS: For the case's "political" segment: Robert Kempner (chief/deputy chief of counsel), Alexander Hardy, William Caming, Alvin Landis, Dorthea Minskoff, John Lewis, Arthur Petersen, John Posner, and Ralph Goodman. For the "economic" segment: Charles Lyon (chief/deputy chief counsel initially), Morris Amchan (chief/deputy chief counsel—took over for Lyon), Paul Gantt, James Fitzpatrick, Walter Rockler, and Walter O'Haire.

NO. 12, THE *HIGH COMMAND* CASE: *US vs. Wilhelm von Leeb, et al.* (Trials Dates: February 5 to October 28, 1948)
DEFENDANTS: High-ranking German military officers and members of the High Command accused of planning/facilitating acts of aggression (entailing crimes against peace/conspiracy charges) as well as bearing responsibility for atrocities in countries occupied by their subordinates during the war. PROSECUTORS: Paul Niederman (chief), James McHaney (deputy chief counsel), Walter Rapp, Arnost Horlick-Hochwald, George Baucom Fulkerson, Morton Barbour, Eugene Dobbs, James Higgins, and Paul Horecky.

AS THE ABOVE list indicates, these cases were being indicted by the fall of 1946 and going to trial by the end of that year and the beginning of 1947. By the spring of 1947, five trials were already under way. This meant that, as perhaps the most important font of evidence supporting charges in court, the Berlin Branch was under great pressure to get results, almost from the moment it was created. As Ben Ferencz later explained: "Time was of the essence. My job, as organizer and Chief of the Berlin Branch, was to scour the official German records in the Nazi capital to supplement evidence previously assembled in Paris and Frankfurt. It kept me and the supporting staff of researchers and investigators hopping. . . . The Berlin office had to deduce what evidence might be persuasive. Incriminating documents had to be found and rushed to eager attorneys preparing the 'Subsequent Proceedings.'"[26]

This meant that Ferencz had to keep "a tight watch on the work produced by each employee, and [maintain a] close liaison with the lawyers in Nuremberg."[27] Surviving archival documents from the activities of the Berlin Branch fully attest to this. Prosecutors in Nuremberg would let Ferencz know what they were looking for as they prepared for trial. The branch chief would then dispatch investigators to a series of locations to find the needed evidence. The biggest repository, in this regard, was known as the Berlin Document Center. It had been created by the Americans from enormous tranches of Nazi files rescued from destruction in May 1945, when they were discovered by US Counter Intelligence Corps agents at a paper mill in Freimann, Germany, where they had been shipped by Hitler's lieutenants to be pulped.

The documents were organized into general categories and placed in a series of buildings in Berlin. There, investigators could find SS rosters, a central index of Nazi Party members, as well as reams of Nazi Party correspondence and documents generated by various branches of Hitler's government. Another important repository was the Ministerial Documents Branch, for which contemporaneous memos from Ferencz's office indicate regular drop-off and pickup times. Other locations often visited by investigators included the French Document Center, the British Field Security Office, the OMGUS Library, and the German Patent Office. Memos also indicate that investigators conducted interrogations (in coordination with the OCCWC's Interrogation Section) and that the Berlin Branch adopted the procedures and protocols used in Nuremberg for such purposes (witnesses could range from suspected Nazis, to German professionals who survived Nazism and the war, to war crimes victims in UNRAA camps).[28]

Ferencz indicated via memos and correspondence that the Berlin Branch could screen documents, conduct interrogations, select incriminating evidence, and send authenticated interrogation transcripts or reproductions of original documents, together with accompanying Staff Evidence Analysis (SEA) documents to any interested parties in Nuremberg. Documents were transported from Berlin to Nuremberg by plane twice weekly.[29]

To ensure evidence retrieval and processing were running at peak speed and efficiency, Ferencz held frequent staff meetings (even on weekends).[30] A big issue for the branch was to ensure that SEAs were generated for each piece of evidence and that the quality of the SEAs was high—otherwise, the evidence might not have been usable for the Nuremberg attorneys. Contemporaneous memos suggest that there was an office-wide SEA deficit, and it was adversely affecting operations in Nuremberg. (The archival record also suggests, though, that Ferencz's efforts were getting the problem cleaned up in Berlin.)

But the branch chief was not dealing only with evidence harvesting and analysis. He had his fingers in every aspect of the office's operations, including decisions related to hiring, firing, promotions, benefits, and leave, as well as liaising with OMGUS.[31] He was working around the clock. Gertrude was also extremely busy, serving not only as an analyst but also moonlighting with respect to a diverse range of branch functions, including document distribution, office supply organization, and file system maintenance.

DESPITE ALL the hard work, Mr. and Mrs. Ferencz still managed to find some time for themselves—a honeymoon in spurts, as it were. Berlin had not yet quite emerged from its smoldering ruins, but the bomb-scarred Opera House in the Soviet sector had been quickly restored, and singers and dancers from the Bolshoi came "to show that Russian artists had more 'Kultur' to offer than the murderous Nazis."[32] Gertrude and Ben spent "many happy evenings" watching "splendid Soviet opera and ballet" that they never could have afforded in New York. The audience included high-ranking French, British, Soviet, and American officers. "Some tickets were also reserved for Germans," Ben later noted, "who could be seen in the cold hall during intermission munching pieces of bread. They all recognized that it's bad to lose a war; nations should consider the consequences before they start one."[33]

There were also occasional excursions outside of Berlin in buses filled with American army wives and schoolteachers. In them, Ben and Gertrude visited scenic spots such as Garmisch and Berchtesgaden. They even took a tour through Switzerland's most picturesque cities. A trip to Italy in December 1946 was particularly memorable. In Milan, they did more than visit the city's renowned cathedral and famous La Scala opera house. The two war crimes–oriented tourists also photographed the gas station where Hitler's partner in crime, Benito Mussolini, met his end—strung up by partisans from the rafters by his heels, with his mistress, Clara Petacci, hanging by his side.[34]

Meanwhile, back in Berlin, Ben Ferencz was having issues with his assigned branch chief car, a German Maybach limousine, "of Rolls Royce caliber, cherished by Hitler's top henchmen."[35] If the bus trips around Europe had contributed to marital bliss in the Ferencz household, the Maybach, which came with a German chauffeur named "Barrs," had the opposite effect. Festooned with American flags on each front fender, which fluttered ostentatiously as the vehicle negotiated Berlin's bombed-out thoroughfares, the pate of the pint-sized Ferencz, when settled down in the deep, plush leather passenger seat, barely cleared the convertible's lower chassis, and he was comically dwarfed by the wind-whipped red, white, and blue pennants. Even worse, his wife considered these wheels far too ostentatious and resented his millionaire commute when she was being herded to the office every morning with other staff members, freezing on the exposed flatbed of a truck. He explained it had to be this way thanks to the government's strong antinepotism policy. But Gertrude would have none of it—she wanted to be next to him on the Maybach's capacious passenger seat.[36]

But the limo ended up wreaking far more havoc on his life than this intrusion on "domestic tranquility."[37] On New Year's Eve 1946, Ben Ferencz hosted Patricia ("Patty") Bull, a reporter who had come up from Nuremberg to do a story on the Berlin Branch (and whose father had been Eisenhower's assistant chief of staff during World War II—Lieutenant General Harold R. Bull). Ferencz wanted to impress her. Flouting army rules that forbade using an official car for nonofficial purposes, and frequenting German premises that were not authorized, he decided to take the Maybach out for a grand night in a forbidden part of town. The focal point would be Café Wien on the Kurfürstendamm (in the British sector), "Berlin's leading cabaret," a nonauthorized German establishment.[38] Joining them would be Eugene Klein, a Hungarian refugee who was Ferencz's personal aide but had served in the US Air Corps and "knew his way around" (Klein had secured the tickets for the Café Wien gala).[39] Also in the party that night was OCCWC-military liaison Lieutenant Colonel Bill Wuest and Barrs, the chauffeur. The latter was invited into the cabaret, to keep warm on a cold night, despite regulations that forbade drivers from leaving official cars.

At one point, Barrs went outside to check on the Maybach—and it was gone! Ferencz suspected the Russians had stolen it, and he spent the balance of the evening racing around the Soviet sector border with British MPs searching for it, but to no avail (the car was eventually returned but completely trashed and unusable). In short order, Barrs was arrested and Ferencz was charged with, among other things, using a military vehicle for an unauthorized purpose, illegally frequenting off-limits German premises, and causing damage to high-value government property (Ferencz successfully interceded on Barrs's behalf, claiming, ironically, that his chauffeur was only following orders).

A short time later, a JAG lieutenant visited Ferencz in his office with a file containing sworn witness statements and the charge sheet itself. He asked the branch chief to sign a statement admitting the facts, but the latter refused, inquiring whether he could keep the file to "study the charges carefully and give him a detailed written reply."[40] The gullible lieutenant agreed, and Ferencz later wrote that "since the file was too thick to fit in the shallow center drawer of my desk, I carefully deposited the entire folder for safekeeping in the spacious wastepaper basket."[41] Thus, the complete case file had been destroyed, and the naïve JAG lawyer "could not possibly duplicate the affidavits of all of the witnesses since many were no longer in Berlin."[42] The young lieutenant, likely unwilling to disclose that he had moronically left the full file, with all copies, in the suspect's custody, probably reported that he had simply lost it. Thus, in full Hell's Kitchen mode, Ferencz had dodged yet another army bullet.

THE FOLLOWING month, the Berlin Branch chief received a memo from one of his newer investigators, a diligent Swiss Germanophone by the name of Frederick Burin. In the February 5, 1947, document, addressed to all "Section Chiefs," Burin summarized a request from prosecutor Peter Walton (of the SS Division in Nuremberg) regarding searches for evidence related to a potential large case against the Reich Security Main Office (Reichssicherheitshauptamt, or RSHA), the umbrella agency covering all security and police forces in Germany. Apart from brief mentions of the Gestapo and the Criminal Technical Institute (a unit that conducted medical experiments on concentration camp inmates), the memo focused on Otto Ohlendorf and the Einsatzgruppen (as well as the SS Intelligence Service [SD]).

It will be recalled that Ohlendorf had already testified at the IMT trial and admitted that his Einsatzgruppe D unit murdered approximately 90,000 Jews. But there was only his confession in court without documentary or other evidence to back it up—that is, there was *a res gestae* problem (insufficient evidence beyond a lone confession that would not support guilt beyond a reasonable doubt). Thus, the memo requested that investigators focus on Ohlendorf's activities related to economics (that is, exploitation of slave labor) as head of RSHA Amt III (or Office III—another major gig Ohlendorf had during the war), the "internal spying" version of the SD.

With regard to the Einsatzgruppen, the memo requested details of activities of the following individual commanders and functionaries: Ohlendorf himself, Heinz Jost (Einsatzgruppe A commander), Otto Rasch (Einsatzgruppe C commander), Max Thomas (who took over for Rasch as Einsatzgruppe C commander), Walther Bierkamp (who took over for Ohlendorf as Einsatzgruppe D commander), and Walter Schellenberger (who served as a liaison for the Einsatzgruppen with the rest of the SS and dealt with the unit's supplies and logistics). As this memo indicates, at this point, even if sufficient evidence corroborating what he testified to at the IMT could be found to indict Ohlendorf, Taylor "had not [anticipated] prosecuting [him] with [exclusively] other Einsatzgruppen leaders." Rather, "he intended to include Ohlendorf in a more general SS case."[43] Indeed, a number of OCCWC lawyers were opposed to an Einsatzgruppen-centered trial because "notwithstanding Ohlendorf's testimony at the IMT—they did not fully grasp the enormity of the crimes committed by the mobile killing squads."[44]

For the next month, the hardworking Burin scoured the various Berlin locales, keeping Ohlendorf and the Einsatzgruppen in the back of his mind. In general, though, his primary research objective was evidence that would incriminate a wide swath of RSHA war criminals.

But then he made a discovery that changed everything. Sometime in March, while searching through a Foreign Ministry annex located near the Tempelhof Airport, he stumbled across an enormous cache of documents that had been slated for pulping but somehow got overlooked. Bug-eyed, he realized he was staring at a nearly complete set of secret dispatches that had been sent by the Gestapo office in Berlin to a hundred or so top officials of the Nazi regime. These were Einsatzgruppen daily reports from the Soviet Union (styled "*SS-Ereignismeldungen aus der UdSSR*") chronicling in minute detail all the activities of these mobile murder units. Burin then raced back to the Armed Forces Building and hurried into Ferencz's office with bated breath.

"You'll never guess what I just found!" the Swiss blurted out. Ferencz listened, thunderstruck, to Burin's description of the enormous trove of documents. He wanted to take a gander for himself. Armed with a little adding machine, he pored over the reports and started totaling the numbers. Once the figure exceeded one million murdered, he put the calculator away and decided to hop on the next Douglas C-47 twin-engine plane from Tempelhof to Nuremberg to report these findings to Telford Taylor.

One can only imagine the astonishment of the chief of counsel when one of his youngest lawyers showed up unannounced on his doorstep from Berlin, with samples of the most complete and damning evidence anyone in his office had found to that point (and would find for the rest of the OCCWC's existence). As we have seen, Taylor had been contemplating a general SS trial, but "most of the high-ranking SD, Gestapo, and RSHA officials that the [OCCWC] wanted to prosecute were either missing (most notably Adolf Eichmann) or known to be dead."[45] Thus, it seems he had already made his peace with not adding a twelfth trial, and, in any event, he presently lacked the personnel and resources for it. Even had he opted to do the general SS trial, he would have needed the Pentagon's blessing and largesse. And that is where things stood when Ben Ferencz burst into his office that day in March 1947 and the two had a confrontation that would change the history of international criminal justice. Ben summarized the encounter:

> I [went] to Telford and I said, "We have to put on a new trial." He said, "We can't." I said, "Look, I've got this evidence here. It's all together here in a big binder—a million murders!" He said, "We can't put on a new trial now, Ben. We've already got . . . all the lawyers . . . assigned. The Pentagon is not going to approve of a new thing. As it is, they're not very happy with this dragging out."

> So I blew my cool. . . . I said, "You can't let these guys go. This is mass murder! On a scale never before seen in human history. You're going to say 'no, you can't put on a new trial'?!?" He said, 'Well, can you do it in addition to your other work?' I said, "Sure." So he said, "OK, you do it."[46]

And in that moment, perhaps the most seminal of his many years, Benjamin Berell Ferencz became the chief prosecutor of what would come to be known as the "biggest murder trial in history." He was all of twenty-seven years old and had never tried a case before. But by June, he had already relocated to Nuremberg and was preparing for the signature event of his life: *United States vs. Otto Ohlendorf, et al.*

12

THE *EINSATZGRUPPEN* TRIAL, PART 1

> The sad truth is that most evil is done by people who never make up their minds to be good or evil.
>
> —HANNAH ARENDT, *The Life of the Mind*

> Members of Sonderkommando 4A, operating along the high banks of the Desna River in the Ukraine, like nimrods seeking wild ducks, reported from Chemigov that on October 23, 1941, 116 Jews were shot; and that on the following day 144 Jews were shot.
>
> —MICHAEL MUSMANNO, *The Eichmann Kommandos*

THERE HAD been justifiable pressure on Telford Taylor to include a Holocaust-focused trial among the Subsequent Proceedings, but the stars were not aligning as access to both suspects and evidence had been lacking.[1] The diligence of the Berlin Branch, however, and the forceful intervention of its chief, came to the rescue. And the timing was felicitous because the OCCWC's Apprehension and Locator Branch "had been able to find a number of Einsatzgruppen commanders and subordinate officers."[2] Moreover, the Berlin Branch had begun to analyze the Einsatzgruppen Daily Reports, "a massive collection" of eight to nine million documents that detailed the murder squads' crimes "with chilling precision."[3] Thus, the evidence demonstrating guilt was overwhelming, and the big issues initially revolved around defendant selection and trial team composition.

By June 1947, having deputized Bill Wuest to run the Berlin Branch, Ben Ferencz was back in Nuremberg and putting it all together. He focused first on selecting a trial team. Given his mandate to make do with personnel already in place, this meant cannibalizing existing OCCWC groupings. In effect, he would have to settle for the other teams' "cast-offs."[4] The requisitioned lawyers included Peter Walton, who had been on the *Pohl* case trial team and whom presiding judge Michael Musmanno would later describe as "some forty years of age, with gray touching his temples and with a slight pleasant drawl which confirmed the biographical note that he was born in Georgia."[5] Another poached lawyer was John E. Glancey, "born and reared in Washington, D.C.," and "tall and broad-shouldered . . . like a football player."[6]

While Ferencz may have considered Walton and Glancey "decent people" but "not competent lawyers,"[7] Arnost Horlik-Hochwald was different—a good chap but also a skilled advocate, whom Musmanno characterized as an "intellectual." Born in Czechoslovakia, he was "of medium height with a shock of gray hair and wearing glasses with thick lenses . . . soft-spoken, polite and extremely courteous."[8] An experienced lawyer from the Moravia region, he had served in his home country's army during the war, escaped capture, and linked up with the Czechoslovak government-in-exile. He was in his birth country's delegation at Nuremberg's initial IMT proceeding, but as Czechoslovakia began receding behind the Iron Curtain, Horlik-Hochwald managed to escape by volunteering his services to the Americans. And he became a well-respected NMT prosecutor, having already acquitted himself admirably in the *Medical* case.

The final addition to Ferencz's team of podium prosecutors was James Heath, a handsome and genteel Virginian with a charming drawl, who was by far the oldest lawyer among them. He had fallen on hard times since his early OCCWC days when he headed one of the Industrialist Divisions and had been Ben Ferencz's supervisor. He was revealed to be a serious alcoholic, struggling to perform his duties adequately. In fact, he had been on Taylor's chopping block when Ben Ferencz became chief prosecutor for the *Einsatzgruppen* case. The younger man never forgot their early friendship, so he saved Heath's job, convincing Taylor to assign him to *Einsatzgruppen* and give him one more chance. The veteran attorney would be designated as a "consultant" and focus strictly on preparing the cross-examination of the trial's chief defendant, SS-Gruppenführer (Major General) Otto Ohlendorf. Ferencz conditioned his appointment on his giving up the sauce cold turkey. During the life of the case, at least, Heath regained his sobriety and his health.

Further support for the *Einsatzgruppen* case chief prosecutor would come from the erstwhile job-hunting team of Gertrude Ferencz and Nancy Fenstermacher. Ben's wife, who had never learned how to drive, had bought a 1938 Mercedes Benz in the former Nazi capital and asked one of the Berlin Branch staff to chauffeur her down to Nuremberg in it. In the meantime, her husband had secured for them a beautiful little villa in Fürth, on the edge of a lush meadow with the Pegnitz River flowing idyllically in the background. The residence had an impressive garden tended by one Ludwig, an amiable groundskeeper with a thick Bavarian accent and a serious green thumb, who arrived every day on a rusty bicycle and taught "a boy raised on the sidewalks of New York" how to garden.[9] Once Gertrude arrived from Berlin, Ferencz came as close to the kind of domestic bliss that he thought he needed to face the trial ordeal that awaited him.

The other half of the Washington, DC, job-hunting duo, Nancy Fenstermacher, came to provide additional support on the *Einsatzgruppen* trial team as a research analyst. In the run-up to the trial, she prepared an extensive report on the paramilitary killing squads that was quite useful during the proceeding's initial phases. (Charles Ippen would also serve as a research analyst, and the team would benefit too from the services of Walter Rapp, Rolf Wartenberg [a central figure during the trial], and Alfred Schwarz of the Evidence Division, as well as the guidance of James McHaney, head of the SS Division, and General Taylor himself.)[10]

Once the team was in place, Ferencz got down to the difficult business of target selection and drafting the indictment. At first, he was overwhelmed at the thought that "There were about 3,000 members of the Einsatzgruppen who spent practically every day on the Eastern front murdering innocent men, women, and children."[11] So he started to reflect on the nature of these Nuremberg Trials and how they differed from the proceedings conducted by the army at Dachau, for example, or the Denazification courts (Spruchkammern) or the Allied military commissions or the national domestic tribunals trying lower-level war criminals throughout various parts of liberated Europe. The trials at Nuremberg were about the high-level perpetrators. And so, he resolved to indict only those fitting that description—the upper-echelon officers and the educated elite of the mobile killing units.

The other consideration, in terms of numbers limitation, was, as Ferencz humorously summarized it, "the furniture." He elaborated: "No Nuremberg tribunal could try more than 24 defendants in the same trial. The reason was that there were only 24 seats in the dock. Historians may not believe it, but it's true. It really wouldn't look nice to have to jam killers together or to have some of them sitting around on the floor during the trial."[12] In the end, as the Einsatzgruppen had four main divisions—A, B, C, and D—a certain number of high-ranking and well-educated officers were chosen from each. Moreover, each of the main units was subdivided into smaller operational commands: starting with Einsatzkommandos (Detachments); then the smaller Sonderkommandos (Special Purpose Detachments); below them the even smaller Teilkommandos (Unit Detachments); and Vorkommandos (Advance Unit Detachments).[13] These were the on-site teams consisting of, depending on the size of the unit, dozens, or hundreds of the actual triggermen in the killing fields. Based on this, the group of twenty-four defendants (all members of the SD, unless otherwise noted) broke down as shown in the tables below (giving the pre-SS education/profession and chief defense attorney of each).

INSATZGRUPPE A

ttached to Army Group North and operated in the Baltic region

efendant	Rank/Function	Background	Defense lawyers
einz Jost	SS-Brigadeführer (brigadier general); overall commanding officer	Worked as a civil servant and in law, after specializing in law and economics at the Universities of Giessen and Munich	Alfred Schwarz Paul Wiessmath
artin Sandberger	SS-Standartenführer (colonel); commanding officer, Sonderkommando 1a	Studied jurisprudence at the Universities of Munich, Freiburg, Cologne, and Tübingen; assistant judge in Inner Administration of Wuerttemberg	Dr. Bolko von Stein Dr. Kurt Mandry
duard Strauch	SS-Obersturmbannführer (lieutenant colonel); commanding officer, Einsatzkommando 2	Graduate of Erlangen University	Dr. Karl Gick Dr. Karl Jaeger

INSATZGRUPPE B

ttached to Army Group Center and operated in the area around Moscow, just south of insatzgruppe A's jurisdiction

efendant	Rank/Function	Background	Defense lawyers
rich Naumann	SS-Brigadeführer (brigadier general); overall commanding officer	Left school early, entered a commercial firm, and then became a police officer	Dr. Hans Gawlik Dr. Gerhard Klinnert
anz Six	SS-Brigadeführer (brigadier general); overall commanding officer	Full-time university professor and dean, journalism and political science	Hermann Ulmer Dr. Konrad Vökel
alter Blume	SS-Standartenführer (colonel); commanding officer, Sonderkommando 7a	Graduated in law at University of Erlangen and was police inspector	Guenther Lummert Rudolf Blume

Eugen Steimle	SS-Standartenführer (colonel); commanding officer, Sonderkommando 7a (took over for Blume)	Studied history, Germanic languages, and French at the Universities of Tübingen, and Berlin; became a schoolteacher	Dr. Erich Mayer Dr. Ferdinand Leis
Adolf Ott	SS-Obersturmbannführer (lieutenant colonel); commanding officer of Sonderkommando 7b	Began career in administrative office of German Workers' Front in Lindau	Josef Koessl Dr. Rudolf Meyer
Waldemar Klingelhöfer	SS-Sturmbannführer (major); officer of Sonderkommando 7b	Opera singer and voice teacher	Dr. Erich Mayer Dr. Ferdinand Leis

EINSATZGRUPPE C

Attached to Army Group South and operated in Ukraine, except for the extreme south of Ukraine

Defendant	Rank/Function	Background	Defense lawyers
Otto Rasch	SS-Brigadeführer (brigadier general); overall commanding officer	Doctor of law and economics; former mayor of Wittenberg	Dr. Hans Surholt
Paul Blobel	SS-Standartenführer (colonel); commanding officer, Sonderkommando 4a	Former architect	Dr. Willi Heim Ludwig Kohr
Waldemar von Radetzky	SS-Sturmbannführer (major); deputy chief of Sonderkommando 4a	Former linguist; worked with import firm	Dr. Paul Ratz Heinrich Rentsch
Walter Haensch	SS-Obersturmbannführer (lieutenant colonel); commanding officer of Sonderkommando 4b	Studied law at Leipzig University; trained as "Referendar" (clerk to a judge)	Dr. Fritz Riedeger Max Krause
Lothar Fendler	SS-Sturmbannführer (major); deputy commanding officer of Sonderkommando 4b	Former doctor in dentistry	Dr. Hans Fritz Dr. Gabriele Lehman

rwin Schulz	SS-Brigadeführer (brigadier general); commanding officer of Einsatzkommando 5	Studied law at the University of Berlin; later became staff member of Dresden Bank; came from the Gestapo, not the SD	Ernst Durchholz Dr. Hermann Müller
rnst Biberstein	SS-Obersturmbannführer (lieutenant colonel); commanding officer of Einsatzkommando 6	Former clergyman	Dr. Friedrich Bergold Oskar Ficht

INSATZGRUPPE D

ttached to the Eleventh Army and operated in southern Ukraine, the Crimea, and the Caucasus

efendant	Rank/Function	Background	Defense lawyers
tto Ohlendorf	SS-Gruppenführer (major general); overall commanding officer	Graduated in law and political science from the Universities of Leipzig and Göttingen; former practicing barrister	Dr. Rudolf Aschenauer Dr. Konrad Öhlrich
illi Seibert	SS-Standartenführer (colonel); deputy commanding officer	Graduated from the University of Göttingen in economics; former stonemason	Dr. Gerhard Klinnert Heinrich Klug
atthias Graf	SS-Untersturmführer (second lieutenant); officer in Einsatzkommando 6	Former independent businessman and civil servant	Dr. Eduard Belzer Joseph Mayer
einz Schubert	SS-Obersturmführer (first lieutenant); Ohlendorf's adjutant	Former apprentice to lawyer; worked in civil service administration	Josef Kössl Rudolf Meyer
lix Rühl	SS-Hauptsturmführer (captain); officer of Sonderkommando 10b	Former commercial clerk; previously lived in England; came from the Gestapo, not the SD	Heinrich Link Dr. Kurt Helm

Werner Braune	SS-Obersturmbannführer (lieutenant colonel); officer, Sonderkommando 11b	Graduated in law from the University of Jena; obtained doctor of juridical science	Dr. Erich Mayer Oskar Stübinger
Gustav Nosske	SS-Obersturmbannführer (lieutenant colonel); commanding officer, Einsatzkommando 12	Studied banking, economics, and law; former lawyer and assessor; came from the Gestapo, not the SD	Dr. Karl Hoffmann
Emil Haussmann	SS-Sturmbannführer (major); officer, Einsatzkommando 12	Former schoolteacher	Deceased right after indictment so no defense counsel

Once the identity of the defendants was determined, and each was verified to be in American custody, it was time to draft the indictment. In theory, this might have been a fairly straightforward task. The substantive crimes enumerated in Control Council Law No. 10, Art. II, were nearly identical to those set out in the IMT Charter's Article 6. If anything, Law No. 10, whose language was a bit more expansive, provided prosecutors with a wider charging berth. In particular, with reference to crimes against humanity, it excised the IMT's so-called "war nexus," that is, proving that the offense be linked to one of the other substantive crimes. At the IMT, prosecutors were aware that crimes against humanity were being codified and charged for the first time in history and they were sensitive to ex post facto law censure; the "war nexus" helped give them cover. After the major Nazi war criminals trial, though, NMT prosecutors had the benefit of precedent on their side and thus could dispense with that unwieldy mandate.

Plus, in the case of the *Einsatzgruppen* defendants, the substance of the crimes against humanity charges was entirely self-evident. In accord with Law No. 10, these murder squad goons had committed "Atrocities and offenses, including but not limited to murder, extermination . . . or other inhumane acts committed against any civilian population, or persecutions on political, racial or religious grounds whether or not in violation of the domestic laws of the country where perpetrated."[14] The same was true of war crimes, given that the mobile killing units were responsible for "Atrocities or offenses against persons . . . constituting violations of the laws or customs of war, including but not limited to, murder."[15] As well, the *Einsatzgruppen* defendants had "Membership in categories of a criminal group or organization declared criminal by the International Military Tribunal," in particular, the SS, SD, and Gestapo.

(Crimes against peace were not implicated because, although they followed the Wehrmacht into Soviet territory to kill civilians, the defendants were not involved in planning, preparing, initiating, or waging aggressive war.)

Ben Ferencz's challenge in drafting the indictment had less to do with formulating potential charges in respect of language explicitly found in Law No. 10; rather, it had to do with formulating potential charges in respect of language *not* explicitly found in Law No. 10. More specifically, the trouble revolved around one term—"genocide." It was a new portmanteau word coined only three years previously by Raphael Lemkin, a Polish-Jewish jurist who had fled his home country but lost most of his family in the Holocaust. He introduced the concept of "genocide" ("genos," from the Greek word for race or tribe, and "cide," from the Latin word for killing) in his 1944 book titled *Axis Rule in Occupied Europe.* He defined it as "a coordinated plan of different actions aiming at the destruction of essential foundations of the life of national groups, with the aim of annihilating the groups themselves."[16]

The reason the term was so vexing for Ben Ferencz at this juncture was due to Lemkin himself, who had endured an incredible odyssey to find himself at the Nazi war crimes trials in Nuremberg. Having always lived as a child under the specter of the anti-Jewish pogroms then endemic to his corner of eastern Europe (in and around the town of Wołkowysk, now a part of Belarus), he developed sympathy for minority-group rights and a burning sense of indignation regarding government complicity in mass violence. In 1926, he earned a law degree from Lwów University in Poland, about one hundred miles south of Wołkowysk (now called Lviv and part of Ukraine). Lemkin began thinking of ways to channel his intense feelings regarding state-sponsored violence against minority groups to effect transnational normative change. In 1933, the year of Hitler's ascension to power, he proposed to the League of Nations criminalizing what he termed "barbarism," that is, "acts of extermination directed against the ethnic, or social collectivities whatever the motive (political, religious, etc.)."[17] The proposal, the seed that would later germinate into the concept of "genocide," was rejected, and Lemkin was discriminated against by antisemitic forces in Poland for having put it forward.

In 1939, as the Wehrmacht was rolling over the Polish military, Lemkin fled, first to Lithuania and then to Sweden, where he lectured at Stockholm University. In 1941, he left for the United States, where he had secured a law professorship at Duke University. He moved to Washington, DC, the following year to join the War Department as an analyst. Then, in 1944, he published *Axis Rule in Occupied Europe* and eventually joined Justice Jackson and his staff (in an unofficial capacity), first in London and, after a return to Washington, DC, later at Nuremberg. During the spring of 1946, when Ben

Ferencz had first arrived in Nuremberg and was attending IMT trial sessions, he had many encounters with Lemkin in the halls of the Palace of Justice. Ben later recalled, "Like the Ancient Mariner of Coleridge's poem, he collared anyone he could, to tell them the story of how his family had been destroyed by Germans."[18] Lemkin had given Ben a copy of *Axis Rule in Occupied Europe*, which the younger man read with great interest and diligence.

And, in the end, as he worked on the indictment the following year, he could not banish from his thoughts the image of the "somewhat lost and bedraggled fellow with the wild and pained look in his eyes."[19] In fact, it was as a "tribute and [in] respect for him" and "the validity of his argument" that he included the term "genocide" in the *Einsatzgruppen* indictment and used it in the trial's opening statement.[20] Thus, paragraph 2 of Count 1 of the indictment, for Crimes against Humanity, avers that the charged conduct was carried out "as part of a systematic program of genocide, aimed at the destruction of foreign nations and ethnic groups by murderous extermination."[21] Count 2 of the indictment charged War Crimes, and Count 3, Membership in Criminal Organizations. This document was originally filed on July 3, 1947, but was amended on July 25 to include six additional defendants.

Beyond drafting the indictment, another pretrial issue involved the potential involvement of the Soviet Union. After all, every charged crime had taken place on Soviet soil. Ferencz tasked Fred Burin, the investigator who made the monumental discovery of the Einsatzgruppen daily reports, to discuss the possibility of a joint prosecution with the Soviets. They were initially "intrigued" by the idea but later in the meeting took the position that they would be satisfied prosecuting, on their own, the suspects already in their custody.[22] Thus, the best chance for an NMT international prosecution died with that decision.

Now officially on their own, and with pressure already mounting to bring the Subsequent Proceedings program to a close, the Americans worked feverishly over the summer to prepare *Einsatzgruppen* for trial. On September 15, 1947, they were ready for the first official court session, the arraignment, where the charges would be read, and the defendants would enter pleas. And this was the first time the parties would see the men in robes who would adjudicate the guilt or innocence of the accused.

Two members of the bench, both soft-spoken and from the US Deep South, did not make too much of an impression. Richard D. Dixon, a World War I veteran and North Carolina superior court judge, had initially been recruited as deputy secretary general for all the Subsequent Nuremberg proceedings but moved into a judicial role and had previously served as an alternate judge on the *Flick* bench. He was considered "a capable jurist."[23] John J. Speight, reputed to be "a prominent Alabama attorney," had had no previous judicial experience before Nuremberg but had been a special assistant to the attorney general of Alabama and had served as an alternate judge for the *Milch* and *Pohl* trials.[24] Speight was apparently not born for the bench, with colleagues describing him as "incompetent," "ineffective," and "a mere cipher." Ferencz later shared his impression that Speight and Dixon figuratively "slept through the entire eight-month trial."[25]

But the third judge, Michael A. Musmanno, who, not surprisingly, was chosen to preside, made quite a different impression. If the pre-Nuremberg careers of Speight and Dixon might not be described as the stuff of legend, the opposite was true of their brother on the *Einsatzgruppen* bench. Born in 1897 to a devout Catholic Italian immigrant couple in Stowe Township, Pennsylvania, a mill and manufacturing community six miles outside of Pittsburgh, he was the seventh of the couple's eight children. His father was a hard worker and made steady upward career progress—advancing from coal miner to railway worker to policeman. He passed on his impressive work ethic to his kids but seemed to have noticed something special about Michael and urged him to strive for higher education. The son took his dad's prodding to heart—after serving in the army in World War I and then holding down a series of jobs (including coal miner) and paying his own way, he earned a remarkable seven degrees from five different universities before even reaching the age of thirty. This included various bachelor of arts and master's degrees from George Washington, National, and American Universities, as well as a law degree from Georgetown University.

Photos and film reveal that Musmanno, like Ferencz, was short of stature, and in his relentless drive for self-improvement and self-promotion, one detects the hallmarks of a Napoleon complex. During his time as a student and lawyer, he wrote fiction and nonfiction almost obsessively, churning out dozens of short stories and legal articles. One of his fictional pieces, "Jan Volkanik," about a Pennsylvania coal mining strike and related murder, was turned into the 1935 Academy Award–nominated film *Black Fury*, directed by Michael Curtiz (later of *Casablanca* fame) and starring Paul Muni. (Musmanno ultimately wrote a total of sixteen full-length books.) In 1932, he challenged the legendary lawyer Clarence Darrow to a debate on the topics of immortality and reincarnation at Carnegie Hall, Pittsburgh, and a review of the proceedings demonstrates that Musmanno held his own.[26]

At one point, he moved to Italy, wrote for Rome's English daily newspaper, taught English, and studied under former Italian prime minister Vittorio Emmanuel Orlando at the University of Rome, where he earned yet another doctorate degree in jurisprudence. While in the Italian capital, he also worked as a bit-part actor for the first film treatment of *Ben Hur*, sang in an opera, and made the acquaintance of Benito Mussolini.

But Musmanno's careers as a lawyer and a politician were equally colorful. He liked to represent the underdog, often serving as a labor attorney for coal miners and other blue-collar workers in Pennsylvania. His championing of the working-class underdog led to his representation of two of the most famous defendants in the annals of American justice—Nicola Sacco and Bartolomeo Vanzetti. The two Italian immigrant anarchists had been convicted for murdering a Braintree, Massachusetts, shoe company paymaster and security guard. Many thought their 1921 trial was a miscarriage of justice tainted with anti-immigrant prejudice. Musmanno moved to Massachusetts and served as their lawyer for the appeal, which was unsuccessful. The two men were executed in 1927, sparking protests around the world. As a result, Musmanno became a lifelong opponent of the death penalty.

In 1928, after the *Sacco-Vanzetti* case, Musmanno ran for a seat in the Pennsylvania House of Representatives and won, being reelected in 1930. The following year, he was appointed as a judge for Allegheny County and was elevated to the Court of Common Pleas in 1934. He served on that bench until the US entry into World War II, when he enlisted in the navy. After being wounded twice during the Italian campaign, his star began to rise, and he became naval aide to General Mark Clark, who commanded the American Fifth Army and later the Allied Fifteenth Army Group. With the liberation of the southern Italian city of Sorrento, Clark appointed Musmanno military governor of the Sorrentine Peninsula. The two were then stationed in Vienna, where the general named his aide president of the United States Board of Forcible Repatriation, which passed on Soviet demands for repatriation of Russian refugees.

From there, Musmanno was transferred to Nuremberg to review the cases against German naval commanders Karl Dönitz and Erich Raeder in advance of the IMT trial. Flowing from this experience, he was recommended for an NMT judge position, and he went on to serve on both the *Milch* and *Pohl* benches before being promoted to the role of presiding judge for the *Einsatzgruppen* trial. And now, on September 15, 1947, at 9:30 a.m., as the arraignment opened, he faced the prosecutors, the defendants, and their attorneys for the proceeding's inaugural court session. In a stentorian voice, the marshall proclaimed, "The Honorable, the Judges of Military Tribunal II-A. Military Tribunal II-A is now in session. God save the United States of America and this honorable Tribunal."[27]

While an attendance roll call of the defendants' names was being read by the Tribunal "Secretary General" (the NMT registrar), the proceeding experienced its first dramatic moment. One of the announced names was met with silence, followed by murmurs in the courtroom. The name was Emil Haussmann, and the silence prompted Ben Ferencz to inform the judges that the former Einsatzgruppe D officer had committed suicide soon after being served with the indictment. Now there were only twenty-three defendants.

The chief prosecutor then started reading the charging instrument. Soon, however, there was more drama. Defendant Eduard Strauch suddenly bolted up out of his seat in the dock, crashed to the floor, and then began writhing wildly like a moray eel yanked out of the sea and dropped on the deck of a ship. The military guards jumped forward with their clubs raised but soon realized the former Einsatzgruppen officer was having an epileptic seizure. He was removed from the courtroom and arraigned separately a week later.

Ferencz continued reading the indictment, but, in no time, there was yet another interruption. Otto Rasch's attorney, Dr. Hans Surholt, raised his voice and addressed the Tribunal. His client, he explained, could no longer be in court that morning as he was suffering from Parkinson's disease and experiencing terrible fits of trembling. The previous week, Surholt had visited Ferencz at the Palace of Justice and requested that Rasch's case be dismissed because of the affliction. Ben immediately recollected that Surholt's client was in overall control of Einsatzgruppe C, which had conducted one of the most infamous operations of the Holocaust—the Babi Yar massacre, where, in two days, roughly 34,000 innocent Jewish civilians, including women and children, were shot in cold blood at a ravine on the outskirts of Kiev. The young man told Surholt that if he had murdered as many innocent civilians as Rasch, he too would be shaking. "Is he breathing?" Ferencz then asked rhetorically. "If so, I am going to indict the son-of-a-bitch."[28]

Surholt then filed a motion to sever/suspend proceedings that was denied. Musmanno, however, excused Rasch for that day and ordered that he be arraigned later. On September 22, 1947, Rasch was brought back to the courtroom on a stretcher carried by two African American MPs; the irony of this brutal Nazi butcher being helped by two persons whom he considered "racially inferior" was not lost on Ben Ferencz. With Rasch still lying on the stretcher and Strauch placed back in the dock, both defendants pled "Not guilty" consistent with their former Einsatzgruppen colleagues. And with that, the case was finally ready for trial.

On the morning of September 29, 1947, Ben Ferencz woke at first light, showered, quickly ate his breakfast, put on his best suit (a double-breasted navy blue with pinstripes, a white handkerchief in the breast pocket, and a US military Honorable Service button pinned to the lapel), white shirt (crisply starched), burgundy tie, and thick woolen overcoat, kissed his wife, and directed his chauffeur, an Estonian national, to drive him to the Palace of Justice.[29] It was a crisp, bright early fall day but, for the rest of his life, he would have little recollection of how he felt or how he perceived his physical surroundings that morning. He had no specific memory of his arrival at the Palace of Justice, his last-minute preparations in his office, his entry into the courtroom, or of the presence there of his wife or many friends and colleagues, including his boss, General Taylor, as the case was called. He was vaguely aware of the judges on the bench and the defendants in the dock. Otherwise, with the great Robert Jackson as his inspiration, his sole preoccupation that morning, and what he remembered most clearly, was that he wanted to deliver his opening statement with as much power and eloquence as he could muster.[30]

With his thoughts fixed on that one objective, he solemnly approached the podium, figuratively, if not literally, following in Jackson's footsteps. He positioned himself before the judges, laid out his notes, and put his finger on the text. "May it please your Honors," he began, and the words started flowing from him as fluidly and effortlessly as he had written them on that legal pad, in the same empty chamber, less than twenty-four hours before. After his stirring first paragraph, which he concluded by invoking his "plea of humanity to law," he continued: "We shall establish beyond the realm of doubt facts which, before the dark decade of the Third Reich, would have seemed incredible. The defendants were commanders and officers of special SS groups known as Einsatzgruppen—established for the specific purpose of massacring human beings because they were Jews, or because they were for some other reason regarded as inferior peoples. . . . Genocide, the extermination of whole categories of human beings, was a foremost instrument of the Nazi doctrine."[31]

He then explained how the Einsatzgruppen started preparing in the spring of 1941 for Operation Barbarossa, the invasion of the Soviet Union. Before coasting through conquered Russian territory on the contrails of the Wehrmacht's *Blitzkrieg*, the mobile units were ordered to "destroy all those denominated as Jew, political official, gypsy, and those other thousands called 'asocial' by the self-styled Nazi superman."[32] He described the mass shootings at the beginning of the macabre campaign and the later asphyxiation of victims in "gas vans"—"vehicles which could receive living human beings and discharge corpses."[33] He went into greater detail regarding the Nazi doctrine of race superiority and genocide as well as the organization of the Einsatzgruppen.

He then sat down and, for the first time that morning, could genuinely concentrate on his immediate surroundings.[34] The great courtroom seemed alive with a kind of electricity he had never experienced before. On so many previous occasions he had seen the chamber's somber mahogany paneling, its thick, white-veined Brunswick-green marble arches framing the entryways (the one on the east wall supporting, on its apex, two statues kneeling with swords of justice), its large ornamental plaques propped atop the upper wainscoting with symbols of mortality/morality (a winged hourglass, Eve offering Adam the apple, and the Ten Commandments), and the almost otherworldly glow of the overhead fluorescent lamps, bathing all in hot, white, bright light. These sights were so familiar. But now, somehow, they all seemed different. Before he had only gazed at them passively, from afar; now he was a part of them, enveloped by them.

And all the other sights and sounds were also starting to come into focus. He glanced at the judges' bench along the west wall, framed on either side by thick sage-green velvet draping over the enormous casement windows, and spotted the stern-faced Musmanno, behind whom the Star-Spangled Banner, presumably suspended on a flagpole not visible, hung in elegant folds. The brass buttons of the presiding judge's white navy uniform were poorly concealed under his robes. Facing him and his brethren on the east wall was the defendants' dock, which consisted of two benches hewn of birch and walnut. On the front one, closest to the east wall door, sat Otto Ohlendorf, in the same seat occupied by Hermann Göring the previous year. Like the former Reichsmarschall, Ohlendorf was the highest-ranking and most notorious defendant, and to his left were placed the other Einsatzgruppen chief butchers in order of descending rank: Jost, Naumann, Rasch, Schulz, Six, Blobel, Blume, and Steimle. On the back bench, directly behind Ohlendorf, was Biberstein, and to his left were Braune, Haensch, Nosske, Ott, Strauch, Klingelhöfer, Fendler, von Radetzky, Rühl, Schubert, and Graf.

Each defendant looked straight ahead, stone-faced, while wearing headphones so as to take in the German translation of the English opening statement. Standing guard behind them, and to their right flank, were six American soldiers clad in olive-green, whose drab Eisenhower jackets stood in sharp contrast to the gleaming jade helmets on their heads. In front of the dock were the four defense tables, piled high with documents and law books that partially obscured the twenty-three German jurists in black robes, most former members of the Nazi Party, sitting behind them.

To their right sat the prosecutors, with Ben Ferencz at the front on the right side of the trial counsel table. To his left, he glanced at Arnost Horlik-Hochwald, whose eyes were trained intently on a document laid out before him. Across from him was John Glancey, and to Glancey's right was Jim Heath. To Glancey's left, sitting across from Ferencz, was Peter Walton. No sooner had Ferencz taken his seat at counsel table than Walton rose and approached the podium. If it had been time to present evidence, he would have looked straight ahead, toward the witness stand, for purposes of examination. Instead, he looked toward his right, and up at the three judges, to continue the prosecution's opening statement. Walton laid out the specific activities of each Einsatzgruppe and the numbers of people they murdered as well as the involvement of each specific defendant.

By this point, Ferencz had taken in all the remaining sights and sounds of Courtroom 600. He had noticed the headphones covering the ears of defense counsel, and that caused him to glance at the glass enclosure in a corner to the left of the dock. Inside it was housed a corps of interpreters, using special IBM simultaneous translation technology, who were "specially trained to integrate their translations so that an auditor could listen in any one of four languages by simply setting the switch on the chair arm to English, French, German or Russian."[35] Given the alleged brutality of the defendants and the high stakes of the trial, the sounds one heard seemed strangely muted: "Since all speaking was done into a microphone, no one raised his voice and, as a consequence, anyone stepping into the large courtroom, and not wearing earphones, encountered a curious effect of dead silence. Such a visitor, seeing the lawyers stand up, extend their arms and move their lips-yet hearing no words . . . could not fail to get the sensation of watching a motion picture with the sound track shut off."[36]

Thus, the seamless and rapid whoosh, click, and hum of the film cameras recording the proceedings stood out. So did the coughs, murmurs, and occasional harrumphs and gasps, of the many hundreds of press members and spectators in the seats to the rear of the prosecution tables and those in the specially built balcony behind and above them, which, together, could accommodate four hundred spectators.[37]

Now Ferencz was at one with his physical surroundings, and, as he stood up on Walton's conclusion, he took a moment to appreciate that he was making history and speaking for posterity. Even though it was his first trial, and the defendants were some of history's worst mass murderers, who only a couple of years previously would have shot him on sight based on his religion, the twenty-seven-year-old was not nervous. Rather, it was the genocidaires in the dock who "were nervous. I didn't murder anyone," he later recalled. "They did. And I would prove it."[38] He stood up again and then slowly strode to the lectern with great purpose; he was ready to close the prosecution's opening with a flourish.

For that, three more key points were to be made: an explanation of the basis of the Tribunal's jurisdiction, the nature of the charges vis-à-vis the notion of individual criminal responsibility, and the defenses the prosecution anticipated. Regarding jurisdiction, he explained that, in narrow terms, it derived from the quadripartite enactment of Law No. 10. But in a larger sense, to paraphrase Justice Jackson, the real complaining party at the bar was civilization itself, humanity writ large. With regard to the nature of the charges, he stressed to the court that the defendants could not hide behind the veil of the state—they needed to be found guilty for their conduct as individuals. He also touched on potential defenses and emphasized that assertions of "*nulla poena sine lege*" (no use of ex post facto laws) and following superior orders could not constitute legitimate shields to liability—that had already been determined at the IMT proceeding. Moreover, he wondered, "Was it not within the knowledge of the accused that the mass murder of helpless people constituted crime? Moral teachings have not so decayed that reasonable men could think these wrongs were right." And thus, he concluded his opening by eloquently reminding the Tribunal, "The judgment of the International Military Tribunal declares that 2 million Jews were murdered by the Einsatzgruppen and other units of the Security Police. The defendants in the dock were the cruel executioners, whose terror wrote the blackest page in human history. Death was their tool and life their toy. If these men be immune, then law has lost its meaning and man must live in fear."[39]

Musmanno later told him: "When you first got up to speak, we hardly saw you over the lectern. But as you began your opening, you became much more visible. And by the end, you were a giant."[40]

AFTER FERENCZ sat down, the Tribunal stood in recess until 11:20 a.m. At that time, Musmanno stated, the Tribunal would hear the prosecution's presentation of proof. Once back in session, though, Ohlendorf's counsel, Dr. Rudolf Aschenauer, objected to Musmanno's previous order that, inconsistent with the other tribunals' practice, there would be no break between the prosecution and defense cases. The defense attorneys were not, contrary to Musmanno's assertion, better prepared than those in the other cases because they had had earlier access to the evidence. The evidence was not, Aschenauer argued, available in the room where the prosecution had claimed it was deposited. Thus, Aschenauer moved for a fourteen-day post-prosecution-case recess.

Ferencz responded forcefully, arguing that the rules required merely that the defense be given copies of prosecution documents only twenty-four hours before they were to be moved for admission into evidence. And he could present receipts proving that each defense counsel had received translated copies of every prosecution document to be admitted into evidence the previous week, well in advance of the twenty-four-hour requirement. Besides, for weeks, most of the evidence, much of it in German, the native language of defense counsel, was available to the attorneys in a specially designated room. Musmanno was persuaded by Ferencz and ruled in favor of the prosecution. It was then time for Ben's team to begin its case.

If the opening moments of the trial bristled with drama, the same could not be said for the prosecution's case-in-chief. This is because Ferencz, supported by Taylor and McHaney, opted not to put witnesses on the stand. Ben later explained why: "I knew that every survivor of a concentration camp would be eager to testify that any one of the defendants was responsible for the murder of his or her family. But I also knew that witness testimony can be fallible, and I did not have to risk it. I would rely upon the captured official German documents to prove the guilt of each defendant."[41]

Thus, the presentation would consist of Ferencz, Glancey, Horlik-Hochwald, and Walton reading Einsatzgruppen reports, defendants' affidavits, and related documents into the record. The process began with Ferencz explaining to the Tribunal the basis for finding that the Einsatzgruppen daily reports were authentic documents—largely an exercise in establishing chain of custody (through "captured document" certificates and various affidavits indicating the documents were found in German archives). He explained that, on a daily basis, each chief officer of the individual paramilitary death squads would radio in a report to the Reich Security Main Office (RSHA) and then follow it with a written report. Copies of these reports were made and distributed to various offices within the Nazi government, and the OCCWC had found the only surviving set of complete reports among the German archives. Judge Musmanno gave his impression of how the reading of one of these reports in the courtroom affected him:

> A chronicler for Einsatzgruppe B, marching through Byelorussia, could almost have been speaking of shooting rabbits or squirrels when he stated that on December 19, 1941, one of the organization's sub-units apprehended, on a road out of Mogilev, industrial and transportation center, "135 persons mostly Jews," of which 127 "were shot." It was not asserted that the Jews had attacked the Einsatz unit, or that they were enemies, or had demonstrated a hostile attitude, or that they had committed any crime. They were simply on the road, some on their way home to their families, some hurrying to their places of employment—most, certainly, minding their own affairs. But they were Jews, and they were shot.[42]

At various junctures, defense lawyers would object vehemently that a certain prosecution exhibit was a photostatic copy. On such occasions, Ferencz later recalled, "[I] invited [them] to inspect the original in my office and I promised to correct any error."[43] In any event, the contents of the reports were further verified by the affidavits of various defendants, including Ohlendorf himself. For example, pursuant to Ohlendorf's sworn declaration (Prosecution Exhibit 9), the Einsatzgruppen routinely worked as follows:

> In the implementation of this extermination program . . . the unit selected for this task would enter a village or city and order the prominent Jewish citizens to call together all Jews for purposes of the resettlement. They were requested to hand over their valuables to the leaders of the unit, and shortly before the execution to surrender their outer clothing. The men, women and children were led to a place of execution, which in most cases was located next to a more deeply excavated anti-tank ditch. Then they were shot—kneeling or standing—and the corpses thrown into the ditch.[44]

These documents, as first introduced, applied to the criminal activity of all four Einsatzgruppen in general and thus to all the defendants. So, afterward, the prosecution would need to specify how particular admitted documents inculpated individual defendants. The prosecutors divided this task. Ferencz assigned each attorney on his team an individual Einsatzgruppe for purposes of admitting evidence for the case-in-chief, cross-examining defendants and witnesses and making evidentiary objections for the defense cases. That division broke down as follows: Einsatzgruppe A—Glancey (although Ferencz took a portion of Jost's cross-examination); Einsatzgruppe B—Ferencz; Einsatzgruppe C—Horlik-Hochwald; and Einsatzgruppe D—Walton. Ferencz was tempted to take D because he "would have loved to cross-examine Ohlendorf" but decided to make that Jim Heath's sole task for the trial because, in light of his medical condition he did not want to overwhelm him, and "his mature stately manner and southern drawl might make a better impression on the Germans, and avoid any taint of Jewish vengeance."[45]

Ferencz later explained that, aside from the unique case of Heath, the assignments were made according to his estimation of each attorney's capabilities.[46] Einsatzgruppe A had only three defendants, so for that one he tasked Glancey, the lawyer with seemingly the lowest skill level. Einsatzgruppe B had six defendants, and he assigned that to himself. Einsatzgruppen C and D had seven and eight defendants respectively, and those were assigned to the barristers with previous NMT courtroom experience, Horlik-Hochwald (for C) and Peter Walton (for D—which would be reduced to seven defendants after Haussmann's suicide).

Thus, once Ferencz, followed by Glancey, finished admitting into evidence the "general" documents contained in Evidence Books 1 and 2, Glancey began with the case against the defendants in Einsatzgruppe A. His first order of business was detailing the breakdown of Einsatzgruppe A into four Sonderkommandos—1A, 1B, 2, and 3. Then he laid out specific criminal acts committed by the Einsatzgruppe A defendants in the dock—Jost, Sandberger, and Strauch. By way of example, with respect to Jost, a former lawyer, Glancy referred to Prosecution Exhibit 55, consisting of Operational Situation Report No. 193, which described the conduct of Einsatzkommandos acting pursuant to Jost's directions in Lithuania: "In Olita, 22 people were shot on 7 April 1942, because of communist activities. . . . The same day, 22 persons, among them 14 Jews, who purportedly had spread communist propaganda very recently, were shot in Kauen [that is, Kaunas]."[47]

Similar proof was offered in respect of defendant Sandberger, also a former attorney, as well as a judge. Prosecution Exhibit 34 was a report dealing with Einsatzgruppe A's activity through October 15, 1941, in an area of Estonia under the control of Sandberger's Sonderkommando 1a. The document revealed that "The arrest of all male Jews of over 16 years of age has been nearly finished. [They] were executed."[48] Various reports of this ilk were read into the record, and the case against Sandberger brought the first day of trial to a close at approximately 4:30 p.m.

Day 2 of the trial was held in Courtroom 2, in Room 581 (throughout the trial, sessions were divided between this chamber and Courtroom 1, that is, the iconic Courtroom 600). Glancey began where he left off, taking up the case against Strauch. Similar kinds of reports were read into the record, including one concerning a November 30, 1941, massacre of 10,600 Jews in Riga by Einsatzkommando 2 under Strauch's supervision.[49] With that, Glancey concluded, and Ben Ferencz began the case against Einsatzgruppe B.

Much as Glancey started with the defendant who was the top officer in Einsatzgruppe A, and worked his way down in rank in terms of the order of presenting evidence, Ferencz used roughly the same approach for Einsatzgruppe B, which had operated in the area south of Einsatzgruppe A, in and around Moscow (and including what is now Belarus). Thus, he started with Naumann, the overall chief (who formerly worked in a commercial firm and as a policeman). To contextualize Naumann's responsibility, Ferencz began by reading from documents that explained that Einsatzgruppe B consisted of Einsatzkommandos 8 and 9, Sonderkommandos 7a and 7b, as well as Vorkommando Moscow. Then he read an excerpt from Prosecution Exhibit 72, Naumann's own affidavit where the defendant confessed that "while I was its chief, Einsatzgruppe B carried out executions."[50]

Exhibit 67, an affidavit from defendant Ott, further inculpated Naumann, referring to 80 to 100 executions carried out by Sonderkommando 7b in the vicinity of Bryansk. It went on: "The people to be executed were handed over to my unit by the local commandant. The corpses were temporarily buried in the snow and later buried by the army. The valuables which were collected from those people were sent to Einsatzgruppe B. This was ordered by command of NAUMANN, the head of Einsatzgruppe B, and the same was true of the other executions."[51] After going through several more of these reports, Ferencz concluded: "Naumann's personnel record in the operational reports cannot be denied. The thousands of murders we have described were committed by Einsatzgruppe B while the defendant was its commanding officer."[52]

Ferencz then worked his way through the evidence against Blume, Steimle, Ott, Klingelhöfer, and Six (the latter should have been next in order in terms of rank, but the chief prosecutor saved him for last—so Six went sixth). Blume, who had been an attorney and served as chief of Sonderkommando 7a, confessed in his affidavit (Exhibit 10) that in May or June 1941, as the Operation Barbarossa Einsatzgruppen were being formed, he was instructed by both RSHA Chief Reinhard Heidrich and RSHA Head of Personnel Bruno Streckenbach that a core objective of the paramilitary squads was "exterminating the Jews."[53] In the affidavit, Blume went on to admit that he fulfilled this task. For example, he recounted that "As Chief of the Sonderkommando 7a . . . I remember one occasion on which between 70 and 80 people were executed in Witebsk (Vitebsk) and another occasion on which a similar number were executed in Minsk. . . . In both cases, a kind of trench was dug; the persons destined to die were placed in front of it and shot with carbines."[54]

In early September 1941, Defendant Steimle took over for Blume as head of Sonderkommando 7a; however, it was clear from the pretrial record that Steimle would deny his unit committed any executions and/or that he was responsible for any. But Ferencz was able to identify reports demonstrating the Sonderkommando continued massacring civilians in the same way it had during Blume's stewardship. Thus, Prosecution Exhibit 65, reporting Sonderkommando 7a's activities, indicated that "272 Jews and Jewesses" of the village of Belowschtschina were "liquidated" on October 25, 1941.[55]

This was followed by the case against former labor front head Ott, a fairly straightforward task as a portion of it had already been offered against Naumann. So Ferencz simply doubled back and then added new evidence. Klingelhöfer's case was next. Here, once again, the former opera singer's own affidavit, admitted as Exhibit 124, was damning. In it, he reported that, as head of Vorkommando Moscow (having taken over for Six), he went "from Smolensk to Tatarsk and Mistislawl to get furs for the German troops and to liquidate part of the Jews there. . . . The executions proper were carried out by Noack under my supervision. Those Jews, who were going to be executed, were led to the edge of a pit . . . and shot from behind. These people mostly fell into the graves. . . . In case it was noted that someone in the pit was still alive, he received the coup de grace."[56]

Finally, Ferencz led evidence against Six, a former professor of journalism and political science and the original chief of Vorkommando Moscow. Like Steimle, Six denied his unit was responsible for murdering civilian Jews, Roma, commissars, or the mentally ill. His unit was only supposed to locate "files and documents," he averred. But Six's affidavit also admitted that, as head of Vorkommando Moscow, he was present in Smolensk. Ferencz was then able to show through other documents that, on August 20, 1941, when Vorkommando Moscow was in Smolensk under Six's command, it executed 46 persons, of whom 36 were "Jewish intellectuals."[57] After marshaling more evidence of this sort, Ferencz concluded: "In view of the extermination function of all Einsatz units, the pattern of whole-sale murder, and the number of executions shown to have occurred in Vorkommando Moscow while the defendant Six was in command, we submit that his contention that he was merely there to collect archives is quite incredible."[58]

Horlik-Hochwald and Walton then engaged in a similar procedure, laying out the documentary cases against the officers of Einsatzgruppen C and D, including evidence of mass murder via gas vans. By this point, Day 2 of the trial was nearing its end. One last piece of evidence remained for the prosecution to present—a film of mass graves filled with Einsatzgruppen victims discovered by Russian soldiers. Defense counsel collectively objected to the film's showing, arguing that it lacked probative value. But the Tribunal accepted its admission on the grounds that it could help establish the *res gestae* (physical evidence apart from the reports and affidavits) of the charged crimes.

The film, which had previously been shown at the IMT trial and whose authenticity was verified by a certificate separately admitted into evidence (from the Russian filmmakers), was shown in Courtroom 600. It was accompanied by English commentary explaining the images on the screen. The excavation of the mounds of cadavers was visually horrifying and served as a powerful coda to the prosecution's case-in-chief.[59] It was now the evening of Tuesday, September 30, 1947—Judge Musmanno partially reversed his earlier decision and opted to grant defense counsel a short recess for the balance of the week. Trial would resume with the defense opening statements the following Monday morning, October 6, 1947.

In the meantime, Telford Taylor, who had been present for the two days of presentation, sent a letter to Chief Prosecutor Ferencz expressing his gratitude. Addressing him by the familiar "Benny," Taylor told his rising young star:

> The presentation of the prosecution in the *Einsatzgruppen* case was, I believe, a remarkable success which reflects great credit on you and your colleagues and assistants. The whole enterprise was exceedingly well-planned and even better executed. The opening statement received very widespread favorable comment, and the presentation of evidence has set a standard for crispness, economy, and expedition which will be very hard to match. Allow me to extend to you and all of your staff my congratulations and thanks for a distinguished performance.[60]

In a written portion of his IMT opening statement, which he spontaneously elected not to read in court, Robert Jackson had famously noted, "We must never forget that the record on which we judge these defendants today is the record on which history will judge us tomorrow. To pass these defendants a poisoned chalice is to put it to our own lips as well. We must summon such detachment and intellectual integrity to our task that this trial will commend itself to posterity as fulfilling humanity's aspiration to do justice."[61] To do that, the Allies had to offer robust due process protections to the defendants at Nuremberg.

Ben Ferencz was convinced that they had. In a 1948 article titled "Nuremberg Trial Procedure and the Rights of the Accused," which he published in the *Journal of Criminal Law and Criminology,* he laid out the full panoply of due process protections, which flowed from the NMTs' rules of procedure and evidence, Military Government Ordinance No. 7 (promulgated by OMGUS).[62] This included the defendant's right to (1) select *two* attorneys paid for by the NMTs (and every defendant in the *Einsatzgruppen* trial had two); (2) receive indictments stating the charges plainly, so as to give sufficient notice, with at least thirty days between service and the trial's start; (3) be present at trial with translations and recordings of the proceedings to check for inaccuracies; (4) marshal evidence in his favor and testify on his own behalf; (5) receive the prosecution's evidence—to be furnished to the accused, and translated, at least twenty-four hours in advance (again, routinely exceeded); and (6) cross-examine all prosecution witnesses.

There was also a presumption of innocence, an attendant burden on the prosecution to prove its case beyond a reasonable doubt, a review of all sentences by the US military governor as well as the right of subsequent petition for review to the US Supreme Court. Hearsay evidence and the death penalty were featured, and juries were not, but, within the relative procedural vacuum of 1945, Nuremberg's fledgling due process standards adequately paid respect to the rights of the accused.[63]

Moreover, apart from hearsay, the rules of evidence were interpreted very generously in favor of the defendants. At the *Einsatzgruppen* trial, this incredibly lax regime came to be summed up in one colorful and metaphoric principle, Judge Musmanno's so-called "Penguin Rule." As explained by the Tribunal president himself:

> [I] ruled that in view of the serious penalties which could accompany conviction, I would allow any evidence which could possibly have a bearing on mitigating the momentous accusations the defendants faced. I made only one exception. I would not permit any evidence on the social life of the penguins in the Antarctic. Later on I removed even that far-extending peripheral limitation and said that if defense counsel could show how such a subject could be relevant, we would listen to what they had to expound. In time this assertion became known as the "Penguin Rule."[64]

With such a liberal procedural and evidentiary framework in place, the courtroom's black-robed Germans individually rose to take up the defense of their clients on the morning of October 6, 1947. The opening statements revealed a wide array of justifications and excuses, both legal and factual. Regarding the former, it was understood among defense counsel that, although specific defendants may have asserted them individually, they applied to all defendants across the board insofar as they all faced similar/overlapping factual circumstances. Moreover, there were threshold attacks on the Tribunal's jurisdiction, including "victor's justice" and ex post application of law (especially in respect of crimes against humanity).

Of the overall set of defenses, the most popular by far was following superior orders—fourteen of the twenty-three defendants asserted it explicitly (only the "blanket denial" defendants, described below, did not separately invoke it). Another asserted legal justification was self-defense—that is, the National Socialists needed to destroy the Bolshevists before they could destroy them. Ohlendorf, Sandberger, and Braune explicitly put this before the Tribunal.

Apart from following superior orders, the most popular legal defense was military justification, that is, those shot by the defendant's unit were partisans, spies, saboteurs, and looters. Rasch, Schulz, Blobel, Sandberger, Biberstein, Haensch, Ott, Nosske, and Klingelhöfer explicitly availed themselves of this argument. Biberstein, a former priest, even had the audacity to assert that, in his case, executions took place only pursuant to individualized fair trials.

Another legal defense, formally embraced by Naumann, Jost, Schubert, and

Seibert, was to invoke the recently developed doctrine of "command responsibility." This meant arguing, in the first instance, that the defendants neither participated in nor ordered any executions. Thus, they wanted to be proactive in countering any suggestion of liability by omission, that is, guilt by virtue of permitting their subordinates to commit atrocities. Such liability might have been possible under the recent US case of *In re Yamashita* (1946).[65] Per that decision, a superior's "command responsibility" for the acts of his subordinates could attach if the superior had knowledge that the crimes were being committed and had the power to prevent them from being committed but failed to do so. The defendants argued the second condition could not be met. In the cases of Jost and Naumann, this was because their predecessors, Franz Walter Stahlecker and Arthur Nebe, respectively, had previously issued the orders to kill for Einsatzgruppen A and B. Jost and Naumann claimed they could not countermand them. For Schubert and Seibert, the argument was that only Ohlendorf would have had the power to rescind his own orders for execution in Einsatzgruppe D.

Finally, defendant Blume raised the German legal defense of *Unzumutbarkeit,* which was translated by Blume's lawyer, Dr. Lummert, as "unexpectability." It roughly equates to a duress defense to the effect that, under such unusual circumstances of danger to the defendant, he would not be expected to act in accordance with law and his crime can therefore be excused. In this case, Blume was ordered by the Nazi state to engage in mass murder under penalty of death to himself if he did not comply. International law, which contained no codified version of crimes against humanity at that point, and pursuant to which the defendant was being prosecuted, could have given him no shield against the state that ordered him to commit murder.

Otherwise, many of the defendants took refuge behind a string of factual defenses and evidentiary/criminal procedure attacks. For example, Seibert and Klingelhöfer argued that the Einsatzgruppen Daily Reports, the most important source of evidence establishing guilt, were unreliable because they covered a wide area of activities, were only summaries of individual reports, and thus were replete with errors. Plus, relatedly, they had not been compiled based on the personal knowledge of those reporting to Berlin, who only received information secondhand.

Biberstein attacked perhaps the most important piece of evidence offered against him, his affidavit. First, he argued that it represented "only a completely one-sided excerpt" from all the various statements he made to interrogator Rolf Wartenberg—exonerating statements were not included.[66] Independently, he claimed the affidavit should be excluded, since he was not told it could be used against him (he thought he was only a witness, not a suspect)—so he was denied a basic right afforded in American criminal proceedings, that against self-incrimination.

Other defendants, such as Jost, Naumann, Schulz, Steimle, Haensch, Strauch, and Fendler, quibbled with the time frames alleged by the prosecution, arguing that they were in the killing fields for shorter periods or that executions did not take place during certain stretches. Others pled mitigating circumstances: Jost testified that he had serious medical issues in the field (e.g., a thyroid disease and spinal stenosis); similarly, Blobel, an alcoholic who directed the Babi Yar massacre, asserted that he was in the hospital for long intervals or not fit for duty at other times; and Schulz argued that, for a spell during his alleged culpability, he was in Berlin, not Ukraine.

Finally, there were the "blanket denial" defendants—Six, Haensch, Rühl, Fendler, von Radetzky, and Graf—all lower-ranking commanders (except for Six). Graf testified that he felt that he must have been included in the case by mistake—his job was simply to report on the local population regarding medical conditions, education, agriculture, and culture. He had absolutely no part in the executions, he asserted. According to von Radetzky, he was deployed for his language abilities and helped gather intelligence. Fendler was also strictly involved in harvesting information, he informed the judges. Rühl was merely a Sonderkommando administrative officer—he neither participated in nor attended executions, he explained, and even helped save Jews. Six helmed Vorkommando Moscow so he could not plead low rank. Still, he issued a flat denial of any involvement in executions—his sole responsibility, he informed the Tribunal, was for capturing and assuring the safety of archives in the Soviet capital and its environs (although Nazi forces never reached Moscow).

Defense cases were presented, with various breaks along the way, from October 8, 1947, through the beginning of February 1948. Of significant interest was the testimony of the lead defendant, Otto Ohlendorf, the first to take the stand. Ferencz described him as "a fairly handsome man, father of five children, [who] had earned a degree in economics."[67] Many spectators piled into the courtroom "just to see him," a former IMT witness who had admitted to murdering 90,000 civilians, "a mass murderer whose story had been widely reported in newspapers."[68] Musmanno painted him as a kind of dark prince sex symbol, with women flocking to Courtroom 600 so as "to marvel at him [and] pass him notes offering encouragement and endearment."[69]

Not surprisingly, he was formidable on the witness stand. Along with IMT defendant Hjalmar Schacht, the former Nazi finance minister, Ohlendorf tested highest on the IQ charts among the Nuremberg prisoners. Ohlendorf's testimony was "erudite and profound, and resembled a philosophy professor more than a man pleading for mercy. [As] hard as the prosecution tried, they could not get him to admit he had done anything wrong let alone break his defense of superior orders."[70]

From a substantive perspective, his superior orders plea was a pillar for the defenses of most of the other men in the dock. And it may have been historically significant beyond the trial itself. According to Ohlendorf, one month before they were deployed, the Einsatzgruppen recruits were gathered at Pretzsch, a small German town on the Elbe River near the Soviet border, the location of a training school for police.[71] Here, the men were trained and briefed about their assignments. Of extreme significance, he testified that on June 22, 1941, Bruno Streckenbach (head of Office I Personnel in the RSHA) and Heinrich Müller (chief of the Gestapo) informed Ohlendorf and other Einsatzgruppen officers that they were transmitting Adolf Hitler's order (having been passed through Himmler and Heydrich) that their paramilitary units were to exterminate all Jews, Roma, and Communist functionaries (as well as the insane and incurably ill, called by the Nazis "useless eaters," "Asiatic inferiors," and "asocials").[72] This was routinely referred to by the defendants as the "Führerbefehl," or Führer Order. If accurate, Ohlendorf's account was of great historical significance since it meant the Holocaust began as early as June 1941 (as opposed to later in 1941, or at the beginning of 1942, the time of the infamous Wannsee Conference, when the bureaucratic organization of the extermination was planned).[73]

In terms of the *Einsatzgruppen* trial itself, Ohlendorf's testimony was critical as the bedrock of a master defense strategy to negate or mitigate the defendants' crimes via obedience to an order issued by the supreme authority in Nazi Germany, Adolf Hitler. Jim Heath, who cross-examined Ohlendorf, sought to elicit testimony such that there were limits to the defendant's adherence to the Führerbefehl and thereby create cracks in Ohlendorf's superior orders defense. But "Ohlendorf did not buckle under Heath's questioning."[74] Musmanno, who took a very active part in examining witnesses throughout the trial, tried his hand at nudging Ohlendorf from his position. He asked the former Einsatzgruppen leader whether he would have murdered his own sister pursuant to the order. Ohlendorf did not flinch—yes, he replied, he would have.[75]

But the defense was badly compromised via Ohlendorf's Einsatzgruppe D deputy commander, Willi Seibert, who wilted under the intense heat of a Musmanno examination on the same subject the following month. For Seibert, the question was somewhat different, whether he would have shot his own parents. It came late in the afternoon of November 19, 1947. Seibert seemed flustered on the stand, "looking out the window at the diminishing light of the dying afternoon," and he refused to answer the question.[76] But Musmanno would not let it go—he ordered him to think about it overnight and provide a response the following morning.[77]

At 9:30 a.m. on November 20, the courtroom was standing room only, abuzz with curious spectators eager to learn whether the Führerbefehl would have compelled Ohlendorf's lieutenant to commit parricide. The Tribunal was called into session, the witness was sworn in, Musmanno gave him a moment to compose himself, and then he repeated the question. "Would you have killed your parents if Adolf Hitler had ordered you to do so?" One could have heard the proverbial pin drop in the chamber. Seibert, looking haggard and trapped, dejectedly muttered, "Mr. President, I would not do so."[78] His fellow defendants in the dock, who had been on tenterhooks, "heaved a collective, heavy grunt of disgust."[79] What they had perceived as the most impregnable bulwark against the charged crimes had just crumbled.

13

THE *EINSATZGRUPPEN* TRIAL, PART 2

> [It] is ordinary people, like you and me, who commit genocide and mass killing.
>
> —James Waller, *Becoming Evil*

> The judge . . . should have learned to know evil, not from his own soul, but from late and long observation of the nature of evil in others.
>
> —Plato, *The Republic*

The testimony of Einsatzgruppe D chief Otto Ohlendorf and his deputy, Willi Seibert, provided some of the trial's truly dramatic moments. In general, though, the proceeding settled into a kind of routine. The defendants presented their cases in the order of their positioning in the dock, starting with Ohlendorf and working their way from right to left on the front bench and then snaking back to the rear pew and following the same order. On direct examination, each lead defense attorney would elicit testimony from his client consistent with what was promised in his opening statement. He would then pose questions to any supporting witnesses. Direct examinations would be followed by cross-examinations conducted by the other defense attorneys, and then by the prosecution. If necessary, there would be redirect and recross in the same order.

The cases of the Einsatzgruppe B defendants, Ben Ferencz's assigned group, provide a good representative sample. After Otto Ohlendorf, the Tribunal skipped over Heinz Jost, and Einsatzgruppe B chief Erich Naumann took the stand on October 16, 1947. His backstory is illustrative of those of many of the other Einsatzgruppen officers. Embittered by Germany's loss in World War I, these men, all born between 1900 and 1910, were inclined to "far right-wing politics."[1] Naumann explained that he joined the Nazi Party in late 1929, at age twenty-four, in response to Germany's being plunged into the Great Depression. He rose in the party rather quickly, becoming an SA leader in 1933, an SD leader in 1935, and then the chief of Einsatzgruppe B on November 30, 1941, taking over for Arthur Nebe by order of Reinhard Heydrich (not on November 1, he claimed, as certain official documents indicated). He asserted that he was against the assignment but had to follow Heydrich's order on pain of being shot. After he reached Smolensk (about five hundred miles west of Moscow) for his new assignment, he overlapped with Nebe for about one week, during which time the departing chief instructed him on how to run the unit. He was in command, with an administrative staff of about sixty, until roughly March 1942.

While there, he claimed, he was subordinate to the commander of Army Group Center and the Higher SS and police leader in the region. Moreover, he asserted that the Einsatzkommandos under his command did not carry out executions of Jews, Roma, and Communist functionaries pursuant to his order, but pursuant to that of Security Police Chief and Gruppenführer Bruno Streckenbach. To the extent the order was transmitted by Nebe, though, it was in place before Naumann arrived, and he could not countermand it.

In particular, he "had no possibility of preventing the execution of a Führer Order [or] Himmler would have [had him] shot."[2] As for the reports submitted by the prosecution showing liquidations, Naumann testified that those occurred before he assumed command of the unit. Moreover, the area covered by Einsatzgruppe B was vast, and the individual units, all far from one another and Naumann's location in Smolensk, acted independently, including in deciding when to conduct executions and against which people. Finally, during his time as chief, he averred that the unit's main preoccupation was dealing with partisans, not executing persons pursuant to the Führer Order. He flatly stated, in response to a direct question asked by his attorney, that he did not commit any crimes. During the examination, Ferencz objected forcefully that attorney Gawlik was leading the witness but was overruled.[3]

The chief prosecutor's cross-examination of Naumann took place on October 17, 1947, and he scored some important points. He began with Naumann's efforts, immediately after the war, to forge documents, assume an alias, and move from farm to farm, working as a laborer. If he had committed no crimes, Ferencz asked, why did he conceal his identity and hide? Naumann responded that, just by virtue of being "an old National Socialist," he feared being apprehended and imprisoned.[4] The answer did not ring true.

He also pressed Naumann on his November start date as chief of Einsatzgruppe B—his claim that November 1 was an official, not actual, start date was contradicted by a later document, as well as the testimony of Eugen Steimle, with which Ferencz confronted him. Along the way, through dogged questioning, the chief prosecutor was able to wring a concession to the effect that Naumann specifically received from Heydrich the Führer Order to kill all

"Jews [including women and children], gypsies and Soviet officials."[5] And he got him to admit that he "accepted the order" of his "supreme commander."[6] Naumann also conceded that he understood he was taking over a unit that would "continue killing defenseless people" and that he discussed carrying out the Führer Order with the individual Kommando leaders in his unit as he was traveling from command post to command post. This included discussions with codefendants Steimle and Ott.[7]

During the cross-examination, Ferencz was also able to show Naumann documents that had only recently been unearthed in Berlin, which indicated that the Einsatzgruppe B leader ordered the execution of a group of Russians at a "Camp Wisoskoje," on December 5, 1942.[8] Naumann tried to deflect, but the documents were facially damning. Finally, Ferencz asked Naumann about whether he tried to coach his former subordinate, codefendant Waldemar Klingelhöfer, about his upcoming testimony before the Tribunal. He produced Naumann's letter to his former subordinate, which began with, "Don't let them bluff you," provided instructions on what Klingelhöfer should say on the stand, and then previewed Naumann's own testimony (including his position on the supposed later November start date) so their stories would mesh.[9] It came off as quite incriminating.

Ten days later, Ferencz cross-examined his next witness, Franz Six, a "blanket denialist," who claimed that his unit, Vorkommando Moscow, which he led from June through the end of August 1941, was solely concerned with collecting and preserving documents. Once again, Ferencz was able to put some chinks in his armor. He got Six to confess his learning of the Führerbefehl to annihilate the Jews in July in Minsk,[10] his unit's presence in Smolensk in late August, and then he confronted him with a report notifying Berlin that on August 20, 1941, when Vorkommando Moscow was in Smolensk under Six's command, it executed forty-six persons, of whom thirty-six were "Jewish intellectuals."[11] Later, Six asserted, he asked to be sent back to Berlin in late August 1941 because he objected to being in charge of the unit. He explained that this created tension between him and Heydrich, but Ferencz presented documents demonstrating that he was promoted twice after his return from the Eastern Front (once by Heinrich Himmler personally) based on "outstanding service" in the Einsatzgruppen.[12]

Walter Blume's cross-examination, conducted on November 4, 1947, was next. From late June through mid-August 1941, Blume held the reins of Sonderkommando 7a. This was a rather straightforward exercise for Ferencz since, as we have seen, Blume conceded his supervision of massacres in Minsk and Vitebsk pursuant to the Führerbefehl. But Ferencz used the examination to elicit helpful testimony regarding Vorkommando Moscow and other Einsatzgruppe B defendants. Eugen Steimle replaced Blume as chief of Sonderkommando 7a, and Ferencz cross-examined him two days later. Like Six, Steimle was a blanket denialist. He testified in court that reports indicating the massacre of Jews by Sonderkommando 7a under his command referred not to Holocaust victims but to partisans. There were no Perry Mason moments here, but Ferencz's tenacious line of questioning made Steimle's bald-faced denials seem absurd, and the chief prosecutor was able to elicit testimony bolstering his case against Naumann.

That left Adolf Ott and Waldemar Klingelhöfer as the final two Einsatzgruppe B defendants Ferencz would cross-examine. Ott took the stand on December 9, and Ferencz started questioning him the next day. He had taken over Sonderkommando 7b from Günther Rausch in February 1942. Again, this was not as challenging an examination because, as we saw previously, Ott had already confessed to carrying out executions ordered by Naumann. During direct examination, he also testified that his unit executed numerous Jews who all happened to be partisans, but Ott admitted under questioning from Judge Musmanno that they would have been murdered regardless, pursuant to the Führerbefehl.[13] Moreover, through the cross-examination, Ferencz elicited testimony that helped corroborate Naumann's guilt, including directing Ott to follow the Führerbefehl and collect execution victims' valuables and send them to Einsatzgruppe B headquarters.[14]

Fittingly, Ferencz's cross-examinations were bookended by Naumann and Klingelhöfer, the two defendants who were linked via one's written communication to the other. Klingelhöfer, the recipient of that communication, was one of the more interesting accused butchers in the dock, having had a previous career as an opera tenor and music teacher. Prosecution exhibits indicated that he took over leadership of Vorkommando Moscow from Six. But during his December 11, 1947, direct examination, he claimed he was only an interpreter and staff analyst. He explained that Prosecution Exhibit 124, the July affidavit signed by him after Wartenberg's interrogation, and indicating his position as Vorkommando Moscow chief and his supervision of 1941 executions of Jews in Tatarsk and Mstislavl, was inaccurate. He drafted his own affidavit in September, which was submitted as a defense exhibit, to the effect that he was never chief of Vokommando Moscow (which he admitted carried out thousands of executions of Jews) and was only in Tatarsk and Mstislavl to collect furs, not direct the person in charge of the executions, Hauptsturmführer Egon Noack, a supposed "expert" on the "Jewish Question."

Ferencz's cross-examination was effective on many levels. First, he was able to show that Klingelhöfer's work as an analyst directly contributed to the murder of defenseless civilians via the Führerbefehl:

Q. So, therefore, you found some lists giving you the names of all the Party functionaries in that area and you just gave that list to [Sonderkommando 7b leader Günther Rausch], is that correct?
A. Yes, that was my duty.
Q. Now, you knew that Hitler had given the order that all Party functionaries were to be exterminated, did you not?
A. Yes. I knew. . . .
Q. Didn't you know at that time he was going to exterminate all those people he could catch?
A. [Of] course, I did.[15]

He was also able to demonstrate Klingelhöfer's responsibility for the murder of innocent Jews through his subsequent leadership role in Vorkommando Moscow. After confronting the witness with a report regarding "38 intellectual Jews" who were shot in Smolensk by the Vorkommando, an incident about which Klingelhöfer claimed to be ignorant, the following terse but effective line of examination ensued:

Q. But you were in Vorkommando Moskau at that time, were you not?
A. Yes, I was in Advance Kommando Moskau.
Q. [You] were [its] deputy [leader]?
A. I was appointed deputy.[16]

Regarding the discrepancies in the July versus September affidavits—crucial as the earlier document laid blame squarely on the defendant's shoulders—through sharp, rhythmic questions, Ferencz was able to draw out the following testimony regarding external circumstances supporting the reliability of the crucial July affidavit:

Q. Do you remember the circumstances under which you gave this affidavit on the 2nd of July?
A. Yes.
Q. Was there any duress in connection with the taking of this affidavit?
A. No.
Q. Was there any threat made in connection with the taking of this affidavit?
A. No.
Q. Was there any force used in connection with the taking of this affidavit?
A. No.
Q. Was there any promise of immunity made in connection with the taking of this affidavit?

A. Promise for reward—no. . . .
Q. Were you reminded before you signed this statement that you were under oath?
A. I was put under oath before—yes.[17]

Ferencz then found another discrepancy between Klingelhöfer's affidavit and a report submitted by his unit. In his affidavit, he admitted to shooting thirty civilian Jewish men in Tatarsk but stated that he had no women shot. The report, which the former opera singer received after signing his affidavit, indicated that he had three Jewish women shot. Ferencz pounced on the divergence:

Q. I am just asking you [to] study this report. Here it says that "all male Jews and the three women who were in Tatarsk at that time were shot." You stated [in your affidavit] that no women were shot. Here it says three women were shot. What is your explanation for the discrepancy?
A. [I] had forgotten about these three women. I cannot give you any other explanation.[18]

Ferencz also elicited damaging testimony from Klingelhöfer regarding ghettoized Jews who were targeted for murder by the Einsatzgruppe in which the defendant served as an officer:

Q. Now, I am trying to find out from you for what purpose did they put the Jews [of Tatarsk] in the Ghetto who were too old or too weak to work?
A. I do not know, Mr. Prosecutor.
Q. Did you ever hear of the Fuehrer Order?
A. Yes.
Q. Did you know that the Einsatzkommandos were supposed to murder all the Jews?
A. Yes, that was the Fuehrer Order.[19]

Even better, through a barrage of piercing questions, Ferencz wore Klingelhöfer down and got him to concede that "whether or not the Jews had violated any order, whether they left or stayed in the ghetto, and whether or not they contacted the partisans, they were all killed."[20]

The cross-examination also ended on a dramatic note, with Ferencz looping back to Naumann's attempt to coach Klingelhöfer. The former voice instructor testified that he had not opened Naumann's note and immediately turned it over to Wartenberg, accompanied by a July 3 letter. In a powerful moment of the trial, Ferencz had the defendant read the letter out loud in court. After stating in the missive that he did not want to be complicit in what he suspected was Naumann's attempts to fabricate testimony, he noted that "after the collapse I gained full insight into the horrible blasphemy which was carried out here. . . . I am fully conscious of the fact that I must bear the consequences completely for my personal attitude and my acts."[21]

After composing this note, Klingelhöfer had attempted suicide. Under questioning from Ferencz, he admitted that, having betrayed Naumann, he felt that his "honor was lost." And Ferencz sharply responded, "You did not think you lost your honor when you shot Jews, did you?" The defendant responded, "I shot Jews, Mr. Prosecutor, because during the war . . ."[22] But he did not complete his sentence. Ferencz tried, but ultimately failed, in eliciting a plea for absolution in open court. Nevertheless, the defendant's maudlin whimpering must have reminded all present of his former career on the opera stage. And the cross-examination soon ended in that pathetic atmosphere of self-pity.

According to Andrew Nagorski, the chief prosecutor's work had impressed Judge Musmanno: "[He] was . . . persuaded that Ferencz 'had not been engaging in figures of speech but in numerals of cast-iron reality.' And he described the diminutive barrister as 'David taking Goliath's measure' as he demolished the defendants' attempts to shift the blame for their killing sprees to anyone but themselves."[23]

By then, it was nearly time for the Christmas recess, and Musmanno announced a break in the proceedings from December 22 through January 3, 1948. The Ferenczes, both exhausted from the intense work of 1947, took advantage and went on an abbreviated vacation in the Alps region, tooling around in Gertrude's 1938 Mercedes. When the tour finished in Merano, Italy, the trial was soon to resume. So a quick departure for Germany was scheduled, as they would have to climb over the Italian Alps. Normally they would have traveled via the Brenner Pass, but, due to the season's inclement weather, it was closed. Conscious of the time, Ben searched for a comparably efficient alpine route on his military map and found one—"a very thin red line leading from where they were to where they wanted to go."[24]

This turned out to be an incredibly steep fissure through the mountains, and it seemed to narrow more and more as they climbed, and the weather worsened. Along the way, they passed foresters who shouted "*Ritornate! Ritornate!*"[25] Gertrude strongly concurred, but Ben thought the Italians badly "underestimated the power of the American spirit to stay the course" and pushed on.[26] As they neared the mountain's apex, the path could barely accommodate the hulking Mercedes, and, in a moment of horror, Ben realized how wrong he had been. The car suddenly skidded toward the edge of the road and was within inches of plunging over the side and dropping them to their death more than ten thousand feet below.

Gertrude peered down into the abyss, speechless and trembling, tears welling up in her eyes. Ben tried to stay calm and consider their options. Cresting the ridge was out of the question as they were precariously balanced on the edge on one side and mired in snow on the other. Walking back would have also meant certain death given the subarctic temperatures that were only continuing to drop. Traveling on foot in those conditions for a very short distance might have been possible, but the nearest town was more than twenty miles behind them. And calling for help would have been equally futile—no living soul was anywhere near them. Somehow, all by themselves, Ben concluded, they had to find a way to extricate the car from the snow without tumbling over the edge of the cliff, turn it around, and try to drive back to the closest town. Was that even possible?

Ben felt a sudden burst of confidence thinking about all the miles he had logged driving over nearly every kind of terrain as a war crimes investigator. With Gertrude as his guide, he felt he could get them out through deft manipulations of the engine and steering wheel. Mrs. Ferencz slipped out of the car in the pitch black and gave him verbal cues. He put the Mercedes in reverse and, coming within a whisker of going over the side, managed to move it away from the precipice. But just as it was about to reach safety on the constricted snow-covered path, the tires caught some ice and skidded farther into a ditch alongside the mountain wall. His efforts "to rock the car out of its trap" were in vain. If they had to remain stationary like that, they would freeze to death just as certainly. Then inspiration hit:

> [I recalled that the great escape artist, Harry Houdini, could get out of any locked box] by concealing a small jack on his person and using [it] to press the nails out of the side. [The] Mercedes had a small jack that could lift the car to repair flat tires. I slid under the car and placed one side of the jack against the mountain and the other against the hubcap. By slithering under the car from front to back for about two hours, jacking it inch by inch, I was able to move the car back on to the road. Hocus Pocus![27]

After a multitude of little steering wheel movements, Ben was able to maneuver the car around so that it was facing downhill. His practice on the path to Hitler's Eagle's Nest in 1945, he reflected, had proved invaluable. The vehicle was finally positioned to descend, and the terrified couple idled glacially down the dark, slippery road to the labored sound of the Mercedes heater chuffing. With Ben's foot on, or never far from, the brake, they silently prayed that they had encountered the last patch of treacherous ice. After what seemed like an eternity, they finally reached the town, hugged each other, and cried. Then they checked into the first hotel with a vacancy and slept like babies. The next day they would take no chances—crossing into Germany via the much longer, but safer, Gotthard Pass. The Mercedes rolled into Fürth just in the nick of time—an exhausted Ben Ferencz was back at the prosecution table in Courtroom 600 on the morning of January 5, 1948, ready for the trial's home stretch.

THE PROCEEDING resumed much as it had before the break. Perhaps of greatest significance was former Einsatzgruppe C leader Otto Rasch attempting to testify on January 12, 1948. His Parkinson's disease had been growing worse by the month, and he began displaying serious symptoms of dementia. Still, he attempted to testify and got through the very first part of his direct examination. Seeing the frail Rasch on a stretcher was quite the spectacle considering that he was recognized "as one of the most brutal executants of Hitler's extermination program, often appearing personally on the field of execution to supervise the slaughter."[28]

Quite feebly, "with one shaking hand [trying] to still the shaking of the other," he pushed out the incongruous story of a happy childhood with a father who taught him how to hunt and respect animals. The macabre and ironic implications of this ruthless genocidaire's tale of killing animals with dignity was lost on no one in the chamber. But that was as far as Rasch got—his body and mind finally gave out. Musmanno had various doctors testify regarding his condition and decided, on February 5, to sever his case from the main proceeding and discontinue it. Rasch was then able to escape the hangman's noose, succumbing to his illness on November 1.

By the time the motion to sever was granted, the defense attorneys were already making their closing submissions. Rudolf Aschenauer had begun for Otto Ohlendorf on February 4, and he was followed by colleagues in the same order that their clients testified. These arguments essentially mirrored their opening statements but with specific reference to testimony sprinkled throughout them as well as more extensive citation to legal authority. They lasted eight days.

On February 13, 1948, the prosecution was finally ready to make its closing argument. This time, the attorney at the podium would not be Ben Ferencz but his boss and benefactor, Telford Taylor. The younger man might have preferred to do the closing himself, but, by then, he had already been the dominant prosecution figure during the trial. In addition to handling the bulk of the opening statement and the Einsatzgruppe B defendants, he argued most of the motions and spoke for the prosecution with respect to calendaring and general evidence issues. And apart from Naumann, Six, Blume, Steimle, Ott, and Klingelhöfer, he had cross-examined the medical witnesses supporting Rasch's motion to sever, as well as an alibi witness for Six (Veronika Vetter). Moreover, lending a hand to Glancey, he had also handled a portion of the cross-examination of Einsatzgruppe A leader Heinz Jost. He was more than magnanimous about letting Taylor take on the trial's last bit of heavy lifting.

Still, the OCCWC chief counsel consulted with his deputy on the closing, and the latter gave the final draft his blessing, subsequently noting that the general's words "summarized the evidence and the arguments in his usual elegant way."[29] Thus, Taylor approached the lectern 137 days after the trial had begun in late September. Alluding to the "conclusive documentary proof in support" of the prosecution case, he immediately signaled that he would refrain from "a tedious rehearsal of the details of the record."[30]

He noted that the position of the blanket denialists, in light of the overwhelming documentary evidence, was "preposterous" and concluded indignantly: "the very idea that the defendants did not know of both the order and of the executions is so ridiculous that we have already dignified it overmuch."[31] Even if certain of the defendants were not present at the massacres because only fulfilling an administrative function, they were at the very least complicit. "The cook in the galley of a pirate ship does not escape the yardarm," Taylor analogized, "merely because he himself does not brandish a cutlass."[32]

And the higher-placed defendants were guilty under the doctrine of command responsibility. For those Einsatzgruppen officers claiming justifiable homicide under the laws of war because the victims were partisans, guerrillas, spies, or saboteurs, the rules required executions pursuant to trials satisfying basic due process standards. Any assertions that proceedings of that nature took place stood against the overwhelming weight of the evidence.

Taylor then turned to the defense of superior orders. He was able to refute it, quite convincingly, by pointing out that the defense does not lie "where, on its face, the order is palpably criminal."[33] Such was the case here when the command was to exterminate defenseless civilians strictly based on their status. Moreover, per Law No. 10, that defense did not negate responsibility but could only mitigate punishment. And, given the gravity of the crimes and the high education level, rank, and professional station of each defendant, such mitigation was unwarranted in the case at bar.

Finally, Taylor addressed the issue of self-defense. He did not take on directly Ohlendorf's claim that the work of the Einsatzgruppen was necessary to take out Bolshevism before it could do the same to National Socialism. Rather, he engaged with the defense through the prism of the genocide committed against the Jews, even invoking the term "holocaust" before the collective conscience had ever capitalized its first letter and placed it into its lexicon of evil to describe that cataclysm:

> The Einsatz massacres of Jews have been defended here as if it were sincerely believed that the killing . . . was a military necessity in order to achieve military victory over the Russian Army. But in point of fact this argument is not sincerely made. [Will] any defendant dare to suggest to us that the execution of the Jews in Russia would have stopped if Russian military resistance had collapsed? On the contrary, the evidence is compelling that a German victory would have enormously widened the scope of operations of the Einsatzgruppen and the holocaust would have been even more staggering.[34]

Taylor then finished eloquently, again revealing the prosecution's view that, despite the Nazi murder of other "subhuman" groups, more than anything, this trial was about the Shoah. And, echoing Ferencz's plea of humanity to law, it was about meting out the proper punishment to assure such horrors could never repeat themselves:

> Some of these defendants still believe that what they did was not murder because the victims were Jews. No system of domestic or international penal law could possibly survive under which the determination of guilt for murder is governed by the political or religious creed or racial origin of the victim. It is vitally important . . . that no such doctrine gain currency among nations. We earnestly suggest to the court that true judicial wisdom in this case counsels firmness rather than leniency to those adjudged guilty of this terrible crime against humanity.[35]

All that remained were the final remarks of the defendants themselves. Ohlendorf went first and, betraying no remorse whatsoever, presented a highfalutin apologia for National Socialism. He spoke in rather abstract terms of spiritual and political decay due to a pluralism brought on by the granting of religious and social freedoms in modern times. This fraying of Christian hegemony yielded a swarm of competing ideologies, attacking one another in the public arena like Roman gladiators, desperately fighting for survival. Thus, he intoned, his generation "searched for new religious values" beyond the anarchic group fighting and found National Socialism, which "was based on the conception of totality in relation to every single individual" and would "furnish the basis of a new order."[36] It sought to reject "bolshevism" as the false "idol."[37] But, according to this Social Darwinist account, National Socialism lost the war, and now the situation had become even direr.

"I have been now in the Palace of Justice in Nuernberg for 2½ years," he reminded those assembled. "What I have seen here of life as a spiritual force . . . has increased my fear."[38] The defendants in the dock, Ohlendorf complained, had let "the power of the victors" strip them of their faith in National Socialism and concede to letting it be "called criminal." As a result, they had given up "their human dignity."[39] And so, remaining an unrepentant Nazi to the end, Ohlendorf concluded: "Not one nation alone is guilty, but ideas and the weight of concrete conditions among the nations fighting for their survival and future find human representatives who are capable of unloosening the pent-up tension. . . . May the verdict of this Court take into account the reality of historic conditions and developments and give the Germans, individually and collectively, the opportunity of true self-realization."[40]

In language less abstract and lofty, but sprinkled with a bit more contrition, certain of the other defendants echoed these sentiments but spoke more of their personal circumstances and comportment. Jost stressed that he had been made chief of Einsatzgruppe A "against [his] will and without [his] agreement."[41] And he said that he felt "conflicted" about carrying out his duties in that assignment. Naumann described an "enormous collision between duty and conscience."[42] But, he added, he did not regard the Nazi invasion of the Soviet Union as aggression because, per the information available to him, it was about to attack Germany. He went on to explain that he was genuinely concerned about "bolshevism" as a threat to Germany and Europe. And thus, he couched his last substantive thoughts in Cold War rhetoric: "How right this attitude has been proved by the subsequent period. The causes which led to the cooling off of the inter-Allied relationship between the U.S.A. and the U.S.S.R. prove, I believe, the accuracy of my original point of view."[43] Seibert emphasized that he voluntarily surrendered to the British and cooperated. Otherwise, the denialists continued to deny, and certain defendants, such as Sandberger, refused to add anything to what their lawyers had already pled.

Mathias Graf spoke last and reminded the panel that, of all the men sitting on the two benches before them, he was the only noncommissioned officer. His last words were the trial's final ones, preverdict: "I have confidence that a [benevolent] destiny will restore my honor and my freedom to me, thanks to the objective and righteous judges." It was the end of the day on February 13, 1948, and the parties had completed their cases. The accused would be returned to their prison cells, waiting for Tribunal II to determine what justice required. (By trial's end, Tribunal II-A had been redesignated Tribunal II.)

WHILE THE defendants remained in place during this period of deliberation, the *Einsatzgruppen* chief prosecutor left Nuremberg. Ferencz's relationship with Telford Taylor was, by then, stronger than ever; he had worked his way into the general's professional inner circle. And so it was that the month after the cases were presented in the *Einsatzgruppen* trial, Ferencz found himself on a work trip to Berlin with his boss and another of Taylor's favorites, Jim McHaney. Ferencz was still Berlin Branch chief and wanted to check up on the goings-on there. McHaney was supervising Berlin-based investigations and appreciated the opportunity to peruse the original documents and speak with the analysts in person. And Taylor traveled to Berlin regularly to meet with General Lucius Clay and other army brass. On this occasion, they would mix in a little pleasure by bringing their wives and taking advantage of Berlin's nightlife offerings, far superior to those of provincial Nuremberg.

The trip went swimmingly, but, on the way back, as with the Ferenczes' recent swing through the Italian Alps, they flirted with disaster. There were omens of it on the eve of the flight—Gertie reported to Ben on the morning of their departure that she had dreamed of dead pigeons. Things did not seem much more auspicious once they arrived at the airport—their transportation was an old two-engine C-47 propeller plane that had seen better days. The weather at Tempelhof Airport was miserable—bitter cold with heavy rain and gusts and limited visibility. But there was even more portentous foreshadowing. The inappropriately cheery pilot, Lieutenant Tom Squires of Texas, strapped each passenger into a harness with two large rings in the front where a parachute could be attached in case of emergency. Then he had them sign a waiver of all possible claims. Ben then tempted fate even more brazenly when he said to Squires, "Be careful, the life you save may be my own."[44] He took it even further once each of them was strapped in. Gertie complained that the harness was too loose. "Don't worry," Ben quipped jocularly, "you probably won't fall out."[45]

Cue the ominous music—within minutes after takeoff, Taylor told the others he spotted oil spewing out of the right engine. Then a stream of smoke poured along the fuselage and the engine began to backfire, rocking the plane with its explosions. Lieutenant Squires immediately shut down the engine. "The old workhorse was supposed to fly on one engine," Ferencz later wrote; "it didn't." The aircraft started plummeting toward the rubble and rebuilding of postwar Berlin. Ben described what happened next:

> Gertrude took her official army identification card from her purse and put it into her pocket so that her body could be identified. I grabbed her hand and we rushed to the rear. Crew members were struggling to get the door open. . . . I managed to get my left knee outside. The rest of me was still inside. Suddenly the door opened wider and I fell out into the clouds. I could see the plane continuing downward out of sight. I . . . yanked the ripcord. A large billowing parachute exploded above me as I swayed wildly with the wind. My first reaction was of relief that I was out of the aircraft and not lying in pieces on the ground. Then came the realization that my wife and my friends were trapped in a plane that was about to explode or crash. . . . When I broke through the clouds I could see that I was dropping fast into the ruins below. . . . Suddenly, I slammed into the ground. I was in the middle of a soccer field.[46]

A group of boys kicking around a ball in the vicinity stared agog at this tiny man suddenly falling from the heavens. He hollered for help and, on their approach, asked them in broken German to take him to the nearest phone. He soon realized that he was in Berlin's Soviet sector. He managed to reach the control tower at Tempelhof and discovered that Squires had managed an emergency landing at Gatow Airport in the British sector, but the fate of the other passengers was unknown. The soccer kids summoned the police, who took him to the nearest police station, where he soon learned that, not far from them, an American woman in a checkered jacket had landed on a roof in a parachute and injured herself sliding off the tiles. "That's my wife!" Ferencz shouted, and he implored the officers to take him to the tall apartment building where she was sheltering. Once there, he burst into the edifice's main entrance, galloped up the many flights of stairs and raced into the designated unit, where he saw Gertrude laid out on a couch, looking banged up and disheveled. Her damaged legs, scraped and battered, were immobile, wrapped in crimson-soaked rags that had once been all white. But her face was contorted with a mix of emotions—pain, relief, fatigue—as she cried convulsively upon seeing her spouse. She had truly taken him for dead and wondered whether she was looking at an apparition.

Unfortunately, their joyful reunion was short-lived as they were soon reminded that they were in the Soviet sector. American medics had arrived and administered first aid and were ready to accompany the Ferenczes out of the building. But no sooner had they set foot out of the door than they were surrounded by a horde of Russian jeeps. The medics were shunted aside, and the married couple forcibly convoyed to a Soviet hospital, where Gertrude was brought in on a stretcher and then dumped on the floor. Ben, violently protesting that he needed to be by his wife's side, was taken to Soviet headquarters for interrogation. Once inside, he was grilled by a "fat Russian Major" as part of what turned into a proto–Cold War tête-à-tête. Ferencz let the Soviet hit him with his best verbal shots, and then he counterpunched: "I told him that we were Nuremberg prosecutors out to convict 24 leading Nazis of murdering over a million Soviet citizens. Did he really think my wife and I were planning an aerial attack on the Soviet Union? It didn't take too long to convince him that it was in his best interest to let me go."[47]

The American military was summoned, and Ferencz was taken to what became the assembly point for all the crash survivors—the US Army's 279th General Hospital. As it turned out, Taylor had also landed in the Soviet sector, but his touchdown had not been as soft as Ben's—he injured his back slamming into a concrete intersection. Miraculously, his wife, Mary, then five months pregnant, had landed on a French sector roof, fallen three stories to the street, and did not lose the baby (she gave birth to a healthy boy a few months later). The McHaneys also parachuted into the French zone and escaped relatively unscathed. Gertrude, having survived her ordeal at the Soviet hospital, soon joined them at the 279th. (The damage to her legs was serious but not permanent—she would make a full recovery.) Once all members of Taylor's party had sufficiently recovered, they returned to Nuremberg via a different, and much preferred, mode of transportation—train. Within a couple of months, though, that would no longer be possible—on June 24, 1948, the Soviets blocked the Western Allies' railway, road, and canal access to the sectors of Berlin under their control, which necessitated the Berlin Airlift. The Cold War was entering a new and more bellicose phase.

MEANWHILE, THE emerging East-West twilight struggle was not as much on the minds of Judge Michael A. Musmanno and his *Einsatzgruppen* trial brethren. They were sifting through the thousands of pages of trial transcript and accompanying exhibits and contemplating what justice ought to look like for the Nazi killing-unit leaders whose fate they would decide. And they were unanimous in finding that the evidence of guilt was overwhelming. But certainly, some were less culpable than others. They reached a tentative agreement for the judgment and individualized punishments and penned a draft of their opinion capturing the points of tentative consensus. Unfortunately for Musmanno—former lawyer for Sacco and Vanzetti, a lifelong opponent of the death penalty—the list of amercements in the judgment included execution by hanging. He was not sure he could sign off on the draft.

The devoutly Catholic jurist was horribly conflicted. Could he vote to snuff out the lives of several fellow human beings, regardless of whether, for a certain portion of those lives, they were mass murderers? He needed spiritual guidance. So he researched the environs and discovered a Cistercian monastery in Seligenporten, built in 1215 and some thirty miles from the Palace of Justice. There, Father Abbot Stephan Geyer assigned him a small but comfortable room overlooking a beautiful garden. For the next several days, he meditated, prayed, conversed with the monks, and eventually made his peace with what he had to do. This was not like Sacco and Vanzetti, he realized, where proof of guilt was murky. The root of his opposition to the death penalty, he came to understand, was the concern that innocent men could be sent to the gallows, even if the chances of innocence were infinitesimal. Here, the defendants' own reports and confessions of cold-blooded mass murder damned them beyond any doubt. He was ready to sign on to the provisional panel recommendations. The abbot sent word to Nuremberg that Judge Musmanno could join his judicial brethren in the judgment and would be with them on the bench for the morning of April 8, 1948, to deliver it—the premonastery draft would be the final draft.

Before leaving Seligenporten, Musmanno took communion and then stepped into a military vehicle that transported him back to the Palace of Justice. Once there, he slipped into his navy uniform and robes and joined Judges Dixon and Speight on the bench. The packed courtroom would hear the reading of the judgment, 175 printed pages, by all three men, taking turns. Musmanno began. And his eloquence soon notified those in attendance that the considered opinion of the Tribunal would be equal to the enormity of the crimes and the historic significance of the occasion.

> [The] facts with which the Tribunal must deal in this opinion are so beyond the experience of normal man and the range of man-made phenomena that only the most complete judicial inquiry, and the most exhaustive trial, could verify and confirm them. . . . [The] charge of purposeful homicide in this case reaches such fantastic proportions and surpasses such credible limits that believability must be bolstered with assurance a hundred times repeated. . . . If what the prosecution maintains is true, we have here . . . a crime of such unprecedented brutality and of such inconceivable savagery that the mind rebels against its own thought image and the imagination staggers in the contemplation of a human degradation beyond the power of language to adequately portray.[48]

Mussmanno then comprehensively chronicled the murderous Einsatzgruppen rampage through the Soviet Union from 1941 through 1943. Innocent civilians were not just slaughtered via bullets through their entrails and esophagi—they were made to slowly rot away in ghettos; they were worked to death out in the elements; they were ripped to shreds by the locals in orgies of violence incited by the Einsatzgruppen men; and they were cruelly asphyxiated in gas vans driven on the streets of their hometowns. No detail of Einsatz sadism was spared in Musmanno's account.[49]

The catalogue of unhinged crimes was not limited to civilians—POWs who were Jewish and/or Soviet functionaries/intellectuals were also systematically searched for and slaughtered. Musmanno, incredulous at what he was reading, then broke in: "How can all this be explained? Even when Germany was retreating on all fronts, many troops sorely needed on the battlefield were diverted on this insane mission of extermination. In defiance of military and economic logic, incalculable manpower was killed off, property of every description was destroyed—all remained unconsidered as against this insanity to genocide."[50]

It remained for the panel to opine on the law, to which another fifty-five pages were devoted. It upheld the validity of its own jurisdiction and the IMT precedent and rejected claims of victor's justice and retroactive application of new law. In respect of the latter, as regards crimes against humanity (murder), the Tribunal held: "Certainly no one can claim with the slightest pretense at reasoning that there is any taint of ex post factoism in the law of murder."[51]

The judgment then took up the defendants' individual justifications and excuses. Its rejection of self-defense came first, and it was unequivocal: "But in killing, e.g., Jews, the defendants did not succor Germany from any real danger. . . . Although they declared that the Jews were bearers of bolshevism, it was not explained how they carried that flag. Nor did anyone attempt to show how, assuming the Jews to be disposed towards bolshevism, this per se translated itself into an attack on Germany."[52] Superior orders did not fare much better. The opinion mocked the notion of applying this defense unquestionably in all circumstances, as the defendants urged:

> It is a fallacy of wide-spread consumption that a soldier is required to do everything his superior officer orders him to do. A very simple illustration will show to what absurd extreme such a theory could be carried. If every military person were required, regardless of the nature of the command, to obey unconditionally, a sergeant could order the corporal to shoot the lieutenant, the lieutenant could order the sergeant to shoot the captain, the captain could order the lieutenant to shoot the colonel, and in each instance the executioner would be absolved of blame. The mere statement of such a proposition is its own commentary.[53]

The claims of the denialists were then taken up and equally spurned. The treatment of Walter Haensch's account is illustrative: "Haensch declared that, during the entire time he served in Russia, he never saw a Jew, and that he never heard of the Fuehrer Order. Although his Kommando, prior to his arrival in Russia, had admittedly slaughtered thousands of Jews, no one ever told him of this nor did he ever hear of it. This is simply incredible."[54]

Nor did the Tribunal give credence to the argument that the great bulk of homicides were justifiable "partisan" executions. First, many of these so-called "partisans" were in units sufficiently well-organized that, when captured, they should have been treated as POWs, not unprivileged combatants. Regardless, even partisans, saboteurs, and spies should have been entitled to trials (or at least investigations) with minimum due process standards before being sentenced to death and executed. The Tribunal did not find credible the claim that there were any such trials, let alone investigations. For example, it noted that "Kommando leaders were not only empowered but encouraged to execute a man more on his looks than on evidence" and that "many of the so-called investigations . . . were . . . for the purpose of obtaining from the victim information which would enable the executioners to locate and seize other victims."[55]

With the conclusion of the general opinion, the panel read out the individual judgments for each defendant. As a prelude to this, the Tribunal stressed the impressive educational and professional pedigrees of the men in the dock. There was little drama, then, when the judges announced the convictions of twenty of the twenty-two defendants on all three counts; Rühl (due to low rank and holding a mere administrative position) and Graf (owing to low rank and no direct proof of participation in executions) were convicted only of criminal membership.

Of note, in the judgments against Naumann and Jost, the Tribunal gave no weight to the defense that no liability for command responsibility could attach because those men replaced unit chiefs who had previously issued orders that could not be countermanded. The judges held that a superior must take effective steps to prevent subordinates from continuing to commit crimes, pursuant to an existing illegal order.[56] He was also obligated to rescind the order as soon as possible.[57]

In the judgment against Blume, the Tribunal acknowledged (by the name of "necessity") his lawyer's assertion of the *Unzumutbarkeit* German legal defense. But it dispensed with it briefly, stressing why such justifications rang particularly hollow in this case: "For let it be said once for all that Hitler with all his cunning and unmitigated evil would have remained as innocuous as a rambling crank if he did not have the Blumes, the Blobels, the Braunes, and the Bibersteins to do his bidding—to mention only the B's."[58]

Up until the reading of the judgment, Ferencz had harbored feelings of animosity toward Judge Musmanno. Much of it was due to the "Penguin Rule" and his belief that Musmanno hypocritically, and systematically, overruled "well-founded objections by the prosecution."[59] But the judgment disabused him of his view that Musmanno had been a "showman" and shoddy jurist:

> What I didn't quite realize, and discovered only later, was that the learned judge could afford to be tolerant because he wanted to give the accused every possible right. He was confident that he would not be deceived by spurious submissions. [In reading the judgment, Musmanno expressed] that "where law exists a court will rise." He saw an international criminal court as a means [of] diminishing crimes against humanity and combating hatred and violence between ideologies. He expressed the hope that mankind, with intelligence and will, would be able "to maintain a tribunal holding inviolable the law of humanity, and by doing so, preserve the human race itself."[60]

But the real drama was saved for the next day, April 10, 1948, when the defendants would come to know their ultimate fates. Ferencz arrived early and sat in solitude, reflecting on all that had happened the past half year. He had come full circle—having been alone in this same space just before the trial opened, when so much burden had been placed on his young and slender shoulders. And now, he realized, he had survived the ordeal and was on the other end of a truly liminal experience. It *had* been a rite of passage—he had done all the hard work, negotiated each phase of the proceeding, answered all the challenges; it had transformed him. And now it was about to end. Like the strong autumnal afternoon light in late September when he had sat there in seclusion and composed his opening statement on the eve of trial, the soft vernal morning light in early April shone through the great chamber as he awaited the trial's finish. The radiance of fall that he had perceived as hope was now the luminescence of spring that he knew was peace.

Soon, Courtroom 600 stirred to life. Ben's prosecution colleagues, the German defense counsel, the translators, the clerks, the guards, the reporters, and a throng of spectators in the visitors' galley streamed in. At 10:00 a.m., the marshal, Colonel Samuel L. Metcalfe, called the case. Musmanno, Dixon, and Speight entered and took their places. From their perspective, surrounded by this sea of humanity, the two benches across the well of the courtroom stood out—the dock was entirely empty. Directly underneath it, in the bowels of the Palace of Justice, the defendants were gathered near the shaft of a lift that would, one by one, take them three floors up to learn whether they would live or die. Once all were seated and a calm had settled over the courtroom,

Judge Musmanno announced, "The Marshal will produce the defendant Otto Ohlendorf."[61]

Ingenious prewar German engineering then stirred to life. The wheels, axles, and gears of the elevator machinery began to rumble within the belly of the massive edifice. The cage, with its human cargo, was now being hoisted up by the pulleys. As if by magic, the old, burnished wood of the rear-dock wall panel, an elevator door hidden in plain sight, slid open, and out stepped former SS general Otto Ohlendorf. Flanked by two African American guards in military duds clutching white truncheons, he bowed respectfully as had been his daily wont since the previous September, picked up the headphones, carefully fitted them over his ears, and then looked up expectantly at the judges, "with a clear, unafraid gaze."[62] As was *his* daily wont since September, Musmanno seized the bench's collective voice first. "Otto Ohlendorf," he began, "you have been found guilty on all counts which charged you with crimes against humanity, war crimes, and membership in criminal organizations. And . . ." Here he paused, later revealing his fleeting thought that, "Ninety thousand murdered souls were perhaps listening."[63] Then he peered into Ohlendorf's impenetrable eyes and continued, "The Court sentences you to death by hanging."[64] On hearing this, as Adolf Eichmann would do thirteen years later, Ohlendorf bowed his head. But he otherwise remained stoic, calmly removing the headphones and, with the slightest enigmatic smile at the corner of his lips, returned to the lift, with shoulders thrown back and head erect. "Then [he] slowly descended," Ferencz later wrote, "as if into Hell."[65]

The elevator machinery paused briefly, the cage was opened and closed, and then the wheels, gears, and axles whirred again. Jost appeared this time, and the same process repeated itself, but with a sentence of life imprisonment. Musmanno then turned over the microphone to Speight, who sentenced Naumann to death and Schulz to twenty years' imprisonment. Dixon then flipped those punishments for the next two defendants—Six got twenty years and Blobel, death. The microphone then rotated back to Musmanno, who pronounced death sentences for Blume and Sandberger. Alternating the same way for every two defendants, fourteen additional sentences were announced. In all, fourteen defendants were condemned to death (in addition to those already mentioned, the list included Steimle, Seibert, Biberstein, Braune, Haensch, Ott, Strauch, Klingelhöfer, and Schubert)—this number of capital punishment determinations far exceeded that of any other Subsequent Proceeding or even the IMT trial itself. There were also terms of incarceration. Like Schulz, Six and von Radetzky were sentenced to twenty years' imprisonment. Fendler and Rühl each got ten-year terms. And Graf's punishment was limited to time served—he walked out of the Palace of Justice that day as a free man. Within only a matter of hours, the sentences were affirmed by the military governor of the United States, General Clay. And then the US Supreme Court denied all petitions for review on May 2.

For the trial's chief prosecutor, the sentencing was more of an ordeal than a triumph. As the judges read each sentence, Ferencz notated a list he had drawn up beforehand, which contained each Einsatz man's name and his predicted punishment. The panel was much more severe than his estimates—this was a hanging bench. "It is not an easy thing to condemn another human being to be hanged," he noted years later.[66] Each time Ferencz heard "Death by hanging" it was like a "hammer blow" that "shocked" his brain. "I had never asked for the death penalty," he added, "although such a recommendation from the Prosecutor was widely expected and it was surely deserved by these unrepentant mass murderers." Ferencz felt that it might trivialize the magnitude of the crimes "by suggesting that it could be settled, and perhaps then forgotten, by executing a handful of genocidal killers."[67] Thus, even though at the close of each Nuremberg trial it was customary for the chief prosecutor to invite his staff to his home to celebrate, the man who held that position for *Einsatzgruppen* "asked to be excused from [his] own party."[68]

Of all the defendants, it would seem that Ohlendorf's death sentence affected Ben Ferencz the most. Despite the lead defendant's nefarious deeds, the prosecutor had developed a grudging respect for him. Unlike most of the other men in the dock, he had been scrupulously honest. And as Einsatzgruppe D commander, he had at least shown a small modicum of humanity in helping perpetrate the Shoah. He wanted to carry out the Führer Order in as military a manner as possible, eliminating any wanton or sadistic violence, inflicting on the victims only the minimum amount of suffering. Thus, for instance, unlike the killers in other units, Ohlendorf's men were under strict orders never to use infants for target practice or to smash their heads against trees. He also ordered his executioners to allow mothers to hold their infants to their breasts and to aim for their hearts so both would die instantly.[69] In this regard, Ferencz recalled that Ohlendorf was the father of five children. This weighed heavily on him after the sentencing, and he wondered if he might be able to do something for Ohlendorf, "such as telling his family that he loved them."[70] Ferencz had listened to months of evidence confirming the potential of human beings to lose their humanity. He was not going to lose his. He resolved to pay a visit to the former SS-Gruppenführer in the holding cell beneath the courtroom.

They met in a small cubicle with a thick glass partition through which they could speak. It was hot, and there was little air. Ferencz asked Ohlendorf, in

German, whether there was anything he could do for him. Some small favor perhaps? The Nazi's bitter reply, consistent with his closing address to the Tribunal, was that the Jews in America would suffer for what Ferencz had done. The *Einsatzgruppen* trial chief prosecutor, apparently having initially tuned out or subsequently forgotten Ohlendorf's unrepentant valedictory message to Judge Musmanno and his brethren, was stunned by this answer. "The man had learned nothing, and regretted nothing. I looked him in the eye, stood up and said slowly, in English, 'Goodbye, Mr. Ohlendorf.'"[71] It was a watershed moment for Ben Ferencz. Not only was the young man saying goodbye to one of history's great monsters, whom he helped send to the gallows; he was also saying farewell to one of history's great proceedings, an event that would turn out to be the most seminal of his life.

A young Benjamin Ferencz with his father and sister, Pearl, 1924. (United States Holocaust Memorial Museum Photo Archives)

Ferencz with Pearl and half brothers David and Eddie. (Courtesy of Keri Ferencz)

Ferencz and his family at the beach, his mother seated beside him, right, with Dave Schwartz behind her, 1940. (United States Holocaust Memorial Museum Photo Archives)

Ferencz and Gertrude Fried at the beach, 1940. (United States Holocaust Memorial Museum Photo Archives)

Ferencz at Harvard Law School, 1942. (United States Holocaust Memorial Museum Photo Archives)

Ferencz in the US Army, 1944. (United States Holocaust Memorial Museum Photo Archives)

Ferencz in the “Immer Allein” as a war crimes investigator for Patton’s Third Army, 1945. (United States Holocaust Memorial Museum Photo Archives)

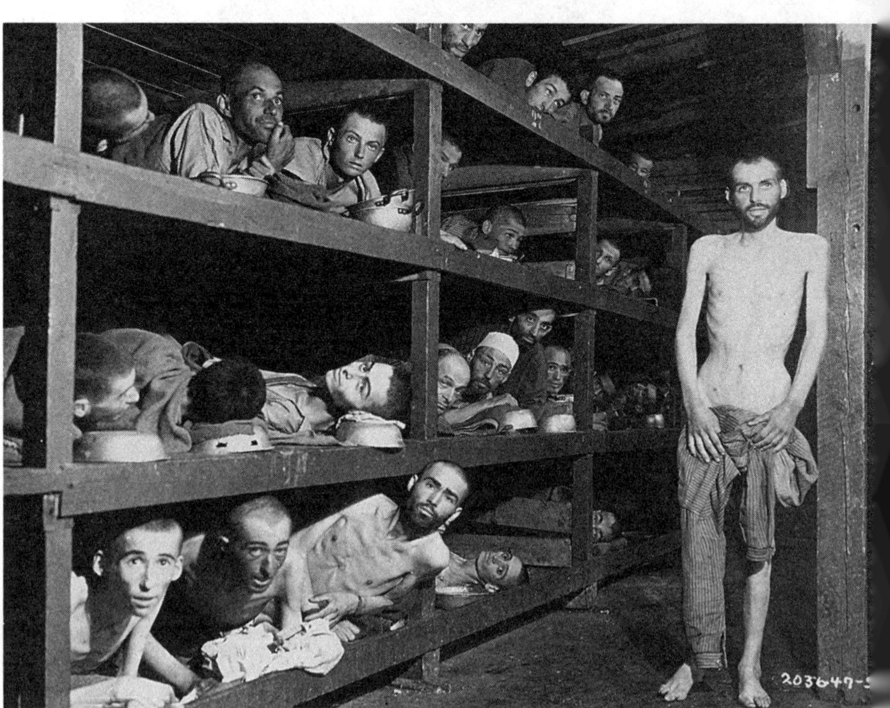

The liberation of Buchenwald (with Elie Wiesel in the second row from the bottom, seventh from the left), 1945. (United States Holocaust Memorial Museum Photo Archives)

ıe courtroom at Dachau during the trial of former camp personnel and prisoners from e Dachau concentration camp, December 4, 1945. (United States Holocaust Memorial ıuseum Photo Archives)

:fendants in the dock at the International Military Tribunal war crimes trial in Nuremrg, November 1945/1946. (Photo by United States Army Signal Corps; Wikimedia, ırtesy of National Archives and Records Administration, College Park [292562])

Robert Jackson, the American chief prosecutor at Nuremberg, February 1946. (Photo by Raymond D'Addario; Wikimedia)

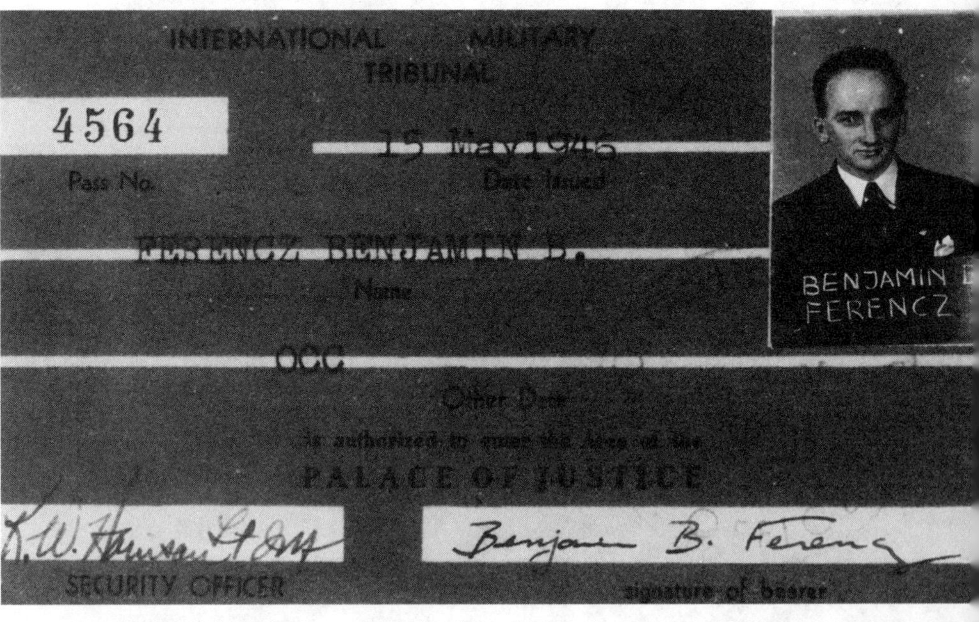

Ferencz's OCC ID card for the International Military Tribunal, 1946. (United States Holocaust Memorial Museum Photo Archives)

rencz at the podium for the *Einzatzgruppen* trial, 1947. (United States Holocaust Memorial Mu-
um Photo Archives)

rencz at the podium for the *Einsatzgruppen* trial with defense attorneys Friedrich Bergold and
dolf Aschenauer, 1947. (United States Holocaust Memorial Museum Photo Archives)

Otto Ohlendorf at the *Einsatzgruppen* trial, October 9, 1947. Ohlendorf was the trial's lead defendant and commander of Ensatzgruppe D, which murdered nearly one hundred thousand innocent civilians in Bessarabia, southern Ukraine, and the Caucasus in 1941–42. (United States Holocaust Memorial Museum Photo Archives)

Telford Taylor gives the *Einsatzgruppen* trial closing statement as Judge Michael Mu manno takes notes and Ferencz listens, in Courtroom 600 of the Nuremberg Palace Justice, 1948. (United States Holocaust Memorial Museum Photo Archives)

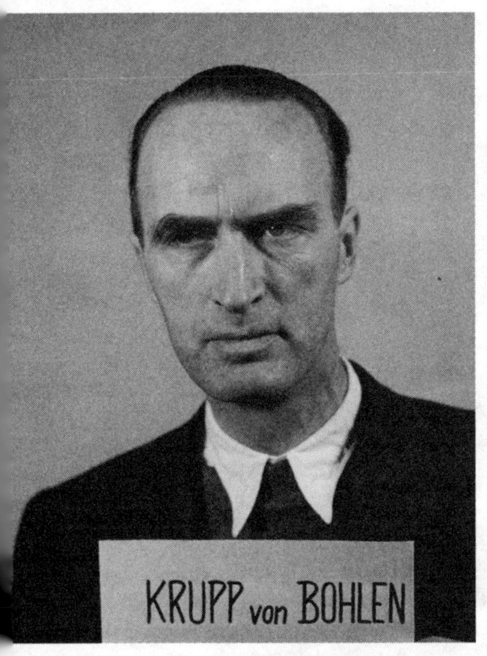

Alfried Krupp von Bohlen und Halbach, who was convicted of war crimes and crimes against humanity at Nuremberg based on his armament firm's use of slave labor and exploitation of occupied countries. His twelve-year sentence was later commuted to time served and his forfeited property restored to him. (Wikimedia, courtesy of National Archives and Records Administration, College Park [169157420])

ertrude Ferencz in a Palace of Justice office in Nuremberg, 1948. (United States Holocaust Memorial useum Photo Archives)

Hannah Arendt, who as executive director of Jewish Cultural Reconstruction (JCR) worked with Ferencz in his capacity as director of the Jewish Restitution Successor Organization (JRSO), as JCR operated under the auspices of JRSO. (Munich City Museum, Collection of Photography, Archive Barbara Niggl Radloff, CC BY-SA.4.0)

President Harry S. Truman with John J. McCloy, United States High Commissioner for Germany (*center*), and Secretary of State Dean Acheson, in the Oval Office of the White House, 1950. (Photo by Abbie Rowe, courtesy of National Archives and Records Administration, Office of Presidential Libraries, Harry S. Truman Library [338957664])

ɛrencz with members of the Claims Conference negotiating team and the Israeli delega- on in Wassenaar, the Netherlands, 1952. *Front row, from left:* Alexander Easterman, Felix ainnar, Moses Leavitt, Giora Josephthal; *second row, from left:* Seymour Rubin, Ferencz, i Nathan, Morris Boukstein, Jacob Robinson, Gershon Avner; *third row, from left:* Jerome ckson and Nehemiah Robinson, unidentified. (United States Holocaust Memorial Mu- um Photo Archives)

nrad Adenauer signs the Luxembourg Agreement while Ferencz, with Nahum Gold- ann seated to his right, looks on, 1952. (Axel Springer/Ullstein Bild)

Ben, Gertrude, and children, 1957. (Courtesy of Joey Kotfica)

Adolf Eichmann, inside the glass booth, is sentenced to death by the court at the conclusion of his trial, December 15, 1961. Ben Ferencz consulted wit the prosecution regarding victims' issues pretrial. The proceeding featured much victim testimony and marked a turning point in the world's awarene of the Holocaust. (Courtesy of the National Photo Collection of Israel, Pho tography Department, Government Press Office)

erencz (*third from right*) with the UN Special Committee on the Question of Defining Aggression as
reaches consensus, 1974. (United States Holocaust Memorial Museum Photo Archives)

erencz at the ICC ratification ceremony, with (left to right) Bill Pace, A. N. R. Robinson, M. Cherif
assiouni, Philippe Kirsch, and Hans Corell, 2002. (United States Holocaust Memorial Museum Photo
rchives)

Ferencz with the ICC's first prosecutor, Luis Moreno Ocampo, and Angelina Jolie, as well as the rest of the prosecution team for the Lubanga trial, 2011. (United States Holocaust Memorial Museum Photo Archives)

Bust of Ben Ferencz by Bjørn Okholm Skaarup in Courtroom 600 of the Nuremberg Palace of Justice. (Courtesy of Leon Greiner)

14

KRUPP TRIAL ATTORNEY AND EXECUTIVE COUNSEL

Every new beginning comes from some other beginning's end.

—SENECA

BY THE SECOND week of April 1948, things were going quite well for Nuremberg prosecutor Benjamin B. Ferencz. Of the nine Subsequent Proceedings tried to that point, he was the chief prosecutor in the only one without a single acquittal (and, of all twelve, his alone would retain that distinction). As well, the *Einsatzgruppen* sentences were, collectively, the harshest handed down (this would also remain true by the NMT program's end). The OCCWC's accomplishment was covered widely, with the *New York Post* describing the overall result as "the most all-embracing in the history of the Nuremberg war crimes trials."[1] Even former First Lady Eleanor Roosevelt was aware of the outcome and sent the trial's chief prosecutor a brief letter expressing her appreciation.[2] Historian Hilary Earl has noted the watershed nature of the trial, describing its "significant and lasting impact on our understanding of the Holocaust" and its having become "a template for later atrocity trials including those of major perpetrators such as: Adolf Eichmann (1961), Slobodan Milošević (2006) and Radovan Karadžić (2016)."[3]

Although, in the immediate aftermath, he might not have appreciated the trial's eventual significance for posterity, Telford Taylor knew what it meant for his office at that moment, as the Cold War was closing in, and support in Washington, DC, for the war crimes trials program was waning. In an April 12, 1948, letter to Ferencz, he "heartily" congratulated his twenty-eight-year-old rising star on "so successful an outcome." He went on: "You directed the prosecution with efficiency, dispatch, and great economy of means, and the judgment and verdict should be a source of satisfaction to you for the rest of your life."[4]

By then, it was clear that Ferencz had become the office "golden boy," and Taylor was going to need him to rise to the occasion once again. The *Einsatz-*

gruppen trial sentencing was on a Saturday, April 10. The first working day after that, Monday, April 12 (the same date as the congratulations letter), Taylor issued "General Orders No. 6," whose various injunctions included directing "Mr. Benjamin B. Ferencz" to "participate as counsel in Case No. 10 (*Krupp*)."[5] So he went right back into the courtroom and advanced sequentially—from Case No. 9 to Case No. 10.

Why the *Krupp* case? Numerical sequencing aside, one reason certainly suggests itself—Ferencz had worked on industrialist matters during the first phase of his Nuremberg experience and had specifically investigated the Krupp firm and its directors. As we saw in chapter 10, he had expressed to Gertrude that his sleuthing was meaningful insofar as it would yield truth and justice with respect to the role of the industrialists in initiating and waging aggressive war. So motivated, he had done yeoman's work during that first Nuremberg phase, and it was on the strength of those efforts that he had been promoted to chief of the newly formed Berlin Branch. Moreover, during his time as OCCWC lead investigator in the former Nazi capital, he naturally gained insights into *all* the office's active files, including *Krupp*.

Still, the timing was a bit odd. Ben was assigned to the trial after the prosecution's case-in-chief had already been presented. Yet things had not been going well. Tribunal III had recently granted the Defense Motion for Acquittal on Charges of Crimes against Peace. Thus, a large chunk of the prosecution's case, and the one that Ben cared most about, was lost. As Kim Priemel has noted, "the counts of crimes against peace and conspiracy [were] at the heart of the prosecution strategy."[6] So Taylor was shaking things up on the team. Thus, also pursuant to General Orders No. 6, he replaced H. Russell Thayer as chief prosecutor and replaced him with Rawlings Ragland. Moreover, Joseph Kaufman, one of the lead attorneys on the case, had previously departed as the result of "tensions due to Kaufman's stubbornness and his inability to balance the different factions within his team."[7] So it would appear that Ben's transfer to *Krupp* was, at least in part, about adding ballast to help right a listing ship.[8]

Moreover, in any event, the *Krupp* defendants had notified the prosecution that they intended to introduce an enormous amount of evidence into the record and call a multitude of witnesses to the stand. Additional manpower was needed, and with Ben having recently come off *Einsatzgruppen*, Telford Taylor wanted one of his best pitching in for *Krupp*. Thus, an OCCWC draft press release from that period announced that Benjamin B. Ferencz, of Arverne, New York, had joined the trial team (that is, Rawlings Ragland, Cecilia Goetz, Max Mandellaub, Herbert Goldenberg, and Maximilian Koessler) to assist in the "preparation and argument of the closing phases of the prosecution's case."[9]

BUT MOVING from *Einsatzgruppen* to *Krupp* was still an adjustment for the diminutive New Yorker. Case No. 10 was quite different from Case No. 9. If the defendants in the latter could be described as Himmler's roving mobs of assassins, those in the former were Hitler's regal makers of armaments.[10] The Krupp family dynasty began manufacturing weapons during the Thirty Years' War.[11] Several generations later, in the early 1800s, Friedrich Krupp established a steel foundry in the Ruhr Valley. Headquartered in Essen, it became one of Europe's premier industrial concerns when Friedrich's son, Alfred, brilliantly devised a technique for casting seamless, no-weld carriage wheels. Thereafter, train manufacturers relied on Krupp to achieve efficient locomotion.[12]

Still, the family's great renown, if not its wealth, continued to derive largely from weapons production. Over time, the name Krupp became intimately associated with the modern rise of Prussian militarism, which was, in turn, entwined with Teutonic imperial ambitions. Krupp, under the aegis of Otto von Bismarck's leadership, supplied the Prussians with innovative breech-loading cannon that proved superior to their French counterparts (many of them still muzzle-loading) and led to Napoleon III's defeat in the 1870–71 Franco-Prussian War. This, in turn, gave rise to a unified German nation.

Thus, the birth of Kaiser Wilhelm I's empire was wet-nursed via Krupp armaments, and the firm came to be known as the "Arsenal of the Reich."[13] This moniker gained greater currency during the First World War, when the weapons manufacturer produced the conflict's most formidable artillery piece of its initial phase—the Big Bertha (named after Alfred's granddaughter, sole owner of the company after 1902). This gargantuan howitzer, weighing 42 tons, was the largest, most-powerful mobile artillery piece in use by any army at that time.[14] But Krupp's most redoubtable weapon was not the only one it produced—it supplied the Kaiser with all the necessary materiel to pursue Germany's aggressive designs, including U-boats, battleships, trains, railway guns, cars, tanks (in particular, the Tiger 1), machine guns, and other howitzers (including the Paris Gun, which bombarded the French capital toward the end of the war and replaced Big Bertha as the largest artillery model of World War I).

During the 1914–18 conflict, as well as the interwar years, the Krupp concern was run by Bertha's husband, Gustav. With Germany's defeat, the company had to give up overt arms manufacturing and publicly focused instead on consumer products. Behind the scenes, though, Krupp secretly resumed arms design and manufacture. Gustav and Bertha were initially skeptical of Adolf Hitler, whom they perceived as below their social station. But gradually, over the course of the 1930s, their resistance gave way, and they cast their lot with the Führer. They purged the company of Jewish managers and significantly ramped up armaments production, which later became the foundation of the Nuremberg aggression case against the company's directors. Toward the end of the decade, Gustav's health declined, and his eldest son, Alfried, started assuming control of the firm. When Gustav suffered a stroke in 1941, Alfried began taking over entirely, a process completed by 1943.

Unlike his parents, though, Alfried was a fanatical Nazi from the outset, having gladly joined the SS in 1931. During the war, Hitler encouraged the company to seize industries in occupied nations, which eventually became the basis for plundering charges at Nuremberg. Additional indictment counts stemmed from the company's practice of using slave labor. At Alfried's behest, Krupp representatives were sent to Nazi concentration camps to select workers; and the Jewish ones were targeted for "extermination through labor."[15] As well, ordinary, law-abiding citizens in Nazi-occupied countries were shanghaied from the streets, treated as criminals, and sent to Germany for compulsory labor. As many as 100,000 enslaved people worked for Krupp, a great portion of whom were Jewish (including women and children).[16]

One of the defendants indicted for the Nuremberg IMT proceeding was the ailing company patriarch Gustav Krupp. But he filed a motion to sever based on his poor health, and it was granted. Thus, like Rasch in *Einsatzgruppen,* Gustav was deemed medically unfit for trial, his case was severed, and the charges against him were technically still pending when he expired in 1950. In response to Gustav's successful motion, Allied prosecutors filed their own motion to substitute in Alfried for his father. But the IMT denied the motion. As a result, any chance of justice against Alfried and his corporate henchmen would have to be via an NMT prosecution.

AND TELFORD TAYLOR was ready and willing. On August 17, 1947, the OCCWC indicted Alfried and eleven of his colleagues, including executives (Ewald Löser, CFO; Friedrich Janssen, Löser's successor as CFO) and the heads of steel works (Eduard Houdremont; Heinrich Korschan, deputy head of steel plants), arms fabrication (Erich Müller), sales (Karl Pfirsch, Karl Eberhardt), labor procurement (Werner Lehmann), intelligence (Max Ihn), plant police (Friedrich von Bülow), and worker camps (Hans Kupke). The charges of the indictment consisted of (1) crimes against peace; (2) war crimes and crimes against humanity (plunder and spoliation); (3) war crimes and crimes against humanity (deportation, exploitation and abuse of slave labor); and (4) conspiracy to commit crimes against peace.[17] Counts 1 and 4 were integral to the prosecution's case, which focused on "the long, historical trajectory of Krupp's involvement in German aggression and the longing of the family and managers to return to the 'halcyon times of Bismarck and Wilhelm II.'"[18] Indeed, the prosecution's prearraignment press release referred to the defendants as "Twelve officials of [the] gunmakers to Bismarck, Kaiser Wilhelm and Hitler."[19]

The trial opened on December 8, 1947, and the prosecution rested its case during the first part of the following March. Then, on March 12, 1948, the defendants filed a Motion for Acquittal on the Charges of Crimes against Peace (that is, Counts 1 and 4). And, as we have seen, much to the surprise and vexation of the OCCWC, it was granted on April 5, 1948. Ben Ferencz was livid about the termination of the aggression counts, lamenting to his old mentor, Sheldon Glueck, that "the tribunal's decision left a mere torso of the case and 'badly wounded the prosecution.'"[20]

So when Ferencz joined the prosecution team the following week, there was much to be done. On April 13, 1948, the Tribunal granted the prosecution's request for leave to file a supplemental brief with respect to the decision on the Motion for Acquittal. and it was granted. Thus, the *Krupp* prosecutors, with Ben on board, put together and filed a new motion to reconsider the aggression-related acquittal. And the newly reconstituted team worked on various responsive pleadings (including an Answer to Motion to Terminate Proceedings Based on Defects in the Appointment of Tribunal III and Answer in Opposition to Defendants' Motion to Strike "Conspiracy" Testimony). Some of these prosecution filings were successful, but much to Ben's chagrin, the Tribunal would not change its position on dismissing the crimes against peace charges. So the team began to focus on spoliation and slave labor—Counts 2 and 3. And that is where Ben concentrated his efforts.

As those in the dock were fewer in this case (only twelve defendants), his efforts would be exerted in Room 196 of the Palace of Justice, not the more ornate (and famous) Courtroom 600, two floors below. William Manchester described the barren fourth-floor chamber as looking "much like an American police court."[21] In an attempt to relieve its bleakness, MPs had hung a silken canopy across the ceiling. "The gesture was well meant," Manchester noted, "but the effect was ghastly; more and more the cloth resembled a shroud."[22] Sitting on the bench were Hu Anderson (presiding judge), Tennessee Court of Appeals; Edward Daly, Connecticut Superior Court; and William Wilkins, Washington Superior Court. Manchester noted with levity that the bench seemed surrounded by "hated" steam pipes and that "each time a member of the tribunal spoke, his listeners were distracted by the valve cock behind Justice Anderson's left ear."[23]

Sitting somewhat off to the side of the bench was the newly constituted prosecution team, into which Ben Ferencz had apparently integrated quite well: "Despite its barren props the room had become a stage for high theater. The tribunal was sober and majestic, and certain performers provided color. Ragland was the southern gentleman, Taylor the New England Aristocrat . . . Benjamin Ferencz . . . slumping carelessly like a preoccupied college instructor, was really an idealist with a first-rate mind and extraordinary dedication. Cecilia Goetz—casually mussed, dressed in a checked wool blouse—smiled easily and thought grim thoughts."[24]

Notwithstanding his bitter disappointment over the demise of the aggression charges, having just come from *Einsatzgruppen,* Ben was well-equipped to handle the crimes against humanity portion of *Krupp.* And through his cross-examinations, he displayed his growth as a trial attorney. Many of the witnesses he questioned were involved with forced labor procurement or served as SS guards for Krupp.[25] Thus, on May 21, 1948, Johannes Dolhaine, a former assistant to defendant Heinrich Lehmann (Krupp's labor procurement chief), who worked in the firm's "Labor Allocation Unit A," testified that, in March 1945, a group of Hungarian Jewish women, enslaved at the Krupp Rolling II plant in Essen, were transferred away from the premises supposedly to protect them from being seized and murdered by the SS.[26]

But on cross-examination, Ferencz established that Krupp actually coordinated with the SS to send the enslaved Jews to Buchenwald in freight cars so they would be prevented from "giving damaging testimony of mistreatment."[27] Further, he got the witness to admit that Krupp supplied the freight trains and "sent a representative to the SS to expedite the transfer."[28] It was one of the dramatic moments in the trial, and *Stars and Stripes* reporters referred to it as "something hot in the *Krupp* case."[29] Ferencz felt that the trial testimony imputed to Alfried Krupp knowledge of the murder of these Jewish women. He would later confess that the fate of these victims was particularly meaningful for him:

> [My] wife had a cousin, two cousins, who were working for Krupp in Essen. One of them had been injured during a bombing raid. And so I was particularly interested in what happened to the 520 Hungarian girls who were taken from Buchenwald and sent to Essen. And the Buchenwald commandant said, "Get them back here because I'll take care of them here," which meant he would kill them. . . . That was the plan. And that's what they did. . . . Alfried

Krupp, the lead defendant in that case, the son of Gustav Krupp, was personally responsible for sending inmates back to a camp in which they were to be killed.[30]

Still feeling that sense of righteous indignation, four days later, Ferencz cross-examined Karoline Geulen, one of the SS guards at the Rolling II facility. On direct examination, Geulen testified that she had worked for Krupp as a "supervisor" of the Hungarian Jewesses, who lived in the adjoining Humboldtstrasse Camp. Geulen maintained that the women were treated well, with good living facilities, adequate food and clothing, and not subject to any injurious or degrading treatment.[31] Ferencz began his cross-examination by stressing Geulen's ties to the SS, her training at Ravensbrück concentration camp, and her resulting incarceration in Ludwigsburg Internment Camp as a suspected war criminal. The cross-examination began quite strongly—the witness's credibility immediately being called into question, with Ferencz exerting excellent control:

MR. FERENCZ: Miss Geulen, how long were you interned . . . in Ludwigsburg internment camp?
WITNESS GEULEN: [Let] me think—about 6 months.
Q. Why?
A. Because we were supervisors.
Q. Because you were a Krupp supervisor and member of the SS?
A. Yes, SS.
Q. You were employed by the Krupp firm in Rolling Mill II from 7 March?
A. Yes.
Q. Until August 1944. Is that correct?
A. Yes.
Q. And at that time the Krupp chief of Rolling Mill II, Mr. Hammerschmidt, told you—
A. Yes.
Q. Just a moment, Witness, just wait until I put my question before you answer it. Now I am asking you if the Krupp chief of Rolling Mill II told you that he was gathering Krupp employees to serve as SS guards for Krupp laborers? Is that correct?
A. Yes.
Q. And then he sent you with some other Krupp employees to Ravensbrück concentration camp for training. Is that correct?
A. Yes.[32]

Ferencz then concentrated on Geulen's training at Ravensbrück. Through superior interrogation technique and timing, he made her evasive and incomplete responses seem comical and, through detail stacking and repetition, tied them to her Ravensbrück training:

Q. What kind of training did you get at the Ravensbrück concentration camp to enable you—
A. I was—
Q. Just a moment, Witness, just let me finish my question. I am asking you what kind of training you got from this concentration camp to enable you to perform your work as a Krupp guard.
A. How am I to understand this question?
Q. You were there you say for 2 weeks?
A. Yes.
Q. What kind of training did you get?
A. We were only told that we were not to beat the women.
Q. So for 2 weeks, every day, 8 hours a day, they told you not to beat the women?
A. No.
Q. Did it take them 2 weeks, 8 hours a day in order to teach you not to beat women?
A. Two weeks? I was only there for not quite 2 weeks.
Q. And after the 2 weeks Krupp requested your return from Ravensbrück. Is that correct?
A. Yes.[33]

Having unsettled the witness about her affiliation with the SS, her training at Ravensbrück, and her incarceration during the Allied occupation, Ferencz got her to crack regarding the living conditions of the Hungarian Jewish women during their period of Krupp enslavement. Then, when the witness tried to prevaricate, Ferencz pounced—expertly using her affidavit to impeach her.

Q. Now, you saw these girls in the Humboldtstrasse camp, did you not?
A. Yes.
Q. Do you remember that the sanitary facilities were so inadequate that the girls had to relieve themselves in the open?
A. Not at the beginning; towards the end, that is correct.
Q. And isn't it true they had no opportunity to wash themselves in the camp?
A. Yes. At the beginning they had opportunities to wash.
Q. But later on they had none?

A. No. Later on they no longer had them.
Q. Do you remember that they were allowed to wash themselves in the showers of the factory, don't you?
A. Yes.
Q. And those who didn't leave the showers in time were beaten, weren't they?
A. I do not know anything about that.
Q. Did you suddenly forget?
A. No.
Q. Do you remember a sworn statement that you gave to Mr. Koessler?
A. Yes.
Q. And do you remember that at that time you swore that those girls who didn't leave the shower quickly were beaten?
A. Yes, they were beaten.
Q. So that they actually were beaten, weren't they?
A. Yes.
Q. Now you remember that these girls had to live in the cellar in Humboldtstrasse [that is, Camp Humboldtstrasse]?
A. Yes.
Q. And it was so cold there and so damp that the beds on which these girls had to sleep were frozen, weren't they?
A. Yes.
Q. And for a long time they had only to sleep on wooden boards. Isn't that correct?
A. I do not know whether they had to sleep on wooden boards. I think they had iron beds.[34]

Until this point, via each segment of the cross, Ferencz had been drawing out progressively darker details regarding the Krupp slave labor experience. And so, having boxed Geulen in by demonstrating that he could effectively impeach her if she lied, he appropriately finished by eliciting the most damaging testimony.

Q. Do you remember that the camp commander [Oskar] Rieck carried a rubber hose?
A. Yes.
Q. And do you also remember that he carried a long leather whip?
A. Yes.
Q. And do you remember that Rieck was particularly brutal to these Jewish girls?
A. Yes.

Q. And he ill-treated them in an inhumane manner?
A. Yes.[35]

In sum, Ferencz destroyed Geulen as a defense witness and actually turned her into a prosecution asset. The superb quality of this cross-examination is evident—the questions were appropriately leading and laconic; the use of outside evidence for impeachment was handled with aplomb; the indirect manner of making the witness's lies seem foolish, even humorous, was devastatingly effective; the overall pacing and buildup was perfect; overall, then, the command over the witness was complete and impressive (with Ben even showing he was well aware that the colloquy was being recorded such that he consistently instructed the witness not to speak over him). This may seem remarkable given that it was only Ferencz's second trial. But that is a misleading statistic.

It must be recalled that Ben had been observing trials as soon as he graduated from Harvard Law School. Before his induction into the army, while working with the New York Legal Aid Society, he had been able to watch criminal proceedings in Big Apple courtrooms. In England, he had observed cases being litigated at the Old Bailey. He had studied the work of war crimes prosecutors at the Dachau Trials and had even been subject to extensive cross-examination himself as a witness at that program's Flossenbürg Trial. And, at Nuremberg, he had sat in on the portions of the IMT proceeding where Allied prosecutors were cross-examining defendants and their witnesses. Also, as chief prosecutor of *Einsatzgruppen*, an inquest that lasted several months, he had to pay attention to numerous cross-examinations and conducted quite a few of them himself. We saw in chapter 13 how his cross-examinations of Einsatzgruppe B defendants had gotten progressively better. He had been carefully taking notes since earning his law degree. And by the end of his time in the *Krupp* case, he had become quite a skilled trial advocate.

On June 24, 1948, as in *Einsatzgruppen*, Telford Taylor delivered the prosecution's closing argument for *Krupp*. His submission focused on the two extant charges—Counts 2 and 3. As to Count 2, war crimes and crimes against humanity via plunder and spoliation, he stressed Krupp's illegal seizure of factories in France as well as Holland, Austria, Greece, and Yugoslavia, and acts of spoliation committed on Soviet territory. The defenses that the property expropriation and territorial exploitation were via Hitlerian decree or under duress, Taylor argued, were unavailing as comparable justifications had already been raised and rejected in the *Flick* case.[36]

As for Count 3, crimes against humanity owing to Krupp's use of slave labor, Taylor submitted: "It is not contended that [the defendants] enslaved or mistreated workers for either sadistic or ideological reasons. [They] used slave workers because the war created a labor shortage in Germany, and prisoners of war, foreign workers, and concentration camp inmates furnished an available supply of a badly needed commodity. . . . Their crime is perhaps the greater because, in the pursuit of a normal economic objective they were cool and ruthless in their utilization of criminal methods."[37]

Over the next week, defense attorneys made their closing arguments, stressing that their clients were pillars of German industry, only following Third Reich policy, and did these things under duress or out of necessity. Finally, on June 30, 1948, the *Krupp* defendants themselves made their closing personal statements to Tribunal III, with Alfried Krupp addressing the judges on behalf of not only himself but also everyone in the dock. Slowly rising from his chair, Krupp peered down at his notes, paused, and turned to the judges. In his expensive, double-breasted suit and striped tie, standing erect with his aquiline nose and broad forehead framing deeply recessed and weary-looking hazel eyes, his body language, sallow cheeks, and thinning hair seemed to convey a rapidly aging aristocrat's displeasure at being unnecessarily burdened with mundane matters others should be dealing with. He cleared his throat and addressed the panel: "[The] essence of which we are charged with is this: You cooperated. No one will be able to hold it against us that in the emergency of war we took the part of duty, a part which millions of Germans had to take at the front and at home, and which led them to death."[38]

The Tribunal was not persuaded, as set forth in its judgment of July 31, 1948. Regarding Count 2, it held: "The defendants cannot . . . contend that, since the acts of spoliation . . . were authorized and actively supported by certain German governmental and military agencies or persons, they escape liability for such acts. It is a general principle of criminal law that encouragement and support received from other wrongdoers is not excusable."[39] That said, the panel deemed the evidence insufficient to support convictions for plundering/spoliation against Karl Pfirsch, Heinrich Korschan, Max Ihn, and Friedrich von Bülow. They were acquitted of that charge.

As for Count 3, whose gravamen was the use of slave labor, the panel was even more dubious of defense claims and deeply troubled by the treatment of the victims. The judgment referenced "the undisputed evidence [showing] that the firm of Krupp participated extensively in [the Nazi slave] labor program."[40] According to the testimony and documentation marshaled by the prosecution at trial, between 1940 and 1945, at eighty-one separate plants within greater Germany, Krupp enslaved a total of 69,898 foreign civilian workers and 4,978 concentration camp inmates, most of whom were dragooned and forcibly brought to Germany to toil in hellish conditions in Krupp enterprises. During the same period, Krupp similarly exploited 23,076 prisoners of war.

The only plausible defense that could be asserted, per the Tribunal, was that of necessity (comparable to duress, that is, that the defendants used the slave labor because Nazi authorities forced them to under threat of terrible consequences). But the Tribunal found that the "Krupp firm had manifested not only its willingness but its ardent desire to employ forced labor."[41]

For an industrialist case, not only was the judgment stern, "so were the sentences, at least if compared to previous cases."[42] Only Pfirsch and Kupke exited the Palace of Justice that day—the former was acquitted, and the latter got away with time served. But Lehmann and Korschan were sentenced to prison for six years and Löser for seven. Eberhardt and Ihn got nine years each and Janssen, ten. Von Bülow, Müller, and Krupp were each punished with twelve-year prison sentences and all of Krupp's property was ordered confiscated. Krupp's failure to testify at trial and his final statement to the Tribunal confirmed "the impression of the haughty magnate" whose "evident unwillingness to show any regret or remorse for this company's actions . . . sat ill with the judges."[43] A later appeal to General Clay, wherein Krupp "blamed his rank and file employees" and "complained bitterly about the biased judges," similarly fell on deaf ears. It only reinforced the impression that "the industrialist utterly failed to understand the moral bankruptcy of German business in the Third Reich."[44]

At least the remaining parts of *Krupp* were salvaged, and, in that regard, Ferencz had made a valuable contribution. But there was no time to savor the salvaging—no sooner had *Krupp* concluded than he was already burdened with new, and in some ways more pressing, concerns. Around the time he had moved from Berlin to Nuremberg to take over *Einsatzgruppen*, Telford Taylor's executive counsel, one William Raugust, was planning to leave Nuremberg. Raugust had been the first person to occupy this "executive counsel" position (previously, Thomas Ervin had served as Taylor's "deputy" before becoming *Flick* chief prosecutor, and then Taylor changed the title and gave the position to Raugust).[45] Analogizing the OCCWC to a newspaper, if chief of counsel was the editor in chief, then executive counsel was his managing editor, the person most responsible for day-to-day operations.

When Raugust announced his departure in the summer of 1947, Taylor urgently needed to identify his replacement. Ben Ferencz was a logical candidate. He had just come from running the Berlin Branch, where he would have had to deal with personnel, administrative, and related legal strategy matters. Additionally, given that the Berlin Branch was the focal point of most investigations supporting the office's prosecution efforts, Ferencz had to be acquainted with the substance of every case the office was trying. He could easily step into Raugust's shoes. Of course, he was also assuming leadership of the *Einsatzgruppen* prosecution at that time and was technically still in charge of the Berlin Branch. But, by then, Taylor was quite confident that Ferencz could successfully multitask, and he was entirely comfortable adding the executive counsel position to the young man's growing portfolio.

Given that the OCCWC was operating under the aegis of the US Army, the job came with a new "simulated rank"—ironically, the man who had nothing but scorn for the military and all its pomp and circumstance went from the civilian equivalent of "colonel" to "brigadier general." Fully grasping the absurdity of this, Ferencz observed: "Since the War Department had discharged me as a sergeant of infantry when the war ended, my meteoric rise in ranks may have set an army record. At a height of 5 feet 1/2 inches, I may also have been the shortest 'General' since Napoleon Bonaparte."[46]

OCCWC interoffice memoranda from as early as September 1947 already show Ferencz being addressed with the title "executive counsel" and dealing with management matters outside *Einsatzgruppen*.[47] For instance, a January 9, 1948, memorandum from Paul Gantt confirmed Executive Counsel Ferencz's decisions regarding personnel for the *Ministries* case team, including hiring, staffing, promotions, and transfers into the team (for example, Arnost Horlik-Hochwald, Ferencz's *Einsatzgruppen* comrade in arms, being assigned to *Ministries* once the former trial concluded).[48]

In all likelihood, though, Ferencz was not able to fully plunge into the role until the last preverdict court day in *Krupp*, that is, June 24, 1948. By then, apart from *Krupp* itself, only *IG Farben* (judgment issued on July 30, 1948), *High Command* (judgment issued on October 28, 1949), and *Ministries* (judgment issued on April 13, 1949) remained on the active docket. In other words, the NMT program was winding down. And the bulk of impending personnel decisions reflected that; it was time to let people go.

Handing out pink slips was the hardest part of the job for Ferencz. Many of those being made redundant were German Jewish refugees who had been persecuted and suffered before and during the war. For them, the Nuremberg Trials meant redemption—a return to the land from which they had been banished and an opportunity to get back on their feet. "I did whatever I could to steer them in the direction of replacement employment," Ben later recollected. "But when that wasn't available, it was really tough sending them away with nothing."[49]

Other unpleasant personnel matters came up, too. One involved the threatened termination of a staff member's life. There was an unspoken "Golden Rule" among OCCWC prosecutors—all evidence was to be shared across cases. In that regard, during the life of the office, one crucial piece of evidence that had implications for more than one case stood out—the infamous Wannsee Protocol. This consisted of the minutes of a January 20, 1942, conference, where high-level Nazis, led by Reinhard Heydrich, assisted by his amanuensis, Adolf Eichmann, drew up the detailed plan for "The Final Solution of the Jewish Problem." From the standpoint of the historical record, like investigator Burin's discovery of the Einsatzgruppen Daily Reports, unearthing this blueprint for the implementation of the Holocaust by investigator Von Eckert (first name unknown) was one of the OCCWC's key investigative finds.

Understanding its importance for *Ministries,* Von Eckert had shared the document with chief prosecutor Robert Kempner. But as *Justice* was being tried during the course of 1947, Von Eckert became aware of the prosecution's failure to rely on the Protocol, which seemed strange as Justice Ministry officials had been present at the Wannsee Conference, and the Protocol had implications for the administration of justice, however warped, in the Third Reich. Von Eckert asked *Justice* chief prosecutor Charles M. La Follette, a former US congressman, about the omission. The feisty La Follette was at first incredulous, as he had not heard of the Protocol's existence. Then, once he realized that Kempner, a glory hound known for hoarding important investigative finds only to later claim credit for them in the press, had concealed the Protocol, La Follette asked Kempner for the document. But the latter feigned ignorance.

La Follette exploded. The executive counsel was then called in as the *Justice* chief prosecutor was seriously threatening to kill the *Ministries* chief prosecutor. "First I called Taylor," Ferencz later recalled, before launching into deadpan humor, "and I said, 'Telford, I got a problem. Charlie wants to kill Bob Kempner.' And Telford says . . . 'Well, we can't let him do that.'" Ferencz recounted what happened next: "So, I go to see Bob Kempner. I said, 'Bob, Charlie's here on a rampage. He says you're holding out on him.' He says: 'Who me? No. No, I don't have it.' 'Yes [you do]. It's an item that lists the defendant on the first page. It's a description.' He said: 'No. No.' I said 'Well, what's in the drawer here?' He went and had locks put on the drawer! He unlocked it. 'Oh, you mean that?!?' and he takes it out."[50]

After having thus "coaxed" Kempner to hand over the Wannsee Protocol from his locked drawer, Ferencz presented it "personally to La Follette with apologies."[51] But La Follette, still incensed, wanted blood. He stormed off to Taylor's office and demanded that he "fire the bastard!"[52] Ferencz followed and was able to convince his boss that *Ministries* would fall apart without

Kempner, so Taylor kept him on.[53] (Significantly, it was later revealed that Kempner, a prominent Jewish jurist in the Weimar Republic who had been persecuted in and then had to flee from Nazi Germany, had appropriated, smuggled into the United States, and kept hidden for the rest of his life, the diaries of IMT defendant and top Nazi ideologist Alfred Rosenberg. These were among the most historically important documents of the Third Reich. The diaries were eventually tracked down and recovered by the US Holocaust Memorial Museum.)[54]

In addition to personnel and related legal strategy matters, there was also a public relations aspect to the executive counsel job. In general, Ferencz was tasked with assisting General Taylor in creating a favorable impression of the Nuremberg Trials among the German public. Thus, by way of example, Ben was kept in the loop regarding the OCCWC's relations with the American-German Club.[55] And he would accompany Taylor, and speak with him, in public appearances, providing information about the Nuremberg Trials. For instance, in May 1948, Ferencz and Taylor (along with fellow prosecutor Sandy Hardy), made an appearance at a German-American Youth Club Forum about the fairness of the Nuremberg Trials.[56]

But perhaps Ferencz's most important accomplishment as executive counsel had nothing to do with the impression the OCCWC was making during the course of its operations; rather, it related to the lasting impact the office would make after shutting down. As early as March 1947, around the time the Berlin Branch chief was being appointed to the position of *Einsatzgruppen* prosecution chief, he floated by Telford Taylor the idea of setting up a "Special Projects Division."[57] Here he showed great vision and insight as a pioneer international criminal prosecutor. He had rightly anticipated that the gargantuan tranches of documents amassed and generated by the Nuremberg Trials would have to be treated specially so as to carry on the Nazi prosecution project after the OCCWC's work had ended and to preserve them for the historical record.

Good examples were the Wannsee Protocol itself, as well as the Einsatzgruppen Daily Reports, whose availability to the public would assure that none "could ever doubt, or dare deny, the authenticity and horrors of the Holocaust."[58] Thus, Ferencz believed, via the Special Projects Division, "Nuremberg's preservation of the historical record of incredible deeds" could become "its most lasting contribution." (A perfect example of his dream end result was "the German government [converting] the villa at Wannsee into a museum that displays in shocking detail the original minutes of the Wannsee Protocol and the biography of all the murderous participants.")[59]

Taylor greatly appreciated this forward thinking and approved the proposal, tapping Ferencz to be its first director.[60] The Division was small, with only a staff of five, and it had three main tasks: (1) gather, organize, sort, and index all evidence for transfer to regional German prosecution and denazification offices as well as to Allied prosecutors in other occupation zones;[61] (2) send all trial materials, amounting to 150 tons, to Washington, DC, for preservation, with "duplicates, in English and German, going to various educational institutions"; and (3) assist the OCCWC's Publications Division (during the initial phase), in compiling accurate and objective summaries of each of the twelve NMT trials—this compilation, in fifteen volumes, would come to be known as the Green Series.[62]

Ferencz played a very active and foundational role in each of these three Special Projects Division tasks. For example, in relation to the transfer of evidence to German domestic jurisdictions, he recalled the good working rapport he established with Bavarian prosecutors: "[We] began first with Munich. We [had] a good [prosecutor] there. I think he was mixed Jewish. . . . [In any event,] he was not a Nazi. . . . And I had a good relationship with him. So, I sent him a lot of stuff, which he could use there."[63]

Ferencz also supervised the transportation of all the trial materials to the US capital. He later recollected that "General Taylor sent me to Washington to coordinate the transfer of records to the Judge Advocate Division of the War Department where a Colonel Young was to offer assistance. Since I have a terrible sense of direction, a good part of each morning was spent wandering through the maze in search of my office in the Pentagon."[64] He also served as the initial editor of the Green Series, which was soon taken over by Drexel Sprecher, assisted by Paul Gantt and Gertrude Ferencz, who stayed on at the OCCWC long after Ben had left. Overall, then, Ben Ferencz was a pioneer in what is today known as the "legacy" field of international criminal law.

By the spring of 1949, once *Ministries* was tried to verdict, the NMT trials had all been completed. Summarizing the program's quantitative accomplishments is a relatively straightforward task. In twenty-eight months, the twelve panels tried 177 defendants, convicting 142 of them and sentencing 25 to death. Of the others found guilty, dozens were sentenced to life in prison or lengthy incarceration periods. In terms of paper memorialization, the twelve trial transcripts combined run 132,855 legal-size pages and include the testimony of more than 1,300 witnesses and the contents of more than 30,000 separate documents.[65] The jurisprudential fruit of those proceedings, the twelve judgments themselves, totals 3,828 pages.[66]

From a more qualitative perspective, as the single judgment by the IMT "against two-dozen culprits could not adequately portray the full extent of

Nazi criminality," the wide swath of Nazi conduct covered in the NMT decisions went a long way toward filling in the lacunae.[67] The nefarious deeds of industrialists, SS executioners, military men, racial policy enforcers, doctors, concentration camp builders and administrators, lawyers, judges, police, diplomats, bureaucrats, governors of occupied territories, propagandists, and bankers were all put under the microscope. In the opinion of Robert Kempner, the trial narratives constituted "the greatest history seminar ever held."[68] They chronicled everything from Hitler and his paladins transforming Germany's courts into a "nationally organized system of injustice and persecution"[69] (*Justice*) and its medical profession into a cabal for euthanasia and inhumane experimentation (*Medical*) to their implementing the concentration camp system (*Pohl*), carrying out racial cleansing and resettlement (*RuSHA*), and initiating the Holocaust (*Einsatzgruppen*) to their working with German industrialists to equip the Nazi war machine (*Flick, Farben, Krupp*), with German ministers to plan and execute the war machine's invasions (*Ministries*), and with military officers to perpetrate and sanction the war crimes committed pursuant to those invasions (*Hostage* and *High Command*).

Based on all that history presented in the courtrooms, there were convictions with respect to all of the delicts (crimes against peace, war crimes, and crimes against humanity) within Law No. 10's subject matter jurisdiction (other than conspiracy). And there were important procedural rulings generated in interpreting the program's governing due process instrument, Military Government Ordinance No. 7. Via all the NMT judgments issued, an impressive foundational body of jurisprudence was developed.[70]

But there was also a negative side to the NMT experience, especially in its end phases. As Ben pointed out to Sheldon Glueck in a letter written after his disappointment over the early 1948 dismissal of the aggression charges in *Krupp*:

> In general, things in Nuremberg are going very badly. . . . The case against fourteen members of the Nazi high command will be completed around June while literally hundreds of their colleagues remain at large. It is unfortunately a fact that we have in our files clear evidence of mass murder on the part of Generals now working with the Americans and we are prevented from doing anything with it. The feeling is that these Generals, even though they be mass murderers, know more about the Russians than we do and it is best not to antagonize them if we hope to make use of their talents in the future.[71]

As Ferencz was suggesting, the impact of the Cold War was, by then, unmistakable and it would become more pervasive over the course of 1948. One important yard marker for the conflict dates back to 1946, when the United States adopted its core policy toward the Soviet Union informed by Moscow-based diplomat George Kennan's famous "Long Telegram." Kennan had warned that the Soviets perceived themselves in a "perpetual war" with capitalist states and that the United States needed to adopt a policy of Soviet containment and anticommunism.[72] The next month, on March 5, accompanied by President Harry Truman, former UK prime minister Winston Churchill delivered his famous "Iron Curtain" speech in Fulton, Missouri. "From Stettin in the Baltic to Trieste in the Adriatic," he began famously, "an iron curtain has descended across the Continent."[73] A year later, the US decision to back the Greek government against Communist-led insurgents marked the adoption of the "Truman Doctrine," that is, the explicit policy of containment of Soviet geopolitical expansion. It was soon economically supplemented via the "Marshall Plan," a $13 billion assistance program for rebuilding Western Europe to shield its countries from Communist influence.

In March 1948, the Soviets engineered a brutal coup in Czechoslovakia that resulted in a Communist takeover. Three months later, they initiated their Berlin Blockade, and, over the next year, the United States overcame it via the Berlin Airlift. By the spring of 1949, when Nuremberg's *Ministries* case was nearing its end, the US spearheaded the establishment of the North Atlantic Treaty Organization (NATO) to provide for Western European collective security against any Soviet threat. And it pushed forward the creation of the Federal Republic of Germany (that is, West Germany) to integrate into the Western Bloc the non-Soviet-controlled portions of the former Reich.

Against this backdrop, the NMTs operated from 1946 through 1949. And, as the program neared its end, the United States became more focused on currying favor with the Germans, who could help fight Stalin, than punishing those same Germans who had fought for Hitler. Thus, echoing Ferencz's lament in his spring 1948 letter to Glueck, there was unquestionably a Cold War–induced "American leniency toward Nazi crimes."[74]

But it was about to get a lot worse. If one name is associated with the nadir of Cold War–diluted Nuremberg justice, it is John J. McCloy, twentieth-century America's ultimate behind-the-scenes power broker and the very definition of éminence grise. After a career advising the American power elite and serving as a top official in the War Department, he was US high commissioner for Germany when the NMT-convicted Nazi war criminals were making clemency pleas. McCloy's 1895 Philadelphia birth to an insurance salesman and a hairdresser might not have foretold that he would ever be in such a position, especially given his father's death when he was only five. But Mrs. McCloy coiffed the hair of Philadelphia's Main Line matriarchs and used her clients to acculturate her son to their blueblood world. And thanks to his mother's thrift and connections, as well as scholarships and his own hard work at odd jobs during school, he got a first-class education at Amherst and then Harvard Law School (Class of 1921, having previously served as a US Army artillery captain in World War I). Via meritocracy, as the Jazz Age was getting under way, this even-tempered and amiable man, already portly and balding, conservative but always with an incongruously impish look in his eyes, began his steep ascent through the socioeconomic strata of interwar America.

During that time, McCloy worked as a Wall Street lawyer at two of the nation's most prestigious firms—Cadwalader, Wickersham & Taft, to begin, and then Cravath, Henderson, & de Gersdorff, where he continued to represent tony corporate clients, including the Rockefellers, until the outbreak of the Second World War. With a winsome, low-key personality and a "fixer's" practical approach to getting things done, he became an indispensable advisor and laid the foundations for a network that, by career's end, would place him in positions that now seem almost cartoonish in their over-the-top indicia of power: councilor to seven presidents, from FDR through Ronald Reagan; president or chair himself of, among others, the World Bank, Chase Manhattan Bank, Chase National Bank, the Ford Foundation, E. R. Squibb & Sons, the UN Development Corporation, the Council on Foreign Relations, the Atlantic Institute, and the Salk Institute; co-creator (along with William Donovan) of the Office of Strategic Services (predecessor to the CIA); member of the Warren Commission, among other powerful government posts and, later, name partner at the Wall Street powerhouse firm that bore his name, Milbank, Tweed, Hadley & McCloy. In his sunset years, his moniker became Chairman of the American Establishment.[75]

But it was his activities in the lead-up to World War II, as well as actions during the war itself, that should have been cause for concern in relation to the judgments at Nuremberg. During his time at Cravath, he worked on matters with German themes or for German clients—and one case in particular occupied him for most of the 1930s: the Black Tom matter. By the middle portion of the decade, while representing Bethlehem Steel, through indefatigable sleuthing, McCloy was able to link damages from a massive 1916 explosion at the Black Tom munitions depot in New York harbor to the sabotage of Imperial German agents seeking to hamper US assistance to Britain and France during World War I. In negotiating a settlement for Second Reich damages, he spent time with Third Reich leaders in Munich, including Rudolf Hess. While negotiations were ongoing in Munich, Hitler and Göring personally invited him to Berlin, where he was a spectator with the Reichsmarschall in the Führer's private box at the 1936 Olympic Games. During the same decade, "McCloy represented I. G. Farben's American subsidiary in the US."[76] And, during this time, "McCloy and his wife [who came from a prominent German American family and spoke fluent German] also socialized with leading Nazis."[77] Owing perhaps in part to these previous Nazi associations, he would eventually be "called by some . . . a racist and an anti-Semite."[78]

If his affiliations and attitudes in the 1930s were cause for concern, his actions in the 1940s, arguably connected, were much worse. McCloy entered government service in 1940, invited by Secretary of War Henry L. Stimson to become a consultant. By April 1941, he was made assistant secretary of war. In that capacity, he was responsible for US policies that would clearly contravene the spirit of the Nuremberg Trials—quite ironic, as he was one of the men who supported and helped design the trials program. Most egregiously, with the Black Tom sabotage on his mind, McCloy overrode the constitutional objections of US Attorney General Francis Biddle, and "more than any official . . . guided and sanctioned the internment of Japanese Americans."[79] And convinced that he could not afford to divert Allied airplanes from military objectives, many view him as responsible for the US refusal "to allow American bombers to blow up the rail heads at Auschwitz," which might have saved tens of thousands of Jews from the gas chambers.[80]

After the war, McCloy served as president of the World Bank. But in September 1949, after the Soviets had developed the atom bomb and the Cold War entered a new and more perilous phase, he was appointed US high commissioner for Germany, when General Clay stepped down as military governor. Despite his already noted contribution, as assistant secretary of the army, to US efforts to prosecute Nazis at Nuremberg, as high commissioner, McCloy became receptive to the complaints of West German politicians, including President Konrad Adenauer, that the convicted war criminals had been treated too harshly, especially the top industrialists, such as Alfried Krupp and Friedrich Flick. And this was at a time when the United States was making a concerted effort to integrate the Federal Republic more fully into the Western alliance.

In March 1950, McCloy established what came to be known as the Peck Panel, an advisory group consisting of three American lawyers, headed by New York Supreme Court Justice David Peck, which would assist him with pleas for clemency or revision of sentences. None of these lawyers had specific expertise in the burgeoning field of international criminal law and would examine only the judgments themselves while hearing from defense lawyers.[81] There would be no review of the original evidence or consultation with OCCWC prosecutors, including Ben Ferencz, who requested an audience.[82]

He "received a curt acknowledgement from the panel's secretary, informing him that the board would let him know if they wanted him. They didn't."[83]

Under such skewed ground rules, the board unsurprisingly found fault with the NMT findings, most notably in the white-collar cases, and advised significant sentence reductions. McCloy then pondered the recommendations, formally walling off the insights of the prosecutors, including the *Einsatzgruppen/Krupp* trial attorney. Ferencz "dropped into the high commissioner's office from time to time." There he saw the records of the *Krupp* trial, which "were packed in crates six feet long and shaped curiously like coffins. Knowing the evidence that lay inside, he kept wondering when the lids would be removed. They never were."[84]

Still, Ferencz never gave up and was at least finally able to speak to McCloy and convince him not to spare the most heinous convicted Einsatzgruppen leaders (especially Ohlendorf) from the gallows. As McCloy later recollected in a recorded conversation with Ferencz: "I know you pressed very hard for Ohlendorf's hanging. I remember talking to you about Ohlendorf a great deal. . . . You convinced me on Ohlendorf."[85]

But, in the end, Ferencz had only limited success. By the time McCloy issued his *Landsberg: A Documentary Report* (hereafter "Landsberg Report") on January 31, 1951 (named for the prison where NMT convicts were being incarcerated), Communists had seized power in China. And the two Koreas were at war with one another. The Cold War had gotten quite hot, and "McCloy believed that a 'solution' to the war-criminals problem was necessary, because the growing Soviet threat . . . had put a premium on improved German-American relations."[86]

The Landsberg Report, which "overturned the bulk of the NMT's findings," reflected that.[87] Of those convicts who had submitted clemency petitions (that is, those not already released under a "good conduct" scheme McCloy had instituted, or for health reasons), seventy-seven out of a total of eighty-nine had their sentences reduced. Of the sixty-nine men sentenced to terms of imprisonment, only five were denied clemency: Wilhelm List and Walter Kuntze from the *Hostage* case (although found by McCloy to be potentially eligible for medical parole); and Hermann Reinecke, Hermann Hoth, and Hans Reinhardt from the *High Command* case. Of those Nazis sentenced to death, the so-called Red Jackets (based on the distinctive apparel they wore in Landsberg Prison), only five ended up hanging: Oswald Pohl and, thanks in part to the efforts of Ben Ferencz, four of the *Einsatzgruppen* convicts, Otto Ohlendorf, Paul Blobel, Erich Naumann, and Werner Braune.

Some of the individual outcomes in the Landsberg Report were astonishing. From the *Pohl* case, SS-Standartenführer Franz Eirenschmalz, who ordered and supervised the construction of concentration camp crematoria knowing they would be used to carry out the Final Solution, had his death sentence commuted to only nine years' imprisonment. McCloy claimed it was based on new evidence but never revealed what the supposed evidence consisted of.[88]

Unfortunately, some of the worst, and most perplexing commutations affected the two cases on which Ben Ferencz had been a podium prosecutor, *Einsatzgruppen* and *Krupp.* In terms of the former, despite Ferencz's efforts, McCloy commuted ten of the fourteen death sentences of the extermination squad leaders. In three of those—Martin Sandberger (Einsatzgruppe A), Waldemar Klingelhöfer (Einsatzgruppe B), and Adolf Ott (Einsatzgruppe B)—he went beyond the recommendations of the already lenient Peck Panel, which had been content to affirm the orders of execution, and commuted the execution sentences to life. Sandberger, a lawyer who had been the leader of Sonderkommando 1a, supervised the slaughter of tens of thousands of innocent civilians in the Baltics,[89] such as liquidating Riga's entire Jewish population.[90] Klingelhöfer and Ott, for their part, had shown no remorse, and, when grilled by Ben Ferencz, Klingelhöfer brazenly prevaricated on the stand.

As for the other Red Jacket Einsatz leaders, after McCloy's intervention, the lightest commutation was life in prison. But the other defendants benefited from serious reductions—one got twenty-five years; another, twenty; two got fifteen years, and a final one got a mere ten years. For some of these, McCloy again alluded to "new evidence," but, as before, that was never identified.[91] Moreover, the *Einsatzgruppen* death row defendants were not the only ones to benefit from McCoy's largesse. Heinz Jost, the chief of Einsatzgruppe A, and the vicious Gustav Nosske, member of the Gestapo and sadistic leader of Einsatzkommando 12 (within Einsatzgruppe D), had been sentenced to life imprisonment, but McCloy commuted these to ten years each. The twenty-year sentence of Erwin Schulz was knocked down to fifteen. Waldemar von Radetzky and Felix Rühl had their respective sentences of ten and twenty years shortened to time served. Franz Six, a former university dean, who led Vorkommando Moscow when it massacred Jews, had his twenty-year prison sentence reduced to fifteen—purportedly due to the crimes not being proved beyond a reasonable doubt. Yet "there was no review of the trial transcript or any of the evidence submitted by the prosecution."[92]

The mercy shown the *Krupp* defendants was equally jaw-dropping. Despite all the horrific evidence of the firm's slave labor practices, undertaken with zeal, as well as Ben Ferencz's attempted interventions, each defendant had his sentence reduced to time served. And, most galling of all, Alfried Krupp was not only released from Landsberg Prison but he had all his wealth restored to him.[93] On reclaiming his liberty and possessions, Krupp returned to generating enormous wealth through the old family business and, in the final corruption of the justice process, according to Ferencz, could later be seen playing golf with McCloy.[94]

For those who could appreciate what was at stake in the NMT proceedings, as well as the volume and complexity of the evidence undergirding its judgments, McCloy's unprincipled, blunderbuss approach to clemency was inexcusable and appalling. Eminent international law scholar Hersch Lauterpacht, who worked with Robert Jackson to define "crimes against humanity" in the IMT Charter, "railed against the indignity done to millions of victims [including his own family, which had been slaughtered in Poland] by the release of convicted Nazi killers."[95] Jackson himself grumbled that "The policy of winning German support against Communists by releasing Nazis, goes on apace."[96] Taylor fumed that "the retreat from Nuremberg [was] on"[97] and that "McCloy had rendered his efforts superfluous."[98]

Ben Ferencz was equally aghast at what he called a "perversion of justice."[99] Referring to the Landsberg Report decisions as "Christmas Amnesties," he could not believe the leniency accorded to so many Einsatzgruppen head honchos, especially Gustav Nosske, "the man whom the other defendants called the biggest bloodhound of them all."[100] And then there was the windfall for Alfried Krupp, whom his trial team had "proved was a murderer too."[101] Not only had he walked out of Landsberg Prison on January 31, 1951, but on that same day, as his chauffeur drove him back onto his old villa's palatial grounds, he again became one of Europe's wealthiest men. In an article written for the *New York Times Magazine*, Ferencz decried the clemency decisions and called for the creation of a permanent international criminal court.[102]

Still, despite unrelenting West German cries for mercy, McCloy stood firm on the five death sentences he had upheld, and they were carried out on June 7, 1951. Beginning at a little after midnight, led to the gallows one by one, Paul Blobel, Werner Braune, Erich Naumann, Otto Ohlendorf, and Oswald Pohl met their ends.

Over the next few years, in dribs and drabs, whether for good conduct credit or medical considerations, more NMT convicts had their sentences commuted as others were still being released pursuant to McCloy's 1951 dilutions of justice. By the end of 1958, all war criminals convicted by NMT panels were free. While persons found guilty of only one murder in US courts were being routinely sentenced to death or life in prison, genocidal mass murderers convicted in US courts in Germany were incarcerated for fewer than fifteen years.

Ferencz, who was still in Germany while many of them were being released, thought it was eerie that they lived among the ordinary citizens he would see on the streets. He could have run into any of them at a restaurant or on a tram. "This was very much on my mind," he later recounted. "I traveled a lot by rail in those days and I would always take a close look inside a train compartment before feeling comfortable enough to step in."[103]

But he was only one of the prosecutors. What must the survivors have experienced? he wondered. How traumatic must such encounters, or even the prospect of them, have been for them? With the NMT trials program coming to its end, the survivors of the Holocaust were increasingly on his mind. In his work as an investigator and as a prosecutor, the powerful, spectral presence of the victims had hovered over everything he had been doing—but they had not been the focal point. All that was about to change.

PART V

PROVIDING

15

THE CONNECTIVE TISSUE BETWEEN RETRIBUTION AND RESTITUTION

> He who profits by villainy, has perpetrated it.
>
> —Iain Pears, *An Instance of the Fingerpost*

If the Nuremberg Trials proved anything, they proved that the combined political and administrative machinery of the Third Reich was an enormous cabal engaging in what was, arguably, history's most profligate and concentrated orgy of mass criminality. But the central focus of those proceedings was the responsibility of the malefactors, not the subsequent well-being of their surviving victims. In contrast, in domestic settings, punishing criminal conduct routinely entails consideration of victim welfare and recompense. By way of example, France and Belgium, victim-friendly civil law jurisdictions, make crime victims civil parties, who can themselves initiate prosecutions, participate in and be heard as parties at trial, and pursue claims for civil damages as part of the criminal case.[1] Even in less victim-centered common law jurisdictions, such as the contemporary United States, victims can provide "impact statements" in court postconviction and presentencing, and punishment may include restitution, that is, compensation paid by a criminal defendant to the victim.[2]

Such victim considerations were entirely lacking at the Nuremberg Trials. Of course, the tragic fate of survivors (as well as that of their deceased loved ones) had been explored in considering the defendants' liability during each proceeding. During the *Einsatzgruppen* trial, for instance, Ben Ferencz knew that he was "the voice of the victims in the courtroom."[3] But that was as far as it went—once proceedings were wrapped up in Nuremberg, what became of the survivors was not part of the justice calculus. Like his fellow OCCWC prosecutors helping to birth international criminal law, Ferencz's job had been to prove each Nazi defendant's individual responsibility, full stop. But as the NMT proceedings were wrapping up, fate intervened and revealed to him an entirely new, and vital, facet of dealing with mass atrocity: posttrial victim welfare.

And there were many victims to care for. At war's end, more than a quarter million Jewish displaced persons (DPs), who had been liberated from Nazi imprisonment, bondage, and persecution, were streaming into locations in Germany, Austria, and Italy. Their final destinations in those countries were primarily DP camps run by the United Nations Relief and Rehabilitation Administration (UNRRA), which had offered Ferencz a job toward the end of his time in the army.

Other Jews were returning to their former hometowns in Poland, Hungary, Slovakia, Romania, and Ukraine, and, incredibly, dealing with new paroxysms of antisemitic violence. Given the unstable situation in Europe, many DPs and victims of postwar persecution sought to immigrate to Mandatory Palestine, which was then under British control and would eventually include the state of Israel, founded in 1948. But, in the immediate aftermath of the war, Great Britain imposed draconian entry quotas for Holocaust survivors. Many of them therefore entered Palestine illegally or were detained trying to do so and then held on the island of Cyprus. Finally, large numbers emigrated to the United States via the Displaced Persons Act of 1948 or to other nations, such as Canada, Australia, South Africa, and Argentina, where they tried to move on from the devastation and build new lives.

Finding safe havens for new beginnings was imperative, but having the means to survive in the long run was equally crucial. Thus, the other postwar reckoning concerned the disposition of stolen Jewish property. Chapter 9 featured one aspect of Hitler's economic war against the Jews—his looting of art—but this was just a small part of the mass plundering. The Nazis had been stealing all manner of things from Jews as soon as Hitler's tentacles reached every apparatus of the German state—tax laws, for example, heavily discriminated against Jews as of 1934. But a systematic program of property crime began on April 26, 1938, only weeks after the German Anschluss of Austria. On that date, Hitler issued the Decree for the Reporting of Jewish-Owned Property, requiring all Jews in both Germany and Austria to register any property or assets valued at more than 5,000 Reichsmarks (about US$2,000 at that time, or US$34,000 today).[4] Within months, Nazi bureaucrats had compiled a registry of assets reported by some 700,000 Jewish citizens worth about 7 billion Reichsmarks. This wealth would be larcenously absorbed into the German exchequer in a process dubbed "Aryanization."

As the Wehrmacht started conquering large chunks of surrounding territory, this policy of theft extended across the continent. In effect, Aryanization was "a gigantic, trans-European trafficking operation in stolen goods."[5] Real property, furniture, paintings, religious relics, vehicles, life insurance, and stocks—nothing was exempt from the clutches of this persecution-driven vampire regime. Some have estimated that Hitler's henchmen pilfered property worth US$230 to $320 billion today and that this ultimately financed a whopping 30 percent of German armed forces expenditures during World War II (not to mention the contribution of slave labor dealt with in previous chapters).[6]

Germany's conquerors recognized that Hitler's asset-stripping had gone hand in hand with the murder of six million Jews in the Holocaust, which is why restitution of looted property to its rightful owners was an important feature of Allied policy during and after the war. As early as January 1943, Great Britain and the United States spearheaded issuance of the Inter-Allied Declaration against Acts of Dispossession Committed in Territories under Enemy Occupation or Control, better known as the London Declaration.[7] In light of Nazi persecutory forced sales or confiscations, the measure announced that the Allies would thenceforth refuse to recognize the transfer of any property in Nazi-occupied countries even if it appeared legal.

Then, at the conclusion of the Potsdam Conference in August 1945, the "Big Three"—Harry Truman, Winston Churchill, and Joseph Stalin—agreed to divvy up German "external assets," Nazi-confiscated property found in neutral countries (primarily Switzerland, Sweden, Portugal, and Spain). The allocation of these assets was between East (that is, the USSR and countries friendly to it in Eastern Europe) and West (that is, the United States, United Kingdom, and Western countries aligned with them). Then, from the Western pot, Article 8 of the December 1945 Final Act of the Paris Conference on Reparation allocated $25 million to reparations, 90 percent of which was to be used to rehabilitate and resettle Jewish victims. Two Jewish organizations were then selected to administer the funds: the Jewish Agency for Palestine (JAP), based on the belief that a large number of Jewish refugees would emigrate to Palestine, which proved to be the case; and the American Joint Distribution Committee (AJDC), the largest Jewish field relief and resettlement organization with a program of wide and varied scope in countries other than Palestine.[8]

Article 8 of the Paris Conference Final Act set aside two other types of money for purposes of "restitution": "non-monetary gold" (for example, jewelry, gold teeth, ornaments) and "heirless assets" (property that had belonged to persons who, with their entire families, were exterminated by the Nazis). Other than the neutral country of Sweden, the best place for finding heirless property for restitution was in Germany, and the United States played a leading role in effectuating "internal" restitution of these assets in its zone of occupation there.[9]

OMGUS achieved this via promulgating Military Law No. 59, titled "The Restitution of Identifiable Property," in November 1947. This law required restoring property to its previous owners when they had been dispossessed of it "for reasons of race, religion, nationality, ideology or political opposition to National Socialism."[10] When said owners, or their heirs, were still alive and could be located, the property would simply be returned to them. But what if they had been killed by the Nazis and had no heirs?

In his book *Indemnification and Reparations: Jewish Aspects* (1944), the attorney Nehemiah Robinson, director of the Office of Indemnification for the World Jewish Congress, contended that the property of murdered Jews with no heirs should not escheat to the German state. Rather, these assets should be applied to ease the physical and economic hardships of survivors via a Jewish welfare organization.[11] Law No. 59 was in accord with Robinson's recommendation. Much as a large portion of collected *external* asset funds were distributed, pursuant to Article 8 of the Paris Conference Final Act, as reparations to the JAP and the AJDC, *internal* asset heirless property collected in Germany was designated, via Law No. 59, for distribution to the Jewish Restitution Commission (JRC). This entity consisted of representatives from various American and Jewish organizations (including the JAP and the AJDC) and was incorporated on May 15, 1947.[12] By the time heirless property could first be distributed in 1948, the JRC had changed its name to the Jewish Restitution Successor Organization (JRSO). (The French and British hewed to the American model and soon promulgated comparable restitution laws in their respective occupation zones—in general, the Soviets did not follow suit in the area they controlled.)[13]

On the lips of the key players whose groups constituted the JRSO was the name of Benjamin Ferencz, owing primarily to his leadership role in the *Einsatzgruppen* case, the most Holocaust-focused proceeding at Nuremberg. When these organizational directors convened to determine who should lead the JRSO, they tapped the OCCWC executive counsel. But they were well aware that recruiting him was no fait accompli. So they approached his wife first. The AJDC lawyer Joel Fischer traveled to Nuremberg from AJDC headquarters in Paris and paid a social visit to Gertrude Ferencz, who described what happened next:

> He said, "Gertrude, I have to talk to you. We'd like you to stay on, but we won't talk to Ben until we talk to you first. Are you willing to stay on, because we want to set up a restitution program for the survivors of the Holocaust." I said, "I don't want to, but for this . . . I have to. I don't have a choice." How could I say no? I knew my husband was the best qualified person at the time to run

> a program like that because he knew what happened. He knew the ropes. He knew the military. He knew how to deal with problems that crop up.[14]

Ben was then approached, and he described the recruitment pitch as follows:

> I was then a high ranking muckey-muck with the U.S. Army, and this was all military occupation at the time. "We don't think anything will come of it," [Fischer] said, "but we have a moral obligation to try. And, of course, we don't have any money to put into this, we need our money for relief of the survivors. We have enough to pay your salary for six months" which was, I think, six or seven thousand dollars all together.[15]

Ben then sat down with his wife, and they discussed whether he should take the job: "Although she had eagerly joined me for our honeymoon in Germany in 1946, she never felt comfortable in Germany. Yet, the moral imperative of possibly being able to help Holocaust survivors (including some of her own relatives) could not be turned down."[16]

So their plans to return to the United States, joining most of the other OCCWC prosecutors, including Telford Taylor himself, had to be put on hold. And for good reason. Aside from his appreciation of the righteousness of the cause, Ben Ferencz was the ideal person for the job. Gertrude had put her finger on some of it—he knew the details of the Holocaust, he knew the military, he knew how to solve problems. But it was more than that. By then, he had arguably become a veritable logistics genius. Whether it was learning how to survive as a student with little to no money; supplying an army battalion through creative resource management; conducting war crimes investigations with limited personnel; scrounging for viable office space in Berlin; pinching spare lawyers and beer in Nuremberg; or running the day-to-day operations of an OCCWC already actively shedding personnel—all of it had trained Ferencz to rely on his resourcefulness, cunning, and can-do attitude to get results in resource-deprived environments. And he had honed it to an art. Much as his Harvard and army experiences had prepared him for Nuremberg, those experiences combined with Nuremberg and, by then, his deep-seated desire for justice, prepared him to take over the JRSO.

And, in a more profound sense, the Nuremberg experience also linked him to two separate aspects of Holocaust justice—retribution and restitution. In fact, he was about to become a unique individual in history: an innovator and leader in three separate phases of the Holocaust justice process—investigation, prosecution, and reparation. In one person, he would be the connective tissue between and among these three stages. And that was symbolically apparent in the location of his initial meeting with Joel Fischer, the Palace of Justice, where he had started as an investigator at the beginning of his Nuremberg career, then become a prosecutor, and now was agreeing to take the laboring oar on Holocaust restitution. In fact, quite fittingly, he began his JRSO job working out of his Nuremberg prosecutor's office.

On being officially hired in August 1948, he persuaded Fischer to designate him as director-general of the JRSO, "knowing that Germans would be impressed by someone who was both a Director and a General."[17] This new title gave him more access, but it did not give him more time, of which, in the late summer of 1948, he had very little. For Law No. 59 had not only set up the JRSO and its mandate, it also imposed a hard deadline in its Article 56: "A petition for restitution pursuant to this Law shall be submitted to the Central Filing Agency in writing on or before 31 December 1948."[18] So he had little more than four months to hire staff, train them, and then locate, compile, and present what surely must have been tens of thousands of claims throughout the American occupied zone of Germany.

He knew this was impossible given the resources at his disposal in August. His best option, he concluded, was to travel to Berlin and ask General Lucius Clay, the US military governor in Germany—that is, the head of OMGUS—for an extension. Ferencz had gotten to know Clay when he had headed the Berlin Branch, and their respective offices had been in the same building. It was appropriate that Ferencz was approaching him now. Clay was famous for being a logistical wizard himself, a Ben Ferencz writ large, as it were. The youngest son of a US senator from Georgia who was close to President Theodore Roosevelt, Lucius graduated in 1918 from West Point as an engineer. He was then assigned to the US Army Corps of Engineers and narrowly missed serving in the First World War.[19] Beginning in 1933, he spent four years in Washington organizing and managing New Deal public works projects. And in 1937, he was transferred to the Philippines, where he worked with General Douglas MacArthur and his chief of staff, Lieutenant Colonel Dwight D. Eisenhower, impressing both.[20]

Clay then moved back to the continental United States and became an expert in airport construction as part of a national defense program. At the start of World War II, in a very compressed time frame, he orchestrated the crash construction of five hundred airfields and was soon promoted to the role of army chief of procurement. In that post, he arranged for the purchase of 299 million pairs of pants, 50 million field jackets, 2.3 million trucks, 178,000 artillery pieces, 88,000 tanks, and billions of rounds of ammunition. Secretary of

State James Byrnes reportedly told President Roosevelt that, given six months, Clay "could run General Motors or U.S. Steel."[21] Shortly after D-Day, General Eisenhower called on him to untangle the flow of supplies at Cherbourg, the Allies' principal port of entry in Normandy. Clay doubled the flow in one day and had supplies moving rapidly toward the front before leaving three weeks later. He continued to shine as Ike's chief logistics fixer through the end of the war.

He was appointed military governor in 1947 and announced that his job was "to run Germany, not ruin it."[22] And his logistical prowess was put to the test again in June 1948 as he began directing the Berlin Airlift. This ultimately consisted of 277,804 flights carrying 2.3 million tons of food and fuel to West Berlin, which broke the Soviet blockade by May 1949 and for which Clay was hailed as a hero in Germany.

In August 1948, Ben Ferencz came in on one of those flights, was chauffeured to his old Berlin Branch digs at the Armed Forces Building, walked into General Clay's office, told him of the Herculean restitution task placed on his shoulders, and came straight to the point—he needed an extension of the claims filing deadline. But World War II's most capable resource manager was not moved. "No, I don't want to extend the law," he explained, "because the sooner we get this problem over with the better off we're going to be. This will be a thorn in Germany's side."[23] Ferencz was ready with a quick, and bold, rejoinder: "All right . . . I'll make a deal with you. I will try to get it done, and I will only come back to you if it's impossible, but I will try. But in order to get it done, I need money . . . I need staff."[24]

Clay was still unmoved. "Well," he said, "Didn't the organization know that when they wanted to get this written into the law that it would cost money to do that?" By now Ferencz was feeling a sense of righteous indignation. "You can't ask the Jewish organizations," he shot back, "which are now spending every penny they can raise to save the lives of these D.P.s, to move them out of here and to rescue them, to put money into trying to get restitution of Jewish property."[25] Ferencz then added, "I think we can take the money out of occupation funds."[26] The army was running on occupation funds, which meant the German treasury printed the money, and the United States used it to pay for whatever it needed. But Clay held firm. "You know I can't get occupation funds because that requires Quadripartite approval," he said. "The Russians are going to have to agree. They'll never agree to using their money for private property claims. I don't think the French will agree and I don't think the British will even agree. And I can't do it on my own."[27]

But Ferencz refused to give up. "Well, I have another proposition," he offered. "Let me borrow the money from the American segment of the occupation funds, and when I get restitution, I'll repay the money." Clay's antennae went up. "Can I do that legally?" he asked. The well-prepared Ferencz had a ready reply: "I have a memorandum here which says you can." Clay, trusting the former Nuremberg prosecutor, never asked for the details and finally just broke. "Well, okay, if you say it's legal and I can do it, go down and talk to my finance man and tell him that it's okay and that whatever money you need to get going, but get going because I want to get this program over with."[28] Of course, Ferencz had no such memorandum, but Clay never called his bluff. So Ben walked down the hall, took care of all the paperwork, and left Berlin with a million marks.

The Jewish civil society leaders who appointed him thought they were just going through the motions of retaining a JRSO head to file a few symbolic restitution claims. Even they underestimated the resourcefulness and stick-to-itiveness of the wily Ferencz, who was motivated, and now had the means, to work around the clock, to generate as many filings as he might have, had he been given triple the time.

Newly flush with cash, he was able engage the services of a small cadre of Jewish lawyers, including Saul Kagan (named as Ben's deputy), who, in turn, put out the word that German-speaking sleuths were needed. Soon they hired a veritable army of Teutonic gumshoes. And they were deployed in jeeps Ferencz requisitioned using his old army war crimes investigator authorizations—vehicles were vultured from every military motor pool he could track down. In them, the investigators sought out all of Germany's real estate registries with instructions to scour every line or stray note and copy down the names of any seemingly Jewish property transfers from 1933 onward.

Fortunately, the Germans had been unwittingly helpful, stamping *J* for *Jude* (Jew) on the property. Even absent this antisemitic scarlet letter, if the name sounded remotely Jewish, it was to be included. Thus, the JRSO dragnet even managed to trawl up and file a claim for a property transaction involving Nuremberg defendant Alfred Rosenberg. Also helpful was the fact that Military Government law mandated that persons who had acquired property during the Third Reich report the transfer. Ferencz's investigators were finding tens of thousands of transfers.

Once the transfer information was brought to Nuremberg, the claims had to be written up on a "big, complicated" form,[29] a very labor-intensive process. So Ferencz needed an enormous pool of secretaries working around the clock in a large space dedicated to processing these cumbersome documents. Across the street from the Palace of Justice was a large building used by Latvian expats as a dance hall. Ferencz later speculated that "many of them [had been] very busy killing Jews before they retreated with the Germans and were captured by the Americans and then used by the Americans [mostly as drivers]." So, he concluded, "We'll throw them out of that building. I need it for restitution."[30]

All unneeded furniture and fixtures were also removed. Ferencz then transferred his OCCWC desk, chairs, filing cabinets, and other office accoutrements across the street and used them to set up his own office—again, the link between prosecution and restitution was as physical as it was symbolic. He filled the rest of the cavernous space with as many tables, chairs, and typewriters as he could requisition from across Nuremberg, a town whose nooks and crannies he had gotten to know quite well. A brigade of secretaries was then brought on board, and the former Latvian dance hall became a claims processing factory, with approximately three hundred people worked in rotating eight-hour shifts.[31] Twenty-four hours a day, seven days a week, investigators were coming back from the field with property transaction information, and secretaries were typing up claim forms. Even Ben, Saul Kagan, and Gertrude chipped in, regularly filling eight-hour shift slots. In all, they were filing about 2,000 applications a day.

And they worked nonstop right up until the deadline. On Friday, December 31, 1948, Ferencz and his JRSO colleagues stuffed a capacious US Army ambulance with the remainder of what turned out to be more than 163,000 forms filed. They drove them to the filing center and had them registered just in the nick of time. Ferencz was confident that he had missed no significant claims—he had achieved in less than four months what should have taken well over a year, if not more. He called General Clay and, with great pride, told him he would not be needing that extension. World War II's premier chaos-into-order expert was duly impressed with his junior counterpart, who later wrote, "I think I gained [Clay's] confidence on all restitution problems thereafter."[32]

BUT PRESERVING the claims was only the first step. They still had to be approved by a specially designated US administrative agency. And the JRSO's claims were often far from straightforward. In particular, the purchasers of the property for which the JRSO sought restitution could file a responsive pleading with the agency requesting that the claim be rejected. Arguments for denial were many but could include the purchaser having (1) been an innocent third-party recipient of a deed in good faith; (2) given greater than fair market value to help a persecution victim raise funds to emigrate; (3) repaired and improved the property far beyond its original value; or (4) paid off a mortgage encumbering the property at the time of purchase. Sometimes, the property had already passed to the purchaser's heir, raising other sticky issues. And even if the purchaser lost at the administrative level (or a settlement could not be reached), there were several layers of appeal (including chambers of the German judicial system, largely staffed with former Nazis, and then its appellate courts) all the way up to the Court of Restitution Appeals (CRA), an American chamber (although German judges were later added for "mixed" panels).[33]

Over the years, Ferencz and his team of lawyers litigated many important cases before the CRA. At the outset, a threshold matter to be resolved was who would bear the risk of devalued property, the persecuted seller or the "Aryan" buyer? Ferencz asked for an advisory opinion, and, crucially, the CRA decided that the buyer would bear the risk. Thus, if the buyer had paid the equivalent of 100,000 marks for the property in 1938 and would only receive the equivalent of 10,000 marks in 1949, the persecuted seller (or any heirs) would not have to make up the difference in reacquiring the property—quite equitably, the risk of devaluation would rest with the victim who sold under duress, not with the German who acquired the property under such circumstances. This was a momentous decision and literally had existential implications for the JRSO. "If the opinion had gone the other way," Ferencz later explained, "there would have been no restitution program in Germany."[34]

Another foundational matter Ferencz litigated before the CRA was fraught with personal drama for him. Known as the *Augsburg* case, it concerned the disposition of property claimed on behalf of a Jewish community in the eponymous city. When Hitler took power in Germany, each city had a legally recognized Jewish *Gemeinde,* or congregation, that paid taxes and owned property, including schools, cemeteries, houses of worship, and other real estate. The Nazis had dissolved these congregations, seized the property, and murdered those members of the *Gemeinde* who had been unable to flee. Under Law No. 59, the *Gemeinden* were able to reclaim such property. Survivors coming from all parts of the world, who were not previously connected to the community but aware of the law, would arrive at the location in question and make a claim for the property on behalf of the *Gemeinde.* According to Ferencz, "Some of them, having been forced to survive using all kinds of means were less than the most honorable or credible people."[35] This is what happened in *Augsburg,* and the case was litigated all the way up to the CRA. Quite powerfully, if not symbolically, the hearing was held at the Palace of Justice, in the august Courtroom 600. Ben described how it unfolded:

> I [had] stood on this spot . . . literally the same spot, and argued against the Nazis—[had prosecuted] the Nazis who had murdered the Jews. I never thought I would stand here and argue against the Jewish community, but I [had] to, because those who [were] entitled [could not] speak for them-

> selves.... And I won the case. Some of those who argued against me ended up in jail. But there again, if that case had gone the other way all the Jewish properties in Germany which had belonged to congregations, would have been dissipated and would have disappeared.[36]

But the JRSO's work was not only in the courts. Once property was finally recovered, the organization had to find people to repair it, maintain it, and manage it. And real property was not the only type of asset awarded to the organization. There were "hundreds of businesses of all kinds which had to be managed and run," Ferencz later observed. "And for all of this we had to train people."[37] This was time-consuming and labor-intensive; applicants had to be screened not only for the proper skills but also for any potential past Nazi affiliations. Millions of Nazi Party files had to be checked. The JRSO was getting the job done but burning through the borrowed occupation funds.

By the fall of 1949, General Clay's initial largesse was no longer enough to pay the bills, and there was a new person in charge of the US occupied zone—High Commissioner John J. McCloy. So Ferencz traveled to the West German capital of Bonn, where McCloy had his headquarters. His pitch was simple. Clay's cash had run out, and although restitution assets were coming in, they were needed to help Jewish DPs and refugees. But there was still important restitution work to be done. If McCloy's assignment was to bring West Germany firmly into the fold of democratic nations, Ferencz argued passionately, restitution would play a crucial role.

But repaying General Clay's loan would stop ongoing restitution efforts dead in their tracks, he added. Besides, Ferencz pointed out, it would be politically and morally untenable to give priority to the wrongdoers by returning borrowed funds to the now prospering West German state while its victims remained in such dire straits. Without a further infusion of German currency, the JRSO could not continue fulfilling its baseline mandate for much longer. But a new million-mark loan would solve the organization's problems, he concluded with a flourish. If Ferencz the logistician was able to persuade Clay the logistician, then Ferencz the lawyer was able to persuade McCloy the lawyer. His advocacy carried the day, and the high commissioner lent Ferencz the same sum as Clay had. The following year, Ferencz repeated his arguments to McCloy, and they were still as effective—the loan amount was tripled.

Then came another moment of reckoning. As detailed in chapter 14, Ferencz did what he could to oppose McCloy's commutations of punishment meted out to the NMT-convicted Nazi war criminals. This was largely to no avail (with the exception of the highest-ranking Einsatzgruppen officers), and he was deeply disturbed, across the board, by McCloy's excessive leniency.

But he was particularly embittered by the decision to free Alfried Krupp and return to him all his ill-gotten gains, and he immediately flashed on the millions of marks in loans he needed to repay McCloy. Ferencz was soon back in the high commissioner's office in Bonn, and, as before, he came straight to the point. He could repay the JRSO loan if McCloy insisted. But as the latter had just given back to a convicted major war criminal assets worth probably more than the amount of money the JRSO borrowed, he asked him to cancel the debt "owed" by the victims of Nazi persecution.

In fact, McCloy had begun feeling a sense of guilt over his "decision to follow a lenient path toward the Nazi war criminals."[38] So he listened to Ferencz quite intently and then asked, "Can I do that [cancel the debt] legally?" As with Clay, Ferencz was ready with a quick retort, and he once again alluded to a phantom document in his possession. "I have a memo in my pocket that says you can," he told McCloy. The latter looked up and said, "The debt is cancelled."[39] Ferencz suppressed his emotions at that moment but left Bonn absolutely elated.

WITH FUNDING no longer an issue, Ferencz extended the reach of the JRSO's restitution efforts and began to focus on the return of looted Jewish cultural objects, including Torahs, religious ceremonial decorations, prayer books, and other sacred texts and objects. Einsatzstab Reichsleiter Rosenberg had amassed these treasures for eventual display in a contemplated Third Reich museum to "prove the perfidy of the Jewish race, religion and ideology."[40] The JRSO was now collecting this "captured booty" with the goal of its "legal and equitable distribution" among surviving or newly established Jewish communities around the world.[41]

Aiding the JRSO in this effort was the Commission on European Jewish Cultural Reconstruction, which eventually shortened its name to Jewish Cultural Reconstruction, Inc. (JCR). It had had been established before the JRSO to serve as a central research and coordinating body for all American activities concerning European Jewish cultural reconstruction. Its founders were concerned American Jewish religious leaders, scholars, and teachers, headed by Professor Salo Baron of Columbia University. Once the JRSO was up and running, the JCR was placed under its aegis, becoming, in effect, the JRSO's "cultural arm."[42] And it had been waiting in the wings to fulfill that function for quite some time. As early as 1946, the Commission had published its "Tentative List of Jewish Cultural Treasures in Axis-Occupied Countries." Prepared under the directorship of the budding philosopher Hannah Arendt, the compilation served as a kind of treasure map for locating Nazi-looted Judaica across Europe.

Arendt had been recruited by Salo Baron and, after compiling the Tentative List, served as JCR executive director from 1948 to 1952. Those turned out to be seminal years in the life of one of the twentieth century's greatest political theorists. Born to a progressive Jewish family in 1906, Arendt had been raised in the Königsberg of Wilhelmine Germany. The Baltic seaport on the Russian border, a great crossroads for travel and trade, had been the hometown of Immanuel Kant, who had written it was "the right place for gaining knowledge concerning men and the world even without travelling."[43] The precocious Arendt soaked it all up and matriculated to the University of Marburg in 1924, where she famously had an affair with her mentor, the married philosopher Martin Heidegger. Heidegger put an end to the relationship in 1926, and Arendt transferred to the University of Heidelberg, where she graduated and wrote a thesis under another great German philosopher, Karl Jaspers, Heidegger's friend. By 1933, with Hitler's ascension to power, Arendt fled the Third Reich and ended up in Paris. In the meantime, Heidegger had embraced Nazism, joining the party and revealing himself to be a rabid antisemite. Despite her still strong romantic feelings for Heidegger, Arendt cut off contact with him. And, with the outbreak of war and France's defeat, she was placed in a French concentration camp but escaped. Via travel to Spain and then Portugal, she was able to secure passage to the United States in May 1941 and remained in New York for the duration of the war.

While compiling the Tentative List of Jewish Cultural Treasures, she was increasingly reflecting on Nazism and Stalinism and turning toward political philosophy. She had begun drafting her first masterpiece, *The Origins of Totalitarianism* (1951). During this time, in 1949, Arendt set out to find the objects identified in the Tentative List and help reclaim and distribute them. In fact, her work on cultural restitution helped her develop ideas for her study on totalitarianism.[44] It also had her working with Ben Ferencz, who was running the JRSO, under whose auspices Arendt would work in Europe on behalf of the JCR.

From Fererncz's perspective, the relationship was not a positive experience. Quite simply, the wisecracking lawyer/logistician and the world-weary philosopher/cultural curator were not a match made in heaven. That was apparent from their first meeting. Ben was responsible for securing Arendt's housing in Germany. On her arrival, he had her over for dinner, and it did not go well. Upon seeing the presumably jet-lagged and haggard Arendt for the first time, Ferencz was struck by how "ugly" she appeared. She "smoked like a chimney," he later recalled, and it negatively affected her countenance. This sense of the "ugly" side of Arendt was also accentuated by what he felt was emanating from inside of her: "My impression was that she was an arrogant bitch. . . . We were having dinner and she smoked through dinner. And then she was very aloof. She sort of treated me like a little boy, you know. . . . And so Hannah and I didn't get along."[45]

Ben also had the impression that she accomplished little for the JRSO/JCR on those trips. He thought she viewed them as a boondoggle to "screw around" with Heidegger, who was, by then, a reputation-damaged emeritus professor at the University of Freiburg.[46] While it is true that Arendt visited Heidegger during her German sojourns on behalf of the JCR (as well as her other old mentor Karl Jaspers, in Basel), her first trip to Freiburg was motivated by legitimate restitution business.[47] Still, she did summon Heidegger to her hotel. Remarkably, she decided to put aside his Nazi past, such that they were able to have a "joyous moment of reconciliation, an instant recognition of continuity of interest, affection, and attraction."[48]

While an additional visit to Germany for JCR also had Arendt passing through Freiburg and spending more time with Heidegger (as well as visiting Jaspers again in Basel), it would not seem, as Ferencz speculated, that there was any sexual liaison between the two philosophers. Moreover, Arendt's work in Jewish cultural restitution probably deserves more credit than Ferencz gave her. Arendt's efforts on behalf of the JCR eventually led to the recovery of "1.5 million volumes of Hebraica and Judaica, thousands of ceremonial and artistic objects, and over a thousand scrolls of law."[49]

These religious treasures were being amassed in an enormous depot in Wiesbaden. The JRSO, assisted by the JCR, next had to identify the appropriate or worthy recipients. In certain cases, this was quite easy. The origin of many of the Torahs (God's law as revealed to Moses in the Bible's first five books) could be traced to well-known synagogues in Poland, Lithuania, Latvia, Estonia, Ukraine, and other centers of Jewish learning. This was true of the other religious objects as well—the place from which they had been looted, if there were still a functioning congregation, would be their ultimate destination. Unfortunately, the vast majority of Jewish communities in occupied Europe did not survive National Socialism. So the JRSO/JCR looked for nascent communities, especially those budding in the new country of Israel.

But even when an existing or newborn congregation could be located, damaged Hebraica presented yet another set of challenges. This was especially true of the Torahs. Once marred, they could not be used in prayer. Certain deformities owing to rough treatment were considered irreparable—if the Lord's name, as printed on the consecrated parchment, had been defaced in even the slightest way, it had to be sent to Israel for burial per ancient Hebrew rituals. Even absent disfigurement of the Creator's written name, physically compromised scrolls would have to be repaired before Jewish clerics could again use them. Ferencz therefore engaged a team of scribes to redeem the holy books under the supervision of the AJDC in Paris. But he soon realized that, during shipment, a good number of the Torahs were disappearing and likely being purloined. Was he dealing with rapacious rabbis? What could one do about a pinched Torah? He asked the rabbi running the repair operation: "I said I suspected that some of the Torahs may have disappeared, and I didn't know whether purloining a Torah was a blessed act or a criminal offense. I asked, 'Do I have to look up to heaven or down to the Devil to find the culprit?' He replied in Yiddish, 'Do not look up or down—take my advice—kik vek!' (Look away!) I learned from that rabbi that sometimes the best thing to do may be to do nothing."[50]

Damaged objects other than Torahs—such as candelabra, silver plates, wine goblets, Torah crowns, and all related paraphernalia used in a variety of Jewish rituals and holidays—presented other problems. Missing parts of ceremonial objects could be scattered among several different boxes. The JRSO brought in two experts from Israel's Bezalel National Museum, Shlomo Shunami and Mordechai Narkiss, and they "searched long and diligently, trying to restore every object."[51] In the end, there were too many broken pieces, including table silver and candlesticks, which were beyond repair and "had to be considered as scrap metal."[52]

But what should be done with this hallowed detritus? Ferencz and his team consulted experts and undertook extensive deliberations. They ultimately resolved to ship the fragments to England, where a well-reputed silver smelting company run by the Jewish family Goldsmith (incongruously) was instructed to melt down the silver for eventual distribution to the neediest Holocaust survivors.

Unfortunately, upon learning of this disposition, a prominent member of the JRSO board of directors soon had a meltdown of his own. When Ferencz was in New York making his report to the board, Rabbi Isaac Lewin, the respected head of the orthodox Union of American Hebrew Congregations, rose slowly, fiercely glowering at Ferencz. His voice trembling, he could barely contain his rage. "Do my ears believe me?" he asked contemptuously. "Did I hear you say that you took these sacred Jewish objects, the last remnant of our murdered ancestors, and you sent them to a CREM-A-TORRIUM??"[53] One could have heard the proverbial needle drop. Stunned, Ferencz stuttered that they had done the best they could under the circumstances. The rabbi would have none of it, and the rest of the meeting was terribly awkward.[54]

Also within the JRSO's cultural restitution remit were Jewish cemeteries—even the dead had not been immune from Nazi kleptomania and desecration. And there were hundreds of such violated holy plots scattered throughout

West Germany. Once again, effective stewardship demanded priestly counsel, and Ferencz engaged the services of three Jewish clerics, one the chief rabbi of Israel. From them, the JRSO director-general was soon privy to a whole new set of arcane, necropolis-related mores and canons: once a cemetery, always a cemetery; no flowers can be placed on the casket or grave; if a tombstone falls, it must be left lying where it fell; nothing can ever be done to profane the bodies or memory of the deceased.

Under the rabbinical council's tutelage, the JRSO was able to carry out its burial ground mandate with few complications. But there were a couple of outlier cases that even the council struggled with. The first related to a cemetery in the central German town of Fulda, not far from Cologne, in the state of Hesse. Having been defiled by the Nazis during the Holocaust, it was reclaimed postwar by a handful of Eastern European survivors, who sought to establish a new Jewish community in the town. Mortuary records revealed that a large portion of the graveyard had never been used, and it was clear that the small group of new settlers would never need it. So, could the unused grounds be sold to raise funds for the needy Shoah survivors? The council replied in the affirmative.

So local authorities purchased the unused section and built a five-story customs office, or *Zollamt.* Unfortunately, Ferencz later learned that a number of bones, presumed to be from Jewish bodies, had been disinterred during the parking lot excavations. He hightailed it to Fulda to confront its city leaders, with the new Jewish community members in tow:

> Having recently prosecuted SS leaders who had murdered over a million Jews, I was in no mood to tolerate the desecration of Jewish graves by any Germans. I demanded that the building, which was already five stories high and near completion, be torn down immediately and the area restored. The leaders of the new Jewish community in Fulda asked to speak with me privately. They . . . implored me not to take such a harsh position. [The] city officials were anti-Nazis who had been most accommodating to them. . . . It was only a small area . . . and there was even no certainty that the bones [were human]. They argued that their lives in Fulda would be made unbearable if I forced the city to tear down the expensive building. I reluctantly agreed to refer the entire file to the rabbinical council in Jerusalem for its recommendation.[55]

The council came up with a very creative solution. Normally, no building of any kind could be placed on top of a Jewish cemetery, with one exception—a chapel where prayers for the dead could be recited. And there was nothing in the Talmud that forbade placing a building on top of such a chapel. So they built a chapel under the corner of the building that trespassed on the old cemetery. As a result, that corner of the building would not be resting on the cemetery itself but only on the roof of a little synagogue in the cellar. The tiny place of worship itself was a "dignified triangular room no larger than about 15 feet in any direction" with small stained-glass windows near the ceiling (affording a partial view of the parking lot) and a Hebrew inscription adorning the wall. The tiny chamber, although little used and quite dusty, can still be found within the bowels of the *Zollamt*.

The second cemetery-related crisis soon followed, and it had far broader implications. Ferencz was due to meet in Bonn with representatives of the West German Finance Ministry and the Ministry of Social Affairs to discuss the care and maintenance of unused Jewish cemeteries. The meeting started well, with the Germans readily acknowledging Hitler's responsibility for the desecration of Jewish cemeteries and the destruction of the communities attached to them. As Germany's successor government, they would see to it that, for a period of twenty years, the grass was cut, and the Jewish graves tended—the same benefits and rights, for the same time period, accorded to publicly maintained German gravesites.

Ferencz could not believe what he was hearing. Jewish law, he explained, called for the maintenance of a Jewish cemetery in perpetuity, not just twenty years. But the Germans stood firm, insisting that the JRSO could not expect German taxpayers to assume an indefinite burden for Jews that they did not even give to their own German citizens. Ferencz exploded: "I shouted at them that if they hadn't murdered the Jews and driven them out, they would not have any problem with Jewish cemeteries. It was only because of the horrendous Nazi crimes that the subject had to be discussed."[56]

Now he was even more enraged. He reached into his pocket and pulled out a set of tiny bones he had been carrying with him since a recent visit to Auschwitz. He had spotted the skeletal fragments under a clump of grass he accidentally kicked over while taking a tour of the former death camp. From their small size, he had surmised they were from the fingers of babies. He kept the "gruesome remnant" in an envelope in his pocket "to be a close and constant reminder of why I had to continue the work I was doing." Soon the bones were out of the envelope, and he slammed them on the table. Then he really came unglued:

> Shaking with anger, I screamed, "Who shall pay? Shall these pay? Then you go and ask them!" [Dr. Ernst] Katzenstein [a JRSO deputy], fearing that we would come to blows, ran from the room. The Chairman called a recess and also left the room. I cannot recall any other time in my life when I gave way to such an

> outburst of anger. . . . When the parties reassembled, some 20 minutes later, the German representatives quietly said that they would accept the obligation to honor the Jewish traditions.[57]

BUT THE cemetery maintenance meeting with German officials was only a microcosm of the confrontational and hostile environment in which the JRSO carried out its mission. As we saw earlier, the organization's property claims were routinely contested, typically all the way up to the Court of Restitution Appeals. Not only was this time-consuming, but a JRSO victory meant that German citizens, many having purchased Jewish property, in part, to help distressed neighbors, were being stripped of their acquisition and bearing the devaluation loss. Collective deep-seated resentment began bubbling to the surface, and there were legitimate concerns about new waves of antisemitism. For a long time, organization members weathered the storm, always mindful of the Holocaust and the inherently coercive environment of the "duress sales" that were the object of their litigation efforts. They would simply buck up and repeat their mantra: "Thou shalt not kill and be allowed to retain the possessions of your victim."

A few years in, though, the situation was becoming untenable. They brainstormed various possible exit strategies and finally hit on one that seemed viable—a "global settlement." The idea was to persuade the German state governments (or *Länder*) to "buy" all the JRSO claims for a fair price. The *Länder* could then take their time disposing of the claims and, where appropriate, make equitable concessions to their citizens. There would be no allegations of "unjust enrichment," and the JRSO would have immediate cash on hand to carry out its urgent charitable obligations.

So Ferencz started reaching out to *Länder* officials and, over time, managed to sell them on the idea. But the negotiations that ensued were quite thorny. The parties had to come to terms on tricky fair value appraisals for thousands of properties. But, as in so many other instances in Ferencz's career, patience paid off, and they eventually hammered out a deal that offered benefits to all. Appropriately, perhaps, the first state to sign an official agreement was Hesse, which had consented to the little Jewish chapel on the old cemetery grounds within the bowels of the *Zollamt*. At the February 13, 1951, signing ceremony, Ferencz was joined by his deputy, Dr. Ernst Katzenstein, in the state capital of Wiesbaden.

The day before, Ferencz and Katzenstein had driven there together, each carrying a beautiful new red attaché case in leather that had recently been put on sale at the Nuremberg PX. Ferencz purchased his first. Inspired by its beauty and reasonable price, Katzenstein followed suit. For the Wiesbaden trip, Ferencz was using his to carry the documents to be signed. The day of the ceremony, after lodging at the same hotel, both men loaded their luggage into the car trunk and drove to the Hessian Royal Palace. Ferencz made a point of brandishing his gorgeous burgundy satchel before the state officials before placing it at the center of the table in the ornate drawing room, where the ceremony was about to take place. After speeches by various high-level ministers, Ferencz popped open the crimson case to pull out the documents of "such . . . historic [importance on] behalf of Nazi victims."[58] But his face soon turned the color of the leather—in his hands, dangling for all the dignitaries to see, were Katzenstein's pajamas! After some hearty guffaws, the correct attaché case was fetched, and the contracts were inked.

Soon, the other West German *Länder* officially signed on too. Overall, restitution in the three Western Allied occupation zones in Germany was impressive. By decade's end, approximately 100,000 private individuals had assets returned to them worth around 3.5 billion marks.[59] Compensation payments by the Federal Republic of Germany amounted to about DM 5.2 billion.[60] Ben Ferencz's organization had gotten everything in place in the American occupation zone and was finally able to focus on providing assistance to Holocaust survivors rather than engaging in litigation and property management. That said, assistance via restitution was only one piece of the complex victim aid mosaic. The JRSO "director-general" was now ready to start filling in the other pieces.

16

MORAL AND MATERIAL INDEMNITY

> Let other nations think of retribution and the letter of the law, we will cling to the spirit and the meaning—the salvation and the reformation of the lost.
>
> —Fyodor Dostoevsky, *The Brothers Karamazov*

The centrality of persecution victims had been a defining feature of Ben Ferencz's entire life, whether as an infant refugee, Hell's Kitchen denizen, Harvard Law research assistant, Third Army investigator, Nuremberg prosecutor, or JRSO director. Fate, perhaps intermingling with his own aspirations, kept him tethered to this core theme. Most recently, Jewish civil society had come calling, and restitution had been his brief for several years. But the issue of property stolen from Jews, along with providing for its return—the focus of restitution—was only one facet of caring for Shoah survivors. Those who staggered back from the charnel houses, camps, factories, quarries, tunnels, and hideouts had not only been robbed and fleeced; most of them had been tortured, starved, enslaved, or deprived of their loved ones. What, if anything, could be done to bind up their wounds or account for their psychic suffering? There was another legal concept being bandied about to cover this: "reparations" An umbrella term that could also include restitution, "reparations" can be defined as the "act of making amends for a wrong" or "compensation for an injury or wrong."[1] The term in German, *Wiedergutmachung,* or "to make good or well again," was soon to become the object of Ben Ferencz's new mission.

Western occupation authorities in Germany had already made strides in this regard. In the first part of 1949, for instance, the British promulgated the "Military Government Law on Compensation for Detention on Political, Racial or Religious Grounds" and the Americans, the "Act on Compensation for National Socialist Injustice."[2] But on May 23, 1949, through unification of the Western occupation zones, the Federal Republic of Germany (FRG), commonly known as West Germany, was created (as a Cold War counterbalance, the German Democratic Republic [GDR], known as East Germany, a Soviet satellite entity, began operating as a state on October 7, 1949). As West Germany began to assume the functions of a sovereign nation, many wondered whether the initial efforts at reparations made by the former Allied occupiers would be taken up by the new republic.

Much of this would hinge on the acumen and efforts of the FRG's outstanding political personality, Konrad Adenauer. Seventy-three years old at the time of West Germany's founding, he was known as "Der Alte" (The Elder) and had been in politics since the time of Kaiser Wilhelm II. Adenauer was a devout Rhineland Catholic born in Cologne, a western riverine city in Teutonic wine country that strangely found itself included within Prussia, albeit on its far western periphery. Like many other Rhinelanders who were geographically closer to France and felt out of place in Frederick the Great's home region, his family had nothing but contempt for Prussian militarism. Adenauer followed in his father's footsteps and earned a law degree. Then he practiced as an attorney in Cologne before being elected to the city council in 1906. His quick rise in local politics had been impressive; he was already lord mayor of Cologne during World War I. His stewardship of the city, both during and after the war, was exemplary, earning him admiration in greater Germany for fiscal responsibility and civic innovation.[3] His staunch anticommunism further burnished his national credentials, and he served as president of the Prussian State Council during the Weimar Republic. By the beginning of the 1930s, his name was being floated as a serious contender for German chancellor.

But the rise of the Nazis put an end to his political ambitions. For Adenauer, the pace of dark events at the beginning of 1933 was dizzyingly rapid: in January, Adolf Hitler became chancellor; in February, his goons set fire to the Reichstag and blamed the Communists; and in March, he used the fire to push through the Enabling Act, allowing legislation by fiat, bypassing parliament, and effectively making him a dictator. Reichstag elections were scheduled for the same month, and, by then, Adenauer realized that his Catholic conservatism was incompatible with Hitler's racist fascism. Formerly blinded to this danger by the specter of communism, he now fully grasped how serious a threat National Socialism posed to the public weal. He refused to meet with Hitler during his Reichstag campaign swing through the Rhine region or allow him to adorn one of Cologne's most prominent bridges with swastika standards. Relying on fraud and coercion, the Nazis achieved the result they needed to maintain their control of parliament, and Adenauer became a marked man. Stripped of his city executive post by decree from Berlin, he was warned by one of his deputies that a unit of Brownshirts was en route to his office to defenestrate him. Leveraging his Catholic connections, he narrowly escaped to a monastery.

Nevertheless, the Nazis eventually found him and threw him in prison. Relying on his network once again, he managed to get out and then lived on the lam in a string of hideaways, never wanting to find himself in Hitler's crosshairs again. Still, after the 1944 assassination attempt on the Führer, Adenauer, by then quite sickly, was hunted down by the SS, incarcerated, and, once again, sentenced to death. This time he was saved by a former Cologne municipal worker, who found his name on an execution list and arranged for him to be admitted to a hospital. By war's end, he had just managed to survive National Socialism.

Then, after a brief convalescence, both his physical and political rehabilitation were swift. He was soon reinstalled as mayor of Cologne, and, this time, his ascent in national politics was unimpeded. He founded the Christian Democratic Union, whose excellent results in West Germany's inaugural Bundestag (parliament) election carried him to the new country's first chancellorship in September 1949. Ever the ardent anti-Communist, he was prepared to brook Germany's division while looking for seamless assimilation into the Western Alliance (and eventual inclusion within NATO). More importantly, on a broader scale, he looked for the Third Reich's non-Soviet successor state to be reintegrated into the family of nations. Atonement for Hitler's sins, in the form of reparations, he soon came to realize, would go a long way toward achieving that end. Thus, addressing the Bundestag on September 27, 1951, Adenauer acknowledged that "unspeakable crimes have been committed in the name of the German people, calling for moral and material indemnity." He then offered "to bring about a solution of the material indemnity problem, thus easing the way to the spiritual settlement of infinite suffering."[4]

But where would the "material indemnity" be disbursed? As we have seen, the greatest number of Jewish refugees who survived the Holocaust had emigrated to Israel. The allure was rather obvious. In Genesis, God promised Abraham, Judaism's first patriarch, a homeland for his people, which they cherished as the "Promised Land" or the "Land of Milk and Honey." After Moses led the Jews out of bondage in Egypt, they eventually settled in that area, today known as Israel. But their wanderings were not over—nearly two millennia later, they challenged Roman subjugation of the region and were expelled, with many exiled to the European continent.

After centuries of European antisemitic persecution, certain late nineteenth-century Diaspora Jews, led by Theodor Herzl, formed a movement called Zionism, hoping to create a Jewish state in the ancestral homeland from which the Romans had exiled them. Some Jews had remained there despite the Roman expulsion, and small streams had already returned over the centuries, with larger waves of "Aliyah" immigrants entering in the late nineteenth and early twentieth centuries. Still, Jews were a distinct minority among the Arab inhabitants. When the British seized control of the area from the Ottomans in 1917, UK foreign secretary Arthur Balfour issued a statement announcing support for the establishment of a "national home for the Jewish people" in Palestine. The so-called Balfour Declaration galvanized the Zionists, and the subsequent rise of Nazism brought even larger waves of Jewish immigration until World War II intervened.

So, from these origins, how did a sovereign Jewish state of Israel come into being? The intersecting life stories of two men—David Ben-Gurion and Nahum Goldmann—help explain. The former was born in Poland in 1886 and in his youth became passionate about the idea of founding a Jewish state in the Holy Land. In 1906, having studied at the University of Warsaw, he emigrated to Ottoman-controlled Jerusalem, worked as an agricultural laborer while laying down Zionist organizational roots, and then moved to Constantinople in 1912 to study law. He returned to Jerusalem during the First World War and became a Zionist leader, but, expelled by the Ottomans for his pro-Jewish activism, he took refuge in the United States. In the wake of the Balfour Declaration, Ben-Gurion sailed back to the Middle East and joined the British army's Jewish Legion to help liberate Palestine from the Ottomans. After the war, he worked to build and organize the Jewish community in Mandatory Palestine and eventually became head of the Jewish Agency for Palestine, the executive branch of the World Zionist Organization, which took the lead in advocating for and organizing a Jewish state. After clashing with the British, who turned against Zionism and Jewish immigration to Palestine in the late 1930s, Ben-Gurion became a resistance leader and helped devise the United Nations' 1947 partition plan, which called for independent Arab and Jewish states.

Nine years after Ben-Gurion, Nahum Goldmann was also born in eastern Europe—in Lithuania—but his family soon relocated to Frankfurt, Germany. He too became an ardent Zionist. During World War I, he served as one of Kaiser Wilhelm II's bureaucrats, working in the Information Department of the German Foreign Office, where "he attempted to enlist the Kaiser's support for the Zionist idea."[5] During the Weimar Republic, Goldmann took an increasingly active role in international Zionist politics and served as the liaison officer with the League of Nations for the Jewish Agency for Palestine. Naturally, he drew the ire of the Hitler regime, and he was stripped of his German citizenship by 1935. At first, he found refuge in Honduras, but he later migrated to the United States, where, with Rabbi Stephen S. Wise, he founded the World Jewish Congress (WJC) to help their coreligionists around the globe deal with the Nazi menace. After the war, with Ben-Gurion directing operations on the ground in Palestine, Goldmann served as an ambassador for the Jewish Agency, helping drum up support at the UN and in national capitals for partition and then creation of a Jewish state.

Goldmann lobbied "effectively for partition," which the UN voted for via General Assembly Resolution 181(II), on November 29, 1947.[6] And on May 14, 1948, after months of postpartition sectarian fighting in Palestine between Jews and Arabs, David Ben-Gurion issued Israel's Declaration of Independence. The following day, armed forces from Egypt, Transjordan, Syria, Lebanon, and Iraq invaded the territory. We saw previously that Mickey Marcus, the American-Jewish soldier/lawyer who recruited Ben Ferencz for war crimes work, was later recruited himself to help Israeli forces, becoming the new state's first general. Marcus and other Jewish military leaders used brilliant tactics and great resolve to overcome superior numbers and equipment and won the War of Independence by the spring of 1949, around the same time the West German state was being established. Two years later, Adenauer was pledging indemnity to Israel on behalf of the Jewish victims of Nazi Germany. As with partition, Ben-Gurion looked to Goldmann as his international negotiator, this time for reparations. And Goldmann, in turn, called on the expertise of Ben Ferencz.

IN BRINGING Ferencz on board, Goldmann told him, only partly in jest, that he defined an "expert," as "one who knows everything, but nothing else."[7] While Ben had built up an impressive knowledge base regarding Holocaust survivor issues, and he was confident he could play an important role in the negotiations, he was well aware that he was only one part of a larger team. At the top, Goldmann served as the indispensable leader of what Ferencz soon came to understand was an initiative fraught with controversy. Many Jews perceived the prospect of reparations from West Germany as "blood money," while many conservative West Germans viewed them as an unjustified windfall. In a way, Goldmann was the glue that held everything, and everyone, together. He had been supporting Ben-Gurion, who first needed to convince his own political party, Mapai, and then the Knesset (Israeli parliament) to approve of reparations negotiations with the West Germans.[8]

Eventually, the Knesset's affirmative vote was secured "after the stormiest session in the history of Israel's parliament."[9] Ferencz later noted that the Israeli parliament "was stoned when the subject was raised. Many Knesset members were convinced that negotiating with Germans would lead only to more betrayals. Ben Gurion, Israel's prime minister, passed the hot potato to Goldmann."[10]

In the meantime, Goldmann had also been working behind the scenes to prepare Adenauer, both diplomatically and psychologically, for the negotiations. The two men met at Claridge's Hotel in London on December 6, 1951.

The main agenda item that day was the Jewish state's claim of US$1 billion as the reparations target figure for the forthcoming negotiations. The Israelis wanted to start acclimating Adenauer to that sum and needed to know whether, in principle, he could come to accept it as a sine qua non baseline. Goldmann, by then a savvy diplomat whose résumé included advanced degrees in German law and philosophy, was able to speak to Adenauer directly and effectively in his mother tongue and the meeting "inaugurated a relationship of mutual respect."[11] The West German chancellor got over the initial sticker shock and, by meeting's end, was on board.

At the same time, wearing his WJC president hat, Goldmann was also busy organizing Jewish civil society, which, collectively, would be the other key party opposite Adenauer at the negotiations table. In late 1951, Goldmann convened an assembly in New York City's Waldorf-Astoria Hotel of twenty-three major Jewish national and international organizations and worked out the terms of their involvement. Collectively, the group would be known as the Conference on Jewish Material Claims against Germany, or the Claims Conference for short. The board of directors of the new organization consisted of the Jewish civil society groups that took part in its formation, with each member agency having two representatives. The Claims Conference had the task of negotiating with the German government a program of indemnification for Holocaust-related material damages to Jewish individuals and to the Jewish people.

Ben Ferencz participated in that gathering, his first active involvement in the project. And, given Jewish ambivalence about taking money from the Nazi successor government, the meeting got off to quite a dramatic start. As the former Nuremberg prosecutor described it in his memoirs:

> [A] meeting to discuss reconciliation soon turned into a battleground. The doors were forced open and a large group of young men, many with flowing curls under their skull caps, stormed into the room. They brandished placards and shouted at the delegates to disperse since they were disgracing Jewish honor by talking about taking blood money from murderers. [One] of the delegates, a rabbi, [was] cringing under a table. There was no need for him to fear. With the help of a few Irish cops, the intruders were firmly escorted from the room.[12]

After the tumultuous organizational kickoff event in New York, there was a follow-up meeting at the Grosvenor Hotel in London. The Jewish delegates were then ready, and a site had to be chosen for the negotiations. West Germany was soon ruled out, since as noted, tensions regarding compensation were running high there too. In fact, given the potential for terrorist attacks, the location the parties opted for was kept secret. Thus, Ben Ferencz left London without the foggiest idea of his next destination. And his passage turned out to be a series of cloak-and-dagger movements with a rather unpleasant ending. On his departure, Israeli Security agents responsible for the safety of Claims Conference delegates directed Ferencz to follow instructions that he would receive in a sealed envelope when he checked out of the Grosvenor. In the taxi, he ripped open the envelope, which, in perfect espionage-speak, read: "Proceed to Hoek van Holland. You'll be met."[13]

He then made his way from London to the English coast and caught the channel ferry in the direction of Rotterdam. Once off the boat, he presented his passport, was given a serious once-over by Dutch officials, and was then sternly told to wait. The tension was thick. Soon, still as if out of a spy novel, a man clad in black appeared, refusing to identify himself, and Ferencz was whisked into a black Buick sedan that screeched off with urgency into the darkness. As dawn was breaking, Ferencz insisted the driver identify himself and reveal their destination. The burly chauffeur, still obscured in the shadows, refused to offer specifics but replied that he was with the Dutch Security Police. The passenger started to let his guard down a little but soon noticed that the car had turned onto a network of small, circuitous, capillary roads and was slowing down considerably.

Then panic set in. In the pale auroral light, he was startled to find the vehicle surrounded by what he thought were uniformed SS men with dogs. "My memory flashed back to the concentration camps where I had last seen such guards," he later recounted. "[And] my heart pounded in fear that I had fallen into an SS trap."[14] But as the car pulled through the gate, he noticed, upon closer inspection, that the men in black uniforms with black boots did not have the SS Death's Head insignia on their collars. As it happened, the Dutch police uniforms were remarkably similar to those worn by Heinrich Himmler's terror cadres. There were still covert SS organizations being operated in various parts of the world at that time, but Ferencz breathed a sigh of relief upon realizing that these men were not a part of them. He had survived this dark passage, but the flash of terror he experienced was revelatory of the air of menace and tension hanging over the negotiations.

Ferencz soon realized that he had arrived at the mystery site. Wassenaar, where the negotiations would take place, was just outside Holland's capital, The Hague, in an isolated, sylvan setting. The parties would meet in the Kasteel Oud-Wassenaar, a nineteenth-century aristocratic abode. Lending further credence to Ferencz's SS fears, during World War II, the estate had been commandeered by the Nazis to accommodate foreign dignitaries. It was also later used by Allied luminaries, such as Winston Churchill and General Bernard Montgomery.

The spectacular palace and grounds starkly contrasted with the gruesome subjects on the negotiations agenda. Located in a lush, green copse bordered by a lake, the stately structure's crow-stepped-gable facade was topped by a pyramidal "stork's nest" tower rising above the castle's arched central structure. Below the tower's apex was a gilded clock, to either side of which, on the building's wings, were circular turrets crowned by cupolas. Arriving inside via the arcaded entrance, delegates walked onto the Great Hall's exquisite black-and-white marble floor, splashed with color from an overhead stained-glass atrium and rimmed by tessellated borders. A grand staircase led to a vaulted mezzanine overhead. And passages jutting out from the majestic hall took delegates to other sumptuous parlors—a white salon, a rustic hunting room, and an ornate ballroom, with adjacent rooms. The ballroom and its salons would serve as the principal negotiation venues.

But once the Jewish-German encounters there began, in March 1952, the magnificent setting in no way dissipated the sense of fear and tension that had seized Ferencz in being transported to it. The castle was crawling with security. Incongruously, given the visual splendor, Dutch and Israeli police and military personnel, armed to the teeth, ubiquitously stood sentry among and within all the palace's marbled and gilded nooks and crannies. Given ongoing developments, these security measures hardly seem surprising today. Both Adenauer and Goldmann had been receiving death threats, and there were credible suspicions of letter bombs. As the meetings were about to begin, an explosive device placed in a hollowed-out German encyclopedia sent to Adenauer had killed two policemen in Munich. Ferencz and his team were informed that a gang of Jewish "terrorists," one led by future Israeli prime minister Menachim Begin (Herut Party), had entered the Netherlands with plans to kill all those who "disgraced Jewish honor."[15]

Over time, though, the tension and hypervigilance eased up. In his memoirs, Ferencz explained how his own situation helped in that regard:

> [While] in the midst of negotiation, an Israeli Security agent . . . gingerly showed me a soiled envelope . . . and asked if I recognized the handwriting of the sender. I said, "of course.". . . I ripped it open and the [guard] jumped away. It was a letter from my wife [enclosing] two strips of antacid pills to help ease my tensions and . . . two rows of film taken of our two infant children.

> Security had detected the powders and the strips of celluloid and concluded that it might be a letter-bomb. They soaked it in oil . . . before they dared hand it to me. Instead of being blown up, we all had a needed laugh.[16]

WITH THE initial sense of hysteria lessening, the parties got down to the tricky business of establishing a legal framework and agreeing on numbers. As the delegates became enveloped in the fine points of law and compensation, Ferencz soon realized that he would be playing a critical role for the Claims Conference. Goldmann, although nominally its leader, was himself more of a facilitator than a negotiator—he was not taking part in the nitty-gritty details of the daily discussions. But, given his excellent relationship with Adenauer, he would be called in to help facilitate breakthroughs or smooth over rough patches. The Israelis, led by Gershon Avner and chief negotiator Felix Shinnar, both of the Foreign Ministry, were present and participating, but they were mostly interested in a separate agreement with West Germany.

The heavy lifting on the Diaspora side was performed by a team of Claims Conference lawyers, led by Moses Leavitt of the AJDC and Nehemiah Robinson, the WJC's international law advisor and director of its Institute of Jewish Affairs.[17] Leavitt nominally headed the delegation, but Robinson was its principal legal advisor. As we saw in chapter 15, Nehemiah Robinson was a brilliant theoretician, having played a leading role in formulating the global Jewish community's legal position regarding restitution. He was joined on the team by his older sibling, Jacob, "arguably the most important and prolific legal scholar-activist in the Jewish world in the middle decades of the twentieth century."[18]

Thus, Benjamin Ferencz was in good company, and he knew it, naturally gravitating toward the Robinson brothers, whose sartorial trademark—a bow tie—further enhanced each sibling's scholarly mien. Other lawyers on the team, including Saul Kagan, Ben's deputy, who would go on to represent the Claims Conference for years to come, made significant contributions during the negotiations as well. But the Robinsons, especially Nehemiah, and Ferencz were at the forefront of devising strategy and proposals. If, behind the scenes, Nehemiah was the Claims Conference's éminence grise, then further behind the scenes the young Ferencz was the not-so-gray éminence grise. In fact, by working very closely together during the negotiations, Ben and Nehemiah forged a special bond. "[He] was like a brother to me," Ben later recalled. "[He] was quiet. He never married."[19] But he became an honorary member of the Ferencz family. Over the long months of dealing with the Germans at the bargaining table, during breaks, Nehemiah would travel with Ben back to

Nuremberg and stay at his house. By then, Ben and Gertrude had three young children (Carol [now Keri], born in 1949; Robin, born in 1950; and Donald, born in 1952), and the bachelor Robinson brother enjoyed spending time with the young couple and their tots.

What Nehemiah and Ben, along with Nehemiah's brother Jacob, were doing is best understood by describing how the structure of the negotiations ultimately evolved. On one hand, the West Germans and the Israelis were working on the draft of a separate agreement that would provide financial assistance to the Jewish state for taking in and caring for Holocaust survivors. At the same time, the West Germans and the Claims Conference were trying to hammer out two separate agreements—one for a global settlement that would allow the Claims Conference to provide general assistance to Diaspora survivors and another that would create a fund and procedures for submission of individual claims to be processed through German courts.

It was particularly with reference to the individual claims agreement that knotty issues arose. Ferencz later summed up the problem:

> No one on the Jewish side ever suggested that any payment should be requested, or accepted, for this senseless genocide. [It] was recognized that we should not try to place any monetary value on a human life. It was just too painful to consider whether papa was more valuable than grandma or a baby sister. . . . The Claims Conference title referred only to "material claims." We were trying to fit into a legal frame some measure of redress based on concepts developed among civilized people accustomed to civilized behavior. The crimes of the Holocaust could not be pressed into such a mold. Blinded by outrage and the desperate needs of impoverished survivors who cried out for justice, we embarked on a mission impossible.[20]

But the mission was not entirely impossible—rather, the team needed to formulate more particularized questions to be answered. Ferencz specified: "What do you ask for loss of limb?"[21] What was the current value of stocks and bonds that Germans seized from Jews during the Third Reich, some of which were now worthless and others of which had increased in value? According to Ben, these issues would come up at the negotiations table, and the calm, cerebral Nehemiah Robinson would ably represent the Jewish side, often quoting ancient proverbs or great philosophers. The Germans would be impressed. And then, like a tag team with Nehemiah, Ben would "chime in," and they would slowly win over the Germans.[22]

If issues were more complex or needed further strategic consideration, Ben and Nehemiah would brainstorm together in the evenings or on weekends to come up with solutions for the next day or the next scheduled session. "I was conversing with him about things, [brainstorming,] How about this? Can we do this? Can we do that? [I] mean, we discussed every substantive thing . . . often."[23] In the meantime, based on these discussions, and the progress they would make in daily sessions with the Germans, Nehemiah was drafting the treaty provisions.[24] Ben and Jacob Robinson were reading over these provisions, making comments, and suggesting edits.

Ferencz also made valuable contributions beyond helping to craft the legal strategy and draft the treaty. Through his years of restitution work in West Germany, he had gotten to know many of the leading legal and political personalities. Much of the impact he made was between the negotiation sessions. According to him, his most effective verbal cues "were not at the conference table [but] after the conference meeting [with] several friends among the delegates. I would take them aside and say, 'Look, we can't accept this. I mean, look, it's impossible.' And then, if our position was reasonable, they would recognize it and say 'I'll see what I can do.' . . . It was in the hallways. By the time we come back to the table we would reach agreement."[25]

Even more important was the relationship Ferencz had cultivated with US High Commissioner John J. McCloy, whom he had gotten to know quite well over the years via the Nuremberg Trials and restitution. During the Wassenaar negotiations, each man was able to rely on the other. As the Germans seemed to balk on overall compensation sums, the Israeli ambassador in Washington, DC, Abba Eban, appealed to US Secretary of State Dean Acheson to intervene.[26] Acheson then cabled McCloy, instructing him to notify the Germans that "unfortunate repercussions would ensure [*sic*] if they now appear to have been insincere on their offer to negotiate."[27] McCloy then requested a memorandum from Ferencz on whether any aspect of US policy directives militated against his intervening in the German-Israeli talks to facilitate an agreement.[28] Ferencz assured him that "if a breakdown of negotiations between Israel and Germany were threatened US policy would favor taking steps to avert such a breakdown, provided no other US interest was seriously threatened."[29]

Having thus assured the high commissioner, if there were truly important and sticky issues, Ferencz would call on him to help achieve breakthroughs. And McCloy had plenty of clout given Adenauer's strong dependence on American largesse and goodwill at that time. We have already seen that the Marshall Plan provided $13 billion to help rebuild Western Europe as a bulwark against Soviet encroachment. Assessing this American initiative, Adenauer noted, "Probably for the first time in history a victorious country held out its hand so that the vanquished might rise again."[30] Adenauer was also grateful for the significant American military presence in the region—by 1952, there were more than 257,000 US military personnel stationed throughout Europe[31]—and was eager for West Germany to join NATO, which it eventually did in 1955. So he wanted to be in the US high commissioner's good graces, and Ferencz was able to exploit that for the Wassenaar negotiations.

For example, when the parties came to an impasse on the valuation of stocks and bonds purchased during the Third Reich, Ferencz put in a call to Bonn and explained the problem to McCloy. The following Sunday morning, while Ferencz was still in bed, he received a call from the high commissioner. "I'm just coming from church with Adenauer," he said. "And he promised he'll give you two billion on the bonds."[32] Ferencz then took that to Moe Leavitt and Nehemiah Robinson, and the path was cleared for an agreement on this issue. (Leavitt, a gruff and cynical man who had earned the sobriquet "No Leavitt," wryly met Ferencz's good news with the rejoinder that they had hoped to squeeze three billion out of Adenauer, not just two.)[33]

Little by little, in this way, the parties were able to make steady progress. Perhaps lost in the thicket of day-to-day negotiations was any appreciation for the monumental nature of what they were trying to do. Nothing like this had ever been contemplated, let alone undertaken. In the past, warring parties that lost had paid reparations to other states. But never in military annals had a defeated belligerent agreed to provide compensation directly to natural persons on an *individual* basis. Working out the principles, setting up the machinery, putting it into legislative form so that it would be sanctioned and adopted by a parliament and enforced by an array of judicial instruments and courts and agencies on an enormous scale so as to process millions of claims—never in human affairs had such a thing been attempted. There were simply no previous reference points. However, little by little, they were managing to work it all out, and, by the end of August, they had crafted a global agreement.

The end products were a treaty, between the Federal Republic of Germany and the State of Israel, and two protocols. The treaty was unprecedented and historic given that one of the countries did not even exist at the time the acts giving rise to the reparations had been committed. Chief Israeli negotiator Shinnar called it "the most memorable in history."[34] Foreign Minister Moshe Sharett characterized the signing as a "political fact of enormous international significance, something quite unprecedented, which has taken a most momentous place in the history of Israel and of Germany."[35]

This Luxembourg Agreement (named for the treaty's signing locale), or Shilumim Agreement, as the Israelis called it (*shilumim* being the Hebrew word for "material reparations"—they rejected the broad term *Wiedergutmachung* as arguably covering nonmaterial reparations)—furnished Israel over a twelve-year period with 3 billion DM (US$7 billion today), as goods in kind rather than cash payment. This permitted the Israelis to build up their new nation's infrastructure and economy. The figure was based on the amount the Jewish state estimated it needed to absorb 500,000 refugees at a cost of US$3,000 per person. Its impact on the fledgling country, according to Ben Ferencz, was inestimable:

> It was a global sum, which at that time was vital for the salvation of Israel. . . . The first payments were oil shipments. . . . From [subsequent] payments . . . the Israeli railroads were built. The Israeli electrical system was built in Germany. If anybody's been in Israel they know that taxi cabs are all made by Mercedes. This was a great help, and it was rather ironic that the state which had set out to destroy the Jews was so helpful in fact in enabling the only Jewish state to survive.[36]

The two agreements with the Claims Conference were protocols (or legal agreements that supplement a treaty) to the West Germany–Israel pact. They have come to be known as the Hague Protocols. Hague Protocol No. 1 permitted filing of individual claims, pursuant to contemplated German law to be enacted, which would compensate Nazi victims directly via indemnification and restitution arising from Nazi persecution. Protocol No. 2 consisted of a pledge by the West Germans to provide the Claims Conference with DM 450 million for the relief, rehabilitation, and resettlement of Jewish victims of Nazi persecution, according to the urgency of their needs as determined by the Conference.

Once the formal documents were drawn up, the ceremony for their official signing was scheduled to take place on the morning of September 10, 1952, in Luxembourg City, the capital of the Grand Duchy of Luxembourg, a tiny country sandwiched among the borders of Belgium, Germany, and France. In anticipation of this event, as a preliminary legal step, the Claims Conference tasked Ben Ferencz with having the papers initialed by the negotiating heads for the Germans and the Diaspora Jews. Departing from Nuremberg in the old family Mercedes, he began his journey by driving to Frankfurt, where German chief negotiator Franz Boehm initialed for the Federal Republic. Then he chauffeured Boehm to The Hague, where an ailing Moe Leavitt initialed on behalf of the Claims Conference. Ferencz and Boehm then drove through the night and arrived in Luxembourg just before the break of dawn. En route, the car passed through Bastogne, Ferencz's destination during the Battle of the Bulge, where Americans and Germans had been locked in mortal combat only a few years previously. Now he was there in the company of a top German official deputized to sign a reparations treaty related to the German loss in that battle. "How things had changed!" he thought, and, for a moment, he took a slightly more charitable view of his travails in the army.

On arriving in the Grand Duchy's capital, they checked into a hotel and managed a little sleep before reaching the Luxembourg City Hall soon after sunup. Photographs suggest Ben Ferencz's importance on the Claims Conference negotiating team—he was seated right next to Nahum Goldmann, close to Moshe Sharett, and almost directly across from Konrad Adenauer. Despite his twenty-four-hour sprint through Germany, Holland, Belgium, and Luxembourg, with next to no sleep, the thirty-two-year-old JRSO chief looked remarkably composed and alert, a little pudgier and balder than in his Nuremberg photographs but still with a veneer of youth, especially in contrast to the septuagenarian West German chancellor on the other side of the table.

"Der Alte" was showing the ravages of time and the burdens of office—like an arroyo rotated ninety degrees, his face was vertically striated, with deep furrows that seemed to pinch and constrict his right eye and cheek. Still, he exuded a kind of dignity and firmness of purpose that, fissures notwithstanding, gave one the impression that he had been chiseled out of granite. The grandeur in his movements seemed to emanate from a well of honor and decency deep within that betrayed not the slightest disequilibrium, when, as he began to sign the first treaty, he realized that his pen had run dry. With alacrity, Ferencz produced the one that Gertrude had bestowed on him as his Harvard Law School graduation gift, "an old Wattermann [*sic*] with a lifetime guarantee."[37] He had carried it with him ever since, in all the battles through France, Belgium, and Germany, through the liberation of the concentration camps, and during the courtroom skirmishes in Nuremberg. Now it was in Adenauer's hand, destined to become a more visible instrument of history.

Soon they were exiting triumphantly from city hall, and, as had Bastogne, Luxembourg started evoking powerful wartime memories for Ben. The next day, in an early fall mist, he wandered by the old bank building whose cold stone floor had served as billets for him during his Third Army days. He flashed back to a young lady whom he had escorted home in the midst of a blackout. She and her family had shown him great hospitality, including some overnight stays, before Patton's lawyers moved on. He recalled that the family name was Schneider, and he looked for the building. For a while, he wandered around the streets of Luxembourg City, admiring the trees whose leaves were already turning autumnal amber and crimson, and taking several wrong turns while waxing nostalgic. He was on the verge of giving up and returning to his hotel but then recognized a couple of landmarks. And then he found the building, and then the apartment, and then he knocked on the door:

> It flew open and a cheer went up from a flock of neighbors who crowded the apartment. The living room was filled and decorated with balloons and signs saying "Benny Welcome!" The morning papers had carried a story of the signing of the reparations treaty, and my photo was included with the article. The Schneiders had alerted all of their neighbors that the GI who slept on their carpet during the war would surely show up. I didn't disappoint them. I was the one, however, who was the most surprised. It was a touching and memorable conclusion to a historical event.[38]

THE SOLEMN Luxembourg ceremony might have been a fitting climax to a momentous, paradigm-shifting process. But for Ben Ferencz it was only the end of a preliminary chapter. A lot of hard work remained. Although Protocol No. 1 had allotted a certain sum for individual claims, those claims would have to be pursued via a German judicial/administrative framework. A Federal Republic law needed to be drafted, and Ben Ferencz was on the Claims Conference committee that would negotiate with the West Germans to get it done. The contemplated objective was a "federal indemnification law" that would pass muster in the Bundestag and be accepted by the West Germany citizenry.

Despite the consensus forged in Wassenaar, the process of formulating the legislation was fraught with division. On the Claims Conference side, committee members who were ostensibly protecting overall Jewish interests seemed more concerned with serving their own constituencies. Thus, pre-Hitler civil servants demanded reinstatement of all lost civil service–related benefits. At the same time, Jews from the non-German Diaspora, who had resettled in Germany, insisted on compensation for their new communities. By and large, these Yiddish-speaking Jews from Eastern Europe were viewed as "interlopers" by their more "enlightened" German coreligionists. In turn, those representing these "resettled Jews" seemed at odds with those representing the Jews who had been left behind in the east. Ferencz felt bound to no constituency, and he soon emerged as a mediator who was able to help forge "unity among the disunited Jewish representatives."[39]

Of course, the committee also had to negotiate with the West Germans. And that presented its own set of challenges. Many on the Bonn team were carryovers from the Third Reich who felt no moral or legal obligation "to impose onerous costs on patriotic German taxpayers" who had loyally supported their government.[40] Their party line was, "That's what all good citizens are expected to do in time of war, isn't it?"[41] The conservative finance minister, Fritz Schaeffer, for his part, relied heavily upon the simple argument that Jewish demands exceeded Germany's capacity to pay. Matters were complicated even further by the fact that other victims of Nazi persecution, such as Roma and Seventh-day Adventists, would be entitled to submit claims.

At times, the negotiations proved quite acrimonious as "beneficiaries competed for a bigger slice of the meager pie." Still, "vague compromises" were "hammered out in a hurry," and the new Federal Indemnification Law was finally agreed to. The West German Bundesentschädigungsgesetz (known by the initials BEG), a word that Ferencz wryly noted "non-Germans could neither spell nor pronounce," was enacted in October 1953. It stipulated that the indemnification program would come to its conclusion by 1963. That turned out to be a ridiculous understatement—after German reunification and the dawn of a new millennium, $50 billion had been paid out to more than 500,000 survivors, and the program survived until 2010.[42]

But in 1953 it was not entirely clear how the claims permitted by the new law would be processed. The legislative schema required initiating legal action, and claimants would need lawyers. Who would represent them? Holocaust survivors could hardly "be expected to turn to a former Nazi lawyer for help or be able to pay for legal assistance."[43] The Claims Conference turned to Ferencz, who had brilliantly helmed the restitution program in West Germany. The JRSO chief seemed the logical candidate to run a related reparations operation. And Leavitt, whose "No" nickname stemmed as much from being cheap as from being gruff, wanted him to do it for no additional remuneration.

He met with Ferencz, and the two plotted out a strategy: they would take over the work of an existing entity called the United Restitution Organization (URO), which had been providing legal aid to Holocaust survivors, and repurpose it to pursue Nazi persecution–related claims of restitution and compensation in West Germany. The URO had been originally sponsored by the British Foreign Office and was headquartered in London.[44] However, with the money now available from the Hague Protocols/BEG, the Claims Conference would take over its operation, move its seat to Frankfurt, and put Ferencz in charge. Ramping up operations with the new infusion of Hague Protocol cash, the organization was tasked with assisting tens, if not hundreds, of thousands of claimants as soon as possible.

Ben then moved his family, which would soon include a fourth child, a daughter named Nina (born in 1954), from Nuremberg to Frankfurt. The Ferenczes found new digs at 14 Liliencronstrasse, just north of the city center and close to the Old and New Jewish Cemeteries. As was customary for all projects he took on, Ferencz soon threw himself into the work and, as usual, achieved big results in little time. Under his energetic leadership, URO offices mushroomed in locations where large numbers of Nazi persecution victims resided. Eventually, there were URO branches in nineteen countries, including Argentina, Belgium, Brazil, Sweden, the United States, Canada, Australia, Chile, South Africa, France, and Uruguay, as well as offices in the major cities of West Germany. While still running the JRSO and acting as Claims Conference chief in the FRG, Ferencz hired and supervised staff and managed resources for all these far-flung URO operations.

Still, the URO job had tremendous challenges that could not be overcome by mere dint of hard work. In the major cities of West Germany, special Finance Ministry agencies were put in place to deal with the new flood of indemnification claims. Soon, hundreds of thousands of cases were being filed. Not by any stretch were the demands easily honored or paid in full in German marks, despite the dedicated work of a 1,000-plus URO staff, "including 250 carefully screened German lawyers."[45] Each one of the claims they filed had to be accompanied by persuasive evidence, including affidavits, historical records, and medical examination documents, which had to be translated and verified. The German agencies were being swamped with literally millions of claims.

Moreover, the Claims Conference pot was not unlimited, and given issues of thin evidence and attenuated causality, many claims were rejected or assessed at lower-than-requested values. Others became the object of protracted litigation. And some regional adjudicators were more reasonable than others. The Berlin-region adjudicators, for instance, were munificent, but the Bavarian ones were miserly.[46] Ferencz fought the bad decisions and litigated them through the German court system, sometimes all the way up to the German Supreme Court. But at times he would lose.[47] Traumatized survivors, seeking symbolic justice but turned away or strung along, were soon seething with anger and resentment. And they were venting their spleen on Ferencz and his "reasonably competent and underpaid staff."[48] DPs in Germany resented that Ferencz was driven around in "American sedans" with "unserem Gelt" (our money) even though the cars, and their maintenance, were paid for out of separate funds by the US government.[49]

But there were complaints coming from jurisdictions outside of West Germany too. In Stockholm, the local URO representative phoned "in a panic" about the clients "rioting in the office." Ferencz told him to convene a meeting of the "rioters" in the main synagogue. He then took the next plane to the Swedish capital. On arriving at the Jewish house of worship, he took off his jacket and "addressed the unruly crowd." He listened to their complaints in

English, German, French, Hungarian, and Yiddish. Then he invited all who felt they could get better service elsewhere "to please come to the office in the morning" and the URO would be happy to return the file "with our best wishes." Of course, "not a single complainer showed up."[50]

But there were also some unexpected triumphs. One of the bottlenecks in the Wassenaar negotiations had been the issue of pensions for Jewish clerics and synagogue administrators. The Weimar Republic had treated all religious congregations in Germany, including Jewish ones, as official government entities. On taking power, Hitler dissolved all governmental links between the Hebraic communities and the government, stripped them of their organizational status, and confiscated their assets. At the Wassenaar negotiations table, the parties could not reach agreement on responsibility for the resulting forfeited pensions of Jewish officials. According to Ferencz: "The German negotiators balked, saying they had no way to confirm which officials would have been entitled to what pension. Wearing my Claims Conference hat, I proposed that we cap the obligation at 30 million marks. They still refused. We countered with a proposal to set up a committee to certify each claim and if the Social Ministry did not agree, no payment need be made. That was so reasonable that they dropped their objections. Then the fun began."[51]

With Ben again put in charge, the Claims Conference set up a Pensions Advisory Board (PAB) office "in a rickety old building [in Bonn] that was inexpensive because the landlord rented rooms by the hour."[52] Besides Ferencz, who served as chairman, the other Advisory Board members consisted of knowledgeable persons drawn from the JRSO, URO, and Claims Conference. The board was fairly generous in its decisions, and it would always give the benefit of the doubt to the claimant.

And, in the rare cases when the board would reject a claim, the Social Ministry would overrule it. Ferencz noted the example of a rabbi who had been on the verge of being fired for cause before Hitler became chancellor based on his occasional failure to appear at funerals "because he may have been [too] busy privately consoling the widow." The board had been "strict" and rejected the pension claim. But the Social Ministry disagreed and approved the pension request of the "rabbinical Romeo." Ferencz later wrote that his greatest satisfaction came when he realized that the pension program cost the German government at least ten times more than the DM 30 million he had offered to settle all pension claims. "The only thing dumber than my proposal," he later wrote, "was Germany's rejection of it."[53]

By 1956, Ferencz was at a crossroads. Life in Germany had been pleasant but somehow strange, and at times unsettling. "It was a colonial, cloistered existence," he later explained. "The Americans fraternized only with the Americans. Germans were used as servants. . . . Everything was very cheap. It was a comfortable life like the British living in India."[54] But it could also be very unwelcoming, even dangerous: "There were some tensions before the *Einsatzgruppen* defendants were executed [in the summer of 1951]. I received several death threats. I took the name off my door. We had death threats later in connection with the [Wassenaar] negotiations. . . . [It] was not a happy place to be. You always felt beleaguered. . . . You were surrounded by persons that regarded you as vermin the years before."[55]

There were issues in his work and family life too. For the previous few years, simultaneously, he had been running the JRSO, the URO, and the Pensions Advisory Board, and he was the representative of the Claims Conference in Germany. His was the life of a workaholic but without commensurate pay—he had been wearing all four hats for essentially his JRSO salary, barely adjusted for inflation. He had never looked at being a Holocaust victims' lawyer as a pathway to wealth. But now, with a large brood in tow and commensurate financial burdens, he felt it was time to put the well-being of his household ahead of his reparations crusade. Part of this was his concern, shared by Gertrude, that if they stayed any longer their "offspring [would start] school in the land that held so many nightmares."[56]

On one of his periodic trips to New York to report to his board of directors, Ferencz gave notice of his decision to resign from his various posts in Germany. "No" Leavitt offered him a slight increase in salary if he remained, but he declined the "kind and ungenerous offer."[57] As a result, Dr. Ernst Katzenstein, Ferencz's deputy at the JRSO, was tapped to take over that organization. Dr. Kurt May, Ferencz's number two at the URO, and Dr. Herbert Schoenfeldt, May's equivalent at the Claims Conference, took over the respective director positions in those organizations, with May also taking over the Pensions Advisory Board. Each man received the same salary that Ferencz had earned doing all those jobs combined. But he took it all in stride:

> Thus, with all three competent men promoted, I was content to begin my search for a new career and a suitable new home. My wife's only requests were that it be in America, in a house small enough for her to manage without help, and without fear of anti-Semitism. We hoped that our combined life savings might be adequate to meet those modest requirements. I looked forward to finally starting to earn my living as a New York lawyer. After a diligent search . . . I found a little house in the suburbs [at] 14 Bayberry Lane, New Rochelle. . . . [We arrived] the first day of spring 1956. When we sailed into New York harbor on the SS United States, expecting to be greeted by singing

> birds and sun-drenched flowers, we found the port completely shrouded in 18 inches of snow. God bless America! We were happy to be home.[58]

They spent the night sleeping on his sister Pearl's apartment floor in the Bronx before striking out for New Rochelle, "where a charitable neighbor had left a shovel in the snow."[59] As he was clearing his new driveway, Ben Ferencz could reflect on the tremendous legacy of his post–Nuremberg Trials work in Germany, especially his part in the international law revolution wrought by the West Germany–Israel/Diaspora treaties and their enforcement. In fact, this seemed of a piece with his Nuremberg Trials achievement. As noted by Ferencz expert Philipp Gut:

> In a certain sense, "Luxembourg" stood next to "Nuremberg": Just as new standards were formulated in 1948 for dealing with the perpetrators of major crimes committed by the state, this was also done in 1952 with a view to dealing with the victims. In this respect, the agreement can be read as a founding document of "historical justice," the effect of which continues to this day. And in the person of Ben Ferencz, these legal developments come together in a unique way.[60]

17

FINISHING THE REPARATIONS REVOLUTION

> [The] most important of all revolutions . . . [is] a revolution of sentiments, manners and moral opinions.
>
> —Edmund Burke, *Reflections on the Revolution in France*

> A revolution can be neither made nor stopped. The only thing that can be done is for one or several of its children to give it a direction by dint of victories.
>
> —Napoleon Bonaparte

Something deep inside of Benjamin Berell Ferencz had been yearning to be a New York attorney for as long as he could remember. Since the 1930s, a diagonal thread running over the warp and weft of his Hell's Kitchen and Bronx memories was a dream of representing clients in the Empire State's halls of justice. Viscerally, since his City College days, he had known that he and Gertrude would create the kind of stable, child-friendly household that neither of them had ever known. At the core of this idyll was his role as Big Apple barrister and breadwinner. All of that might have begun in the early 1940s had World War II not intervened. But it did, and it changed everything. Now, in the latter part of the 1950s, were his travails connected to that conflagration finally over? He proceeded as if they were.

And choices seemingly abounded. He could join an old-line, white-shoe Wall Street law practice. Or he could be recruited by one of Midtown Manhattan's biggest and best up-and-coming firms. He could even go in-house with one of the top corporations. It was 1956, the year rock and roll swept the country and Elvis Presley became a megastar. America had emerged from the hardships of armed conflict. Dwight D. Eisenhower, who first moved into the White House in 1952 and had negotiated the end of the Korean War, was running for reelection. The economy was booming. And America had become a land of freeways, suburbs, and televisions. Anything was possible.

But nothing panned out. In Germany, among the international elites, he may have rubbed elbows; but in New York City, among the law profession's gatekeepers, he got nothing but cold shoulders. Corporate America's legal titans, it turned out, "seemed to have no use" for his talents.[1] Sure, he had a Harvard Law School degree, and his career to that point had been impressive and colorful. But where was his book of business? His cohort of fellow HLS grads had already been practicing domestically for over a decade. Many of them were already rainmakers. Ferencz could tell great stories, but he could offer no clients. He was assured, however, "that if the big law firms had to prosecute mass murderers or cope with . . . claims for Nazi victims, they would be happy to consult [him]."[2] Even John McCloy's firm had nothing to offer him.

Still, he was not entirely bereft of options—the firm of Guzik & Boukstein had been recruiting him. Leo Guzik and Maurice Boukstein had been actively involved with Holocaust reparations issues. Guzik had served as counsel to important Jewish organizations, such as the Jewish Agency for Israel (the name change owing to the founding of the Jewish state) and Hadassah, a women's group. Boukstein, for his part, had also advised the Jewish Agency and the World Zionist Organization. And he had represented Holocaust survivors in the infamous Hungarian Gold Train case, negotiating the transfer to JRSO coffers of a decent portion of stolen Jewish assets found on that Nazi train.[3] The Ferencz-Boukstein relationship was then strengthened when the latter served as a Claims Conference representative at the Wassenaar negotiations. So, when Big Law spurned Ferencz, he was finally ready to accept Guzik & Boukstein's offer.

In May 1956, the small Wall Street firm, with an address of 150 Broadway, New York 38, was sending out the following announcement: "We are pleased to announce that BENJAMIN B. FERENCZ, former Executive Counsel, U.S. War Crimes Trials, Nürnberg, having resigned as Director General of the Jewish Restitution Successor Organization (JRSO) and Director, United Restitution Organization (URO), and Claims Conference in Germany, is now associated with us in the general practice of the law."[4]

Despite the fanfare, the association did not go well. Ben resented the "beginner's salary" and access to only a "smattering" of the firm's "unimportant matters."[5] It was quite the comedown for the Nuremberg Wunderkind. And the daily work routine did little to leaven the sense of humiliation. He soon discovered that plying his trade in New York's lower courts was "definitely not to [his] liking." He found the "coarse and greedy clerks" and the "crowded and unruly dockets" to be "particularly distasteful." "It was, to put it mildly," he later recollected, "a very far cry from the lofty ideals taught at Harvard."[6]

Disillusioned with his marginal lot at Guzik & Boukstein, by 1957 he was ready to "strike out on his own" and hang up a shingle. He was on retainer with the Claims Conference and the URO and continued to handle some of their matters. But he was still clinging to that old vision of himself as a truly local New York practitioner. His new strategy was to build up a successful non-Holocaust-related client roster via the jack-of-all-trades solo practitioner route. He associated with fellow shingle-hanger Nathan Eisner, his sister Pearl's husband, and the two brothers-in-law rented space together at 21 East Fortieth Street, New York 16. To help drum up business, Ferencz joined his local synagogue, a move that "of course had little to do with a devotion to religion."[7]

And he represented whichever clients came his way. Those involved in divorce cases? He was signing them up, even though it always "pained" him to see "how love could sometimes turn to hate, particularly when children were involved."[8] His strategy in such matters was to "urge reconciliation" or at least a "civilized separation" without "getting lawyers involved if it could be avoided." Slip-and-fall plaintiffs? Some of those were his clients too, but "exaggerated negligence claims left [him] cold."[9] He handled real estate closings but found them to be "a total bore."[10]

By the late 1950s, he was struggling "in the lowlands of the legal profession" and "found himself in a long period of professional drought."[11] According to Ferencz experts Constantin Goschler, Marcus Böick, and Julia Reus, Ben's previous "activities for the American military government as well as for Jewish organizations hardly helped him to gain a foothold in the competitive New York law business. He was not established in professional networks and, above all, had no solvent client base."[12] By 1958, "he decided to write a letter in which he retrospectively described his career in Germany with the bitter remark: 'Can it be that at age 37 my future is behind me?'"[13]

Ferencz slogged his way through to the end of the decade. Then, in 1960, everything started to change. And it coincided with, or was, in part, sparked by, a reunion with his old Nuremberg boss, Telford Taylor. The erstwhile OCCWC chief and his executive counsel had managed to stay in close touch during the first half of the 1950s as Ferencz, on his "many trips to the United States," had always made a point of visiting Taylor.[14] While Ben had been blazing new Holocaust justice trails in Germany, Telford, who had joined the prestigious New York firm of Paul, Weiss, Wharton & Garrison, was reinventing himself as a celebrated American lawyer for the underdog. And those whose causes he championed most vigorously at first were the opponents of US senator Joseph McCarthy.

Starting in 1950, the Republican legislator from Wisconsin had issued a string of unsubstantiated claims suggesting that an invisible "Communist" Fifth Column had infiltrated various branches of the US government, including the State Department and the army. So he launched a series of investigations to expose these supposed Soviet moles. This brought McCarthy to prominence, and the higher he rose, the more he abused his newfound power—the number of allegations mounted, and, in his fulminations, the extent of supposed Communist subversion grew. For the next few years, he destroyed the careers of countless innocent Americans with his baseless allegations, but many were afraid to stand up to the witch hunt, including President Eisenhower himself.

Telford Taylor, though, was different. The man who had tangled with the most monstrous Nazi war criminals led the charge against what people started referring to as McCarthyism. In a November 1953 speech before the Cadet Corps at West Point, when "McCarthy was one of the most feared men in Washington," Taylor accused the Wisconsin legislator of "a shameful abuse of congressional investigating power."[15] He even rebuked President Eisenhower for failing to stand up to the GOP senator's persecution campaign.[16]

McCarthy retaliated by accusing Taylor of disloyalty. But the latter did not flinch.[17] In seeming defiance of the Republican demagogue, the former Nuremberg prosecution chief took on the defense of various leftist figures, including Harry Bridges, the Australian-born leader of the International Longshoreman's and Warehouseman's Union, who was prosecuted for false statements based on a US immigration declaration that he had never been a member of the Communist Party.[18] Eventually, in December 1954, McCarthy was censured by the US Senate, and his power dissipated.

During his old boss's anti-McCarthy travails, Ferencz, who had always hated bullies and opportunists, remained a dogged supporter. And he dreamed of joining Taylor in the practice of law. In 1955, he told Saul Kagan of his early-1950s desire to be hired by Taylor's firm; impossible then, given that "Taylor's own practice was rather limited."[19] But Taylor's professional situation soon changed. He left Paul, Weiss and went into partnership with Ferencz's old HLS dean, James M. Landis.

Apart from his academic role, Landis had held an impressive list of government posts, including chairman of the Securities and Exchange Commission and member of the Federal Trade Commission. With the former OCCWC chief and progressive-minded attorney David E. Scoll, he formed the firm of Landis, Taylor & Scoll. But it later came to light that the lead name partner was a serious alcoholic and had failed to pay his federal income taxes during the mid-1950s. Landis, who had served as an advisor to John F. Kennedy's administration in its initial phases, was eventually prosecuted and pled guilty to tax evasion charges in the early 1960s.

As the 1950s were coming to an end, Landis announced that he was leaving the firm. And Ben Ferencz finally got the call he had been waiting for—Taylor invited him to join the practice, and the letterhead was changed to Taylor, Scoll, Ferencz & Simon. That last name belonged to Kenneth Simon, a member of Taylor's circle and lawyer for accused Communist Alger Hiss. Ben was elated. And 1960 turned out to be a seminal year for him. JFK was elected president of the United States on November 8 of that year. A member of Ferencz's generation, the young and dashing Kennedy introduced his New Frontier program, infusing the country with a sense of vitality and optimism.

Even more important for Ferencz, though, was the date May 11, 1960. That evening, Argentina time, Israeli intelligence officials captured the war criminal Adolf Eichmann in an industrial community twelve miles north of the Buenos Aires city center. The new Israeli prisoner had headed Gestapo Department IV, B4 for Jewish Affairs and was notorious for his role in organizing the logistics for the deportation of Jews to extermination camps.

Before headlines around the world announced the arrest, Ben Ferencz had already been quite familiar with Adolf Eichmann. In August 1938, mere months after the German Anschluss of Austria, the Gestapo logistician had devised a "conveyor-belt system" for effectuating Jewish expulsion from the land of Adolf Hitler's birth. He set up an office at the former Rothschild Palace at 22 Prinz Eugen Strasse, in Vienna. There, Jews passed from one Nazi bureaucrat to another, being stripped of their property, livelihood, and dignity in the process.[20]

It had occurred to Ferencz that he and Eichmann were, in a certain sense, bookends of the same process—Eichmann, the destroyer, stripping the Jews of everything they had in the Holocaust's nascent phase, and Ferencz, the restorer, trying to return it all in the genocide's aftermath.[21] Based on his initial success in Vienna and then his subsequent efforts to deport Jews from the Nazi-acquired territories of Czechoslovakia and Poland, Eichmann was sent to Berlin and put in charge of overseeing Jewish affairs. When Hitler decided to exterminate the Jews after the 1941 invasion of the Soviet Union, Eichmann helped organize the Wannsee Conference for Nazi security services chief Reinhard Heydrich. Before the Conference, to facilitate efficient planning for the coming genocide, Eichmann compiled statistics regarding Jewish inhabitants in occupied territories. During the Conference, he took the meeting minutes, recording how the genocide was to be organized among the various German government departments. This document came to be known as the Wannsee Protocol (the one later discovered by Robert Kempner). After the Conference, pursuant to the Protocol, Eichmann was put in charge of overseeing large-scale deportations of Jews to the various Nazi extermination centers, becoming a central perpetrator of the Holocaust.

Not long after Eichmann's capture in Argentina and transfer to Jerusalem, Ben Ferencz wrote a letter to the Israeli minister of justice, Dr. Pinhas Rosen. Dated May 25, 1960, and bearing the letterhead of "Taylor, Scoll, Ferencz & Simon, Counselors at Law (400 Madison Avenue, New York 17)." The missive's opening paragraph noted that "As Chief Prosecutor at Nuremberg against the Einsatzgruppen, I know the reports flowing from Eichmann's office about the extermination of millions of Jews and had long been gnawed by the injustice that this man might have escaped. My first reaction of the news, therefore, was one of excitement and vicarious pride that Jewish forces had succeeded where everyone else had failed."[22] The balance of the letter, citing fairness considerations and the agreement of his "colleague" Telford Taylor, largely focused on persuading Israel to turn Eichmann over to the West Germans for trial before an international tribunal. However, citing his extensive reparations work, Ferencz also emphasized "the need to provide redress for surviving victims insofar as it is humanly possible."[23]

Rosen responded by letter on June 8, noting that Ferencz's epistle impressed "by reason of its obvious sincerity," and acknowledged an "appreciation for it and the spirit in which it [was] written."[24] But Rosen emphasized Israel's legal basis for prosecuting Eichmann on "universal jurisdiction" grounds under its 1950 Nazi and Nazi Collaborators (Punishment) Law, pursuant to which the Holocaust logistics master was indicted on fifteen counts, including crimes against humanity, war crimes, crimes against the Jewish people (akin to the crime of genocide), and membership in criminal organizations (the Gestapo, SD, and SS). And, perhaps in part responding to Ferencz's stated concerns about the centrality of victims in the proceeding, Rosen assured Ferencz that Israel would "try Eichmann properly" and "demonstrate this to the world at large."[25]

Following up on this, over the next year, as Ferencz traveled to the Jewish state on reparations business, he met with Israeli chief prosecutor Gideon Hausner and his team, Deputy Attorney General Gabriel Bach, and Tel Aviv District Attorney Yaakov Bar-Or. They "came together on different occasions" and discussed trial strategy as well as the importance of victims in the proceeding within the context of Ferencz's restitution advocacy.[26] Although, in light of his law practice schedule, Ben was not able to attend the trial itself, which took place from April 11 through August 14, 1961, he could take satisfaction in knowing that Hausner's strategy "placed survivors at the center of the trial, the first time the world had heard from them at length."[27] In stark contrast to the *Einsatzgruppen* trial, which relied entirely on documents to prove Nazi guilt, Hausner's strategy was to shine "the spotlight on the witnesses" to "help paint the broad picture of the entire destruction process."[28] The Eichmann trial was therefore the moment "survivors acquired their moral stature."[29] And their testimony, covered in a "packed courtroom [by reporters] from South America, North America, and, of course, Europe,"[30] was the "reason the Eichmann trial so shook the world."[31]

The inquest, which was held in a specially constructed courtroom at the Beit Ha'am, an auditorium in central Jerusalem, featured Eichmann in an iconic bulletproof glass booth. And, in retrospect, the proceeding seemed like something of a reunion for so many important figures in Ben Ferencz's professional life. Taylor was there covering the case for the British magazine the *Spectator.* Kempner was there to testify as an expert witness regarding, inter alia, the Wannsee Protocol.

From a Ferencz perspective, another noteworthy presence at the trial was Judge Robert Musmanno. Since Nuremberg, among other literary endeavors, he had undertaken a book project titled *Ten Days to Die* (1950), documenting Hitler's final phase in the bunker, for which he had interviewed many surviving intimates of the Nazi dictator.[32] He had also since been appointed as a Pennsylvania Supreme Court judge but had sullied his reputation somewhat by becoming a local anti-Communist crusader, something akin to a watered-down, Keystone State version of Joseph McCarthy (although this was arguably counterbalanced by Musmanno's ardent support for and involvement in the American civil rights movement).

By 1960, it would appear that Musmanno had been missing the international limelight that had come with being a Nuremberg judge and Nazi expert. He notified the *Eichmann* prosecutors that, through his previous work, he had collected information demonstrating that Eichmann was the invisible hand in Berlin operating the levers of the Einsatzgruppen murder machine. Of course, that did not square with the historical record, and Musmanno's testimony at the trial was not credited by the *Eichmann* court. That record in Jerusalem, along with a subsequent account of the *Einsatzgruppen* trial misleadingly titled *The Eichmann Kommandos* (1961), put a cloud over Musmanno's otherwise excellent Nuremberg reputation.

Also present at the trial was another of Ferencz's former colleagues, Hannah Arendt. Since beginning her work with the JRSO/JCR, she had published, to great acclaim, *The Origins of Totalitarianism* (1951). Already a famous philosopher by the time of Eichmann's capture, she was in Jerusalem to report on the case for the *New Yorker.* Her subsequent book based on that coverage, *Eichmann in Jerusalem: A Report on the Banality of Evil* (1963), only brought her greater acclaim and transformed the volume's subtitle into a celebrated encapsulation of the Third Reich's extermination bureaucracy culture. But the book was not without controversy. Eichmann was not an evil genius thirsty for

Jewish blood, Arendt posited, but rather a compliant bureaucrat, a transportation specialist, not rabidly antisemitic; more of a "clown" than a monster.[33]

Jacob Robinson, Ben's comrade in arms in Wassenaar, who had worked with the Israeli prosecutors to prepare for the trial and served as their international law expert, was also there, seated right next to Hausner throughout the proceeding. He would go on to write the lesser-known book *And the Crooked Shall Be Made Straight: The Eichmann Trial, the Jewish Catastrophe, and Hannah Arendt's Narrative* (1965), a direct refutation of Arendt's thesis regarding Eichmann's "banality" and "normalcy." It effectively put the lie to Arendt's suggestion that Eichmann lacked genocidal intent or awareness of the evil of his actions.[34]

The trial judges, Moshe Landau (presiding), Benjamin Halevy, and Yitzhak Raveh, were more swayed by Robinson's version of Eichmann's role and rejected his "following orders" defense.[35] On December 12, 1961, having deliberated since August, they read their verdict in open court. They convicted Eichmann on all counts. Four days later, the former SS-Obersturmbannführer was sentenced to death, and the Israeli Supreme Court rejected his appeal on May 29, 1962.[36] Eichmann was hanged on June 1, 1962.

THE EICHMANN TRIAL marked a turning point regarding worldwide awareness of the Holocaust and inspired a newfound desire to do justice in reference to it.[37] Around the same time, one can arguably trace a subtle change in Ben Ferencz's attitude as well. Perhaps it was based on his reunion with Taylor or the new global consciousness regarding the victims of the Holocaust and concern for their welfare. But instead of doggedly trying to redeem his old pledge to make it as a lawyer handling domestic matters in New York, he seemed to embrace what fate actually had in store for him—seeking justice around the world as a lawyer for victims of the Holocaust. As he later acknowledged in his own words, "I decided to stick to the subjects I knew best."[38]

Granted, he had no clean moment of epiphany in this regard—it was not necessarily a linear process. He had been on retainer with the Claims Conference and URO since his return from Germany. But, at first, he regarded the URO/Claims Conference work as only a sidelight to help pay the bills while he cut his teeth on negligence, property, and family law cases. Eventually, however, the domestic cases largely faded away, and Ferencz fully accepted the reparations work as his primary professional pursuit. He ultimately discovered, he later observed, that "my traumas of World War Two and the work I had been doing in Germany thereafter could not simply be discarded and forgotten."[39] In many ways, this gradual trajectory toward exclusive Holocaust justice pursuits can be charted via his work with survivors seeking civil damages against German industrial firms that had used them as slave laborers. Initially, this involved a new opportunity to seek justice against two Nazi commercial concerns that had been the object of his investigative and prosecutorial efforts at Nuremberg—IG Farben and Krupp.

IG Farben

For many, the name IG Farben evokes two of the most chilling terms in the Holocaust lexicon: Auschwitz and Zyklon B. The former came to symbolize Nazi mass industrial extermination. And the latter was the substance responsible for much of the murder there—the gas that cruelly asphyxiated two thousand naked Jews at a time, made to raise their arms so they could be crammed like sardines into an underground chamber where the toxin was released.

Within the overall Auschwitz complex, the Monowitz facility was "connected with the initiative by the German chemical concern IG Farbenindustrie AG (a large German conglomerate of chemical firms) to build [a] plant for synthetic rubber [known as 'Buna-N']."[40] In February 1941, after negotiations with the company, Heinrich Himmler signed an order permitting construction of an IG Farben Buna-N (synthetic rubber) plant—known as Monowitz Buna Werke (or Buna). (Monowitz/Buna was later dubbed "Auschwitz III"; Auschwitz I was the complex's administrative center, and Auschwitz II-Birkenau was the extermination camp.)

The Buna plant's workforce consisted of Auschwitz slave labor, leased to the company by the SS for a low daily rate of three to four marks. At its peak in 1944, approximately 11,000 unfortunates, mostly Jews, toiled there under the IG Farben/SS whip. Given subsubsistence rations, they were meant to be worked to death within months. In a letter to his colleagues about IG Farben's arrangements with Himmler, director Otto Ambros wrote that "our new friendship with the SS is very fruitful."[41]

At the same time, IG Farben subsidiary Degesch supplied Zyklon B, a cyanide-based pesticide, to Auschwitz and other Nazi death centers. This combined with the conglomerate's appropriating property in occupied territories, its use of slave labor beyond Auschwitz, medical experimentation on prisoners, and its provision to the Reich of industrial goods permitting the manufacture of weapons, explosives, artificial rubber (for tires) and synthetic fuel, gave rise to charges against twenty-three company executives at Nuremberg of crimes against peace, war crimes, crimes against humanity, related conspiracy counts, and membership in criminal organizations.

Despite the compelling evidence of these crimes presented at trial, thanks to the poorly reasoned majority opinion of conservative midwestern judges Curtis Grover Shake (Indiana Supreme Court) and James Morris (North Dakota Supreme Court), only nine of the twenty-three *IG Farben* defendants were found guilty of spoliation in occupied territories, and a mere five were convicted of the slave-labor-related charges. The third judge on the panel, Paul M. Hebert, dean of the Louisiana State Law School, disagreed with his brethren in respect of the slave labor charges. He dissented, lamenting:

> The important fact is that Farben's *Vorstand* [managing board] willingly cooperated in utilizing forced labor. They were not forced to do so. . . . The conditions at Auschwitz were so horrible that it is utterly incredible to conclude that they were unknown to the defendants, the principal corporate directors, who were responsible for Farben's connection with the project. . . . Each defendant who is a member of the *Vorstand* should be held guilty.[42]

Those defendants not convicted of spoliation or slave labor–related charges were acquitted. And those adjudged guilty were sentenced lightly, with none receiving more than eight years' imprisonment (and others as little as a year and a half). Ferencz, who, at the time, was serving as OCCWC executive counsel, was in the courtroom when these results were announced. His was among the "sad . . . faces" on the prosecution team that day because "the accused had gotten off lightly."[43] He subsequently groused in a letter to Sheldon Glueck that the "political considerations of not antagonizing the Germans . . . clashed with moral principles urging the correction of Nazi wrongs."[44]

This injustice was experienced most bitterly by one of IG Farben's direct victims, Holocaust survivor Norbert Wollheim. In March 1943, the German Jewish native, his sister Ruth, his wife Rosa, and their three-year-old son Uriel had been arrested in Berlin and were soon shipped to Auschwitz. Upon arrival, Ruth, Rosa, and Uriel were "selected" for the gas chamber. Norbert was placed in bondage to IG Farben and slated to be worked to death. He managed to survive the torturous existence of starvation rations, beatings, sleep deprivation, exposure to the elements, and disease until January 1945, when he and other surviving slaves were taken out of the camp on a death march. Somehow, he was able to break away from the phalanx of the condemned and seek shelter. Eventually, he found his way back to Germany and settled in Lübeck. After the July 1948 verdict in the *IG Farben* trial, Wollheim looked for another way to seek justice. This eventually led him to attorney Henry Ormond.

Born as Hans Jacobson, by 1938 Ormond was going by the name Hans Oettinger. After Kristallnacht, in November of that year, Gestapo agents arrested the former practicing lawyer and incarcerated him in Dachau. He was released in 1939 and fled, first to Switzerland and then to the United Kingdom. Upon his postwar repatriation to Germany, having changed his name to Henry Ormond, he set up a law practice in Frankfurt. Still scarred from his time at Dachau, Ormond represented Wollheim for only a nominal fee, filing suit against the postwar version of the IG Farben entity (then being split up by German authorities into separate entities) in the Frankfurt Landgericht (regional court).

Given the Cold War climate in West Germany, and a clash with high-priced IG Farben lawyers, the odds were entirely stacked against Wollheim and Ormond. But in 1953, after IG Farben overplayed its hand at trial by describing Auschwitz as a "convalescent camp" with reasonable work conditions and "delicious" food served to the workers, the court ruled in Wollheim's favor and awarded him DM 10,000 and attorneys' fees.[45]

The decision was a rude awakening for all German industrial concerns that had profited from concentration camp labor under National Socialism, not merely IG Farben. But the chemical giant was the object of this test case and decided to fight it, not just for itself but also, implicitly, on behalf of all the other Hitlerian corporate slavers. Not only would IG Farben bring in even bigger legal guns to fight, but thousands of other potential plaintiffs were ready to sign up for litigation. Ormond knew he needed help.

So he turned to the Claims Conference, and that is when Ferencz joined the fray. "Because of my Nuremberg connection," he later wrote, "it was natural that I should accept primary responsibility for proceeding against IG Farben on behalf of all those who had toiled for the firm at Auschwitz and other camps."[46] First, Ferencz arranged for the Claims Conference to provide a pool of money for Wollheim's legal fees and make available the assistance of URO attorneys whenever necessary. Then, he and Bonn Claims Conference lawyer Herbert Schoenfeldt met with IG Farben attorney Walter Schmidt to see if a settlement could be negotiated. But quite the chasm separated the two sides at the outset—Ferencz was asking for a total of DM 100 million, and Schmidt was offering DM 10 million.

Ferencz and his team of lawyers then used whatever tools they had at their disposal to push IG Farben closer to a reasonable settlement number. First, they received figures from Israel indicating that there were about six thousand survivors of the IG Farben Auschwitz plant. At the next hearing of the pending appeal, Claims Conference lawyers explained the situation, and the bench leaned on IG Farben to increase its counteroffer. In light of all this, at the subsequent meeting with Schmidt, Ferencz argued that each IG Farben survivor should receive DM 10,000 and that an additional 10 percent should be added for cases of extreme hardship; Ferencz thus reduced his demand from DM 100 million to DM 66 million. IG Farben then doubled its number to DM 20 million, but it was still much too little.

At the next appellate hearing, IG Farben's lawyers included Otto Kranzbühler, Alfried Krupp's Nuremberg advocate (as well as that of Grand Admiral Karl Dönitz before the IMT)—considered by many as the Nuremberg Trials' finest German defense attorney. However, thanks to the efforts and funding of Ferencz and his Claims Conference team, Wollheim's representation, in addition to Ormond, included non-Jewish German lawyer Otto Küster. Ferencz later described the power of Küster's advocacy in court: "Küster, a lay leader of the Evangelical Church, was a man of rigid moral principles. . . . A towering man of stern visage, Küster began his summation in a low voice. It was a duty of honor, he said, to defend in its entirety the decision of the lower court. He went on to describe the many grisly abuses to which the inmates had been subjected and the 'slavery of those who had been humans.'"[47]

On March 2, 1955, under the headline "Slave Laborers Find a Champion," the *New York Times* lauded Küster's courage in joining Wollheim's fight and denouncing IG Farben. In its ruling of March 15, the appellate court refrained from deciding the merits and told the parties to return to the negotiations table. Discussions continued, and, by the end of 1956, the parties had closed the gap, with IG Farben characterizing its softening position as a "gesture of goodwill" rather than "the discharge of an obligation."[48] Ferencz and the other Claims Conference counsel, "fed up with the indignity . . . about how much should be paid to which Auschwitz survivors," were also ready to resolve matters.[49]

On February 6, 1957, the parties entered into an agreement pursuant to which IG Farben would pay out DM 30 million. The settlement was hailed in prominent American newspapers, with one describing it as "One of the most significant [and] encouraging . . . events since the formal cessation of hostilities of World War II."[50] Ferencz later explained its historical magnitude: "For the first time in history, a settlement had been concluded between a worldwide Jewish organization and a German company for the company's use of concentration camp inmates as forced laborers."[51]

The Claims Conference established a supplemental adjudicative body, the Kompensations-Treuhandgesellschaft (Compensation Trust Society), to examine applications submitted by individuals for fund compensation. Ferencz would spend the next several years helping administer this process. By 1968, 5,855 claimants had received compensation, mostly DM 5,000 each. It made their lives, Ferencz noted, "just a little bit easier."[52] Now armed with this important precedent and a long list of extant German slave labor profiteer companies, Ferencz spearheaded additional Claims Conference litigation efforts.

And his most prominent new target was "Friedrich Krupp, AG," still run by none other than convicted war criminal Alfried Krupp.

Krupp

As a Nuremberg investigator and prosecutor, Ben Ferencz had sought justice in reference to the contributions of IG Farben and Krupp to Germany's planning and prosecution of aggressive war. Much to Ben's profound disappointment, the NMT aggression counts against the men who directed these corporations were dismissed. And though many of these same men were convicted of spoliation and slave labor-related charges, by the early 1950s they were out of prison thanks to McCloy's amnesties. Particularly galling for Ferencz, in this regard, was the case of Alfried Krupp, whose fortune was also restored to him. Krupp placed approximately 100,000 people in bondage, most of them perishing in the process or being sent back to concentration camps to be finished off by the SS. In addition to his other concentration camp–fueled enterprises, Krupp ran a slave labor operation adjacent to the Auschwitz complex. In a 1943 letter, he assured Nazi authorities that "a very close cooperation exists between this office and Auschwitz, and is assured also for the future."[53]

After Alfried Krupp was amnestied and made financially whole, by the mid-1950s, *Time* magazine, which featured him on its cover, was describing Krupp as "the wealthiest man in all of Europe—and perhaps the world."[54] Ferencz was distraught over Krupp's release and regained riches. And he was certainly not alone. In 1954, inspired by Wollheim's efforts against IG Farben, a Polish Jew by the name of "Mordechai S." sued Krupp in the Essen District Court. The plaintiff, his wife, and three children had been arrested in 1941 and transported in packed cattle cars to Auschwitz. There, his wife and children were murdered straightaway, but he was selected for slave labor and survived the brutal conditions and the torture. He was now the lead plaintiff in litigation against Krupp.

But Mordechai was impecunious, and as soon as Krupp demanded that cash be posted to cover court costs (the DM 40,000 asked for in the complaint), he "was stopped in his tracks."[55] So the claim was essentially held in abeyance. But as the *IG Farben* case was being resolved, Ferencz convinced the Claims Conference to pursue "test cases" against other German corporate slavers. When Ben and the Claims Conference became aware of *Mordechai S. v. Krupp*, they helped resuscitate that lawsuit and combined it with filing other cases to create a viable global reparations litigation strategy.

For Ferencz, this new pursuit of justice was gratifying as there were post-Nuremberg scores to settle with Krupp for his logistical enabling and exploitation of Hitler's war and the Holocaust. In a June 9, 1958, letter to Saul Kagan, Ben noted that, in seeking justice via civil litigation for the crimes of Krupp (and other Nazi corporate exploiters), "It would give me a great deal of *personal satisfaction* to meet the challenge and reach a settlement for the slave laborers."[56] Later that month, in a letter to his old Nuremberg colleague Drexel Sprecher, Ben clearly revealed his mindset:

> I am going for a gentleman called Alfried Felix Alwyn von Bohlen und Halbach, more commonly known to us intimates as "Alfie the Drip." The plan simply is to start one or more cases in a German court seeking to hold Alfie and the firm liable for personal injuries, pain and suffering or other damages inflicted upon concentration camp inmates laboring for them. This endeavor is designed to be the key opening the way to an overall settlement on behalf of all similarly situated concentration camp inmates. . . . For this purpose, I will require as a starting point our old Nuernberg documents. . . . Do you have, or do you know where I can obtain the materials I need to build my bonfire?[57]

Ferencz and the Claims Conference also helped kindle the Krupp justice "bonfire" through the good offices of John J. McCloy. Ben was not the only prominent figure in Jewish civil society who had influence with McCloy. Claims Conference senior vice president Jacob Blaustein, an oil company magnate with VIP access to the White House, was also on very good terms with the former high commissioner and similarly took advantage of the relationship to persuade McCloy to intercede with Krupp so as to facilitate a settlement. Krupp was in McCloy's debt and assigned the new chairman of his corporation, Berthold Beitz, to negotiate with McCloy and the Claims Conference.

After a series of fruitless meetings, the combination of the incriminating Nuremberg evidence assembled by Ferencz, along with McCloy's influence, which extended to having Adenauer also exert pressure, eventually persuaded Krupp to settle. At the end of 1959, as Ben was transitioning to his new practice with Telford Taylor, the parties reached an agreement. Pursuant to its first paragraph, Krupp denied having any legal liability and claimed that he was acting "without prejudice to any other German firm."[58] Nevertheless, he would make "money available to ameliorate the suffering endured by Jewish concentration camp inmates 'as a result of National Socialist action' while they were employed in plants of Krupp or its subsidiaries."[59]

The "available money" consisted of DM 6 million set aside for Jewish claimants who could demonstrate to the Claims Conference that they were Nazi prisoners forced to work for Krupp. If the DM 6 million proved insufficient to compensate each eligible claimant, Krupp would pay up to DM 4 million more. But the agreement specified that Krupp's total obligation would not exceed DM 10 million and that the Claims Conference would guarantee that no further claims would be made against the firm in respect of World War II forced labor.

The Krupp agreement made headlines around the world. On Christmas Eve day 1959, the *New York Times* carried a front-page story under the headline "Krupp Will Pay Slave Laborers."[60] The article quoted a Krupp spokesperson expressing hope that the arrangement would "help 'heal the wounds suffered during World War II.'"[61] The *London Sunday Dispatch* was far less charitable, condemning the agreement as "mean spirited and tawdry" and characterizing it as "the most grasping, clutching, derisory 'gift' in recent memory." The *Dispatch* slammed Krupp for having made a fortune on "the blood and misery and starvation of 12,000 Jewish slaves who worked for him during the war."[62]

As it turned out, and as the Claims Conference feared, the allocated funds were entirely insufficient. There were far too many survivors than Krupp had allowed for in the negotiations. In the end, 3,090 applicants from thirty-three different countries received a total amount of DM 10,050,900. The maximum amount paid out to individual survivors was DM 3,300 marks (about US$825 at the time). About 4,000 applications had to be rejected. Over the 1960s, in the post-*Eichmann* world of heightened concern for Holocaust victims, Ferencz and the Claims Conference pleaded with Krupp to increase the allotted amount due to the unforeseen high number of survivors. Krupp was entirely indifferent and would not make a single additional mark available.

The Quest for Compensation from Other Nazi Slavers

During the first part of the 1960s, with IG Farben and Krupp checked off the list, Ben Ferencz set his litigation sights on obtaining reparations from other Nazi corporate slavers. In large part, the directors of these concerns had not been prosecuted at Nuremberg. Among these was a trio of electrical companies (AEG, Siemens, Telefunken), another weapons manufacturer (Rheinmetall), and the businesses of one former Nuremberg defendant, Friedrich Flick. The pattern for obtaining compensation followed the IG Farben/Krupp template—after Ferencz and the Claims Conference initiated litigation, they "conducted negotiations with the company bosses."[63]

The Electric Companies

As AEG (Allgemeine Elektricitäts-Gesellschaft) had taken over Telefunken in 1941, its chairman of the board, Hans C. Boden, was able to speak for both corporations. Boden had been a Rhodes Scholar at Oxford, a post–World War I reparations diplomat for Germany, and had a reputation for being anti-Nazi. All of that boded well for the Claims Conference's prospects and, indeed, precipitated a swift conclusion to the negotiations in the spring of 1960. The agreement consisted of a simple exchange of letters that stressed confidentiality. AEG recognized no legal liability but, without prejudice to other German firms, promised to pay DM 4 million "to ameliorate the suffering" of Jewish concentration camp inmates who had toiled for AEG or Telefunken during the war. So as to alert potential applicants without revealing the company's name, an ad went out requesting persons to come forward who had engaged in forced labor for any German company during the war. Eventually, 4,000 submitted claims, of which 2,223 were paid the equivalent of US$500 (in early 1960s dollars).

The Siemens negotiations were much trickier. The company, which had without qualms profited from Jewish slaves provided from Auschwitz, Flossenbürg, Sachsenhausen, Buchenwald, Gross Rosen, Ravensbrück, and Mauthausen, initially offered the Claims Conference a meager DM 2 million. Company representatives claimed that they were forced to use the slaves, and, in any event, there were very few of them. Ferencz and his colleagues indignantly rejected Siemens's whitewashing and paltry compensation offer. And they unearthed an internal wartime report, whose existence the business had tried to cover up, titled "The Use of Foreign Civilian Workers, Prisoners of War, Jews, and Concentration Camp Inmates in the House of Siemens."[64]

This new evidence pinned on Siemens the voluntary exploitation of thousands of slaves and brought the company to its senses. Citing mere "moral considerations" but no *obligation*,[65] the firm tripled its initial offer, and the parties signed an agreement on May 24, 1962. Nearly 6,000 forced labor survivors submitted claims against Siemens, but only about one-third could qualify for payment under the restrictive terms of the contract. In the end, with accumulated interest, the Kompensations-Treuhandgesellschaft paid out a total of DM 7,184,100, which, when divvied up, amounted to no more than DM 3,300 per former prisoner.

Rheinmettal Berlin AG

Second only to Krupp in terms of arms production for the Third Reich, Rheinmetall Berlin AG had also been a slave-labor profiteer during the war. In the late 1950s, the Claims Conference filed cases against the company, this time on behalf of Irene Reinharcz and Judith Buls, two Czech Jews selected to be Rheinmettal slaves in Sömmerda, not far from Buchenwald, after the rest of their family members were dispatched to Auschwitz's gas chambers. During the early 1960s, the cases were litigated all the way up to the German Constitutional Court while, simultaneously, the Claims Conference parried with Rheinmettal company officials at the negotiations table.

Significantly, and conveniently, by 1964 the German arms manufacturer was being considered by the US Department of Defense for an important weapons purchase contract. The wily Ben Ferencz and his team figured they could use this as leverage in the negotiations. Thus, in February 1965, the *Einsatzgruppen* trial chief prosecutor was in the Pentagon meeting with Defense Secretary Robert McNamara's top lieutenant, Cyrus Vance. The US government sent subtle messages that a movement in favor of settlement in the slave labor compensation negotiations would be "desirable." But later in 1965, Rheinmettal wrote to the Claims Conference that it could not recognize the "justification" of the claims. The strategy of quiet, back-channel diplomacy, the Claims Conference's typical modus operandi, was then abandoned.

Sharply worded telegrams were sent directly to McNamara and Secretary of State Dean Rusk protesting the purchase of arms from Rheinmettal. The press was also informed, and the *New York Times*'s Sunday edition for February 6, 1966, carried a front-page article whose title featured the words "Pentagon Denounced for Plans to Buy Guns in West Germany." These and other headlines had the desired effect in Washington, DC.[66]

Ratcheting up the pressure publicly got Rheinmettal to move. As if out of a film noir, Ben was soon sizing up an exotic woman who arrived unannounced at his New York office and who, by all appearances, could have passed for the classic femme fatale. As he later recounted:

> An attractive lady of regal appearance, wearing a mink coat with matching mink hat and carrying an alligator handbag over her arm, said she wanted to talk to me about the Rheinmetall guns. She introduced herself as Mrs. John R. Hecht of Vancouver, British Columbia, and said she had some information that I might find of interest. . . . Mrs. Hecht informed me that she had been authorized to transmit an offer from the . . . firm [which] was willing, she said, to pay [DM 2,000] to each inmate who had worked in a Rheinmetall plant in West Germany.[67]

After this Sam Spade–style breakthrough, it finally took a meeting between McNamara and his West German counterpart, acting as proxies for the parties, to conclude an agreement. Rheinmetall's Pentagon contract was in consideration of setting up a fund of DM 2.5 million (about US$650,000 at that time) to compensate slave laborers. As with the other firms, Rheinmettal refused to acknowledge its responsibility and insisted on strict confidentiality. The limited allocation meant that payments would be forthcoming only to Buchenwald-supplied Jewish female slave laborers who had toiled at the Rheinmetall plant of Sömmerda as well as those from the Lodz and Warsaw Ghettos forced to work at the Unterlüß and Hundsfeld plants.

This is why Ferencz considered it a Pyrrhic victory when the May 18, 1966, edition of the *New York Times* picked up the story under the headline "Nazi Victims Win Pay with U.S. Help—Arms Maker to Reimburse Jews Used as Slave Labor." And he felt the sting of Rheinmettal's meager gesture even more when right-wing media, such as the *Deutsche National-Zeitung und Soldaten Zeitung* published stories with headlines such as "Rheinmetall Gave in to B'nai B'rith, 3% of the Armaments Contract Went to a Zionist Organization."[68]

The Return of Flick and a "Medley" of Disappointments

If Rheinmettal's paltry gesture provoked Ferencz's scorn, he was even more outraged by the complete absence of concern from convicted Nuremberg industrialist Friedrich Flick, whose NMT liability stemmed in large part from exploiting slave labor. Flick had accumulated vast wealth by establishing a major industrial conglomerate in the coal and steel industries. He fanatically embraced Nazism—even contributing to a personal fund for Himmler, who once gave him a VIP tour of Auschwitz—and expanded his empire by "seizing companies in Nazi-occupied territories . . . through Aryanizations—the expropriation and forced sale of Jewish-owned businesses."[69] A 2008 study estimates that as many as 40,000 laborers may have died working for Flick companies during the war.[70] At Nuremberg, the industrial baron was found guilty of crimes against humanity and war crimes via spoliation and use of slave labor. But he served not even quite half of a seven-year sentence and was allowed to retain much of his previous wealth. Like Krupp, Flick expanded his empire postrelease, focusing on steel, buying a controlling interest in Daimler-Benz, and becoming a rival to Alfried for the title of Europe's wealthiest man.

To enhance their likelihood of obtaining reparations, Ferencz and the Claims Conference homed in on only the most egregious of Flick's slave labor–fueled enterprises: Dynamit Nobel AG, a company that used Jewish captives to manufacture gunpowder and in which Flick owned a controlling interest. After years of tricky, seesaw negotiations during the late 1960s, an agreement in principle to pay DM 5 million in compensation was reached. But, in the end, Friedrich Flick simply refused to transfer the funds, concluding curtly that there was simply no basis for doing so. "You will never convince us," he coldly intoned.[71]

Other slave labor–tainted German businesses were even less receptive to the Conference's outreach efforts, including those in the aviation industry (Junkers, Messerschmitt, and Heinkel), energy and construction sectors, and a whole host of others participating in the Federation of German Industries. They never meaningfully responded to the inquiries.

Ferencz later referred to these last efforts as a "medley of disappointments."[72] And he might very well have filed them away in his memory to be forgotten. But after concluding his work on the slave labor cases, he was urged by the great Holocaust historian Yehuda Bauer to write a book about his efforts. For the resulting tome, *Less Than Slaves: Jewish Forced Labor and the Quest for Compensation* (1979), Ben collected all his research and notes and reviewed the efforts of the Claims Conference.

In verifying the contents of the resulting manuscript, he reached out to the one person then living with perhaps the greatest inside knowledge regarding the Nazi slave labor program, its coordinator and overseer, the former German armaments minister Albert Speer. It was 1976, and Hitler's former architect and confidante, who at trial had expressed remorse for his actions, had been a free man for a decade after serving his twenty-year sentence at Spandau Prison. The Speer-Ferencz meeting in a lounge near the Frankfurt Airport was cordial, with the erstwhile Nazi bigwig expressing "his satisfaction that he could exchange views with a former Nuremberg prosecutor who was a Jew."[73]

Despite the evidence of hundreds of thousands of them grinding away in impossibly dangerous conditions, underfed, ill-clad, and often tortured, Speer would not acknowledge that Jews were targeted for murder via inhumane toiling (per Speer, it would have been "inefficient to train a man for several months and then work him to death").[74] But he admitted that compensation was justified and that industrialists, such as Friedrich Flick, were wrong in refusing to make funds available (he also later reviewed the manuscript of *Less Than Slaves* and affirmed all of Ferencz's factual claims, often writing reaffirming comments in the margins).

Upon its release in 1979, *Less Than Slaves* was widely praised, winning the 1980 National Jewish Book Award (Holocaust Category). In the tome's powerfully written foreword, Telford Taylor described as "appalling" the response to requests for modest compensation from the "wealthy, powerful" German industrialists who profited from slave labor. He assigned much of the blame to McCloy's clemency decisions and noted, "Despite the ingenuity and tenacity of the campaign that Mr. Ferencz and his colleagues waged, its fruits were a miserable pittance—barely a token."[75] In the volume's conclusion, Ben detailed the pathetic harvest: "Of the hundreds of German firms that used concentration camp inmates, the number that paid anything to camp survivors could be counted on the fingers of one hand. Less than 15,000 Jews received any share of the combined total of under $13 million paid by the few German companies. Even the severe hardship cases of those who had survived work for I.G. Farben at Auschwitz got no more than $1,700 each."[76]

Still Ferencz finished the book on a note of hope and strength: "The evils here recounted, and the failure of so many to recognize them, stemmed not so much from hatred as from an indifference that made it possible for otherwise decent people to accept or ignore what was happening. The last word, as in Genesis, is not hate but what we owe one another."[77] Although the limited reparations of his Cold War–era efforts were not what he had been looking for, Ferencz and his colleagues had, as Edmund Burke described, laid the groundwork for "a revolution of sentiments, manners and moral opinions."

In the post–Cold War world, in class action lawsuits filed in the last years of the twentieth century, inspired, in part, by Ferencz's earlier efforts, former Holocaust slave laborers sought remedies in American federal courts against many of the corporations that had snubbed Ferencz and the Claims Conference previously. The litigation led to a settlement and the creation of a DM 5.4 billion reparations pool called the German Foundation Fund, which was meant to pay about $7,300 each to nearly 200,000 Jewish slave laborer survivors.[78] Ben later put his earlier work into perspective: "The paltry sums eked out for former slave laborers would cost the German firms dearly about thirty years later. . . . There is no doubt that the [Cold War–era slave labor settlements] set a historical legal precedent that those who abuse others in their power have an obligation to make amends."[79]

As Ferencz began rededicating his professional life to Holocaust-victim justice, another important client emerged: B'nai B'rith (the Hebrew term for "Children of the Covenant"). The organization began in New York City in 1843 with the goal of providing economic and social assistance to low-income Jewish citizens, gradually developing into a system of fraternal lodges and chapters throughout the United States and, eventually, the world. When Hitler came to power, he shuttered and seized all the organization's German properties. As Ben Ferencz was ramping up his 1960s reparations practice, he took cognizance of a restitution opportunity that no one had yet considered. Pursuant to the War Claims Act (WCA) of 1948, the United States had a fund consisting of money from the sale of properties on American territory, owned by German enemy nationals, which had been seized by the alien property custodian. The funds were to be distributed to Americans to compensate them for what they lost via Third Reich property seizures.

Ferencz thought B'nai B'rith, which was headquartered in Washington, DC, qualified based on its lost German lodges. So he approached the organization's president, Philip Klutznick (who would later become Jimmy Carter's secretary of commerce), and the latter authorized him to pursue the matter under a contingency fee arrangement.

Ferencz then filed a case with the relevant adjudicative body, the War Claims Commission, which was "very impressed by the creative legal arguments" and issued an award, subsequently affirmed and increased by the Foreign Claims Settlement Commission.[80] The final amount earmarked for B'nai B'rith was nearly $1.5 million, but it came with a big disclaimer: the likelihood that it would never be paid out. Thanks to the adroit lobbying of certain privileged corporate interests, the 1948 War Claims Act had been amended in 1962 to provide them with priority allocation of nearly the entire pot. The evident unfairness of this situation toward nonprofit claimants, such as B'nai B'rith, viscerally offended Ferencz's sense of justice, and he later recalled his mindset: "The wrath of Ferencz was upon the culprits!"[81]

He soon devised a two-pronged attack: initially, he would formulate an amendment to change the law; then, he would develop and employ a lobbying strategy of his own to assure the amendment's adoption. The first part, accomplished early in 1966, was relatively easy. For the second, he decided to bring on board a Christian/Charitable Organization coalition to support his efforts, convening a meeting of various denominations and organizations at Riverside Church in Morningside Heights, near Columbia University (the twenty-nine participants would eventually be known as the Coordinating Council of Religious and Welfare Agencies). Ferencz's "sermon" that day inspired them, and Catholics, Protestants, and secular charities alike agreed to join forces with B'nai B'rith and hire Ferencz as their attorney. The standout among those present was a certain Sister Celestine of the order of the Sisters of Charity, a nun cum lawyer tasked with looking out for Catholic interests.[82]

Next, Ferencz arranged for his amendment, a bill that would have to be passed by both houses of Congress, to be introduced in the lower chamber via Baltimore representative Sam Friedel. Then, with Sister Celestine in tow, he set out for Washington, DC, where he canvased the offices of all the legislators whose support he needed.

More important than Ferencz's lobbying on Capitol Hill, though, was Celestine's away from it. As it happened, the wife of the devout Catholic Speaker of the House, John McCormack, was ill and convalescing in a DC hospital run by the Sisters of Charity. The nun who carried the evening tray, Sister Rosa, had been briefed by Sister Celestine in terms of communicating with McCormack at his wife's bedside. Rosa, tray in hand, would gently ask him,

"And how, pray tell, is our War Claims Bill coming along?"[83] Then she would smile beatifically as she fed the ailing spouse of the influential House Speaker, who would look on in gratitude. Rosa's light-touch lobbying seemed to work. A fired-up McCormack was soon bringing to bear his considerable power in lining up a coalition for passage of the amendment in the House. Ferencz sat in the balcony of that august chamber when the Speaker called the bill for a vote. Everything had been well choreographed in advance. Soon, McCormack slammed down his gavel and shouted, "Passed!"

A delighted Ferencz and team were halfway there, but they still needed to secure passage in the Senate, a much more daunting task. Still, things started well—Ben arranged for New York senator Jacob Javitz to introduce the bill and for Massachusetts senator Ted Kennedy (whose brother, the president, had been tragically assassinated in November 1963) to be its prominent sponsor. The Catholic Kennedy's support was further annealed in meetings with Ferencz and Celestine, whose pious charm won over JFK's youngest sibling.[84]

But despite Kennedy's assistance, and that of Javitz, it soon emerged that the bill was being bottlenecked in the Senate Judiciary Committee, which needed to sign off before it could be presented to the full body for a vote. Kennedy, who was on the Judiciary Committee, met with Ferencz and informed him that the problem was the committee's ranking Republican member, Nebraska's conservative senator Roman Hruska, who had close ties to the corporations counting on taking the lion's share of the seized German-property funds (and who had introduced the 1962 legislation giving them priority). Now the legislator from the Cornhusker State was in Ferencz's crosshairs. Unfortunately for Hruska, his Senate term was expiring that year, which made him more vulnerable than usual.

The former Nuremberg prosecutor fully intended to exploit the situation. First, he met with one of Hruska's aides and advised him that, when his boss returned to Nebraska over the weekend to campaign, he would be met by an eager gaggle of Coordinating Council church representatives asking for his help with passage of the War Claims Act amendment bill. A positive response would likely generate favorable campaign publicity; a negative one, he hinted menacingly, could have the opposite effect. That weekend, Hruska was polite to the church representatives but noncommittal.

Feeling the heat, though, he invited Ferencz to lunch in the Senate dining room the following week. There, over white bean soup and sour milk, they talked about a potential compromise on the bill. In the end, however, after consulting with the corporate lobbyists, Hruska would not budge. Ferencz then called for the Coordinating Council to go all out and use its extensive network to petition as many congressmen and senators as possible to lean on the Nebraskan in advance of an impending vote of the Senate Judiciary Committee.

The following week, Hruska spotted Ferencz in the Senate anteroom and approached him menacingly, demanding, "Who is putting all this pressure on me?" He glared at the diminutive lawyer, and his face grew red as he shouted, "I'd like to know who is putting all this pressure on me?!?" Ferencz replied coolly, "Senator, you have your responsibilities, and I have mine."[85] The Judiciary Committee vote was scheduled for the next day, and Hruska finally conceded to the compromise that he and Ferencz had discussed at lunch. Ben and Sister Celestine were waiting intently in the corridor outside the door of the committee room. Several minutes later, Kennedy threw it open and rushed over to the two Coordinating Council representatives. "What did you do to Hruska?!?" he asked Ferencz with a mix of excitement and bemusement. "I never saw such a flip-flop!"[86]

The bill then sailed through the full Senate. President Richard Nixon signed it into law on Christmas Eve of 1970. For most of the Coordinating Council, it was a great Christmas gift; for B'nai B'rith, it was a Hanukkah present, as December 24 happened to be the third day of the Jewish Festival of Lights. For Ben Ferencz, who had contingency fee arrangements with the various Coordinating Council groups, it would be the biggest payday of his legal career. The scrappy Hell's Kitchen product, the master logistician, the never-say-die lawyer had battled for a decade against the odds and yet again found a new and innovative way of seeking restorative justice for some of Hitler's victims. It only seemed like poetic justice, then, that it also meant he could now afford to put all his kids through college.

In fact, breaking new ground in Holocaust restorative justice became Ferencz's abiding professional passion. As part of working in this survivors' milieu, he would often intersect with the person he thought of as the "spokesman of the victims," Elie Wiesel, his Jewish Transylvanian compadre. They had crossed paths at Buchenwald as, respectively, Holocaust liberator and prisoner. Wiesel had become a world-renowned writer, having penned dozens of Shoah-focused books, including his powerful memoir of survival at Auschwitz and Buchenwald, *Night* (1960). Now the two men often found themselves invited to similar events in the United States, such as Holocaust commemorations and radio shows, interacting, respectively, as Holocaust lawyer and survivor. Ferencz was impressed by Wiesel, whom he described as a living "symbol" who became a remarkably effective "spokesperson" (Wiesel would win the Nobel Peace Prize in 1986).[87]

In the meantime, Ferencz had become a remarkably effective victims' attorney. Continually surveying the reparations landscape in search of Holocaust survivors who had been overlooked or left behind, he was always at the ready for new rounds of outreach, negotiation, or litigation with Hitler's former abettors or the Third Reich's successor states. Reflecting on the discussions that gave rise to the Luxembourg Agreement, it occurred to him that, although West Germany had agreed to bear the direct expense of medical treatment for Shoah survivors, there was no recognition given to private citizens who, or entities that, at great personal expense, had already provided care to those physically and psychically abused by Nazi Germany and its agents. These medical Good Samaritans had been entirely forgotten at Wassenaar. Ferencz decided to take up their cause.

And his initial inquiries to relevant West German ministries bore fruit. The Federal Republic agreed to consider reimbursement if individual victims were legally obligated to repay the charitable organization that had incurred medical expenses on their behalf. Ferencz then got to work examining the voluminous medical records for such organizations and found that many Nazi victims had signed hospital paperwork agreeing to assign monies they might receive to pay for costs. This legal obligation would be the basis for a multitude of Good Samaritan compensation claims. Of the many charities Ben helped make whole, it was particularly gratifying for him to present a sizeable check to the Hebrew Immigrant Aid Society, which had provided succor to his family on their arrival in America.

An even more important segment of victims who had slipped through the figurative reparations cracks were those living behind the Iron Curtain. As a private lawyer, Ferencz first took up their cause in the late 1950s, when "a very nice lady named Caroline Ferriday showed up at [his] office with an interesting plea."[88] A former actress and passionate Francophile, Ferriday had worked on behalf of the French Resistance during the war. Via her relationships with former imprisoned female Resistance fighters, she came to know a group of Polish Catholic women who had been tortured and disfigured through gruesome Nazi medical experimentation at the Ravensbrück concentration camp. These women were known as the "Rabbits of Ravensbrück" for both "the experiments they underwent as well as how they hopped around the camp after sometimes fatal procedures in which dirt, rusty nails, [glass], and other items were inserted into their flesh to test the efficacy of sulfa drugs."[89]

Ferriday had a master plan for helping these unfortunate survivors and wanted Ben's help. Part of the arrangement involved recruiting Norman Cousins, the influential editor in chief of the *Saturday Review,* to bring the women to the United States for plastic surgery. Cousins, a staunch opponent of nuclear weapons, had previously helped arrange for Japanese atom bomb victims—the so-called "Hiroshima Maidens"—to travel to the United States for medical treatment. Cousins was on board, and now he and Ferriday wanted Ferencz to seek German compensation for these expenses as well as for the future medical care of the "Rabbits." Ben enthusiastically accepted the engagement on a pro bono basis and went right to work.

He started flipping through his Rolodex of West German government contacts and making the necessary inquiries. This led to the proposal of a quick, global settlement, but it was a nonstarter for the Germans—they refused to compensate victims within the Soviet sphere. This was the usual lousy start to most Ferencz projects, but his response was equally typical—he refused to brook this Cold War cold shoulder. Thus, once the "Rabbits" arrived in America and received treatment, on Ben's advice, they went on a "tour" across the country, telling their harrowing and heartwarming tale to thousands. The enormous publicity surrounding their visit, in the national and international press alike, stoked great interest in their plight—so, from Ferencz's perspective, mission accomplished. Soon, Ben was contacted by West Germany's ambassador in the United States, followed by an invitation for negotiations in Bonn. The parties then hammered out an agreement setting up a compensation fund.

On June 22, 1960, Adenauer's government passed a special resolution authorizing payments to victims of medical experiments from the East. The FRG, at its own expense, would examine each applicant and pay agreed-upon sums to three different categories of claimants, with the payment amount determined by the severity of the injuries. Ferencz successfully negotiated for compensation in Swiss francs at a favorable exchange rate. As a result, the beneficiaries could spend the money directly for medical care in Switzerland.

The FRG was soon flooded with claims from Nazi medical experiment victims throughout the Eastern Bloc, including Hungarians, Czechs, and more Poles. Several years later, one of Ferencz's West German government inside connections, who was privy to Finance Ministry statistics, reported to him the final amount actually paid to these medical experiment victims. It turned out to be at least ten times more than what he had suggested for a quick global settlement in the first instance.

Of course, hovering in the background of all this was the question of why the East Germans were not contributing. It was not for lack of effort by Ben Ferencz and the Claims Conference. Overtures had been made but rejected. Finally, by 1974, the German Democratic Republic (GDR), the other successor state to the Third Reich, was willing to negotiate with the Claims Conference about Holocaust victim compensation. The US State Department was fully informed and even offered to intervene if needed. Ferencz represented the Claims Conference in these negotiations and would dutifully trudge through Berlin's famous Checkpoint Charlie and back for heated sessions wherein the East Germans would complain that, as Communists, they were also victims of Hitler and should not have to pay anything.

But there was eventually a breakthrough. The GDR lead negotiator had been imprisoned at Mauthausen. As we have seen, Ben Ferencz had been with the forces that liberated that camp. Based on this, he made a heartfelt appeal: "I told him that we were both acting as representatives of others, but since I had risked my life to save his, I hoped we could at least be honest with each other. He agreed."[90] The East Germans were soon asking for the Claims Conference's bank account numbers, indicating that a transfer of funds was imminent.

On Ferencz's next visit, in November 1976, there were liquor bottles and glasses on the bargaining table, and cameramen in the room. The GDR representative read a statement in the name of their "Head of State," to the effect that the East Germans were donating $1 million to the Claims Conference to benefit needy Jews in the United States. They offered a toast. Ferencz replied that he would relay the message. He called Nahum Goldmann in Paris, and the Claims Conference president was insulted by the GDR's paltry, token gesture ("like throwing the dog a bone"). Goldmann called a press conference and blasted the GDR's cheap propaganda stunt while Ferencz hightailed it back to the West through Checkpoint Charlie. Not surprisingly, negotiations were temporarily put on ice.

But Ferencz persevered, and the dialogue eventually resumed. By the late 1980s, after years of tough negotiations, the gap between the parties started narrowing. In October 1988, after secret meetings in New York with GDR foreign minister Oskar Fischer, who had just addressed the UN General Assembly, the East Germans, and the Claims Conference reached an agreement whereby the former would pay the latter $100 million in installments. Ferencz immediately shuttled to Washington, DC, to draw up the necessary legal documents. During this time, the Claims Conference kept the administration of then President Ronald Reagan fully apprised of the negotiations. When Ferencz reported the agreement through the appropriate channels, he received a sharp rejoinder from National Security Advisor Colin Powell vetoing any accord with the communist government.

The Claims Conference was shocked and bitterly disappointed by the response but had no desire to tangle with the US government. Thus, after getting so heartbreakingly close to meaningful GDR reparations after over a decade of great persistence and patience, Powell's injunction effectively killed the deal.

Soon the Berlin Wall would be coming down, and the East German regime collapsed without ever having paid a single pfennig of Holocaust reparations. By then, however, Ferencz had long since shifted his main focus from providing for the victims of the Holocaust to preventing the occurrence of another Holocaust. Those efforts would occupy him for the rest of his days.

PART VI

PREVENTING

18

THE NEW LEMKIN

An ounce of prevention is worth a pound of cure.

—BENJAMIN FRANKLIN

Peace and justice are two sides of the same coin.

—DWIGHT D. EISENHOWER

FOR BEN FERENCZ, if the 1950s and 1960s were about the quest for reparations, the 1970s and 1980s were about the quest for peace. The change in emphasis began even before the presidency of Richard Nixon and reflected an evolution of events and circumstances both external and internal to the life of the former Nuremberg prosecutor. In the world around him, the great awakening for Holocaust victims, which coincided with and was affected by the *Eichmann* trial, became more seamlessly, and progressively, integrated into the collective consciousness. But on November 22, 1963, within eighteen months of Eichmann's ashes being scattered over the Mediterranean, President John F. Kennedy was assassinated in Dallas, Texas. In the aftermath, his White House successor, Lyndon B. Johnson, concerned that he would be considered "too soft on Communism," deepened America's involvement in what came to be known as the Vietnam War.

Since the 1800s, Vietnam had been a part of a Gallic Southeast Asian colonial empire known as French Indochina. After the Second World War, as European possessions in Asia and Africa began liberating themselves from the shackles of colonialism, Communists in Vietnam's northern portion organized a national liberation movement that would morph into a civil war between north and south. After the former's 1954 victory at the Battle of Điện Biên Phủ, per the Geneva Accords, which established an armistice, French Indochina was divided into three new countries: Vietnam as well as the kingdoms of Cambodia and Laos. Vietnam was further subdivided into northern and southern administrative regions, pending elections scheduled for 1956, which were meant to reunite the country under popularly elected Vietnamese leadership. But in 1955, via a fraudulent referendum, the corrupt southern Vietnamese politician Ngô Đình Điệm proclaimed himself president of the

"Republic of Vietnam" and was supported by the Eisenhower administration. North Vietnam, helmed by Communist leader Hồ Chí Minh and backed by the Soviet Union and China, then began referring to itself as the "Democratic Republic of Vietnam." The Vietnam War, the conflict between the two sides, developed into a Cold War proxy battle between East and West. Eisenhower sent advisors to help the staunchly Catholic Điệm and slowly escalated America's involvement in the conflict.

By early November 1963, with Buddhist protests on the rise and general unrest also escalating, the venal and feckless Điệm was killed in a US-condoned military coup, as President Kennedy was ostensibly planning America's gradual withdrawal from Vietnam. But JFK's own murder in Dallas later that month changed all that, and Johnson's escalation of American involvement after winning the 1964 presidential election disenchanted citizens at home. Tensions gradually ratcheted up as greater numbers of young men came back in body bags, leading to large-scale civil unrest, which dovetailed into the concerns of the civil rights movement. The latter, which had been envisaged by Ben Ferencz in his World War II diaries, had begun under the leadership of Dr. Martin Luther King Jr. in the 1950s. But by the mid-1960s, MLK would denounce a war that was "taking the black young men who had been crippled by our society and sending them eight thousand miles away to guarantee liberties in Southeast Asia which they had not found in southwest Georgia and East Harlem."[1] As America looked to the 1968 presidential election, protests spread and turned more violent. After North Vietnam's January 1968 Tet Offensive, punctuated by Dr. King's April assassination, followed two months later by that of JFK's brother Robert, then a New York senator who had been running for president on an anti–Vietnam War platform, the country arguably stood on the brink of a new civil war.

Those were the external events that began to shift the professional and humanitarian concerns of Ben Ferencz. Both he and his law partner, Telford Taylor, decided to take a stand against the war. Following Jane Fonda, Taylor even went to Hanoi with folk singer Joan Baez and others to denounce US involvement in the former French colony. He defended those "charged with conspiring to counsel young men to violate the draft laws" and wrote a book titled *Nuremberg and Vietnam: An American Tragedy* (1970),[2] in which he drew comparisons between the Nazi war crimes prosecuted in Courtroom 600 of the Palace of Justice and those then being committed by American forces in Southeast Asia. (Ben Ferencz would contribute a foreword to a future edition titled "Will We Finally Apply Nuremberg's Lessons?")[3]

Ferencz was "disgusted" by the war, which he later called "crazy" and "illegal,"[4] and he lent his pen to the protest movement. That began rather subtly with a June 1968 article, "War Crimes and the Vietnam War," which appeared in the *American University Law Review.* In it, he published a list of war crimes allegations against the United States, including "wanton destruction of villages, the dropping of napalm bombs, devastation not justified by military necessity, the mistreatment of prisoners and the use of poison gas against old people, women and children."[5] He implicitly reminded American servicemen of the Nuremberg principle "that there is no duty to obey an order which is manifestly illegal."[6] And he similarly warned their superiors that any leader who plans or conspires to commit "inhumane acts" or "political, racial or religious persecution" may be "condemned a criminal."[7] Invoking Nuremberg again, he added, "The fact that an act was done by order of the State or a superior officer will offer no defense if the doer knew or should have known that the act done was in fact unlawful."[8] He concluded by calling for the creation of a permanent "international penal court."[9]

The need for such a court was soon apparent. Not long after the 1968 Tet Offensive, a US Army unit (Charlie Company of the First Battalion, under the aegis of the Twenty-Third Infantry Division) entered the village of Son My, including the hamlet known as My Lai 4. They were tasked with rooting out Viet Cong (South Vietnamese Communist rebels collaborating with the north) in what was thought to be an enemy stronghold. But when no Viet Cong were found, the enraged soldiers nonetheless murdered some five hundred noncombatants, including infants and toddlers, while gang-raping women, slaughtering livestock, and burning huts to the ground.[10] The US Army tried to cover up what came to be called the My Lai Massacre, but certain brave soldiers, cognizant of the horrific war crimes, refused to keep silent.[11] Despite the clear awareness, participation, and complicity of higher-ups, including Captain Ernest Medina, only Lieutenant William Calley, at the bottom of the command chain, was ever successfully prosecuted. Although sentenced to life in prison, three days after his conviction President Nixon had him removed from the stockade and placed under house arrest. And in 1974, Nixon's successor in the White House, Gerald Ford, released Calley on parole.[12]

During Calley's 1970–71 trial, disclosure of the atrocities further galvanized public opinion against America's involvement in the Vietnam War and inspired Ben Ferencz to take up the pen more forcefully. His 1972 article "Compensating Victims of the Crimes of War," appearing in the *Virginia Journal of International Law,* decried the "wrongs on a massive scale [that] have been committed in Southeast Asia," where "large numbers of innocent persons have been the victims."[13] And he urged the United States to "start to plan and prepare the measures which will be required to compensate the victims of war crimes."[14] He even met with Warrant Officer Hugh Thompson, whom

Ferencz described as the "Forgotten Hero of My Lai." A helicopter pilot who had witnessed the massacre from above, Thompson landed in the hamlet and intervened, saving a handful of civilians and reporting the crimes.[15] Ferencz was subsequently supportive of the campaign to belatedly award Thompson the Soldier's Medal for Bravery, which finally happened in 1988.[16]

Also in 1972, Ferencz took on the pro bono legal representation of three Vietnam War protesters in Honolulu, Hawaii. The defendants were known as the "Hickam 3" and included University of Hawaii religion professor Jim Douglas, peace activist and teacher Jim Albertini, and Vietnam War protester Chuck Giuli. They were charged with destroying government property after breaking into Hickam Air Force Base and pouring human blood onto secret Vietnam War files. These peace activists were represented at trial by Ferencz and fellow former Nuremberg prosecutor Mary Kaufman (of the *IG Farben* trial).

At this Hawaii federal court proceeding, held before US District Judge Martin Pence, "Ferencz argued the defendants 'believed crimes were about to be committed by an agency of their government and took such steps as were reasonably possible to prevent the commission of the crimes.' [And he] cited the Hague Convention of 1907 prohibiting 'the use of weapons, such as antipersonnel bombs that cause unnecessary suffering.'"[17] The former *Einsatzgruppen* trial chief prosecutor explained that, in arguing that the defendants were preventing the commission of war crimes, he and co-counsel were presenting the "Nuremberg Defense" by comparing "the defendants to good Samaritans who, on passing a house in flames, must break down the door to rescue the children cowering on the roof. Surely they lacked any criminal intent."[18]

Ferencz and Kaufman were quite successful. Thanks to expert cross-examination, the case against Giuli fell apart and was dropped.[19] In respect of Douglas and Albertini, the prosecutors withdrew the felony charges, which could have resulted in maximum prison sentences of fifteen years. Instead, the protesters were convicted only of misdemeanors, their six-month sentences were suspended, and they ended up paying no fines.[20] Moreover, per Douglas, the former Nuremberg prosecutors were able to get admitted into evidence against the government very damaging documents and testimony.[21]

In the aftermath, the defendants were extremely grateful, with Jim Albertini later writing: "I remember former Nuremberg prosecutors Ben Ferencz and Mary Kaufman with much gratitude and aloha for volunteering to come to Hawaii and help defend our resistance to the U.S. war in Vietnam. Their voice and presence is a blessing I will never forget."[22]

Rewinding the clock a bit to the late 1960s, as Ben Ferencz's attention was being more and more diverted to America's widening military entanglement in Southeast Asia, and the larger issues of war and peace, he was still working as perhaps the world's leading reparations lawyer for victims of the Holocaust. He may not have realized it, but with the new decade of the 1970s on the horizon, he was about to reach a life-altering junction in his life. And at the exact moment he would stand before the proverbial crossroads, Ferencz was in, of all places, Puerto Rico.

It was the winter of 1969, and New York was in the throes of a brutal arctic freeze. The workaholic Ferencz promised Gertrude and their youngest daughter, Nina, that he would get off the road and take them somewhere sunny by the sea. In terms of convenience, proximity, and cost, Puerto Rico fit the bill. So he booked a flight for its capital, San Juan, and, with spouse and child in tow, drove from New Rochelle to John F. Kennedy Airport in Queens. And that is when the Empire State's horrible winter turned even more horrible. The infamous "February 1969 Nor'easter" dumped more than twenty inches of snow in three days (February 8–10), paralyzing New York City and grounding all regional flights. Ben and family were stuck in the JFK terminal, sleeping on benches and scrounging for food. This massive blizzard ultimately took the lives of forty-two New Yorkers.[23] In such awful conditions, the Ferencz paterfamilias "tramped through deep snow searching the airport for food for [his] hungry family."[24]

After three days of such exertion, on little sleep and fewer calories, the San Juan–bound traveler finally found himself on the designated aircraft and felt its measured movement as it taxied on the icy runway and achieved liftoff in the frigid air. Now nearly fifty years old, Ben Ferencz was utterly, profoundly exhausted—so thoroughly depleted that he had never experienced anything quite like it before, not on the battlefields or in the concentration camps or in the courtrooms where his exertions had been so complete, so draining, so overwhelming. By the time of the plane's turbulent descent into the Puerto Rican capital, he thought he felt the life draining out of him.

Quite fortuitously, Ben had learned of a doctor's presence in his cabin section, and he hailed the man for help. On seeing the patient's drawn complexion and dilated pupils, the physician immediately checked his wrist for a pulse. But there was none. The doctor thought the afflicted traveler "was possibly having a heart attack" and "should be rushed to the hospital as soon as possible."[25] On landing, he was taken off the plane in a stretcher, placed in an ambulance, and then rushed to the nearest hospital. But that facility, unfortunately, "had no room. The Intensive Care unit was also completely occupied. The best they could do was to put me on a gurney in the hall."[26]

There, alone in the empty corridor, lying completely immobile in the dark, bracing for the worst, he began contemplating not his next life, but his current one. If, indeed, this was his time to go, what would he be leaving behind? There was much to be proud of, he reckoned: an impressive educational pedigree; an historic contribution to justice as a war crimes investigator, Nazi prosecutor, and Holocaust victims' attorney; and the creation of a beautiful family, with a lovely, adoring wife and four physically healthy children he loved with all of his now weakened heart.[27]

Could his spirit hover over the ceremony, that would have been the panegyrical account he might have hoped to hear at his funeral. But he knew there was more. The calamitous event that had shaped, if not defined, most of his life, World War II, had been both a wellspring of opportunity and achievement and an abyss of pain and dysfunctionality. His time in the army had been pivotal, not just for how it formed him as a war crimes investigator and future prosecutor but also for how it marked him emotionally and, to a certain extent, socially.

Liberating the concentration camps had taken a terrible toll on him. And that had repercussions for his family life. In many ways, in terms of being a parent, he had been able to overcome the psychological scarring from that trauma. His kids have fond recollections of their early years with him. On Saturday mornings, they would wake up and watch cartoons, their ears on alert for the unlocking of the master bedroom door. On hearing it, the four tykes would burst in, jump on their parents' bed, and they would all lovingly tussle and wrestle, laughing and having fun. At other times, Ben would play "King of the Mountain" with the children. He would dangle a handkerchief in front of them, daring them to pry it from his hand. And they would end up in a huge pile on the floor, laughing and squealing with delight.

In addition to making sure his children were having fun for fun's sake, he was equally concerned with mixing education into their amusements. He would buy them books with great works of art, and they would affix stickers to the pages to identify the Great Masters and the titles of their creations. And, to give them a grounding in classical music, he would put them in front of the television to take in Leonard Bernstein's *Young People's Concerts* with the New York Philharmonic. No doubt with fond recollections of his own childhood excursions on the town with "Uncle Dave," Ben would take each child on a "date" to Manhattan, rotating weekends among the four little ones, often treating them to lunch at the Horn & Hardart automat.

When not overseas for his job, Ben would cook the children meals on the evenings Gertrude was at school (she attended classes at night for degrees in social work from Hunter College [bachelor's] and Herbert Lehman College [master's] throughout the 1960s). Ben's evening culinary specialty was hamburgers. And he would prepare breakfast for the kids on the weekends, typically including his signature dish of sardine salad. Eldest daughter Keri later observed that it was "a weird thing for breakfast, but, you know, we were used to it."[28]

Thus, Ben's early days of parenthood were relatively pleasant and tranquil. As the children started maturing and taking on more individualized personalities, though, tensions arose. The onset of adolescence within the Ferencz brood inevitably brought emotional highs and lows. But "Pop," as the kids called him, had trouble dealing with the latter. And much of it could be traced back to his wartime experience. His daughter Keri has explained, "In our household, we always . . . had to be happy because, you know, we weren't in a concentration camp. What did we have to complain about?"[29] She added, "My dad is not very supportive. [He] can really ridicule people and make them feel small. And my mom would always say, 'Oh, you know, he loves you. He doesn't mean it that way.' But . . . that never gave me any support at all. . . . I would bring home my grades and he would always say, 'You can do better than that.'"[30]

Robin, born the year after her older sister, recalls that, as teenagers, she and Keri would go out at night and return later than Ben thought was appropriate. She notes that he "thought we were punishing him. . . . He used to threaten us, would hit us and [yell], saying, 'Why are you doing this to me?' He had his own view [that] children should be seen and not heard. . . . He didn't want to know us as individuals."[31]

Keri and Robin were sent away to St. Christopher's, a Quaker boarding school in England. But they returned after only one year, and so did the children-parent problems. At one point, the two girls ran away, hitchhiking to a commune in Maryland. But they never reached their destination. In Virginia, they unwittingly asked an off-duty police officer for a ride, and he arrested them for truancy because, per Keri, like their father, they were very short of stature.[32] Before coming to their rescue, Ben let them stay in juvenile detention for a few days to "scare them straight." But it was the 1960s—Keri continued to rebel and was experimenting with drugs. She was again sent to boarding school, this time in Connecticut. And, once she reached majority age, she distanced herself from her family, taking up a peripatetic "hippie" existence, eventually settling in Berkeley, California.

The two younger children, Don and Nina, were also affected. The latter describes certain traumatic childhood experiences related to her father that were grounded in his work on the Holocaust:

> My mother was in college at night. . . . [My] father would come home, and he fixed us dinner. And he'd tuck us into bed. And he would tell us bedtime sto-

> ries that went like this: "I tuck you in bed. Two men come into the house with bayonets. They throw you and your brother out the window because you're too small to bother with. They shoot me in the head. They take your sisters away. And have a good night. . . ." So one of the other things that he used to do [was] take us individually [Don and Nina] into the bedroom. He locked the door. He pulled out the suitcase [with graphic photos he had taken at the concentration camps]. When I was eight years old, he gave me an envelope of bones from Auschwitz and said, "Happy Birthday! Take good care of these. It's probably one of your cousins."[33]

Don confirms being shown the gruesome concentration camp photographs as a child. And his dad would often "describe the horrors of the Holocaust—graphic details such as Jewish families being massacred and babies having their heads smashed against trees."[34] All of this took a toll on the younger siblings as well. Nina admits that she would often "sleep under the bed so when the Nazis came they wouldn't find me."[35] She adds, "My entire framework hinged on this notion that . . . I'm supposed to be dead."[36] For years, Don would wake up in the middle of the night screaming from nightmares of being attacked by Nazis.

But Ben's focus on World War II affected more than just his relationship with his children. His marriage suffered as well. We have seen that, during the war, when he was away from Gertrude and, for certain stretches when her letters were not arriving regularly, the lonely GI found solace in the arms of other women. That pattern continued as he worked as a Holocaust reparations lawyer, back on the road again in Europe, still immersed in the dark mental milieu of World War II. According to his daughter Robin: "[We] were living in New Rochelle and he was going to Europe. He asked my mother to go with him. And she didn't. He always asked her, 'Will you come with me?' . . . And she didn't go with him. . . . When we were young, and my father was frequently absent, my mother really held the family together."[37]

On these grim voyages, while ensconced in the minutiae of the Shoah, his loneliness intermingled with powerful childhood memories. In later discussing his extramarital affairs, Ben pointed to his upbringing in a home with parents in a miserable, arranged marriage and a mother, whom he adored, ultimately taking one of their former boarders as her lover.[38] His father had dalliances, including with a patient of the doctor who lived with them. And, for a small but formative portion of his boyhood, right after his parents' divorce, he lived in a home where his mother's sister, Tante Fani, who was also in an unhappy, arranged marriage, was sleeping with one of her boarders.[39]

These early life remembrances impacted him, he later confided.[40] Intimacy outside of matrimony did not seem terribly taboo.

And so, during his bleak, solitary days of Holocaust reparations work, there were "opportunities," he later acknowledged, to be intimate with women while "on the road."[41] And at times he took advantage of them. His youngest daughter, Nina, who, of all the children, developed the closest relationship with Gertrude, relates that her mother told her that she was aware of her husband's infidelity.[42] Ben himself acknowledged that he had been forthright with Gertrude about his dalliances (one of which was with a particular German woman over a period of many years).[43] And Nina said that her mother "was telling me in the course of these various conversations that [my dad] was a player."[44] At one point, Nina explains, "she was . . . crying, telling me she wanted a divorce."[45]

But Gertrude thought better of it. She told Nina she wanted her "children to have the best life they could have, and they wouldn't have the best life they could have if I was divorced."[46] And Ben never stopped adoring his wife, always putting her on a pedestal whenever they were together. According to Nina, "there is no doubt in my mind that my father worshipped my mother" and loved her "fully."[47] And this was not lost on Gertrude, who told Nina that she knew eventually Ben would have to get off the road. And then, she added, "he'll be all mine."[48]

So, as he lay there on the gurney in that dim Puerto Rican hospital corridor, taking stock of all that had been good and bad in his half century of existence, it would seem he had an epiphany: much of what had been so troubling in his adult life could be traced back to World War II and the Holocaust. Of course, those pivotal events in history had been equally pivotal to his own growth and development—in fact, his entire professional identity had been forged in the fires of those cataclysms. They made him who he was and gave him a central mission in life. But he had been on that mission now, much of it on the road, away from his family, for nearly thirty years. Maybe it was time to stop. Maybe it was time to leave that dark place. He had given much. He had learned much. He had achieved much. Perhaps now was the opportunity to change course. But, all the same, he knew how crucial his work had been to those seeking justice for the horrific crimes of the Shoah. He needed more time to think.

Somehow, despite his serious brush with death, he made it through that long, tenebrous night, seemingly suspended in time and space. By morning he could feel his body starting to heal. Later that day, while reclining on a chaise lounge on a patch of lawn adjacent to the hospital, a bandaged boxer was sprawled out on a similar wicker contraption next to him. He had just been beaten to a pulp in a prizefight and was nursing his wounds. Grousing to Ben about his lot in life, he let on that he was thinking of getting out of pugilism. There had to be a better way to earn one's keep, he said, than getting physically abused all the time. And then the proverbial light bulb went off in Ben's head—he realized that, from a mental perspective, he felt the same way about his own work.

Whether consciously or not, he was returning to his nocturnal thoughts on the gurney and developing them further. At great personal cost, he had given his all to seek justice for the victims of the Holocaust. But the defendants convicted of crimes against humanity by the Nuremberg Military Tribunals (NMTs) who were still alive had by then been set free.[49]

And, more specifically, those NMT defendants whose supply of armaments had been responsible for enabling Hitler's crimes against peace, including Alfried Krupp and Friedrich Flick, had never even been convicted of those particular offenses. It will be recalled that in May 1946, while working on the industrialist cases in Nuremberg, he had told Gertrude that, among other reasons, "IG Farben and Krupp and their officials should be hung as war mongers." He added, "I'm sure we'll be able to prove that they desired and planned for war." And he then he concluded, "I feel a certain satisfaction in the work as though we are groping for the roots of war causes. And perhaps we may move a little closer thereby toward permanent peace."[50]

Ferencz had given his all in preparing those cases as an investigator (and as chief of the Berlin Branch), and he was then a courtroom prosecutor for the *Krupp* trial. But the acquittal of these industrialists for crimes against peace, as well as their early releases for crimes against humanity, had infuriated him. And, despite his recent litigation efforts, those corporate enslavers still alive were now paying only a pittance or, like Friedrich Flick, nothing at all for their exploitation of innocent Jews so Nazi Germany could carry out its acts of aggression.

His hopes at Nuremberg for criminal justice in reference to this genocidal enabling of Hitler's war machine, and in the 1950s and 1960s for related civil justice, had been dashed (with failed negotiations with Flick as recent as the previous year and into the beginning of 1969).[51] And now the Vietnam War was responsible for even more depredations committed by his adoptive country. But why focus on all that? Those wars, and their attendant crimes, had not been prevented. It was too late. What might be done about potential wars in the years ahead? It dawned on him that "the only satisfactory solution to the problem of having to compensate victims for war crimes is to avoid warmaking itself."[52]

And so, at last, he began to see things clearly. He knew what course he would be taking. Like the battered boxer next to him, it was time for a major career change. He had been in the dark hospital corridor thinking about the dark aspects of his career. Now he was in the light, and he could feel somewhere deep inside that it was time to stop working on the crimes against peace and humanity of the past and apply himself to preventing those of the future. War, he realized, was the breeding ground for atrocity and so much other misery. War was a scourge that had to end. He would work toward making that happen. He would work for peace. "The next two weeks," he later wrote, "were spent lolling in the sun, chatting with my family, and watching the waves. I spent the time on Candado Beach contemplating life and death, and the possibility that my time had run out; and perhaps I had been given another chance."[53]

THE REVELATION in San Juan did not translate into a sudden and stark change in Ferencz's professional life. But a favorable financial situation permitted a gradual scaling back of the Holocaust reparations work. As he later observed, "By living frugally, we had managed to save some money which we had invested cautiously [primarily through the stock market]. I had no fear about striking out in a new direction."[54]

The real challenge for the transition lay more in mastering the new subject matter and successfully engaging with it. He began in the library.[55] Having done some foundational reading, he then contacted his erstwhile Wassenaar negotiating partner, Jacob Robinson, for advice on next steps. The great jurist expressed regret that Ferencz would be phasing out the reparations work but was encouraging of the younger man's idea of establishing a permanent international criminal court with jurisdiction over the crime of aggression. Giving Ferencz his blessing, Robinson, who had been a member of the Israeli delegation to the United Nations, cautioned him that the idea of creating such an institution had been the brief of the UN's International Law Commission (ILC), even while the Nuremberg Trials were unfolding. The project had stalled, though, and Robinson was not sanguine about its long-term prospects.

Undeterred, Ferencz picked the brains of human rights experts as well. He had met René Cassin, Nobel Peace laureate and a principal drafter of the 1949 Universal Declaration of Human Rights, at a ceremony honoring the latter in New York City. Ben had served as the French Jewish jurist's interpreter that night, and they had remained in touch. He was very encouraging of his former translator's proposed endeavor.

His law partner, Telford Taylor, was equally enthusiastic and advised him to consult with Yale law professor Myres McDougal, whose 1961 publication *Law and Minimum World Public Order: The Legal Regulation of International*

Coercion (cowritten with Florentino Feliciano) had inspired Ferencz. At the start of their meeting in New Haven, the former Nuremberg prosecutor described his tentative plan of going back to school to earn an advanced degree and pursue peace advocacy as a legal academic. McDougal counseled against it, offering that Ferencz was likely too long in the tooth to secure a law professor post. He suggested writing books and lobbying policymakers about the subject instead. So that is exactly what Ferencz resolved to do. This "led to an intense and extremely productive career as a publicist, lecturer and unpaid advocate for peace."[56]

WITH HIS newfound focus, a second round of intensive study led him to the locked basement three stories below the UN's main library at its headquarters on the Hudson River, where he found a vast collection of books and archives devoted to peace studies. He was able to gain access to this subterranean treasure trove, otherwise off-limits to the public, as a member of a nongovernmental organization accredited to the UN (initially via the Coordinating Board of Jewish Organizations and then the American Society of International Law). Within the bowels of its successor, then, he immersed himself in the historical minutiae of the League of Nations' efforts to maintain peace and security during the interwar years. And then he traced the progression of the still-fledgling UN's similar efforts in the aftermath of World War II and during the Cold War. As well, he consumed all the legal scholarship on the topic he could. He was soon nearly as conversant in the history, language, theory, and law of peace studies as he had been on atrocity prosecution and reparations.

But his time as a budding peace advocate was more than just academic. With practically unfettered access to UN Headquarters, he took full advantage by attending official meetings and conferences related to his new area of expertise. He even participated in a peace studies conference at Wingspread, a Frank Lloyd Wright–designed estate in Wisconsin, where discussions were led by Chair Louis Sohn (a Harvard law professor whose 1958 book, coauthored with Grenville Clark, *World Peace through World Law,* was part of the peace advocacy canon). And activities were not limited to the United States either, with Ferencz also spending time at the Max Planck Institute in Heidelberg and going to UN meetings in Geneva.

Via his studies and engagement with UN committee work, he started getting a handle on the key initiatives related to the global community's normative efforts to maintain peace and prevent war. From his library and archival work, he knew the League of Nations had botched its mission "to achieve international peace and security"[57] largely because it failed to flatly revoke the right of states to resort to war; rather, member states were merely required to submit any interstate disputes for arbitration or seek other forms of judicial settlement at the League's Council. Assuming such procedures came up short, the nations of the world could still legally wage war against one another.

The UN Charter was better, outlawing the use of force in Article 2(4) absent Security Council authorization (with a limited right of self-defense enshrined in Article 51), and authorizing the Security Council to act in cases of "aggression" (roughly, the unauthorized use of force by one state against another). But there was no definition in the Charter of the key term "aggression," which would inform the Security Council as to when it would need to act. And such guidance was crucial. For example, the Council needed to know exactly what was meant by "use of force." And even if that aspect could be fleshed out, use of force vis-à-vis what? Was it as against "territory" only? And which state agents would be responsible for wielding the force? These were among the many questions that had to be answered.

Some work on the definition had begun, but the project had stalled given the Cold War's polarizing effects. Various martial flashpoints, such as the Suez Crisis (1956), the Cuban Missile Crisis (1962), the Congo Crisis (an early to mid-1960s civil war with US/Soviet proxies, after the Belgian colony achieved independence), the Vietnam War, and the Soviet occupations of Hungary (1956) and Czechoslovakia (1968), gave rise to opposing notions regarding the desirability of defining aggression. Thus, the ILC's nascent efforts to date had come to naught.

But, as fate would have it, when Ben Ferencz had his career-changing epiphany in Puerto Rico, serious efforts were finally under way at the UN to define exactly what was meant by unauthorized state use of force—not coincidentally, perhaps, while the Americans and Soviets were engaged in the talks that would lead to the 1972 Strategic Arms Limitation Treaty (SALT) and usher in a period of Cold War "détente." Thus, his timing was propitious, and he decided to throw himself into the project entirely: to become, in effect, a one-man lobbying campaign for the adoption of a consensus UN definition of aggression. As he later described it: "I began . . . regular attendance at various UN aggression committees [and would collar] diplomats in UN corridors [and would] write memos and law review articles exposing what was happening, and suggesting various ways to get out of the quagmire in which distinguished representatives were wallowing."[58]

His persistent and aggressive (as it were) tactics certainly ruffled feathers. Much of the UN effort centered on the work of the Special Committee on the Question of Defining Aggression. During one tension-filled 1971 Special Committee meeting Ferencz attended in Geneva, the Egyptian delegate, whose country was then contemplating how to take back by armed force territories it lost to Israel in the 1967 Six-Day War, rose in anger, referencing in a raised voice the fact that it was a closed meeting, and requesting the former Nuremberg prosecutor's eviction. The delegation from Cyprus intervened and "saved the day" by inviting Ben to join them.[59]

And so it went for the next couple of years, with Ferencz becoming more and more active in the process (with many calling him "Mr. Aggression").[60] He began crafting and circulating compromise proposals and publishing these in high-profile outlets, such as the *American Journal of International Law*, the *Columbia Law Journal*, and the *International and Comparative Law Quarterly*. Practically stalking officials and experts in the world assembly's corridors and meeting rooms, drafting proposals, and lobbying delegates, he had unwittingly become a kind of new Raphael Lemkin in respect of aggression.

Like the great Polish jurist, psychologically scarred from World War II and obsessively making efforts to speak to anyone he could regarding genocide, a similarly scarred Ferencz was engaged in comparable efforts in New York and Geneva regarding what Robert Jackson and his prosecutors saw as the "supreme international crime."[61] That Ben had personally been on the other end of such efforts vis-à-vis Lemkin at Nuremberg, and had helped Lemkin via his references to the crime of genocide at the *Einsatzgruppen* trial, made his early 1970s campaign seem all the more fitting and poignant.[62]

And, like Lemkin, Ferencz saw his dream realized. By 1974, as he was ratcheting up the pressure (and, quite helpfully, after the Americans had withdrawn combat troops from Vietnam the previous year), the pace had quickened. Between March 12 and April 11, 1974, the Special Committee on the Question of Defining Aggression held nine meetings to hammer out a final definition. All signs pointed toward the members reaching consensus, which they did, on April 12, auspiciously Good Friday. Ferencz, who had been there in the thick of the debates, told Gertrude that history was about to be made and to join him at UN Headquarters. Thus, the formidable husband-and-wife team of Nuremberg was there in New York to partake of international law history again when the Special Committee at long last signed off on a definition of aggression.

The key provisions of the end product were, at once, supple and comprehensive. The document's Article 1 began with a broad description of aggression: "the use of armed force by a State against the sovereignty, territorial integrity or political independence of another State, or in any other manner inconsistent with the Charter of the United Nations." Article 3 then enumerated specific examples, including invasion, attack, occupation, annexation, bombardment, and blockade. Article 4 specified that the list was not exhaustive and that the Security Council could determine that other acts constituted aggression.[63]

That Ferencz played a prominent role in the crafting of such a wide-ranging but legally sound definition was evidenced by the Special Committee's asking him to join them for the official photograph commemorating the achievement. He was the only nonofficial to be so included. And the fruits of that group's efforts were realized on December 14, 1974, when the UN General Assembly adopted by consensus Resolution 3314 (XXIX), annexing the Definition of Aggression formulated by the Special Committee.

Paragraph 4 of Resolution 3314 drew the attention of the Security Council to the Definition and recommended that the Council "should, as appropriate, take account of that Definition as guidance in determining, in accordance with the Charter, the existence of an act of aggression."[64] In the years since, the Definition has been an essential link in the chain of doctrinal development. The International Court of Justice, the UN's judicial arm, has held that a portion of it reflects customary international law.[65] And, over three decades later, the Definition became "a crucial building block for the crime of aggression" within the jurisdiction of the International Criminal Court.[66] In that, once again, Ben Ferencz would play a central role.

In the meantime, Ferencz sought to solidify and promote the gains made at the UN. He took up his pen once more to produce what turned out to be a trilogy of books on aggression and the law enforcement infrastructure needed to prosecute it (and related crimes) and maintain peace. At the same time, by the mid-1970s, his reparations work was being slowly phased out. His law partner, Telford Taylor, had also been transitioning out of law practice and into a full-time professorship at Columbia Law School. Over the nearly thirty years that the two men had known each other, they had grown quite close.

And the depth of their relationship was about more than just work. In the mid-1960s, for example, when Taylor's extramarital affair with a Danish diplomat resulted in a pregnancy, Ferencz became Taylor's closest confidante.[67] With Ben's guidance, Telford decided to come clean about the situation with his wife, Mary, and support his lover in whatever decision she made about the pregnancy. Thus, a daughter was born to them in 1965 and, with Ben's encouragement, became a loved and accepted part of Telford's family.[68] In the end, his law partner and most trusted advisor at Nuremberg proved equally invaluable as his wise friend. So when Telford's marriage with Mary finally crumbled in the early 1970s, Ben was there for him in a similar capacity (Telford and Mary finally divorced in 1972).[69]

But by the mid-1970s, both men were moving in different directions professionally and slowly drifting away from their law partnership. By the early 1980s, when Taylor, Ferencz & Simon was finally winding down,[70] Ben was working from a dedicated office in his New Rochelle home. He had already written the seminal first tome of what I will refer to as his "aggression trilogy," the two-volume *Defining International Aggression: The Search for World Peace—A Documentary History and Analysis* (1975).[71] In this sense, he was different from Lemkin—the great Polish jurist wrote his seminal book on genocide—*Axis Rule in Occupied Europe: Laws of Occupation, Analysis of Government, Proposals for Redress* (1944)—*before* undertaking his lobbying campaign for legal codification. Ferencz flipped the script with aggression. In 1974, as the UN was finally adopting the definition to which he had contributed so much, he was writing *Defining International Aggression.*

This was a great summative work encapsulating the fruits of his intensive 1970s research, and it included all the key source documents. The digest's first volume chronicled the watershed moments in the League of Nations' futile quest to define as well as assure international peace and security as well as the UN's mission to do the same in the immediate aftermath of World War II. The second volume then examined the UN's Cold War efforts to define aggression leading up to the adoption of General Assembly Resolution 3314. The nearly 1,300-page book has become "a practical and indispensable working tool for experts, politicians and students,"[72] which provides an insider's perspective on the "crafting and honing" of aggression's definition.[73]

After taking a break to write *Less Than Slaves* (1979), Ferencz followed up *Defining International Aggression* with its necessary complement, a treatise on creating an enforcement mechanism. *An International Criminal Court: A Step toward World Peace—A Documentary History and Analysis* (1980) traced the history of proposals relating to the establishment of a permanent world penal tribunal. Volume 1, titled *Half a Century of Hope,* chronicled efforts to establish such an institution in the half century leading up to World War II; volume 2, titled *The Beginning of Wisdom,* covered efforts from 1945 through the end of the 1970s. Based on this comprehensive account, Ferencz suggested how the global community could move forward in converting prior proposals into modernly feasible doctrinal and procedural architecture.

In the book's introduction, sizing up this second part of Ferencz's aggression trilogy, Louis Sohn included the author among a pantheon of giants in the discipline: "The efforts in this field in the inter-war period by such eminent lawyers as Elihu Root, Henri Donnedieu de Vabres, Vespasien V. Pella, Constantin T. Eustathiades and Antoine Sottile, have now been joined by a new group, to which belongs the author of these volumes, Benjamin B. Ferencz."[74] The trilogy's second volume "helped [our] understanding [of] how the creation of a permanent international criminal court could generalize and operationalize the individual criminal responsibility for the crime of aggression, which the creative precedent of Nuremberg had introduced into the international legal order."[75]

Importantly, the book exerted a profound influence on one of international criminal law's most significant contemporary figures, David Scheffer, America's first ambassador-at-large for war crimes issues and its chief negotiator for what turned out to be the International Criminal Court treaty. Before that, as chief advisor to UN Ambassador Madeleine Albright, Scheffer also played a significant role in the creation of the ad hoc tribunals for the former Yugoslavia and Rwanda. And, later on, he innovatively helped devise other "hybrid" international criminal courts (mixing domestic and transnational personnel and features), including the Special Court for Sierra Leone (prosecuting atrocities committed after November 30, 1996, during Sierra Leone's 1991–2002 civil war) and the Extraordinary Chambers in the Courts of Cambodia (prosecuting Khmer Rouge crimes). In the early 1980s, while based in Asia, Scheffer was breaking in as a junior international lawyer with the Coudert Brothers firm. The books of the second volume of the Ferencz trilogy helped educate him on international criminal law and courts and how the latter should be constructed. According to Scheffer, "Those books were inspirational to me. . . . As a practicing international lawyer, I would turn from my usual corporate and banking work . . . and I would sort of escape to Ben Ferencz. . . . I didn't know Ben; I just knew the books. Little did he know that there was this international lawyer sitting in Singapore [educating himself] with Ben's transformative books."[76]

The final book in the trilogy, *Enforcing International Law: A Way to World Peace—A Documentary History and Analysis*, was published in 1983. If the first book helped define the substantive crime of aggression, and the second book demonstrated how to set up a court to prosecute that crime (and others flowing from it), then the third explained how such a court could be backed up through enforcement mechanisms. It concluded with suggested nostrums for strengthening existing enforcement mechanisms and deploying new ones. It proved invaluable for putting "the prospect of integrating the first two books' doctrinal and procedural recommendations into the larger framework of the greater international system of enforcement."[77]

In fact, the trilogy has been a cornerstone in the development of the law of aggression and related enforcement mechanisms. Professor Claus Kress, who played a pivotal role in negotiations leading to the criminalization of aggression in the Statute of the International Criminal Court, puts this into perspective:

> Ben's 1975–1983 "aggression trilogy" represents one of the foundational works in the history and scholarship on the development of the law against aggression. . . . When the issue of the crime of aggression was prominently put back on the international community's agenda in the post–Cold War period, and leading up to the negotiation of the Rome Statute in 1998 and the Kampala Amendments in 2010, the Ferencz trilogy served as one of the important bedrocks upon which new generations of scholarship on aggression could be developed. . . . [H]e has made groundbreaking and lasting contributions on multiple levels.[78]

After the publication of *Enforcing International Law,* Gertrude, who had provided invaluable assistance researching and proofing the trilogy, "suggested that [her husband] stop producing such big tomes and write something that normal human beings could understand."[79] Ben could only chuckle, but he wholeheartedly agreed. Inspired by Thomas Paine's 1776 Revolutionary War pamphlet *Common Sense,* which, in a mere forty-seven pages, used simple but persuasive prose to encourage the American colonists to break from Great Britain and fight for an egalitarian government, Ferencz next published *A Common Sense Guide to World Peace* (1985). Its message, delivered in a comparably compact manuscript, was the opposite—urging its readers *not* to fight.

As such, the small paperback was dedicated to "those leaders of the United States and the Soviet Union who will have the courage and the wisdom to overcome their fears and reconcile their differences, so that all who dwell on this planet may live together in peace and dignity regardless of their race or creed."[80] Part 1 of the book summarized the history covered in the trilogy's weighty tomes within forty-two pages. Part 2 covered the policy recommendations of the trilogy in fewer than thirty pages. Part 3 rounded out the book and set out practical measures (such as engaging in arms control, educating the public, and reforming the Security Council). The entire work came in at under one hundred pages (minus the endnotes and index).

The follow-up book was *PlanetHood: The Key to Your Future* (1988), cowritten with Ken Keyes Jr. The genesis of the work was noteworthy. Soon after publishing *A Common Sense Guide to World Peace,* Ben's home office phone rang, and, when he picked it up, he heard a strange voice on the other end say, "This is Ken Keyes calling from Coos Bay, Oregon, and you are the hundredth monkey!"[81]

At first Ben thought it was a prank call and nearly hung up. But the caller immediately, and efficiently, launched into an explanation, saying that fundamental changes in collective thinking and behavior were brought about by groups reaching a critical mass pursuing a common goal. He cited the example of monkeys and sweet potatoes. The primates struggled for generations, he explained, to learn the best way to remove sand from the sugary tubers. The hypothetical "hundredth monkey" discovered how to do it by rinsing them with water. This last primate achieved cognitive critical mass among the world's collective simian population—almost simultaneously, through some unexplained process, monkeys all over the globe independently arrived at the same conclusion (a kind of "sweet spud synchronicity," as it were). Keyes said this process applied to humanity in terms of discovering how to end the nuclear arms race (as expressed in his book *The Hundredth Monkey* [1982]). Having just read *A Common Sense Guide,* Keyes, who had also written dozens of spiritually oriented self-help empowerment books, felt that Ferencz was the "hundredth monkey" for nuclear disarmament and world peace.

Keyes then proposed that he and Ferencz write a book together. The wisecracking New Yorker took a dim view of this apparent hippie-dippie self-help guru from the West Coast. "Never having met a monkey before, I concluded he was crazy. Hoping to avoid further involvement, I asked Mr. Keyes to send me a memo. To my surprise, a few days later, his response arrived."[82]

Keyes laid out a serious proposal, and, much to his own surprise, Ferencz agreed to the partnership. In 1988, they published *PlanetHood* (riffing on the word "nationhood" to inspire persons to see themselves as "global" citizens rather than just national ones).[83] The book's cover posed a list of eight questions: "Do you want to: (1) Reduce your tax burden? (2) Create world prosperity? (3) Eliminate international war? (4) Rescue the environment? (5) Stop terrorists and hostaging? (6) Preserve your liberty and freedom? (7) Give your children a future? (8) Reform the United Nations to enforce international law?" The bottom of the cover read, "PlanetHood shows how!"

In parallel, the book was then divided into eight "steps to lasting peace and prosperity." Those self-help measures involved various individual actions to protect the environment, prevent war (via instituting a world government), establish a leadership role in the community to effectuate those goals, recognize and promote the twentieth century's advances, such as the human rights movement, reform the UN (such as by abolishing the Permanent Five's veto in the Security Council), communicate with fellow global citizens about these measures, and give oneself credit for doing all of the above (via awarding oneself a peace prize).

As this rather folksy approach indicates, the paperback was meant to appeal to the largest reading public possible. Its introduction stressed that the work was not copyrighted and could be reproduced without any obligation to the authors. And the text featured thematically appropriate quotations from famous persons inserted in large boxes at the margins of every page. As its eye-catching cover suggested, Keyes was adept at promoting the book—hundreds of thousands of copies were soon distributed, and it was eventually translated into several languages. Through it all, Ferencz had never met his coauthor in person—their communication had been strictly via telephone and written correspondence. A couple of years after *PlanetHood*'s publication, Ferencz was finally able to lay eyes on the man who had dubbed him the "hundredth monkey." And his later description of the encounter is touching:

> [Ken] called to say that he was coming to lecture in New York and he would be pleased if we could meet.... When I arrived to pick up my guests, Ken's wife, a robust and smiling young lady, met me at the door and asked me to wait until she came back with her husband. In a few minutes she returned, carrying in her arms a beaming old man with a neatly trimmed beard and sparkling eyes. Ken Keyes, the man who was so full of love, hope, and optimism, was quadriplegic. He weighed 70 pounds and was completely paralyzed [due to polio].[84]

Ferencz's final sole-authored work on peace was *New Legal Foundations for Global Survival: Security through the Security Council* (1995). The book struck a balance between the Brobdingnagian proportions of the aggression trilogy and the Lilliputian scale of the two peace books that followed. Updating the previous works of the 1970s and 1980s with a post–Cold War perspective, Ferencz called it "the culmination of over 20 years of intensive study."[85] And UN Secretary General Kofi Annan praised it as "a remarkable work that could 'further the cause of the United Nations and its aims of peace and justice.'"[86]

For twenty years, Ferencz the author had compiled an impressive body of work on how to define aggression, how to punish it, how to enforce the punishment, and how to prevent the crime from being committed in the first place. Along the way, he sought to disseminate his scholarship through the lecture circuit and classroom teaching. In fact, by the mid-1980s, he had a regular adjunct professor gig at Pace Law School in White Plains, New York. A member of its law faculty, Blaine Sloan, had urged him to lecture there, and it seemed like a good fit. During the 1980s, Ben's son Don and his daughter Nina earned law degrees from the same institution. So the paterfamilias thought it made sense to expand the Ferencz presence there. From 1985 through 1996, he taught a course titled "The International Law of Peace" one evening a week.[87]

But he wanted to do more and later noted: "The third-year law students who chose to study 'The International Law of Peace' were generally grateful for the inspiring experience. . . . [But i]t was always clear that it would take more than teaching a few students for a few hours a week to bring about the changes needed to save civilization from its own annihilation."[88] What was needed, he decided, was a kind of peace institute. Thus, he worked with the law school administration to establish the "Pace Peace Center."

The potential was there, but the project never really took off. Its major stumbling block was fundraising. Modest donations came in from some former law clients. But efforts to bring in serious money from the big charitable foundations and the US government (via the US Institute for Peace—an organization whose 1984 establishment Ferencz supported and for which he testified before Congress) came to naught. Still, the Center managed to survive by running a scaled-down operation out of the Ferencz homestead, with Gertrude serving as executive assistant.

Through such economizing, Ben and Gertrude were able to scrape together enough cash to organize the Center's flagship event: a June 1990 weeklong colloquium with Soviet experts, UN officials, and prominent peace advocates to discuss Soviet premier Mikhail Gorbachev's proposals for peace. However, to put it mildly, the event did not live up to expectations. In particular, the focal point for the colloquium, the USSR's experts, were not up to snuff. "They had all written books related to law," Ferencz later noted, but, at dinner on the night of their arrival, "they seemed more interested in getting drunk."[89]

Over the next few days, meetings at the Pace satellite campus in Pleasantville, New York, as well as a roundtable at UN Headquarters, yielded recordings in "heavily accented Russian-English" that amounted to "20 reels of unintelligible gibberish."[90] Ferencz extracted the best of it and put it in manuscript form, which resulted in *World Security for the 21st Century: A Colloquium between American and Soviet Legal Experts* (1991). It soon drew bad reviews, which provoked no animosity in its editor, who later quipped, "Conferences among persons with no authority, with other people who have no authority, might be a way to pursue peace, but not to attain it."[91] Even worse, the Peace Center was by then cash-strapped and being accorded pariah status by the university; the Ferenczes decided to shut it down.

But new opportunities were appearing on the horizon. If 1991 saw the demise of the Pace Peace Center, it also saw the birth of US-Russian peace. The Soviet Union was dissolved in December after a failed August military coup against Gorbachev by Communist hard-liners inspired Boris Yeltsin to rally democrats and establish the Russian Federation. The Cold War was finally over. And there was an arguable ascendency of Western liberal democracy, an apparent final flourishing in the evolution of human government, which Francis Fukuyama famously, and prematurely, called the "end of history."[92]

But the irenic veneer was not to last. With the dissolution of the bipolar order, internecine tensions at the local level, which had been put on ice during the Cold War, started to heat up. Soon, ethnic cleansing in the Balkans and genocide in Rwanda would awaken the world to an ugly new reality of the multipolar world. And Ben Ferencz would be transformed from largely forgotten Nuremberg prosecutor to celebrated prophet for peace. Remarkably, before the decade was out, and owing much to his efforts, his dream of a permanent international court with jurisdiction over the crime of aggression would be realized.

19

CREATING A PERMANENT COURT IN THE ETERNAL CITY

> Yes, I have finally arrived in this city, the capital of the world. . . . All the dreams of my youth now seem alive.
>
> —Johann Wolfgang von Goethe

It is hard to imagine even the most impassioned and credible seer convincing Ben Ferencz at the start of the twentieth century's last decade that a permanent global court with possible jurisdiction over the crime of aggression would be created before the dawn of the new millennium. As the calendar pages turned to January 1990, the world had only once experienced the creation of true international criminal tribunals—the then-seeming anomalies at Nuremberg and Tokyo in the aftermath of World War II. And they had been temporary.

In 1947, the year after the IMT's judgment at Nuremberg and before the IMTFE's in Tokyo, the United Nations General Assembly charged the International Law Commission (ILC) with drafting a "code of offences against the peace and security of mankind" (Draft Code of Offences). The ILC was also tasked with codifying the "Nuremberg Principles"—the key norms to be titrated from the IMT's Charter and Judgment, such as recognition of the core crimes and individual responsibility for committing them, rejection of superior orders and head of state immunity as defenses, and the right to a fair trial.[1] As well, within a couple of years, the task of drafting a Statute for the Establishment of an International Criminal Court (Draft ICC Statute) was assigned to two UN special rapporteurs.

The ILC's draft of the Nuremberg Principles, whose norms, in general terms, the UN General Assembly had already embraced as international law via Resolution 95(I) (December 11, 1946), was without controversy and saw the light of day by 1950. The other two projects did not fare as well. As Jacob Robinson had broadly suggested to Ben Ferencz when they met post–Puerto Rican epiphany, the Draft Code of Offences eluded completion due to a lack of consensus on defining "aggression."

To surmount this hurdle, the task of formulating the definition was farmed out to the Special Committee on the Question of Defining Aggression. In the meantime, Cold War conventional wisdom called for a finalized Draft Code of Offences before the formulation of a Draft ICC Statute. This was presented as "cart-before-horse-avoidance" logic since, as the argument went, a criminal enforcement mechanism should not precede the crimes it was meant to enforce. More plausibly, this inefficient fragmentation of codification efforts was the product of global Cold War bureaucratic sabotage in that, seeking to avoid subordinating "their sovereignty to an international criminal tribunal," the world's two major hegemons and their allies implicitly agreed that "neither one of these endeavors should proceed in a cohesive and coordinated fashion."[2] And thus, both projects languished for the balance of the 1950s and 1960s.

Ben Ferencz helped inject new life into the undertaking through his work with the UN Special Committee and their success in finally defining aggression in 1974. The former Nuremberg prosecutor then got to work on his "aggression trilogy" of books, hoping that it would help prod the UN into finally completing the Draft Code of Offences and then the Draft ICC Statute. But fundamental Cold War realities had not changed, and the codification projects stalled once again.

In the meantime, despite Nuremberg and the "Never Again" pledge, and in addition to the war crimes committed in the Korean and Vietnam Wars, government-sponsored mass murder of innocent civilians continued, seemingly unabated. Many refer to President Sukarno's 1965–66 bloody anti-Communist purge, in which up to one million people were killed, as the Indonesian Genocide.[3] The 1970s arrived, and nothing changed—with the new decade bringing fresh outbreaks of state-sponsored mass violence. In 1971, as the majority-Bengali-speaking exclave of East Pakistan sought independence from the central-government-controlling and majority-Urdu-speaking West Pakistan, the latter's military forces and local militias, trying to foil the breakaway attempt, murdered up to three million civilians and raped up to 400,000 women, as part of the Bangladeshi Genocide (whose victims also included Hindus).[4]

In Burundi, a minority-Tutsi-controlled government crackdown on Hutu dissent in the spring and summer of 1972 led to "one of the most gruesome genocides experienced by an African state" when up to 300,000 Hutus were massacred.[5] From 1975 through 1979, Pol Pot and the Khmer Rouge, seeking to impose a utopian agrarian society by force, murdered more than one million urbanites, the well-educated, and ethnic minorities in the "Killing Fields" of the Cambodian Genocide.[6] Starting in 1975 and lasting into the 1980s, Operation Condor, a coordinated campaign among right-wing South American dictatorships (including that of Chile's Augusto Pinochet) to disappear, torture, and murder "leftists," claimed the lives of approximately 80,000 civilians and put a half million political prisoners into brutal detention centers.[7]

There were similar bloodbaths in the 1980s. During the decade's first three years, the Guatemalan army and its right-wing paramilitary allies slaughtered more than 100,000 Mayan peasants.[8] And in the "Anfal" campaign, Saddam Hussein targeted northern Iraq's Kurds for destruction, via chemical weapons, as part of his Iraqi Arabization program—during the first few months of 1988, the attacks destroyed 2,600 villages and put between 50,000 and 100,000 gassed civilians in mass graves.[9]

By 1990, the fall of the Berlin Wall and the crumbling of the Soviet Union might have signified that the international community was ready to start normatively addressing such horrors. But the state of paralysis would have likely endured had not two fresh paroxysms of intercommunal violence in the early part of the new decade, one in the Balkans and the other in Africa, galvanized public outrage and engagement. Unlike the Cold War atrocities, ethnic cleansing in the former Yugoslavia and genocide in Rwanda took place as the world was basking in the perceived glow of Francis Fukuyama's "end of history" moment, enhanced by a global-consensus military expulsion of Saddam Hussein's invading Iraqi army from Kuwait. It was a rare instance of world harmony that was shattered, in part, by the Balkan and African atrocities. So, the planet's citizens were paying attention this time. And their calls for action were intensified, and sustained, by another post–Cold War phenomenon, the so-called "CNN Effect," whereby instant images transmitted via 24/7 news coverage increased "the impact" and inspired the public "to demand that 'something be done,' and done now."[10]

Finally awakened by these calls from the Cold War carryover lethargy that rendered it a passive bystander during the carnage in the former Yugoslavia and Rwanda, the United Nations began mobilizing. The Security Council dispatched to the Balkans a Commission of Experts, led by the international criminal law guru M. Cherif Bassiouni, and soon learned that the origins of the crisis there could be traced to the 1980 death of Yugoslavia's Josip Broz Tito. The ethnically mixed war hero's legend and outsize personality had been the glue holding together the nonaligned Communist country's diverse Serbian, Croatian, Muslim/Bosniak, Slovenian, Macedonian, and Albanian peoples. But with Tito's passing, and the waning of Cold War unity, old irredentist enmities began flaring up. By the early 1990s, as the Soviet Union was coming apart, so too was the Socialist Federal Republic of Yugoslavia. The regions of Slovenia and Croatia declared independence in June 1991 and Bosnia and Herzegovina followed suit the next March.

In response, the Serb-dominated Yugoslav People's Army lashed out, and Serb politicians, such as Yugoslav president Slobodan Milošević and Bosnian-Serb leader Radovan Karadžić, sought to carve out Serb-only living spaces. Army and paramilitary units enforced this through "ethnic cleansing" in Bosnian enclaves peopled with Muslims and Croats. Subjecting these groups to threats and violence (including murder, rape, torture, imprisonment, and destruction of property), they drove them out of their homes.

Soon, what had been the Socialist Republic of Bosnia and Herzegovina was convulsed by atrocity—concentration camps were set up to detain those being ethnically purged, the new government's seat, Sarajevo, was subject to the longest siege of a capital city in the history of modern warfare (with Bosnian-Serb army snipers picking off scurrying civilians from the tops of the hills ringing the urban center), and Croat and Bosniak forces were engaging in ethnic cleansing of their own. By the beginning of 1993, the death toll from war crimes and crimes against humanity in the former Yugoslavia was mounting into the six figures. The ghosts of the Holocaust were returning to Europe, and world leaders, persuaded by the recommendations of the Commission of Experts' February 1993 report calling for the creation of an international penal body, agreed that the UN should do something about it.

On May 25, 1993, via Resolution 827, the Security Council established the International Criminal Tribunal for the former Yugoslavia (ICTY). As part of its remit to maintain peace and security, the Council empowered the ICTY to prosecute "persons responsible for serious violations of international humanitarian law committed in the territory of the former Yugoslavia" from January 1, 1991, through a date to be determined by the Council. The Resolution contained the Statute of the Tribunal, which laid out its structure, procedure, and prosecutable offenses.

And, indirectly, Ben Ferencz played a role in its creation. In particular, one of the Statute's principal drafters, Virginia Morris,[11] an attorney with the UN Office of Legal Affairs, was guided in her efforts by the second installment of Ferencz's aggression trilogy, *An International Criminal Court: A Step toward World Peace.*[12] Ben later recounted a special moment of recognition for his influence: "Within a matter of months, the formation of such a court was approved. I happened to be in Geneva visiting the International Law Commission when the Security Council text was faxed to them. As soon as it was received, the administrative assistant, Armella Ferrara, handed the copy to me, saying, 'Here, this is your work.' I was grateful for her kind consideration and I felt richly rewarded."[13]

The fruit of that work would soon be needed to deal with even more ferocious internecine violence on the African continent. On April 6, 1994, an airplane carrying the president of Rwanda, Juvenal Habyarimana, was shot down as it was about to land in the nation's capital, Kigali. The Rwandan leader, a member of the majority Hutu ethnic group, had been returning from a UN-sponsored summit in Arusha, Tanzania, with leaders of a rebel group of the country's Tutsi minority. The rebels were part of a large Tutsi diaspora that had fled the country after it gained independence from Belgium in 1962. Serving as Belgium's local managers, the Tutsis had held power during the colonial period. But once Rwanda gained sovereignty and the Hutus took the governmental reins, the resentful majority group massacred large numbers of its former overlords, causing many of them to flee to neighboring countries.

By 1990, an armed group of these Tutsi refugees, the Rwandan Patriotic Front (RPF), invaded from Uganda. The incursion was ultimately repulsed, but it sparked new rounds of violence against Tutsis who had remained in the homeland. Undeterred, the RPF continued its military efforts until Habyarimana was ready to sign a peace deal, the Arusha Accords, which would have allowed the rebels to be integrated into the government and armed forces. When the presidential plane was shot down on returning from Arusha in April 1994, Hutu extremists appeared responsible.

What followed was one of the most horrifying orgies of mass violence in human annals. The extremists formed a rump government, armed militias with machetes, fired them up with hate speech on government-sponsored radio stations, and then unleashed them on innocent Tutsi civilians with instructions to destroy the entire ethnic group. The RPF resumed fighting, and by the time it reached Kigali and put an end to the slaughter in late July, approximately 800,000 Tutsis and moderate Hutus had been butchered, many of them brutally hacked to death. A small UN peacekeeping mission, which had been stationed in Rwanda to help enforce the Arusha Accords, witnessed this ninety-day spasm of genocide and called for international assistance but got none.

By year's end, the awful magnitude of what had happened in Rwanda at last penetrated the international community's conscience, and the Security Council established the International Criminal Tribunal for Rwanda (ICTR) via Resolution 955 (November 8, 1994). In large part, the ICTR Statute, which focused on prosecuting those most responsible for genocide and "other such violations" during the calendar year of 1994, and which was attached to Resolution 955, was a replication of its sister tribunal, the ICTY (with which it would share an appeals chamber). Thus, once again, Ben Ferencz's handiwork, via the influence of his magnum opus on creating a world tribunal, played a role in the post–Cold War revivification of the international criminal law project to whose initial launch he had contributed so much at Nuremberg.

BUT THE creation and operation of these new ad hoc tribunals constituted only part of global penal law's rebirth. The main project Ferencz had been assiduously pushing since Nuremberg—the establishment of a *permanent* international criminal court via the UN's various drafting endeavors—also played its part. He had made important contributions to the UN's formulating a definition of aggression, believing that filling in this lexical lacuna would lead to the completion of the Draft Code of Offences against the Peace and Security of Mankind (and then, logically, a draft ICC Statute). But, despite his best efforts, as well as those of others in the field, the nations of the world could not be shaken from their collective inertia. And then an interesting opportunity presented itself.

At the 1972 Wingspread peace studies conference in Wisconsin, Ferencz had met and befriended Arthur Napoleon Raymond (A. N. R.) Robinson, a politician from Trinidad and Tobago who asked his new friend to call him "Ray." After the conference, Ben and Ray stayed in touch, and the latter kept abreast of the former's work on aggression and the proposed creation of an international criminal court. The Trinidadian became a staunch supporter of the ICC proposal and, with Ben's encouragement, decided to contribute toward kickstarting the stalled UN work on the Draft Code of Offences and Draft ICC Statute. Ferencz and German law professor Robert Kurt Woetzel worked with Robinson, by then the prime minister of Trinidad and Tobago, to draft a proposal for the creation of a permanent ICC that was presented to the 44th Session of the UN General Assembly in late 1989.[14] The Trinidadian leader pitched the proposal as a means of dealing with "growing narcotics related terrorism" that threatened to overwhelm "the resources of small countries and could intimidate law enforcement and judicial officials."[15] He argued that "international action was necessary for prosecuting and punishing offenders who command the means to evade the jurisdiction of domestic courts."[16]

It worked. The matter was then referred to the International Law Commission, where the project was slowly brought back to life. It initially aimed to reprise work on the Draft Code of Crimes (changed from "Offences" and then possible thanks to the 1974 Definition of Aggression). And the project picked up steam after the world became aware of the atrocities in the former Yugoslavia and the Security Council had created the ICTY. The Europeans began pressing for the establishment of a judicial institution to enforce the Draft Code of Crimes. Finally, in 1993, the General Assembly obliged them, instructing the ILC to give priority to the preparation of a permanent ICC draft statute.[17] This time, the ILC, which had already been engaged since the Commission of Experts' 1993 report on Balkan atrocities and had been quite active behind the scenes, worked quickly and delivered a Draft Statute the following year. Accompanying it was a recommendation that a conference of plenipotentiaries be convened to conclude a treaty to set up this new penal institution.

Upon receipt, the General Assembly set up an Ad Hoc Committee, which met for a couple of sessions in 1995 to iron out some issues in the ILC's Draft Statute. Then, in December 1995, the Assembly established a Preparatory Committee, which solicited the views of UN member states and prepared a "widely acceptable consolidated" treaty text as the springboard for negotiations at the envisaged conference.[18] Between March 1996 and April 1998, the Preparatory Committee (Prep Com) met for six separate sessions that lasted a total of fifteen weeks. During this time, it solicited the views of UN member states, taking into account a wide array of proposed amendments.

Ben Ferencz was an active participant in this process. And his involvement was through various channels and manifested itself in various ways. One of his most symbolically powerful avenues for contributing was in confederation with his fellow American Nuremberg prosecutors. In 1996, Whitney Harris founded the Committee of Former Nuremberg Prosecutors for a Permanent International Criminal Court, which, in addition to Ben, included Ted Fenstermacher, Cecilia Goetz, Bill Jackson (Justice Robert Jackson's son and one of his chief lieutenants at Nuremberg), Henry King, and Drexel Sprecher.[19] Harris, Ferencz, and the other IMT/NMT veterans offered to assist the UN based on its "collective experience at the Nuremberg Trials . . . to contribute to the negotiations currently underway . . . calling for the establishment of an International Criminal Court and also to hearings which will follow in the Senate of the United States if a treaty is ultimately proposed."[20]

Ferencz also participated in his individual capacity via the Coalition for the International Criminal Court (CICC), a network of nongovernmental organizations (NGOs), including, among others, Amnesty International and Human Rights Watch. The CICC was headed at the time by Bill Pace, who had had a long history of working with NGOs and the World Federalist Movement on human rights and international criminal law issues. Its headquarters were across the street from the UN building in Manhattan.

Through his involvement with the CICC, Ferencz was able to take part in Prep Com sessions and impart his insights to key state representatives, such as David Scheffer, senior advisor to Madeleine Albright (then US ambassador to the UN). According to Scheffer, Ferencz was a tireless and valuable advisor: "I became head of the U.S. delegation [and] he would intersect with me. [He] was a relentless lobbyist for the accountability of the exercise of creating an International Criminal Court. And so, he was sort of the memory of Nuremberg that was always with us as we worked our way through."[21]

Given his Nuremberg stature, Ferencz also operated outside of the CICC's framework, meeting with government officials on his own initiative, including on trips to the Netherlands, France, and Germany. Via these activities, he was able to make an impact in three primary ways: (1) urging incorporation of aggression into the court's subject matter jurisdiction; (2) advocating for inclusion of victim provisions (that is, for participation in proceedings and compensation), along with ideas on how best to draft them; and (3) using his celebrity to persuade state delegations to generally embrace the idea of a permanent court and fight for its creation. Regarding the last of these, one of Ferencz's most noteworthy endeavors was to act as a liaison between civil society and the ad hoc tribunals, especially the ICTY. Thus, in May 1997, he wrote that his "recent international penal activities center around obtaining support for the ad hoc tribunals for Yugoslavia and Rwanda and working for a permanent [ICC]."[22] Toward that end, he made efforts to cultivate a relationship with the ICTY president (that is, chief judge), the great Italian jurist Antonio Cassese.

In August 1996, Ferencz met with Cassese, and they discussed how the former Nuremberg prosecutor could raise awareness and support for the creation of the ICC by engaging in activities that would strengthen the ICTY. Ferencz believed this was a top priority because "a vital step toward a permanent international criminal court requires a successful ICTY," and, thus, he would do everything in his power to "further both objectives."[23]

Undertaking a brand-new and resource-deprived mission whose success was against the odds had always been his specialty. And even though he was now in his late seventies, he still had the energy for it. Thus, as he had done as a new war crimes investigator for General Patton, as a prosecutor at Nuremberg, as a reparations lawyer for Holocaust victims, and as an advocate for defining and criminalizing aggression, Ben dived into this new assignment headfirst. In short order, he arranged for a pro-ICTY broadcast on Dutch TV, news stories in Agence France-Presse, a letter in the *New York Times*, a lecture at the UN, commentary on CNN International, and messages posted on the internet.[24]

In response to Ferencz's beehive of activity, Cassese wrote him a letter noting that he was "delighted" with and "grateful" for his efforts and agreed that "a successful ICTY would represent an important step towards a permanent Criminal Court."[25] And he responded positively to Ferencz's suggestion during their meeting that, in order to boost awareness of its work, the ICTY start posting its publicly available documents online.[26] The relationship between the two men grew over the next year (and beyond—in 2009, the two jurists would be chosen as cowinners of the prestigious Erasmus Prize, awarded to those who make "especially important contributions to culture, society, or social science in Europe").

As Ferencz was working hard to support the ICTY, Cassese found a way to express his appreciation in a most august and public setting. On September 18, 1997, in delivering the ICTY's Fourth Annual Report to the UN General Assembly, the Italian jurist paid tribute to Ferencz by quoting from his *Einsatzgruppen* trial opening:

> It should also not be forgotten that the persons remaining at liberty who have been indicted by the Tribunal have been charged with extremely serious crimes—genocide, "ethnic cleansing", mass rape, murder of defenceless civilians. In the words of Benjamin Ferencz, Prosecutor before the United States Military Tribunal II sitting at Nuremberg: "If these men be immune, then law has lost its meaning and man must live in fear."[27]

Ferencz responded with a letter to Cassese on November 18, 1997, expressing his appreciation and providing an update on his activities:

> I wanted to thank you personally for [quoting] from my opening in the *Einsatzgruppen* trial. . . . Last night, at the annual Blaine Sloan Lecture at Pace Law School, I used your report to illustrate that it may take fifty years before dreams can move closer to realization but young people should never stop trying to make this a more humane world.
>
> Upon the success of the ICTY depends the hopes for a permanent international criminal court. Last week I met with [former] President [Jimmy] Carter as well as David Scheffer and President [Bill] Clinton's representative on the National Security Council and others discussing what can be done to create an effective permanent international court. [Such] meetings . . . are designed to stimulate public interest and support. Yesterday, a fax from our friend [then ICTY prosecutor] Judge [Richard] Goldstone in Braamfontein contained invi-

tations to attend high-level meetings in Europe and Washington to campaign for the arrest of those indicted by the ICTY. You should know that you do not stand alone.[28]

As for advocating in favor of inclusion of the crime of aggression in the ICC treaty, the evidence of Ferencz's efforts during the Prep Com phase is ample. For example, in his notes taken during the August 1996 sessions, he wrote, "I pitched for inclusion of aggression as core crime and cited new French position paper and Draft Code of Crimes by the [International Law Commission]."[29] Those familiar with Ferencz, the man whose early 1970s campaign to define illegal war had earned him the moniker "Mr. Aggression," would be little surprised to learn of these efforts in the lead-up to the diplomatic conference for a negotiation of a permanent international criminal court.

But that perception of Ferencz obscures an equally important mission he undertook during the Prep Com phase: ensuring that the court recognize and take care of victims' interests. In accord with the common law tradition (for example, the legal culture of the United Kingdom and its former colonies and consistent with the Nuremberg Trials constitutional documents), the ad hoc tribunals for the former Yugoslavia and Rwanda had essentially ignored victim participation/reparation, focusing instead on the guilt and due process rights of the accused. Granting victims an official juridical role at trial and awarding them compensation is a feature of civil law countries, such as France, Germany, and numerous states in Asia, Africa, and Latin America, where Continental European influence rubbed off via colonialism and/or admiration.

The key victims' rights provisions of what would become the treaty for the permanent international criminal court, Articles 68(3) ([Victim] Participation in the Proceedings) and 75 (Reparations to Victims), were inserted/supported by the French during the Prep Com phase (Egypt, in line with France, was the initial proponent of Article 68[3]).[30] In the words of one of the key members of the French negotiating team, Gilbert Bitti, of the French Justice Ministry, France "played a significant role in ensuring a new, and, as far as possible, central place for victims before the ICC."[31] In his own words, "within that delegation, this author was in charge of monitoring the victims' rights negotiations."[32]

Ferencz's contemporary notes reveal that he met with Bitti during the Prep Com phase in 1996.[33] Then, in June 1997, he traveled to Paris and met with French officials there (his notes suggest a meeting with Bitti at the Justice Ministry, as he jotted down Bitti's address there on a separate piece of notepad paper,[34] and he explicitly recalled meetings at the Foreign Ministry). He reported to Bill Pace that he met with the head of the French delegation, Marc Perrin de Brichambaut (then head of the French Foreign Ministry's Legal Division), with whom he was able to have "substantive discussions."[35] In respect of these meetings with the French regarding victim provisions, Ferencz later noted that he "was pushing because, you know, [concern for victims] was . . . in my blood."[36] He also described how he was able to contribute:

> There was a recognition that victims should be compensated. . . . I was already highly experienced, the most experienced man in the world on that topic. And so mostly it was just done through . . . meetings. . . . I said, "Put something in. Put something in." And the—it never occurred to them, Who's going to pay for it? And how much? And where? Who is going to qualify? Who's going to check out whether the conditions have been met? How do you do it organizationally? How do you do it worldwide? All of which we had gone through.[37]

In the meantime, Ferencz was closely tracking the progress of the victims' reparations provision of the developing drafts of the ICC treaty. Toward the end of the Prep Com phase (that is, April 1998), in a document with various provisions of the ICC draft treaty that bore the date "Monday 15 March 1998" at the top, Ferencz marked the entry "A/AC.249/1998/DP.19; Proposal by France and the United Kingdom of Great Britain and Northern Ireland [by then, the United Kingdom had joined France in pushing for this provision]; Article 66 [45 bis], Compensation to victims" with the words "Barely Adequate."[38]

By then, the UN General Assembly had scheduled the diplomatic conference of plenipotentiaries to be held in Rome, Italy, from June 15 to July 17, 1998. For Ben Ferencz, it was another opportunity to return to Europe and help make history. Gertrude, who had steadfastly supported him during all his struggles and triumphs on the continent of their birth, would be there by his side. Those gathered in Rome knew how important he had been as a living symbol of the Nuremberg Trials and as a "voice in the wilderness" advocate for a permanent international criminal court through the darkest days of the Cold War. Since the final 1949 NMT judgment, alone among Courtroom 600's podium prosecutors, Ferencz had vociferously, persistently, and single-mindedly championed the creation of a permanent global penal court, right up until that pivotal moment in Rome.

The delegates wanted to give him a place of honor where he could inspire them from the outset. So he was asked to address the conference as it was opening. And, picking up on his concerns about proper provision for victims as he prepared to depart for Rome, he led off his speech invoking them:

> I have come to Rome to speak for those who cannot speak—the silent victims of monstrous deeds. . . . Over fifty years ago, I stood in a courtroom at Nuremberg and accused 22 high-ranking German Storm Troopers of deliberately murdering more than a million men, women and children. The defenseless victims were slaughtered because they did not share the race or creed of their executioners. I asked the tribunal to affirm the legal right of every human being to live in peace and dignity. It was a plea of humanity to law—a plea that needs repeating.[39]

Then, reprising his opening sentence and faintly echoing Shakespeare's version of Marc Anthony's great "I have come to bury Caesar" speech in the same city more than two thousand years previously, but with a view toward ICL *resurrection* rather than burial, Ferencz continued:

> I have come to Rome to plead for a more humane world order.
>
> Nuremberg was the beginning of a process. Failure to build on its precedents has cost the world dearly. Once the political will was aroused, the Security Council was able—in 1993 and 1994—to establish competent criminal courts quickly to bring perpetrators of genocide and crimes against humanity in the former Yugoslavia and Rwanda to trial. But limited ad hoc courts created after the event is hardly the best way to ensure universal justice. A permanent court is needed for permanent deterrence. The time for decisive compromise has come.[40]

He then invoked the subject that mattered to him as much as taking care of past atrocity victims, the very thing he thought would prevent there being *future* such victims, criminalizing aggression to ensure world peace:

> I have come to Rome to speak for Peace.
>
> Ever since the judgment at Nuremberg, it has been undeniable that aggressive war is not a national right but an international crime. War is the soil from which the worst human rights violations invariably grow. The UN Charter prescribes that only the Security Council can determine when aggression by a state has occurred but it makes no provision for criminal trials. . . . Excluding aggression from international judicial scrutiny is to grant immunity to those responsible for "the supreme international crime"—omission encourages war rather than peace.[41]

He then concluded with rousing words to inspire the delegates to see their mission through to the end:

> I have come to Rome to encourage your noble efforts.
>
> [Never] lose faith that the dreams of today for a more lawful world can become the reality of tomorrow. Never stop trying to make this a more humane universe. If we care enough and dare enough, an international criminal court—the missing link in the world legal order—is within our grasp. The place to act is here and the time to act is now![42]

Ferencz later noted that, at the speech's conclusion, the audience "broke out in sustained applause."[43] And the "stirring peroration" had its intended effect.[44] According to Liechtenstein's current ambassador to the United Nations, Christian Wenaweser, who served as his country's representative at the Rome Conference:

> [Of] course, his time as a prosecutor made him unique and combined with his wartime experience and the fact that he had worked years and years and years before, tirelessly, when he was a lone voice. He had always said "We need this." And that gave him such an immense credibility. . . . I mean, the Rome conference, in some ways, was a unique event, as far as . . . the collective energy and the dynamic that prevailed . . . this enormous sort of collective feeling "We can get this done." [And] you know, of course, [Ben's speech played] a very important part there.[45]

Soon, the hard-core negotiations started. And the challenges were daunting. The point of departure was a massive document—the ILC's 128-article Draft Code of Crimes with proposed alternative language provided by states in 1,700 brackets across the collective text. This behemoth, a dissonant jumble of conflicting proposals, needed to be reconciled among the 160 participating countries in a mere five weeks.[46] But the conference organizers, led by chair Philippe Kirsch of Canada (known as "The Magician" for "the many compromises he seemed to pull out of thin air"),[47] organized the work quite efficiently. Much of it proceeded at the lower level in "working groups" and "informal negotiating bodies" toiling on various issues and subissues "from early morning until late at night."[48]

And it was in "walking the corridors" and "making interventions" with these working groups,[49] informal negotiating bodies, and at times, high-level diplomats, that Ferencz was able to impart the message of his opening speech directly into the ears of individual actors working around the clock to transform his decades-long dream into reality. Besides helping delegates forge ahead on aggression and victims' rights, he also inspired them with foundational issues, which, in his view, would be integral to the court's future success, for example, rejection of a "consent regime" (that is, additional approval by a state for prosecutions beyond its ratifying the treaty), inclusion of a prosecutor who could initiate investigations on her own, and limits on Security Council interference with the court's functioning. These more "progressive" positions (including codification of the aggression offense), opposed by superpowers such as the United States and China, were championed by the so-called "like-minded" states from Africa, North and South America, Asia, western and eastern Europe, and Oceania.

Ferencz became a symbolic ambassador for this group. In one sense, as an American citizen, he was "taking his own delegation to task."[50] But, in another (with him often humorously describing himself as a "nongovernmental individual"), he transcended national identity, acting as he did in opening the *Einsatzgruppen* trial, as a representative of all humanity. In the words of Morten Bergsmo, a leading expert in international criminal law who was the ICTY's representative at the Rome Conference and later became chief of the ICC Prosecutor's Legal Advisory Section:

> [Ferencz] was a man with real moral authority during the meetings of the Preparatory Commission and also at the Conference and at the inter-sessional informal meetings and bilateral processes that took place. . . . He was not just the embodiment of the legacy of the Nuremberg tribunal and judgment and the efforts to codify firm principles of international law and to build an International Criminal Court, but he was a person who transcended the limitations of states, their delegations, and formal manner of communicating in a multilateral forum like this. He was not there as an American. He was not there as a member of the western European [delegations] or as a member of the like-minded group. He was there, in a way, representing another form of sovereignty, mainly that of the aspirations of people around the world.[51]

But his participation also had a concrete impact on specific issues. In particular, apart from his support of French efforts regarding victims' provisions, his most important contribution was using his celebrity and influence to assure that the crime of aggression was within the treaty's ambit. Christian Wenaweser described this quite succinctly, and powerfully, in addressing Ben Ferencz at an event commemorating his 101st birthday: "It was because of you, with [chief German representative] Hans Peter Kaul, that we had an aggression provision. Without you, we would not have had the crime of aggression in the Rome Statute."[52] Crucially, according to Bergsmo, Ferencz helped empower, inspire, and guide Kaul (who would go on to become an ICC judge) during the negotiations (both with respect to including aggression and victim reparations):

> [Hans Peter Kaul] would frequently refer to Mr. Ferencz's . . . views. [I] think for [Kaul] Mr. Ferencz [represented] the ultimate rationale and justification for the Nuremberg Tribunal, the Nuremberg Judgment, the Nuremberg principles, the reparations regime that Germany accepted. And all these historical facts and their values which led to the Germans playing perhaps the most principled role during both the Preparatory Committees and the Rome Conference and in the subsequent years, in terms of creating an effective International Criminal Court and not just a paper court.[53]

By July 16, 1998, the Conference's penultimate day, a fully negotiated draft had emerged. But on the following day, scheduled to be the Conference's last, the delegations from India and the United States (much to Scheffer's regret but driven by the Pentagon and conservatives putting pressure on Bill Clinton) tried to sabotage consensus adoption of that draft. India went first, seeking a vote on its request to exclude Security Council referral of cases and requests for suspension of cases and to add nuclear munitions to the list of prohibited weapons as part of the war crimes provision. The United States then requested a vote on twin proposals meant to limit the scope of the court's jurisdiction in respect of nonparty states. With only one day left, it looked as if the Indian and American delay tactics would derail consensus adoption.

But the Norwegians intervened and saved the day, moving for a "no-action" vote on India's proposed amendments. The initiative was killed, with 144 delegations voting yes. So when the American amendment proposals came up for discussion, Norway used the same tactic. A "no-action" vote once again carried the day, with 113 delegations supporting it, 17 voting against it, and 25 abstaining. On July 17, 1998, 120 countries voted to adopt the Statute, with 7 voting against it (the United States, China, Iraq, Israel, Libya, Qatar, and Yemen) and 21 abstaining.

Ben Ferencz later described what happened once the American proposals were shot down:

> The hall went wild with joy. Me too. . . . But it pained me when the victors did not let up but continued their rhythmic clapping while circling and glaring at the U.S. delegation defiantly. I had known and respected our Ambassador, David Scheffer, for many years. He sat glumly with representatives from the Pentagon and the Senate. My joy at the victory for the rule of law was tem-

> pered by my sorrow that the U.S. was in opposition, and my friend David, who represented the United States as a loyal public servant, had to bear the burden of international humiliation.

Scheffer, who had idolized Ferencz as a young lawyer and, as we have seen, used his "aggression trilogy" as his early-career bible, powerfully described what it looked like from the other end of the telescope:

> My personal recollection of Ben that night is very vivid. . . . There was that moment when the entire room rose and applauded and there was a celebration because at that point the [most recent proposed] draft was going to be adopted as the draft of the treaty. And it was at that very moment that Ben became a symbol of celebration in the room. And he went up to the top podium and stood with [UN Legal Counsel] Hans Corell, Philippe Kirsch, and, I think, [UN Secretary General] Kofi Annan, [among others]. And so he went up and stood among them and it was a very odd moment for me, because I was the head of the US delegation. I [officially represented approximately] 310 million people . . . I remained seated. And here was the famous American, Ben Ferencz, essentially seizing the mantle of the United States and putting it up at the front area [of] the podium . . . standing with the leadership of the conference . . . as if, in a sort of odd way, he was saying, "yes, the United States is here," which is great. . . . And here was a man whom I had known for years, who had influenced me from the earliest years of my being an international lawyer. And yet, he was the one standing up there and I was seated . . . in the last row.[54]

Before his triumphant departure from Rome, Ben took Gertrude on a tour of the Italian capital, reliving parts of their 1946 "belated honeymoon," a time when he was still the Berlin Branch chief. How much had transpired since that wintry sojourn amid the war ruins: *Einsatzgruppen* trial chief and *Krupp* trial podium prosecutor; executive counsel of the American prosecution team at Nuremberg; pioneer and leader of the Holocaust reparations program; advocate and architect for defining and criminalizing aggression; visionary for a permanent international criminal court—and now a wizened idealist who had lived long enough to contribute to the realization of his half-century-old dream.

BUT THE celebration was tempered; Ben knew that critically important work lay ahead—the terms of the treaty had been agreed on, but to go into effect, it still needed a minimum of sixty ratifications. And, apart from that, the former Nuremberg prosecutor still wanted the United States to sign on. So, in conjunction with other supporters, and to counter Republican propaganda to the effect that the court would be controlled by a "runaway Prosecutor" who would destroy American sovereignty, Ferencz embarked on a "one-man campaign" to "tell the truth to the American people."[55]

> Despite many concessions made to keep the U.S. on the team, America's defiant opposition . . . was led by Senator Jesse Helms, Chairman of the powerful Foreign Relations Committee. . . . [He] adamantly declared that no American would ever be tried by a foreign court. . . . I wrote articles, launched e-mail tirades, appeared on radio and TV, and lectured at universities and institutions, but it was no match for [this conservative] propaganda [which stressed] that an uncontrolled Prosecutor could bring unwarranted accusations against Americans, inhibiting our humanitarian or military goals. The truth is that no Prosecutor in human history has ever been subject to more controls than the Prosecutor for the ICC. . . . The Prosecutor cannot file any charges without approval by panels of judges. The Security Council can suspend prosecutions indefinitely. All proceedings must be open to public scrutiny.[56]

On his end, Ambassador Scheffer was similarly trying to keep the United States engaged in post–Rome Conference developments, such as participating in the drafting of the court's Rules of Procedure and Evidence (RPE) and Elements of Crimes (EOC)—documents that formed a crucial procedural/doctrinal framework for the court. In conjunction with this, he worked to drum up support for the United States signing the treaty. With the Clinton presidency in its lame-duck end phase, and thus the days of Scheffer's watch dwindling, he ramped up his campaign. But his efforts were still being stymied by Senator Helms, who continued to "bulldoze" him.[57] Thus, his pleas to the White House were falling on deaf ears, and the United States had only until December 31, 2000, to sign on to the treaty (per the terms of the treaty itself). The prospects were not encouraging.

Then, at the eleventh hour, the tide turned. It began with an unexpected intervention from former US defense secretary Robert McNamara. During his 1965 efforts to seek Jewish slave labor reparations from German arms manufacturer Rheinmettal Berlin AG, which had been trying to secure a US weapons purchase contract, Ferencz had indirect dealings with McNamara via his deputy, Cyrus Vance. Ferencz, representing the Claims Conference, had then sent a sharply worded telegram directly to McNamara (as well as Secretary of State Dean Rusk) protesting the purchase of arms from Rheinmettal. The strategy had worked, and McNamara eventually helped broker a reparations agreement between the Claims Conference and the German firm. Ferencz and McNamara had never met in person, but the latter had apparently remembered the former's written powers of persuasion.

One day in the late fall of 2000, while Ferencz was out running errands, Gertrude took a call from McNamara asking that her husband call him back. On his return, Ferencz dialed the number scrawled on the notepad, and he soon had the former Pentagon chief on the line. McNamara proposed that they cowrite an op-ed for the *New York Times* urging President Clinton to sign the Rome Statute. "Mr. Secretary," Ferencz replied, "you must be aware that some people have been calling for your trial as a war criminal for having sent troops to fight in Vietnam even after it was clear that the war was lost. Why do you want to support the ICC?"[58] McNamara explained that, had he known his conduct had been illegal, he would have acted otherwise. "The Court was therefore important to put the public and officials on notice."[59]

With that, Ferencz happily agreed to the request and wrote a draft, which McNamara quickly approved. It was published in the *New York Times* on December 12, 2000. Titled "For Clinton's Last Act," it began, "With the stroke of a pen, President Bill Clinton has a last chance to safeguard humankind from genocide, crimes against humanity and the ravages of war itself. He must simply sign a treaty, finalized in Rome in 1998, to create a permanent International Criminal Court."[60] The op-ed went on to explain why Jesse Helms's fearmongering about the court was unjustified—there were serious checks on the prosecutor. And, under the court's core principle of "complementarity" (domestic prosecutions being favored in the first instance with the ICC only serving as a stopgap mechanism), Americans could bring their own nationals to justice, if warranted. Besides, the signature itself would not signify American membership (that would require the advice and consent of two-thirds of the Senate, which Helms had vowed to block). Rather, an American "John Hancock" on the Rome Statute would only secure US assurances to support, and not thwart, the court's fundamental objectives. McNamara and Ferencz then concluded by again focusing on Clinton:

> The president must help deter future atrocities. At the United Nations and elsewhere, he and Secretary of State Madeleine Albright have repeatedly called for an international court to carry forward the lessons of Nuremberg. Now, he has a chance to take action. More than 100 nations, including all our NATO allies, have already signed. . . . If President Clinton fails to sign the treaty, he will weaken our credibility and moral standing in the world. We will look like a bully who wants to be above the law. If he signs, however, he will reaffirm

> America's inspiring role as leader of the free world in its search for peace and justice.[61]

It worked. Clinton read the piece and, as Ambassador Scheffer later recounted:

> Leave it to the wonders of a prominently published op-ed to finally awaken a president to action. [Advisor Eric] Schwartz immediately informed me that Clinton had written on the margins of the op-ed that he wanted to be kept informed on the issue, as if I had not been trying to do that for years. One can write countless memoranda and hold the highest-level meetings on an issue, and yet what galvanizes a president is often what the rest of the world sees along with him on a cold winter's morning.[62]

Then, as if successfully taking the baton from McNamara and Ferencz, Scheffer himself, or through the good offices of others (such as Elie Wiesel, Nelson Mandela, Jimmy Carter, and Steven Spielberg) adroitly lobbied Clinton.[63] Still, the president waffled until the very end. Not knowing how Clinton would ultimately decide, Scheffer hedged his bets by boarding Union Station's first New Year's Eve Amtrak train bound for New York City. He arrived at Penn Station midmorning, still in the dark about Clinton's intentions. But as he was ascending the escalator into the light of day on his way out of the building, his cell phone rang, and he nervously whipped it out of his pocket. It was Secretary of State Albright. She got straight to the point, confirming that the president of the United States had just decided that his country would sign the Rome Statute.[64] "Congratulations," Albright said with genuine warmth (her surname now seeming so symbolically apt).

Scheffer, who decades previously had first dreamed of a permanent international criminal court thanks to Ben Ferencz's writing, was now about to sign his country onto such a court, thanks again to Ben Ferencz's writing. And he was instructed by the secretary of state to do so forthwith. Unfortunately, there had been a snowstorm raging, and the American diplomat could not find a cab. So he dramatically trudged through the snow to the United Nations building (about an hour-long walk in such conditions). There, UN Legal Counsel Hans Corell was waiting for him. After ushering the cold and tired Scheffer into the building, Corell arranged a small ceremony, "complete with flags and a signing table."[65] Then the US ambassador-at-large for war crimes, still in his hiking boots and covered in snow, finally signed the Rome Statute on behalf of the United States. Israel, having been informed of this, decided to sign on as well.

Ferencz, who had once again made an historic contribution to the advancement of international justice, was ecstatic. But the euphoria was short-lived. After a much-disputed election wherein he lost the popular vote, George W. Bush was soon sworn into office as the forty-third president of the United States. "W," as he was known, urged on by the likes of Helms, the Pentagon, and prominent conservative lawyers such as John Bolton, "unsigned" the Rome Statute and took an aggressively hostile stance toward the ICC. Bolton was soon appointed as Bush's under secretary of state for arms control and international security (later becoming US ambassador to the UN). As under secretary, using various types of military assistance/cooperation as leverage, he negotiated with ICC member states so-called Article 98 agreements (named after the relevant provision in the Rome Statute), which prohibited them from surrendering Americans to the ICC. The new millennium New Year's Eve signing at the UN now seemed only a Pyrrhic victory.

20

TIME MACHINE MOMENTS

The distinction between past, present and future is only an illusion, however persistent.

—Albert Einstein to Michelangelo Besso

The ephemeral nature of the Clinton administration's New Year's Eve 2000 Rome Statute signing was underscored after the events of September 11, 2001. On that dark day in American history, al-Qaeda, a militant Islamist organization led by the former fanatical mujahideen fighter Osama bin Laden, carried out four coordinated terrorist attacks by hijacking commercial airplanes and crashing them into symbolically important American sites. Two of the aircraft were flown into the upper floors of the North and South Towers of the World Trade Center complex in New York City. One of the jets was hurtled full force into the Pentagon, just outside of Washington, DC. And the fourth, now infamously known as Flight 93, whose passengers bravely rose up against the hijackers (foiling their attempts to direct the United Airlines plane into the White House), crashed into an empty field in western Pennsylvania, about twenty minutes by air from the nation's capital. The attacks took the lives of 2,977 people, including the forty heroic passengers killed on Flight 93—it was the deadliest day on US soil since the Civil War's Battle of Antietam (resulting in more deaths than even the Pearl Harbor attack). The operation was planned and coordinated from Afghanistan, a brutally oppressive theocracy controlled by the Islamist Taliban.

In response, President Bush announced that the United States had been the victim of an "armed attack," signaling his belief that the United States Armed Forces could legally be used in self-defense.[1] This would be part of a declared "global war on terror," and Congress supported it by enacting the Joint Resolution Authorizing the Use of Military Force against the 9/11 perpetrators (and covering any potential future attacks they might launch). Now essentially empowered to use whatever force he deemed necessary, Bush demanded the Taliban surrender bin Laden. The request was promptly denied, and the United States launched Operation Enduring Freedom, an invasion of Afghanistan wherein numerous suspected Taliban and al-Qaeda operatives were captured. The president soon issued Military Order Number 1, establishing a detention facility at the leased US naval base in Guantánamo Bay, Cuba, to try captives suspected of committing war crimes before military commissions at the same location.

Ben Ferencz believed this was the perfect opportunity to prosecute these suspects using the new machinery of international justice. He was to be bitterly disappointed, later recollecting: "Osama bin Laden, the leader of Al Qaeda, a loose organization of militant Moslem fundamentalists, appeared on world-wide television to boast of the successful attack. President Bush vowed to bring the criminal to swift justice. No mention was made of the International Criminal Court."[2]

Instead, the Bush administration largely dispensed with many basic domestic guarantees of due process (let alone *international* ones). As the US-leased facility in Guantánamo Bay was not on American territory but also not subject to Cuban jurisdiction, the president and his advisors reasoned that American justice standards did not apply. Thus, these so-called "illegal combatants" (a term Bush used to justify extralegal measures but not found in the Geneva Conventions or customary law)[3] could be interrogated using brutal and degrading methods (such as waterboarding), warehoused without the right of habeas corpus, and eventually tried before bare-bones military tribunals using antiquated procedures resurrected from the 1940s, utterly inconsistent with modern courts-martial.

Ben Ferencz, in chorus with many other legal experts around the world, condemned America's seemingly indefinite detention and apparent torture of these men, with their proposed eventual proceedings before the kangaroo-court commissions, as war crimes, human rights breaches, and/or violations of the Due Process Clauses of the US Constitution—points mostly affirmed by the US Supreme Court in cases such as *Rasul v. Bush* (2004), *Hamdan v. Rumsfeld* (2006), and *Boumediene v. Bush* (2008), where the Court recognized the detainees' rights to habeas corpus and due process.[4]

Despite its domestic Orwellian justice measures, the Bush administration proved incapable of persuading the world to abort the embryonic ICC during its post-1998 gestation period. Following the required sixty ratifications, the Rome Statute entered into force, and the International Criminal Court was officially established on July 1, 2002. During the first week of February 2003, the Court (via its Assembly of States Parties, or ASP, that is, the treaty signatories) elected the members of its judicial branch—eighteen judges hailing from countries as diverse as Cyprus, Italy, Brazil, Ireland, Samoa, Latvia, Ghana, Finland, South Korea, France, Trinidad and Tobago, the United Kingdom (UK), and Costa Rica. They included six women and such Rome Conference luminaries as Hans Peter Kaul of Germany and Phillipe Kirsch of Canada, with the latter being chosen to serve as the Court's first president.

On March 11, 2003, appropriately Ben Ferencz's eighty-third birthday, the newly elected judges were sworn in during the inaugural session of the Court. The ideal birthday present had been offered to the former Nuremberg prosecutor, as he was invited to the ceremony in The Hague, and then to the Dutch Royal Palace for a lunch hosted by Queen Beatrix. Between the investiture ceremony and the royal repast, Ferencz agreed to join a pro-ICC NGO's demonstration against US opposition to the Court. In particular, the group's bile was to be vented on a piece of Bush-sponsored legislation known as the Servicemembers Protection Act of 2002, which authorized the use of military force to "liberate" any American citizen in the ICC's custody.[5] Derided in many quarters as the "Hague Invasion Act," it was "intended to intimidate countries that [ratified the ICC] treaty" and revealed that the Bush administration would "stop at nothing in its campaign against the court."[6]

The protest featured construction of sand barricades along the beach at nearby Schevinengen, with life-sized cardboard soldiers erected to stand guard behind their national flags, symbolically poised to repel any invasion by US troops. Ferencz, who had brought a large American flag with him, was the event's keynote speaker. He later summarized his remarks, which closed the event:

> [I] noted that I had landed at nearby Normandy Beach during World War Two, wearing the uniform of the U.S. Army. I had come then to fight for freedom. Now I had come not to attack the U.S., but to defend the reputation of the American public that believed in the Nuremberg principles and the rule of law. I cited Tom Paine that the duty of a true patriot is to have the courage to stand up for what is right when his country has gone astray. As I hoisted the Stars and Stripes into the wind, I asked the audience to join me in reciting the concluding sentence of the pledge of allegiance that calls for "liberty and justice for all"—not just for Americans.[7]

Soon, he was brushing off the sand and rushing to the Royal Palace. At the luncheon hosted by Queen Beatrix, the Dutch prime minister, Jan Peter Balkenende, stood up and, after congratulating the new judges, "announced that it was an extra special occasion" because of Ben Ferencz's presence. After "effusive praise," he proposed a toast to the former Nuremberg prosecutor. There was warm applause, and Ferencz later recounted that it was "a most unexpected and impressive birthday celebration," adding, with a bit of his signature humor, "even more memorable than my Bar Mitzvah."[8]

Now that the ICC's judicial branch had been sworn in, it would be officially serviced by a Registry, whose staff had been hired and whose activities were being ramped up. Led by Registrar Bruno Cathala (a French magistrate, elected by the ICC's judiciary), its brief was to handle the Court's nonlegal, administrative matters. Otherwise, the ICC's most important organ would be the Office of the Prosecutor, charged with conducting investigations and bringing prosecutions. On April 21, 2003, the ASP elected Luis Moreno Ocampo as the ICC's first prosecutor. Moreno Ocampo had played a major role in Argentina's 1980s transition to democracy as, among other roles, a prosecutor for the "Trial of the Juntas" (members of the Argentine dictatorship most responsible for the country's massive human rights violations between 1976 and 1983).

Ferencz also attended Ocampo's June 16, 2003, swearing-in ceremony, warmly praising the new prosecutor and taking advantage of the occasion to excoriate yet again the Bush administration's anti-ICC policy. Thumbing its nose at such superpower animosity, the Court remained unfazed. By the middle of 2005, it was already issuing its first arrest warrants (against leaders of the genocidal Ugandan rebel group the Lord's Resistance Army).

Meanwhile, the United States found other ways to pursue its policy of American exceptionalism. Thus, more Bush administration erosions of international justice standards followed with the US invasion of Iraq on March 20, 2003, which Ben Ferencz considered an act of aggression.[9] Using the well-respected Secretary of State Colin Powell as his mouthpiece before the global community, Bush justified the invasion on supposed evidence (later proved false) that Saddam Hussein had at his disposal, and was likely to use, weapons of mass destruction (WMD).[10] Such WMD were never found. Nonetheless, unlike his father in the prior Gulf War, *this* President Bush would not permit the survival of the Hussein regime (in fact, some believed that was the principal motivation for the attack, that is, the son making up for the father's mistake, especially after Hussein's failed attempt to assassinate the father in 1993).[11] So US forces toppled the brutal Ba'athist dictator and, in conjunction with local Iraqis, put him and his henchmen on trial before the American-created Iraqi High Criminal Court (IHCC). This was established by occupation authorities under Iraqi national law but used substantive international criminal law provisions to prosecute charges of genocide, crimes against humanity, war crimes, and other serious offenses committed between 1968 and 2003.

Pursuant to a trial lacking many customary international guarantees of due process, Hussein himself was convicted and sentenced to death by the IHCC in November 2006 for crimes against humanity in connection with the 1982 massacre of 148 Shiites in Dujail. His appeal was quickly rejected, and he was hanged in December, despite his other pending trial on much more serious genocide charges in connection with the extermination of close to 200,000 Kurds in the infamous 1988 Anfal Campaign. Ben Ferencz had advised that the best solution for trying Hussein would be "a tribunal competent to try all international criminals" and warned against "summary judgment and prompt execution."[12] With the United States having ignored Ferencz, "UN human rights experts and international human rights organizations, including Amnesty International, concluded that the executions [of Saddam Hussein and his codefendants] were carried out after a trial which failed to meet international fair trial standards, and an appeal process which was fundamentally flawed."[13]

In the meantime, the International Criminal Court continued to go about its business and gain momentum. In fact, in March 2005, the United States softened its stance on the ICC and permitted the UN Security Council to request Moreno Ocampo to open an investigation into atrocities in Darfur and investigate Sudanese leader Omar al-Bashir and his lieutenants in connection with the allegations of genocide committed against non-Arab Sudanese in that region. The following year, the Court indicted Thomas Lubanga Dyilo, leader of a rebel group in the Democratic Republic of the Congo that was suspected of committing massacres in the country's Ituri province in 2002–3. Although the group was accused of massive human rights violations, including ethnic massacres, murder, torture, rape, mutilation, and conscripting and using child-soldiers to participate actively in hostilities, only the latter two crimes were the object of the indictment. Ben Ferencz would eventually play a role in the trial of this case, the first to be held before the ICC.

But at the time of Lubanga's indictment in 2006, Ferencz was more focused on the issue that had pulled him away from the practice of law in the first place: the crime of aggression. In the summer of 1998, Ferencz had lobbied hard for the inclusion of the offense in the Rome Statute. And, in the Conference's waning hours, the crime was added to Article 5, joining genocide, crimes against humanity, and war crimes as "the most serious crimes of concern to the international community as a whole."[14]

To have preserved the crime for inclusion in the treaty was quite a feat—but much remained to be done as aggression was not defined therein, and the parameters for charging it were in no way laid out. In fact, paragraph 2 of Article 5 specified that the Court would "exercise jurisdiction over the crime of aggression once a provision is adopted in accordance with articles 121 and 123 defining the crime and setting out the conditions under which the Court shall exercise jurisdiction with respect to this crime. Such a provision shall be consistent with the relevant provisions of the Charter of the United Nations."[15] In essence, when read together, Articles 121 and 123 specified that, seven years after the Statute's entry into force, amendments to Article 5 could be proposed and voted on by the ASP at a Review Conference. That meant that the earliest such a conference could be held was after July 2009. Those pushing for the Court to define aggression and activate jurisdiction over it started to look at 2010 as the best time for the necessary Review Conference.

So, not long after Rome, the nascent ICC started to lay down the groundwork for the contemplated gathering. Over the course of ten 1998–2002 Preparatory Commission meetings, during which States Parties drafted the Rules of Procedure and Evidence, the Elements of Crimes, and other vital documents supporting the Rome Statute, a definition for the crime of aggression was discussed but not agreed on. A more dedicated Special Working Group on the Crime of Aggression was then established, and Prince Zeid Ra'ad Al Hussein of Jordan, ASP president at the time, appointed his good friend and colleague Christian Wenaweser as chair. The selection may have been based on a sense of trust built up between the two men over the years. But putting the Liechtensteiner in charge proved to be a brilliant move by Zeid on many levels.

Wenaweser not only provided great leadership and initiative but also made sure to do so in the proper setting. He soon realized that that the delegates needed to be removed from the many distractions of UN Headquarters and placed in an environment more conducive to successful negotiations. Thus, taking advantage of an Ivy League connection in neighboring New Jersey, Wenaweser scheduled Special Working Group meetings on the idyllic campus of Princeton University. On an annual basis between 2003 and 2009, in this more contemplative and intellectually vibrant setting, the Special Working Group, which included NGOs and individual experts, chatted and wrangled in relative seclusion, hashing out the language needed to define aggression and specify the conditions for activation of the Court's jurisdiction over the crime.

Ben Ferencz played a crucial role in this so-called Princeton Process. As its first meeting was getting under way, he delivered a keynote address, firing up the stakeholders for the work that lay ahead. Liechtenstein's then legal advisor to the UN mission (and later, deputy ambassador), Stefan Barriga, has noted that Ferencz's speech was vital to "put us in the right mood."[16] And, according to Wenaweser, this positive influence was a steady and necessary presence throughout the Process:

> Ben sat through every single session. . . . He was a great part of the process. . . . And the discussion, even among those who were, in a way, very skeptical and were on the very conservative side. . . . [I]t was a really, really difficult discussion—but without [Ben helping allay the concerns of these people] we wouldn't have had half the success in Kampala [at the eventual Review Conference] that we did. I think over time the atmosphere, in my view, was . . . that [this] was an inevitability. So, okay, we're doing this; we will find a conclusion. And Ben certainly was a big part of that.[17]

According to the aggression expert Noah Weisbord, who participated in the Princeton Process, Ferencz's contribution was critical right up to the very end, as his speeches bookended the gatherings: "When negotiations stalled, Wenaweser invited Ferencz to speak, to remind diplomats why they were there. 'It is so obviously correct that law is better than war and that it is better to live in peace with human rights than to live in war, killing people who you don't even know,' Ferencz said."[18]

At last, the long-awaited Review Conference was scheduled to begin in Kampala, Uganda, on May 31, 2010. Ben Ferencz was there, accompanied by his son, Don, who had become a well-respected expert on the crime of aggression in his own right, having left a tax law practice in 2005 and then participating in and significantly contributing to the Princeton Process himself. Ben welcomed Don's crucial involvement, but it also dredged up certain underlying tensions in their relationship. On one hand, Ben had always encouraged his kids to strive for excellence and serve society in an impactful way. Don reports: "I grew up in a family where . . . my dad used to [go around the table and] ask us every night, 'What have you done for mankind?'"[19] And, as the only son, there was particular pressure on Don in this regard. According to his sister Nina, because he was a boy, he had "greater burdens placed upon him in terms of expectations."[20]

At the same time, and somewhat paradoxically, Ben was leery of his son overshadowing him—as though he wanted to make sure that, despite Don's accomplishments, Ben remained the center of attention. Nina acknowledges a "weird combination" of higher expectations for Don but a "greater sense of competition." She indicates that the father-son dynamic was "a really tough thing [for Don] to navigate."[21] For his part, Don explains that he "always got along" with his dad and felt great "affection" and "respect" for him. But he admits that, at times, there had been "extreme tension in the relationship."[22] This seemingly schizophrenic vibe between father and son surfaced during the Kampala Conference, where Ben was, all at once, beaming with pride at his son's contributions while evidently concerned that his boy might be stealing the limelight. At one point during the proceedings, Don and Ben met some diplomats neither of them knew, and Ben said, "Oh, meet my son Don. He's along for the ride."[23]

THAT "RIDE" ended up being quite rocky. But it began smoothly enough—with the Conference adopting a consensus definition of the crime of aggression that was hammered out during the Princeton Process and based on the UN General Assembly's 1974 definition to which Ben Ferencz had contributed so much. It had been updated and modified to include liability for responsible political or military leaders only when use of force constitutes "a manifest violation" of the UN Charter (this would become Article 8 *bis* of the Rome Statute). That said, it was still a "conservative law" focused on the armed conflicts "of a bygone era" given the modern loss of "[the state's] monopoly on combat forces, the diminishing importance of conventional war, and the rise of super-powerful rogue individuals and groups."[24] But such a definition was needed to "garner the widest possible support and insulate [the] proposed law from attack."[25]

Nevertheless, the Conference soon revealed a deep divide over an issue much more inherently thorny—the conditions for the exercise of jurisdiction. Delegates would have to determine how ICC members and nonmembers would be subject to the crime that was the object of this conservative consensus definition. What, exactly, would be the specific ways an aggression case could be brought to the ICC for prosecution of political or military leaders?

This key question roughly cleaved the delegations into two opposing camps, which Noah Weisbord dubs "Camp Consent" and "Camp Protection."[26] At the heart of their disagreement was the interpretation of the poorly drafted Rome Statute provision governing how the treaty could be amended. Camp Consent, comprising the Security Council P5—the United States (which had become much more positively ICC-engaged since the election of Barack Obama, who sent a large delegation to Kampala), Europe, Canada, Australia, and New Zealand—interpreted the provision such that both aggressor and victim states needed to ratify the Kampala outcome to permit ICC prosecutions. This would be tantamount to a "nonaggression pact excluding the great powers and their close allies [thus suffering] from similar weaknesses [as] the League of Nations."[27]

In contrast, Camp Protection, which represented the world's less powerful nations (especially those from the Global South, such as Africa, Latin America, and the Caribbean), interpreted the provision as requiring ratification by the victim state alone to allow ICC prosecutions in cases of aggressive use of force. The two camps were also divided in terms of how aggression cases could be initiated at the ICC. Camp Consent wanted initiation strictly via Security Council referral (meaning P5 approval would be necessary). But Camp Protection wanted initiation possibilities to include referral by ICC state parties or at the initiative of the prosecutor (that is, via so-called *proprio motu* investigations).

According to Stefan Barriga, Ferencz was an important presence at Kampala in terms of opening the minds of Camp Consent delegates to the viewpoints of Camp Protection: "Ben Ferencz was just always—such a figure! He would just capture the attention of absolutely everyone in the room. . . . [From] the beginning until the end, the P5 countries were very, very skeptical. . . . But . . . he was really helping us to put people into a cooperative mode and to see the bigger picture, and then to see that there is a purpose we were pursuing. So he definitely helped move the needle."[28]

Still, as the Conference headed into its final days, the parties remained deadlocked. So Christian Wenaweser, who was now ASP president himself and running the show in Kampala with Prince Zeid's crucial assistance (the latter now serving simply as Jordan's diplomatic representative at the Conference), decided to maximize the "Ben Ferencz Effect" and asked him to inspire the gathering with a final oration. Luis Moreno Ocampo, who was there in his capacity as ICC prosecutor, described the speech as "very strong" because Ferencz had been a voice in the wilderness for so many years, and this "was the peak of his efforts."[29] Barriga characterizes it as a "big speech" wherein "[Ferencz expressed] that he's just running out of patience and really calling on people to put their squabbles behind and to focus on finding a compromise. [He] was really . . . showing us the big picture of what we were doing. . . . It was just easier to then follow up with concrete ideas and concrete suggestions on how we can move forward on the crime of aggression after he had prepared the ground."[30]

So roused and focused, the delegates finally saw movement via a proposal to create separate jurisdiction and entry-into-force mechanisms for Security Council referrals and state referrals/*proprio motu* investigations. On one hand, Security Council referrals, relatively uncontroversial and favored by Camp Consent, would be available as soon as the first state party ratified what were now being referred to as the Kampala Amendments (this referral mechanism was eventually codified in Rome Statute Article 15 *ter*). The more contentious state referral/*proprio motu* investigation amendments (ultimately codified as Article 15 *bis*) would enter into force only after seven-eighths of the state parties ratified them, which could take time. But it would yield a more protective jurisdiction regime not requiring the consent of the aggressor state or a Security Council referral. Moreover, the parties agreed on an opt-out mechanism whereby the ICC could, by default, exercise jurisdiction over an alleged aggressor state unless that state had previously opted out of the Kampala Amendments. Further, aggression prosecutions would not be possible against states that were not ICC members.

The compromise on the table helped bring the two sides closer together, but, as the final grains of sand were dropping from the top of the hourglass, they were still too far apart. Wenaweser and Zeid were frantically shuttling between them as the Conference was winding down, trying to iron out any remaining differences. And, as in Rome, at the eleventh hour, they seemed to achieve a final workable arrangement. Per the compromise hammered out, absent Security Council referral, the leaders of all ICC member states would automatically be subject to the aggression law once seven years had passed, thirty states had ratified the Kampala Amendments, and the Assembly of States Parties had agreed to activate the jurisdiction (the specific seven-eighths approval proviso had dropped out). But ICC member states could subsequently opt out, and nonmember states were not covered by the law.[31] Thus, only Security Council referrals would open the door to prosecution of political and military leaders of nonstate parties.

In the early-morning hours of June 11, 2010, with the Conference wearily and anxiously gathered for its final plenary session, Wenaweser asked the delegates, "Do I take it there is a consensus on the adoption of this text?" There was a pregnant pause, broken only by the brittle voice of the chief Japanese representative: "The delegation of Japan has serious doubts about the legal integrity of the amendment," he said.[32] One could feel the room's ebbing energy drain away completely, as it seemed the meticulously cobbled-together agreement was about to come undone. Fortunately, the Japanese diplomat added one more sentence, with a whiff of resignation: "But we will not stand in the way of consensus."[33]

Wenaweser took a moment to process this final reprieve and then brought down his gavel. The cavernous auditorium broke into ecstatic applause. Don Ferencz, who had taken up the bagpipes over the years and had brought his set to Kampala, removed the instrument's parts from its case, assembled them, and joyously piped "Nkosi Sikelel' iAfrika" (Lord lift up Africa), as the delegates whooped it up, exchanging handshakes and hugs.

But the elder Ferencz did not join in the revelry. Noah Weisbord describes approaching the former Nuremberg prosecutor as he sat glumly off to the side ("looking all his ninety years old"), in stark contrast to his demeanor in the final moments in Rome, twelve years previously. "Congratulations," Weisbord said. "What do you mean congratulations?" Ferencz barked back, thinking of the byzantine set of conditions grafted on to the exercise of the new aggression jurisdiction. "There are three new locks on the courthouse door," he added.[34] According to his son Don, the three new "locks" consisted of (1) initially, the need to secure thirty ratifications; (2) even if the thirty ratifications could be secured, and seven years had passed, the lack of guarantee that the matter would actually be brought back for a vote before the ASP (nothing in the Kampala Amendments guaranteed this, and the head of the US delegation, Harold Koh, had vowed to do whatever he could to prevent it); and (3) even if brought back for a vote seven or more years later, there was no guarantee that the amendments would actually be adopted at that time.[35] And this was apart from the fact that the only jurisdictional lever available against nonmembers and opt-outs was in the hands of the politicized Security Council, where only one P5 veto could upend what might otherwise be a legitimate prosecution.[36] In such a case, nonmembers and opt-outs would be shielded—giving their leaders immunity to pursue acts of aggression.

So Ferencz was quite disappointed with this so-called Kampala Compromise. But he did not remain deflated for long. Resilient, resourceful, and relentless as ever, he was already thinking about how to work around the problem. As others were still celebrating in the auditorium, it occurred to him that prosecuting use of illegal force as aggression might not be the only way to seek justice against responsible state leaders. What about crimes against humanity? Although the relevant provision of the Rome Statute (Article 7) had a specific list of offenses covered (for example, murder, rape, torture), there was a "residual" clause that allowed for prosecution of "other inhumane acts." Remarkably, "Mr. Aggression" began embracing the idea that leaders responsible for crimes against peace could be brought to justice for crimes against humanity.

And the more he thought about it, the more it made sense. For many years, apart from prevention, his central international justice concern had been victims. The name of the offense itself, crimes against *humanity,* betokened the centrality of *human* victims in charging it. In contrast, the direct "victim" of the aggression offense is another state (as the crime focuses on breaching the territorial integrity/sovereignty of another state)—in other words, it is a "state-centric" offense, not as directly or immediately concerned with human victims. Thus, Ferencz began thinking, prosecuting illegal use of force as crimes against humanity was the way forward. As he had declared before the judges in Courtroom 600 of the Nuremberg Palace of Justice and before the world's representatives in Rome, he would be the voice of the victims. When it came to seeking justice for state mass crimes, *human* victims were what mattered, whether their plight was due to an external state's illegal use of force or their own state's internal infliction of violence.

Ferencz described his idea of charging "illegal use of force" as a crime against humanity, and not just as aggression, to ICC prosecutor Luis Moreno Ocampo. And then, invoking one of his trademark metaphors, he added with bravado, "They closed the door on aggression, but I will open the window!"[37] The Argentine could only marvel at the nonagenarian's creativity and stick-to-itiveness: "So, I think, my God, this guy is 90, so brilliant and so resilient. So, for me, from that day, I said, look, 'My job is to understand that Ben is opening doors [and windows!], I have to follow him.'"[38]

Moreno Ocampo's resolution soon had real-world manifestations. Six months after Kampala, in December 2010, he crossed paths with Ferencz at the Ninth Session of the ICC's Assembly of States Parties at UN Headquarters in New York. By then, the case against Thomas Lubanga, the Congolese rebel charged with the enlistment/conscription and use of child-soldiers to participate actively in hostilities, was wrapping up. Moreno Ocampo realized that, at the proceeding's very end point, Ferencz could "open the door" to the legacy of Nuremberg and remind the judges that they were connected to the origins of a living, growing body of law and justice. He asked Ferencz if he could join the prosecution team in The Hague and participate in the trial's closing arguments. Patton's founding war crimes investigator immediately grasped the importance of this request from the ICC's founding prosecutor. It was history coming full circle. With a great sense of honor and duty, he accepted the invitation.

Significantly for Ferencz, pursuant to Article 68(3) of the Rome Statute, which he helped inspire and craft, victims of Lubanga's child-soldier exploitation had participated in the trial and presented their views. By then, all the witnesses had been led and the exhibits admitted. So the prosecution's closing arguments were scheduled for August 25, 2011. In advance of this, Moreno Ocampo had Ferencz appointed as special counsel to the Office of the Prosecutor (OTP). He arrived in The Hague a week before the appointed date and began working with the team. Moreno Ocampo and his lawyers were thrilled to have the Nuremberg legend assist them in drafting, refining, and rehearsing their arguments. "This was an amazing part of my tenure," the chief prosecutor later explained, "because there was a feeling that Ben is Nuremberg supporting us . . . really closing the gap."[39]

At the same time, Ferencz worked on his own closing, reviewing trial transcripts and conferring with OTP special assistant to the prosecutor Joanna Frivet, who helped him understand the finer points of the case, while appreciating the sum of its parts. International criminal law's elder statesman was a perfect fit on the team, using his trademark sense of humor to put everyone at ease. Just after his arrival, Moreno Ocampo recalls, one of his female staff helped Ben find the restroom and, out of respect and concern for his age, held the door open for him. With his New York–accented gravelly voice at highest volume, he blurted out with a chuckle, "I'm sorry lady, I'm married. Please leave this bathroom at once!"[40] Those within earshot burst out in laughter at the salty curmudgeon's hijinks.

Of course, at the very beginning of his career, there had been another humorous bathroom encounter, when the young corporal accidentally walked in on Marlene Dietrich luxuriating in a tub at General Patton's headquarters. In yet another parallel all these years later, a famous actress would arrive on the scene of his war crimes work in the new millennium. This time it was Angelina Jolie, not only a star among the upper tier of Hollywood royalty but also widely admired for her humanitarian work as a goodwill ambassador for the UN high commissioner for refugees. Jolie was an ardent supporter of the ICC and had become friendly with Moreno Ocampo, who invited her to attend the trial; she accepted, arriving with two of her children in tow.

As with Dietrich in 1945 Germany, Ferencz had lunch with Jolie in 2011 Holland. Instead of General Patton being at the head of the table, this time it was Prosecutor Moreno Ocampo. They talked about Ben's contributions at Nuremberg, his representation of Holocaust victims, and his role as a visionary advocate for a permanent international criminal court. They also discussed the Lubanga trial and the child-soldier problem in Africa, with Jolie describing some of her inspiring work as a UN goodwill ambassador. Later that afternoon, before the court session began, she wished him luck and gave him a kiss on the cheek.[41] Then she took a seat with her two kids in the audience section's front row. If the future *Judgment at Nuremberg* star inspired Ferencz as he was beginning his war crimes investigation service, the *Lara Croft: Tomb Raider* star inspired him as he was preparing to end his war crimes prosecution service.

The OTP was now ready for its closing. First to address the bench was the Gambian deputy prosecutor Fatou Bensouda (who would later become chief prosecutor herself). She provided an overview of the evidence demonstrating Lubanga's 2002–3 war crimes—systematically recruiting and using children under the age of fifteen as soldiers in combat for his Union of Congolese Patriots/ Patriotic Force for the Liberation of the Congo (known as the UPC/ FPLC based on its French names). The Belgian attorney Olivia Struyven then presented a summary of the prosecution's video evidence, including an infamous film of Lubanga holding a Kalashnikov as he stood before a large assembly of youngsters and encouraged them to fight. Then law professor Tim McCormack of Melbourne University, special advisor on international humanitarian law, argued that the armed conflict in which the UPC/ FPLC had been engaged should be characterized as noninternational in character (thus helping the court apply the proper legal criteria).

Finally, it was time for Ben Ferencz to address the court. Fortunately, in contrast to barely clearing the large wooden lectern in Nuremberg's Courtroom 600, merely by standing up, the diminutive advocate easily cleared the prosecution's low-lying and tech-friendly blond-wood table, equipped with computers, from which location he would address the bench. He then moved a couple steps to his left, where he placed his notes on a Plexiglas stand. Microphones and monitors and other sophisticated electronics were ubiquitous, and spectators were separated from the chamber via a thick glass barrier. "It was not the Nuremberg courtroom," Ferencz later recounted, "it was a [much] smaller [and more modern-looking] room."[42] He took it all in and then turned to face Judges Adrian Fulford (United Kingdom, presiding), Elizabeth Odio Benito (Costa Rica), and René Blattman (Bolivia).

"May it please your Honors," he began, exactly as he had almost sixty-five years previously in opening the *Einsatzgruppen* trial. But the baby-faced twenty-seven-year-old lawyer of 1947, then dressed in an American navy-blue suit and silk tie, was now the craggy-faced dean of international prosecutors, covered in a European black *toge d'avocat* with a ridged, white linen *jabot* around his neck that was rectangular and reached his chest. His thinning gray hair in no way covered the large hearing aids protruding from his ears. But this old man, who had dreamed for decades about the creation of this court he was now addressing, had in no way lost any of the passion or vigor that had sustained him through the many travails that brought him to this magnificent moment.

Ferencz was asked to go last because Moreno Ocampo wanted the lawyer's towering stature and inspiring eloquence to convey the "gravity of the crime"; in other words, to convince Judges Fulford, Benito, and Blattman that this case was not just about recruiting and using child-soldiers but, rather, about transforming child-soldiers into mass murderers and rapists as well as victims of physical abuse and sexual slavery.[43] Ferencz wasted no time in getting to the point. After explaining why, from his perspective, this first trial of the ICC was an "historic moment," he briefly detailed his personal journey, from Nuremberg to Rome, and how human rights advocacy had blossomed since the end of World War II. And he explained how the ICC, whose remit was to deter crimes to protect victims, was an integral part of that blossoming. Then he tied it all to the case at bar:

> The evidence showed that waves of children, recruited under Mr. Lubanga's command, moved through as many as 20 training camps, some holding

> between eight and sixteen hundred children under age 15. Words and figures cannot adequately portray the physical and psychological harm inflicted on vulnerable children who were brutalized and who lived in constant fear. The loss and grief to their inconsolable families is immeasurable. Their childhood stolen, deprived of education and all human rights, the suffering of the young victims and their families left permanent scars. We must try to restore the faith of children so that they may join in restoring the shattered world from which they came. Imagine the pain of mothers crying and pleading at the door of the camps still suffering and wondering what happened to their children. Picture the agony of the father who said: ". . . he is my first son. All of my hopes were laid on him. . . . the child was ruined. . . . Today he can do nothing in his life.". . . All of the girls recruited could expect to be sexually violated. All of these events which the Prosecution has carefully presented have been proved beyond reasonable doubt.[44]

Films of his remarks, now available online, show the intense reaction of those present. The bearded and graying Moreno Ocampo, himself a figure of great stature, is seen looking up at Ferencz, beaming with pride and admiration. From the bench, Judge Fulford's bare pate is cocked at a discernable angle, and his deeply inset eyes betray the wonder of beholding this time machine moment connecting Nuremberg to his courtroom. That connection was intensified as Ferencz started wrapping up his ICC closing with the words that began his Nuremberg opening:

> Once again, "the case we present is a plea of humanity to law." It is a call for human beings to behave in a humane and lawful way. The hope of humankind is that compassion and compromise may replace the cruel and senseless violence of armed conflicts. That is the law as prescribed by the Rome Statute that binds this Court as well as the UN Charter that binds everyone. Vengeance begets vengeance.

Then he updated his Nuremberg plea to address his two chief post-Nuremberg concerns, ending aggressive war and protecting victims. And he was directing this eloquence to the institution that was so much the product of his vision and hard labors—these might as well have been the valedictory words of his Methusalean career:

> The illegal use of armed force, which is the soil from which all human rights violations grow, must be condemned as a crime against humanity. International disputes must be resolved not by armed force but by peaceful means

only. Seizing and training young people to hate and kill presumed adversaries undermines the legal and moral firmament of human society. Let the voice and the verdict of this esteemed global court now speak for the awakened conscience of the world.

And with that, Benjamin B. Ferencz moved two steps to his right, sat down, and ended his career as a war crimes prosecutor. The speech, a powerful coda to Moreno Ocampo's solid case, seemed to have had its intended effect. On March 14, 2012, Lubanga was found guilty of all the charges in the indictment and later sentenced to fourteen years of imprisonment. Moreover, in further proceedings pursuant to Article 75 of the Rome Statute, and in conjunction with the Court's Trust Fund for Victims (TFV), Lubanga was found liable for US$10 million in reparations to be paid to his victims. The Court also imposed collective reparations in the form of provisions of services, including needed health care, education, and job training. Yet another important part of the Ferencz legacy, taking care of victims in the aftermath of international crimes, was bearing real fruit while he was still alive to appreciate it.

BUT AS BEN FERENCZ approached his hundredth year, he found it impossible to slow down. In 1996, he and his son Don had cofounded the Planethood Foundation, a tax-exempt charitable organization whose mission statement was "educating to replace the law of force with the force of law." Since its founding, and by using money Ben had saved through thrift and wise investments over the years, Planethood had been funding a myriad of transnational and transitional justice initiatives. Early on, the main recipient of its largesse was the Coalition for the International Criminal Court, as it lobbied for the creation and ratification of the ICC.

Over time, Planethood expanded its charitable contributions. For example, it started funding the American Society of International Law's Helton Fellowships, "micro-grants" for law students/young professionals to pursue fieldwork and research on significant issues in, among other areas, international criminal law (ICL). Kip Hale, a noted ICL expert who has investigated and prosecuted atrocity crimes in conflict zones across the globe, cut his teeth at the Extraordinary Chambers in the Courts of Cambodia (ECCC) through a grant funded by Planethood. After serving as a prosecutor with the ECCC for three years, Hale was appointed director of the ABA's International Criminal Court Project, which Planethood (along with other organizations) has funded generously. The ABA ICC Project seeks to educate and advocate on international criminal justice and US-ICC relations.

Similarly, Planethood made grants to educational institutions, such as Harvard and Oxford, seeding internships to study ICL or work on it in hot spots around the world, such as Myanmar, where Rohingya Muslims have been the victims of government-sponsored/sanctioned atrocity crimes. Other grants assisted the Centre for International Law Research and Policy to fund scholarships for non-Western students (especially those in China and India) to work on ICL issues.

More recently, Ben Ferencz gave financial assistance to the government of Liechtenstein in its efforts to raise awareness about and secure ratifications of the Kampala Amendments. This eventually helped generate the thirty ratifications needed to bring the Kampala Amendments before the ICC Assembly of States Parties for a vote in 2017. And on December 17 of that year, the ASP voted to accept the Kampala Amendments and activate the aggression jurisdiction. It may not have been Ben Ferencz's ideal justice regime, but his vision, writing, lobbying, and money nevertheless played an integral role in the international criminalization of the illegal use of force.

But just as atrocity victims were a key focal point for Ferencz's justice and education efforts, the same was true of his philanthropy. From its founding in 2005 by Cardozo Law professor Sheri Rosenberg as the Holocaust, Genocide and Human Rights Program (HGHRP), Planethood contributed money for various ad hoc HGHRP projects. In 2013, the contributions were beefed up to establish the Telford Taylor Human Rights Clinical Teaching Fellowship (to honor Ferencz's former boss, partner, and friend) funding a young professional to work with students as part of the clinical wing of Rosenberg's program, which had been renamed the Cardozo Law Institute in Holocaust and Human Rights (or CLIHHR).

In 2016, Ferencz endowed the clinic with a $1 million gift, and it was renamed the Benjamin B. Ferencz Human Rights and Atrocity Prevention Clinic. Its victim advocacy projects run the gamut, from litigation assistance for a genocide reparations case on behalf of the Waimiri-Atroari people in Brazil, to help with gender violence and torture cases pending before the judicial mechanisms of the inter-American human rights system, to working with attorneys in European domestic courts seeking reparations for Yazidi survivors of ISIS atrocities. In respect of these victim-oriented projects, Ben Ferencz took an active role in meeting with students and providing advice.[45]

At the same time, Planethood donated directly to victims. In 2013, it contributed $50,000 to the ICC Trust Fund for Victims (TFV), the TFV's first major private contribution. TFV chair Motoo Noguchi said the gift showed "the need to recognize the plight of the victims of [ICC] crimes" and would give a "strong boost" to the Trust Fund's "ability to engage with victims within the Rome Statute's reparative justice framework."[46]

But Planethood's largest gift was earmarked in 2016 for the US Holocaust Memorial Museum's Simon-Skjodt Center for the Prevention of Genocide. After consulting with various experts in the field, Ferencz decided to give the Skjodt Center an annually renewable gift of $1 million to establish the Ferencz International Justice Initiative. Anna Cave, who had recently left the Obama administration, where she had worked in different posts on high-level international criminal law issues, was appointed the Initiative's founding director. According to Cave, the Initiative's focus on atrocity victims' issues was based on what mattered most to Ferencz:

> You know he gets the glory and the recognition for his [prosecution] work. . . . But the work he was most proud of was . . . this work for victims [that] is hard, it's messy. And yet, that is the work he was most proud of. So, I felt like of what I had seen for many years in my own work this really dovetails. And where I saw this huge gap in international justice [assisting atrocity victims], he had forged . . . a new path, and that would be an exciting place for the Ferencz Initiative to go.[47]

In human rights disaster zones such as South Sudan, where a civil war (and its aftermath) has fueled atrocities since the country's independence from Sudan in 2011, the Ferencz Initiative has worked at a grassroots level to bring together victim communities and experts to form Justice Advisory Groups (JAGs). Cave explains that the JAGs are effective because "having different people around the table . . . a huge number of perspectives in the room . . . allows you to have divergent thinking."[48] The Initiative's website adds that the project "brings together coalitions of change-agents—from affected communities and from the halls of power—to incubate new strategies to advance justice."[49] In the end, Cave notes, the Ferencz Initiative "equips and supports victims and local . . . advocates to . . . take concrete steps toward justice at home."[50] And Cave is eager to add that Ferencz, with his years of experience in dealing with victims' issues, proved invaluable in providing quality-control feedback.

The *Einsatzgruppen* trial chief prosecutor contributed $5 million to the Initiative (although he decided to cut funding toward the end of the first Donald Trump administration based on his many profound disagreements with Trump's policies). Still, the foundation had been laid, and the Initiative's work goes on. In 2021, director Sarah McIntosh (Cave left in 2019) spearheaded the publication of *Pursuing Justice for Mass Atrocities: A Handbook for Victim Groups,* which sets out the blueprint for the Initiative's JAGs-oriented victim advocacy projects. Fittingly, in the handbook's introductory pages, there are back-to-back photographs of and quotations from Elie Wiesel and Ben Ferencz. Once again, the two sons of Transylvania's rural Jewish community—one who spent his entire childhood in the region and became a celebrated Holocaust survivor and the other who left early and became a celebrated Holocaust liberator—found their paths crossing. Sadly, Wiesel, the survivor, ultimately passed away in 2016, the year the Ferencz Initiative was launched. But his neighbor from the Old Country, the liberator, lived another seven years and kept fighting for justice.

APART FROM his continuing philanthropy, Ferencz's main way of continuing to fight the good fight was through the projection of his voice in various media from his home in Delray Beach, Florida. As Nuremberg's last living prosecutor, who turned one hundred years of age in March 2020, he generated somewhat of a media frenzy in his final years with features covering his life and work in the *Washington Post,* the *Independent,* and the *Guardian.* Just before his one-hundredth birthday, Netflix released, to great acclaim, the documentary *Prosecuting Evil: The Extraordinary World of Ben Ferencz.* He was also featured on *60 Minutes* and in Michael Moore's documentary *Fahrenheit 11/9.*

Through these outlets, he continued to support the International Criminal Court and the global rule of law. And Ferencz never ceased to call on the carpet its enemies, such as Donald Trump and John Bolton, who served as Trump's national security advisor from 2018 to 2019. Through it all, his overall message remained constant. As he told National Public Radio:

> I have boiled everything down into a slogan: Law not war. Three words. If you could do that, how you would change the world. You'd save billions of dollars every day to be able to take care of the students who can't pay their tuition, take care of the refugees who don't have homes. And the next question is, how do you do it? I have also three words: Never give up. And that's what I'm doing. And all I can do as an old man [is] sit here in a little bungalow in Florida and urge the world to come to its senses. Good luck, world.[51]

POSTSCRIPT

LAW, NOT WAR

As DAWN broke on February 24, 2022, armed forces of the Russian Federation, which had been massing for months, launched an invasion of its neighbor Ukraine, with Russian leader Vladimir Putin falsely claiming the attack against this supposed "artificial" country was necessary to thwart an alleged NATO invasion as well as "genocide" against Russians in the frontier areas.[1] This massive ground assault, a follow-up to the Russian annexation of Crimea and incursions into eastern Ukraine in 2014, was widely condemned as criminal aggression. On March 2, 2022, Sergiy Kyslytsya, Ukraine's UN ambassador, addressed an emergency special session of the General Assembly and called on the international community to stand against Russian aggression, invoking the life and example of Benjamin B. Ferencz. To conclude, he pulled out his cell phone and played a video of the Nuremberg prosecutor reciting his mantras "Law, not war" and "Never give up," along with related words of inspiration. Kyslytsya then asked that the august chamber "show respect" to the UN Charter, the secretary general, and Benjamin Ferencz.[2] And then he sat down. Via a lopsided 141–5 vote (35 abstentions), the General Assembly went on to issue Resolution A/RES/ES-11/1 condemning Russian aggression in Ukraine and demanding that it be terminated.[3] Thus, well into the twenty-first century, Ben Ferencz was still educating, still inspiring, still leading.

Kyslytsya's allusion to Ferencz and the UN Charter in the same breath was apt, not just for the centenarian's contributions to defining the references to "aggression" in the global body's founding document. Fittingly, this pioneer of international justice was born in 1920, the year the Covenant of the League of Nations, the UN Charter's predecessor, went into effect. Thus, he came into the world at the inception of a new international order and came of age as it was being torn apart. He helped construct another one that still governs us today. But does the conflagration in Ukraine presage its end? And if so, what can we learn from the life of Ben Ferencz that, as we potentially transition into a new era, might give us hope that peace and respect for human rights will not disappear?

Certainly, through his long life, Ben Ferencz, a living symbol of the struggle for the rule of law over the last century, never faded away—his "never give up" motto is borne out by his own life experience. Somehow, completely against the odds, a preternaturally tiny, dirt-poor, non-English-speaking immigrant kid in a dysfunctional family survived the Great Depression on the rough streets of New York City, gained admission to an elite tuition-free prep school and college, and then parlayed that into a spot at Harvard Law School, Patton's Judge Advocate Section, Nuremberg, the Claims Conference, and then Telford Taylor's law firm.

But he faced obstacles every step of the way—no grammar school would enroll him in his early years, no address was permanent in the wake of his parents' divorce, no job would stick during the Depression, no branch of the military would take him at the war's onset, no legal work was available during his first years in the army, no prosecutor positions were open to him when he began at Nuremberg, no resources were provided for his Holocaust reparations work, and even Telford Taylor was not able to hire him on his return from Germany. And despite being one of international criminal law's most respected elder statesmen, post-Nuremberg, he was never asked to work on behalf of his own country's government and had to operate as an outsider, a lone wolf.

And yet, in the long run, he was always the great beneficiary of such struggles. If the elementary schools rejected him based on language ability and physical stature, then he would study harder than everyone else and strengthen his body (eventually even becoming a boxer)—and that extra effort would eventually carry him to the nation's premier law school. If his early family life was marked by marital discord and a peripatetic existence, then he would make sure his marriage survived (despite all the challenges it faced—many, admittedly, of his own creation). And, once he bought his family a home in New Rochelle in 1956, it remained the Ferencz homestead until it was sold in 2021. If he could not hold down a job during the Depression, he would make sure his finances were sound during his adult life, and he became a millionaire through savvy investments and then a great philanthropist. If he had to serve as a supply clerk for an anti-aircraft artillery battalion during the war, then he would cultivate an expertise in, if not a genius for, logistics that would prove invaluable for his career as a war crimes investigator, prosecutor, reparations advocate, and peace activist.

If he had to start as an investigator in Nuremberg, then when he got his chance in the courtroom it was as chief prosecutor for one of the most heralded and impactful cases of the Nuremberg Trials. And his investigator experience allowed him to run the Office of Chief of Counsel's most important operation outside of Nuremberg—the Berlin Branch—and later become executive counsel, working with Taylor to oversee all prosecutions as well as establish the Special Operations Division (the birth of the "legacy" subfield in international criminal law). In fact, piecing together the impressive range and importance of these various activities, it is safe to say that Benjamin Ferencz was one of Nuremberg's most important figures post–International Military Tribunal.

If Jewish organizations thought they were hiring a short-term figurehead with no funding to run the Jewish Restitution Successor Organization for a few months, their underestimation of this scrappy underdog fueled a remarkable drive to redeem all possible claims for ill-gotten heirless property in the American sector of occupied Germany and then the birth of a reparations revolution. If he had to wait to join Taylor in law practice, he was soon the second name on the firm letterhead, and the bond between the two men deepened appreciably during the next two decades, especially with America's growing involvement in the Vietnam War. And if he remained outside of official US circles during the post–Cold War renaissance of international criminal law, then it allowed him to assume the mantle of humanity's representative, free to speak his mind and take bold action on behalf of all the world's citizens. His fight to criminalize aggression at Rome in 1998 and activate its jurisdiction in Kampala in 2010, in defiance of American policy, is ample proof of this.

Thus, over the course of more than a hundred years, what this indomitable spirit achieved, the overall body of work, is remarkable. However, quite surprisingly, as we have seen, Ferencz's recounting of it was selective. For example, in his memoirs, he summarily described his 1945 art looting investigative work almost comedically, ignoring his collaboration with the famous Monuments Men and his interrogation of such important witnesses as Gisela Limberger, Hermann Göring's personal secretary. And he concluded that his investigations "didn't amount to much," even though they contributed toward the prosecution of a portion of the case against Göring at the IMT.[4]

Similarly, one might say that he trivialized his significant investigative contributions to the Dachau Trials by unreservedly impugning the integrity of those prosecutions (calling them "terrible" and harping on their summary nature),[5] which over the course of three years (1945–48) resulted in the conviction of more than 1,500 Nazi war criminals. While not ideal from a due process perspective (given defense attorneys representing multiple clients, for example), the justice at Dachau has been commended as a "laudable" effort, supported by defense lawyers whose "total dedication" stands as a "tribute to the military's commitment to fairness."[6] That many of those prosecutions were supported by evidence collected by Ben Ferencz should not be overlooked or underappreciated. Nor should the fact that, despite his censuring them as unfair, hasty proceedings, he spent two days on the stand for one of them, the *Flossenbürg* trial, which lasted from June 1946 through January 1947.

Ferencz similarly trivialized certain of his important post-Nuremberg contributions, such as his powerful courtroom defense of Vietnam War protesters. Or he ignored certain ones entirely, such as his encouraging and codrafting Trinidadian prime minister A. N. R. Robinson's 1989 address to the UN General Assembly requesting creation of an international criminal court, which resuscitated the International Law Commission's then-moribund drafting efforts and ultimately led to the 1998 adoption of the Rome Statute.

But by far the most glaring, and shocking, omissions are on his Nuremberg résumé. According to his standard account, soon after his spring 1946 arrival in the Franconian capital, he was dispatched to Berlin to run Telford Taylor's most important investigative unit. In fact, as research from previously unavailable archives has revealed, his departure for Berlin was not until late summer. In the meantime, he served as an investigator on the *Krupp* and *IG Farben* cases, which, among other activities, led him to various parts of the German-speaking world, including Vienna, Linz, and Frankfurt, and had him interrogating top IG Farben executives. This experience not only had an impact on his being selected as chief of the Berlin Branch; it also helped prepare him to run that office effectively.

Even more puzzling, though, he never spoke about his work as a podium prosecutor for the *Krupp* trial. Having spent the better part of three days speaking with Ben Ferencz in great detail about his career, one of the most dramatic moments in my research for this book was coming across a document in the Telford Taylor Papers at Columbia University that indicated Ferencz was cross-examining witnesses in the *Krupp* trial. I could not believe my eyes! In great excitement, I zipped out of the Butler Library's Rare Book and Manuscript section and onto the grounds of the main campus, where I made cell phone calls in the frozen winter air to fellow Nuremberg experts. They had similarly been ignorant of Ferencz's *Krupp* trial exploits and were equally astonished.[7]

So I decided to travel back to Florida and ask Ben Ferencz himself about this. Why had he always left out this important part of his biography? His response: "It was marginal to my other work."[8] But this seems hard to square with the historical record. First, his courtroom service in *Krupp* shows him at the apogee of his trial advocacy skills (recall the masterful cross-examination featured in chapter 14) and helps show the connection with his earlier investigative efforts for the industrialist cases at Nuremberg before he took over the Berlin Branch. Second, it helps put in perspective his prominent role post-

Nuremberg in directing the Claims Conference's Nazi slave labor civil litigation program (which included a case against Krupp) during the 1950s and 1960s. Ferencz told Saul Kagan in 1958 that it would give him "a great deal of *personal satisfaction* to meet the challenge and reach a settlement for the slave laborers."[9] That said, remarkably, Ferencz never even mentioned his Nuremberg work related to the *Krupp* case in *Less Than Slaves,* his 1979 memoir detailing the slave labor litigation campaign.

Most importantly, however, Ferencz's work on the industrialist cases arguably helps explain, in part, his later passionate crusade to define, criminalize, and prevent aggression. He was well aware that a coterie of key German magnates, the likes of Alfried Krupp, Friedrich Flick, and the directors of IG Farben, had enabled Hitler's military conquests. We have seen that, in May 1946, while investigating the industrialist cases in Nuremberg, he expressed to Gertrude that "IG Farben and Krupp and their officials should be hung as war mongers." He elaborated, "I'm sure we'll be able to prove that they desired and planned for war." And then he concluded, portentously: "I feel a certain satisfaction in the work as though we are groping for the roots of war causes. And perhaps we may move a little closer thereby toward permanent peace."[10]

Of course, much to Ferencz's dismay, the munitions masters tried at Nuremberg were acquitted of the aggression counts. And it was at the end of his civil litigation work against the industrialists, as he likely contemplated the justice deficits in reference to monsters such as Krupp and Flick, that Ferencz decided to phase out of his Holocaust reparations work and devote himself fully to the cause of peace, and, by extension, atrocity prevention. Thus, we might consider Ben's powerful May 1946 communication to his wife as the "missing link" between his Nuremberg work and his ultimate transformation into a peace advocate.

So one gains significant perspective in connecting the dots—from investigation to prosecution to reparation—when focusing on the dovetailing between Ferencz's labor on the industrialist cases and his eventual crusade to help define and criminalize aggression. But why, in later years, when he wrote his memoirs and gave many interviews, did he excise this from his curriculum vitae? I think there could be a couple of reasons. Part of it may be owing to memory loss. During the life of the American trials program, Ferencz's first few months in Nuremberg were relatively inconsequential compared to his time in Berlin and then his stint as *Einsatzgruppen* trial chief prosecutor and Taylor's executive counsel. Over time, this early period may simply have receded in his memory or been conflated with his time in Berlin.

And this would not be the only instance when, presumably, fading recall prevented him from summoning up other important details in his life. We have seen this in many instances, including the particulars regarding his transfer from the Third Army's 115th AAA Gun Battalion to its Judge Advocate Section (initially facilitated by his own application, not merely Sheldon Glueck's intervention, as he would later suggest), his appointment as the OCCWC's executive counsel (pre-*Einsatzgruppen* trial, not posttrial per his standard account), or his role in advocating against John J. McCloy's contemplated clemency/commutation decisions (a limited role with some success rather than no role at all). For similar reasons, his engagement with the *Eichmann* case on the margins and his distaste for Hannah Arendt might have resulted in the gradual elision of any associated memories over the years.

But Ferencz excluding his work on the industrialist cases in telling his life story cannot be chalked up to senility alone. In interviewing him, it was evident to me that he remembered his work on the *Krupp* trial. So why the complete silence over the years? I think the answer is simple—a perception (even if subconscious) that involvement with the *Krupp* Nuremberg proceeding might muddy his Nuremberg legacy. The more streamlined narrative he honed over the years is cleaner and much more powerful: he arrived in Nuremberg and was immediately (and impressively, for his young age) put in charge of the OCCWC's new investigative nerve center in Berlin. While there, he found the evidence that allowed for the *Einsatzgruppen* trial, fought for the proceeding to take place, and then served as its chief prosecutor. It was arguably Nuremberg's most black-and-white, most good-versus-evil case, for which more death sentences were issued than any other trial (and one of only three NMT proceedings pursuant to which defendants were executed).

Compare this to the *Krupp* trial's legacy. All of the defendants in that proceeding were acquitted of crimes against peace, and even those convicted of crimes against humanity (for slave labor/spoliation) received relatively light sentences. And they were soon released thanks to McCloy's absurd clemency/commutation decisions. Even worse, Alfried Krupp regained all his wealth and, via resuming the old family business, soon became one of Europe's wealthiest men. Perhaps, in the end, Ferencz asked himself (again, even if only subconsciously), "Why be associated with such tainted justice?"

And Ferencz's careful curation of his life story went beyond professional endeavors. He assiduously cultivated the image of a man in an idyllic, monogamous marriage with his childhood sweetheart. But we have seen that, owing to his extramarital activities, the relationship with Gertrude was not exactly as he described it. That was the other big shock for me in researching this book. My goal in undertaking the project was to examine the life of a pioneer in my field who achieved great things and to better contextualize that life and those accomplishments, with a particular emphasis on his work for ICL victims. I fully intended to take a "warts and all" approach, always conscious of steering clear of hagiography. Still, I never doubted the veracity of the fairy-tale romance between Ben and Gertrude (and, in my mind, had analogized it with the model relationship of a man I deeply admire, Harry Truman, with his wife, Bess).

But I had always intended for the research to be wide-ranging and thorough, and it eventually led me to revelations about Ben's personal life that I wish I had never encountered. So what was I to do? In pondering this, I turned to the insights of one of history's greatest biography subjects, Samuel Johnson, the famed English man of letters. His life was brilliantly chronicled by his good friend James Boswell, a lawyer, same as I. According to Dr. Johnson:

> I have often thought that there has rarely passed a life of which a judicious and faithful narrative would not be useful. But biography has often been allotted to writers who seem very little acquainted with the nature of their task, or very negligent about the performance. They rarely afford any other account than might be collected from publick papers, but imagine themselves writing a life when they exhibit a chronological series of actions or preferments; and so little regard the manners or behaviour of their heroes, that more knowledge may be gained of a man's real character, by a short conversation with one of his servants, than from a formal and studied narrative. . . . [There] is danger lest his interest, his fear, his gratitude, or his tenderness, overpower his fidelity, and tempt him to conceal, if not to invent. . . . [There] are many who think it an act of piety to hide the faults or failings of their friends . . . we therefore see whole ranks of characters adorned with uniform panegyrick . . . yet [there is] more respect to be paid to knowledge, to virtue, and to truth.[11]

With this guidance in mind, I knew quite clearly that my instinct to report what I had found was grounded in nothing prurient or sensationalistic. I was not interested in flaunting sordid details that might sell more books; I was interested in exposing basic truths that might deepen understanding. Toward that end, I realized that the point of bringing to light Ben's infidelity was to develop the reader's appreciation for his struggles as a child and his traumas as an adult. In other words, it would show how very human he was and, as I realized had been my goal from the outset, better contextualize his accomplishments, if not make them more relatable. How encouraging, if not inspiring, to realize that a man of such amazing achievements was not perfect. We can all do great things even if we sometimes make mistakes.

And there were mitigating circumstances beyond a rocky upbringing, probable PTSD, and abject loneliness. From all accounts, every day of their relationship, Ben never stopped loving Gertrude passionately, fully, utterly; he genuinely adored her. And I got a taste of that when I spent time with the couple in their Delray Beach bungalow, while interviewing Ben for this project. Despite Gertrude's Alzheimer's, Ben doted on her, letting her know in so many little ways how much he loved her. Somehow it was true that he had been adulterous and uxorious all at once.

And he had a similarly complicated relationship with his children. Their father's suffering certainly filtered into their upbringing. But his true love and basic decency, supplementing the nurturing parental foundation laid down, and always vigilantly tended to by Gertrude, is what has marked them more than anything else in the end. After years of wandering, Keri, a brilliant polyglot, discovered her center, got married, reconnected with her family, and found great success as an interpreter/translator in the San Francisco Bay Area. Robin Ferencz-Kotfica, a math whiz, earned degrees at SUNY Stony Brook and Stanford, taught college math (later working as an accountant), got married, and had a daughter, Joey (as well as a stepson, Keith). Don and Nina became lawyers, with the former having first worked as a teacher, tax attorney, and, later (as we have seen), as an expert/activist with respect to the crime of aggression. He also got married (but has since divorced and remarried), had a daughter (Kate), and adopted a son (Jude) with his first wife. Nina Dale also began her career as a schoolteacher but transitioned to law and had a distinguished career with the US Environmental Protection Agency.

Over the years, each of the children, now the age of pensioners themselves, has bought a dwelling in the same Delray Beach, Florida, gated community (Kings Point) as their father, which facilitated their spending time with him when they were in town: Keri and her husband Jim and Robin (now widowed) are based in California; Don in Wales (where he lives with his Welsh/Italian wife, Valentina); and Nina in Maryland. But toward the end of Ben's life, even when they were not in Florida, every Friday at 1:00 p.m. (EST) the children (and sometimes grandchildren) would have a weekly Zoom chat with "Pop." Sadly, Gertrude passed away on September 14, 2019. But the powerful spirit of this remarkable woman, loved by all, an accomplished social worker and selfless mother who contributed so much to her husband's life and career, was always with them. Ben followed her in death on April 7, 2023.

Some might say that Ben Ferencz made his mark through the extremes of chronological age in reference to Nuremberg. In 1947, as a cherub-faced twenty-seven-year-old, he stood out as the youngest chief prosecutor of any of the Nuremberg Trials. And until 2023, as a Yoda-faced 103-year-old, he stood out as the last living Nuremberg prosecutor. But how will he be viewed by posterity in the decades and centuries to come? If this chronicling of his years has anything to do with it, I would hope that his life will be studied and celebrated more for what he did leading up to and in the aftermath of Nuremberg. The Holocaust was the ineffable calamity through which justice for mass atrocity initially took form and developed. And only one man in history, Benjamin Berell Ferencz, can be said to have been a pioneer and major participant in all three of its phases—investigation, prosecution, and restitution. And his work since then may yet spare us from other Holocausts whose horrors we will never know.

In his memoirs, Ferencz tells the story of the inquisitive Danish astronomer Tycho Brahe, who was supported by the equally curious King Frederick II, both eager to know more about the origins of the universe.[12] The king built Brahe a royal astronomical observatory, Uraniborg, on the Island of Hven. Over the years (1576–97), the astronomer used his naked eye, aided by the instruments of pretelescope technology, to mark the position of all the stars he could see in the universe. By the time Frederick II died some two decades later, his successor, Christian IV, asked for an accounting of Brahe's work at Uraniborg. When the new king's bureaucrats questioned this watcher of the sky about his accomplishments, he pointed to his charts painstakingly fixing the position of seven hundred stars. And "if I live long enough," he added, "I hope to reach a thousand."[13] "But what is the use of it?" asked his irritated inquisitors. Tycho confessed that he had "not yet fathomed the mystery of the stars." But he was confident that, in attempting to do so after this own passing, his successors would be saved twenty years of labor.[14]

Ferencz concludes by noting his hope that, at the very least, like the Danish stargazer, vis-à-vis humanity's efforts to achieve justice and peace, his eighty years of labor will have laid a foundation upon which future generations can build. In this sense, Nuremberg's citizen prosecutor, who became the world's citizen peacemaker, will be remembered for more than the extremes of his age; he will be remembered for his extraordinary contributions to the ages. He never gave up—and he will never be forgotten.

NOTES

Prologue

1. Certain accounts state that he was so small he needed to stand on a pile of books to clear the lectern (see, e.g., Sanjeeta Bains, "War Hero Who Brought Nazi Death Squads to Justice at Nuremberg Passes Away Aged 103," *The Mirror*, April 10, 2023). However, photographs of Ferencz at the podium on that day do not depict him standing on any elevated surface.
2. Karen Heller, "The Improbable Story of the Man Who Won History's 'Biggest Murder Trial' at Nuremberg," *Washington Post*, August 31, 2016.
3. Benjamin B. Ferencz, interview by author, Delray Beach, FL, January 18, 2019.
4. Robert H. Jackson, "Opening Statement before the International Military Tribunal, November 21, 1945," Robert H. Jackson Center, https://www.roberthjackson.org/speech-and-writing/opening-statement-before-the-international-military-tribunal/.
5. Benjamin B. Ferencz, "Opening Statement, Einsatzgruppen Trial, September 29, 1947," Famous Trials, https://www.famous-trials.com/nuremberg/1917-einsatzopen.
6. Benjamin B. Ferencz, "Starting Life in America," Stories, https://benferencz.org/stories/1920-1943/starting-life-in-america/.
7. Ibid.
8. Ferencz, interview, January 18, 2019.
9. Bjorn Okholm Skaarup, "The Last Prosecutor," *AJC Global Voice*, May 5, 2020.
10. Federica D'Alessandra, *"Law Not War": Ferencz' 70-Year Fight for a More Just and Peaceful World*, TOAEP Occasional Paper Series (Brussels: Torkel Opsahl Academic EPublisher, 2018), 13–14.
11. Benjamin Ferencz, interview by Joan Ringelheim, United States Holocaust Memorial Museum (USHMM), August 26, 1994, transcript, 32, https://collections.ushmm.org/oh_findingaids/RG-50.030.0269_trs_en.pdf (hereafter cited as USHMM interview); Benjamin B. Ferencz, "Detained for Impersonating an Officer," Stories, https://benferencz.org/stories/1946-1949/detained-for-impersonating-an-officer/.
12. Ferencz, USHMM interview, August 26, 1994, 16, https://collections.ushmm.org/oh_findingaids/RG-50.030.0269_trs_en.pdf.
13. Benjamin Ferencz, "Investigating Nazi Concentration Camps," Stories, https://benferencz.org/stories/1943-1946/investigating-nazi-concentration-camps/.
14. Ferencz, USHMM interview, August 26, 1994, 13–14; Benjamin Ferencz, "Trials by US Military Commissions," Stories, https://benferencz.org/stories/1943-1946/trials-by-u.s-military-commissions/.

15. Benjamin Ferencz, "Introduction," Stories, https://benferencz.org/stories/introduction/introduction/.
16. Benjamin B. Ferencz, interview by author, Delray Beach, FL, January 17, 2019.
17. When I discovered this in my research, it came as a complete surprise. And when I asked other Nuremberg experts about it (even Ferencz's son, Don), they were equally surprised and had been unaware of his role as a *Krupp* trial attorney. This was reported in his *New York Times* obituary (Robert D. McFadden, "Benjamin B. Ferencz, Last Surviving Nuremberg Prosecutor, Dies at 103," *New York Times,* April 8, 2023) and then reported in subsequent obituaries. But I believe that information was acquired by the *Times* writer via interviews with one or more persons who knew about this through my informing them. Indeed, it appears nowhere in Philipp Gut's 2020 biography of Ferencz in German (Gut, *Jahrhundertzeuge Ben Ferencz* [Munich: Piper Verlag, 2020]).
18. See, e.g., Michael Scharf and Benjamin Ferencz, "Last Living Nuremberg Trial Prosecutor Recalls His Work on the Einsatzgruppen Trial," *Judicature* 105, no. 3 (Fall/Winter 2021–22): 11–17, 12–13: "I landed on the beaches of Normandy. I got five battles stars when the war was all over, for not having been killed in any of the major battles, beginning with Normandy beach." Based on this impression he has given, it has been reported that he fought there on D-Day. See Heike Mund, "How 100-Year-Old Ben Ferencz Spent a Lifetime Making Legal History," *Deutsche Welle,* November 18, 2020: "On June 6, 1944, D-Day, he and his comrades jumped from a landing craft and pushed toward Omaha Beach, on the northern French coast of Normandy."
19. See, e.g., Benjamin B. Ferencz, "A Prosecutor's Personal Account: From Nuremberg to Rome," *Journal of International Affairs* 52, no. 2 (Spring 1999): 455, 456: "Following the defeat of Adolf Hitler, Allied leaders were determined to hold war criminals accountable. . . . Washington turned to Professor [Sheldon] Glueck, [who] suggested that the army try to locate me to help set up a war crimes branch." That said, as will be demonstrated in chapter 6, on applying to the JA Section, and at their request that he provide a letter of recommendation, Ferencz did supply one from Professor Glueck.
20. Hilary Earl, email to author, August 14, 2019.
21. Justice Rosie Abella, interview, in *Prosecuting Evil: The Extraordinary World of Ben Ferencz,* dir. Barry Avrich (Melbar Entertainment Group, 2018).
22. Martin Weil, "Telford Taylor, 90, Dies," *Washington Post,* May 24, 1998.
23. Robert Mcg. Thomas Jr., "James M. McHaney Dies at 76; Prosecuted Nazis at Nuremberg," *New York Times,* April 26, 1995, D25.
24. "Charles Marion La Follette," United States House of Representatives Archives, https://history.house.gov/People/Detail/16576.
25. Eric Pace, "Robert Kempner, 93, a Prosecutor at Nuremberg," *New York Times,* August 17, 1993, B6.
26. Kim C. Priemel, *The Betrayal: The Nuremberg Trials and German Divergence* (Oxford: Oxford University Press, 2016), 159 (describing Taylor's staff as a

young "motley crew" of Ivy Leaguers, New Dealers, socialists, Jewish émigrés, lawyers from prestigious Wall Street firms, recent small law school graduates, and individual acquaintances of Taylor).

27. *Collins Dictionary*, s.v. "Citizen," https://www.collinsdictionary.com/us/dictionary/english/citizen (noting that, in an adjectival form, a "citizen journalist" or a "citizen scientist" is an "ordinary person" engaging in such jobs).
28. Tanya Somander, "'The Most Important Title Is "Citizen"': President Obama on the Significance of a Civil Society," Obama White House Archives, September 23, 2014, https://obamawhitehouse.archives.gov/blog/2014/09/23/most-important-title-citizen-president-obama-importance-civil-society.

1. From Dracula's Castle to Hell's Kitchen

1. Andràs Boros-Kazai, "Hungary," in *Eastern Europe: An Introduction to the People, Lands, and Culture*, ed. Richard C. Frucht (Santa Barbara, CA: ABC-CLIO, 2005), 2:353–408.
2. "Romania: Transylvania," The Cultural Guide to Jewish Europe, https://jguideeurope.org/en/region/romania/transylvania/.
3. Pinkas Hakehillot, "Romania," in *Encyclopedia of Jewish Communities* (Jerusalem: Yad Vashem, 1980), 2:269.
4. Ben Ferencz's online memoirs indicate that he was named "Berrel" at birth but changed his name to "Berell" in his later life.
5. Many sources, including the US Holocaust Memorial Museum's Finding Aid for the "Benjamin B. Ferencz Collection," list his birthplace as "Soncutta-Mare, Romania" (a misspelling, as the true name is "Şomcuta Mare"). These references are almost certainly due to the fact that Ciolt is just outside of Şomcuta Mare. It would seem that the larger town is referenced rather than its smaller satellite village.
6. Benjamin Ferencz, "Starting Life in America," Stories, https://benferencz.org/stories/1920-1943/starting-life-in-america/.
7. Ibid.
8. Ibid.
9. Ibid.
10. Ibid.
11. John Strausbaugh, "Turf of Gangs and Gangsters," *New York Times*, August 17, 2007, E23.
12. Ibid.
13. Ferencz, "Starting Life in America."
14. Ibid.
15. Ibid.
16. Ibid.
17. Benjamin Ferencz, "Education on the Sidewalks of New York," Stories, https://benferencz.org/stories/1920-1943/education-on-the-sidewalks-of-new-york/.

18. Benjamin Ferencz, interview by author, January 17, 2019.
19. Benjamin B. Ferencz, interview by Martha Minow, "Dean Minow Interviews Benjamin B. Ferencz '43," Harvard Law School, October 1, 2013, https://youtu.be/skmQgtaFjRM.
20. Ibid.
21. Ferencz, interview, January 17, 2019.
22. Ferencz, "Education on the Sidewalks of New York."
23. Ferencz, interview, January 17, 2019.
24. Ibid.
25. Ibid.
26. Benjamin Ferencz, "Growing up Feeling Lost," Stories, https://benferencz.org/stories/1920-1943/growing-up-feeling-lost/.
27. Ibid.
28. Ibid.
29. Ibid.
30. Ibid.

2. Divorce, Depression, and Deliverance

1. Benjamin Ferencz, "Growing up Feeling Lost," Stories, https://benferencz.org/stories/1920-1943/growing-up-feeling-lost/.
2. Benjamin Ferencz, interview by author, Delray Beach, FL, January 17, 2019.
3. Ibid.
4. Ferencz, "Growing up Feeling Lost."
5. Ibid.
6. Ibid.
7. Benjamin Ferencz, "Starting Life in America," Stories, https://benferencz.org/stories/1920-1943/starting-life-in-america/.
8. Ibid.
9. Benjamin Ferencz, interview by author, January 17, 2019.
10. Heikelina Verrijn Stuart and Marlise Simons, *The Prosecutor and the Judge: Benjamin Ferencz and Antonio Cassese—Interviews and Writings* (Amsterdam: Pallas, 2009), 28.
11. Ferencz, "Starting Life in America."
12. Ferencz, interview, January 17, 2019.
13. Ferencz, "Growing up Feeling Lost."
14. Ibid.
15. Ibid.
16. Ferencz, interview, January 17, 2019.
17. Ferencz, "Growing up Feeling Lost."
18. Bernard Baruch, "The Present Morass: How America Can Pull Herself Out," *Vital Speeches of the Day* 4, no. 11, (March 15, 1938): 322–25.
19. Ferencz, interview, January 17, 2019.
20. Ibid.

21. Ferencz, "Growing up Feeling Lost."
22. Ferencz, interview, January 17, 2019.
23. Ibid.
24. Ferencz, "Growing up Feeling Lost."
25. Benjamin B. Ferencz and Ken Keyes Jr., *Planethood: The Key to Your Survival and Prosperity*, introduction by Ferencz (Coos Bay, OR: Vision, 1988), xxxii.
26. Marty Friedman and Frederick Allen, "The Parkway All-Stars Come Home," *New York Magazine*, June 14, 1982, 16.
27. John Gaynor, "Growing up in the Bronx from 1928 to 1957," *Bronx Board*, https://bronxboard.com/diary/diary.php?f=Growing%20Up%20in%20the%20Bronx%20from%201928%20to%201957.
28. Ibid.
29. Ferencz, "Growing up Feeling Lost."
30. Ferencz, interview, January 17, 2019.
31. Ferencz, "Growing up Feeling Lost."
32. Ibid.
33. Benjamin Ferencz, "The Happy Man Moves On," Stories, https://benferencz.org/stories/1920-1943/the-happy-man-moves-on/.
34. Ibid.
35. Autograph Book, 1933, RG-12.001.01*01, series 1, box 1, Benjamin B. Ferencz Collection, 1919–1994, United States Holocaust Memorial Museum Archives, Washington, DC.
36. Ibid.
37. Ferencz, "The Happy Man Moves On."
38. Ibid.

3. Of Resilience, Romance, and Revolutionaries

1. William L. Silber, "Why Did FDR's Bank Holiday Succeed?," *Economic Policy Review* 15, no. 1 (July 2009): 19–29, https://www.newyorkfed.org/medialibrary/media/research/epr/09v15n1/0907silb.pdf.
2. Benjamin Ferencz, "No High School Diploma for Me," Stories, https://benferencz.org/stories/1920-1943/no-high-school-diploma-for-me/.
3. Ibid.
4. Ibid.
5. Ibid.
6. Ibid.
7. Ibid.
8. Ibid.
9. Ibid.
10. Ibid.
11. Ibid.
12. Ibid.
13. Benjamin Ferencz, "Address upon Receiving the Harvard Law School Medal

of Freedom," Harvard Law School, November 12, 2014, https://youtu.be/BXZcQKnHO-o.

14. Carol Smith, "Free Speech at CCNY, 1931–1942," CUNY Digital History Archive, https://cdha.cuny.edu/collections/show/182.
15. Ibid.
16. Benjamin Ferencz, "Life at City College and the Beginning of Romance," Stories, https://benferencz.org/stories/1920-1943/life-at-city-college-and-the-beginning-of-romance/.
17. Ibid.
18. Gertrude Ferencz, interview by Leslie Frank, October 16, 1995, transcript, University of Connecticut Center for Oral History, Witnesses to Nuremberg, http://hdl.handle.net/11134/20002:860389821.
19. Ibid.
20. Ferencz, "No High School Diploma for Me."
21. Ferencz, "Life at City College and the Beginning of Romance."
22. Ibid.
23. Ibid.
24. Ferencz, interview, January 17, 2019.
25. Ferencz, "Life at City College and the Beginning of Romance."
26. Ibid.
27. Ibid.
28. Ibid.
29. Benjamin Ferencz, interview by Martha Minow, "Dean Minow Interviews Benjamin B. Ferencz '43," Harvard Law School, October 1, 2013, https://youtu.be/skmQgtaFjRM.
30. Heikelina Verrijn Stuart and Marlise Simons, *The Prosecutor and the Judge: Benjamin Ferencz and Antonio Cassese—Interviews and Writings* (Amsterdam: Pallas, 2009).
31. Ferencz, "Life at City College and the Beginning of Romance."
32. Ibid.
33. Ibid.
34. Ibid.
35. Ibid.
36. Ibid.
37. Sarah Kate Kramer, "When Nazis Took Manhattan," National Public Radio, February 20, 2019, https://www.npr.org/sections/codeswitch/2019/02/20/695941323/when-nazis-took-manhattan?t=1580516538440.

4. The World War II Waiting Game at Harvard

1. Benjamin Ferencz, interview by Martha Minow, "Dean Minow Interviews Benjamin B. Ferencz '43," Harvard Law School, October 1, 2013, https://youtu.be/skmQgtaFjRM.

2. Ibid.
3. Drake Bennett, "Crimson Tide," *Boston Globe,* October 19, 2008, http://archive.boston.com/bostonglobe/ideas/articles/2008/10/19/crimson_tide/.
4. Bruce A. Kimball and Daniel R. Coquillette, "History and Harvard Law School," *Fordham Law Review* 87, no. 3 (2018): 883, 894.
5. Ibid., 896.
6. Ferencz, interview, October 1, 2013.
7. Winthrop K. Twombly d, "Around the Yard," *Harvard Crimson,* August 9, 1945, https://www.thecrimson.com/article/1945/8/9/around-the-yard-pmid-term-hour-exam/.
8. Benjamin Ferencz, "Lessons Learned at Harvard Law School," Stories, https://benferencz.org/stories/1920-1943/lessons-learned-at-harvard-law-school/.
9. Ibid.
10. Ibid.
11. Ibid.
12. Robert S. Summers, *Lon L. Fuller* (Stanford, CA: Stanford University Press, 1984), 1.
13. Lon L. Fuller, "Positivism and Fidelity to Law—A Reply to Professor Hart," *Harvard Law Review* 71, no. 4 (February 1958): 630, 660.
14. Albert M. Sacks, "Lon Luvois Fuller," *Harvard Law Review* 92, no. 2 (December 1978): 349, 349.
15. Ferencz, interview, October 1, 2013.
16. Ferencz, "Lessons Learned at Harvard Law School."
17. 250 U.S. 616 (1919).
18. Ferencz, "Lessons Learned at Harvard Law School."
19. Ibid.
20. Ferencz, interview, October 1, 2013.
21. Ferencz, "Lessons Learned at Harvard Law School."
22. Ibid.
23. Ibid.
24. Ibid.
25. See Peter Rees, "Nathan Roscoe Pound and the Nazis," *Boston College Law Review* 60, no. 5 (2019): 1313.
26. Benjamin Ferencz, interview by Joan Ringelheim, United States Holocaust Memorial Museum, August 26, 1994, transcript, 4–5, https://collections.ushmm.org/oh_findingaids/RG-50.030.0269_trs_en.pdf.
27. There is no explicit reference to the von Hagenbach trial in the book that Glueck eventually published, *War Criminals: Their Prosecution and Punishment.* On the von Hagenbach precedent, see Gregory S. Gordon, "The Trial of Peter von Hagenbach: Reconciling History, Historiography and International Criminal Law," in *The Hidden History of War Crimes Trials,* ed. Kevin Jon Heller and Gerry Simpson (London: Oxford University Press, 2013): 13–49.
28. Department of State, "France, Great Britain, and Russia Joint Declaration,

1915," Facing History, May 29, 1915, https://www.facinghistory.org/resource-library/totally-unofficial-raphael-lemkin-and-genocide/france-great-britain-and-russia-joint-declaration-1915. It should also be noted that the Joint Declaration is not explicitly cited in *War Criminals: Their Prosecution and Punishment.* And the book's explicit focus is war crimes rather than crimes against humanity.

29. Sheldon Glueck, *War Criminals: Their Prosecution and Punishment* (New York: Alfred A. Knopf, 1944), 38.
30. Ibid., 17.
31. Ibid., 10.
32. John B. Pope, review of *War Criminals: Their Prosecution and Punishment,* by Sheldon Glueck, *Virginia Law Review* 31, no. 3 (1945): 739, 743.
33. Glueck, *War Criminals,* viii.
34. Benjamin Ferencz, "Getting into the Army," Stories, https://benferencz.org/stories/1943-1946/getting-into-the-army/.
35. Ibid.
36. Ibid.
37. Ibid.
38. Ibid.
39. Ibid.
40. Ibid.
41. Ibid.
42. Ibid.
43. Ferencz, interview, October 1, 2013.
44. Ferencz, "Getting into the Army."
45. Glueck, *War Criminals,* viii. Ferencz does not specifically recollect being in the seminar, but the Harvard Law School Registrar's Office has confirmed that Professor Glueck taught "Legal History/ Criminal Justice Administration," and the end date of the course as noted on Ben's transcript, and "1/43" corresponds with Glueck's description of the time period in which he conducted the seminar (Benjamin Berell Ferencz, Harvard Law School transcript, on file with author).
46. Ferencz, "Getting into the Army."

5. Private Benjamin

1. Benjamin Ferencz to Sheldon Glueck, May 27, 1943, HOLLIS601626, box 74, Sheldon Glueck Papers, Harvard Law Library, Cambridge, MA.
2. Ibid.
3. Benjamin Ferencz, interview by Global Brief, August 20, 2015, https://www.youtube.com/watch?v=Kcu78HgaexY&t=381s; Benjamin Ferencz, "Lessons Learned at Harvard Law School," Stories, https://benferencz.org/stories/1920-1943/lessons-learned-at-harvard-law-school/.

4. Benjamin B. Ferencz, "Basic Training," Stories, https://benferencz.org/stories/1943-1946/basic-training/.
5. Ferencz to Sheldon Glueck, May 27, 1943.
6. Benjamin B. Ferencz, interview by Joan Ringelheim, United States Holocaust Memorial Museum, August 26, 1994, transcript, 7, https://collections.ushmm.org/oh_findingaids/RG-50.030.0269_trs_en.pdf.
7. Ferencz, "Basic Training." Over time, Ferencz forgot his name, and I did not find it in my research for this book.
8. Diary of Benjamin Ferencz, September 9, 1943, to April 22, 1944, series 1, RG-12.001.01*02, box 1, Benjamin B. Ferencz Collection, 1919–1994, United States Holocaust Memorial Museum Archives, Washington DC.
9. Ibid., 5.
10. Ibid.
11. Ibid., 12 (emphasis in the original).
12. Ibid., 6.
13. Ibid., 6–7.
14. Ferencz, "Basic Training."
15. Ibid.
16. Ibid.
17. Ibid.
18. Ibid.
19. Ibid.
20. Ferencz Diary, 1943–1944, 1.
21. Ibid., 2.
22. Ibid.
23. Ibid., 3.
24. Ibid., 10.
25. Ibid., 9.
26. Ibid., 10.
27. Ibid., 13.
28. Benjamin B. Ferencz, "Rehabilitation of Army Offenders," *Journal of Criminal Law and Criminology* 34, no. 4 (1944): 245, 247.
29. Ferencz Diary, 1943–1944, 19.
30. Ferencz, "Basic Training."
31. Ferencz Diary, 1943–1944, 15.
32. Ibid., 19.
33. Ibid.
34. The original plan for invading France called for a two-pronged attack, in Normandy and Southern France. But there were not enough ships for both landings, so the invasion of Southern France was delayed. That happened later, in August 1944, via Operation Dragoon.
35. Ferencz Diary, 1943–1944, 28–29.
36. Ibid., 30–31.

37. Ibid., 32.
38. Ibid., 32–33.
39. Ibid., 34–36.
40. Ferencz Diary, 1943–1944, 37.
41. Ibid., 39.
42. Ferencz, "Basic Training." It should be noted that this incident is nowhere recorded in Ben Ferencz's contemporary diary.
43. Ferencz Diary, 1943–1944, 42.
44. Ibid.
45. Ibid., 24–25.
46. Ibid., 47.
47. Ibid., 53.
48. Benjamin Ferencz, "Mutiny on the HMS Strathnaver," Stories, https://benferencz.org/stories/1943-1946/mutiny-on-the-hms-strathnaver/.
49. Ibid.
50. Ibid.
51. Ibid.
52. Ferencz Diary, 1943–1944, 73.
53. Ibid., 74.
54. Ibid., 75.
55. Ibid.
56. Ibid., 79.
57. Ibid., 84–85.
58. Ibid., 81.
59. Ibid., 92–93.
60. Ibid., 94–95.
61. Benjamin Ferencz, "England as a Staging Area," Stories, https://benferencz.org/stories/1943-1946/england-as-a-staging-area/.
62. Ibid.
63. Benjamin Ferencz, "Preparing for War," Stories, https://benferencz.org/stories/1943-1946/preparing-for-war/.
64. Ibid.
65. Ibid.

6. Patton's Soldier

1. Diary of Benjamin Ferencz, May 13, 1943 to August 15, 1945, 22, series 1, RG-12.001.01*03, box 1, Benjamin B. Ferencz Collection, 1919–1994, United States Holocaust Memorial Museum Archives, Washington, DC. Ferencz also noted in his diary that the "sea-sick pills and vomit bags I had issued to everyone on board ship were completely wasted" (ibid.). In direct contrast, in his later "Stories," Ferencz refers to "turbulent seas" and a "bunch of seasick Americans"

(Benjamin Ferencz, "The Liberation of France," Stories, https://benferencz.org/stories/1943-1946/the-liberation-of-france/).

2. Apparently, the troops spent the night of July 4 on the SS *James B. Weaver* and actually disembarked on July 5 (ibid., 24).
3. Ibid., 26.
4. Ibid.
5. Ibid., 30.
6. Cleve C. Barkley, "Key to the Normandy Breakout: The Hill over St. Lo," *WWII History* magazine, https://warfarehistorynetwork.com/2016/11/23/key-to-the-normandy-breakout-the-hill-over-st-lo/.
7. Benjamin Ferencz, "Farewell Artillery, Hello General Patton," Stories, https://benferencz.org/stories/1943-1946/farewell-artillery-hello-general-patton/.
8. Ferencz, "The Liberation of France."
9. Ibid
10. Christopher Klein, "10 Things You May Not Know about George Patton," History.com, updated April 26, 2019, https://www.history.com/news/10-things-you-may-not-know-about-george-patton.
11. Ferencz Diary, May 1943–August 1945, 39–40.
12. Victor Davis Hanson, "George Patton's Summer of 1944," Real Clear Politics, July 24, 2014, https://www.realclearpolitics.com/articles/2014/07/24/george_pattons_summer_of_1944_123439.html.
13. Ferencz Diary, May 1943–August 1945, 40–41.
14. Ibid., 43–44. In the diary, there is a misspelling, and the town is referred to as "Avrances" and not by its proper name, Avranches.
15. Ibid., 42–43.
16. Ferencz Diary, May 1943–August 1945, 48–49.
17. Ibid., 49.
18. Ferencz, "Farewell Artillery, Hello General Patton."
19. Ferencz Diary, May 1943–August 1945, 50.
20. Ibid., 51.
21. Ibid., 47–48.
22. Ibid., 50. The diary states that the chateau was located on top of a "mountain," but it would appear that there are no mountains in this area of France.
23. Ibid., 53.
24. Ibid., 54–55.
25. Ibid., 55–56.
26. Ferencz, "The Liberation of France."
27. Ferencz Diary, May 1943–August 1945, 53.
28. Ibid., 59.
29. Ibid., 59, 61.
30. Hanson, "Patton's Summer."
31. Ferencz Diary, May 1943–August 1945, 70–71.

32. Ferencz, "The Liberation of France."
33. Benjamin Ferencz, "Advancing into Germany," Stories, https://benferencz.org/stories/1943-1946/advancing-into-germany/.
34. Ibid.
35. Ibid.
36. Benjamin B. Ferencz, "Hostile French Civilians," *Journal of Criminal Law & Criminology* 35, no. 4 (1945): 228–32.
37. Ferencz Diary, May 1943–August 1945, 77.
38. In the " Stories," Ferencz did not mention his JA Section transfer application. Rather, he indicated the transfer notice came as a complete surprise since, unbeknownst to him, he had been recommended to the Pentagon by, he speculated, Sheldon Glueck and was transferred as part of the army setting up a war crimes investigative unit: "What brought about this sudden attack of sanity on the part of the army, I may never know. I suspect that following the Allied Leaders Declaration, the army . . . turned to . . . Professor Sheldon Glueck . . . and I believe that he gave my name" (Ferencz, "Farewell Artillery, Hello General Patton"). That said, Ferencz's diary stated that he was "really surprised" when notified of the transfer (Ferencz Diary, May 1943–August 1945, 81). Perhaps the diary/Benny Stories discrepancy can be reconciled by considering that Ben was initially told there were no JA Section openings. It may be that, in the intervening two weeks, Glueck did communicate with decision-makers in the Pentagon such that a position was created for Ferencz. After all, Glueck had already provided a recommendation letter—he may very well have followed up with a phone call. Either way, the army ultimately realized that Corporal Ferencz was of more value in the JA Section.

7. War Crimes Investigator

1. Diary of Benjamin Ferencz, May 13, 1943, to August 15, 1945, 81, 22, series 1, RG-12.001.01*03, box 1, Benjamin B. Ferencz Collection, 1919–1994, United States Holocaust Memorial Museum Archives, Washington, DC.
2. Ibid. This is at odds with Ferencz's account in the Benny Stories of his arrival at the Judge Advocate Section. There, he wrote that Patton's headquarters were in Luxembourg, not Nancy (Benjamin Ferencz, "Farewell Artillery, Hello General Patton," Stories, https://benferencz.org/stories/1943-1946/farewell-artillery-hello-general-patton/).
3. Ferencz Diary, May 1943–August 1945, 81.
4. Ibid., 82.
5. Ibid.
6. Ibid. Similarly, this is inconsistent with Ferencz's Stories description of his first days at the Judge Advocate Section. There, he wrote: "When I reported [there,] I was greeted by a Lt. Colonel Joseph who confirmed that . . . they had received orders to set up a war crimes branch [and that he] had never been

trained to deal with foreign persecutions. . . . He asked in all seriousness, 'Tell me Corporal, what is a war crime?' My hour had finally come!" (Benjamin Ferencz, "Farewell Artillery, Hello General Patton," Stories, https://benferencz.org/stories/1943-1946/farewell-artillery-hello-general-patton/). One wonders how a superior officer in the Judge Advocate Section of the Third Army at that time would not know what a war crime was. Someone in that position would have been quite familiar with War Department's *Field Manual FM 27-10*, "Rules of Land Warfare," whose most recent edition at that time had been issued in October 1940. Chapter 11 ("Penalties for Violations of the Laws of War"), paragraph 347, of that document defined "Offenses by Armed Forces" (War Department, "Rules of Land Warfare," *Field Manual 27-10* [Washington, DC: War Department, 1940], 86–87, https://tile.loc.gov/storage-services/service/ll/llmlp/rules_warfare-1940/rules_warfare-1940.pdf).

7. War Department, *Field Manual 27-10*, 83.
8. Ibid.
9. Evan Andrews, "8 Things You May Not Know about the Battle of the Bulge," History Stories, last modified December 6, 2019, https://www.history.com/news/8-things-you-may-not-know-about-the-battle-of-the-bulge.
10. Benjamin Ferencz, "Trials by U.S. Military Commissions," Stories, https://benferencz.org/stories/1943-1946/trials-by-u.s-military-commissions/.
11. Ibid.
12. Ibid.
13. Ibid. Ferencz's diary, written around the time of these events, does not present this kind of detail regarding his time in the Ardennes Forest. In the diary, on January 12, 1945, Ferencz recounts: "The Germans had launched a counter-offensive just before Xmas and had succeeded in making quite a dent in our lines and wiping out most of the First Army. To slow down their drive and fill in the gap, General Patton rushed Third Army forces up to attack at the flanks. We moved along also, to be nearer our fighting lines. So far we have not seen any action at all. We are comfortably located in a fine office building and Luxembourg seems to be as good a place as France" (Ferencz Diary, May 1943–August 1945, 85–86). Of course, it is possible that the initial movement toward the German flank with Patton took JA soldiers as far as Bastogne. Perhaps after that, then, they started heading back and returned to headquarters in Luxembourg, where they were located when Ferencz wrote the January 12 passage in his diary. Still, it is odd that the compelling account of his time in Bastogne was not recorded contemporaneously in the diary.
14. Hannah Tindle, "Ten Things You Might Not Know about Femme Fatale Marlene Dietrich," *AnOther,* April 10, 2018, https://www.anothermag.com/fashion-beauty/10744/ten-things-you-might-not-know-about-femme-fatale-marlene-dietrich (emphasis in the original).
15. Danielle DeSimone, "Why Marlene Dietrich Was One of the Most Patriotic Women in World War II," *United Service Organizations,* March 5, 2020, https://

www.uso.org/stories/2414-marlene-dietrich-most-patriotic-women-in-world-war-ii.

16. Benjamin Ferencz, "An Entertaining Tale," Stories, https://benferencz.org/stories/1943-1946/an-entertaining-tale/.
17. Ibid.
18. Ibid.
19. Judge Advocate General's Corps, *Army Lawyer: A History of the Judge Advocate General's Corps, 1775–1975* (Washington, DC: United States Army, 1975), 181, https://commons.wikimedia.org/wiki/File:The_Army_lawyer_a_history_of_the_Judge_Advocate_General%27s_Corps,_1775-1975.pdf.
20. Convention Relative to the Treatment of Prisoners of War, Geneva, 27 July 1929, International Committee of the Red Cross, pt. 1, art. 2, https://ihl-databases.icrc.org/ihl/INTRO/305.
21. Oliver Clutton Brock, *Footprints on the Sands of Time: RAF Bomber Command Prisoners of War in Germany 1939–1945* (London: Grub Street, 2003), 472.
22. Ibid.
23. Ibid. (emphasis added).
24. Traugott Vitz, "The Murder of Allied Airmen," Aircrew Remembered, https://www.aircrewremembered.com/VitzArchive/.
25. Ibid.
26. Ibid.
27. Ibid.
28. Ferencz, "Trials by U.S. Military Commissions."
29. Ibid.
30. Ferencz Diary, May 1943–August 1945, 81–82. It should be noted that the diary does not spell out the words "enlisted men." Rather, it reads, literally, "the officers & EM have been very friendly."
31. Ibid., 82. It may be that Cheever and the four lieutenant colonels, along with Ferencz, were assigned to a new war crimes investigation subunit within the JA Office. That would explain the seeming discrepancy between Ferencz's description of the size of the entire JA Office in his memoirs versus his diary. He was likely referring only to the war crimes investigation subunit in his memoirs.
32. Ferencz Diary, May 1943–August 1945, 91.
33. Ferencz, "Trials by U.S. Military Commissions."
34. Benjamin Ferencz, interview by author, Delray Beach, FL, January 17, 2019.
35. Ferencz, "Trials by U.S. Military Commissions."
36. Ferencz, interview, January 17, 2019.
37. Ferencz, "Trials by U.S. Military Commissions."
38. Ferencz, interview, January 17, 2019.
39. Ibid.
40. Ibid.
41. Ibid.

42. Ferencz, "Trials by U.S. Military Commissions."
43. Ferencz, interview, January 17, 2019.
44. Ferencz, "Trials by U.S. Military Commissions."
45. Ibid.
46. Ferencz, "Trials by U.S. Military Commissions."
47. Ibid.
48. Ibid. Ferencz Diary, May 1943–August 1945, 102.
49. Ferencz, "Trials by U.S. Military Commissions."
50. Ibid.

8. Liberating the Concentration Camps

1. Edward Raczynski, Stanislaw Mikolajczyk, and Jan Karski, *The Mass Extermination of Jews in German Occupied Poland* (London: Hutchinson, 1942).
2. C. Peter Chen, "Discovery of Concentration Camps and the Holocaust: 24 Jul 1944–29 Apr 1945," World War II Database, https://ww2db.com/battle_spec.php?battle_id=136.
3. Stephen E. Ambrose, *The Supreme Commander* (Garden City, NY: Doubleday, 1970), 659.
4. Benjamin Ferencz, "Trials by U.S. Military Commissions," Stories, https://benferencz.org/stories/1943-1946/trials-by-u.s-military-commissions/.
5. Ibid.
6. Ibid.
7. Bruce Nickols, "Report from the Ohrdruf Liberation," Stories, https://remember.org/witness/ohrdruf.
8. Robert H. Abzug, *Inside the Vicious Heart: Americans and the Liberation of Nazi Concentration Camps* (Oxford: Oxford University Press, 1987), 21.
9. Benjamin Ferencz, "Investigating Nazi Concentration Camps," Stories, https://benferencz.org/stories/1943-1946/investigating-nazi-concentration-camps/.
10. Ibid.
11. When I asked him about it, Ferencz stated that he had no conscious recollection of seeing Wiesel there (Benjamin B. Ferencz, in discussion with author, January 2019).
12. *Prosecuting Evil: The Extraordinary World of Ben Ferencz,* dir. Barry Avrich (2018; Portland, OR: Collective Eye Films, 2021), DVD.
13. Ferencz states definitively, in his correspondence with Trudy, that he found the lampshades. On human skin lampshades, see Tim Rutten, review of *The Lampshade,* by Mark Jacobson, *Los Angeles Times,* October 27, 2010, https://www.latimes.com/archives/la-xpm-2010-oct-27-la-et-rutten-20101027-story.html.
14. Ferencz, "Investigating Nazi Concentration Camps."
15. Ibid.
16. Ibid.

17. Ibid.
18. Benjamin Ferencz to Gertrude Fried, April 16, 1945, series 1, RG-12.001.03*01, box 3, Benjamin B. Ferencz Collection, 1919–1994, United States Holocaust Memorial Museum Archives.
19. Benjamin Ferencz to Gertrude Fried, April 20, 1945, series 1, RG-12.001.03*01, box 3, Benjamin B. Ferencz Collection, 1919–1994, United States Holocaust Memorial Museum Archives.
20. Benjamin Ferencz to Gertrude Fried, April 27, 1945, series 1, RG-12.001.03*01, box 3, Benjamin B. Ferencz Collection, 1919–1994, United States Holocaust Memorial Museum Archives, Washington, DC.
21. This may seem at odds with his earlier refusing the sergeant stripes (as recounted in the Stories). Perhaps this can be explained by the fact that, had the promotion resulted in a rank much higher than sergeant, the insignia would not have been a hindrance. And likely his sense of duty regarding the unit's needs would have trumped his distaste for higher rank.
22. Benjamin Ferencz to Gertrude Fried, April 27, 1945, series 1, RG-12.001.03*01, box 3, Benjamin B. Ferencz Collection, 1919–1994, United States Holocaust Memorial Museum Archives, Washington, DC.
23. Ibid.
24. Benjamin Ferencz to Gertrude Fried, April 16, 1945, series 1, RG-12.001.03*01, box 3, Benjamin B. Ferencz Collection, 1919–1994, United States Holocaust Memorial Museum Archives, Washington, DC.
25. Benjamin Ferencz to Gertrude Fried, April 29, 1945, series 1, RG-12.001.03*01, box 3, Benjamin B. Ferencz Collection, 1919–1994, United States Holocaust Memorial Museum Archives, Washington, DC.
26. Ibid.
27. Ibid.
28. Ibid.
29. Ibid.
30. Ibid.
31. Ibid.
32. Ibid.
33. Ibid.
34. Ibid.
35. Ferencz, "Investigating Nazi Concentration Camps."
36. Ibid.
37. In addition to Gauleiter von Oberdonau (a Nazi Party regional command for Upper Austria), Eigruber also carried the titles of SS-Obergruppenführer (lieutenant general) and Landeshauptmann von Oberösterreich (provincial governor of Upper Austria) (see Mario Morgner, *Verlorenes Weltwund—Das Bernsteinzimmer* [Norderstedt, Germany: Herstellung und Verlag, 2011], 153).
38. Benjamin Ferencz to Gertrude Fried, May 15, 1945, series 1, RG-12.001.03*01,

box 3, Benjamin B. Ferencz Collection, 1919–1994, United States Holocaust Memorial Museum Archives, Washington, DC.

39. Ibid.
40. Ibid.
41. Ibid.
42. Ibid.
43. Diary of Benjamin Ferencz, May 13, 1943, to August 15, 1945, 99, series 1, RG-12.001.01*03, box 1, Benjamin B. Ferencz Collection, 1919–1994, United States Holocaust Memorial Museum Archives, Washington, DC.
44. Ibid.
45. Benjamin Ferencz, interview by Joan Ringelheim, United States Holocaust Memorial Museum, August 26, 1994, transcript, 32, https://collections.ushmm.org/oh_findingaids/RG-50.030.0269_trs_en.pdf.
46. Benjamin Ferencz to Gertrude Fried, May 15, 1945, series 1, RG-12.001.03*01, box 3, Benjamin B. Ferencz Collection, 1919–1994, United States Holocaust Memorial Museum Archives, Washington, DC.
47. Lucien Vanherle, sworn statement, May 1945 (French translation into English by Benjamin B. Ferencz; provided to author by Don Ferencz).
48. Ibid.
49. Ibid.
50. Ibid.
51. Mark Vasdaz, "Concentration Camps: Ebensee (Austria)," Jewish Virtual Library, https://www.jewishvirtuallibrary.org/ebensee-austria.
52. Ibid.
53. Ibid.
54. Ferencz Diary, May 1943–August 1945, 99.
55. Benjamin Ferencz to Gertrude Fried, May 27, 1945, series 1, RG-12.001.03*01, box 3, Benjamin B. Ferencz Collection, 1919–1994, United States Holocaust Memorial Museum Archives, Washington, DC.
56. Ferencz, "Investigating Nazi Concentration Camps."
57. Ibid.

9. Monuments Man at the Eagle's Nest and the Dachau Trials

1. Diary of Benjamin Ferencz, May 13, 1943, to August 15, 1945, 81–82, series 1, RG-12.001.01*03, box 1, Benjamin B. Ferencz Collection, 1919–1994, United States Holocaust Memorial Museum Archives, Washington, DC.
2. Stephen E. Ambrose, *Band of Brothers: E Company, 506th Regiment, 101st Airborne: From Normandy to Hitler's Eagle's Nest* (New York: Simon and Schuster, 1992), 353.
3. Ibid., 353–54.

4. Benjamin Ferencz, "Looking for Hitler and Looted Art," Stories, https://benferencz.org/stories/1943-1946/looking-for-hitler-and-looted-art/.
5. There are significant discrepancies between Ferencz's account of this investigation in the Stories and one given in a roughly contemporaneous letter written to Gertrude Fried on May 23, 1945 (e.g., conducting the investigation alone versus with others). The account in this book reconciles the Stories with the May 23, 1945, letter (on file with author, provided by Keri Ferencz). Moreover, based on certain details in the narrative (e.g., reference to a verandah), it is possible Ferencz was mistaking the Eagle's Nest for Hitler's residence in the Obersalzberg, the Berghof, which was relatively close to the Eagle's Nest.
6. Ferencz, "Looking for Hitler and Looted Art."
7. Ibid.
8. Kenneth D. Alford, *Nazi Plunder: Great Treasure Stories of World War II* (Cambridge, MA: De Capo, 2003), iii.
9. Mary Kate Farber, "The Art Looting Investigation Unit: Finding Their Place in World War Two History" (honors thesis, Union College, 2015), 60, https://digitalworks.union.edu/cgi/viewcontent.cgi?article=1297&context=theses.
10. In the Stories, Ferencz's narrative gives one the impression that he conducted the mission by himself—there is no mention of McKay. Moreover, he suggests that Würzburg was still burning as a result of the British firebombing (Ferencz, "Looking for Hitler and Looted Art"). This is not plausible as the British firebombing of Würzburg took place on March 16—Ferencz arrived in Würzburg approximately three months later, in June.
11. Benjamin Ferencz to Gertrude Fried, June 6, 1945, series 1, RG-12.001.03*01, box 3, Benjamin B. Ferencz Collection, 1919–1994, United States Holocaust Memorial Museum Archives, Washington, DC.
12. Ibid. Presumably Haberstock was speaking in German.
13. Ibid.
14. Ibid.
15. Benjamin Ferencz to Gertrude Fried, July 21, 1945 (letter provided to author by Keri Ferencz).
16. Felix Bohr et al., "Hildebrand Gurlitt's Deep Nazi Ties," *Spiegel International*, December 23, 2013, https://www.spiegel.de/international/germany/hildebrand-gurlitt-and-his-dubious-dealings-with-nazi-looted-art-a-940625.html. Ferencz's contemporary reports of the hoard have not been located.
17. Ibid.
18. Ferencz, "Looking for Hitler and Looted Art."
19. Benjamin Ferencz to Gertrude Fried, May 23, 1945.
20. Michael Hussey, Michael J. Kurtz, and Greg Bradsher, "OSS Art Looting Investigation Unit Reports," Holocaust-Era Assets, National Archives and Records Administration, Washington, DC, https://www.archives.gov/research/holocaust/art/oss-art-looting-investigation-unit-reports.html.
21. Ferencz Diary, May 1943–August 1945, 104–5.

22. Ibid., 105–6.
23. Ibid., 106–7.
24. Ibid.
25. See Thomas S. Hinkel, "Interrogation of Karl Haberstock, November 6, 1945," Donovan Nuremberg Trials Collection, Cornell Library, http://s3.amazonaws.com/cul-hydra/nur/nur00780/pdfs/nur00780.pdf.
26. "Theodore Rousseau, Jr. (1912–1973)," Monuments Men and Women Foundation, https://www.monumentsmenandwomenfnd.org/rousseau-lt-theodore-jr.
27. Benjamin Ferencz to Gertrude Fried, August 8, 1945 (letter provided to author by Keri Ferencz).
28. Michael J. Bazyler and Frank M. Tuerkheimer, *Forgotten Trials of the Holocaust* (New York: NYU Press, 2014), 79.
29. Durwood "Derry" Riedel, "The U.S. War Crimes Tribunals at the Former Dachau Concentration Camp: Lessons for Today," *Berkeley Journal of International Law* 24 (2006): 554, 571.
30. A scattering of prosecutions for the murder of downed U.S. pilots had been conducted in various parts of Germany even before the *Hadamar* trial, as early as June 1945. These were very small proceedings and will not be the object of greater exposition here.
31. The Moscow Conference: Joint Four-Nation Declaration, October 1943, https://avalon.law.yale.edu/wwii/moscow.asp.
32. James Larry Taulbee, *War Crimes and Trials: A Primary Source Guide* (Santa Barbara, CA: ABC-CLIO, 2018), 78.
33. Joshua M. Greene, *Justice at Dachau* (New York: Broadway, 2003), 29.
34. Benjamin Ferencz, interview by Joan Ringelheim, United States Holocaust Memorial Museum, August 26, 1994, transcript, 15, https://collections.ushmm.org/oh_findingaids/RG-50.030.0269_trs_en.pdf.
35. Bazyler and Tuerkheimer, *Forgotten Trials of the Holocaust*, 95–96.
36. See, e.g., Benjamin Ferencz, interview by author, Delray Beach, FL, January 17, 2019.
37. Benjamin Ferencz to Gertrude Ferencz, July 18, 1946 (letter provided to author by Keri Ferencz).
38. Bazyler and Tuerkheimer, *Forgotten Trials of the Holocaust*, 95–96.

10. From the Pentagon to the Palace of Justice

1. Benjamin Ferencz, "Starting a New Life," Stories, https://benferencz.org/stories/1943-1946/starting-a-new-life/.
2. See Sheldon Glueck to Dean Frederick K. Beutel, November 14, 1947, Sheldon Glueck Papers 1916–1972, box 74, Harvard Law School Library, Harvard University, Cambridge, MA.
3. Benjamin Ferencz, "Starting a New Life," Stories, https://benferencz.org/stories/1943-1946/starting-a-new-life/.

4. Ibid.
5. Ibid.
6. Benjamin Ferencz, interview by author, Delray Beach, FL, June 8, 2020. In the numerous accounts I had heard/read of Ferencz describing this momentous encounter, he had never mentioned this detail. But it came out spontaneously during one of our discussions.
7. Ibid.
8. Based on anecdotal evidence, Ben stopped referring to his significant other as "Trudy" after the war.
9. Keri Ferencz, interview by author, Berkeley, CA, April 11, 2022.
10. Ibid.
11. Ibid.
12. Nina Dale, interview by author, Delray Beach, FL, April 10, 2022.
13. Telford Taylor, *The Anatomy of the Nuremberg Trials: A Personal Memoir* (New York: Alfred A. Knopf, 1992), 61.
14. Ibid.
15. International Military Tribunal, "Judgment," in *Trial of the Major War Criminals before the International Military Tribunal,* vol. 1 (Nuremberg: Secretariat of the Tribunal, 1946), 223, https://tile.loc.gov/storage-services/service/ll/llmlp/2011525338_NT_Vol-I/2011525338_NT_Vol-I.pdf.
16. Robert H. Jackson, "Opening Statement before the International Military Tribunal, November 21, 1945," https://www.roberthjackson.org/speech-and-writing/opening-statement-before-the-international-military-tribunal/.
17. Ibid.
18. Ibid.
19. Ibid. As we shall see in chapters 12 and 13, these "excuses" for massacres (e.g., fires, epidemics) were fabricated and inserted to help salve the consciences of the executioners. These massacres took place pursuant to a policy of genocide.
20. "Testimony of Otto Ohlendorf, January 3, 1946," in *Trial of the Major War Criminals before the International Military Tribunal,* vol. 4 (Nuremberg: International Military Tribunal, 1946), 314–16, https://tile.loc.gov/storage-services/service/ll/llmlp/2011525338_NT_Vol-IV/2011525338_NT_Vol-IV.pdf.
21. Benjamin Ferencz to Gertrude Ferencz, May 13, 1946 (letter provided to author by Keri Ferencz).
22. Ibid.
23. Benjamin Ferencz to Gertrude Ferencz, May 11, 1946 (letter provided to author by Keri Ferencz).
24. Benjamin Ferencz to Gertrude Ferencz, May 16, 1946 (letter provided to author by Keri Ferencz).
25. Ibid.
26. Benjamin B. Ferencz, "Detained for Impersonating an Officer," Stories, https://benferencz.org/stories/1946-1949/detained-for-impersonating-an-officer/.
27. Ibid.

28. Telford Taylor, *Final Report to the Secretary of the Army on the Nuernberg War Crimes Trials under Control Council Law No. 10* (Washington, DC: US Government Printing Office, 1949), 36, https://tile.loc.gov/storage-services/service/ll/llmlp/NT_final-report/NT_final-report.pdf.
29. Telford Taylor, "Organizational Memo No. 1, May 17, 1946," RG 238, entry NM-70 202, Office of Chief of Counsel, Subsequent Proceedings Division, National Archives and Records Administration, Washington, DC.
30. Telford Taylor, "Office of Chief of Counsel, Subsequent Proceedings Division, Organizational Memo No. 2, June 25, 1946," series 5, box 26, Telford Taylor Papers, Columbia University Rare Book and Manuscript Library, New York.
31. Ibid.
32. Benjamin Ferencz to Gertrude Ferencz, May 24, 1946 (letter provided to author by Keri Ferencz).
33. Benjamin Ferencz to James Heath and/or Drexel Sprecher, June 15, 1946, RG 238, box 1, folder 4, National Archives and Records Administration, Washington, DC.
34. Benjamin Ferencz to Gertrude Ferencz, June 9, 1946 (letter provided to author by Keri Ferencz).
35. Benjamin Ferencz to Gertrude Ferencz, June 12, 1946 (letter provided to author by Keri Ferencz). It is not clear what offense Tibby committed, and Ben Ferencz could not recall. It was certainly very serious and may have been desertion.
36. Benjamin Ferencz to Gertrude Ferencz, June 3, 1946 (letter provided to author by Keri Ferencz).
37. Benjamin Ferencz to Gertrude Ferencz, July 18, 1946 (letter provided to author by Keri Ferencz).

11. The Berlin Branch

1. Benjamin Ferencz to Gertrude Ferencz, August 14, 1946 (letter provided to author by Keri Ferencz).
2. Ibid.
3. Kevin Jon Heller, *The Nuremberg Military Tribunals and the Origins of International Criminal Law* (Oxford: Oxford University Press, 2011), 32.
4. Benjamin Ferencz to Gertrude Ferencz, August 14, 1946.
5. Ibid. My research did not reveal the reasons for the animosity. In later years, it would seem, Ferencz developed a much more charitable view of King.
6. Benjamin Ferencz, "Life in Berlin 1946," Stories, https://benferencz.org/stories/1946-1949/life-in-berlin-1946/.
7. Ibid.
8. Ibid.
9. Ibid.
10. Ibid.
11. Ibid.

12. Ibid.
13. Carlos D'Este, "The Final Days," review of *The Fall of Berlin 1945*, by Antony Beevor, *New York Times*, September 8, 2002.
14. Ibid.
15. Benjamin Ferencz, interview by author, Delray Beach, FL, January 18, 2019.
16. Ibid.
17. Ibid.
18. Ibid.
19. "Lucius D. Clay Headquarters," Liberation Route Europe, https://liberationroute.com/germany/spots/l/lucius-d-clay-headquarters.
20. "Organizational Chart for the OCC's Berlin Branch," undated, RG 238, entry NM-70 202, box 6, Office of Chief Counsel for War Crimes (OCCWC) Berlin Branch Correspondence Memoranda, National Archives and Records Administration, Washington, DC. This document was clearly created soon after the Berlin Branch's creation in August because it refers to the "Subsequent Proceedings Division" (still within Robert Jackson's organization, Office of Chief Counsel for Prosecution of Axis Criminality, or OCCPAC), which was used early on but eventually replaced by Office of Chief Counsel for War Crimes (OCC or OCCWC), a part of OMGUS, in October.
21. Telford Taylor, *Final Report to the Secretary of the Army on the Nuernberg War Crimes Trials under Control Council Law No. 10* (Washington, DC: Superintendent of Documents, 1949), 14–15, https://tile.loc.gov/storage-services/service/ll/llmlp/NT_final-report/NT_final-report.pdf.
22. Heller, *Nuremberg Military Tribunals*, 45, quoting John Mendelsohn, *Trial by Document: The Use of Seized Records in the United States Proceedings Nurnberg* (New York: Garland, 1988), 58.
23. Ossip Flechtheim to Carl Schmitt, RG 238, entry NM-70 202, box 4, Office of Chief Counsel for War Crimes (OCCWC) Berlin Branch Correspondence Memoranda, National Archives and Records Administration, Washington, DC. Schmitt was arrested on March 23, 1947, but released from custody on May 6, 1947 (see Kevin Jon Heller, "Carl Schmitt's Nuremberg Near-Miss," Opinio Juris, October 1, 2010, http://opiniojuris.org/2010/01/10/carl-schmitts-nuremberg-near-miss/). Schmitt had been contemplated as a possible defendant in a possible "Propaganda and Education Case" that, given resource constraints and concerns about success in the courtroom, never saw the light of day (see Gregory S. Gordon and Ryan Mitchell, "Carl Schmitt and Ossip Flechtheim at Nuremberg: A Crossroads for International Justice and Intellectual History," *German Law Journal* 25, no. 4 [2024]: 597–634, www.cambridge.org/core/journals/german-law-journal/article/carl-schmitt-and-ossip-flechtheim-at-nuremberg-a-crossroads-for-international-justice-and-intellectual-history/B9E48B6FEC46732191DC875DEC9F9764).
24. Technically, over time, the Economics Division was eliminated, and separate teams formed for each of the individual cases just mentioned. Another case

that was investigated and contemplated for trial was "Dresdner Bank," but it was dropped.

25. For purposes of this list, the prosecution's opening statement marks the trial's start date. The Tribunal's issuing its sentence marks the end date.
26. Ferencz, "Life in Berlin 1946."
27. Ibid.
28. In a January 2020 interview by the author, Ferencz stated that he had no recollection of the Berlin Branch conducting interrogations. But the archival record suggests otherwise. See, e.g., Edmund H. Schwenk, "Memorandum to Benjamin B. Ferencz, January 10, 1947," RG 238, entry NM-70 202, box 2, Office of Chief Counsel for War Crimes (OCCWC) Berlin Branch Correspondence Memoranda, National Archives and Records Administration, Washington, DC (noting that Berlin Branch vehicles have been traveling "to various places in Berlin to interrogate individuals who might be witnesses in the trials in Nuremberg").
29. See, e.g., Benjamin Ferencz, "Memorandum to OCCWC, December 30, 1946, Subject: Interrogations," RG 238, entry NM-70 202, box 2, Office of Chief Counsel for War Crimes (OCCWC) Berlin Branch Correspondence Memoranda, National Archives and Records Administration, Washington, DC.
30. See, e.g., Benjamin Ferencz, "Memorandum to All Personnel, Berlin Branch, December 5, 1946," RG 238, entry NM-70 202, box 2, Office of Chief Counsel for War Crimes (OCCWC) Berlin Branch Correspondence Memoranda, National Archives and Records Administration, Washington, DC.
31. See, e.g., Benjamin Ferencz, "Memorandum to Thomas Ervin, October 14, 1946," RG 238, entry NM-70 202, box 2, Office of Chief Counsel for War Crimes (OCCWC) Berlin Branch Correspondence Memoranda, National Archives and Records Administration, Washington, DC (dealing with "Promotion or Reclassification of Mrs. Olga Lang"); Benjamin Ferencz, "Memorandum to All Personnel, January 20, 1947," RG 238, entry NM-70–202, box 6, Office of Chief Counsel for War Crimes (OCCWC) Berlin Branch Correspondence Memoranda, National Archives and Records Administration, Washington, DC (dealing with "Leave Policy").
32. Ibid.
33. Ibid.
34. Ferencz, "Life in Berlin 1946."
35. Ibid.
36. Ibid.
37. Ibid.
38. Benjamin Ferencz, "The Case of the Missing Maybach," Stories, https://benferencz.org/stories/1946-1949/the-case-of-the-missing-maybach/.
39. Ibid.
40. Ibid.
41. Ibid.

42. Ibid.
43. Heller, *Nuremberg Military Tribunals,* 71.
44. Ibid.
45. Ibid., 71–72.
46. Ferencz, interview, January 18, 2019.

12. The *Einsatzgruppen* Trial, Part 1

1. Kevin Jon Heller, *The Nuremberg Military Tribunals and the Origins of International Criminal Law* (Oxford: Oxford University Press, 2011), 80 (noting that the World Jewish Congress would have preferred that the OCCWC hold a "special Jewish trial" as the "NMT trials had simply not focused enough on the architects of the Holocaust"). Unfortunately, however, "most of the high-ranking SD, Gestapo, and RSHA officials that the OCC wanted prosecuted were either missing (most notably Eichmann) or known to be dead" (ibid., 71–72).
2. Ibid., 72.
3. Ibid.
4. Hilary Earl, *The Nuremberg SS-Einsatzgruppen Trial: Atrocity, Law, and History* (Cambridge: Cambridge University Press, 2009), 204.
5. Michael A. Musmanno, *The Eichmann Kommandos* (Philadelphia: Macrae Smith, 1961), 96–97.
6. Ibid., 97.
7. Hilary Earl, "A Judge, a Prosecutor, and a Mass Murderer: Courtroom Dynamics in the SS-Einsatzgruppen Case," in *Reassessing the Nuremberg Military Tribunals: Transitional Justice, Trial Narratives and Historiography,* ed. Kim C. Priemel and Alexa Stiller (New York: Berghahn, 2012), 63n109.
8. Musmanno, *Eichmann Kommandos,* 97–98.
9. Benjamin Ferencz, "The Making of a Prosecutor," Stories, https://benferencz.org/stories/1946-1949/the-making-of-a-prosecutor/.
10. During the defense opening statements, on October 6, 1947, Rolf Wartenberg was requested by defense counsel to take the stand and testify regarding his interrogations of the defendants and the resultant affidavits. Musmanno allowed it, and there was an initial direct examination by Peter Walton followed by cross-examination of various defense counsel. The cross-examination did not seem to damage Wartenberg's credibility or the affidavits' trustworthiness.
11. Benjamin Ferencz, "Preparing for Trial," Stories, https://benferencz.org/stories/1946-1949/preparing-for-trial/.
12. Ibid.
13. Vorkommandos were established to go into capital cities in advance of the other Einsatzgruppen and collect the names of regime targets. Paramilitary task forces could then murder them. Interestingly, Franz Six was meant to lead Vorkommando London when the plans for invading the United Kingdom were being drawn up. As this action, code-named Operation Sea Lion, was never

carried out, and Hitler decided to attack the Soviet Union instead, Six was made head of Vorkommando Moscow.

14. Control Council Law No. 10, art. II, 1(c), reprinted in Telford Taylor, *Final Report to the Secretary of the Army on the Nuernberg War Crimes Trials under Control Council Law No. 10* (Washington, DC: US Government Printing Office, 1949), 251–52, https://tile.loc.gov/storage-services/service/ll/llmlp/NT_final-report/NT_final-report.pdf.
15. Ibid., 250, art. II, 1(b).
16. Raphael Lemkin, *Axis Rule in Occupied Europe: Laws of Occupation, Analysis of Government, Proposals for Redress* (Washington, DC: Carnegie Endowment for International Peace, 1944), 79.
17. L. J. van den Herik, *The Contribution of the Rwanda Tribunal to the Development of International Law* (Leiden: Martinus Nijhoff, 2005), 89.
18. Benjamin Ferencz, "Mass Murderers Seek to Justify Genocide," Stories, https://benferencz.org/stories/1946-1949/mass-murderers-seek-to-justify-genocide/.
19. Ibid.
20. Ibid. It should be noted that Robert Jackson also used the term in his opening at the IMT trial. And the term was used at various junctures during the IMT trial, although not in the indictment or the IMT's judgment.
21. "Einsatzgruppen Indictment," in *Trials of War Criminals before the Nuernberg Military Tribunals under Control Council Law No. 10*, vol. 4 (Washington, DC: US Government Printing Office, 1949), 15, https://tile.loc.gov/storage-services/service/ll/llmlp/2011525364_NT_war-criminals_Vol-IV/2011525364_NT_war-criminals_Vol-IV.pdf.
22. Heller, *Nuremberg Tribunals*, 72.
23. Earl, *The Nuremberg SS-Einsatzgruppen Trial*, 218.
24. Ibid., 219.
25. Ibid.
26. See Michael A. Musmanno and Clarence Darrow, *Does Man Live Again? A Debate on Immortality between Michael A. Musmanno and Clarence Darrow, Held at Carnegie Music Hall, Pittsburgh, Pennsylvania, December 12, 1932* (Girard, KS: Haldeman-Junius, 1936). See also Louis H. Simons, "Looking into Musmanno Personality—A Visit with the Judge," *Beaver County Times*, October 14, 1968, reprinted in *Congressional Record* (October 14, 1968) 114, pt. 24: 31800 (noting that Musmanno "tripped up" Darrow "on a quotation from Voltaire").
27. "Arraignment," United States of America v. Otto Ohlendorf, et al., September 15, 1947, RG 238, M895, roll 2, 1, National Archives and Records Administration, Washington, DC.
28. Ferencz, "Preparing for Trial."
29. Benjamin Ferencz, interview by author, Delray Beach, FL, April 20, 2022.
30. This is based on a composite of the author's impressions after having spoken to Ferencz for hours and having researched other sources, including photographs, related to the details of that momentous day in his life.

31. US v. Ohlendorf, September 29, 1947, 31.
32. Ibid.
33. Ibid., 32.
34. Again, these impressions are based on the author's composite conversations with Ben Ferencz over a series of days as well as relevant photographs.
35. Musmanno, *Eichmann Kommandos,* 90.
36. Ibid.
37. Ann Tusa and John Tusa, *The Nuremberg Trial* (New York: Skyhorse, 2010), 109.
38. Ferencz, "Preparing for Trial."
39. "Trial," *US v. Ohlendorf,* September 29, 1947, 60.
40. Ferencz, interview, April 20, 2022.
41. Benjamin Ferencz, "The Biggest Murder Trial in History," Stories, https://benferencz.org/stories/1946-1949/the-biggest-murder-trial-in-history/.
42. Musmanno, *Eichmann Kommandos,* 67.
43. Ferencz, "Mass Murderers Seek to Justify Genocide."
44. *US v. Ohlendorf,* September 29, 1947, 102.
45. Ferencz, "Mass Murderers Seek to Justify Genocide." Although he has never acknowledged this, it is also likely that Ferencz was mindful of the fact that it was his first trial, and this was the key cross-examination of the trial.
46. Benjamin Ferencz, interview by author, Delray Beach, FL, May 21, 2020.
47. *US v. Ohlendorf,* September 29, 1947, 128–29.
48. Ibid., 130–31.
49. Ibid., 138.
50. Ibid., 147.
51. Ibid., 148.
52. Ibid., 151.
53. Ibid., 152.
54. Ibid.
55. Ibid., 167.
56. Ibid., 172.
57. Ibid., 180.
58. Ibid., 181.
59. At the beginning of the next court session, on the morning of October 6, 1947, having seen the film the previous Friday, Musmanno reversed himself and decided to exclude the film, noting it could not be linked to these specific defendants.
60. Telford Taylor to Benjamin Ferencz, October 2, 1947, series 5, box 26, TTP-5-1-1x: NMT Correspondence (1947–1949), Telford Taylor Papers, Columbia University Rare Book and Manuscript Library, New York.
61. John Q. Barrett, "No Poisoned Chalice," The Jackson List, November 21, 2013, https://thejacksonlist.com/wp-content/uploads/2015/07/20131121-Jackson-List-Poisoned-Chalice.pdf.
62. Benjamin Ferencz, "Nurnberg Trial Procedure and the Rights of the Accused,"

Journal of Criminal Law and Criminology 39, no. 2 (1948): 144; United States Zone Military Government, Ordinance No. 7, October 18, 1946, reprinted in *Trials of War Criminals before the Nuernberg Military Tribunals under Control Council Law No. 10*, vol. 1 (Washington, DC: US Government Printing Office, 1946), xxi.

63. Gregory S. Gordon, "Toward an International Criminal Procedure: Due Process Aspirations and Limitations," *Columbia Journal of Transnational Law* 45 (2007): 647–48.
64. Musmanno, *Eichmann Kommandos,* 246–47. At trial's end, in appreciation of his fairness, the defense attorneys gave Musmanno a three-foot bronze statue of a penguin (Earl, *The Nuremberg SS-Einsatzgruppen Trial,* 88).
65. *In re Yamashita,* 327 U.S. 1 (1946). Yamashita, a Japanese general whose soldiers committed atrocities in the Philippines, was convicted by a US military commission based on "command responsibility." In affirming the result, the US Supreme Court held that the superior must have "some degree of knowledge about the crimes and the opportunity to prevent them" (Jeremy Dunnaback, "Command Responsibility: A Small Unit Leader's Perspective," *Northwestern University Law Review* 108, no. 4 [2014]: 1393).
66. *US v. Ohlendorf,* October 6, 1947, 124.
67. Ferencz, "Mass Murderers Seek to Justify Genocide."
68. Earl, "A Judge, a Prosecutor, and a Mass Murderer," 64.
69. Musmanno, *Eichmann Kommandos,* 107.
70. Earl, "A Judge, A Prosecutor, and a Mass Murderer," 64.
71. *US v. Ohlendorf,* October 6, 1947, 515–16.
72. "Opinion and Judgment," *United States v. Ohlendorf (Einsatzgruppen),* in *Trials of War Criminals before the Nuernberg Military Tribunals under Control Council Law No. 10,* vol. 4 (Washington, DC: US Government Printing Office, 1947), 416.
73. Historians disagree regarding the factual accuracy of Ohlendorf's testimony as well as its implications for the "intentionalist-functionalist debate," which centers on whether Hitler had a master plan from the start for exterminating the Jews (the "Intentionalist School") or whether the plan began as only partially genocidal and then grew organically to become fully genocidal (the "Functionalist School") (see Earl, *The Nuremberg SS-Einsatzgruppen Trial,* 180–81 ["The question arose [given] a lack of clear documentary evidence to prove when and by whom the decision for the Final Solution was made"]).
74. Ibid., 204. Despite this, Ferencz thought Heath performed well. "He lived up to my expectations and even Telford Taylor, who wanted him fired, agreed [he] did a fine job of grilling the Nazi General" (Ferencz, "Mass Murderers Seek to Justify Genocide").
75. *US v. Ohlendorf,* October 6, 1947, 740–52.
76. Musmanno, *Eichmann Kommandos,* 132.
77. "Trial," October 6, 1947, *United States of America v. Otto Ohlendorf, et al.,* RG

238, M895, roll 4, 2673–74, National Archives and Records Administration, Washington, DC.

78. Ibid., 2676.
79. Musmanno, *Eichmann Kommandos*, 133.

13. The *Einsatzgruppen* Trial, Part 2

1. Hilary Earl, *The Nuremberg SS-Einsatzgruppen Trial: Atrocity, Law, and History* (Cambridge: Cambridge University Press, 2009), 59–60.
2. "Trial," October 16, 1947, *United States of America v. Otto Ohlendorf, et al.*, RG 238, M895, roll 2, 813, National Archives and Records Administration, Washington, DC.
3. Ibid., 816.
4. Ibid., 848.
5. Ibid., 852.
6. Ibid., 853.
7. Ibid., 855–56.
8. Ibid., 874.
9. Ibid., 881–82
10. "Trial," October 27, 1947, *United States of America v. Otto Ohlendorf, et al.*, RG 238, M895, roll 3, 1462, National Archives and Records Administration, Washington, DC.
11. Ibid., 1441–44.
12. Ibid., 1450–57.
13. "Trial," December 10, 1947, *United States of America v. Otto Ohlendorf, et al.*, RG 238, M895, roll 5, 3753–54, National Archives and Records Administration, Washington, DC.
14. Ibid., 3770, 3774.
15. Ibid., December 12, 1947, 3900–901.
16. Ibid., 3903.
17. Ibid., 3913–14.
18. Ibid. 3921.
19. Ibid., 3926.
20. Ibid., 3939.
21. Ibid., 3958.
22. Ibid.
23. Andrew Nagorski, *The Nazi Hunters* (New York: Simon and Schuster, 2016), 54.
24. Benjamin Ferencz, "Sliding off the Alps," Stories, https://benferencz.org/stories/1946-1949/sliding-off-the-alps/.
25. In his memoirs, Ben Ferencz reported the word as "Retournado," but "Ritornate" would be the grammatically proper word and the one likely used.
26. Ibid.
27. Ibid.

28. Michael A. Musmanno, *The Eichmann Kommandos* (Philadelphia: Macrae Smith, 1961), 241.
29. Ferencz, "Judgment Day for Mass Murderers," Stories, https://benferencz.org/stories/1946-1949/judgment-day-for-mass-murderers/.
30. *United States v. Ohlendorf (Einsatzgruppen)*, in *Trials of War Criminals before the Nuernberg Military Tribunals under Control Council Law No. 10*, vol. 4 (Washington, DC: Superintendent of Documents, 1947), 369.
31. Ibid., 370–71.
32. Ibid., 373.
33. Ibid., 376.
34. Ibid., 382.
35. Ibid., 383.
36. Ibid., 385.
37. Ibid., 387.
38. Ibid., 388.
39. Ibid.
40. Ibid.
41. Ibid., 390.
42. Ibid.
43. Ibid., 393.
44. Ferencz, "Unplanned Parachuting into Berlin," Stories, https://benferencz.org/stories/1946-1949/unplanned-parachuting-into-berlin/.
45. Ibid.
46. Ibid.
47. Ibid.
48. *United States v. Ohlendorf (Einsatzgruppen)*, 411–12.
49. Ibid., 437–38.
50. Ibid., 451. The judgment did not engage in any legal analysis of "genocide," but it is sprinkled with references to it in describing the Nazi program in passages such as this.
51. Ibid., 459.
52. *United States v. Ohlendorf (Einsatzgruppen)*, 464.
53. Ibid., 470.
54. Ibid., 490.
55. Ibid., 489.
56. Ibid., 517. See also Kevin Jon Heller, *The Nuremberg Military Tribunals and the Origins of International Criminal Law* (Oxford: Oxford University Press, 2011), 269–70.
57. Heller, *Nuremberg Tribunals*, 270.
58. *United States v. Ohlendorf (Einsatzgruppen)*, 464.
59. Ferencz, "Judgment Day for Mass Murderers."
60. Ibid.
61. Musmanno, *Eichmann Kommandos*, 260.

62. Ibid.
63. Ibid.
64. Ibid., 260–61.
65. Ferencz, "Judgment Day for Mass Murderers."
66. Ibid.
67. Ibid.
68. Ibid.
69. Benjamin Ferencz, "Mass Murderers Seek to Justify Genocide," Stories, https://benferencz.org/stories/1946-1949/mass-murderers-seek-to-justify-genocide/.
70. Ferencz, "Judgment Day for Mass Murderers."
71. Ibid.

14. *Krupp* Trial Attorney and Executive Counsel

1. "20 SS Men Guilty of Million Murders," *New York Post,* April 9, 1948, series 1, RG-12.002.01, box 12, Benjamin B. Ferencz Collection, 1919–1994, United States Holocaust Memorial Museum Archives, Washington, DC.
2. Eleanor Roosevelt to Benjamin B. Ferencz, April 29, 1948, series 1, RG-12.002.01, box 3, Benjamin B. Ferencz Collection, 1919–1994, United States Holocaust Memorial Museum Archives, Washington, DC.
3. Hilary Earl, "Legacies of the Nuremberg SS-Einsatzgruppen Trial after 70 Years," *Loyola Los Angeles International and Comparative Law Review* 39, no. 1 (2017): 97.
4. Telford Taylor to Ben Ferencz, April 12, 1948, series 5, box 26, TTP-5-1-1x: NMT Correspondence (1947–1949), Telford Taylor Papers, Columbia University Rare Book & Manuscript Library, New York.
5. Telford Taylor, "General Orders No. 6," series 6, box 28: Document Book VII, Miscellaneous [Volume E], Document 85, Paul H. Gantt Nuremberg Trial Papers, Special Collections and University Archives, Towson University, Towson, MD (hereafter cited as Gantt Papers). Ferencz was officially referred to as "Special Counsel" for the case.
6. Kim C. Priemel, *The Betrayal: The Nuremberg Trials and German Divergence* (Oxford: Oxford University Press, 2016), 178.
7. Ibid., 179n95.
8. See Drexel Sprecher to Cecilia Goetz, March 20, 1950, box 59, folder DASPP-059-001: Publications Project File—Case X—Krupp, Drexel A. Sprecher Personal Papers, Nuremberg Trials, 1945–1951, John F. Kennedy Presidential Library and Museum, Boston, MA.
9. "Background on Krupp Case," July 15, 1948, Public Relations Office, OCCWC, series 5, box 29, file TTP-5-1-4-63 NMT-OCCWC: Press Releases 1948, Telford Taylor Papers, Columbia University Rare Book & Manuscript Library, New York.

10. William Manchester, *The Arms of Krupp* (New York: Bantam, 1983), 30 (quoting Norbert Muhlen, *The Incredible Krupps: The Rise, Fall, and Comeback of Germany's Industrial Family* [New York: Henry Holt, 1959], 7).
11. Stephen Bull, "Krupp, Manufacturer," in *Encyclopedia of Military Technology and Innovation* (Westport, CT: Greenwood, 2004), 146.
12. Günther Birkenstock, "The Krupp Dynasty—Glorified and Vilified," *Deutsche Welle,* October 4, 2012, https://www.dw.com/en/the-krupp-dynasty-glorified-and-vilified/a-15867835.
13. *Encyclopaedia Britannica,* s.v. "Alfred Krupp," https://www.britannica.com/biography/Alfred-Krupp.
14. Marc Romanych, "Big Bertha," in *Encyclopaedia Britannica,* https://www.britannica.com/technology/Big-Bertha-weapon.
15. Stanley Goldman, "A Führer of Industry: Krupp before, during and after Nuremberg," *Loyola Los Angeles International and Comparative Law Review* 39, no. 1 (2017): 189.
16. Roderick Stackelberg, "Krupp, Von Bohlen und Halbach," *The Routledge Companion to Nazi Germany* (Abingdon-on-Thames, UK: Routledge, 2007), 219.
17. "Indictment," in *United States v. Krupp,* in *Trials of War Criminals before the Nuernberg Military Tribunals under Control Council Law No. 10,* vol. 9 (Washington, DC: US Government Printing Office, 1947), 239 (hereafter cited as *TWC*).
18. Priemel, *The Betrayal,* 177.
19. Press Release, Office of Chief of Counsel for War Crimes, October 31, 1947, series 5, box 29, TTP-5-1-4-62: NMT-OCCWC: Press Releases 1947, Telford Taylor Papers, Columbia University Rare Book & Manuscript Library, New York (hereafter cited as OCCWC Press Release).
20. Priemel, *The Betrayal,* 184 (quoting Benjamin Ferencz to Sheldon Glueck, February 16, 1948, box 74, F.9, Sheldon Glueck Papers 1916–1972, box 74, Harvard Law School Library, Harvard University, Cambridge, MA).
21. Manchester, *The Arms of Krupp,* 718.
22. Ibid.
23. Ibid.
24. Ibid.
25. Nürnberg Krupp Trial Papers of Judge Hu C. Anderson, Alyne Queener Massey Law Library Vanderbilt University, Nashville, TN, https://krupp.library.vanderbilt.edu/sites/default/files/transcript%20p.7532-7552.pdf (hereafter cited as Anderson Papers), 7546.
26. Anderson Papers, 8945, https://krupp.library.vanderbilt.edu/sites/default/files/transcript%20p.8926-8945.pdf; OCCWC Press Release, May 21, 1948, series 5, box 29, TTP-5-1-4-63: NMT-OCCWC: Press Releases 1948.
27. Anderson Papers, 8936, https://krupp.library.vanderbilt.edu/sites/default/files/transcript%20p.8926-8945.pdf; OCCWC Press Release, May 21, 1948. See also

Telford Taylor, *Final Report to the Secretary of the Army on the Nuernberg War Crimes Trials under Control Council Law No. 10* (Washington, DC: Superintendent of Documents, 1949), 89–90 (hereafter cited as *Final Report*).

28. Anderson Papers, 8937, https://krupp.library.vanderbilt.edu/sites/default/files/transcript%20p.8926-8945.pdf; "Miscellaneous Documents," Trial 10—Krupp Case, 149, The Gen. Eugene Phillips Nuremberg Trials Collection, University of Georgia Law, Augusta, https://digitalcommons.law.uga.edu/nuremberg/.
29. "Miscellaneous Documents," Phillips Collection, 149.
30. Benjamin B. Ferencz, interview by author, Delray Beach, FL, January 19, 2020.
31. These points were not reflected in as much detail in the direct examination but rather in the affidavit Ms. Geulen gave, which was admitted into evidence.
32. *TWC*, vol. 9, 1185.
33. Ibid., 1185–86.
34. Ibid., 1186–87.
35. Ibid., 1187.
36. "Closing Statement for the United States of America," Phillips Collection, 8–11, https://digitalcommons.law.uga.edu/cgi/viewcontent.cgi?article=1002&context=nmt10.
37. Ibid., 13.
38. Ibid., 1325.
39. Ibid., 1346.
40. Ibid., 1374.
41. Ibid., 1440.
42. Priemel, *The Betrayal*, 184.
43. Ibid., 185.
44. Ibid.
45. Kevin Jon Heller, *The Nuremberg Military Tribunals and the Origins of International Criminal Law* (Oxford: Oxford University Press, 2011), 81.
46. Benjamin Ferencz, "Closing down the Nuremberg Trials," Stories, https://benferencz.org/stories/1946-1949/closing-down-the-nuremberg-trials.
47. See, e.g., "Memorandum from Berlin Branch to Benjamin Ferencz, September 15, 1947," RG 238, entry NM-70 202, Container 6—Nuremberg THRU Memos—General Information, National Records and Archives Administration, Washington, DC; Bert Heilpern, Memorandum to Benjamin Ferencz, October 22, 1947, ibid. In the Stories, Ferencz states he was made executive counsel in April 1948, but this does not square with the record (see Ferencz, "Closing Down the Nuremberg Trials").
48. Paul Gantt, "Memorandum for the Files, Subj. Personnel, January 9, 1948," series 6, box 28: Document Book VII, Miscellaneous [Volume E], Gantt Papers.
49. Benjamin B. Ferencz, interview by author, June 23, 2020.
50. Ibid.
51. Ferencz, "Closing down the Nuremberg Trials."
52. David Kinney and Robert King Wittman, *The Devil's Diary: Alfred Rosen-*

berg and the Stolen Secrets of the Third Reich (New York City: HarperCollins, 2017), 16.

53. Ibid.
54. Charles Fenyvesi, "Mysteries of the Lost (and Found) Nazi Diaries," *National Geographic News,* June 15, 2013.
55. See Telford Taylor to American-German Club, December 29, 1947, series 5, box 26, TTP-5-1-1x: NMT Correspondence (1947–1949), Telford Taylor Papers, Columbia University Rare Book & Manuscript Library, New York (Ferencz is copied in on this letter).
56. OCCWC Press Release, May 14, 1948, series 5, box 29, TTP-5-1-4-63: NMT-OCCWC: Press Releases (1948), Telford Taylor Papers.
57. Herman L. Lang, "Memorandum on History of the Special Projects Division," August 31, 1948, series 6, box 28: Document Book VII, Miscellaneous [Volume E], Document 1, Gantt Papers.
58. Ferencz, "Closing down the Nuremberg Trials."
59. Ibid.
60. Lang, "Memorandum on History of the Special Projects Division." According to Lang, James Heath and then Paul Gantt subsequently served as director.
61. Ibid.
62. Ferencz, "Closing down the Nuremberg Trials." Ferencz indicates in his memoirs, and in the author's discussions with him, that the Special Projects Division assumed the task of compiling the Green Series. But in his 1949 *Final Report* to the secretary of the army, Telford Taylor indicated that it was exclusively the OCCWC's Publications Division, under the direction of Drexel Sprecher, that was at that time compiling the Green Series (see *Final Report,* 41). Still, it is possible to reconcile Ben Ferencz's recollections on this matter if one considers that the Special Projects Division was set up before the Publications Division. It would seem then that the former began the Green Series work before handing it over to the latter, once it was fully established. This supposition is arguably bolstered by the fact that Gertrude Ferencz worked on the Green Series as well and was part of the Special Projects Division.
63. Ferencz, interview, January 19, 2019, 48.
64. Ferencz, "Closing down the Nuremberg Trials."
65. OCCWC, "Statistics of the Nurnberg Trials," March 15, 1949, series 5, TTP-5-1-1-25, 4–6, Telford Taylor Papers.
66. Heller, *Nuremberg Tribunals,* 3.
67. Benjamin Ferencz, "War Crimes Trials at Nuremberg," November 2004, https://benferencz.org/articles/2000-2004/war-crimes-trials-at-nuremberg/.
68. Quoted in Lawrence Douglas, "History and Memory in the Courtroom: Reflections on Perpetrator Trials," in *The Nuremberg Trials: International Criminal Law since 1945,* ed. Herbert R. Reginbogen and Cristoph J. Safferling (Munich: De Gruyter Saur, 2006), 95.
69. Heller, *Nuremberg Tribunals,* 3.

70. Ibid.
71. Benjamin Ferencz to Sheldon Glueck, April 16, 1948, box 74, F.9, Sheldon Glueck Papers 1916–1972.
72. John Lewis Gaddis, *George F. Kennan: An American Life* (New York: Penguin, 2011), 201–8.
73. Larry Wolff, *Inventing Eastern Europe: The Map of Civilization on the Mind of the Enlightenment* (Palo Alto, CA: Stanford University Press, 1994), 1.
74. Ulrike Weckel, "The Power of Images: Real and Fictional Roles of Atrocity Film Footage at Nuremberg," in *Reassessing the Nuremberg Military Tribunals: Transitional Justice, Trial Narratives and Historiography,* ed. Kim C. Priemel and Alexa Stiller (New York: Berghahn, 2012), 236.
75. Kai Bird, *The Chairman: John J. McCloy and the Making of the American Establishment* (New York: Simon and Schuster, 1992), 1.
76. Adam LeBor, "Nazi Blueprint for Postwar Integration: How Walther Funk's 1940 Memo Predicted the Rise of the European Union," *The Critic,* June 2020. See also Scott Christianson, *The Last Gasp: The Rise and Fall of the American Gas Chamber* (Berkeley: University of California Press, 2010), 106.
77. Christianson, *The Last Gasp,* 106.
78. Evan Thomas, review of *The Chairman: John J. McCloy and the Making of the American Establishment, Washington Monthly,* March 1, 1992. See also Bird, *The Chairman,* 101–2 (alluding to McCloy's pre–World War II "passive" "anti-Semitic thoughts" as inclining him to be in favor of the social segregation of the Jews but describing him as being not as virulently antisemitic as his good friend and brother-in-law, politician/businessman Lewis W. Douglas, who believed the Jews "were part of the conspiracy to destroy the capitalist system" and who "blamed the New Deal's faults on the Jewish Race").
79. Thomas, review of *The Chairman.*
80. Ibid. Michael Berenbaum, "Why Wasn't Auschwitz Bombed?," *Encyclopaedia Britannica,* https://www.britannica.com/topic/Why-wasnt-Auschwitz-bombed-717594.
81. See Thomas Alan Schwartz, *America's Germany: John J. McCloy and the Federal Republic of Germany* (Cambridge, MA: Harvard University Press, 2014), 162.
82. Ferencz, "Death by Hanging," Stories, https://benferencz.org/stories/1946-1949/death-by-hanging/.
83. Manchester, *The Arms of Krupp,* 757.
84. Ibid., 757–58.
85. John J. McCloy, "Interview Transcript," April 24, 1984, series 2, RG-12.002.02*12, box 16, 21, Benjamin B. Ferencz Collection, 1919–1994, United States Holocaust Memorial Museum Archives, Washington, DC.
86. Heller, *Nuremberg Tribunals,* 341.
87. Priemel, *The Betrayal,* 366.
88. Heller, *Nuremberg Tribunals,* 352.
89. TWC, vol. 4, 16.

90. Ibid.
91. Heller, *Nuremberg Tribunals,* 354.
92. Hilary Earl, *The Nuremberg SS-Einsatzgruppen Trial: Atrocity, Law, and History* (Cambridge: Cambridge University Press, 2009), 284.
93. It should be noted that Flick had also been freed and allowed to rebuild his vast fortune ("Friedrich Flick Is Dead at 89; Industrialist Who Aided Hitler," obituary, *New York Times,* July 22, 1972).
94. Ferencz, interview, January 18, 2019.
95. David Meyers, *America and the Postwar World: Remaking International Society, 1945–1956* (Oxon, UK: Routledge, 2018), 53.
96. Ibid.
97. Heller, *Nuremberg Tribunals,* 354.
98. Meyers, *America and the Postwar World,* 53.
99. Ferencz, "Death by Hanging."
100. Heikelena Verrijn and Marlise Simons, *The Prosecutor and the Judge* (Amsterdam: Amsterdam University Press, 2010), 24.
101. Ferencz, interview, January 18, 2019, 42.
102. Benjamin Ferencz to *New York Times,* series 2, RG-12.002.02*04, box 13, Nuremberg Supplementary Materials, 1949–1990, Benjamin B. Ferencz Collection, 1919–1994, United States Holocaust Memorial Museum Archives, Washington, DC. The article was attached to a February 25, 1951, letter to the *New York Times Magazine,* but it would appear that the article was never published.
103. Phillip Gut, *Jahrhundertzeuge Ben Ferencz* (Munich: Piper Verlag, 2020), 150.

15. The Connective Tissue between Retribution and Restitution

1. Johana Göhler, "Victim Rights in Civil Law Jurisdictions," in *The Oxford Handbook of Criminal Process,* ed. Darryl K. Brown, Jenia I. Turner, and Bettina Weisser (New York: Oxford University Press, 2019), 276.
2. Beth E. Sullivan, Note, "Harnessing *Payne:* Controlling the Admission of Victim Impact Statements to Safeguard Capital Sentencing Hearings from Passion and Prejudice," *Fordham Urban Law Journal* 25 (1998): 608–13.
3. Benjamin Ferencz, interview by author, Delray Beach, FL, January 18, 2019, 36.
4. Lorraine Boissoneault, "A 1938 Nazi Law Forced Jews to Register Their Wealth—Making It Easier to Steal," *Smithsonian Magazine,* April 26, 2018.
5. Götz Aly, *Hitler's Beneficiaries: Plunder, Racial War, and the Nazi Welfare State* (New York: Holt Paperbacks, 2008), 184.
6. Jason Skog, *The Legacy of the Holocaust* (Mankato, MN: Compass Point, 2010), 37; "Jewish Assets Seized by Nazis Funded 30 Percent of WWII Expenses," *Haaretz,* November 8, 2010, https://www.haaretz.com/jewish/1.5136723.
7. "Declaration Regarding Forced Transfers of Property in Enemy-Controlled Territory," *Department of State Bulletin,* January 9, 1943, 21.

8. Seymour J. Rubin and Abba P. Schwartz, "Refugees and Reparations," *Law and Contemporary Problems* 16, no. 3 (Summer 1951): 380.
9. Ibid., 389.
10. Military Government Law No. 59, Military Government Gazette, Germany, United States Area of Control, November 10, 1947, RG 260, box 167, National Archives and Records Administration, Washington, DC (hereafter cited as Military Government Law No. 59); also available at https://iiif.lib.harvard.edu/manifests/view/drs:6347670$515i.
11. Nehemiah Robinson, *Indemnification and Reparations: Jewish Aspects* (New York: Institute of Jewish Affairs of the American Jewish Congress and World Jewish Congress, 1944), 256–57.
12. Staff of Presidential Advisory Commission on Holocaust Assets in the United States (PACHA), "Restitution of Victims' Assets," in *Plunder and Restitution: Findings and Recommendations of the PACHA and Staff Report* (December 2000), https://govinfo.library.unt.edu/pcha/PlunderRestitution.html/html/StaffChapter5.html.
13. Benjamin B. Ferencz, with Michael J. Bazyler and Kristen L. Nelson, "Seeking Redress for Hitler's Victims: Personal Remembrances," in *Reparations for Victims of Genocide, War Crimes and Crimes against Humanity,* 2nd ed., ed. Carla Ferstman and Mariana Goetz (Boston: Brill|Nijhoff, 2020), 124–25n10.
14. Gertrude Ferencz, interview by Leslie Frank, Nuremberg Trials Oral History Project, The Center for Oral History, University of Connecticut, October 16, 1995, transcript, 4, https://archives.lib.uconn.edu/islandora/object/20002%3A860389821#page/1/mode/2up.
15. Benjamin Ferencz, interview by Joan Ringelheim, United States Holocaust Memorial Museum, August 26, 1994, transcript, 74, https://collections.ushmm.org/oh_findingaids/RG-50.030.0269_trs_en.pdf (hereafter cited as USHMM interview).
16. Benjamin B. Ferencz, "Restitution of Confiscated Property," Stories, https://benferencz.org/stories/1948-1956/restitution-of-confiscated-property/.
17. Ibid.
18. Military Government Law No. 59, art. 56.
19. Richard F. Weingroff, "General Lucius D. Clay—The President's Man," *U.S. Department of Transportation Highway History,* https://www.fhwa.dot.gov/infrastructure/clay.cfm.
20. See Jean Edward Smith, *Lucius D. Clay: An American Life* (New York: Henry Holt, 1990), 82, 456.
21. Weingroff, *General Lucius D. Clay.*
22. Ibid.
23. USHMM interview, 75.
24. Ibid.
25. Ibid., 75–76.

26. Ibid., 76.
27. Ibid.
28. Ibid.
29. Ibid., 77.
30. Ibid.
31. Julie-Marthe Cohen, Felicitas Heimann-Jelinek, and Ruth Jolanda Weinberger, *Handbook on Judaica Provenance Research* (New York: Conference on Jewish Material Claims Against Germany, 2018), 48, http://art.claimscon.org/wp-content/uploads/2017/12/Part-1-Dispersion-of-Jewish-Ceremonial-Objects-in-the-West-JCR-12.12.2017.pdf (hereafter cited as *Judaica Handbook*).
32. Ferencz, "Restitution of Confiscated Property."
33. Military Government Law No. 59, pt. 10; Court of Restitution Appeals Reports, Harvard Law School Digital Collections, https://hls.harvard.edu/library/digital-collections/court-of-restitution-appeals-reports/.
34. USHMM interview, 80.
35. Ibid.
36. Ibid., 80–81.
37. Ibid., 78.
38. Thomas Alan Schwartz, *America's Germany: John J. McCloy and the Federal Republic of Germany* (Cambridge, MA: Harvard University Press, 2014), 175.
39. Ferencz, "Restitution of Confiscated Property."
40. Benjamin B. Ferencz, "Retrieving Sacred Treasures," Stories, https://benferencz.org/stories/1948-1956/retrieving-sacred-treasures/.
41. Ibid.
42. *Judaica Handbook,* 49.
43. Immanuel Kant, *Anthropology from a Pragmatic Point of View,* trans. Mary Gregor (The Hague: Martinus Nijhoff, 1974).
44. Elisabeth Young-Bruehl, *Hannah Arendt: For Love of the World,* 2nd ed. (New Haven, CT: Yale University Press, 2004), 187–88.
45. Ferencz, interview, January 18, 2019, 65.
46. Ibid.
47. Young-Bruehl, *For Love of the World,* 246.
48. Daniel Maier-Katkin, *Stranger from Abroad: Hannah Arendt, Martin Heidegger, Friendship and Forgiveness* (New York: W. W. Norton, 2010), 139.
49. Ibid., 188.
50. Ferencz, "Retrieving Sacred Treasures."
51. Ibid.
52. Ibid.
53. Ibid.
54. Ibid.
55. Benjamin B. Ferencz, "Reclaiming Cemeteries," Stories, https://benferencz.org/stories/1948-1956/reclaiming-cemeteries/.

56. Ibid.
57. Ibid. Ferencz kept the bones for many years after that. They were eventually returned to Auschwitz, where they were given a dignified burial (ibid.).
58. Benjamin B. Ferencz, "Bulk Settlements for Property Claims," Stories, https://benferencz.org/stories/1948-1956/bulk-settlements-for-property-claims/.
59. Phillip Gut, *Jahrhundertzeuge Ben Ferencz* (Munich: Piper Verlag, 2020), 165.
60. Ibid.

16. Moral and Material Indemnity

1. *Black's Law Dictionary,* 11th ed., ed. Bryan A. Garner (Eagan, MN: Thomson Reuters, 2019), s.v. "Reparation."
2. German Federal Ministry of Finance, *Measures to Compensate for National Socialist Injustice* (Berlin: Federal Ministry of Finance, 2020), 4–5, https://www.bundesfinanzministerium.de/Content/EN/Standardartikel/Press_Room/Publications/Brochures/A-timeline-Measures-to-compensate-for-National-Socialist-Injustice.pdf?__blob=publicationFile&v=8.
3. Arnold J. Heidenheimer, *Adenauer and the CDU: The Rise of the Leader and the Integration of the Party* (The Hague: Martinus Nijhoff, 1960), 50.
4. Ronald W. Zweig, *German Reparations and the Jewish World: A History of the Claims Conference,* 2nd ed. (London: Routledge, 2013), 21.
5. "Nahum Goldmann," *Jewish Virtual Library,* https://www.jewishvirtuallibrary.org/nahum-goldmann.
6. Linda Charlton, "Nahum Goldmann, A Leading Zionist, Dies at 87," *New York Times,* August 31, 1982, D17.
7. Benjamin B. Ferencz, "A Treaty to Compensate Victims," Stories, https://benferencz.org/stories/1948-1956/a-treaty-to-compensate-victims/.
8. Shlomo Shafir, "Nahum Goldmann and Germany after World War II," in *Nahum Goldmann: Statesman without a State,* ed. Mark A. Raider (Albany: State University of New York Press, 2009), 214.
9. Ibid.
10. Ferencz, "A Treaty to Compensate Victims."
11. Shafir, "Nahum Goldmann and Germany," 214.
12. Ferencz, "A Treaty to Compensate Victims."
13. Ibid.
14. Ibid.
15. Ibid.
16. Ibid.
17. Karen Heilig, "From the Luxembourg Agreement to Today: Representing a People," *Berkeley Journal of International Law* 20, no. 1 (2002): 180n23; Ronald W. Zweig, "'Reparations Made Me': Nahum Goldmann, German Reparations, and the Jewish World," in *Nahum Goldmann: Statesman without a State,* ed. Mark A. Raider (Albany: State University of New York Press, 2009), 244.

18. Jonathan Bush, "Nuremberg and Beyond: Jacob Robinson, International Lawyer," *Loyola L.A. International and Comparative Law Review* 39, no. 1 (2017): 264.
19. Ferencz, interview, January 18, 2019, 74.
20. Benjamin B. Ferencz, "Seeking Fair Compensation—A Mission Impossible," Stories, https://benferencz.org/stories/1948-1956/seeking-fair-compensation-a-mission-impossible/.
21. Ferencz, interview, January 18, 2019.
22. Ibid.
23. Ibid.
24. Ibid. According to Giora Josephthal, the "Shilumim Agreement was actually drawn up by Dr. Jacob Robinson" (Josephthal, *The Responsible Attitude: The Life and Opinions of Giora Josephthal,* ed. Ben Halpern and Shalom Wurm [New York: Schocken, 1966], 147).
25. Benjamin Ferencz, interview by author, Delray Beach, FL, January 19, 2019.
26. Thomas Alan Schwartz, *America's Germany: John J. McCloy and the Federal Republic of Germany* (Cambridge, MA: Harvard University Press, 2014), 180.
27. Dean Acheson to John J. McCloy, April 4, 1952, D(52) 589, box 39, RG 466, McCloy Papers, National Archives and Records Administration, Washington, DC.
28. Schwartz, *America's Germany,* 180–81.
29. Benjamin B. Ferencz to John J. McCloy, April 4, 1952, D(52) 589, box 39, RG 466, McCloy Papers, National Archives and Records Administration, Washington, DC.
30. David Storey, "Postwar Marshall Plan That Rebuilt Europe Marks 70th Anniversary," *ShareAmerica,* June 2, 2017, https://share.america.gov/marshall-plan-marks-70th-anniversary/.
31. "Should the United States Keep Troops in Germany?" National WWII Museum, New Orleans, https://www.nationalww2museum.org/war/articles/should-united-states-keep-troops-germany.
32. Ferencz, interview, January 19, 2019, 9.
33. Ibid.
34. Lily Gardner Feldman, "The September 1952 Reparations Agreement between West Germany and Israel: The Beginning of a Remarkable Friendship," American Institute for Contemporary German Studies, November 12, 2019, https://www.aicgs.org/2019/11/the-september-1952-reparations-agreement-between-west-germany-and-israel-the-beginning-of-a-remarkable-friendship/.
35. Ibid.
36. Benjamin Ferencz, interview by Joan Ringelheim, United States Holocaust Memorial Museum, August 26, 1994, transcript, 104, https://collections.ushmm.org/oh_findingaids/RG-50.030.0269_trs_en.pdf (hereafter cited as USHMM interview).
37. Ferencz, "A Treaty to Compensate Victims."
38. Ibid.

39. Benjamin B. Ferencz, "Implementing Compensation Agreements," Stories, https://benferencz.org/stories/1948-1956/implementing-compensation-agreements/.
40. Ibid.
41. Ibid.
42. Ibid.
43. Ibid.
44. "United Restitution Organization (URO)," The Central Archives for the History of the Jewish People Jerusalem (CAHJP), http://192.114.7.128/content/united-restitution-organization-uro ("The administrative center, established in London, was headed by Secretary-General Hans Reichmann, a German-Jewish civil servant, from 1949").
45. Ferencz, "A Treaty to Compensate Victims."
46. Ferencz, USHMM interview, August 26, 1994, 108.
47. Ibid., 109.
48. Ibid.
49. Ibid.
50. Ibid.
51. Benjamin B. Ferencz, "Some Unanticipated Consequences," Stories, https://benferencz.org/stories/1948-1956/some-unanticipated-consequences/.
52. Ibid.
53. Ibid.
54. Ferencz, USHMM interview, August 26, 1994, 95.
55. Ibid.
56. Benjamin B. Ferencz, "Returning Home to New York in 1956," Stories, https://benferencz.org/stories/1956-1970/returning-home-to-new-york-in-1956/.
57. Ibid.
58. Ibid.
59. Ibid.
60. Philipp Gut, *Jahrhundertzeuge Ben Ferencz* (Munich: Piper Verlag, 2020), 165.

17. Finishing the Reparations Revolution

1. Benjamin B. Ferencz, "Returning to New York in 1956," Stories, https://benferencz.org/stories/1956-1970/returning-home-to-new-york-in-1956/.
2. Ibid.
3. "Maurice Boukstein, 75, A Lawyer and an Adviser to Jewish Groups," obituary, *New York Times*, November 20, 1980. See also "U.S. Apologizes for WWII Gold Train Case," NBCNews.com, October 11, 2005.
4. Benjamin Ferencz to Gertrude Ferencz, May 1956 (attachment to letter provided to author by Keri Ferencz).
5. Ferencz, "Returning to New York in 1956."
6. Ibid.

7. Constantin Goschler, Marcus Böick, and Julia Reus, *Kriegsverbrechen, Restitution, Prävention: Aus dem Vorlass von Benjamin B. Ferencz,* trans. Lukas Buchholz (Göttingen: Vandenhoeck & Ruprecht, 2019), 35.
8. Ferencz, "Returning to New York in 1956."
9. Ibid.
10. Ibid.
11. Goschler, Böick, and Reus, *Kriegsverbrechen.*
12. Ibid.
13. Ibid., 33.
14. Ferencz, "Returning to New York in 1956."
15. Richard Severo, "Telford Taylor, Who Prosecuted Nazis at Nuremberg War Crimes Trials, Is Dead at 90," *New York Times,* May 25, 1998, A13.
16. Ibid.
17. Tina Rosenberg, "The Lives They Lived: Telford Taylor," *New York Times,* January 3, 1999, sec. 6, 26.
18. Severo, "Telford Taylor, Who Prosecuted Nazis at Nuremberg War Crimes Trials, Is Dead at 90."
19. Benjamin Ferencz to Saul Kagan, July 3, 1955, Benjamin B. Ferencz Collection, 1919–1994, series 1, RG-12.001.03*06, box 3, United States Holocaust Memorial Museum Archives.
20. Deborah Lipstadt, *The Eichmann Trial* (New York: Nextbook-Schocken, 2011), 70.
21. Benjamin Ferencz, interview by author, January 18, 2019 ("[One] way of looking at it [is that I] helped restore what Eichmann took away").
22. Benjamin Ferencz to Pinhas Rosen, May 25, 1960, series 3, RG-12.003.09*10, box 29, Benjamin B. Ferencz Collection, 1919–1994, United States Holocaust Memorial Museum Archives, Washington, DC.
23. Ibid.
24. Pinhas Rosen to Benjamin Ferencz, June 8, 1960, series 3, RG-12.003.09*10, box 29, Benjamin B. Ferencz Collection, 1919–1994, United States Holocaust Memorial Museum Archives, Washington, DC.
25. Ibid.
26. Ferencz, interview, January 18, 2019.
27. Franklin Foer, "Why the Eichmann Trial Really Mattered," *New York Times,* April 8, 2011, https://www.nytimes.com/2011/04/10/books/review/book-review-the-eichmann-trial-by-deborah-e-lipstadt.html.
28. Lipstadt, *The Eichmann Trial,* 53.
29. Foer, *Why the Eichmann Trial Really Mattered.*
30. Lipstadt, *The Eichmann Trial,* 66.
31. Foer, *Why the Eichmann Trial Really Mattered.*
32. Michael A. Musmanno, *Ten Days to Die* (New York City: Doubleday, 1950).
33. Hannah Arendt, *Eichmann in Jerusalem: A Report on the Banality of Evil* (New York: Penguin, 1994), 19. See also Ron Rosenbaum, "The Evil of Banality:

Troubling New Revelations about Arendt and Heidegger," *Slate,* October 30, 2009.

34. Jacob Robinson, *And the Crooked Shall Be Made Straight: The Eichmann Trial, the Jewish Catastrophe, and Hannah Arendt's Narrative* (Philadelphia: Jewish Publication Society, 1965). In Ron Rosenbaum's view, Arendt's "banality of evil" thesis is "fatuous," "fathomless," and increasingly discredited (Rosenbaum, "The Evil of Banality").
35. CrimC (Jer) 40/61 Attorney-General of the Government of Israel v. Adolf Eichmann, 5722, 36 I.L.R. 18 (1961).
36. CrimA 336/61 Eichmann v. Attorney General, IsrSC 16 2033, 36 I.L.R. 277 (1962).
37. "The Eichmann Trial: Shaping Awareness of the Holocaust in Israel and World Public Opinion," Yad Vashem, https://www.yadvashem.org/yv/en/exhibitions/eichmann/awareness-of-the-holocaust.asp.
38. Benjamin B. Ferencz, "You Can't Win Them All," Stories, https://benferencz.org/stories/1956-1970/you-cant-win-them-all/.
39. Ibid.
40. "IG Farben," Auschwitz-Birkenau Memorial and Museum, http://auschwitz.org/en/history/auschwitz-iii/ig-farben.
41. Ibid.
42. *United States v. Carl Krauch, et al.* (*IG Farben*) in *Trials of War Criminals before the Nuernberg Military Tribunals under Control Council Law No. 10,* vol. 8 (Washington, DC: US Government Printing Office, 1947), Dissenting Opinion of Judge Hebert on the Charges of Slave Labor, 1307–25.
43. Benjamin B. Ferencz, *Less Than Slaves: Jewish Forced Labor and the Quest for Compensation* (Cambridge, MA: Harvard University Press, 1979), 35.
44. Benjamin B. Ferencz to Sheldon Glueck, May 20, 1949, box 74, F.9, Sheldon Glueck Papers 1916–1972, Harvard Law School Library, Harvard University, Cambridge, MA.
45. Ferencz, *Less Than Slaves,* 37.
46. Ferencz, "You Can't Win Them All."
47. Ibid., 45.
48. Martin Gilbert, "Working for Farben," *New York Times,* December 9, 1979, BR1.
49. Ferencz, *Less Than Slaves,* 48.
50. Ibid., 49.
51. Ibid., 53–53.
52. Ibid., 67.
53. Ibid., 69.
54. "The House That Krupp Rebuilt," *Time,* August 19, 1957.
55. Ferencz, *Less Than Slaves,* 76.
56. Benjamin Ferencz to Saul Kagan, June 9, 1958, series 4, RG-12.004.01*01, box 30, Benjamin B. Ferencz Collection, 1919–1994, United States Holocaust Memorial Museum Archives, Washington, DC (emphasis added).

57. Benjamin Ferencz to Drexel Sprecher, June 20, 1958, series 4, RG-12.004.14*01, box 42, Benjamin B. Ferencz Collection, 1919–1994, United States Holocaust Memorial Museum Archives, Washington, DC.
58. Ferencz, *Less Than Slaves,* 86.
59. Ibid.
60. Theodore Shabad, "Krupp Will Pay Slave Laborers," *New York Times,* December 24, 1959, 1.
61. Ibid.
62. "British Paper Assails Krupp Compensation Agreement on Slave Labor," *Jewish Telegraphic Agency,* December 29, 1959.
63. Philipp Gut, *Jahrhundertzeuge Ben Ferencz* (Munich: Piper Verlag, 2020), 150.
64. Ferencz, *Less Than Slaves,* 121.
65. Gut, *Jahrhundertzeuge Ben Ferencz.*
66. Ferencz, *Less Than Slaves,* 121.
67. Ibid., 123.
68. Ibid., 149.
69. David De Jong, "The Nazi Shadow behind the World's Youngest Billionaires," *Time,* May 8, 2018.
70. Ibid.
71. Ferencz, *Less Than Slaves,* 194. Flick's heirs later paid out the earmarked money after his death in 1972.
72. Ibid., 171.
73. Ibid.
74. Ibid., 194–95.
75. Ibid., foreword, ix.
76. Ibid., 188.
77. Ibid., 195.
78. Stewart Ain, "Solving the Restitution Mystery," *New York Jewish Week,* September 29, 2000.
79. Ferencz, "You Can't Win Them All."
80. Benjamin B. Ferencz, "Creative Approach to Law Practice," Stories, https://benferencz.org/stories/1956-1970/creative-approach-to-law-practice/.
81. Ibid.
82. Ibid.
83. Ibid.
84. Benjamin B. Ferencz, interview by author, Delray Beach, FL, January 19, 2019.
85. Ferencz, "Creative Approach to Law Practice."
86. Ibid.
87. Benjamin B. Ferencz, in discussion with author, January 2019. At the same time, Ferencz also expressed his view that, over time, Wiesel was affected by his great celebrity and became "arrogant" (ibid.).
88. Benjamin B. Ferencz, "Reimbursing Good Samaritans," Stories, https://benferencz.org/stories/1956-1970/reimbursing-good-samaritans/.

89. Lisa Klug, "How a Book on WWII Rabbits of Ravensbrück Leapt onto Bestseller Lists," *Times of Israel,* May 16, 2017.
90. Benjamin B. Ferencz, "Some Unanticipated Consequences," Stories, https://benferencz.org/stories/1948-1956/some-unanticipated-consequences/.

18. The New Lemkin

1. The Martin Luther King, Jr. Research and Education Institute, "Vietnam War," Stanford University, https://kinginstitute.stanford.edu/encyclopedia/vietnam-war.
2. Telford Taylor, *Nuremberg and Vietnam: An American Tragedy* (New York: Quadrangle, 1970).
3. Benjamin Ferencz, "Foreword: Will We Finally Apply Nuremberg's Lessons?," in Telford Taylor, *A New Introduction to Nuremberg and Vietnam: An American Tragedy,* Foundations of the Laws of War Series (Clark, NJ: Lawbook Exchange, 2010).
4. Karen Heller, "The Improbable Story of the Man Who Won History's 'Biggest Murder Trial' at Nuremberg," *Washington Post,* August 31, 2016.
5. Benjamin B. Ferencz, "War Crimes and the Vietnam War," *American University Law Review* 17 (1968): 403, 411.
6. Ibid., 410.
7. Ibid., 411.
8. Ibid.
9. Ibid., 423. In the article, Ferencz also noted that, in strictly legal terms, without further fact-finding, the US war effort was not in breach of its obligations, either from an international law or domestic constitutional law perspective. Thus, in many respects, this early article provided a more nuanced, balanced legal analysis.
10. David Greenberg, "Editor's Note," in Howard Jones, *My Lai: Vietnam, 1968, and the Descent into Darkness* (Oxford: Oxford University Press, 2017), xxi.
11. Ibid., xxii.
12. William Thomas Allison, *My Lai: An American Atrocity in the Vietnam War* (Baltimore, MD: Johns Hopkins University Press, 2012), 115.
13. Benjamin B. Ferencz, Comment, "Compensating Victims of the Crimes of War," *Virginia Journal of International Law* 12 (1972): 343.
14. Ibid., 356.
15. Greenberg, "Editor's Note," xxii.
16. Ferencz, "A Mélange of Vignettes" (Vignette One: Vietnam War on Mock Trial), Stories, https://benferencz.org/stories/1956-1970/a-melange-of-vignettes/.
17. Ian Lind, "Nuremberg Prosecutor Featured on '60 Minutes' Defended Hawaii Peace Activists in 1972 Case," iLind, https://www.ilind.net/2019/07/01/nuremberg-prosecutor-featured-on-60-minutes-defended-hawaii-peace-activists-in-1972-case/. Judge Pence, appointed by President John F. Kennedy

and Hawaii's first federal judge once the territory became a state, was later replaced as presiding judge by Samuel King, who had recently been appointed by President Richard Nixon.

18. Ferencz, "A Mélange of Vignettes" (Vignette Two: Priests on Trial in Hawaii).
19. Lind, "Hawaii Peace Activists."
20. Terry Messman, "Jim Douglas and Nonviolent Resistance to War and Nuclear Weapons," Street Spirit, https://www.peaceworkersus.org/docs/jim-douglas-and-nonviolent-resistance-to-nuclear-weapons.pdf.
21. Ibid.
22. Lind, "Hawaii Peace Activists" (online post from Albertini attached to article).
23. Rob Frydlewicz, "Recap of Each Winter's Snowstorms in New York (1950–2022)," New York City Weather Archive, https://thestarryeye.typepad.com/weather/2014/11/each-winters-snowstorms-1970-2014.html.
24. Benjamin B. Ferencz, "Contemplating Life and Death in Puerto Rico," Stories, https://benferencz.org/stories/1970-present/contemplating-life-and-death-in-puerto-rico/.
25. Ibid.
26. Ibid.
27. In his memoirs, and in my discussions with him, Ferencz could not recall his exact thinking (or its precise sequence) while lying in the dark hospital corridor that night. But, based on our conversations, the thoughts recorded here generally capture what was on his mind.
28. Keri Ferencz, interview by author, October 13, 2020.
29. Ibid.
30. Ibid.
31. Robin Ferencz Kotfica, interview by author, November 7, 2020.
32. Keri Ferencz, interview, October 13, 2020.
33. Nina Dale, interview by author, October 24, 2020.
34. Don Ferencz, interview by author, January 27, 2021.
35. Nina Dale, interview, October 24, 2020.
36. Ibid.
37. Robin Ferencz Kotfica, interview, November 7, 2020.
38. Benjamin Ferencz, conversation with author, January 25, 2021. Ferencz requested that this conversation not be recorded.
39. Ferencz did not specifically allude to this fact during the January 25, 2021, conversation with the author. But he alluded to it in his memoirs. See Benjamin B. Ferencz, "Growing up Feeling Lost," Stories, https://benferencz.org/stories/1920-1943/growing-up-feeling-lost/ ("Sam's [Fani's husband] marriage had been prearranged [so] he found his happiness in a bottle. Fani had a boarder [a Greek named Albert] who cleaned felt hats. I liked Albert. Fani did too.").
40. Ibid.
41. Ibid.
42. Nina Dale, interview, October 24, 2020.

43. Benjamin Ferencz, conversation with author, January 25, 2021.
44. Nina Dale, interview, October 24, 2020.
45. Ibid.
46. Ibid.
47. Ibid.
48. Ibid.
49. In his memoirs, regarding his decision in Puerto Rico to change careers, Ferencz did not specifically reference thinking about the Nazi industrialists evading justice for their World War II crimes. But his frustrations regarding this have been well documented herein, and his trip to Puerto Rico took place not long after securing minimal or nonexistent reparations against certain industrialists (as noted, there were ongoing fruitless negotiations with Friedrich Flick himself in 1969, when Ferencz left for Puerto Rico). While he may not have consciously focused on the industrialists or the other NMT justice shortfalls while in San Juan, they had been weighing on him for years. And his conversations with me clearly suggested they were at least generally filtering through his mind during those pivotal days.
50. Benjamin Ferencz to Gertrude Ferencz, May 24, 1946 (letter provided to author by Keri Ferencz).
51. See Benjamin B. Ferencz, *Less Than Slaves: Jewish Forced Labor and the Quest for Compensation* (Cambridge, MA: Harvard University Press, 1979), 167–68.
52. Benjamin B. Ferencz, "Epilogue—The Long Journey to Kampala: A Personal Memoir," in *The Crime of Aggression: A Commentary,* ed. Claus Kress and Stefan Barriga (New York: Cambridge University Press, 2017), 1507.
53. Ferencz, "Contemplating Life and Death in Puerto Rico."
54. Ibid.
55. Benjamin B. Ferencz, "Starting a New Career," Stories, https://benferencz.org/stories/1970-present/starting-a-new-career/.
56. Philipp Gut, *Jahrhundertzeuge Ben Ferencz* (Munich: Piper Verlag, 2020), 286.
57. League of Nations, "Preamble," Covenant of the League of Nations, https://www.refworld.org/docid/3dd8b9854.html.
58. Benjamin B. Ferencz, "Getting Aggressive about the Crime of Aggression," Stories, https://benferencz.org/stories/1970-present/getting-aggressive-about-the-crime-of-aggression/.
59. Ibid.
60. Benjamin B. Ferencz, "Where the ICC Stands and Where It Is Going," Stories, https://benferencz.org/stories/global-survival/where-the-icc-stands-and-where-it-is-going/.
61. Jonathan Bush, "The Supreme . . . Crime and Its Origins: The Lost Legislative History of the Crime of Aggressive War," *Columbia Law Review* 102, no. 8 (2002): 2324.
62. Constantin Goschler, Marcus Böick, and Julia Reus, *Kriegsverbrechen, Restitu-*

tion, Prävention: Aus dem Vorlass von Benjamin B. Ferencz, trans. Lukas Buchholz (Göttingen: Vandenhoeck & Ruprecht, 2019), 38.

63. Nevertheless, given the needed compromises, aggression expert Noah Weisbord notes that "Paradox, illusion, and double meaning lay at the heart of the General Assembly's final 1974 definition" (Weisbord, *The Crime of Aggression: The Quest for Justice in an Age of Drones, Cyberattacks, Insurgents, and Autocrats* [Princeton, NJ: Princeton University Press, 2019], 62). Ferencz was frustrated with many aspects of the definition, but, per Weisbord, he still felt it was "a small, cautious and faltering step in the direction of a better world" (ibid., 65).
64. General Assembly Resolution 3314 (XXIX), U.N. GAOR, 29th Sess., Supp. No. 31 (Dec. 14, 1974).
65. *Military and Paramilitary Activities in and against Nicaragua (Nicaragua v. United States of America),* Merits, Judgment, I.C.J. Reports 1986, p. 14, para. 3 (in reference to Article 3(g)).
66. Weisbord, *The Crime of Aggression,* 65.
67. Toby Golick (Telford Taylor's second wife), interview by author, October 31, 2020.
68. Ibid.
69. Toby Golick, email to author, March 29, 2021 (on file with the author).
70. Taylor's personal papers indicate that, as of 1981, he was still using the firm letterhead for correspondence and client invoices for legal work (see, e.g., Telford Taylor Papers, TTP-7-3-54-738-: Special Master–National Basketball Association Labor Agreement: Filings and Correspondence [1981]). Curiously, there is online mention of the firm in the *Martindale-Hubbell Law Directory* as late as 1991.
71. Each book of the trilogy was published by Oceana Publications (Dobbs Ferry, NY).
72. Gut, *Jahrhundertzeuge Ben Ferencz,* 291.
73. Claus Kress, note to author, November 8, 2021 (on file with author).
74. Louis Sohn, introduction to *An International Criminal Court: A Step toward World Peace—A Documentary History and Analysis* (Dobbs Ferry, NY: Oceana, 1980), xv–xvii.
75. Claus Kress, note to author, November 8, 2021 (on file with the author).
76. David Scheffer, interview by author, November 27, 2021.
77. Ibid.
78. Claus Kress, note to author, November 8, 2021 (on file with the author).
79. Benjamin B. Ferencz, "Writing for World Peace," Stories, https://benferencz.org/stories/1970-present/writing-for-world-peace/.
80. Benjamin B. Ferencz, untitled front matter in *A Common Sense Guide to World Peace* (Dobbs Ferry, NY: Oceana, 1985).
81. Benjamin B. Ferencz, "Reaching for the Public," Stories, https://benferencz.org/stories/1970-present/reaching-out-for-the-public/.

82. Ibid.
83. Its publisher was Vision Books (Nagar, India: SAS)
84. Ferencz, "Reaching for the Public."
85. Benjamin B. Ferencz, preface to *New Legal Foundations for Global Survival: Security through the Security Council* (Dobbs Ferry, NY: Oceana, 1995), vii.
86. Kofi Annan to Benjamin B. Ferencz, June 24, 1997 (as chronicled in Ferencz, "Epilogue," 1509n12).
87. Faran Fagen, "97-Year-Old Nuremberg Trials Prosecutor Still Pushes for Peace," *Palm Beach Post*, February 14, 2018.
88. Benjamin B. Ferencz, "Teaching for Peace," Stories, https://benferencz.org/stories/1970-present/teaching-for-peace/.
89. Benjamin B. Ferencz, "The Pace Peace Center," Stories, https://benferencz.org/stories/1970-present/the-pace-peace-center/.
90. Ibid.
91. Ibid.
92. Francis Fukuyama, *The End of History and the Last Man* (New York: Free Press, 1992).

19. Creating a Permanent Court in the Eternal City

1. Principles of International Law Recognized in the Charter of the Nürnberg Tribunal and in the Judgment of the Tribunal ("Nuremberg Principles"), 1950 Report of the International Law Commission to the General Assembly, GAOR, 5th Sess. Supp. (No. 12) U.N. Doc. A/1316, pt. 3, 11–14 (1950).
2. M. Cherif Bassiouni, *A Draft International Criminal Code and Draft Statute for an International Tribunal* (Leiden: Martinus Nijhoff, 1987), 5.
3. See Katharine McGregor, Jess Melvin, and Annie Pohlman, "New Interpretations of the Causes, Dynamics and Legacies of the Indonesian Genocide," in *The Indonesian Genocide of 1965: Causes, Dynamics and Legacies* ed. McGregor, Melvin, and Pohlman (London: Palgrave Macmillan, 2018), 11.
4. Anwar Ouassini and Nabil Ouassini, "'Kill 3 Million and the Rest Will Eat of Our Hands': Genocide, Rape, and the Bangladeshi War of Liberation," in *Genocide and Mass Violence in Asia: An Introductory Reader*, ed. Frank Jacob (Berlin: De Gruyter, 2019), 1:43.
5. René Lemarchand, "Burundi 1972: Genocide Denied, Revised, and Remembered," in *Forgotten Genocides: Oblivion, Denial, and Memory*, ed. Lemarchand (Philadelphia: University of Pennsylvania Press, 2013), 37.
6. Michael G. Vann, "Murder, Museums, and Memory: Cold War Public History in Jakarta, Ho Chi Minh City, and Phnom Penh," in *Genocide and Mass Violence in Asia: An Introductory Reader*, ed. Frank Jacob (Berlin: De Gruyter, 2019), 1:201.
7. B. V. Olguín, *Violentologies: Violence, Identity, and Ideology in Latina/o Literature* (Oxford: Oxford University Press, 2020), 324n5.

8. Greg Grandin, “Politics by Other Means: Guatemala’s Quiet Genocide,” in *Quiet Genocide: Guatemala 1981–1983*, ed. Etelle Higonnet (London: Taylor & Francis, 2009), 1.
9. Choman Hardi, “The Anfal Campaign against the Kurds: Chemical Weapons in the Service of Mass Murder,” in *Forgotten Genocides: Oblivion, Denial, and Memory*, ed. René Lemarchand (Philadelphia: University of Pennsylvania Press, 2013), 107.
10. Nik Gowing, “Inside Story: Instant Pictures, Instant Policy: Is Television Driving Foreign Policy?,” *Independent*, July 2, 1994. See also Babak Bahador, *The CNN Effect in Action: How the News Media Pushed the West toward War in Kosovo* (London: Palgrave Macmillan, 2007), 21–22.
11. Leila N. Sadat, review of *The International Criminal Tribunal for Rwanda*, by Virginia Morris and Michael P. Scharf, *American Journal of International Law* 94, no. 2 (April 2000): 431 (“As an attorney with the United Nations Office of Legal Affairs, Morris helped to draft the Statute of the International Criminal Tribunal for the Former Yugoslavia”).
12. Benjamin B. Ferencz, “Writing for World Peace,” Stories, https://benferencz.org/stories/1970-present/writing-for-world-peace/.
13. Ibid.
14. Philipp Gut, *Jahrhundertzeuge Ben Ferencz* (Munich: Piper Verlag, 2020), 313.
15. Claude E. Welch Jr. and Ashley F. Watkins, “Extending Enforcement: The Coalition for the International Criminal Court,” *Human Rights Quarterly* 33, no. 4 (November 2011): 952.
16. Ibid.
17. Roy S. Lee, “Introduction—The Rome Conference and Its Contribution to International Law,” in *The International Criminal Court: The Making of the Rome Statute—Issues, Negotiations, Results*, ed. Lee (The Hague: Kluwer Law International, 1999), 2–3.
18. Ibid.
19. Whitney Harris to members of the Association, November 28, 1996, Benjamin B. Ferencz Collection, United States Holocaust Memorial Museum (Ferencz’s post-1994 papers have yet to be accessioned by the USHMM; copy of letter obtained from the collection on file with the author). An odd omission was Telford Taylor, but the Subsequent Trials chief was quite ill by then, would be dead by May 1998, and likely could have done little more than symbolically occupy a slot on the Committee’s letterhead.
20. Whitney Harris to NGO Coalition for an International Criminal Court, November 28, 1996, Benjamin B. Ferencz Collection, United States Holocaust Memorial Museum (copy of letter on file with the author).
21. David Scheffer, interview by author, November 27, 2021.
22. Benjamin B. Ferencz to Len Cavise, May 19, 1997, Benjamin B. Ferencz Collection, United States Holocaust Memorial Museum (copy of letter on file with author).

23. Benjamin B. Ferencz to Antonio Cassese, August 3, 1996, Benjamin B. Ferencz Collection, United States Holocaust Memorial Museum (copy of letter on file with author).
24. Ibid.
25. Antonio Cassese to Benjamin B. Ferencz, August 12, 1996, Benjamin B. Ferencz Collection, United States Holocaust Memorial Museum (copy of letter on file with author).
26. Ibid.
27. Antonio Cassese, Fourth Annual Report of the International Tribunal for the Prosecution of Persons Responsible for Serious Violations of International Humanitarian Law Committed in the Territory of the Former Yugoslavia since 1991, A/52/375, September 18, 1997, 46.
28. Benjamin B. Ferencz to Antonio Cassese, November 18, 1997, Benjamin B. Ferencz Collection, United States Holocaust Memorial Museum (emphasis added) (copy of letter on file with author).
29. Benjamin B. Ferencz, "Notes at Meeting for Coalition of an International Criminal Court, August 12, 1996," Benjamin B. Ferencz Collection, United States Holocaust Memorial Museum (copy of document on file with author).
30. Christoph Sperfeldt, "Rome's Legacy: Negotiating the Reparations Mandate of the International Criminal Court," *International Criminal Law Review* 17 (2016): 358; Mark Klamberg, *Commentary on the Law of the International Criminal Court* (Brussels: Torkel Opsahl Academic EPublisher, 2017), 515n557. The full title of Article 68 is "Protection of the Victims and Witnesses and Their Participation in the Proceedings." Rome Statute of the International Criminal Court, U.N. Diplomatic Conf. of Plenipotentiaries on the Establishment of an ICC, art. 68, U.N. Doc. A/CONF.183/9 (1998).
31. Gilbert Bitti, "A Court for Victims?," in *Victims at the Centre of Justice from 1998 to 2018: Reflections on the Promises and the Reality of Victim Participation at the ICC,* International Federation for Human Rights, No. 730a (December 2018), https://www.fidh.org/IMG/pdf/droitsdesvictimes730a_final-2.pdf.
32. Ibid.
33. Benjamin B. Ferencz, "Notes, Meeting with French Delegates, August 20, 1996," Benjamin B. Ferencz Collection, United States Holocaust Memorial Museum (copy of document on file with author).
34. Benjamin B. Ferencz, "Note with the Address of Gilbert Bitti, August 20, 1996," Benjamin B. Ferencz Collection, United States Holocaust Memorial Museum (copy of document on file with the author). The notes do not indicate exactly when Bitti's address was written down. It may very well have been during the Prep Com phase with Ferencz planning a future trip to Paris. The author spoke with Bitti about his interactions with Ferencz during this phase, but Bitti had no specific recollection of the nature and/or content of these discussions.
35. Benjamin Ferencz to William R. Pace, July 10, 1997, Benjamin B. Ferencz Col-

lection, United States Holocaust Memorial Museum (copy of document on file with author).

36. Benjamin B. Ferencz, interview by author, Delray Beach, FL, January 19, 2019.
37. Ibid.
38. "Documents distributed Monday, 15 March 1998," Benjamin B. Ferencz Collection, United States Holocaust Memorial Museum (copy of document on file with author).
39. Benjamin B. Ferencz, "Needed: A World Criminal Court," Archive: Articles, June 1998, https://benferencz.org/articles/1990-1999/needed-a-world-criminal-court/. The speech was delivered on June 16, 1998 (see United Nations Diplomatic Conference of Plenipotentiaries on the Establishment of an International Criminal Court, Rome, 15 June–17 July 1998, Official Records, vol. 2: Summary Records of the Plenary Meetings and of the Meetings of the Committee of the Whole, A/CONF.183/13, 80).
40. Ferencz, "Needed: A World Criminal Court."
41. Ibid.
42. Ibid.
43. Benjamin B. Ferencz, "What Really Happened in Rome," Stories, https://benferencz.org/stories/global-survival/what-really-happened-in-rome/.
44. Ibid.
45. Ambassador Christian Wenaweser, interview by author, September 13, 2021.
46. Roy S. Lee, "Introduction—The Rome Conference and Its Contribution to International Law," in *The International Criminal Court: The Making of the Rome Statute—Issues, Negotiations, Results,* ed. Lee (The Hague: Kluwer Law International, 1999), 2–3.
47. Ferencz, "What Really Happened in Rome."
48. Ibid.
49. Morten Bergsmo, interview by author, August 27, 2021.
50. Wenaweser, interview, September 13, 2021.
51. Bergsmo, interview, August 27, 2021.
52. Christian Wenaweser, "'Law. Not War'—Special Event Honouring Ben Ferencz on His 101st Birthday," Nuremberg Principles Academy, March 11, 2021, https://www.youtube.com/watch?v=QkXBfAmwWFY.
53. Bergsmo, interview, August 27, 2021.
54. Scheffer, interview, November 13, 2021. Photographs do not seem to bear out Scheffer's memory that Kofi Annan was among this group.
55. Benjamin B. Ferencz, "Misguided Fears about an International Criminal Court," Stories, https://benferencz.org/stories/global-survival/misguided-fears-about-an-international-criminal-court/.
56. Ibid.
57. David Scheffer, *All the Missing Souls: A Personal History of the War Crimes Tribunals* (Princeton, NJ: Princeton University Press, 2013), 237.

58. Ferencz, "Misguided Fears about an International Criminal Court."
59. Ibid.
60. Robert S. McNamara and Benjamin B. Ferencz, "For Clinton's Last Act," *New York Times,* December 12, 2000, A33.
61. Ibid.
62. Scheffer, *All the Missing Souls,* 238.
63. Ibid., 239.
64. Ibid., 241.
65. Ibid., 242.

20. Time Machine Moments

1. Mary Ellen O'Connell, "Evidence of Terror," *Journal of Conflict & Security Law* 7 (2002): 19–20.
2. Benjamin B. Ferencz, "Misguided Fears about an International Criminal Court," Stories, https://benferencz.org/stories/global-survival/misguided-fears-about-an-international-criminal-court/.
3. Umesh Kadam, "Contemporary Issues in and Challenges to International Humanitarian Law," *Chinese (Taiwan) Yearbook of International Law and Affairs* 25 (September 2007): 201 (explaining that the United States used the term "illegal combatants" to describe Guantánamo detainees, but "there is no such notion of an 'illegal combatant' in IHL"—instead, such persons should be referred to as "unprivileged combatants").
4. Alka Pradhan and Scott Roehm, "Nuremberg Prosecutor Says Guantanamo Military Commissions Don't Measure Up," Just Security, August 24, 2021, https://www.justsecurity.org/77835/nuremberg-prosecutor-says-guantanamo-military-commissions-dont-measure-up/.
5. "US: 'Hague Invasion Act' Becomes Law," Human Rights Watch, August 3, 2002, https://www.hrw.org/news/2002/08/03/us-hague-invasion-act-becomes-law.
6. Ibid.
7. Benjamin B. Ferencz, "The Overdue Baby Is Born," Stories, https://benferencz.org/stories/global-survival/the-overdue-baby-is-born/.
8. Ibid.
9. Ibid.
10. Based on this intelligence, the administration concluded that Iraq was in violation of the UN Security Council Resolution establishing a cease-fire to end the Gulf War of 1991.
11. Nicholas Lemann, "The Iraq War Decision," *Frontline,* October 12, 2004.
12. Benjamin B. Ferencz, "What to Do with Saddam Hussein Now," Archive: Articles, December 2003, https://benferencz.org/articles/2000-2004/what-to-do-with-saddam-hussein-now/.
13. "Unjust and Unfair: The Death Penalty in Iraq," Amnesty International, April 20, 2007, https://www.amnesty.org/en/documents/MDE14/014/2007/en/.

14. Rome Statute of the International Criminal Court, Art. 5 (1), adopted on July 17, 1998, and in force on July 1, 2002, United Nations Treaty Series Online, 2187, no. 38544, Depositary: Secretary-General of the United Nations, https://legal.un.org/icc/statute/romefra.htm.
15. Ibid., Art. 5(2).
16. Stefan Barriga, interview by author, September 8, 2021.
17. Ambassador Christian Wenaweser, interview by author, September 29, 2021.
18. Noah Weisbord, *The Crime of Aggression: The Quest for Justice in an Age of Drones, Cyberattacks, Insurgents, and Autocrats* (Princeton, NJ: Princeton University Press, 2019), 102.
19. Donald Ferencz, interview by author, September 8, 2021.
20. Nina Dale, interview by author, October 23, 2020.
21. Ibid.
22. Donald Ferencz, interview, September 8, 2021.
23. Ibid.
24. Weisbord, *The Crime of Aggression,* 107.
25. Ibid.
26. Ibid.
27. Ibid.
28. Barriga, interview, September 8, 2021.
29. Luis Moreno Ocampo, interview by author, January 28, 2022.
30. Ibid.
31. In the end, as it turned out, once jurisdiction was activated in December 2017, only State Parties that ratify the amendments can be subject to the aggression jurisdiction (Klaus Kress, "On the Activation of ICC Jurisdiction over the Crime of Aggression," *Journal of International Criminal Justice* 16 [2018]: 12).
32. Weisbord, *The Crime of Aggression,* 108.
33. Ibid., 108–9.
34. Ibid., 109.
35. Donald Ferencz, conversation with author, January 23, 2022.
36. "Indeed, regarding the crime of aggression, the specter of Russia's veto has prevented the Security Council from referring the Ukrainian situation to the International Criminal Court in the wake of Russia's 2022 full-scale invasion" (Graham M. Glusman, "Justice from the General Assembly: An International Tribunal for the Crime of Aggression in Ukraine," *Chicago Journal of International Law Online* 3, no. 1 [Winter 2024]: 5, https://cjil.uchicago.edu/sites/default/files/2024-02/Glusman_Justice%20from%20the%20General%20Assembly.pdf).
37. Luis Moreno Ocampo, January 28, 2022.
38. Ibid.
39. Ibid.
40. Ibid.
41. Benjamin B. Ferencz, interview by author, Delray Beach, FL, January 19, 2019.

42. Ibid.
43. Ibid.
44. Benjamin B. Ferencz, "Ferencz Closes Lubanga Case for ICC Prosecution," Archive: Articles, August 2011, https://benferencz.org/articles/2010-present/ferencz-closes-lubanga-case-for-icc-prosecution/.
45. Jocelyn Getgen Kestenbaum, interview by author, January 4, 2022.
46. International Criminal Court, "Ferencz Family's Planethood Foundation Donates $50,000 to Trust Fund for Victims," March 21, 2013, https://www.icc-cpi.int/fr/news/ferencz-familys-planethood-foundation-donates-50000-trust-fund-victims.
47. Anna Cave, interview by author, January 26, 2022.
48. Ibid.
49. United States Holocaust Memorial Museum, "The Ferencz International Justice Initiative," United States Holocaust Memorial Museum, https://www.ushmm.org/genocide-prevention/simon-skjodt-center/work/ferencz-international-justice-initiative.
50. Cave, interview, January 26, 2022.
51. National Public Radio, "The Last Nuremberg Prosecutor Has 3 Words of Advice: 'Law Not War,'" *Morning Edition,* October 18, 2016.

Postscript

1. Kelsey Vlamis, "Why Is Russia Attacking Ukraine? Here Are 5 Reasons Putin and Others Have Given for the Invasion," *Business Insider,* February 25, 2022.
2. Sergiy Kyslytsya, "Ukraine Ambassador Remarks during U.N. General Assembly Debate," C-SPAN, March 2, 2022.
3. Colum Lynch, "U.N. Denounces Russia's Ukraine Invasion," *Foreign Policy,* March 2, 2022.
4. Benjamin Ferencz, "Looking for Hitler and Looted Art," Stories, https://benferencz.org/stories/1943-1946/looking-for-hitler-and-looted-art/.
5. Benjamin Ferencz, interview by Joan Ringelheim, United States Holocaust Memorial Museum, August 26, 1994, transcript, 15, https://collections.ushmm.org/oh_findingaids/RG-50.030.0269_trs_en.pdf.
6. Michael J. Bazyler and Frank M. Tuerkheimer, *Forgotten Trials of the Holocaust* (New York: New York University Press, 2014), 99.
7. After Ben's passing in April 2023, obituaries referenced his being part of the *Krupp* trial team at Nuremberg. See, for example, Robert D. McFadden, "Benjamin B. Ferencz, Last Surviving Nuremberg Prosecutor, Dies at 103," *New York Times,* April 8, 2023. I believe this is due to persons in Ben's life having been alerted to this via my 2020 research and adding this information when questioned about Ben's life in 2023. This seems to be confirmed by the fact that neither Ben's memoirs (presented in the online "Stories") nor Philipp Gut's 2020 biography *Jahrhundertzeuge Ben Ferencz* makes mention of Ferencz's Nurem-

berg work as a *Krupp* trial attorney. Interestingly, given this lacuna in Ben's account of his service at Nuremberg, the *New York Times* Ben Ferencz obituary reported this fact but, in describing it, confused/conflated Ben's Nuremberg *Krupp* trial work with his 1950s civil litigation efforts against the Krupp firm on behalf of victims.

8. Benjamin B. Ferencz, interview by author, Delray Beach, FL, January 19, 2020. I tried to press him on this point, explaining why it should perhaps not be omitted in considering his life's work, but it was clear he did not want to discuss it further, so I moved on.
9. Benjamin Ferencz to Saul Kagan, June 9, 1958, series 4, RG-12.004.01*01, box 30, Benjamin B. Ferencz Collection, 1919–1994, United States Holocaust Memorial Museum Archives, Washington, DC (emphasis added).
10. Benjamin Ferencz to Gertrude Ferencz, May 24, 1946 (letter provided to the author by Keri Ferencz).
11. Samuel Johnson, "The Rambler No. 60, Saturday, October 13, 1750," in *The Works of Samuel Johnson, LL.D. in Nine Volumes, Volume the Second* (London: Talboys and Wheeler; and W. Pickering, 1825), 291.
12. Benjamin B. Ferencz, "My Guiding Stars," Stories, https://benferencz.org/stories/global-survival/my-guiding-stars/. Ferencz's account is based on Alfred Noyes's telling of the story in his book *The Torch-Bearers: The Watchers of the Sky,* vol. 1 (New York: Frederick A. Stokes, 1922), 2.
13. Ferencz, "My Guiding Stars." In "My Guiding Stars," Ferencz gives a slightly different account, with Brahe using a telescope and reporting to the government officials that he had charted the stars in eighty-nine books and hoped to reach one hundred.
14. Ibid.

INDEX

Page numbers followed by a *t* refer to tables describing the *Einsatzgruppen* case.

Democratic Ideals in Global Perspective

This series seeks to publish scholarship on democracy as a historical practice and as a social and cultural enterprise at work in global, pluralistic societies, including projects that see gender and sexuality-based rights movements as inherently democratic, projects that show how civil struggles and minority rights claims and strategies highlight the limits and possibilities of democracy, and projects that offer profiles of decolonization.